BASIC RETAILING

Carl M. Larson

University of Illinois, Chicago Circle

Robert E. Weigand

University of Illinois, Chicago Circle

John S. Wright

Georgia State University

PRENTICE-HALL, INC., *Englewood Cliffs, New Jersey*

Library of Congress Cataloging in Publication Data

LARSON, CARL M (date)
Basic retailing.

Includes bibliographical references.
1. Retail trade. I. Weigand Robert E., joint author. II. Wright, John Sherman (date) joint author. III. Title.
HF5429.L317 658.8'7 75-29381
ISBN 0-13-068056-7

Printed in the United States of America

10 9 8 7 6 5 4 3 2 1

PRENTICE-HALL INTERNATIONAL, INC., *London*
PRENTICE-HALL OF AUSTRALIA, PTY. LTD., *Sydney*
PRENTICE-HALL OF CANADA, LTD., *Toronto*
PRENTICE-HALL OF INDIA PRIVATE LIMITED, *New Delhi*
PRENTICE-HALL OF JAPAN, INC., *Tokyo*
PRENTICE-HALL OF SOUTHEAST ASIA (PTE.) LTD., *Singapore*

Dedicated to
the late Professor BERNT O. LARSON

and
JANE LARSON, JACKIE WRIGHT, and
ARTHUR A. and NORA L. WEIGAND

CONTENTS

PREFACE

The day of the general merchandise store may be about over; there are one-third fewer such stores today than there were twenty years ago. There are also fewer food and furniture stores now than just a few years ago. On the other hand, Dynamic Classics, Ltd., has opened automobile parts boutiques in several American department stores to cater to women who like cars but are uncomfortable in typical auto supply outlets. And a San Diego restaurant caters to dieters; everything on the menu has a low calorie content. The key to success seems to be making the food tasty without using fattening ingredients. Obviously, the demand for some types of retailers fades, while the demand for others grows.

Lobb's Shoe Shop in London offers a pair of riding boots for about $600, although some are far more expensive. Its customer list reads like an international *Who's Who*, and satisfied patrons often order by mail from throughout the world. But retailers such as Pic 'N Save, Dollar General, Bill's Dollar Stores, and Family Dollar Stores often buy rejects and overruns from major suppliers and resell the merchandise at low but profitable prices. The consumer market is very diverse, and these retailers operate at different ends of the consumer spectrum.

A Cleveland supermarket hired a wine steward to explain to shoppers the differences among wines and what wine should be served with various foods. The supermarket operator is attempting to educate Americans, who have a lot to learn about wine, including learning to accept it as a regular part of a meal. Marketing theoreticians usually argue that major responsibility for performance of the information function shifted many years ago from the retailer to the manufacturer and the consumer, but the Cleveland example is an exception. However, one of Marathon Oil Company's subsidiaries requires the automobile driver to pump his own Speedway gas; the gas station operator no longer does so. What had historically been accepted as a retail function has been shifted to the customer.

A shopping center manager was concerned about morning lulls, so he hired a bus to bring elderly shoppers or browsers from a nearby apartment complex once a week. Many of them do their entire week's shopping at that time, but their presence also gives the illusion of "busyness" that the manager believes is essential. Another retailer, concerned about the number of bad checks he was receiving, devised a technique for placing the check cashers' fingerprints on each check that is cashed. Losses have been reduced to almost nothing. And a manager of a bookstore oriented to black culture faces the seemingly unsolvable problem of being geographically convenient to black customers and simultaneously being accessible to high income white customers who may want to read about the black experience. Retail problems and the ways retailers resolve them come in just about every size and shape.

The Attorney General of New York State has issued a pamphlet entitled "The ABC's of Careful Buying" in English, Spanish, German, French, Italian, Yiddish, Hungarian, and Chinese. Meanwhile, New York City's Department of Consumer Affairs has ruled that repair and delivery men or women must give 24 hours notice if they are unable to keep an appointment. They are subject to a fine if they fail to do so. And retailers throughout the United States are concerned about the "giveaway" programs of banks and savings and loan companies. Retailers of small appliances, calculators, and jewelry are concerned that too many prospective customers are obtaining such goods by putting a few hundred dollars into a checking or savings account. Many of the forces that affect a retailer's future are already identifiable, although their pervasiveness and impact may be difficult to discern.

The above stories suggest some of the real life diversity of twentieth century retailing. They may seem out of the ordinary to outsiders, but they are everyday experiences to those who are involved in retail operations. Such problems and opportunities make up the marrow of retailing and lend authenticity to the basic concepts and theories with which we must deal if we are to have an orderly view of the world of retailing. Without an underlying framework the stories become nothing more than an endless series of yarns and folklore. The above five examples have been chosen because they suggest the direction the authors believe a retailing course should take. In particular, upon completion of the course the student should have accomplished five goals:

1. The understanding that business and other institutions exist to serve society. In a free society where customers vote with their dollars, efficient institutions will offer the right goods and services to their customers, jobs for their employees, and profits for their owners. If a profit-seeking institution fails to serve an economic need, it may fail. Our first example suggests how long term business prosperity is tied to customer needs.
2. An appreciation of the diverse views on the nature of the group(s) that retailers serve. Market segmentation is a generally accepted business practice. No retailer can serve everyone with equal efficiency and customer satisfaction. Rather, a retailer may claim to satisfy "the Hispanic-American market," "the west side suburban market," "the high income, cocktail party-goers market," or "the low income youth market." Unfortunately, data concerning the most profitable market to serve is not always available to retailers. In many instances it must be painstakingly dug out a bit at a time or perhaps even discovered by accident. Some retailers may survive for years without an academically satisfactory definition of their market(s). Lobb's Shoe Store in London and the dollar stores

1 AN OVERVIEW OF RETAILING

America's huge Sears, Roebuck and Company is well known in the United States, but operates in Belgium through Galeries Anspach. And the C. and A. Breunninkmeyer Company, based in the Netherlands, operates not only throughout Europe but also in the United States through Ohrbach's, one of its subsidiaries. Sears, Galeries Anspach, C. and A. (Breunninkmeyer has been dropped in some countries), and Ohrbach's must compete fiercely not only with each other but with many small retailers throughout Europe and in the New York area.

A few years ago, venture capitalists thought they observed that motels were looking more and more like hotels—expensive construction and higher prices to registered guests. They reasoned that there must surely be a large number of people who wanted a low-cost good night's sleep. The result was construction of many motels under such names as Motel 6 and Regal 8. Perhaps the owners had never heard of the "wheel of retailing," to be discussed in this chapter, but they were acting it out.

A group of college students who are tired of the food sold in the university's dining room open a "people's restaurant" just off campus. They discover some of the complexities of satisfying student tastes, discuss the moral implications of serving food with low nutritional content, worry about the city's health and sanitation departments, are astonished at how much ingredients cost, and face some of the same personnel problems that larger businesses do. ("Where were you yesterday when you were supposed to work?" "I had to study for an exam.")

A store in Los Angeles that sells and rents equipment to skydivers decides to invest several thousand dollars in snorkelling equipment that it hopes to sell. Even in a large city the prospective market for skydiving equipment is limited, so the store owner hopes to expand by extending his product line. His argument is that those who are thrilled by jumping out of airplanes can also be encouraged to try water sports.

Such well-known American retailers as Dayton-Hudson, Alexander's, and Giant Stores have attempted to operate discount catalog stores, not always successfully. Customers must review their needs from a catalog either in the store or at home and purchase merchandise, often without seeing it. Partly because labor costs are low, such retailers have been able to underprice even the discount houses, who, in turn, underprice traditional department stores. By 1975 some were advertising "Beat the Recession" prices, an attempt to be sensitive to America's economic problems at the time. Still, many catalog stores were having difficulties earning a profit—perhaps suggesting that the wheel of retailing has not yet made a complete turn.

An artist who paints local scenes of New Orleans sits in front of Saint Louis Cathedral and sells his product to the many tourists walking around Jackson Square; a heroin pusher in Jersey City is the last step in an involved series of middlemen who move the drug from its European source to its American user; and a little boy and girl sell Kool-Aid for a nickel a glass to passersby. They do not think of themselves as retailers in the usual sense—indeed, they probably don't reflect on the question at all—but they are retailers, just as are Gimbels, Shakeys, or the local Ford dealer.

It is obvious from the above examples that a wide range of retailers, with differing problems and responses, exists in a complex society. Retailing itself means different things to different people. To a housewife, it is the source of groceries, clothing, and other household needs. To a manufacturer, retailing is the last commercial link in the marketing channel and the point where products finally reach their users. To retailers, it is a livelihood, as it is to more than 12 million workers.

Each of us is familiar with retail establishments, for we are retailing's customers. Furthermore, at one time or another nearly everyone has engaged in a retail venture similar to the youthful entrepreneurship shown in Figure 1.1. Many of us now serve in retailing's ranks to help finance our educations. But let's look more specifically at retailing from the customer viewpoint.

FIGURE 1.1

Almost everyone has engaged in retail ventures similar to that of these young entrepreneurs

Source: Noel Davis, *The Atlanta Journal-Constitution*, June 21, 1971.

When a customer enters a restaurant, orders, and consumes a steak, he or she demonstrates a fundamental retailing principle. (See Figure 1.2.) The customer acts as the last in a long line of institutions and people who are involved with a product—the farmer who raised the cow, the meat-packing company who bought it and changed it to edible form, the meat wholesaler who delivered the steak to the restaurant, and the restaurant where it was cooked and served. The diner in this case is the ultimate consumer, and retailing is marketing at the level of the ultimate consumer. The retailing industry includes each and every shop and store that sells

FIGURE 1.2
Restaurants are excellent examples of the retailing of services; eating and drinking places account for nearly $30 billion in sales annually

Source: Tony Kelly, Consolidated Foods Corporation, Chicago, Illinois.

consumer products and services—from department stores to drugstores, from barbershops to bars.

RETAILING DEFINED

Even though we all know in a general way from personal experiences what retailing is, we need to define the term and describe it more precisely before embarking on a thorough study of the subject. Inasmuch as retailing is an integral part of marketing, it is helpful to know what we mean by the latter term. The American Marketing Association has developed the following definition:

> Marketing is the performance of business activities that direct the flow of goods and services from producer to consumer or user.[1]

Retailing is one aspect of marketing, and can be defined as follows:

[1]Committee on Definitions, Ralph S. Alexander, Chairman, *Marketing Definitions: A Glossary of Terms* (Chicago: American Marketing Association, 1960), p. 15.

> Retailing includes all activities directly related to the sale of goods or services to the ultimate consumer for personal nonbusiness use.[2]

Three elements of this definition warrant explanation. First, the term *activities* means the core operations of retailing that are described in detail throughout this book. Second, *goods and services* carry the important idea that although physical products are important in today's retailing, personal services are increasingly important in the overall sales total for the industry. This point is illustrated in Figure 1.3. Third, those activities involved in wholesaling are separated from retail activities by the phrase *ultimate consumer for personal nonbusiness use.* If a product is purchased for resale or for use in business pursuits, that sale is deemed to be at wholesale. The distinction between retailing and wholesaling will be amplified shortly.

FIGURE 1.3

The relative importance of services in the retailing mix became evident in 1970, when total sales of services surpassed total sales of goods in the United States

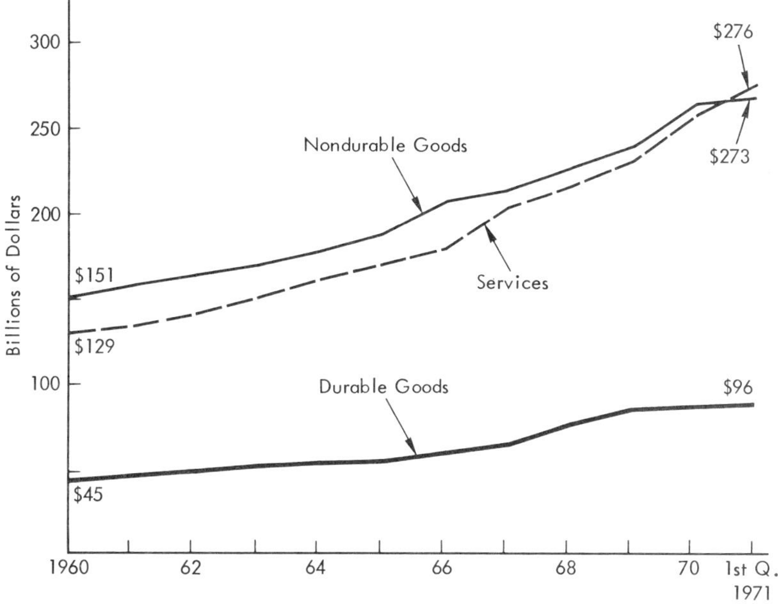

Source: *Sales Management*, May 15, 1971, pp. 70, 71. Reprinted by permission from Sales Management, The Marketing Magazine. Copyright 1971.

A pragmatic, but anonymous, definition of retailing is:

[2]William J. Stanton, *Fundamentals of Marketing*, 4th ed. (New York: McGraw-Hill Book Company, 1975), p. 336.

> Successful retailing is selling merchandise that doesn't come back to customers who do.

This pithy definition highlights the importance of the right assortment of goods and services to retailing success, as well as the centrality of the consumer in retailing.

Two additional observations about retailing should be made. First, the retailer typically sells in small quantities. Second, the end expectation of the retailer's activities is profit. Therefore, we like to think of retailing as:

> all activities involved in the sale of small quantities of goods and services, at a profit, to ultimate consumers for personal use.

It then follows that a retailer is the one who sells the goods or services to the ultimate consumer, and a retail sale is the actual transaction.

What Is a Retail Sale?

A sale may be classified as a retail sale *only* if the buyer of the product or service is the ultimate, or final, consumer and the product is for a nonbusiness use. Let's look at two examples.

1. A wholesaler sells a color television set to a householder who will personally use the set. This is a retail sale even though the seller is classed as a wholesaler, because the product is sold to the ultimate consumer for his or her personal use.
2. A local stationery store sells pencils to a hardware store for use by the clerks to compute customers' sales checks. This is a wholesale transaction even though made by a retailer, because the sale is for a business purpose.

Fortunately, most transactions are not difficult to classify; most institutions that call themselves retailers actually are engaged in retailing, and those that call themselves wholesalers are engaged in wholesaling. The Bureau of the Census classifies business units as retailers if more than 50 percent of their sales are to consumers, and as wholesalers if more than 50 percent of their business is with other businesses.

CHARACTERISTICS OF RETAILING

Consumer Initiates the Transfer of Goods

The retailer offers goods to the public in a variety of ways, but in most instances the consumer initiates the proposed transfer of goods. The major exceptions would be retailing by telephone, door-to-door, direct mail, and vending machines. That the consumer takes the first step is in contrast with marketing on the manufacturer's level, where salesmen seek out their customers to obtain sales. Even though the customer generally initiates the contact, the retailer must have considerable information about the ultimate consumer and his or her desires. The retailer tries to learn why one product is favored by the consumer while other similar products become casualties of the marketplace. Perhaps it is more important to find out why a consumer favors one retailer over another, even though both may be handling the same product and perhaps the same brand.

Sense of Urgency

A sense of urgency is characteristic of retailing. People want the goods soon after they become aware of their own needs. They purchase products at their favorite stores, take them home, and use them. Some products—for example, food—must be obtained almost daily, and the purchasing process is quite routine. The success of the "convenience" store, which sells the most frequently needed grocery items throughout the day and most of the night, caters to the consumer's sense of urgency.

Other products are purchased infrequently, and the buyer may take a considerable period of time to plan the purchase. For example, when a householder decides to buy a color television set, the family members probably will discuss the need for such a product, read literature on comparable sets, and finally inspect models at various stores. However, it is generally true that once contact has been established with a retailer and a decision to buy has been reached, the customer seeks immediate delivery if possible.

Small Quantities

A third characteristic of retailing, as mentioned earlier, is that small quantities of goods comprise the typical transaction. The average sale made by a retailer differs markedly in size from that of a wholesaler, distributor, or manufacturer. Consider these facts from research carried out several years ago. At that time the typical family made food purchases that totaled $26.69 weekly. This amount paid for approximately 57 separate items, which were purchased in three trips to the grocery store. By 1974 the largest supermarket averaged 12,730 transactions per week, and the average transaction was $8.64. The great number of transactions needed to move $131 billion of grocery store sales into the nation's homes is readily perceived from these data.[3] Small quantities are an important characteristic of most other kinds of retailing. Unit values for consumer durables, of course, may be high.

Geographic Convenience

Retailing is generally localized. Most household customers do not have to travel far in order to find products and services that accommodate most of their needs. The food store, gas station, restaurant, and variety store that adequately suit us are generally not far away. This contrasts with many business-to-business transactions where buyers and sellers must seek each other out, perhaps hundreds or even thousands of miles apart. Indeed, many purchasers of industrial goods or raw materials "shop the world" for their needs. However, most successful retailers offer geographic convenience to their customers; those who don't ("Come visit our storeroom out of the high-rent district, and save, save, save!" says the advertisement) must usually offer some other appealing attraction.

[3]"42nd Annual Report of the Grocery Industry," *Progressive Grocer* (April 1975), p. 74.

Analysis of the numbers of retailers and the population of each of our 50 states indicates that establishments are roughly dispersed throughout the country in proportion to each state's population. There are nearly 2,000,000 retail establishments in the United States that serve our more than 211,000,000 population. But it is interesting to note that in 1970 North Carolina contained 2.5 percent of America's retail establishments and the state had 2.5 percent of the country's population. California had 9.8 percent of the nation's retailers and 12.2 percent of the nation's people. And for Alabama the figures were 1.7 percent and 1.6 percent respectively. Further analysis seems to show that retailers are somewhat more attracted to those states with higher disposable personal income figures. Still, population seems to be a powerful determinant of where retailers locate; in short, people with money and an inclination to buy constitute a market, and retailers respond by locating near that market.

HISTORY OF RETAILING

Origin of Trade[4]

At some time during the beginnings of civilization, groups began to trade with one another. How or why this occurred is not known, but various possible explanations have been offered.

One theory holds that trade is as instinctive as the need for food, water, and bodily comforts. Another theory is based on human aggressiveness and hostility. Yet another explanation asserts that trade is the outgrowth of friendly gift giving. A more plausible theory suggests that whenever people have more goods than they care to consume, the surplus is traded away. George W. Robbins thinks trading began when people placed a value on goods in terms of other goods, rather than to value goods in terms of spiritual or mystical beliefs. Robbins also adds that mores and customs had to be receptive to the changes that trading would bring to the people's patterns of living.[5]

Early History of Retailing

Retailers of today are an important element in our economic society, and successful merchants are respected by a majority of their fellow citizens. However, this was not always so. Retailers in the ancient world were looked upon with scorn and contempt, and their services were little appreciated. The retailer was regarded as an unproductive member of society by the government, as unpatriotic by the military, and as unholy by religious leaders. The ideal state of Plato was to have as few retailers as possible so they would do the least possible damage. How were retailers able to climb from this low position to the high status they enjoy today? We can give at least a partial answer to this question.

In the ancient world, trade flourished between peoples simply because some

[4]For a more complete discussion about the origin of trade, see George W. Robbins, "Notions About the Origin of Trading," *Journal of Marketing*, 11, no. 3 (January 1947), 228–36.

[5]Ibid.

had a surplus of one type of good and desired goods they did not have or could not produce—if one believes the "surplus goods" theory of trade. Only luxury goods were traded, and caravans traveled from one area to another carrying silks, spices, and other precious commodities. The earliest traders were the Cretans who sailed the Mediterranean and carried on trade with the people of that area. The Cretans flourished for two thousand years, from 3000 B.C. to 1000 B.C., and their culture is believed to have influenced later civilizations, especially that of Greece.

The Phoenecians followed the Cretans as civilization's major traders, and they distributed the goods of Egypt and Babylonia to the rest of the known world. Tyre, Sidon, and later Carthage were the principal trading cities in this empire. The Phoenecians ranged widely and eventually established a rich trade with Spain. They were said to be so wealthy that they made the anchors of their ships out of pure silver.

Phoenecian traders were succeeded on the world's commercial stage by the Romans, who established a sophisticated form of retailing. Numerous small shops were set up within veritable shopping centers. In fact, ancient ruins indicate that the world's first department store was in Rome. With the fall of the Roman Empire in the fifth century A.D., retailing on any scale disintegrated.

The Dark Ages

During the period following the fall of the Roman Empire, the only retailers of any consequence were peddlers. With their stores on their backs, the peddlers went from village to village selling their wares. They often victimized the villagers by offering inferior merchandise, so it is little wonder that early laws penalized peddlers.

By the thirteenth century fairs and markets flourished. These early fairs often had a religious foundation. On feast days people would gather at their churches and exchange goods they had brought for that purpose. On other occasions they would meet for the sole purpose of exchanging goods. The larger markets were called fairs, and people traveled long distances to participate. Goods from distant lands were sold for gold and silver or simply bartered for other goods. Eventually, fairs became places of amusement as well as trading centers. The practice of holding fairs has survived through the centuries and has culminated in the giant state and world's fairs of today.

By about the twelfth century a new development in the history of retailing occurred. Artisans and tradesmen no longer depended solely on fairs and markets as outlets for their wares, but instead they opened small shops. They then organized themselves into associations called "guilds," which were designed to secure economic and social advantages for the particular trade or craft to which its members belonged. By the fifteenth century the shop system had become quite successful, especially in England. Still, with few exceptions, the shopkeepers as a class were relatively unimportant, both socially and economically.

History of American Retailing

Many American retailing institutions originated after 1850. Prior to that date most Americans lived in rural areas and were largely self-sufficient. Transportation and communication were poor, and, except for the people clustered in cities on the

Eastern seaboard, there was little need for retailers. During this period itinerant peddlers and general stores in frontier communities were popular.

Kelley and Brisco give the following description of this era:

> In the frontier days the Indian trading post also served the adventurous white in its territory and gave way to the general store where settlements located. Itinerant peddlers on horseback and in wagons brought staples, some fancy goods, and news from Eastern seaboard cities to the most remote regions. Wagon trains with merchandise followed every gold rush. As American manufacturers appeared, Yankee notions, textiles, tinware, and clock peddlers brought their products to isolated communities and sold, or often bartered, both to customers and to general stores. Several of these early peddlers opened retail stores that developed into some well-known department stores of today, such as Gimbels, whose first store was in Vincennes, Indiana.[6]

The Department Store. After 1850 the department store became much more important in the United States. For example, Rich's was established in Atlanta in 1867 by four Hungarian immigrants; today the firm operates more than a dozen stores in Georgia. Simon Lazarus, an immigrant from Prussia, opened a men's clothing store in Columbus, Ohio, in 1851; his children and grandchildren kept the tradition going, and today Federated Department Stores operates such divisions as I. Magnin, Shillito's, Ralph's Supermarkets, and Bloomingdale's. And Macy's ("The World's Largest Store") can be traced to 1858 when Rowland Macy, who spent his earlier life on a whaling ship, opened a dry-goods store on Sixth Avenue in New York City.

Department stores evolved in several ways. Occasionally, as towns and villages grew into cities, the local general store expanded by taking on new lines of products until it eventually became a true department store. Others grew out of a single-line store that handled one specialty product. Still other independently owned shops which happened to be under a common roof merged into a centralized operation with a single owner. Sometimes wholesalers added retailing to their operation and did so well that they abandoned wholesaling entirely and concentrated on retailing. By whatever route the department stores emerged, they became giants of twentieth-century retailing and still exert considerable impact on the entire retailing industry; they presently account for 10.4 percent of all retail sales in the United States.

Most of the early department stores attempted to raise the standards of retailing by emphasizing quality at low price. They also made shopping a pleasant and convenient experience by being among the first establishments to use such symbols of progress as central heating, elevators, telephones, and electric lighting. By 1900 the department store was well established in all the principal cities of the United States, and its role as a mass distributor of goods in an urban environment was recognized.

Whenever one mentions department stores, the names of such men as John Wanamaker, Marshall Field, and R. H. Macy are remembered. These men intro-

[6]Pearce C. Kelley and Norris B. Brisco, *Retailing: Basic Principles*, 3rd ed. (Englewood Cliffs, N.J.: Prentice-Hall Inc., 1957), p. 25.

attention to understanding their field. Theory is often disparaged by those who prefer that students learn something "practical." Indeed, professors are occasionally disturbed when asked whether they "teach a lot of theory" or if they deal with "something worthwhile." But when theory is well elaborated and understood it can serve as a worthy basis for understanding real world events. However, much retailing goes on without theoretical explanation and students cannot wait for it to develop. The brief examples at the beginning of each chapter[1] suggest how retailers operate when faced with various opportunities or problems. They are not cited as the best ways to perform, but only as interesting insights into retailer behavior. It is useful to remember that everyone has a "map" of the world in mind, and each individual acts in order to enhance his own position in it. Thus everyone acts on the basis of a theory, though it might be an incorrect map for the situation or too difficult to articulate. Still, we strive for theory—a systematic explanation of seemingly isolated events.

A WORD OF THANKS

The authors are indebted to a number of people. Specifically we wish to thank Professor Adel El-Ansary of Louisiana State University and Professor Richard E. Embertson of Western Michigan University for their excellent criticisms and suggestions. Edwin W. Berg, professor of retailing at Morraine Valley Community College of Palos Hill, Illinois, is the cartoonist whose work is seen on the chapter openings throughout this book. We are grateful that this good friend has used his talents in our behalf. We are also indebted to Maureen Wilson for her expertise in production editing and for her many suggestions that have improved the readability of our book. Without her cheerful assistance, our assignment would have been more difficult.

We also want to acknowledge the kindness of all individuals and companies who provided us with the illustrations that are an integral visual part of this book. Individual acknowledgments accompany each illustration.

Many others, including family, friends, associates, colleagues, and students, gave us their support, confidence, suggestions, and criticisms. We were also blessed with secretaries and typists who worked their magic to transform our handwritten copy into a readable manuscript. Therefore we wish to publicly thank these supporters, contributors, friends, assistants, and typists: Susan Baylen, Steve Cristol, Frank Enenbach, Ramon Greenwood, Sheila Griffin, Barbara Gruenke, Judy Gruenke, Fred Hanson, Shirley Hanson, Elizabeth Hirschman, Roy Kempa, Diane Niedbala, Irving Robbin, R. Rubin, Jackie Sbarboro, Ray Schuman, Joyce Speck, and Lisa Taranucha.

Last—but not least—we wish to thank our families whose contributions are beyond measurement. This special group includes Jane Larson, Jackie Wright, and Arthur and Nora Weigand.

[1]The examples are largely from the experience and observations of the three authors, but have also been drawn from such sources as *The Wall Street Journal, The New York Times, The Chicago Daily News, Advertising Age, Business Week*, Mahoney and Sloan's *The Great Merchants* (Harper & Row), and the Federal Trade Commission's *News Summary*.

throughout the United States clearly appeal to different markets. But to describe the difference as rich people versus poor people may vastly oversimplify the character of each market.

3. An awareness of the functions and structure of retailing and the policies and practices that retailers follow. Retail institutions are highly diverse in terms of how they serve society. These differences can be explained by focusing on the different functions they perform. Some engage in personal selling; others are involved in storing goods; still others in servicing goods. And on it goes through all the functions that might be associated with retailing. This results in differences in the size of the institution, its command over a market, the number of outlets it operates, the power it has over suppliers, its efforts toward vertical integration, and other attributes used to measure an industry's structure. In order to carry out its mission, the retailer must devise and promulgate the policies that will give consistency to the operation. The wine supplier in Cleveland and the Speedway gas station examples hint at how managements are continually defining the role their businesses play in catering to customer needs. Retailing policies and practices will continue to change in response to the opportunities in the marketplace as perceived by the retail manager.
4. An understanding of the problems that retailers face and the tools they use to solve them. It would be foolish to suggest that a single book can outline all the possible problems a retailer might face. Some are highly complicated and technical matters, such as designing computer reports that indicate the inventory position of each outlet fast enough to make buying decisions. Others are nontechnical and are far less certain in outcome, such as what a store manager should do with a fourteen-year-old who has been caught shoplifting for the first time. Such problems are too diverse to imagine or to list. But no retailing student should be unprepared for any future onslaught of different situations.
5. A modest awareness of what lies ahead—or at least the ability to speculate about it. Forecasting is full of hazards, and a favorite sport among business people is to look back at how earlier predictions turned out. Many are downright, laughably wrong. However, there is no alternative to the serious task of trying to decide which political, social, and economic forces will affect the future and in what ways. The roles they will play in affecting a business must be estimated accurately if the business expects to operate profitably and efficiently. Fortunately, there are certain early warning signals that retailers can watch for, which will give sufficient lead time for decision-making purposes. The role of government in protecting the consumer from abuse at the hands of business is watched by astute business people. They are quite aware that the things that are happening in New York may not be isolated events but may be harbingers of the future for all retailers.

A WORD OR TWO ABOUT THEORY

Theory can be defined as an explanation of the order that one sees in otherwise unrelated events. In the absence of theory, the world is nothing more than unexplained phenomena that seem to have no systematic relationship to each other. This book is not heavily steeped in theory, largely because retailing theory is not sufficiently developed to be used as the basis for a text. The authors would like to be able to furnish students with a sound theoretical understanding of retailing, but that will have to wait until more scholars and business people have paid closer duced stability and order into retailing. They also established the one-price policy. Prices were clearly marked on the merchandise, and everyone paid the same price. Marshall Field is given credit for initiating the slogan "The customer is always right." This principle has become one of the most important policies of major department stores throughout the United States.

Mail-Order Houses. Whereas the department stores grew and flourished in the cities, chiefly to the advantage of urban citizens, the mail-order houses catered primarily to farmers and residents of small villages—and at a time when America was a rural nation. The mail-order retailer depended on the transportation system of the nation to carry on his business, because his customers ordered from illustrated catalogs and then received delivery by parcel post, express, or freight. In 1896 rural free delivery (RFD) was adopted by the post office, and the mail-order business was given a very substantial boost.

The reasons for the success of the early mail-order houses was the convenience in buying, the low prices, and the large assortments of goods. The customer needed only the illustrated catalog from which to make his or her selections. It was as if a store was brought into the customer's home. No longer did rural people have to travel over poor roads to shop. Furthermore, the catalog contained a wide assortment of merchandise. Sears, Roebuck and Company sold their catalogs at a dollar a copy, canvassing the rural areas aggressively to sell all they could. Sears knew that sales would increase rapidly if catalogs were widely distributed. The wisdom of this theory is seen in the $234 million sales volume attained by Sears in 1919.[7]

The mail-order houses were able to cut buying costs by buying in large quantities directly from factories. This enabled them to sell the merchandise at low prices to their customers. Furthermore, as they pioneered new merchandising techniques, they cut costs still further and passed the savings on to their customers.

Mail-order houses were also pioneers in sponsoring truthful and informative advertising. Moreover, they granted liberal return privileges and guaranteed complete customer satisfaction. Many customers availed themselves of the privilege of having the goods shipped C.O.D. (collect on delivery), subject to inspection before payment. Thus, this retailing institution introduced retailing policies and procedures that now permeate most forms of retailing.

Retailers who sell solely through the mail today do less than one percent of the business of all retailers; however, many kinds of retailers sell at least a portion of their merchandise by mail. The one percent figure understates the importance of sales by mail in the United States.

Chain Stores. Mail-order sales began to decline after the automobile became a part of the American scene. As automobiles were perfected and as good all-weather roads began to crisscross states, rural buyers found it easy to come to the city to shop. Therefore, the mail-order houses set up retail stores to serve these customers better. Sears pioneered in building retail stores in principal cities and has become one of the world's most successful retailers. In the fiscal year ending Janu-

[7]Ibid., p. 30.

ary 31, 1975, its sales totaled approximately $13.1 billion.[8] Sears' phenomenal growth is a tribute to good management, proper merchandising techniques, and an awareness of changing customer needs and wants. Figure 1.4 shows the Sears' growth story as reflected in company facilities.

Food store chains, which originated in the era immediately preceding the Civil War, were an even earlier form of chain store. For example, the Great Atlantic and Pacific Tea Company (A & P) opened for business in 1859. In 1974 it was the second largest of the food chains, with over $6.7 billion in sales annually.[9] The real drama of the food chains and their impact upon the American scene took place after 1920; the food chains began to grow and for a time it appeared as if chains would drive independent grocers out of business. However, independents organized into voluntary and cooperative groups in order to survive and even prosper. By the end of 1973, chains—defined as organizations operating eleven or more units— accounted for 49.8 percent of all food sales, while independents accounted for 50.2 percent.[10]

Chains account for about 79 percent of the sales by variety stores. One of the most successful of these chains was begun by Frank W. Woolworth, who opened his first five-cent store in Lancaster, Pennsylvania, in 1879. The articles contained in his stores were all priced at five cents. Later, ten-cent items were introduced, and the first five-and-ten cent store came into being. Woolworth catered to mass markets, and his success is most eloquently told by the more than 2,000 stores one still sees today which bear his name. The company also operates approximately 300 Woolco stores, 1,500 Kinney shoe stores, and 260 Richman clothing stores. Changing times, greater prosperity, and inflation have all combined to raise the price ceiling from ten cents in the Woolworth outlets. Yet today one still hears shoppers say they are going to the "dime store."

For all their success, chains have never been important in some kinds of retailing. Less than five percent of the sales in durable goods stores are made by chains. Some kinds of retailing—automobiles and furniture are good examples—are best handled by independent retailers. The reasons often cited are that independents can negotiate prices, take trade-ins, buy for individual customers rather than in large quantities, and give friendlier attention than can a chain. Contrary to popular thinking, the chains are not taking over the country.

The Changing Scene. The period between the two world wars was a time of consolidation and growth in American retailing. Department stores became the backbone of main streets in the principal cities throughout the United States. Variety stores were located next door to one another, and thus confirmed the principle that competitors handling competitive goods can often help one another by attracting larger numbers of people to the main street. It is one form of synergism, or cooperative action.

[8]*Chicago Tribune* (March 26, 1975), section 4, p. 9.

[9]A & P was the largest of the food chains until 1973, when Safeway became number one by a slender margin.

[10]"41st Annual Report," *Progressive Grocer* (April 1974), pp. 71, 106.

FIGURE 1.4

Sears, Roebuck and Co. grew from a Minnesota railroad station in 1886 to an 109-story Chicago skyscraper in 1973.

Source: Sears, Roebuck and Co., Chicago, Illinois.

The winds of change are still blowing. Today's retailers are concerned about discount houses, trading stamps, the decline of the downtown shopping district, the impact of the computer, and a whole host of problems and opportunities that characterize the modern world. Successful retailers are adjusting to these changes and will undoubtedly remain a vital link between the producer and the consumer.

THE WHEEL OF RETAILING

One cannot study the history of retailing without examining the "wheel of retailing," the name given to an explanation of retail development originated by Malcolm P. McNair. His hypothesis is a classic in the literature of marketing. McNair states that new retailers enter the marketing arena as low-price operators with little status and poor facilities, and offer a minimum of services to customers. The establishments are operated by those who are extremely cost conscious and aggressively competitive. Eventually they invest in better stores and more elaborate facilities; they add more services, and increase their prices to cover these additional costs. Ultimately these merchants mature into high-cost, high-price retailers offering merchandise accompanied by considerable service. At this stage they are open to competition from entrepreneurs who aggressively pursue a low-cost, low-price operation. The wheel continues to turn, and each competitor repeats this cycle of growth. For example, the full-service food retailer lay open to the onslaught of the cash-and-carry supermarket; the traditional department store was hit hard by the limited function discount house; and, more recently, the higher priced furniture stores began to feel the pressure from supermarket-type, low-priced outlets such as Levitz and Wickes. (See Figure 1.5.)

FIGURE 1.5
The wheel of retailing thesis

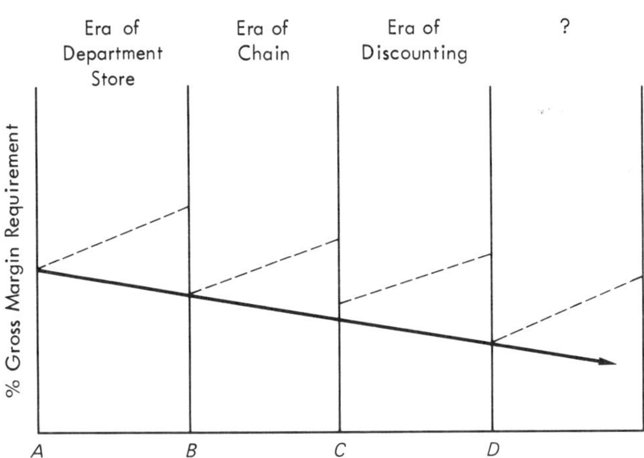

Source: Ronald R. Gist, ed., *Management Perspectives in Retailing*, 2nd ed. (New York: John Wiley and Sons, Inc., 1971), p. 27.

Six Theories Explaining the Wheel of Retailing

Six theories have been advanced as explanations for the movement of the wheel.[11]

1. Aggressive, low-cost, low-price retailers become soft. Businessmen mellow as they mature, and managerial expertise declines. Furthermore, successors are less capable and are unable to cope with changing conditions. This deterioration of management capability causes the wheel to turn another notch.
2. Trade advertisements coax retailers into modernizing and improving their stores and facilities. Modernization raises costs and causes retailers to increase prices. Competition from aggressive low-cost, low-price operators moves in.
3. Retailing, it is claimed, exemplifies imperfect competition. To the extent that this is true, retailers avoid price-competition and engage in nonprice competitive practices, such as free delivery service, extension of credit, customer services, and improved facilities. The addition of the new services is financed through higher prices. Again, the increase in price makes the older retailers vulnerable to competition.
4.  The retailing industry develops excess capacity as it matures. (This theory is advocated by McNair.) Excess capacity refers to the fact that retailers have larger investments in stores and facilities than their sales justify. This hypothesis also assumes imperfect competition. Because of this excess capacity, retailers operate at a higher cost level and thus invite low-cost, low-price competitors into the industry.
5. Secular trend states that people's standards of living increase steadily in the long run. Therefore, as people become more affluent, merchants take advantage of the opportunity and stock more expensive merchandise and add more services. They become high-cost, high-price retailers and are vulnerable to innovative competitors.
6. The wheel phenomenon may be an illusion. Retailers may add new products at higher margins while keeping margins on older items the same. (A margin is the difference between the selling price of an item and its invoice cost.) The result is a higher average margin. As in the previous cases, the higher margin exposes traditional retailers to new competition.

THE MARKETING CONCEPT AND RETAILING

Another important idea from the broader realm of marketing will facilitate a better feeling for what retailing is all about. This idea has become known as the marketing concept.[12]

Prior to World War II most manufacturers produced goods, placed them in a warehouse, and employed salesmen to sell the goods to wholesalers, distributors, other manufacturers, and retailers. In turn, retailers sold the goods to consumers. In many cases the consumers were only moderately happy with the products offered to them, and in many instances products simply did not sell. The result was tension

[11] Stanley C. Hollander, "The Wheel of Retailing," *Journal of Marketing* (July 1960), pp. 37–42.

[12] Ibid., pp. 37, 42.

and chaos for some retailers, losses for others, bankruptcy for still others. The reason consumers accepted as many products as they did under this *production concept* of marketing is that they did not have a wide choice; product lines had not yet proliferated in response to market segments.

Consider the housewife of a few decades ago who went to a local department store to select a ready-made dress. Perhaps there were only two or three dresses in her size. Faced with a limited selection, her decision to choose one of the three was quite easily made. Possibly she disliked all three dresses, but as there was no suitable alternative except to forego the purchase, she made her selection from one of the three.

With the end of World War II, the economy of the United States was geared to turn out great quantities and varieties of products; virtually all types of retailing outlets became competitors of sort. *Scrambled merchandising* is the term given to this broadening of retail offerings. While merchants were offering a greater variety of goods, consumers became more sophisticated in their tastes, and it was natural for competitors to court customers' needs and wants. Manufacturers who did not know why customers preferred to buy specific products faced a precarious existence. One began to hear about motivation research, and explanations of buying motives and attitudes filled the marketing literature of the 1950s. Marketing research came into its own as customers were questioned, analyzed, and studied in countless ways. Likes and dislikes were taken into account before manufacturers produced goods. The term *marketing concept* was coined to explain the new philosophy of marketing strategy.

This focus of attention, which was shifted from the making of goods to satisfying consumer needs, is described in the following quotation:

> The marketing concept of management is a unifying approach marshalling and directing the total resources of a business firm toward the determination and satisfaction of customer and consumer wants and needs in a way planned to enhance the firm's overall profit position.[13]

The marketing concept is so simple that it is strange it was articulated so late in the history of business. Of course, consumers are changeable, and their opinions not easily interpreted. This means that householders sometimes do not buy products which they have indicated to researchers they want. In other cases manufacturers simply misunderstand consumers' wishes and produce the wrong goods. Adopting the marketing concept does not guarantee to the manufacturer perfect information concerning consumers' wants, tastes, and willingness to spend. Interpretation of customers' needs and desires is still more of an art than a science, in spite of the greater employment of scientific methodology, quantitative techniques, and the use of the computer.

Another related point is the belief held by some observers that consumers are

[13]Richard R. Weeks and William J. Marks, "The Marketing Concept in Historical Perspective," *Business and Society* (Spring 1969), p. 25.

exploited by manufacturers and lured through clever advertising into buying products they actually do not want. The most popular treatment of this theory is found in the book *The Wastemakers* by Vance Packard. This belief does not do justice to the vast majority of American manufacturers and retailers who do strive to determine in advance what consumers want. Indeed, one only needs to observe the high rate at which new products fail—some say as high as eighty percent—to refute such a charge. The exploitation concept, if it is true, marks a return to the old production concept and is opposed to the marketing concept. In view of the widespread use of the marketing concept, the exploitation concept is followed by very few marketers, whose ignorance of consumers' wants dooms them to eventual failure. The successful marketers of today serve the consumer, and their financial success depends upon their ability to discern the tastes of those in their markets to produce products that suit those tastes.

Because of their closeness to consumers, retailers have always been more customer-oriented than manufacturers. With the marketing concept being employed by their merchandise sources, it is now easier for retailers to serve customer needs. They do not need to serve as passive conduits for merchandise that does not fully satisfy consumers. On the other hand, with greater variety of products being manufactured and with consumers becoming more discriminating in merchandise selection, retailers must cast a wider net when looking for items to stock. Furthermore, they need to use the modern marketing research techniques developed by market-oriented manufacturers to determine what their customers will buy. Chapter 18 deals with marketing research opportunities for retailers.

THE ECONOMIC IMPACT OF RETAILING

Significant Measurements

There are many ways to gauge the significance of retailing to the economy as a whole. One can cite data showing the number of retail establishments, the total value of all retail sales, or the percentage of total personal income spent on retail sales. Table 1.1 highlights some of these measures. One can see that retail sales grew from $47.7 billion in 1929 to $535.0 billion in 1974. One might expect that total retail sales would increase proportionately with the increase in population. If the population doubled from 1929 to 1969, we would expect retail sales to double, too. But we can see that the population fell short of doubling at the same time that retailing registered more than a sevenfold increase. An easier and more useful method of showing retail growth is to express the total retail sales on a per capita basis. One can see from Table 1.1 that per capita retail sales increased from $392 in 1929 to a total of $2,517 by December 31, 1974.

The last two columns of Table 1.1 show the increase in personal income and the percentage of total income spent by householders on retail sales. The significant feature of these statistics is the declining percentage that the householder allocates to goods and services.

TABLE 1.1
Economic Impact of Retailing as Indicated by Selective Measures

Year	*Population*	*GNP (in billions of dollars)*	*Sales by Retail Establishments (in billions of dollars)*	*Per Capita Sales (in current dollars)*	*Personal Income (in billions of dollars)*	*Retail Sales (as percent of personal income)*
1974	212,530,000	$1416.3	$535.0 (est.)	$2517	$1150.4	46.5
1973	210,400,000	1294.9	503.3	2392	1035.4	48.6
1972	208,840,000	1155.2	448.4	2147	939.2	47.7
1970	205,820,000	989.9	364.6	1769	801.0	45.5
1969	204,000,000	932.1	357.6	1720	747.2	47.0
1968	201,000,000	865.7	339.3	1688	687.9	49.3
1963	188,658,000	583.9	244.2	1254	464.1	52.6
1958	173,320,000	444.5	199.6	1152	360.3	55.4
1954	161,164,000	363.1	169.9	1055	289.8	58.7
1948	146,093,000	259.4	128.8	882	210.4	61.2
1939	130,880,000	91.1	41.4	317	72.9	56.9
1929	121,770,000	104.4	47.7	392	85.5	55.7

Source: *Survey of Current Business*, 51, no. 4 (April 1971) and 54, no. 12 (December 1974).

The data in Table 1.1 may tempt one to conclude that the rising incomes of American consumers, along with the rising value of retail sales, indicates that Americans are enjoying a higher standard of living. This may, in fact, be true, but it cannot be logically deduced from the table. However, some authorities believe that retailing stimulates a rising standard of living. For example, Kelley and Brisco commented:

> Not only are goods made conveniently available to consumers, but the modern retail store is the showplace of the best merchandise producers have to offer. Even supermarket checkout girls have their dresses designed by a leading fashion designer. The public can see, inspect, and have explained or demonstrated any article from the latest fashion creation to every staple and new gadget on the market. Alert retailers constantly seek new merchandise and feature it in their advertising and displays. Consumers not only find it convenient to satisfy their wants, but are continuously tempted to expand their wants or to experiment with improved products to satisfy their dream wants. Easy credit offered by most stores helps to reduce one major barrier to buying, whereas careful credit control tends to maintain a proper balance between spending ability and ability to pay.[14]

Table 1.2 is interesting because it shows the total 1973 retail sales by kinds of retail establishments. For example, passenger car and other automobile dealers had sales totaling $92.8 billion. Retailers with the largest sales volume were in the food group, which includes grocery stores but does not include eating and drinking places.

[14]Kelley and Brisco, *Retailing*, p. 9.

TABLE 1.2

Retail Sales by Kind of Business for the Year 1973
(in billions of dollars)

Automotive Group		100.7
Passenger car, other automotive dealers	92.8	
Tire, battery, accessory dealers	7.9	
Furniture, Appliance Group		24.0
Furniture, home-furnishings stores	14.3	
Household appliance, TV, radio stores	7.9	
Other	1.8	
Lumber, Building, Hardware, Farm Equipment Group		30.9
Lumberyards, building materials dealers	18.0	
Hardware stores	4.7	
Others	8.2	
Apparel Group		24.1
Men's and boys wear	5.6	
Women's apparel, accessory stores	9.1	
Shoe stores	4.2	
Other	5.2	
Drugs and Proprietary Stores		15.5
Eating and Drinking Places		37.9
Food Group		105.7
Gasoline Service Stations		34.4
General Merchandise Group including nonstores		83.3
Department stores	52.3	
Mail-order (department store merchandise)	5.4	
Variety stores	8.2	
Other	17.4	
Liquor Stores		9.6
Unlisted Durable Goods Stores		14.7
Unlisted Nondurable Goods Stores		22.5
Total		503.3

Source: *Statistical Abstract of the United States, 1974*, U.S. Dept. of Commerce, p. 755.

This group had a sales volume totaling $105.7 billion. Eating and drinking retailers had sales equal to $37.9 billion. The data in Table 1.2 can be examined for a better understanding of the structure of American retailing.

Retailers as Employers

Table 1.3 shows the number of Americans employed in nonagriculture establishments. Note that almost as many Americans are engaged in retail occupations as are employed by the federal, state, and local governments.

The Economic Role of the Retailer

The United States has one of the highest standards of living in the world. There is such a vast outflow of goods and services that some authorities are concerned

TABLE 1.3
Nonagricultural Employment, November 1974
(seasonally adjusted)

Employment Field		*Number Employed (in thousands)*
Contract construction		3,855
Federal government		2,747
Finance		4,185
Manufacturing		19,628
Mining		679
Retailing		12,759
Service		13,748
State and local government		11,782
Transportation and public utility		4,703
Wholesaling		4,282
	Total	79,087

Source: *Survey of Current Business*, 54, no. 12 (December 1974), S-14.

about the population's ability to consume all that is produced. In this situation, retailers have the task of selling goods in order to prevent unusual inventory accumulation and consequent unemployment. Thus, the retailer has an important role to play in economic growth.

One of the best measures of an economy's performance is expressed in terms of the gross national product, commonly called the GNP. This is the final value of all the goods and services produced in a year. In order to arrive at the correct total, double counting must be avoided. The total dollar value of all the steel produced should not be added to the market price of automobiles, because the value of the steel would be counted twice. Therefore, GNP includes the price of a product only at its point of final sale, a price that has been arrived at by taking into account the values added in the other stages of production. Table 1.4 shows the growth of GNP for selected years and its relation to national and personal incomes.

National income is the sum of the dollars earned in the productive process; it includes the total of all wages and salaries, interest income, net income, and profits. Personal income is the sum of all dollar incomes earned by all individuals.

Retailing plays an important role in selling part of the nation's GNP. In particular, changes in the dollar volume tied up in inventory can affect employment, especially for short periods. Let us look at a simplified example.

Assume that in Year 1 all the goods produced are sold for a total of $790 billion, and there is no inventory. The relationship to GNP follows.

	Final Sales		*Inventory*		*GNP*
Year 1	$790 billion	plus	0	=	$790 billion

TABLE 1.4
Selected Economic Measurements (in billions of dollars)

Year	*GNP*	*National Income*	*Personal Income*
1929	103.1	86.8	85.9
1933	55.6	40.3	47.0
1941	124.5	104.2	96.0
1950	284.8	241.1	227.6
1962	560.3	457.7	442.6
1963	590.5	481.9	465.5
1964	631.7	517.3	496.0
1965	684.9	564.3	538.9
1966	749.9	620.6	587.2
1967	793.5	654.0	629.4
1968	865.7	714.4	687.9
1969	932.1	771.0	747.2
1970	989.9	800.1	813.3
1971	1055.5	859.4	863.5
1972	1155.2	941.8	939.2
1973	1289.1	1053.9	1035.4
1974 (4th quarter)	1428.6	1169.9 (est.)	1186.4

Source: The 1929–1973 data is taken from *Survey of Current Business*, 54, no. 5 (May 1974), p. S-2; the 1974 data is taken from *Federal Reserve Bulletin* (February 1975), p. A-56.

Assume that in Year 2 the final sales remain constant but retailers hold $10 billion in inventory.

Year 2	$790 billion	plus	$10 billion	=	$800 billion

Note that employment of resources must increase to produce the $10 billion of goods that are held as inventory, if productivity is constant. This can only take place provided the economy has unused resources—labor, capital, and raw materials.

Assume that in Year 3 the final rate of sales still remains constant, but retailers decide not to hold any inventory.

Year 3	$790 billion	minus	$10 billion	=	$780 billion

The sales for Year 3 would be $780 billion of goods produced in Year 3, plus $10 billion of goods produced in Year 2. GNP would decline from $800 billion to $780 billion, a drop of $20 billion. It would take fewer resources, including people, to produce the goods in Year 3; therefore, unemployment would increase.

Through the mechanics of our simplified example, we have shown that retailers must sell all the goods earmarked for the ultimate consumer, except for normal inventory accumulations. If they fail to sell all the goods, it is inevitable that inventory accumulations will occur and unemployment in the production segment of the economy will follow. This is seen clearly in the automobile industry in 1975, which has had a serious inventory glut that has forced layoffs among the workers and has given rise to rebates to sell cars. The retailer's responsibility is enormous when one considers the increase occurring annually in the productivity of both labor and capital. Furthermore, there is usually an annual increase in the capacity to produce goods, which further compounds the problem.

IMPACT OF SOCIETY ON RETAILING

Retailing is subject to the forces of change that are at work within society as a whole. Americans today have more income to spend and more leisure time in which to spend it than any previous generation. This, of course, expands the total number of dollars spent in retailing establishments and forces the nation's retailers to change their methods of operation. Frequently, retailers must trade up and carry a better quality line of products because of the higher incomes enjoyed by households. The affluence of the consumer is apparent to anyone who strolls through the stores of any shopping area and notes the variety of goods offered for sale and the prices asked.

The automobile has affected American society in many ways, but primarily it has made householders more mobile. The impact of this mobility has led to many social changes that in turn have had their effect on retailing institutions. For example, there has been a great migration of citizens from central cities to suburban locations. As we will discuss in Chapter 2, this has forced many retailers to open branches in suburban areas in order to hold on to their former city customers. At this point it is sufficient to point out that the creation of huge shopping centers has been largely a response of retailers to suburban living. The typical suburban housewife can get into her automobile and within fifteen minutes to a half hour can reach several major shopping centers and a half dozen smaller ones. No longer does she remain loyal to stores within walking distance of her home. This fact has caused a revolution on "Main Street" among the various retailers, and has increased the scope of competition that each merchant encounters.

The retailing revolution has had some more visible effects. For example, there has been a building boom in shopping centers located away from the main streets. As a result, shoppers have switched their allegiance to shopping plazas, and many vacant stores testify to the decline of the main street in many cities and towns. This decline has caused much concern among retailers, landlords, and local governments who have a stake or an investment to protect.

There are other visible evidences of change. Stores are open Sundays and many evenings to cater to the changing shopping patterns desired by the consumer. Stores are growing larger and stocking a greater variety of goods. A general trading up in the quality of goods being offered is a sign of the increased affluence of the American family. These and other aspects of the retailing revolution are discussed in detail in succeeding chapters.

SUMMARY

Retailing is marketing at the level of the ultimate consumer and includes all the activities related directly to the sale of goods and services to the ultimate consumer for personal use. Trading has existed in some form since civilization's earliest era. Although there are many theories claiming to explain trade, its origins are unclear. Retailing, an outgrowth of trade, is easier to trace through history. Usually the history of retailing is traced back only to the days following the collapse of the Roman Empire, when peddlers, fairs, and markets were dominant. Shops did not emerge until the twelfth century and actually did not reach importance until the fifteenth century.

In the United States, some of our modern marketing institutions date back to around 1850. Improved transportation facilities started to allow increasing numbers of Americans to migrate to the interior of the country, and more and more small pioneer settlements became true towns and cities. These changes necessitated the development of a system of internal trade, and the department store and mail-order house became significant factors in retailing. Chain food stores and chain variety stores also were established in the middle of the nineteenth century, but reached maturity in the twentieth century.

One cannot study the history of retailing without considering McNair's wheel of retailing. This theory postulated that retailers start as low-cost, low-price retailers and mature to high-cost, high-price retailers. This maturation induces aggressive newcomers to enter the industry to compete as low-cost, low-price enterprises. Evidence indicates the "wheel phenomenon" is characteristic of much of American retailing.

The United States is one of the world's most affluent nations. Retailers have the responsibility for moving goods through the last part of the trade channel and into the nation's homes. This is accomplished in spite of all the economic and social changes that have combined to cause the greatest retailing revolution in history. Because retailing is marketing at the level of the ultimate consumer, it is essential for retailers to adopt the marketing concept. In order to survive financially, the retailer must study the consumer thoroughly and cater to his or her needs. The challenge has been accepted by many retailers, and newer, plush shopping centers testify to the manner in which this challenge is being translated into effective merchandising. A study of retailing proves that the American householder is for the most part a sophisticated shopper, and there is little evidence to substantiate claims that the householder is the victim of clever exploiters. Many changes are occurring that are affecting retailers in their methods of operation, types of goods carried, and their approach to current problems. Retailing is truly a dynamic and fascinating activity.

QUESTIONS FOR DISCUSSION

1. List the various kinds and types of retailing found in all communities.
2. Do you think free choice by consumers is necessary for effective retailing?

3. Discuss the role of retailers in maintaining a high level of employment.
4. What social forces cause changes to take place in retailing?
5. Explain McNair's "wheel of retailing." Cite examples to show that this theory is valid in real life.
6. Do you think the marketing concept is consistent with a free enterprise economy? Why? Is it applicable to retailing?
7. Discuss how mobility of consumers affects retailing.
8. Does retailing increase the standard of living? How?
9. Is the charge valid that retailers exploit consumers by forcing them to buy the products they stock? Discuss.
10. Describe a personal buying experience in a retail store that illustrates some idea discussed in this chapter.

2 THE INSTITUTIONS OF RETAILING

Retailers sometimes are imaginative in ferreting out locations that are unusual and often low cost. In Indianapolis developers have remodeled an abandoned railroad station. In Chicago a movie theater has been converted into a multilevel shopping center right in the middle of a densely populated area. And throughout the country service stations that were closed during the 1973–74 petroleum shortage have been made into restaurants, dry cleaning drop-off stations, currency exchanges, and many other types of outlets.

Demographic factors must be watched by retailers very closely because they often foretell what will happen to particular types of businesses. Lane Bryant was founded in 1900 by a young widow who was particularly skilled at sewing maternity clothes. But with the country's population growth slowing, some of the firm's more than 150 outlets have dropped their maternity departments.

Some argue that increased theft is due to the blurring of the distinction between private and public property, while others think it is largely due to the increased use of narcotics. Whatever the cause, retailers have had to respond. An appliance retailer keeps smaller appliances away from doors and elevators where shoplifters might get away quickly. A book retailer places a small disk in the back of each book in his inventory that must be removed as soon as the book is sold; if a thief carries the book out of the department, it will trigger an alarm. A department store uses in-store television. And a phonograph record and tape retailer places a privately hired armed guard in a conspicuous place in front of the store.

A vending machine manufacturer knows that retail customers around the world face many different kinds of problems. Japanese vendors must adjust their machines so that coffee is about twice as sweet as in the United States, and Scandanavian retailers produce coffee twice as strong as in America; the home folks like it that way. And the automatic vending retailers in Latin America purchase machines that can easily accommodate changes in coin size; rampant inflation in that part of the world makes vending by machine more difficult. Retailing problems certainly are not the same everywhere.

Large numbers of retailers began to follow their customers when Americans moved to the suburbs in such large numbers after World War II. Those retailers who remained in the central city fought back in a number of ways, one of which was to shut off selected streets in the downtown area to vehicular traffic. Thus, "pedestrians only" shopping malls have been created where automobiles and trucks were once so dominant. More recently, Europe has begun to suburbanize. Not surprisingly, Amsterdam, Munich, Cologne, Madrid, and many other cities have created versions of a downtown American shopping mall.

These examples demonstrate the fact that successful retailers are those who are most perceptive about the structural, demographic, and behavioral changes that are going on about them. At the end of Chapter 1 we saw that society has a significant impact on retailing. This chapter amplifies that basic, yet vital, theme.

Retailing institutions are those business enterprises that carry out the tasks of retailing. The gamut of these institutions runs from the most rudimentary to highly complex and sophisticated ventures. The simplest form is shown in Figure 2.1, where the producers sell their wares at roadside. This mountain couple harvests wild berries and converts them into jellies and jams for sale to passing consumers. One step up the retailing ladder, insofar as complexity is concerned, is illustrated in Figure 2.2. There a retailer takes his store of goods, produced by others in this case, to the isolated consumer who has no means of getting to the marketplace. These two examples of retail institutions are, of course, virtual anachronisms in today's retailing system and we will devote little time and space to them. Instead, we will examine modern retailing institutions—how and why they evolved.

A theme that recurs throughout this book can be expressed in a truism: Retailing institutions come into existence when a need for them exists. A corollary to this statement points out that retailing institutions die when they no longer fulfill con-

FIGURE 2.1

The simplest type of retailing institution is exemplified by the roadside stand where this couple sell their homemade goods

Source: *The Atlanta Journal-Constitution*, August 2, 1971.

FIGURE 2.2
This retailer brings the marketplace to consumers who have no means of transportation

Source: *The Atlanta Journal-Constitution*, June 1971.

sumer needs. Implicit in these observations is the idea that someone must recognize that an opportunity for a new approach does, in fact, exist, and that person in turn must develop a retailing business to serve this consumer need. Furthermore, the retailer must remain sensitive to changes in the total environment as they take place, adjusting operations to changing conditions.

RETAILER RESPONSE TO CHANGE

The winds of revolutionary change have blown furiously within the retailing industry since 1945. There are at least eight important forces behind this ferment in the retailing system: (1) explosion in population; (2) rising standard of living; (3) increased mobility of householders; (4) technological innovations; (5) improved communications; (6) impact of youth upon society; (7) urbanization; and (8) political and civil unrest.

Population Explosion

One key element of markets for goods and services is the existence of people to buy and use them. In a 30-year period, population in the United States grew from 131 million in 1940 to over 210 million in 1973. By the mid-1970s the growth rate had slowed appreciably. Indeed, in 1973 the national fertility rate was 1.9 children, considerably below the 2.1 figure needed for replacement. Some say that ZPG (zero population growth) will be achieved by about the twenty-first century. If population growth does taper off in the United States, perhaps the number of retailing enterprises will diminish, although those that remain may do more business.

Rising Standard of Living

Data in Table 1.1 showed that personal income in the United States rose from $72.9 billion in 1939 to $360.3 billion in 1958, a five-fold increase in two decades. The following decade witnessed another near-doubling as personal income rose to $687.9 billion in 1968. By January 1974, the figure stood at $1,035.4 billion (all in current dollars). This rapid rise in personal income permitted sales to burgeon to a total of $530 billion in 1974, even though the percentage of personal income committed to retail store purchases declined. The increase in consumer income allowed consumers to buy an increasing volume of goods collected from the four corners of the earth. Each household has increased its purchase of both semiluxury goods and pure luxury goods. This additional volume led to enlargement of the selling areas of most stores. For example, compare the food supermarket of today with its counterparts of ten and more years ago. Supermarkets that opened in 1973 averaged 32,000 square feet in size, compared with 22,000 square feet in 1970, 10,000 square feet in the early 1960s, or 2,000 square feet in 1942. Larger stores are necessary if a greater variety of goods is to be stocked. Some super stores opened in 1974 with 50,000 square feet of space.

One of the most spirited rivalries in the supermarkets is the competition for shelf space by brand manufacturers. This rivalry can be understood if one considers the fact that typical food supermarket shelves contain approximately 7,500 items. In 1941 the same type of store stocked approximately 1,000 items. A new product explosion characterized our society throughout the '50s and '60s and continued into the '70s. An interesting exercise is to visit your favorite food store and count the goods that have been on the market five years or less. It would probably be easier to count the products that have been on the market five years or longer.

Many shops practice a scrambled merchandising policy, which was mentioned in Chapter 1. It simply means that retail stores add lines of products that are significantly different from their traditional inventories. Let's visit Rita's Food Shop and inspect the merchandise offered for sale. First of all, one notices the usual or customary lines, such as groceries, meats, fruits and vegetables, dairy products, and bakery goods. In addition, Rita's stocks health and beauty aids, a line of toys, a limited line of soft goods such as ladies' hosiery and children's clothing, phonograph records, and greeting cards. Rita's is following a scrambled merchandising policy.

A perennial joke is mentioning the difficulty of locating the prescription department in the typical drugstore. One generally finds it in the back of the store since shopping goods are displayed in high traffic locations. (See Figure 2.3.) On the other hand, there are exclusive specialty shops that have narrowed their lines to one

FIGURE 2.3

"Scrambled merchandising" is being used in this drugstore; in addition to prescriptions, tobacco goods, toiletries, cosmetics, cameras, and housewares are part of the merchandise assortment

Source: Jewel Companies, Inc., Chicago, Illinois.

type of product, or perhaps a single item, examples of which are those handling only candies or those specializing in bathroom accessories. Some of these specialty shops are called "boutiques." The word *boutique* comes from the French and is defined as "a well-stocked shop." Boutiques are especially common in the sale of fashion merchandise to women. And there are even prescription drugstores which sell the compounds prescribed by only the doctors of the store's customers.

Limited-line specialty stores are one response of retailers to increased affluence among America's consumers. In 1965 approximately 23 percent of the families in the United States had incomes of $10,000 and over. Figures for 1975 placed the median family income at $12,000 annually, and it is increasing. One reason for the rise in both aggregate income figures and family income is the fact that almost 44 percent of women aged 14 and over are gainfully employed. Furthermore, 60 percent of working women are married. Working wives boost family income and make for more affluent households.

Statistical data indicate a long-term rising standard of living. However, the affluence of today's shoppers can also be seen by inspecting the quality of the merchandise handled by the larger department stores and better specialty shops. It is no longer a novelty to find customers from the middle classes purchasing mink scarves, stoles, or even full length minks. Many people can indulge in expensive hobbies such as boating, photography, or record collecting; hence, many stores are filled with merchandise to cater to these sophisticated tastes. Merchandise of this type often carries a high price tag; yet during prosperous times it sells easily and often. The generally high incomes of today's families permit most people to live better and often to upgrade themselves culturally.

In sum, retail stores are carrying larger inventories with greater variety of merchandise to serve better the affluent consumer's increased needs. Furthermore, a demand for specialized stores has sprung from this rising standard of living.

Mobility of American Consumers

The mobility of the typical householder has increased conspicuously. Estimates place about 100,000,000 automobiles on America's highways. Traffic jams are commonplace; they are more of a pollution problem than a shopping problem. Inasmuch as most shoppers have automobiles at their disposal, the location of shoping areas must take the automobile into consideration. Most major and minor shopping areas are within a short drive of the shopper's home. This opens up many alternatives to the shopper, and his or her loyalty to the traditional main street shopping has been weakened in recent years.

Some time ago the *Chicago Tribune* studied 2,000 households in the Chicago metropolitan area to ascertain the extent of shopper mobility. They found that:[1]

25.5 percent of the households visited 1 to 3 shopping areas during the year.
49 percent of the households visited 4 to 7 shopping areas.
25.5 percent of the households visited 8 or more shopping areas.

An area is defined as either a neighborhood strip center, a shopping plaza, or the central business district. The *Chicago Tribune* study also stated:[2]

> The shopper of today is visiting considerably more shopping areas than the shopper of five years ago. *The modern shopper is becoming increasingly mobile in her shopping activity.*
>
> As our economy experiences even greater growth in the years to come, with a corresponding rise in personal incomes, one would expect shoppers to become more mobile in their shopping habits. This general rise in the level of mobility will undoubtedly derive a major portion of its impetus from the elevation of lower income families to an economic position where they will, for the first time, have a modicum of discretionary income.

Many retailers are aware of the choices that are open to each household; therefore, they endeavor to present an attractive place to shop with ample free parking.

[1]"How Chicago Shops—The Changing Retail Market," *Chicago Tribune* Research Division (1964), p. 12.

[2]Ibid.

They must also stock the right merchandise in the right brands at the right prices. Those merchants who fail to do a good job of merchandising see their customers going to a competitor. The automobile seems to have forced many merchants to do a better job of merchandising, and the consumer is the winner.

The American family has added another dimension to mobility—one-fifth of all households move every year. It is an unusual individual who grows into adulthood and remains in the same neighborhood, city, or even state for his or her entire life. This mixing of people throughout all fifty states has the effect of creating a more homogenerous market. People now buy consumer products that are produced thousands of miles from their point of consumption, as well as those produced close to home. For example, consider the Mizens, a typical suburban family in northern Illinois. They own two cars, one a model made in Germany and the other an American model produced in Detroit. They watch television on a set made in Japan, often while eating ham sandwiches—the ham is sometimes from Iowa, or sometimes from Poland. The lettuce is from California. The bread is baked in Chicago. The program that they are watching could very likely be a pro football game between the Chicago Bears and the Los Angeles Rams—televised live from Los Angeles. The purpose of this illustration is simply to point out that the retailers of today must handle products produced any place in the world, because the market has become accustomed to a choice and demands it.

Technological Progress

Ninety-five percent of all the scientists who have ever lived are still alive today. Their genius has poured out a stream of new products made from materials that were unheard of not many years ago. All of us are aware of artificial fibers such as nylon, acrilan, dylan, and orlon. We now see "fake" furs and diamonds, artificial eyelashes, head pieces, and falls. We have noticed all the appliances that lighten the homemaker's tasks, and we have amused ourselves with hi-fi, stereo, video tape, and home movies. This list of some of the achievements of the technological world points out the fact that retailers share the responsibility of introducing these items to their customers and encouraging their initial use by the consumers. The technological explosion has had a tremendous impact upon retailing, making it much more complex for the retailer who must be alert to changing flows of merchandise available for stocking. Moreover, retailers must reduce inventories of items that suddenly become obsolete because of technological progress.

Improved Communications

We live in an era of instant information. Wars, plagues, disasters, crises, and other scourges are brought into our living rooms through the medium of television, sometimes aided by a satellite transmitter. This phenomonen has definite implications for retailing. In earlier times knowledge of new products and fashions spread slowly throughout the nation, from coastal cities to the interior and from high society circles to lower socioeconomic groups. Now a new hair style, a new style of men's suits, or a new household appliance is seen by millions at the same instant as they sit in their living rooms viewing their favorite television shows.

Retailers in the past went to central markets where they selected merchandise to stock with knowledge that the items had been tested in more sophisticated cities than their own. It was thus not too risky to take on an item, as the fashion cycle would assure the retailer that it would be acceptable in Dubuque next season if it had been in Chicago this year. The buyer still attends trade shows for the purpose of buying merchandise for resale in his or her store, but with mass communication of the instant variety so characteristic of today's marketing, the buying process is no longer so simple for the retailer, nor is it as fail proof. The fashion cycle moves at a much faster pace. Moreover, as consumers learn of new products quickly, they expect retail outlets to make such goods instantly available for purchase. In part, the retailer must be an observer of mass communications media if he or she is to remain sensitive to consumer needs and wishes.

Impact of Youth

One result of the baby boom after World War II is that approximately one-half of our population is under twenty-five years of age. The large number of young people in society has produced many social issues, but the one which affects retailing is the purchasing power of this group.

In the prosperous 1960s, the younger set had as much money to spend as they wished; their discretionary spending power was truly staggering, as sales of phonograph records and tapes readily reflected. It is anticipated that teen-agers and young adults will continue to provide significant market opportunities for many retailers in the coming years.

The youth movement of the '60s affected consumption patterns of the adult population. Some of the manifestations of the "hippie" culture slowly crept into the mainstream of American life, and we saw movement toward unusual clothing and, in some instances, movement away from an emphasis on material goods altogether. The retailer must be a student of all society, even when a "generation gap" exists between his or her values and those of youth. This sensitivity is necessary if the retailer is to tap the youth market, with its swiftly changing patterns of demand as fads come and go, but also to predict changing wants of the general public. Retailers must also realize that the teen-ager of today becomes the householder and different customer of the future, and that habits of purchasing at certain retailing establishments can carry over in future years. Merchandising policies must reflect the important role played by youth in our society and in the retailer's own business success.

Urbanization and Suburbanization

People have become less willing to live in a rural environment or are unable to earn a living there, and the twentieth century has witnessed the growth of large metropolitan areas. Thirty-six percent of all households in the United States are now in apartments. In central cities traffic congestion has long been a major problem. Not only does it take a long time to get through the central business district by automobile, but if you wish to shop, where do you park? Municipalities are forced to build public garages, provide offstreet parking facilities, or meter onstreet parking. Retailers often must invest in parking lots for the use of their customers if they wish to hold onto their patronage. Some retailers have opened branches in outlying areas where parking facilities are available. Other retailers are becoming part of high-rise apartment projects so that the resident dwellers can conveniently shop without worrying about traffic congestion and the lack of parking facilities.

The '60s saw the growth of suburban areas around all major cities. Retailers followed the people out to the suburbs and built huge shopping complexes to accommodate their needs. Most of these suburbanites are in the middle and upper income segments of our society, so they are families with considerable discretionary purchasing power. Many downtown merchants have opened branch stores in suburban shopping plazas to accommodate this lucrative market.

Political and Civil Unrest

The 1960s and early 1970s were turbulent years filled with tensions and general unrest, all having impact on retailers. Much unrest was due to the war in Vietnam. There also was considerable activity to improve the plight of the disadvantaged, erupting into violence in some instances. Central city merchants were forced to adjust to this turbulent tempo. The retailer's prime responsibility is to see that all customers have the opportunity to purchase quality merchandise at fair prices. This objective is difficult to achieve when conditions are chaotic and turbulent. As a result many chain retailers pulled out of the central city or ghetto areas, leaving the residents in worse condition insofar as shopping facilities were concerned. A debate still goes on as to the best way to serve the disadvantaged consumer.

RETAILER RESPONSE TO CHANGE THROUGH STORE LOCATIONS[3]

One way retailers adapt to changing conditions, such as increased mobility of consumers and urbanization and suburbanization, is to locate retail outlets in new places. Although Chapter 5 goes into retail store location in considerable detail, let us examine briefly at this point how the retail structure of major cities has been altered as retailers seek to respond to consumers' ideas of shopping convenience.

Cities have five types of retail structure: (1) the central business district; (2) the outlying business center; (3) the principal business thoroughfare; (4) the neighborhood business street; and (5) the isolated store cluster. A description follows of each of these types.

[3]This section is based in part on Malcolm J. Proudfoot, "City Retail Structure," in *Modern Marketing Thought*, eds. J. Howard Westing and Gerald Albaum (New York: Macmillan Company, 1964), pp. 54–66.

The Central Business District

Traditionally, the principal cities of the United States possess a retail structure which has at its heart a central business district. There retail stores do the greatest volume of business, both individually and collectively, as compared with other areas of the city. In spite of the changes that have taken place in the retailing industry, the traditional "Main Street" is still very much a part of the scene. Many downtown retailers are experiencing their most prosperous years and are looking forward to even greater years of prosperity. On the other hand, some small independent retailers who cling to their sites on a traditional downtown street are in trouble. The degree of their difficulties varies from city to city and among merchants.

Some traditional main streets have witnessed significant declines in the number of shoppers, and a general deterioration in the appearance of the shops. They contrast sharply to the newer stores in regional and community shopping centers and neighborhood shopping plazes, all located to make shopping more attractive, convenient, and complete.

Nevertheless, the central shopping district, through which Main Street passes, is the heart of the retailing structure of any city. Customers still come from all parts of the city and surrounding suburbs. There the large department stores, specialty shops, and chain variety stores are concentrated. All types of merchandise can be found in the central shopping district. Generally this consists of household goods, appliances, ladies' and men's wear, jewelry, shoes, sportswear, records, cameras, and other shopping or specialty goods. The size of the city dictates to a large degree the size of the central shopping district. In any case the stores are usually larger than similar stores within the city. This is the place where one is directed if he or she asks for the downtown shopping areas. In large cities such as New York, Chicago, or San Francisco, one also finds that the large hotels and restaurants, office buildings, and theaters are located in the central shopping district. Intensive land use prevails, and normally rents are high, as are real estate taxes; both reflect the high cost of land. Into these areas, the mass transportation systems bring workers, shoppers, and fun seekers. Traffic is extremely heavy and parking is a severe problem.

In smaller cities, villages, and towns, the central shopping district may be the only shopping area of the town. There are clustered all the stores of the community, whether they sell shopping goods, convenience goods, or specialty goods.

Outlying Business Centers

The outlying business district is a miniature of the retail structure found in the central business district. There a concentration of stores does considerable business volume, both as individual shops and collectively as a retailing area. However, the volume of business is usually less than that of the central district. The customers who are attracted to these areas do not come from all over the city, but nevertheless are people who are willing to travel long distances to shop in these stores. Frequently, these areas develop where two major streets intersect; in foreign countries, such centers often are located near important railway stations.

The Principal Business Thoroughfare

The principal business thoroughfare is both a business street and a traffic artery. Proudfoot says:

> As a business street it possesses large, widely spaced shopping and convenience goods stores. As a traffic artery it carries a heavy density of mass and vehicular traffic. This dense traffic primarily results from attractive forces exerted on residential population by the central business district or some outlying business center.[4]

Neighborhood Business Street

The neighborhood business street draws its customers from nearby homes, an easy walking distance away. This type of retail structure contains supermarkets, bakeries, drugstores, and other stores handling convenience goods. Occasionally, a few stores handling shopping goods are included.

If the city is very large, one sees a continuous line of shops strung out for blocks along major arterial streets. Often these shops are uncoordinated with each other and unplanned. Sometimes these shopping districts serve an ethnic culture that dominates a particular neighborhood. The string shopping districts are in reality outlying business centers, principal business thoroughfares, and neighborhood streets merged into one continuous line of stores.

Isolated Store Cluster

These stores are located in sparsely settled areas. More often than not there are only a few stores in the cluster, often including a food store and a drugstore.

In a general sort of way we can see that each of the last four types of urban shopping areas materialized because cities grew in size. The new types were established to make certain kinds of shopping more convenient for consumers. But a major question remains: Why did downtown decline?

DECLINE OF DOWNTOWN

The central shopping district, and to a lesser extent the secondary business districts, in most cities are plagued with declining sales and profits. You may have noticed the number of vacant stores in your city's downtown area. Traditional street shopping districts are declining in relative importance as planned shopping centers continue to emerge at all levels of competition. The reasons for the decline of Main Street are:

1. Shift of affluent population to suburban locations.
2. Increased use of automobiles for shopping and, therefore, a need for more convenient parking.

[4]Ibid., p. 55.

3. Development of newer and more attractive buildings in planned shopping areas.
4. Changing buying habits of shoppers.

The decline of Main Street has not gone unchallenged by downtown merchants. These merchants are interested in preserving their place in retailing, and are now taking remedial actions. In community after community, downtown development committees are being set up to study the problem and to offer solutions. Merchants are seeking cooperative actions from local governments to revitalize downtown areas. This often leads to urban redevelopment projects that tear down old slum areas, construct new civic centers, improve traffic flow, construct new parking facilities, and encourage retailers to modernize their stores and facilities. In some cases the downtown areas are beautified by planting trees, constructing flower beds at strategic locations, hanging baskets of artificial flowers from light poles, or blocking off entrances to streets so that mall areas can be constructed.

Not everyone believes that downtown is being revitalized properly. For example, E. B. Weiss thinks the downtown area is suffering from "middle-age bulge."[5] He uses this phrase to show that there are too many older shoppers and too few young shoppers in downtown stores. Weiss claims that the average downtown shopper is 45 years of age. Furthermore, he believes that downtown merchants neglect their own areas because their attention is focused on the suburban shopping centers. As a consequence, the downtown area declined as a place to live, a place to shop, and a place for entertainment. To salvage the downtown area, Weiss thinks retailers must become more youth oriented. He says:

> My only suggestion for downtown retailing will be that it must develop a strategy aimed at persuading the all-important young generations to form the downtown habit—a strategy that should be part of a total concept developed by all interests to increase downtown's appeal to the younger generation.[6]

The strategy to attract young shoppers must take into account the activist role played by young people today. Downtown must offer the opportunity for young singles and young marrieds to live nearby. Entertainment must be available to fit both their tastes and their pocketbooks. It is not enough to hold an occasional rock concert, and expect young people to support the downtown area. If the downtown shopping district is to experience a renaissance, it will come about through combined efforts aimed at revitalizing the total environment of the district.

PLANNED SHOPPING CENTERS

Traditional street shopping areas were not planned but rather evolved. In general they grew as the population expanded and individuals, partnerships, or corporations saw a need for a particular kind of retailing. After World War II there was

[5]E. B. Weiss, "Downtown Retailers Must Think Young," *Marketing Insights*, 3, no. 6 (November 4, 1968), pp. 10–11.

[6]Ibid., p. 10.

a marked decentralization of retail trade as merchants followed people as they moved into the outer reaches of the metropolitan area.

A shopping center is a cluster of stores, arranged in different patterns, that provides off the street parking for customers. In some instances, tenants of the center are chosen to limit direct competition; hence the stores are selected with the market potential of each line of merchandise carefully considered. However, in recent years astute retailers have recognized that the presence of competing retailers is likely to draw more customers to the center, so in the larger centers it is common to see two food stores competing with each other. The architecture of the center is uniform and modern, and each retailer operates an attractive store. Most shopping centers have a name, and in most cases, all merchants participate in promotions designed to benefit the entire center as well as the individual retailers.

Classification of Shopping Centers

Planned shopping centers are classified as follows: (1) regional shopping centers, (2) community shopping centers, and (3) neighborhood shopping centers.

Regional Shopping Centers. The regional shopping center is the largest of the three types and is located outside of a central city on an arterial highway or expressway. People come for many miles to shop here. In Chicago one of the earliest regional shopping centers was Old Orchard, with a primary trading area of over 100 square miles.[7]

To acquaint you with a regional shopping center, we have selected Randhurst as an example. It is located approximately 22 miles northwest of downtown Chicago, in an area that is both heavily populated and prosperous. There are 90 tenant merchants offering a variety of merchandise that can be classified as shopping goods, convenience goods, and specialty goods. Besides retailers, tenants offer professional services, including doctors, dentists, insurance firms, and accountants. There is also a bank on the first floor and a community meeting hall in the lower level.

Randhurst can be classified as a mall-type shopping center, that is, one where the building is placed in the center of the acreage with parking all around. The entire complex is under one roof, thus permitting a 72-degree climate all year. Colorful lockers are placed near all entrances so that shoppers may shop without coats. All stores front onto the center of the mall. A regional shopping center such as Randhurst draws customers from a wide area, perhaps serving and trading an area of 1,000,000 people. There are parking places for 7,500 automobiles. Moreover, the entire shopping area contains 1,250,000 square feet, of which 940,000 feet is selling area. Its three department stores occupy 575,000 square feet of the selling area. Figure 2.4 is a schematic diagram of Randhurst. Notice that the three department stores are at the points of a triangle.

Old Orchard and Oak Brook shopping centers are two other major regional centers in the Chicago area that feature the center mall. However, neither is en-

[7]*Chicago Tribune Study*, p. 33.

FIGURE 2.4

Note the strategic placement of a large department store at each corner of Randhurst, a mall-type regional shopping center

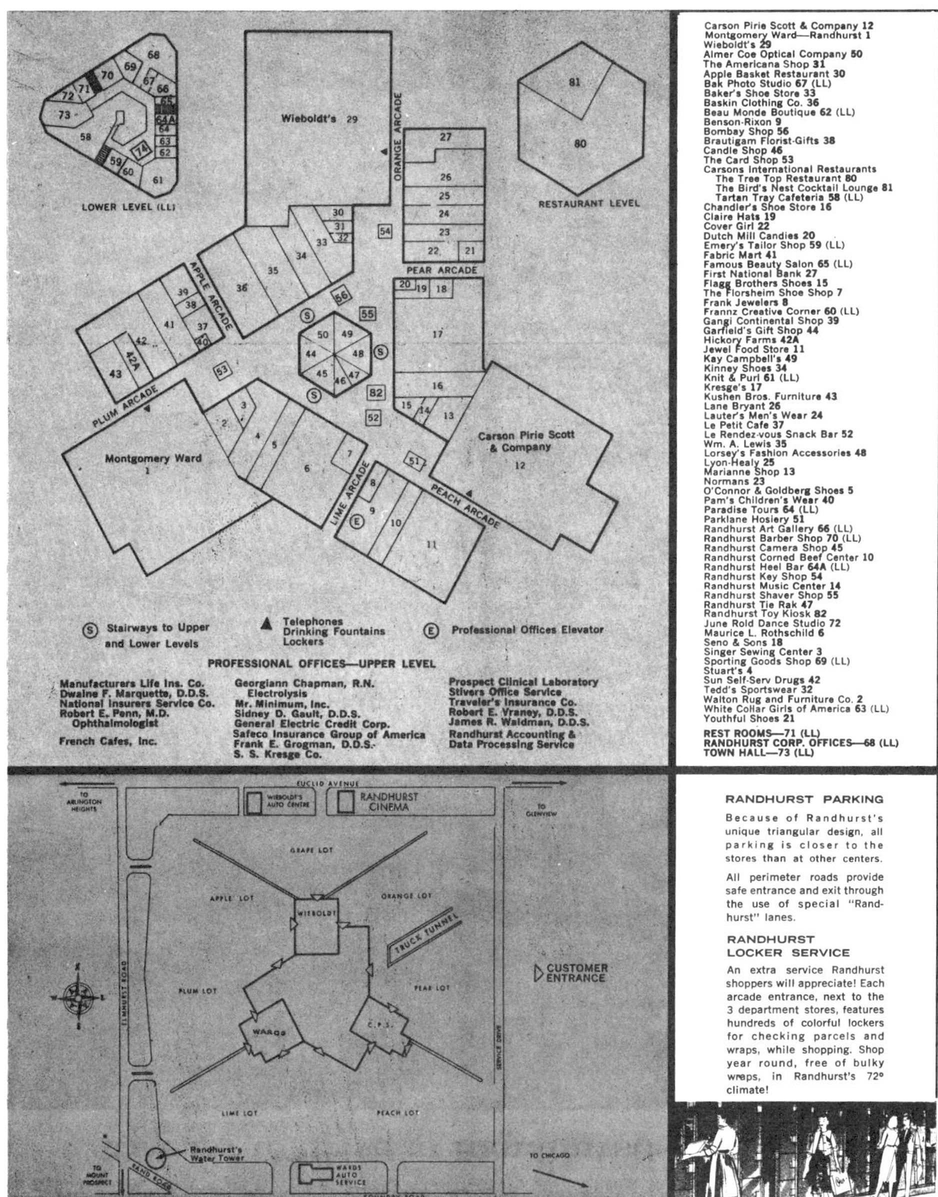

Source: Randhurst Corporation, Mount Prospect, Illinois.

closed, so the shopper must go outside to enter another store. Marshall Field and Company is the leading department store in these centers.

The Community Shopping Center. The community-type shopping center is smaller than the regional center and draws customers from a more limited geographical area. It serves no more than 10,000 families, and the entire complex occupies only 10 to 20 acres. In essence, it is thought of as a junior size regional shopping center, with a small department store at its hub. The center carries a fairly complete line of shopping, convenience, and specialty goods. Like all planned shopping centers, it has ample free parking, and it is located close to heavily populated suburban towns and villages.

The Neighborhood Shopping Center. The neighborhood shopping center is much smaller than the other two and carries a very limited selection of merchandise, generally of a convenience good type. This kind of center is the most numerous and is located throughout the United States. Many are of the "strip type"—that is, the stores are set alongside a major thoroughfare, but far enough from the street to permit front-door parking.

Shopping centers are excellent illustrations of retail institutions emerging to meet changing conditions in the marketplace. The failure of downtown shopping areas to provide convenience to consumers led to the establishment and prosperity of suburban shopping centers. Two other retailing institutions—discount stores and vending—buttress this principle.

DISCOUNT STORES

The discount store is a product of the era immediately following World War II. It developed as manufacturers satisfied the pent-up demands of war-rationed consumers, and surpluses of goods began to build up. By 1950 these surpluses in both "hard goods" and "soft goods" were so large that many manufacturers made merchandise available to anyone who wished to sell it. Davidson and Doody summarize the development as follows:

> During the early 1950s the pent-up demand for consumer goods that followed World War II was almost altogether satisfied, and a "buyers market" prevailed. Generally speaking, merchandising shortages had turned into surpluses. This was especially the case for durable goods manufacturers, who found it difficult to make substantial cuts in production due to their cost structures. Established distribution outlets, wholesale and retail, were provided added incentives to move more goods, but still there were surpluses. It was relatively easy, therefore, for additional stores such as discount houses to obtain merchandise which they could sell at lower prices because of their unorthodox operating methods. For example, merchandising emphasis was predominantly on items that could be bought under exceptionally favorable circumstances, rather than under planned assortments. Services were generally eliminated or if available at all, a separate charge was commonly made. Stress was placed upon low mark-up, minimum expense, higher turnover, and maximum returns for inventory investment.[8]

[8]William R. Davidson and Alton F. Doody, "The Future of Discounting," *Journal of Marketing*, 27, no. 1 (January 1963), p. 36.

This explanation, of course, emphasizes the supply side of the picture. Consumers had to exist on the demand side if the discount movement was to catch on. By looking at what we mean by the term, we can show that side of the discounting coin.

What Is a Discount Store?

Sometimes called a "mass merchandiser," a discount store is a retail establishment that sells merchandise which is usually readily identified by shoppers, at less than traditional prices. Usually the merchandise assortment consists of nationally branded products with high levels of consumer acceptance. The discount store possesses the following characteristics:

1. Price is the major sales appeal.
2. Target customers are economy minded.
3. Buildings and fixtures are inexpensive.
4. Customer service is de-emphasized.
5. Merchandise is advertised aggressively.
6. Merchandise is turned over rapidly.
7. Stores are strategically located to be available to large masses of people.
8. Stores feature long hours and are open Sundays (if legal).
9. Acres of free parking are provided for the convenience of the shoppers.
10. Emphasis is on well-known brands so that price comparison is easier.

Acceptance of Discounting

Discount stores are eagerly accepted by some of the public in spite of the reduction in store services. This is especially true of young married couples who are anxious to stretch their buying dollars. The long store hours appeal to most shoppers, as do Sunday openings. Furthermore, the promotional gimmicks of the discount store give an air of excitement to the entire operation. The major reason for a discount store's popularity is, of course, the lower prices that customers obtain on branded merchandise, as compared with the prices charged by other retailers for the same or similar merchandise. In the beginning, the discounters were given very little competition by orthodox retailers. These merchandisers were more concerned about maintaining list or fair trade prices among themselves than in the prices charged by discounters. Also they were intimately involved in the downtown store location vis à vis the shopping center. In any case discount stores caught the public's fancy, and by 1960 they were well entrenched in retailing.

Sometime during the 1960s the discount store matured and became "respectable." This is evidenced in part by the architecture and fixtures of the new stores, the types and quality of customer services, and their more exacting standards for their salespeople. They are practicing the same type of merchandising techniques that characterize the more orthodox competitor. The wheel of retailing continues to turn.

At this point, you might assume that all discount stores are alike. This is not the case, for substantial differences do exist among them. Some of these differences are:

1. Some stores emphasize "hard lines" (e.g., refrigerators and stoves) while others emphasize "soft lines" (e.g., wearing apparel).
2. Some discount stores have food departments, others do not.
3. Some discount stores own all the departments within the store, others lease out departments.
4. Some stores feature "distress" merchandise (e.g., goods bought from bankrupt firms), others sell more conventional goods.
5. There is a vast difference in locations. Some prefer shopping plazas (although they are sometimes unwelcome), others prefer to go it alone, while still others choose more conventional locations.

Some traditional retailers have adopted the principle that "if you can't beat them, join them." This has been especially true of variety stores. For example, F. W. Woolworth operates the Woolco Discount Store, and S. S. Kresge operates K-Mart. Jewel Tea Company, primarily a food chain, has opened the Turnstyle Center for soft goods; they also operate the Osco Drugstore, a discount drugstore similar to Walgreen's.

Discounting was already a $20 billion business when W. T. Triplett, Jr., president of Bazar, Inc., a West Coast discounter, paid tribute to the discount industry in these words:

> The *discount industry* is the *fastest growing* segment of American retailing. In the span of just 10 years the industry has passed the variety chain volume, the drug chain volume, and last year, the department store volume—sales in this fledgling industry reached $18 billion, are expected to exceed $20 billion this year, and reach $25 billion by 1975. Truly a dynamic situation—unmatched by any other.[9]

Discounters are not without their problems, however. By 1974 a number of large and well-known discounters were experiencing difficulties, and one—Arlan's Department Stores—had petitioned for bankruptcy. The source of the difficulties is hard to identify, but three suggestions have been made. First, the major appeal of discounters is price, a strategy that is easily "neutralized." Price concessions to meet other retailers who compete on a price basis can result in such low gross margins that it is impossible to cover a firm's costs and earn a profit. In short, discounters have selected the strategy that is least likely to result in customer loyalty. Second, it is said that some discounters have not adjusted their ways of doing business in response to changes in their customers. Perhaps this suggests that as Americans grow wealthier they do not respond quite so quickly to those who sell on the basis of low prices. Third, shopping center operators often have refused to lease space to discounters, apparently believing that such stores would adversely affect the sales of more "legitimate" shops. The Federal Trade Commission took note of

[9]W. T. Triplett, Jr., in an address to the Portland Society of Financial Analysts, 1970, p. 4.

this practice, and beginning in November, 1973, initiated a series of moves to open up shopping centers to discount houses. Numerous developers and large leasees have signed consent orders in which they agree not to discriminate on the basis of price policy, type of advertising, or the type or quality of goods sold.

Thus, starting as a device to speed up the distribution of products, the discount house has become a major force in the retailing system of the nation. These mass merchandisers are now an integral part of the consumer's normal shopping pattern. While some services may still be omitted in exchange for lower prices, the latter are now possible more because of huge sales volumes than from the shortage of customer services. The discount store is an example of the retailing system's responsiveness to the natural desire of the general public to want more goods for their money income. In a period of rising expectations, the discount house reduced potential customer frustration.

AUTOMATIC VENDING

The vending industry provides a contrasting illustration of retailing's adaptability. In the case of machine vending, the response is not to consumers' desires for economy, but rather to their desires for convenience. Nearness of merchandise in time and place relative to the customer is the dominant facet of the operation. Prices are often higher than in regular retail outlets.

Although people frequently think that the vending machine is a product of the machine age, ancient Egyptians used coin-activated machines in their temples as early as 215 B.C. There is no evidence that vending machines were in use any place thereafter until the seventeenth century. At that time snuff and tobacco boxes were activated by coins in English inns and taverns. These devices were quite crude, and a few may still be found in museums and private antique collections. In the nineteenth century vending machines were taken seriously for the first time. Throughout Europe various inventors patented machines to sell stamps, candy, gum, and tobacco.[10]

The first product successfully sold through vending machines in the United States was chewing gum. Thomas Adams used machines to sell his gum on New York elevated platforms in 1888. (See Figure 2.5, pp. 44-45.)

The Nature of the Vending Industry

Vending is big business. In 1970 the industry chalked up a record sales volume, exceeding $6 billion.[11] When one considers that in 1946 total industry sales stood at a relatively modest $66 million, the growth that has occurred is evident. In Europe, sales through machines are even more important. A large variety of goods

[10] G. R. Schreiber, "A Concise History of Vending in the U.S.A.," *Vend Magazine* (Chicago, 1961), pp. 9–12.

[11] *Vend, Food Service and Vending Management*, 1971 Census of the Industry (New York, May 1, 1971).

FIGURE 2.5

The postal card vending machine (circa 1886) and the combination cigar and gum vending machine (circa 1900) are part of the history of vending in the United States, where the first patent was issued in 1884

Source: "A Concise History of Vending in the United States," *Vend* Magazine.

are sold "after hours" in front of many retail outlets. For example, in the Netherlands even cut flowers are sold through vending machines.

Vending in America is largely confined to a few standard items, including candies, tobacco products, soft drinks, milk, and prepared foods. Cigarettes are by far the most important product vended, accounting for approximately one-third of all sales through machines. Bottled soft drinks account for about 11 percent of vended sales. It is estimated that 6,000 companies are engaged in vending, with 52 percent of this total in food vending. Plants and factories are the most important

FIGURE 2.5 (cont.)

sites for vending machines, and in 1970 they accounted for 35 percent of all vended sales.[12]

The Future of Vending

The future of the vending industry appears bright. Some people are optimistically forecasting the day when variety stores, department stores, and food supermarkets will consist solely of vending machines. Malcolm Morris, however, believes there are a number of barriers to the growth of automatic vending, and he claims these barriers will act as limiting factors for many years.[13] The chief barrier is the consumer himself. For a variety of reasons—some psychological—the consumer hesitates to accept vending machines wholeheartedly. Morris points out that a vending machine is not an acceptable substitute for a salesperson. He says:

[12]Ibid.

[13]Malcolm L. Morris, "Growth Parameters for Automatic Vending," *Journal of Retailing*, 44, no. 3 (Fall 1968), pp. 31–45.

> Why would a person who buys coffee from a vending machine located at his place of work tend to rebel at the idea of purchasing coffee from a vending machine in a restaurant? And why would this same person not hesitate to purchase cigarettes from a vending machine either at work or in a fine restaurant? The answer lies, at least in part, in the social and psychological elements of the purchase situation.[14]

Regardless of what the future brings, one can conclude that the vending machine is here to stay and that its sales will continue to grow. This is especially true for standard items such as cigarettes, candy, and food. Vending seems to be a natural for hospitals, schools, offices, and factories. Experiments will be run to learn the feasibility of selling different products via vending machines and in varied locations. The vending route to retail innovation holds considerable promise as retailers strive to respond to consumer needs and desires.

THE RETAILING OF FOOD[15]

The retailing of food accounted for more than $130.8 billion in retail sales in 1974; thus, it merits mention in any discussion of retail institutions. Furthermore, the retail food industry furnishes another illustration of the sensitivity of retailing to changing needs of consumers.

The Supermarket

The major impetus for the development of the supermarket was the Great Depression of the 1930s. The early operators in the field of supermarketing were in effect discount sellers of food products long before the current discount house came on the retailing scene. Innovators leased abandoned warehouses and similar structures as retail stores. In them they placed open boxes of canned foods, as well as bulk items and produce staples. Consumers walked through this disarray of merchandise with baskets over their arms. After making their selections, they proceeded to the cashier where the transactions were consummated.

Clarence Saunders experimented with the *self-service principle* in his Piggly-Wiggly stores before 1920, although the idea did not catch on until later. Its standard method of operation was founded upon price appeal, with practically no services being provided by the store—no personal selling, no delivery, no credit.

This retailing innovation caught on rapidly, because other conditions were favorable for its success. By the 1930s a life-and-death struggle was going on between independent food retailers and the giant chain organizations which were beginning to capture the industry. The largest was A & P, as the Great Atlantic and Pacific Tea Company was called. This chain operated as many as 15,000 individual store units at its height. (The number in 1974 was 3,680.)[16] These stores

[14]Ibid., p. 39.

[15]Statistics on supermarkets taken from "41st Annual Report of the Grocery Industry," *Progressive Grocer* (April 1974).

[16]A & P announced in March 1975 that they would shut down one-third of its stores as soon as they could negotiate out of leases and appease unions. (Most of these stores are marginal and in central cities.)

were, of course, really only neighborhood shops within easy walking distance of the household; it was believed that the typical woman would not walk more than six blocks for her grocery needs. The family automobile broke the housewife's dependence on the neighborhood store. Before the supermarket could catch on as a retailing institution, people had to have the mobility that the personal car provided. The auto, along with the economic pressure of the Depression on the family budget, furnished the climate needed for the supermarket to flourish.

Another environmental ingredient was the mechanical refrigerator. Before the consumer could move away from the pattern of daily trips to the grocery store, the household had to have a place to store perishables. Household grocery storage made the costs of trips to more distant stores worthwhile when balanced against price savings offered by the new supermarkets.

What Is a Supermarket? Personal experience tells us what a supermarket is, as all of us patronize such retail establishments with some degree of regularity. One marketing authority defines a supermarket as:

> A large-scale, departmentalized retailing institution offering a wide variety of merchandise (including groceries, meats, produce, and dairy products), operating largely on a self-service basis with a minimum of customer services, and featuring a price appeal and usually ample parking space.[17]

A distinction based on sales volume is often made, with an annual sales volume of $1 million needed to call the store a supermarket. When such terminology is used, a "superette" is then defined as any food store doing between $500,000 and $1 million sales volume. Table 2.1 shows the dominance of the supermarket in the retailing of food, with more than three-fourths of the industry's sales volume occurring in these outlets. This dominance is the continuation of a long existing trend. In 1952, for instance, supermarkets captured only 39 percent of the total food sales, moving to 65 percent in 1960 and 71.8 percent in 1974.

The Struggle between Independent versus Chain Stores. The development of the supermarket played an important role in the fight between chain stores and independent operators in the food retailing industry. (An operator of 11 or more stores is classified here as a chain, with the firm owning 10 or less stores being designated an independent.) The relative importance of both types can be seen in Table 2.1. Chain stores, partially because they had so much money invested in traditional stores, were slow to seize the supermarket opportunity. Not until after World War II did the old line food chains start to move aggressively to the supermarket. This delay permitted independent newcomers to prosper in the field, in many cases developing new chain operations themselves.

Another important factor that slowed the demise of the independent retailer brought by chain store competition was the development of the so-called voluntary and cooperative chains in the 1930s. A voluntary group exists when independent retailers affiliate with a wholesaler at the wholesaler's behest; the retailers joining

[17]William J. Stanton, *Fundamentals of Marketing*, 4th ed. (New York: McGraw-Hill Book Company, 1975), p. 359.

TABLE 2.1
Food Sales by Types of Stores for the Year 1974

	Number of Stores	*Dollar Volume in Millions*	*Percentage of Total Volume*
Supermarkets			
Chain	19,690	$58,760	44.9
Independent	11,740	35,200	26.9
Total	31,430	93,960	71.8
Superettes			
Chain	2,000	1,600	1.2
Independent	9,500	8,075	6.2
Total	11,500	9,675	7.4
Small Stores			
Chain	2,500	880	0.7
Independent	130,000	21,000	16.0
Total	132,500	21,880	16.7
Convenience	22,700	5,320	4.1

Source: "42nd Annual Report of the Grocery Industry," *Progressive Grocer* (April 1975), p. 59.

the voluntary chain adopt common store fronts and merchandising techniques and agree to purchase from the sponsoring wholesaler. Examples are the I.G.A. (Independent Grocers' Alliance) and the Rexall Drug Stores in the drugstore field of retailing.

The cooperative chain comes about when independent retailers band together to perform the wholesaling function. Both initiative and ownership rests with the retailers. An example is Certified Grocers. In 1974 voluntary groups accounted for 52 percent of all independent stores by affiliations; cooperative groups accounted for 35 percent; with unattached independents accounting for 13 percent. The voluntary and cooperative methods have made it possible for independents to compete successfully with chain retailers in food and other retailing lines. Chapter 6 is devoted to further discussion of the advantages and disadvantages of various organizational structures available to retail firms.

Nonfoods

Broadening of merchandise lines is a popular retailing strategy; it is part of the ferment that characterizes a dynamic business environment. Once supermarkets captured the bulk of the public's demand for food products, it was only logical that ingenious retailers would experiment to see if the heavy floor traffic generated by supermarkets could be persuaded to buy nonfood items while food shopping. The price was dramatically lower than was customarily charged in the traditional outlet for the product. We now see more than one-half of all toothpaste being sold in supermarkets rather than in drugstores, formerly the traditional source. Other examples readily come to mind. Customers liked the idea of doing more than just food shopping on a trip to the supermarket.

Nonfoods in 1974 accounted for nearly $7,297,000 of supermarket sales. Table 2.2 shows how that sales volume is divided among various product categories. The Health and Beauty Aids (HBA) group is by far the most important.

TABLE 2.2
Nonfood Sales by Categories for 1974

Categories	*Sales*	*% of Total Nonfood Sales*
Health and beauty aids	$3,666,000	50.2
Housewares, hardware	1,556,000	21.3
Soft goods, pantyhose	570,000	7.8
Magazines and books	413,000	5.7
Stationery, school supplies	193,000	2.7
Sewing notions, yarns	97,000	1.3
Greeting cards	64,000	0.9
Photo films, flash, finishing	124,000	1.7
Pet supplies	146,000	2.0
Continuity, seasonal, and all other	468,000	6.4
Total all nonfoods	$7,297,000	100

Source: "42nd Annual Report of the Grocery Industry," *Progressive Grocer* (April 1975), p. 165.

The Convenience Food Store

The great success of the supermarket led to the opportunity for the convenience, or *bantam*, food outlet. Most householders make one or two trips to one or more supermarkets weekly, where the bulk of the family's food and related needs are purchased. However, items are inevitably left off shopping lists, or emergency needs spring up between trips. Because the typical supermarket is so huge and the checkout lines are usually long and slow-moving, the consumer often dreads another time-consuming trip. Therefore, the old-fashioned grocery store, which had been killed off by the supermarket movement, came back into existence in the form of the convenience store.

What Is a Convenience Store? According to *Progressive Grocer*, there were 22,700 convenience stores handling a full line of grocery products in the United States in 1974.[18] The National Association of Convenience Stores defines the institution in these words:

> A convenience store is as follows: Building size—1,000 to 3,200 square feet and parking for 5 to 15 cars; store hours extend beyond other area markets; self-service offering complete convenience of shopping; balanced inventory for daily needs to include dairy, bakery, beverages, tobacco, frozen foods, delicate items, grocery products, health and beauty aids, limited produce, and nonfood items. A convenience store should not be considered direct competition to the supermarket, but rather complements the larger store.[19]

[18] *Progressive Grocer* (April 1975), p. 59.

[19] *Progressive Grocer* (April 1967), p. 204.

Progressive Grocer makes this further observation:

> In certain ways convenience stores are a revival of the old-fashioned mom and pop grocery store. However, they have the added self-service layout, a complete stock selection, and easy drive-up parking. Their seven-day-a-week policy, late hours, complete with good housekeeping procedures and neighborhood friendliness are other major reasons for their success.[20]

Figure 2.6 illustrates a typical convenience store floor plan.

FIGURE 2.6
This typical convenience store layout is designed so that customers can easily locate goods

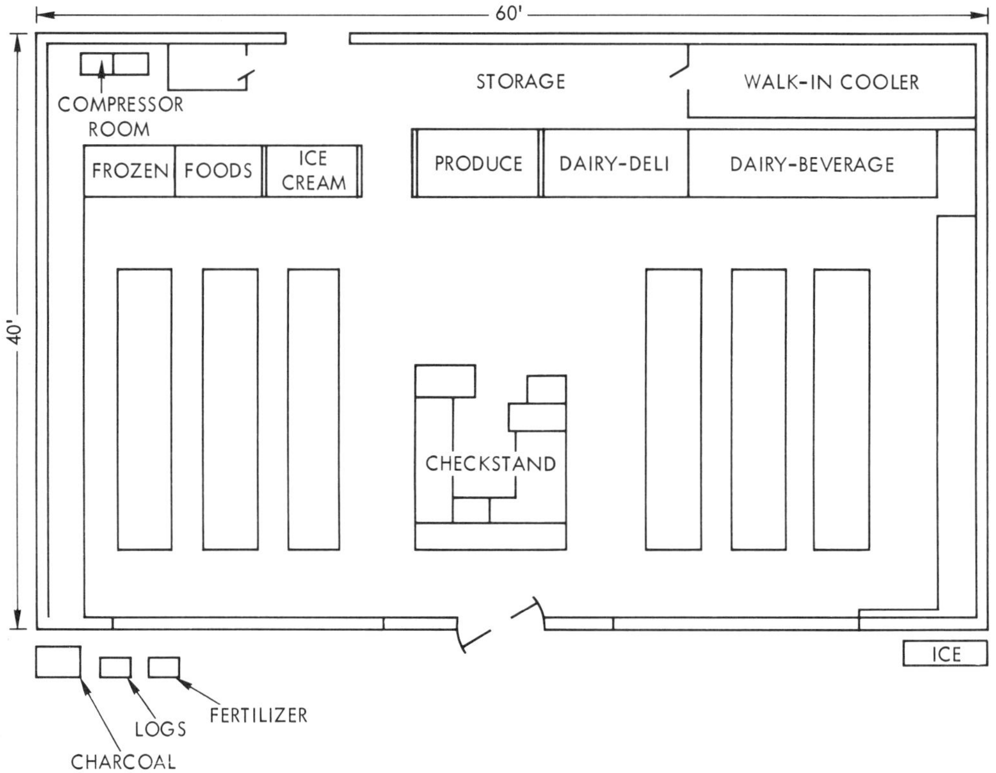

Source: *Supermarketing* Magazine, January 1971, p. 69.

Convenience stores sell the same high volume items found in large supermarkets but their offerings are limited to the most popular brands. Prices charged per item are appreciably higher than those found in supermarkets. The stores achieve

[20]Ibid., p. 204.

higher margins on sales; thus, customers make monetary sacrifices for the kind of convenience that is offered by these outlets. The trade name of one of the industry's leaders, 7–11 Stores, dramatically tells the public that the convenience store is open from 7 A.M. to 11 P.M. (See Figure 2.7). Several major gasoline retailers are

FIGURE 2.7

A pioneer in the convenience store industry, 7-Eleven stores are familiar sights throughout the United States and in parts of Canada

Source: The Southland Corporation, Dallas, Texas.

now combining their operations with convenience food stores; sometimes the bays formerly used for oiling and lubricating automobiles are converted into food selling areas. Table 2.3 provides some operating statistics for convenience stores. We can expect to see more of these stores established throughout the nation as traffic congestion mounts and regular supermarkets get bigger and bigger. In many major

TABLE 2.3

Statistical Data for Convenience Stores, 1974

Average annual sales per store	$234,360
Number of stores	22,700
Total sales	5,320,000,000
Average net profit before taxes	4.81%

Source: *Progressive Grocer* (April 1975), pp. 117–18.

cities supermarkets have lengthened their operating hours, thus neutralizing one of the major weapons of the convenience stores. Where this has happened—usually in densely populated neighborhoods—convenience stores have begun to experience difficulties.

SUMMARY

The dramatic change in retailing institutions over the past two or three decades was the result of many pressures in the nation's environment. At least eight of these forces were discussed in this chapter. Our major goal is to highlight how retailing institutions respond to changes in society.

The physical location of stores and shopping districts furnishes good evidence of this responsiveness on the part of the retailing industry. Whereas most retailing was once carried on in the central shopping district of the city, we now see a retailing mix consisting of outlying business centers, principal business thoroughfares, and neighborhood business streets, as well as isolated store clusters. With the decline in importance of the downtown shopping area came the planned shopping center. This retailing institution changed the retailing of shopping and specialty goods immeasurably.

TABLE 2.4
Where America Spends Its Retail Dollar, 1974

Food stores	22.3%
Automotive dealers	17.3
Department stores	10.4
Other retail stores	12.4
Eating, drinking places	7.8
Gasoline service station	7.4
Lumber, building materials, farm equipment, hardware dealers	4.0
Apparel, accessory stores	4.6
Furniture, home furnishings, equipment stores	4.8
Variety stores	1.6
Drugstores, proprietary stores	3.1
Nonstore retailers	2.3
Liquor stores	2.0
Total	100 %

Source: *Progressive Grocer* (April 1975), p. 62.

Another important innovation of the period was the discount store, which deemphasized personal selling by substituting low prices, store availability, and brand name merchandise as motivating factors in the buying process. In a different way, vending machines serve consumer desires for convenience.

Further examples of retailer responsiveness are found in the supermarket and convenience store methods of selling food products. Both have carved significant niches in the retailing structure of the nation. Other forms of retailing provide additional proof that institutions must adapt to changing conditions. Their reasons for existing are gone if they fail to do so, and the institutions fade from the scene.

QUESTIONS FOR DISCUSSION

1. Why has the retailing mix of the United States changed so dramatically in recent decades?
2. How can a food supermarket implement a scrambled merchandising policy?
3. It is said that affluence is creating a mass market of the upper income consumers. If this is true, what course of action would you advise the proprietor of a specialty shop featuring ladies' dresses to take?
4. Describe the central shopping district with which you are personally familiar.
5. State the major reasons for the decline of "traditional Main Street."
6. Assume that you are called in as a consultant by a group of merchants representing a central shopping district. You are asked for suggestions for the revitalization of Main Street. What would you suggest?
7. Why has the discount store flourished?
8. Discuss the past and future of vending as a retailing institution.
9. Contrast the functions performed by the supermarket and the convenience store in the retailing of food.
10. Define the following:
    a. voluntary chain
    b. cooperative chain
    c. supermarket
    d. superette
    e. independent

3 CONSUMER BEHAVIOR AND RETAILING

Psychological and Physiological Influences

A Ford dealer in Seattle is well aware that a new automobile is a very important purchase to most people, one that requires much agonizing before the transaction takes place and even a great deal of postpurchase thought. The dealer sends a letter to each new car buyer a few days after the automobile is delivered, assuring the buyer that he or she has made a wise decision. He believes that many buyers are looking for confirmation that they were shrewd customers and made a "good deal." The dealer may never have heard of "cognitive dissonance," but he is acting to reduce it among his customers. If he is successful, they probably will come back to him for their next car and even recommend him to their friends.

One of the many road signs outside the Amsterdam Central Railway Station states that it is only 5,397 miles to Wall Drug Store, Wall, South Dakota. Not many Netherlanders give it much attention, but to passing American tourists it stands out in sharp contrast to the other signs. The store is best known for serving free ice water to parched tourists enroute to somewhere else, but is actually a large general store. The sign, because of its location, is an effective and incongruous cue that Americans are likely to see and remember for a long time.

In-store advertising is not new. But a Memphis company places television sets in the aisles of cooperating food stores, and advertisements are shown on the screen. To attract attention, cameras occasionally focus on customers, whose pictures are then shown on the screens throughout the store. The Memphis firm argues that it is a rare customer who won't watch the screen carefully if he or she thinks the camera may pan in his or her direction. We are all egoists. (The system is also used for surveillance by the store's security force.)

The manager of the bridal shop in a Milwaukee department store has not yet found a way to use the findings of a study sponsored by the Bridal Apparel Association, which argues that the divorce rate among couples married in formal wear is only about half that of those whose weddings were informal. The manager would like to use the evidence; marriage is an emotion laden step and one that can be very profitable if the emotional needs are properly satisfied. But getting such information to ministers, priests, rabbis, and other counselors is not easy without making it seem self-serving. Besides, the counselors are sure to point out that correlation does not prove causation.

A large but perhaps declining number of European housewives still perceive themselves as being mainly interested in the home, children, and cooking. To cater to those who believe food is a central part of life, London has Fortnum and Mason, where the salesmen still wear morning coats; Paris has Fauchon; and Munich has Dallmayr's, where a shopper can select from over 100 kinds of wurst, over 50 cheeses, and countless types of bread. But for the other type of shopper—one who seems to get less deeply involved in food—there are the supermarkets. And there are the "hypermarche," vastly larger in sales volume than supermarkets in the United States, carrying only about 2,500 fast-selling items. In America, large supermarkets often carry 10,000 items.

The consumer is at the heart of all marketing activity. This is as true for retailing as for other institutions in the marketing channel. During the 1960s marketing students began to devote greater attention to a new discipline known as consumer behavior. The insights of psychologists, sociologists, and anthropologists were drawn upon to understand better how people act in their role as consumers.

The above illustrations point out that astute retailers often intuitively know a great deal about consumer behavior, and they devise strategies and tactics that they believe are likely to elicit a favorable response. We have devoted the next two chapters to a discussion of various aspects of consumer behavior in order to reinforce this point and emphasize its vital importance to retailing success.

Retail buying decisions begin when a shopper becomes aware of a need and end when the shopper either buys the product or rejects it. For example, when a college student decides to buy a dress for a party, she makes a number of decisions in addition to the major one of buying the dress. She selects a shopping district to visit; chooses the store where she is to make her purchase; decides on the type of dress, color, price, style, and size; and elects to pay cash or charge the purchase. Moreover, the dress-buying decision may lead to others in related product categories, such as shoes, purse, jewelry, and other accessories. Each of these new products requires its own set of decisions.

Even the purchase of a rather simple product such as aspirin requires a number of decisions, often made almost simultaneously. The shopper must decide on the quantity to be purchased, the brand, and the store in which to make the purchase. These decisions are sometimes made easily, and at other times they are agonizingly difficult. Regardless of the complexity of the decision-making process, all decisions are based on such individual factors as motivation, emotion, learning and remembering, traits and attitudes, perception, and personality. In addition, variables such as status, culture, social class, family, and reference groups play important roles.

Interest in consumer psychology is not a new phenomenon. Walter Dill Scott, at one time the president of Northwestern University, is sometimes cited as the outstanding consumer psychologist of the early 1900s. Scott used the experimental method to investigate the problems of consumer behavior, especially those related to advertising, and presented his views in a book titled *The Theory and Practise of Advertising*.[1] Scott was a forerunner of a number of prominent individuals including Daniel Starch, George Gallup, and Elmo Roper. Starch began measuring advertising readership as early as 1931. Gallup and Roper were concerned with public opinion polling as far back as 1936. However, as recently as the end of World War II only about a dozen qualified people were working as full-time consumer psychologists.[2] Therefore, much of the research and writing is of recent origin.

CONSUMER BEHAVIOR AND CONSUMER PSYCHOLOGY DEFINED

As we know, behavioral scientists are interested in all patterns of human behavior, of which consumer behavior is only a small segment. Consumer behavior

[1]Walter Dill Scott, *The Theory and Practise of Advertising* (Boston: Small, Maynard and Company, 1903).

[2]Dik Warren Twedt, "The Consumer Psychologist," in *Consumer Behavior in Theory and in Action*, ed. Steuart Henderson Britt (New York: John Wiley & Sons, Inc., 1970), p. 25.

is limited to those activities associated with the buying of products and services and the reasons underlying these activities. One definition of consumer behavior is the following:

> The acts of individuals directly involved in obtaining and using economic goods and services, including the decision processes that precede and determine these acts.[3]

George Katona says consumer psychology is "the study of the dynamics of the behavior of masses of consumers."[4] Explicit in Katona's definitions is the fact that consumer psychologists are not interested in the behavior pattern of a single individual, but rather the behavior of masses of consumers. In general, there are four principal areas of interest to consumer psychologists: (1) decision making in the marketplace, (2) changes in attitudes and behavior of consumers, (3) influence of time and uncertainty, and (4) studies of group belonging.

Consumer behavior can be explained by identifying and studying all factors that influence behavior. These factors can be classified into two broad groups, which are the focal point of this and the following chapters: (1) individual influences, and (2) social or group influences. Consumer behavior is the result of both kinds of influences interacting with each other; however, for analytical reasons it is necessary to examine each separately.

MOTIVATION

Behavioral scientists are interested in why a human being behaves in certain patterns and whether such behavior can be predicted. Obviously the "how and why" of behavior is complex, and explaining consumer behavior concepts is not easy. Nevertheless it is essential that we explore the subject of human motivation and the forces behind it.

Words such as motives, needs, drives, and urges are used by some experts to explain the same phenomenon; therefore the literature can be confusing. For our purposes it is only necessary to understand that motivation grows out of an individual's awareness of a state of tension within him- or herself. The individual is also aware that this state of tension is not appeased until he or she acts to relieve it. The internal forces that cause an individual to seek a solution to or release from the state of tension is called a *drive*, among which are "hunger drives," "thirst drives," and "sex drives." Once an individual becomes conscious of these physiological drives, as he or she most certainly will, the individual is aware of a need. At this stage the need becomes a want, and the individual takes the necessary steps to satisfy the want.

[3]James F. Engel, David T. Kollat, and Roger D. Blackwell, *Consumer Behavior*, 2nd ed. (New York: Holt, Rinehart and Winston, Inc., 1973), p. 5.

[4]George Katona, "What is Consumer Psychology?" *American Psychologist*, 22 (March 1967), pp. 219–26.

Classifying Motives

Most psychologists are in general agreement as to which drives are physiological in nature. These include hunger, thirst, temperature regulation, sex, and breathing.

Abraham H. Maslow's classification of drives is well known and deserves special mention because he ranks them in a hierarchial fashion. His classification ranked from high to low is:[5]

1. self-actualization—desire to know and understand.
2. esteem and status—desire for reputation.
3. belongingness and love—wanting acceptance by others.
4. safety— over survival and prudence in justifying hunger and thirst.
5. physiological—survival, hunger, and thirst.

Two contemporary marketing educators suggest the following classifications:[6]

1. visceral drives—hunger, thirst, breathing, temperature regulation, and sex.
2. activity drives—exercise, rest, preservation, rhythm, novelty, and curiosity.
3. aesthetic—color, tones, rhythm, and qualities of taste, smell, and touch.
4. emotion—fear, rage, disgust, shame, hate, and love.

A third classification by James Bayton divides motives into two broad areas: biogenic and psychogenic, which he describes as follows:[7]

> Although there is not much disagreement as to the list of specific biogenic needs, there is considerable difference of opinion as to the list of psychogenic needs. However, the various lists of psychogenic needs can be grouped into three broad categories:
>
> 1. Affectional needs—the needs to form and maintain warm, harmonious, and emotionally satisfying relations with others. (See Figure 3.1.)
> 2. Ego-bolstering needs—the needs to enhance or promote the personality; to achieve, to gain prestige and recognition, to satisfy the ego through domination of others. (See Figure 3.2, p. 60.)
> 3. Ego-defensive needs—the needs to protect the personality; to avoid ridicule and "loss of face"; to prevent loss of prestige; to avoid or to obtain relief from anxiety. (See Figure 3.3, p. 62.)

Many advertisements appeal to all three needs; however, one appeal may be dominant. We cite three examples to illustrate Bayton's classification:

[5]See A. H. Maslow, *Motivation and Personality* (New York: Harper & Row Publishers Inc., 1954).

[6]Edward Brink and William T. Kelley, *Consumer Behavior and Demand Stimulation* (Englewood Cliffs, N.J.: Prentice-Hall, Inc., 1963), p. 88.

[7]James Bayton, "Motivation, Cognition, Learning: Basic Factors in Consumer Beravior," *Journal of Marketing*, XXII (January 1958), p. 282.

FIGURE 3.1

This apparently satisfying relationship appeals to the consumer's *affectional* needs

Source: J. B. Williams Co., Inc., New York, N.Y.

1. Automoble—"Continental—The Final Step Up." Lincoln-Mercury, a division of Ford Motor Company, makes an appeal to a potential car buyer's desire for higher status; the ad, as can be seen in Figure 3.4 (p. 63), urges a car buyer to step up to a Continental. This ad is ego-bolstering.
2. Insurance—"We Think You Have Enough to Worry About." Traveler's Insurance Company uses the appeal shown in Figure 3.5 (p. 64) to reduce the anxieties of being underinsured. This ad is ego-defensive.
3. Hair Color—"It Lets Me Be Me." Clairol suggests Nice 'n Easy, as a means to make a woman's hair lovelier while letting her be herself (see Figure 3.6, p. 65). This is ego-bolstering and affectional.

Retailers are aided by manufacturers and others through advertising messages of the kind illustrated. However, the retailer must capitalize on these appeals in his

FIGURE 3.2

This woman suggests that the consumer should use these products to satisfy *ego-bolstering* needs

Source: Avon Products, Inc., New York, New York. © 1970 by Avon Products, Inc.

or her own advertisements or through point-of-purchase display materials. (This will be discussed in Chapter 12.)

Application to Retailers

How can the retailer translate this knowledge of consumer drives into meaningful action? First, the retailer should understand that customers are individuals, each with a unique combination of needs, drives, and emotions that relate to each other and to the environment. The retailer can put knowledge of consumer motivation to use when selecting merchandising techniques. Let us examine some of the products found in the beauty aids section of a typical department store and relate them to consumer motivation.

	Product	*Action*	*Classification*
1.	Mouthwash	Relieves anxiety of bad breath	Ego-defensive
2.	Toothpaste*	Relieves anxiety of cavities	Ego-defensive
3.	Deodorant	Relieves anxiety of perspiration odors	Ego-defensive
4.	Lipstick	Enhances beauty of mouth	Ego-bolstering
5.	Eye makeup	Makes for prettier eyes	Ego-bolstering
6.	Hair coloring	Makes for more attractive hair	Ego-bolstering
7.	Perfumes	Promotes love	Affectional needs
8.	Colognes for men	Promotes love	Affectional needs

*Some toothpastes are sold to whiten teeth (cosmetic effect) and are ego-bolstering rather than ego-defensive.

A retailer should look at every item in the department and relate it to an individual's need for affection, relief of anxiety, or ego-bolstering. The knowledge gained is helpful in planning purchases, promoting the sale of merchandise, preparing advertising copy, or training salespeople.

Just as the retailer in the cosmetic example would study his or her stock in relation to the psychogenic needs of customers, a retailer could study the stock in housewares, furniture, ladies' ready-to-wear, lingerie, men's wear, or any other class of merchandise. A retailer's sales success is directly related to his or her ability to understand consumer behavior, and then to use this knowledge through better merchandising techniques.

Although every customer is a separate individual with different needs, drives, fears, and anxieties, there are sufficient numbers with similar wants to make the job of the retailer somewhat easier than it appears initially. For example, it is said that clothes are a projection of the personality of the person who wears them—they are an extension of one's self. If so, then consider the following advertisement headlines and the type of person to whom they are directed:

"Will serve for years to come." Men's raincoats.
"Lingerie that makes some startling revelations about you." Lingerie.
"A perennial Spring favorite." Men's suits.
"Beautify . . . the French way." Cosmetics.
"A free-spirited sandal." Women's shoes.
"Watch for our 'Budget-maker' special." Food.

Social Motivations

An individual seldom lives in isolation from other members of a society. This gives rise to social motives such as gregariousness, self-assertion, and acquisitiveness. In contrast to biological needs, most experts agree that social motivations are learned. Here we focus our attention on the meaning of motives.

FIGURE 3.3

Chewing gum is sometimes advertised as a way to reduce the anxiety that arises from *ego-defensive* needs

Source: Courtesy of Wm. Wrigley Jr. Company, Chicago, Illinois.

Gregariousness. Gregariousness means that individuals group themselves into clubs, churches, cities, states, or other groups, both formal and informal. The need to associate with other individuals who have similar tastes and goals is very strong. A few years ago Pepsi-Cola used this appeal by suggesting that one should "join the Pepsi-Generation." The appeal of shopping plazas, supermarkets, department stores, and specialty shops is due in part to this tendency. It is true that the goods displayed are the major attraction, but many shoppers enjoy the crowds and the feeling of belonging to a group of shoppers. The excitement generated by people shopping together undoubtedly contributes to increased sales.

Self-assertion. This particular social motive is individualistic. In this instance, the individual does not suppress individual goals to a group; rather, he or

FIGURE 3.4
This ad appeals to the car buyer's desire for improving his status

Introducing a limited edition Lincoln Continental. The Town Car.

Fifty years ago, the first Lincoln offered such amenities as bud vases, mohair upholstery, and a revolutionary 81 h.p. engine.

Today, Lincoln Continental commemorates its first car with a brand new 50th Anniversary model: the Town Car.

This is a very special car. A personal statement. It is not intended for great masses of people. It will be produced in strictly limited numbers.

You see in the picture the Town Car in its special 50th Anniversary Gold Moondust Metallic color. The roof is a stunning new black cavalry twill vinyl.

The interior, except for the Brazilian rosewood grain appliqués and the polished chromium highlights, is black. Black natural grain leathers on seating surfaces. Black vinyl fabrics. Black cut pile nylon carpeting. Black napped nylon headlining.

You may care to note that, in addition to Anniversary Gold, you may custom order your Town Car in 25 other exterior colors. And 7 other interior colors.

Color aside, the Town Car is built to be the most harmonious blend of luxury and engineering excellence the discerning buyer could wish for.

From small niceties such as the vanity mirror mounted in the glove box to major luxuries such as automatic temperature control, most comforts and conveniences are standard equipment.

Michelin steel-belted radial ply tires are standard. And so are automatic transmission, power steering, power brakes, and power front seats.

You may wish to consider the option of Sure-Track, the industry's first computer controlled anti-skid braking system.

At every hand, the Town Car reminds you of your unique and individual choice of motor car. Tasteful gold squares bearing your own initials etched in black are furnished, to be mounted on the outside of the front doors.

The Town Car identifies itself with block letters mounted on each front fender and on the rear deck lid.

In addition, with the special 50th Anniversary Gold Town Car, you are given a Limited Edition plaque that fits discreetly on the instrument panel. You will also receive a boxed set of 22 karat gold finished ignition and door keys.

And as always, there is the incomparable Lincoln Continental ride. A ride as cathedral quiet, gossamer smooth, and reassuringly substantial as you have ever known in any car.

The Town Car. Truly worthy of the proud Lincoln Continental name.

Continental: the final step up.

Source: Ford Motor Company, Detroit, Michigan.

FIGURE 3.5

Consumer anxieties resulting from the worry of being underinsured are appealed to in this ad

Source: The Travelers Insurance Co., Hartford, Connecticut.

FIGURE 3.6

A combination of affectional and ego-bolstering, this ad is aimed at women who want beautiful hair, but also want to be themselves

Source: Clairol, Inc., New York, New York.

she wishes to assert him- or herself. Appeals for luxury goods are good examples (in automobiles, it may be a Cadillac). Retailers of both men's and women's clothes carry a wide assortment and suggest (partially by advertisements) that they have *the* style, *the* color, *the* fabric to appeal regardless of how discriminating the taste of potential customers might be. For example, a woman may dress in the latest fashions and still permit her individuality and personality to be highlighted by clothes selected off racks in her favorite dress shop.

Acquisitiveness. People in our society enjoy acquiring goods and building up their total estates. Many of us are taught the value of thrift at an early age. Often one of the first gifts a baby receives is a piggy bank, and the growing child is taught the principles of saving. It is said that there is no better way to inflate the ego than to possess money, goods, or wealth. Banks and savings and loan institutions appeal to wage earners, urging them to make regular deposits from their paychecks. Acquisitiveness is a learned social motivation.

Emotions

Emotions are best described as those internal forces that stir an individual and cause him or her to react in a certain way. Examples of emotions are fear, anxiety, depression, reverence, tenderness, love, and hate. In traditional marketing textbooks, it is standard procedure to classify buying motives into two basic groups: rational (nonemotional) and emotional. Examples of rational buying motives are such traits as dependability, economy, convenience, quality, and durability. These motives involve an individual's judgment and, therefore, are the result of learned experiences. An appeal to a prospective car buyer to purchase a compact automobile because it is more economical to operate is a good example of a rational buying motive. However, in more recent years the distinction between rational and emotional motives has faded. It is believed that *all* motives are rational in that they make sense to the individual who is acting out his or her needs.

Emotions are the basis for many television commercials. An example is the coffee commercial suggesting that brides can gain their husbands' respect (and love) by brewing a good cup of coffee. All that it takes is the correct brand. An hour watching television will yield many examples of the use of emotional buying motives.

Almost all retailers rely on emotional buying motives in appealing to their customers (usually through advertising). Consider the following examples:

1. *Clyde's Garage and Car Clinic* (Motive used—fear). Ad features the scare headline—"How *Safe* is Your Car?" Readers of Clyde's advertisement are urged to have their brakes checked and repaired if they need correction. The ad attempts to use fear of an accident to motivate the readers to come to Clyde's Garage for service.
2. *Robbin's Cosmetic Boutique* (Motives used—love and reverence). Robbin advertises her products in a variety of ways, but all are designed to strengthen love (in the case of married couples) or to encourage love among singles.
3. *Schultz' Furniture Store* (Motive used—anxiety). Advertisements regularly say, "The home of the homemaker. Send it back if not completely satisfied in every way." This is an anxiety-reducing headline designed to make buying easier for furniture buyers. Many buyers are unsure of their taste and are comforted by the assurance that their initial decision is not a binding one. This is particularly important for expensive products that are desgned to last for many years.
4. *Sheila's Jewelry Store* (Motive used—reverence). Sheila, the owner and manager of the store, teaches her sales people to handle precious gems carefully and to talk with customers in slightly hushed tones. The atmosphere should be one of reverence for such expensive products.

COGNITIVE DISSONANCE

Leon Festinger has proposed a theory of *cognitive dissonance* to explain one aspect of consumer behavior. According to Festinger, it is normal for individuals to behave in a manner that is consistent with their strongly held beliefs or attitudes and to avoid situations where their potential actions would be inconsistent or dissonant with these beliefs and attitudes. But sometimes individuals may change their beliefs so they are more consonant with their behavior. Festinger says:

> In short, I am proposing that dissonance, that is, the existence of nonfitting relations among cognitions, is a motivating factor in its own right. By the term "cognitions," I mean any knowledge, opinion, or belief about the environment, about oneself, or about one's behavior. Cognitive dissonance can be seen as an antecedent condition which leads to activity oriented towards dissonance reduction, just as hunger leads to activity towards hunger reduction.[8]

Festinger says that it is not unusual to find consumer behavior that is inconsistent with an individual's attitudes and beliefs. For example, a man may sincerely believe that smoking cigarettes is harmful to one's health; yet the man smokes. In this situation, if he is uncomfortable about the dissonance, he can take steps to reduce it. The ultimate step is to discontinue smoking, a change in behavior. However, the smoker may find the addiction too difficult to break, so he switches to a filtered cigarette, low in tar, in order to reduce the dissonance. Or he may avoid those sources of information that tell him about the perils of smoking.

Retailers are aware of the dissonance between themselves and their customers through the complaints registered by the customers. Stores may seek to reduce the dissonance by improving their services. For example, they could institute a more liberal return policy. The slogan "the customer is always right" indicates a store's pledge to eliminate dissonance.

The conscientious retailer should address himself to the possibility of dissonance-creating activities. Although it probably does not happen often, he or she may "sell the customer something he doesn't really need," only to have the customer regret the purchase after leaving the store. Rather than make this mistake, most retailers avoid unnecessarily forceful selling; they allow the customer to reconcile the product or service with his beliefs and attitudes. But in other instances the customer may be searching for a reason to justify the purchase of a particular product. The astute retailer may plant the justification seed in the mind of the customer and hope that it grows. When McDonald's used the advertising theme, "You deserve a break today," it was tacitly suggesting that the work ethic of many Americans should be occasionally broken. In short, if the American customer is looking

[8]Leon Festinger, "Introduction to the Theory of Dissonance" in *Consumer Behavior and the Behavioral Sciences*, ed. Steuart Henderson Britt (New York: John Wiley & Sons, Inc., 1970), p. 115.

for a reason to buy a product or service, the imaginative retailer should be able to furnish it—but not without risking postpurchase dissonance.

Retailers must also realize that many buyers suffer from what might be called "postpurchase anxiety." This condition is especially common when expensive durables are bought. The buyer begins to have "second thoughts" about the outlay of cash. This is why people who have just bought cars continue to read ads for the brand they have purchased or notice the number of similar cars on the road. They wish to reinforce their confidence in their recent action. Retailers who have a policy of followup on the purchase of durables understand the rationale behind Festinger's theory and reap long-term benefits from thus reducing the buyer's dissonance.

LEARNING

Most buying decisions are based upon a learning experience acquired in previous problem-solving situations. Consumers repeat the purchase of a product and brand if they have learned that this product and brand is best for them. The learning pattern is very complex, but to understand behavior, one must understand how consumers learn.

The Pavlovian Learning Model

One of the popular models to explain learning behavior is Pavlov's learning model,[9] named after Ivan P. Pavlov, a Russian psychologist famous for his experiments with dogs. In one experiment, Pavlov would ring a bell while feeding a dog. After repeating this experiment many times, Pavlov observed that the dog would salivate when the bell rang even though no food was present. The dog had learned to associate the ringing of the bell with feeding time. This type of study is known as the stimulus-response model and is used by its advocates as the prime model to explain consumer behavior. The key to understanding this model is a knowledge of such concepts as drives, cues, responses, and reinforcement. We have previously discussed drives and indicated that they are the internal forces causing many to seek a solution to his or her state of tension.

Cues. Cues are those stimuli that direct the individual to respond to his or her drives in some suggested way. Advertising messages are external stimuli that are often used effectively as a cue. For example, when a motorist becomes aware of hunger, he or she then becomes alert to roadside signs that suggest lunch or dinner. Store fronts and window displays may provide cues to consumers with respect to the nature of a retailer's business, the quality of products, prices, and services offered. Promotional stores project a "busyness" which is a cue to the consumers seeking bargains, while service-oriented stores attempt to communicate that shopping within will be restful and pleasant. Conversations with neighbors provide in-

[9]The application of this model and succeeding models used in Chapters 3 and 4, as well as some of the discussions, is based on the work of Philip Kotler in *Marketing Management*, 2nd ed. (Englewood Cliffs, N.J.: Prentice-Hall, Inc., 1972), pp. 104–6.

formation about the relative merits of various neighborhood restaurants, the friendliness of nearby stores, and how to fight crabgrass. Some of the information is stored in the individual's memory and will be retrieved when its seems useful.

Response. Response is the action taken by the individual to satisfy a drive. In the example of the hungry motorist, he or she may stop at the sign of the golden arches, pull into a McDonald's, and respond by placing an order for a hamburger, fries, and cola.

Reinforcement. Reinforcement takes place when an individual repeats his or her performance under similar circumstances and is again "rewarded" as before. In the above example, if the hungry motorist was completely satisfied with the choice of McDonald's, he or she is likely to repeat the experience under similar circumstances. Some people repeatedly purchase the same brand of a product because it has consistently been satisfactory. These people are not brand switchers.

Behaviorism. The stimulus–response (Pavlovian) model is frequently referred to as behaviorism because of the attention paid to the stimulus–response syndrome. Many examples may be cited to note the reliance on this model by various kinds of marketers. Manufacturers promote their consumer products repetitively to elicit the proper responses.

The world of retailing also follows the behaviorist school. Food store chains that construct stores of the same architectural design in order to present a familiar face to shoppers, regardless of the city or neighborhood in which they are located, is an example. Other retailers, notably variety chains, gasoline stations, and drug outlets, follow the same principle. (See Figure 3.7.)

Many retailing practices seem to be based on the theories of the behaviorist school. For example, the early F. W. Woolworth stores were all painted red with gold coloring on the signs, regardless of the neighborhood in which they were located. Presumably such a color cue would be interpreted by the experienced consumer as a "Great Five-Cent Store," as they were originally known in Utica, New York, and Lancaster, Pennsylvania. Or, for another example, many food retailers are aware that shoppers think they "know" the price of only a small number of food items—usually frequently purchased staples. They project to unknown items what they know about the very few. Thus a food store may earn a reputation for high or low prices on the basis of how it prices only a handful of items. A shrewd food store manager attempts to learn what the shopper thinks he or she knows about prices and keeps margins low on those items. The retailer earns profits on the unknown items.

The Psychoanalytic Model of Learning

Critics of the Pavlovian behaviorist model claim that it emphasizes stimulus and response but neglects such phenomena as perception, the subconscious, and interpersonal relationships; in short, it centers too much attention on the decision and too little attention on the thinking process that leads to the decision.

Sigmund Freud, the psychologist whose name is most frequently associated with

FIGURE 3.7

This behavioral model for analyzing buyers shows how consumption patterns emerge as outputs from the individual's psyche

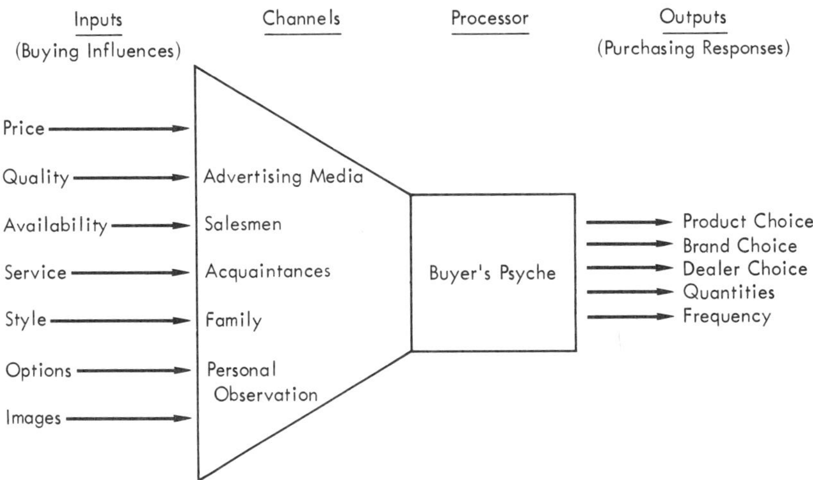

Source: Philip Kotler, "Behavioral Models for Analyzing Buyers," *Journal of Marketing*, October 1965, pp. 37–45. Reprinted from *Journal of Marketing*, published by the American Marketing Association.

the psychoanalytic model of consumer behavior, suggested that every individual has a psyche that is divided into three parts: the id, the ego, and the superego. The id is that part of the psyche where instinctive drives such as hunger, thirst, and sex reside. The ego is that part of the psyche that governs the id according to some intelligent plan. The superego is the conscience of the psyche, and channels the individual's drives in a morally approved manner, thereby helping the individual to avoid guilt or shame.

Freud evidently believed sex to be the most important of all instinctive drives, arguing that sex manifests itself in behavior patterns that might be completely unconscious to the person involved. There have been many psychologists who have since adopted Freud's theory and enlarged or refined it. An important advocate was Alfred Adler, who emphasized man's urge for power and its manifestation in inferiority and superiority complexes.[10]

Critics of the psychoanalytical model believe it has limited application to the marketing environment. They argue that a retailer would not be able to isolate the unconscious drives of an individual consumer and use this knowledge in a meaningful manner. For example, one critic says:

> While unconscious desires can be important, they are virtually impossible to uncover empirically outside of months of psychoanalysis, and, when uncovered, they can be ugly and not lend themselves to effective selling appeals.[11]

[10]Alfred Adler, *The Science of Living* (New York: Greenberg, 1929).

The most important application of the Freudian psychoanalytical model is the implied suggestion that buyers are often motivated to buy a product because of its symbolic meaning, often rooted in sex. An example is the belief by some that a cigar is more masculine if it has an offensive odor.

Modern motivational research is concerned with the hidden things in a buyer's mind which cause him or her to buy a certain good. Ernest Dichter is one of the leading authorities in this field, and marketing authors often call him the father of motivational research.[12]

PSYCHOLOGICAL CONCEPTS

There are a number of concepts that are vital to the understanding of human psychology. We shall discuss briefly traits and attitudes, perception, and personality.

Traits and Attitudes

A trait may be defined as that part of an individual's total personality which arouses a person to a particular kind of behavior. A shopper who has an argumentative trait may well quarrel with a salesclerk over a relatively minor matter while a less argumentative shopper will let the matter pass.

Does a sale appeal to a spender or a saver? Arguments can be given to support both positions, although there is no argument that the saving trait and the spending trait are diametrically opposite.

A housewife with a neatness trait is perhaps a better customer for detergents, polishes, or waxes than is a careless housewife. Other examples of traits are talkative, quiet, shy, bold, timid, and autocratic. One writer suggests there may be as many as 18,000 traits.[13]

Attitudes are the subjective opinions an individual holds about another person, an object, or a concept. Whenever an individual gives an opinion he or she is verbalizing an attitude, which can be either positive or negative. People have attitudes about a variety of subjects, and a person's behavior frequently gives away his or her attitudes. An attitude has a definite object of reference while a trait has none, although attitudes are frequently an outgrowth of a trait. For example, a saver may have a friendly attitude toward banks and other savings institutions. On the other hand, a borrower may have a hostile attitude toward a bank even though he or she received a loan from it. Attitudes become popular and exert considerable influence when masses of people verbalize the same attitude. Ever since the public was made aware of the problems of pollution, people in general have become hostile toward any product that pollutes the environment. Often people have hostile attitudes to-

[11]Engel, et al., *Consumer Behavior*, p. 29.

[12]See Ernest Dichter, *Handbook of Consumer Motivations* (New York: McGraw-Hill Book Company, 1964).

[13]Steuart Henderson Britt, "Behavior Traits," in *Consumer Behavior and the Behavioral Sciences* (New York: John Wiley & Sons, 1970), p. 170.

ward retailers who do not stock pollution-free detergents, who operate a business in the inner city but live in the suburbs, or who do not contribute to community betterment funds.

Perception

Perception is the process by which an individual receives stimuli and interprets their messages. Perception begins through the five senses: sight, smell, sound, taste, and touch. When this occurs it is called a sensation. Psychologists relate perception to memory. For example, when a driver encounters a red traffic signal, he or she stops. This is learned behavior. In a similar maner when a woman pushes her shopping cart through a supermarket she sees items that appeal to her senses. The smell of freshly baked bread in a bakery department may cause the shopper to buy a loaf or two. Daniel Yankelovich says "perception is seeing, apperception is seeing in the light of experience."[14]

There is a relationship between the change in physical stimulus and the change in sensation perceived by an individual. Weber's Law explains it with this simple formula:

$$\frac{\triangle I}{I} = K$$

Weber's Law states that the smallest change in the intensity of a stimulus noticeable to an individual ($\triangle I$) depends upon the amount of the original stimulus (I). For instance, if a manufacturer of a \$5,000 automobile (I) increases its price by \$10.00 ($\triangle I$), it may not be noticed. Yet if the manufacturer of an auto wax increases its price by 25¢ (from \$1.00 to \$1.25), he may encounter considerable sales resistance. This concept has real implication for retail price strategy.

Even though many retailers have never heard of Weber's Law, they are constantly enforcing it. For example:

> A fashionable Pittsburgh department store uses professional models to walk through the store wearing the latest designs and carrying an unobtrusive sign indicating the department the model represents. Such clothes receive extraordinary exposure to shoppers.
>
> When A & P announced an "early warning system" on price increases, the company received much publicity. It promised that price increases would be posted seven days before their effective date so that customers could stock up at low prices. A large number of American shoppers were aware of this step because it was so different from the usual approach.
>
> One of New York City's largest retailers claims it owns and displays the world's largest American flag, brought out only for special occasions. A New Yorker who apparently understood the store's motive said, "Well, you sure can't ignore it."

[14]Daniel Yankelovich, "Apperception," in *Consumer Behavior and the Behavior Sciences*, ed. Steuart Henderson Britt (New York: John Wiley & Sons, Inc., 1970), p. 157.

Not every signal or cue that the retailer sends to the consumer will be fully and accurately received or digested. Hence many advertisements, personal selling comments, and other messages are entirely or partly wasted. The human mind is highly selective with regard to what signals are allowed to contribute to the learning process. Three kinds of selectivity occur: (1) selective exposure—the customer attempts to encounter only those media and messages that are important to him and consistent with his deeply held values and beliefs; (2) selective perception—the customer will "see" or "hear" certain signals and not see or hear others; and (3) selective retention—the retention and forgetting rates will differ among incoming signals. In short, communication with customers requires more than just an ample budget and the sincere efforts of a retailer; the consumer must be receptive to the message. Otherwise he will use the filter that is in each of us to avoid its full impact.

Personality

Personality refers to all the factors that cause an individual to behave in a unique manner. It includes both motives and all of his or her traits and attitudes. Generally speaking, the response traits that one exhibits are a good clue to one's personality. Response traits are of three major types: (1) the traits an individual exhibits when carrying out his or her role, (2) the traits exhibited while relating to others, and (3) the manner in which he or she expresses him- or herself. For example, an individual may be assertive, conspicuous, self-confident, a leader, and a planner. These traits are exhibited in the person's behavior. The individual may also be friendly or unfriendly with others, sociable or unsociable, sympathetic or unsympathetic. Furthermore, the individual may express him- or herself aggressively or competitively. As one can see there are many combinations possible, and all are "windows to a person's personality."

In more recent years, marketers have become interested in using personality measures to predict consumer buying behavior. These are called *psychographic studies*. It has been theorized that personality traits are useful in predicting brand preferences, store preferences, and other types of market behavior.

In 1954, G. P. Stone identified four distinct consumer personalities: (1) the economic, (2) the personalizing, (3) the ethical, and (4) the apathetic.[15]

1. *The Economic Shopper*—This shopper judges both the store and the shopping process by economic criteria. He or she is aware of price, quality, and the selection of goods available. This customer demands efficiency from the store personnel if it is to receive his or her patronage.
2. *The Personalizing Consumer*—This shopper seeks out the store which places value on an individual's personality because he or she likes a warm, intimate relationship. This customer identifies easily with the store's personnel.
3. *The Ethical Consumer*—This shopper has a strong sense of ethics, often favoring the small independent store over the large chain store. The reasoning is

[15]G. P. Stone, "City Shoppers and Urban Identification: Observations on the Social Psychology of City Life," *American Journal of Sociology* (July 1954), pp. 36–45.

that he or she should help "the little guy" regardless of price, brand, or other criteria, rather than give business to the cold, impersonal chain.

4. *The Apathetic Consumer*—This individual actually dislikes to shop, hence he or she makes it as easy as possible. Inasmuch as these shoppers are chiefly interested in their convenience, prices, selection of merchandise, and warm relations with store personnel are of little concern to them.

Some day buyer behavior may be predicted through an analysis of personality characteristics. However, results are inconclusive at this time. One reason is the lack of definitive tests that can measure personality traits. Standardized tests have been less successful in identifying and predicting consumer behavior than tests tailor-made for a specific occasion. However, it has been found that personality traits differ between heavy users and light users of a product. Future research in this important area may offer renewed hope in predicting consumer behavior.

SUMMARY

Behavioral scientists are studying consumer behavior, and their findings are regularly reported in books, journals, and monographs. Retailers are beneficiaries of this vast outflow of literature. Consumer behavior is a complex process and difficult to explain. However, questions regarding purchase decisions are being raised and behavioral scientists are supplying some of the answers.

Every individual behaves in a unique manner, in part because of his or her physiological drives. However, the human being is more than an animal and, therefore, many of his or her motivations are psychological in nature. These drives are difficult to classify; however, there are many excellent classifications available. Bayton's system, which consists of ego-defensive, ego-bolstering, and affectional drives, is useful for retailers.

Most consumer decisions are repetitive and based on past learning experiences. One of the most popular models to explain learning is the stimulus–response, or Pavlovian, model. Critics believe stimulus–response is overemphasized while perception, subconscious, and symbolic meaning are neglected. Therefore the psychoanalytical model is advanced as an alternative.

Buying behavior is also the result of emotions, attitudes, perceptions, sensations, and the personality traits of the individual. Each of these factors contributes in a meaningful fashion to the decision-making process.

QUESTIONS FOR DISCUSSION

1. Why is it important for a retailer to understand consumer behavior? (Isn't it true that all consumers are alike—that is, they are people with similar biological drives?)
2. If you were a retailer, how would you merchandise products whose appeals are basically emotional? In your answer consider advertising, promotion, display, and personal selling.

3. G. P. Stone identifies four distinct types of consumers. What are they? How would this knowledge help you if you were a retailer of women's fashions? A supermarket operator?

4. Trace step-by-step the decisions involved in a purchase which you recently made.

5. Describe how a "state of tension" built up in a consumer's makeup leads to buying action. How can a retailer adapt a merchandising program to benefit from this psychological fact?

6. What are "social motivations"? What implications do they have for the practice of retailing?

7. Explain Festinger's theory of cognitive dissonance. Does the theory have any value for the modern retailer?

8. Contrast the Pavlovian and psychoanalytical learning methods. Give examples of retailing activities which seem to be based on each explanation of consumer behavior.

9. List ten learning cues that department store retailers employ while attempting to motivate consumers to become buyers.

10. Give examples of the way Weber's Law applies to retailing.

4 CONSUMER BEHAVIOR AND RETAILING

Social Influences

The American culture prizes thin bodies, so reducing salons have sprung up all over the country in response. These salons sometimes promise more than they can deliver ("Lose 8 pounds in 5 days," "Eat what you want and still lose," "Wear two sizes smaller in a week"), and many have been the center of attention from the Federal Trade Commission for deceptive promises, and the Food and Drug Administration for using weight-reducing medicines and drugs of unproved value. Many of us will do almost anything to look as our peers think we should look.

On the Rockville Pike near Washington, D.C., the Marriott Corporation operates seven restaurants, none of which is more than two miles from the other. Each is different in decor, menu, service, and price; indeed, the typical customer probably is unaware of the common ownership. The people at Marriott intend to serve different market segments. The man who brings his children to one restaurant for hamburgers may be back to a different restaurant with his wife an hour later for cocktails and dinner. Marriott sees no reason why it cannot serve all social classes—but not necessarily in the same restaurant.

A haberdasher in Nashville noticed several years ago that young women often bought blue jeans, even though denim was once almost exclusively for men; to make the female customers more comfortable in the store he hired his first saleswoman. In Chicago, hairdressers are battling a law that prevents them from styling the hair of people of the opposite sex; they want to operate "unisex" salons. And in Cleveland, a department store executive comments on the huge increase in the number of men who are using a wide variety of cosmetics. This blurring of sex roles means that women are obtaining better paying jobs and winning the freedom that money implies. Younger women almost certainly have more to say about how their families' budgets are allocated than did their mothers. And retailers had better pay attention.

When Sears, Roebuck began retailing in Spain in the early 1960s, it discovered it would be easier to adjust to Spanish customs than to expect the Spanish to change their ways. Although Americans have long been accustomed to credit or installment sales, the Spanish rather resent the idea that they are unable to pay cash. Credit cards have made their way into Spanish life very slowly. Merchandising has also been different. Almost every aspect of the firm's inventory (ladies' suits, swim wear, millinery) has been affected by the conservative outlook of Spanish women.

In Atlanta, Georgia, a convenience food mart has installed a gasoline pump so that customers can buy their food and fill their automobiles with a single stop. In Lincoln, Nebraska, a savings and loan association has installed remote computer terminals in each outlet of a food chain so that customers can engage in elementary financial transactions without visiting the association's home office. And in Tokyo, department stores sell stocks and bonds, travel and theater tickets, and have Buddhist shrines on the roof where a shopper can rest or contemplate. Such scrambling of merchandise and services is partially in response to accelerated life styles where conserving time is often more important than saving money.

Consumer behavior is not determined solely by the physiological and psychological forces within an individual, although these forces are very important. As we can see from the above examples, individuals are also members of various social, political, and economic groups that influence behavior. This chapter deals with how groups help to shape the behavior patterns of consumers.

THE VEBLENIAN MODEL

The importance of social influence on personal consumption patterns was first seen by Thorstein Veblen, an economist prominent at the turn of the century, who is best known for writing about the behavior of the leisure class.[1] In particular, he believed that many consumer goods were purchased by individuals in order to gain prestige and status. His theory introduced the principle called "conspicuous consumption": a person of the leisure class purchases goods which call attention to the user because of their uniqueness and high visibility. Since Veblen's time many behavioral scientists have become interested in consumer behavior, and there is a considerable body of literature available showing the significance of such parts of society as culture, subculture, social status, reference groups, and family in explaining consumer behavior, as shown in Figure 4.1.

CULTURE

Culture is the sum total of behavior responses made by large groups of people when confronted with similar problems. Culture represents the ideas, values, attitudes, artifacts, and symbols governing the behavior of a member of the group. Cultural values endure for long periods of time and are highly resistant to change.

Culture determines the responses that individuals make in given situations. Normally these responses are taught early in the life of children by parents and other adult family members. However, schools, churches, and other institutions reinforce the teachings of the family. Because culture imposes rather rigid behavior patterns upon people when they are young, cultural traits become very stable. It is good retailing strategy to offer products that conform with cultural values rather than attempt to defy culture or change it. Astute retailers are aware, for example, that per capita sales of cosmetics are higher in New York than in the rest of the country; that health foods sell well in California; that Americans buy a disproportionately large number of "how to succeed" books; that coffee and tea do not sell well in Utah; and that original art does not sell equally well among all social classes. Retailers should be persistent observers of the cultural scene and respond to change when it occurs.

[1]See Thorstein Veblen, *The Theory of the Leisure Class* (New York: The Macmillan Company, 1899), and Philip Kotler, *Marketing Management*, 2nd ed. (Englewood Cliffs, N.J.: Prentice-Hall, Inc., 1972), pp. 108–12.

FIGURE 4.1
Individual consumer behavior is influenced by five societal elements: culture, subcultures, social status, reference groups, and family

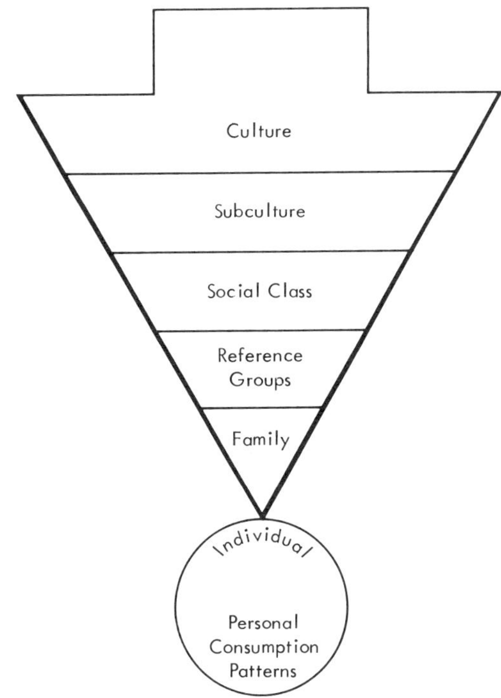

Source: Steven M. Cristol.

We are primarily interested in the American culture, which is a subset of Western culture. The major American cultural values—if, indeed, there are any "universals"—are religion, achievement, security, conformity, leisure, youthfulness, and urbanization. Most of these values are self-evident, and we do not intend to describe them extensively.

Religion

Most Americans who are religious embrace one of the Christian or the Jewish faiths. These faiths stress the worthwhileness of an individual, so individualism becomes an important cultural trait. Furthermore, most of these religions make virtues of goals such as hard work, thrift, and accumulation of wealth; most of us are familiar with the Puritan ethic.

The religious beliefs of the American culture are very important, and consequently they affect not only consumer behavior but the marketing strategy used to sell products and services. One example is the law regulating Sunday openings of retail stores in some areas. Although Sunday openings have become rather commonplace in most states, some communities still resist them vigorously. Other examples of the influence of religion and its effect on the operation of retail stores are federal statutes governing the rates of interest charged by merchants (truth-in-lending), laws governing labels and packaging (truth-in-packaging), and laws governing advertising.

Achievement

The American culture stresses achievement. This accounts for some workers' criticism of those in America who are idle, and thus are not achievers. The stress placed upon this value accounts partly for the purchase of those products commonly referred to as "status symbols," for they indicate achievement to peer group members. The need to achieve stimulates the competitive spirit of both individuals and groups. Many retailers recognize that products are not just valued for their functional ability but also for what they symbolize. Wall-to-wall carpeting, expensive automobiles, fur coats, and original works of art suggest a great deal about the accomplishments of the owner. As a man once said, "Half the fun of going to Florida each year is to subtly lord it over my friends who can't afford to go."

The drive that most Americans have for achievement also raises personnel problems for the retailer. Achievement on the job generally suggests upward mobility, meaning promotions to better jobs and more money. But many employees are not strongly motivated and do not have the training or ability to move upward in the firm. Thus achievement must be defined differently. Imaginative retailers have learned to recognize those employees who have been doing basically the same task for many years through award ceremonies, frequent mentions in the store newspaper, appointment to Store Advisory Councils, and other techniques. It is not easy, but it is essential if a loyal staff is to be maintained.

Security

One of the most important ingredients of the human make-up is security, both emotional and physical. The retailer can play a role in furnishing security to both his customers and his employees. Many customers are unsure of their tastes and look to a trusted retailer for help in making decisions. Few retailers will refuse to sell a product to a customer, but many will attempt to direct their purchases toward products that seem more suited to their needs. This may even include recommending a lower priced product if it seems to be better for the customer. Customers sometimes look upon the retailer as the other half of a buying team that is committed to maximizing the customer's buying dollar. The astute retailer cultivates this feeling and profits from it. Retailers who gladly show customers a variety of merchandise before narrowing down the choice, who take back unsatisfactory merchandise without raising many questions, and who do not high-pressure customers to buy are aware of the insecurities that often are built into some purchasing situations.

Employees also need security. Americans are demanding more help from their employers and the federal government to protect themselves from problems beyond the control of any one person. Social Security, health insurance, unemployment benefits, Medicare, food stamps, and welfare payments are all manifestations of the desire for security. But the retailer can also do many things that generate a feeling of security. For example, Filene's, the world's largest specialty store, inaugurated a Board of Arbitration to adjudicate disputes between management and employees before the turn of the century. Thus employees of the Boston store can be sure that their stories will be heard by an impartial panel that renders a decision. Or for another example, when Marshall Field's large State Street store burned to the ground in Chicago's Great Fire of 1871, employees were notified that they would be paid all that was owed them on the following week. Notice of the payment was posted at the site of the burned out store, even while it was still smoldering.

Conformity

Conformity is that trait which causes people to be like others in dress, talk, and behavior patterns. Most people seemingly want to conform with their peer group, and each group has its symbols that mark membership in it. The strong desire for conformity makes the retailer's task somewhat easier by lending a small element of certainty to a market; it means that the assortment to be offered will necessarily be smaller than if there were no desire to conform. Neither a fashion nor a fad is easy to predict, but once it has become popular it is certain that a large number of people will follow it. Such products as white suede shoes for men or midi-skirts for women were quickly popularized and faded just as fast. The drive to conform means that lower costs are incurred by the businessman and consumer satisfaction is enhanced.

Youthfulness

Youthfulness is another trait stressed by American culture:

> Many of the values that are considered desirable by the society are precisely those that are manifested most strongly in youthful groups. Physical attractiveness, sexual vigor, athletic prowess, and knowledge absorption are examples of values highly cherished in the United States culture, which happens to be distributed most heavily among young people. As a consequence the quality of youth has become highly esteemed even by older persons.[2]

Retailers know that youthfulness appeals even to those who are young only in spirit. Evidence of youthfulness in the consumption of products can be seen in commercials on television and advertisements in newspapers and magazines.

Urbanization and Suburbanization

It is an accepted fact that the American culture is more urban than rural. However, in recent years the big change has been the migration of millions of people to

[2]James F. Engel, David T. Kollat, and Roger D. Blackwell, *Consumer Behavior* (New York: Holt, Rinehart and Winston, Inc., 1969), p. 249.

the suburbs that ring the central cities. Today almost one-third of the nation's population lives in suburban communities. Furthermore, by 1980, 60 percent of the present total metropolitan population will have moved to the suburbs while only 40 percent will remain in the central city. This reshuffling of the population has caused the movement of large numbers of retail stores into regional suburban shopping centers; this movement is expected to accelerate.[3]

Urbanization and suburbanization have raised some interesting questions for retailers. They have affected the character of products demanded by the American consumer, the business facilities through which they are sold, and the personnel policies that the retailer must follow. Movement to the suburban areas has meant an increased demand for lawn care products and services, security devices, different clothes, outdoor entertainment products, and exercise areas that take up little space. It also means location of retail outlets near public transportation, the construction of large retail complexes that do not pollute, and an increased concern that facilities serve social as well as economic needs. Finally, it creates such problems as store security, employee safety, checking the backgrounds of prospective employees, and training salespeople to deal personally with customers whom they do not know.

Inner/Outer/Traditional Directedness

David Riesman has described the social character of any culture as being inner-directed, outer-directed, and/or tradition-directed. Riesman contends that the American culture is a blend of outer-directed and inner-directed values. Inner-directed values are learned primarily from the immediate family while outer-directed values are the result of interaction between the individual and his or her environment. Because Americans are becoming more outer-directed, they are ready to accept the values of others. A retailer may capitalize on the individual's growing tendency to accept outer-directed values through the use of attractive advertisements and imaginative promotions.[4]

DIVIDING THE MASSES

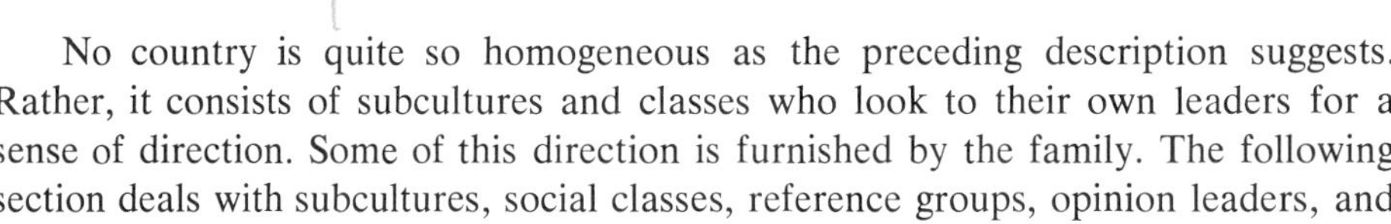

No country is quite so homogeneous as the preceding description suggests. Rather, it consists of subcultures and classes who look to their own leaders for a sense of direction. Some of this direction is furnished by the family. The following section deals with subcultures, social classes, reference groups, opinion leaders, and the family.

[3] *The Suburbanization of Retail Trade: A Study of Retail Trade Dispersion in Major U.S. Markets, 1958–67* (New York: Spindletop Research, Inc., for Dept. of Economics and Research, CBS Broadcasting Group, 1970), p. 8.

[4] David Riesman, Nathan Glazer, and Ruel Denny, *The Lonely Crowd* (New York: Doubleday & Company, Inc., 1956).

Subculture and the Disadvantaged

A discussion of American subcultures is incomplete without a reference to racial subcultures. Blacks, who constitute 92 percent of the nonwhite population of America, are the most important part of this group. There are about 22.7 million black Americans concentrated in the principal cities of the United States.[5] Indeed, such cities as Washington, Newark, Gary, and Atlanta have black majorities and over forty percent of the people in such cities as Baltimore, New Orleans, Detroit, Wilmington, Birmingham, Richmond, and Saint Louis are black. An increasing number of blacks are moving into suburbs in an attempt to move nearer good jobs that are available in suburban industrial parks and to find better housing than is available in the central city.

There has been some controversy over whether or not a black consumer market as such exists. D. Parke Gibson insists that there is and cites four reasons to support his conclusion: (1) the people are identifiable, (2) they have definable purchase patterns, (3) the market is large, and (4) the market is concentrated in large cities.

The 1970s saw evidence that American companies—many of which are owned and operated by blacks—were doing a good job of selling their products to blacks and other minorities. In order to market any products to a subculture, the retailer will find the following questions helpful:

1. Does the subculture need the product?
2. Will the product be used by the subculture as it is in other markets?
3. What is the sales potential of the product?
4. What type of retailing mix must be employed?
5. Can the effectiveness of the selling effort to the subculture be measured?

One of the more important contributions of the civil rights movement is the awareness it caused in American society of the importance of the black person as a consumer. Moreover, blacks increasingly have become aware of themselves, and black consumer patterns are increasingly accepted as valid expressions of behavior.

Social Classes

Social classes are divisions of the total society into which individuals and families can be placed. Within each social class there is a further ordering of individuals and families. Inasmuch as each social class is in a higher or lower position with respect to other social classes, the members of any social class are esteemed according to their ranking in the hierarchy. Membership in a particular social class is determined by such factors as occupation, wealth, income, education, power, and prestige. Occupation is said to be the best predictor of social class membership.

Members of each social class tend to be homogeneous in beliefs, attitudes, and

[5]See D. Parke Gibson, *The $30 Billion Negro* (London: Macmillan Co., 1969).

behavior. That is, people of the same social class tend to dress alike, live in the same kinds of neighborhoods, have similar attitudes and opinions, and *shop in the same stores*. Because this is so, social class membership is important to retailers.

There is no absolute agreement among sociologists as to the number of social classes. However, one of the best-known classifications is that of W. L. Warner, who divided American society into six classes: upper-upper, lower-upper, upper-middle, lower-middle, upper-lower, and lower-lower. Almost 85 percent of the people are concentrated in the three lowest classes; this group constitutes the mass market, although the lower-lower group often is ignored. Mass marketing strategies are made to appeal to those classes rather than to the people of higher classes.

Social Class and Spending Behavior. Pierre Martineau once concluded:[6]

1. There is a social class system in the United States, and it can be isolated and described.
2. There are important psychological differences in the people who comprise different social classes.
3. Consumption behavior patterns delineate social class membership and are significant determinants of economic behavior.

Martineau's psychological contrasts between social groups are shown in Table 4.1. The implications to a retailer are very important.

Retailers must recognize that there is a social class concept, and that psychological differences exist between the classes; these differences often account for different consumer behavior. The retailer must first determine what social class he or she wishes to serve and then be certain that all of his merchandising techniques including the kinds of goods carried, the fixtures in the store, the layout and decor, the selling approaches, and the advertising techniques fit the value structure of the social class. It must also be remembered that membership within a social class is not fixed, and that a person may move from one class to another. Furthermore, as incomes of all classes increase, the mobility within classes change and mobility between classes changes, too. Retailers must alter their policies and practices to remain responsive to all these changes.

Reference Groups

A reference group is any collection of people that helps to shape the attitudes and behavior of an individual. People are attracted to a group because they have similar values and are prepared to accept the norms that influence its behavior. There are two basic types of reference groups: formal and informal. The formal groups include such institutions as churches, fraternities, clubs, schools, country clubs, and unions. Informal groups are usually based on friendships of one kind or another.

[6]Pierre Martineau, "Social Classes and Spending Behavior," *Journal of Marketing* (October 1958), p. 130.

TABLE 4.1

Contrasting Attitudes Found Among the Middle and Lower Classes

Middle Class	*Lower Class*
1. Pointed to the future	1. Pointed to the present and past
2. Viewpoints embrace a long expanse of time	2. Lives and thinks in a short expanse of time
3. More urban identification	3. More rural identification
4. Stresses rationality	4. Essentially nonrational
5. Has well-structured sense of the universe	5. Vague and unclear structuring of the world
6. Horizons vastly extended or not limited	6. Horizons sharply defined and limited
7. Greater sense of choice making	7. Limited sense of choice making
8. Self-confident, willing to take risks	8. Very much concerned with security and insecurity
9. Immaterial and abstract in thinking	9. Concrete and perceptive in thinking
10. Sees him- or herself tied to national happenings	10. World revolves around the family and body

Source: Pierre Martineau, "Social Classes and Spending Behavior," *Journal of Marketing* (October 1958), p. 129.

All products have either positive or negative qualities, and some reference groups identify with one kind of product more than others do. For example, some groups exist solely to participate in some activity that is pleasing to all its members, such as a ski club. In this case, the members may purchase the same brand of skis and equipment and go for skiing weekends to the same slopes. Frequently, there is someone in the group who is the opinion leader or taste maker; others will tend to conform to his or her ideas and behavior.

Opinion Leaders

An interesting theory is that marketing efficiency can be immeasurably improved if opinion leaders can be identified. Elihu Katz and Paul Lazarsfeld are closely identified with this theory.[7] They have found that an opinion leader can influence other consumers in making a buying decision on products such as food, soaps, clothes, and hairstyles. This opinion leader usually influences other customers through normal day-to-day contacts. This theory has been called the "two-step" flow of communication because the route is from the promotional media to the opinion leader to opinion followers.

Opinion leaders are found on all social levels. Unfortunately for marketers the identity of the opinion leader for one product or service may not be the opinion

[7]Elihu Katz and Paul F. Lazarsfeld, *Personal Influence* (New York: The Free Press of Glencoe, Inc., 1955).

leader for other products. Myers and Reynolds make the following statement concerning the identity of opinion leaders:

> Whether or not a person becomes an opinion leader seems to depend upon at least three major factors: who one is (prestige), what one knows (instrumentality), and where one is located (accessibility). In effect, opinion leaders are selected by their followers rather than vice versa, and they may actually be lower in status.[8]

Simply because it is difficult to identify the names and addresses of the opinion leaders does not rule out the creative effort needed to locate these people. Some of the ways that have been used to find opinion makers are:[9]

1. By sponsoring consumer contests and thus obtaining names and addresses of entrants.
2. From warranty cards of purchasers of appliances.
3. From listings from direct mail organizations.
4. From membership lists of community organizations such as the Rotary or Lions clubs.
5. From lists of subscribers to magazines.

Even if the opinion makers can be identified, there is no surefire way to communicate with them. In one famous study undertaken in Philadelphia, it was learned that window air conditioners were likely to be purchased in "clusters." The population in the Overbrook Park area at that time were primarily white-collar workers earning about the same wages and living in nearly identical homes. Yet air conditioners were likely to be purchased by next-door neighbors, meaning that once a unit was purchased and installed it was quite likely that the next-door neighbor would also buy a window unit. However, it was *not* likely that families across the street would be immediately affected.[10] Salespeople have learned that when one family on a block installs a major appliance, the nearest neighbors are the next most logical customers.

Some retail stores have formed panels of opinion leaders to advise on merchandising policy. An example might be Wes's Appliance Store:

> Wes has a very successful appliance store in one of the suburbs of a large city. His customers are quality conscious and interested in service. He regularly consults a panel of 15 advisors that he has personally selected as opinion leaders. Some are customers, others are public officials (village officials or school board members), others are chosen because of their professional standing, still others are heads of households. And some of his panel are women ranging from young marrieds to women whose children are married.

[8]James Myers and William H. Reynolds, *Consumer Behavior and Marketing Management* (Boston: Houghton Mifflin Co., 1967), p. 308.

[9]Ibid., p. 308.

[10]William H. Whyte, Jr., "The Web of Word of Mouth," *Fortune* (November 1954), p. 140.

Three times a year, Wes invites his panel to a dinner and then a seminar is conducted. All types of topics are discussed. He often asks their opinion before placing his order for new merchandise.

Wes is not certain that the panel he has selected contains the true opinion leaders of his community; nevertheless, he has reason to think they are. He has had many inquiries from interested people about opportunities to be on his panel, and he replaces panel members from a list of those who ask about membership. Wes has been successful in the three years that he has used the panel, and he attributes some of his success to the advice that he receives.

Panel members are given expensive presents for their services ($25 to $50).

The Family

The family is the reference group responsible for most of the attitudes held by an individual. Normally it is within the family that one learns; it shapes one's attitudes toward religion, country, education, politics, sex, products, brands, and stores. Each member of a family influences consumer buying decisions in different ways. Retailers are interested in the identification of the influencing member of the family in all buying decisions.

Some retailing decisions are automatic because everyone in the family agrees on what brand to buy. On other occasions, the husband is dominant, in others it is the wife, and in still others it is the children. Each family is different from other families; it is hard to generalize. However, it is sometimes said that the wife is the purchasing agent for the family and she probably accounts for the majority of consumer buying decisions on food, clothing, and household supplies. The husband and wife are both involved in decisions as to the brand of refrigerator, stove, washing machine, or dryer to buy. In short, in decisions that call for the expenditure of large sums of money, both the husband and wife usually play major roles.

Children are often consulted on products that affect their welfare, and consequently they exert considerable influence. Members of a family assume different roles as time passes and the family members are in different stages of their life cycle. For example, a college woman may exert unusual influence on the clothes her mother selects. In the same manner, the college man may have an inordinate influence on the kind and model of car his father buys. Each family's approach to buying decisions reflects the individual characteristics of each person and the interrelations among the family members. The astute retailer tries to distinguish among (a) the buyer—the one who comes into the store to make the transaction, (b) the user —the one or more persons who consume the product, and (c) the influential—the one or more individuals who help make a decision about what will be purchased. The problem is additionally complicated by the fact that individual family members may have great influence on certain aspects of a buying decision but not on others. For example, one study suggests that a decision about a purchase of furniture is not a single decision but a set of decisions; husbands and wives differ in their influence over each part. In particular, the purchase raises such questions as how much to spend; when to buy; where to buy; what to buy; what style to buy; and what color and fabric to select. Husbands wield far more influence over how much to spend than over the other questions where the wife's decisions are more important. The same study indicates that the influence of the wife is important only in selecting the color of a new automobile; the husband dominates the other elements of the decision.[11] The changing role of the female in the family is sure to be the subject of intense research and much speculation in the future.

STORE IMAGE

Just as an individual consumer has a self-image, the individual store also has an image. Most customers are aware of a store's image, and they will patronize that store with which they can identify. A store's image is determined by nine attributes:[12]

1. Merchandise—quality, selection or assortment, styling or fashion, guarantees, and price.
2. Service—presence of self-service, ease of merchandise return, delivery, and credit policies.
3. Clientele—social class appeal, self-image consistency, and store personnel.
4. Physical facilities—elevators, lighting, air conditioning, and washrooms.
5. Convenience—location and parking.
6. Promotion—advertising, displays, trading stamps, symbols, and colors.
7. Atmosphere—customer's feeling of warmth, acceptance, or ease.
8. Institutional—the conservative–modern projection of the store, reputation, and reliability.
9. Post-transaction satisfaction—satisfaction with the merchandise while in use, and with the store.

It may be useful to consider the type of image which each of these two retail dress shops has:

Jane's Fashions	*Avenue B. Dress Shop*
1. Shop is located in large regional shopping center	1. Store is located on a major street in a run-down section of the city
2. Architecture is modern and harmonizes with all the other stores	2. Store was built in early 1900s and needs remodeling
3. Customers are from households in upper 20 percent of income receivers	3. Customers are from low income households
4. Window displays are works of art	4. Windows are clutterered, dirty, and unimaginative

[11]Harry L. Davis, "Dimensions of Marital Roles in Consumer Decision Making," *Journal of Marketing Research* (May 1970), p. 169.

[12]Jay D. Lindquist, "Meaning of Image," *The Journal of Retailing* (Winter 1974–75), p. 31.

Jane's Fashions	*Avenue B. Dress Shop*
5. Decor of interior is in good taste; floors are carpeted	5. Interior is dull, poorly lit; floors are wood
6. Merchandise is expensive, highly styled, and displayed in good taste	6. Merchandise is of poorer quality and priced low
7. Stores features soft sell	7. Clerks use hard sell
8. Charge accounts are invited	8. Cash only is accepted
9. Delivery service is available	9. No delivery service is available
10. Advertisements are stylish, easy to read, and feature only a few items	10. Store seldom advertises

The image of a store is carefully built up through its advertising, and usually this is sufficient to permit easy identification. Pierre Martineau substantiates this observation when he says:[13]

> Whether he realizes it consciously or not, all of his advertising is creating an image of his store. One of the most important functions in the housewife's role is to know the store. She learns to single out certain cues in the advertising which will tell her about the store's status, its sense of styling, its policies on returns and credit, its general atmosphere, its customer body, even its physical qualities; and then she decides intuitively whether this is where she fits in. Far more than by any explicit claims about the store by the store, intuitive judgments are formulated by the new rational symbols; the type, the whiteness or fullness of the ad, the general tone, the sophistication of the art—in other words, by the totality of advertising style.

The modern individual consumer seems to be in revolt against both mass production and mass consumption. There has been an attempt by some large retailers to lump all customers into one class and to present one store image to everyone. Other retailers are becoming aware of the consumer revolt and are attempting to counteract this by catering to smaller groups. An example is the proliferation of boutiques, about which Grey Advertising has this to say:[14]

> The success of boutiques in a large measure demonstrates that a mounting number of customers are in revolt against *two trends* in our mass-production and mass-consumption society.
>
> 1. The *ho-hum service* in the vast barns which are today's mass-merchandising stores. This includes most department stores, which, in whole or in part, have become depersonalized.
> 2. The *"me-too character"* of so much of the merchandise found in today's stores. Product exclusivity is like a flare, it lights up a store and quickly sputters out, just as fast as modern ingenuity fills the marketplace with replicas.

[13]Pierre Martineau, *Motivation in Advertising* (New York: McGraw-Hill Book Company, 1957), p. 175.

[14]"Ideas and Trends in Retail Distribution," *Grey Matter* (retail edition), 13, no. 6 (November 1967), p. 3.

The reasons behind consumer acceptance of boutiques are the needs to be recognized as an individual and to be assured that the consumer is part of a distinct group. Perhaps a case can be made against many modern retailers who prefer to lump all consumers into one giant mold—the mass consumer—and then build one large store to serve all these people with identical, mass-produced merchandise. Actually, there is no such consumer; each is an individual with distinct drives, tastes, emotions, and social patterns. It is necessary for retailers to operate stores that cater to groups, but they must avoid the temptation to include everyone in the same grouping.

Whenever a market is divided into meaningful buying groups, it is said to be segmented. We may speak of the teen-age market, the college market, or the young married market. The purpose of segmenting the market is to find significant differences among buyers, and then group these buyers into meaningful submarkets. Whenever retailers are able to separate their customers into significant groups, they may be able to maximize their retailing opportunities.

TRADITIONAL CLASSIFICATION OF CONSUMER GOODS

In Chapter 3 we examined individual human behavior in order to understand how people act in their role of consumer. In this chapter we have looked at the various social, political, and economic groups that influence behavior. It is appropriate also to look at the way in which customers perceive goods in order to understand the strategies and tactics that the retailer devises in selling merchandise to customers. Marketers and retailers have traditionally classified consumer goods into three categories: convenience, shopping, and specialty goods.

Convenience Goods

Davidson and Doody define convenience goods as:

> Goods that are in habitual use, are of low unit value, and are purchased frequently.[15]

Under most conditions it can be said that convenience goods have the following characteristics:

1. They usually are sold at a low price.
2. They are purchased frequently by the customer.
3. There is usually very little time in planning their purchase (from the consumer's point of view).
4. Very little effort is spent by the consumer in shopping for these goods.
5. The product is sold in many retail stores.
6. There usually is a long channel of distribution.

[15]William R. Davidson and Alton F. Doody, *Retailing Management*, 3rd ed. (New York: The Ronald Press Co., 1966), p. 180.

Examples of convenience goods are razor blades, bread, milk, detergents, tobacco, women's hosiery, and men's socks. (See Figure 4.2.)

FIGURE 4.2
Convenience stores are usually stocked with low-priced frequently purchased products that are classified as convenience goods

Source: Tony Kelly, Consolidated Foods Corporation, Chicago, Illinois.

Retail Application. The retailer may locate convenience goods anywhere in the store. For example, since tobacco products are sold at many outlets, the local drugstore may place cigarettes close to the door so that the customer may enter the store, make a purchase, and leave quickly. On the other hand, a supermarket locates bread and milk at the rear of the store in order to encourage shoppers to pass other goods as they walk through. There is much debate in retailing as to whether the customer should be forced to seek out frequently purchased items or not. The seeking out results in customer exposure to other items along the way, but it may also create such frustrations that the customer soon transfers patronage to another retailer.

Impulse Goods. Impulse goods are convenience goods that consumers purchase on the spur of the moment. The customers have not entered the store explicitly to purchase those items, and a good display is essential to promote the sale. The next time you are checking out the weekly groceries at the supermarket, take notice of all the items that surround the checkout station. As an example, suppose that a woman went to the supermarket to do her weekly shopping. While she was passing the candy section, she was attracted to a package of licorice. She was intrigued because she hadn't seen or tasted this type of licorice since she was a little girl. She put a package into her cart immediately—promising herself a treat that she hadn't enjoyed for a number of years. The licorice is an impulse good. The impulse purchase should never be confused with the "irrational" purchase. Impulse purchases generally are rational; they occur when the item brings to awareness the thought that the goods will fill a need perceived by the customer. Prior to exposure to the product, the need existed; exposure raised the need above the awareness threshold.

Du Pont made a study in 1959 in which they found that only 30.5 percent of all purchases in a supermarket were planned—that is, the shopper had a specific item or brand in mind to purchase before entering the store. The remainder (69.5 percent) were in-store decisions. Fully 50.9 percent of the in-store decisions were impulse decisions. That is, the shopper had made no plans, either by specific item or brand, to make the purchase. The other in-store decisions (18.6 percent) were generally planned or occurred when a substitution was made for a planned purchase. There is no reason to believe that today's purchases would be more planned than was found in the Du Pont study.[16] Figure 4.3 helps to explain this situation. Note that 73 percent of unplanned purchases spring from in-store forces.

Shopping Goods

Shopping goods are those which are so important to the buyer that he or she is likely to take considerable time before making the decision to buy a particular item or brand. Examples of shopping goods are automobiles, refrigerators, men's suits, shoes, and women's apparel. One writer suggests that shopping goods can be divided into two groups—homogeneous and heterogeneous.[17] Shoppers sometimes view goods as being essentially the same, that is, they are highly standardized, and the differences may be only in their prices. In this case the shopper may actually shop around for the best price. These categories of homogeneous products would certainly include such "big ticket" items as refrigerators, stoves, dishwashers, washers, driers, and television sets.

Retailers who handle homogeneous products should be aware that customers view these products as being essentially alike, and therefore customers need the retailers to point out significant differences. Some retailers become successful discounters by displaying all popular brand appliances side by side and inviting the public to come and compare. Because price is extremely important to buyers of homogeneous products, the retailer should be hesitant to quote prices over the telephone because it affords the retailer little opportunity to outline other services and advantages a purchaser could obtain by buying a particular product from the retailer.

On the other hand, a heterogeneous shopping good is one that is nonstandard-

[16]*Today's Buying Decisions* (Wilmington, Del.: E. I. Du Pont de Nemours & Co., Inc., 1959).

[17]E. Jerome McCarthy, *Basic Marketing: A Managerial Approach*, rev. ed. (Homewood, Ill.: Richard D. Irwin, Inc., 1964), pp. 389–99.

FIGURE 4.3

The primary reasons for unplanned purchases (impulse goods) have been charted by a research group

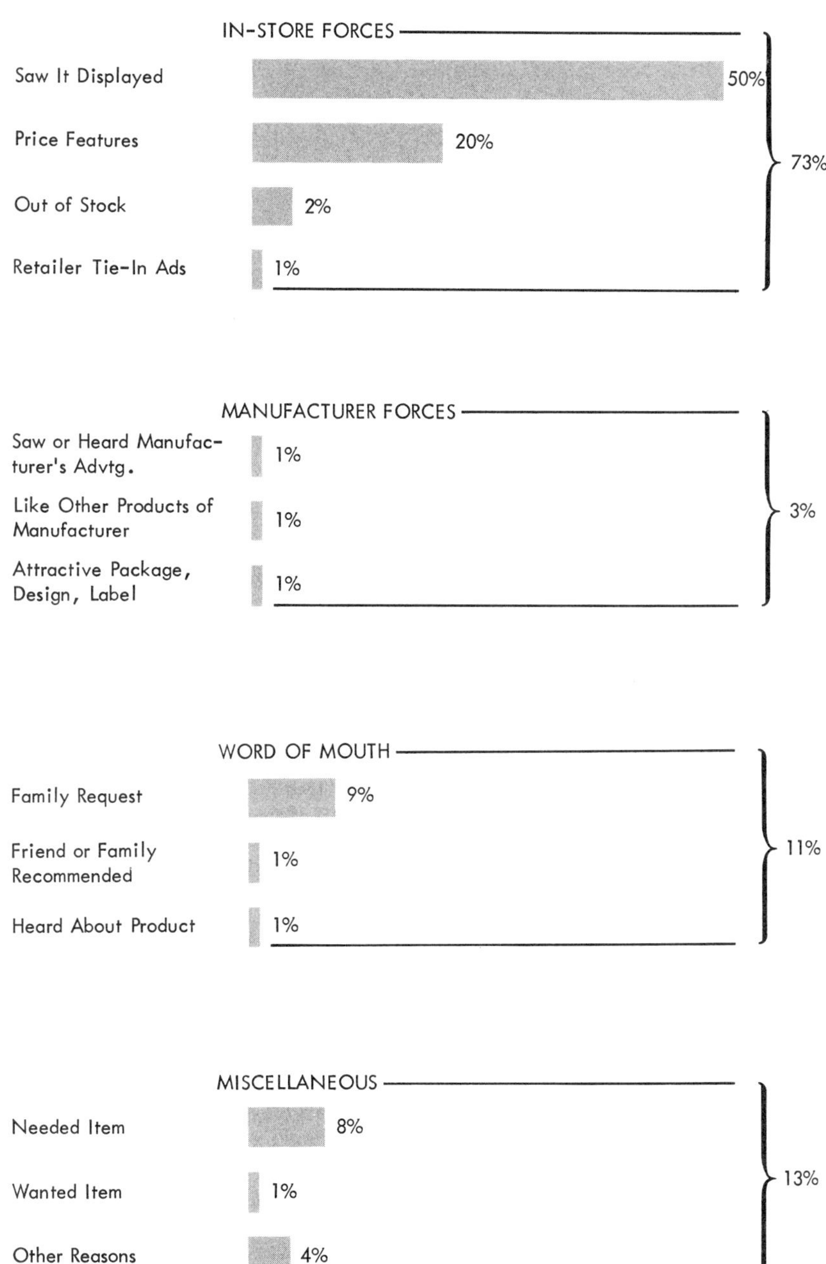

Source: Point-of-Purchase Institute, "Why Shoppers Make Unplanned Purchases in Mass Merchandising Stores," p. 32.

ized. Examples of this type are draperies, furniture, men's clothing, and ladies' fashions. In these cases prices are secondary while the style and quality of the goods are all-important. The shopper is more than willing to spend a great deal of time in comparing items in different stores before making the buying decision.

A retailer often can differentiate from other retailers who market shopping goods by assisting the customers to make a decision. In the case of a furniture store, it might offer an interior decorating service (at no extra cost to the consumer) to help plan the furnishing of the home. A retailer of draperies may agree to hang the draperies in order to assist the buyer. A man may purchase a suit from one retailer because he has learned to appreciate the tailor's expertise in seeing that the suit fits him properly.

Fashion Goods. Fashion goods are shopping goods that are purchased because of their current appeal. Many people confuse the words *style* and *fashion*. A style is a type of good produced by a manufacturer, and it has a distinctive expression so that it may be easily identified. We may speak of a Louis XIV chair, a Dutch colonial house, a sack dress, or a mini-skirt. These styles do not change with the passage of time. In other words, a Dutch colonial house, a ranch house, or a Cape Cod will remain the same 25, 50, or 100 years from now. But fashion indicates a particular style that is currently popular.

Fashion Cycle. It is common for authors of retailing books to refer to a fashion cycle. They usually break the cycle into the following stages: (a) distinctive, (b) emulation, (c) mass consumption, and (d) declining. (See Figure 4.4.)

FIGURE 4.4

The sales curve represents the various stages of the fashion cycle

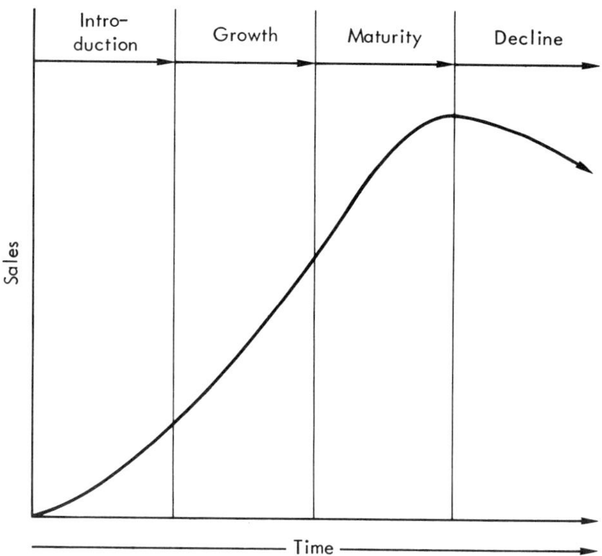

Today there is some disagreement about whether a fashion cycle moves vertically down from a high social economic class to successive lower ones, or whether it moves horizontally across several social economic classes at the same time. The vertical movement is referred to as the "trickle down" process, while the horizontal movement is called the "trickle across."

Historically the trickle down theory has been the primary explanation of the fashion cycle. For example, in the case of a woman's cocktail gown, one would find that an upper class taste maker (usually a leader in the fashion world) would purchase a cocktail dress because it was distinctive for the social group in which she moved. Other women would begin to emulate the fashion leader, and soon this gown would be on display in the fashionable shops across the nation. If this style is accepted, it is likely to trickle down to the shops that cater to the middle class. Generally speaking, once a style becomes mass-produced, its life as a fashion is almost at an end. Long before this, the taste makers will be wearing a different style—and a whole new cycle will have started.

Charles W. King does not think that the trickle down theory actually describes the modern situation. He reasons that this is due to:[18]

1. The changing social environment.
2. The impact of mass media upon all people at the same time.
3. Structural processes within manufacturing and merchandising companies which impede the vertical flow of the fashion.

In other words, a given style will be introduced simultaneously to different social strata. In each of these social classes, the style will be introduced by the innovators, and then if it becomes accepted, it will become fashionable. In support of this theory, note that pant suits were quickly manufactured and marketed at many price levels and sold by stores catering to all social classes. Furthermore, women in all roles of life wear them, thus giving credence to the "trickle across" theory.

George Field offers a third explanation of how fashions are diffused through our culture. He perceives an upward flow of innovative influence from lower- to high-status levels. This process he calls the *status float phenomenon.* To illustrate, he cites conservative males copying the trademarks of both the youth and the black subcultures. The preference of many blacks for vibrant colors has carried into the general male population, as have the hippies' fashions, albeit in modified manner.[19]

Retailing Fashion Goods. It is said that a manufacturer should be able to recognize the stages of the fashion cycle to which a particular good may be directed. This is also good advice for retailers. Furthermore, each retailer should know in which stage of the cycle they prefer to operate. Ordinarily a retailer cannot appeal to all classes of consumers at the same time. A retailer who projects a store image

[18]Charles W. King, "Fashion Adoption: A Rebuttal to the Trickle Down Theory," in *Dimensions of Consumer Behavior*, ed. James A. McNeal (New York: Appleton-Century-Crofts, 1955), pp. 114–27.

[19]George A. Field, "The Status Float Phenomenon," *Business Horizons* (August 1970), pp. 45–52.

that is favorable to high-income shoppers should not attempt to merchandise the same fashion to shoppers of a low social stratum. It all boils down to these two points:

1. A retailer should always know which socioeconomic group is in agreement with his or her store image.
2. A retailer should introduce the fashion to customers to take advantage of their position in the social strata.

Buying Fashion Merchandise. Those retailers who merchandise high fashion styles are forced to buy their stock in advance of the season. The dangers are that the retailer will buy the wrong merchandise or, conversely, will buy too little of a "hot" item and thus will suffer a loss in both sales and profits. In general, fashions are a function of such variables as living habits, economic conditions, and current aesthetic appeal. Buyers from high fashion shops may acquire information from among the following sources:

1. Fashion news from shops of couturiers (especially in Paris and New York). These dressmaking establishments show their collections at least twice a year (February for spring and summer wear and July for fall and winter wear.) Their offerings are accompanied by much publicity in newspapers and magazines, and on radio and television. Some of the leading couturiers are Coureges, Cardin, Gernreich, and Givenchy. Carnaby Street in London was the source for the popularization of the mod fashions of the '60s, particularly of the miniskirt.
2. Trade journals—especially *Women's Wear Daily.* These publications feature the "jet-set" and detail all the fashions that this group finds fascinating.
3. Magazines such as *Vogue, Harper's Bazaar, Modern Bride, Esquire,* and *Better Homes and Gardens.* These publications are important sources because they indicate current fashions and predict trends.
4. Newspapers. Newspapers give publicity to the latest fashions through news stories, features on the women's pages, and through the advertisements they carry.
5. Resident buying offices. These facilities can be helpful to retailers by directing the buyer's attention to specific offerings in central markets such as New York, Hollywood, and Dallas.
6. Fashion shows. Produced in department stores and leading specialty stores, fashion shows present the newest styles to the public.

In spite of all the information that is available, a buyer finds it difficult to predict the success of any article with fashion overtones. Retail shops catering primarily to innovators, opinion leaders, and taste makers also find it difficult to buy the right merchandise in the right amounts. They may have to depend upon intuition, inspiration, and experience to guide them in their buying decisions.

Specialty Goods

Specialty goods are those which are distinctive either because of their unique characteristics or because of their brand name, and consumers will make a special effort to purchase them. Examples are gourmet foods, health foods, expensive clothes, photographic equipment, stereo sets, and branded sporting goods.

Whether there was a classification of goods that could be identified as specialty goods was once the source of a dispute that centered around its definition. Ultimately the differences were resolved when the disputants agreed that there were specialty goods, and such a classification would be helpful to marketers.[20]

Specialty goods have the following characteristics:

1. The prices for these goods are relatively high.
2. Specialty goods are infrequently purchased.
3. Shoppers are likely to spend considerable time in actually making the purchase, although they frequently go directly to the retail outlet and obtain the product with a minimum of time and effort.
4. Shoppers are likely to spend considerable time in planning the purchase.
5. The brand name is usually very important.
6. The retail outlet that sells the product is usually very important to the shoppers.
7. Normally there is a short channel of distribution.

Perhaps the key to understanding the nature of specialty goods is the fact that consumers insist on a particular brand, and they are exceedingly loyal to it. For this reason retailers may not be able to substitute a different brand. A man who has always worn an Arrow shirt may not consider another brand. This type of buyer will spend a great deal of time and effort to search out a retailer who carries "his brand," if his usual retailer is temporarily out of stock.

CONSUMERS AS A MARKET

What is a market? This term is used in many contexts; for example, the urban market, the rural market, the student market, the farm market, the commodity market, the stock market, and so on. It is not unusual, therefore, to believe that the word *market*, as a concept, is confusing. One view is that a market is a physical place where buyers and sellers get together and a transfer of title takes place as goods are exchanged. In this context, it means that there are people, there are goods and services for sale, and there exists a price determination mechanism.

Another view of a market is that it consists of people with buying power with a tendency to buy; unlike the first definition, it is not a physical place. But people are not alike. Rather, all markets are divided into submarkets, each of which is homogeneous within itself. For example, we could speak of the automobile market, yet there exist subsets of that (Cadillac, Buick, Chrysler, Dodge, Ford, or Chevrolet). We may also speak of the market for foreign cars, compact cars, sports cars, or luxury cars.

[20]D. J. Luck, "On the Nature of Specialty Goods," *Journal of Marketing*, 24, no. 1 (July 1959), pp. 61–64; and R. H. Holton, "The Distinction Between Convenience Goods, Shopping Goods, and Specialty Goods," *Journal of Marketing* (July 1958), pp. 53–56.

People

Markets consist of people, and people are consumers; therefore, it is important to examine this segment of the market. There are two major ways in which we can analyze the population—one is quantitative and the other is qualitative. In the first we merely count numbers and express them in that form or convert the numbers into percentages. In late 1967 the population of the United States passed 200 million and it was recognized as a significant event in all news media. It had taken only 52 years to double the population since the 100th million was counted in 1916. The present rate of growth has slowed somewhat as the birth rate has declined from the peaks of the post-World War II years. Some forecasts predict a population of about 250 million Americans by 2000 A.D.

The number of people is interesting as a total, but it becomes more meaningful when it is broken down qualitatively. There is an infinite variety of ways in which the population may be broken down. Take, for example, the population of a large city of the United States. We could find the totals for any of the following categories:

1. Total population
2. Number of adult men and women, and number of children
3. Number of white adults, nonwhite adults
4. Number of teen-agers
5. Number of people with less than 8 years of education
6. Number of high school graduates
7. Number of college graduates
8. Number of homeowners
9. Number of renters
10. Number of marriages

Besides breaking the total population into geographical patterns such as regions, states, cities, counties, and so on, it is useful to break it down into other groupings such as age, sex, race, or educational background. *Progressive Grocer* magazine states it this way:[21]

> This vast army of literally hungry consumers represents a prime merchandising opportunity for creative merchants and marketers, not only by their sheer numbers, but of equal importance, by the way they differ from each other. Age, climate, regional behavior patterns, ethnic differences all exert more or less subtle variations that the successful store operator and food marketer carefully evaluates as part of his selling technique.

One need not be a demographer or a marketing expert to see the value of population statistics broken down into meaningful categories. For example, about 10.2

[21]"U.S. Population, 1967," *Progressive Grocer* (April 1967), p. 171.

percent of our population is over 65 years of age. What effect will this market have on doctor's services, hospital beds, retirement homes, and all the other products that this age demands?

We also have a vast youth market. It is estimated that 45 percent of our total population is under the age of 25, and about 7.9 percent of the total population is under 5. The teen-age market is approximately 17 percent of the total population. We are finding that marketers are focusing their sights on the teen-age market for such things as clothes, records, cosmetics, jewelry, and snacks. When we consider the money that the teen-age market has to spend, it is no wonder that so much attention is being given to this segment.

It is known that the young marrieds are an important market for food, furniture, housing, children's clothes, and household goods. *Progressive Grocer*'s "Consumer Dynamics Study" has defined a young married as someone under 40 years old with children under 13 years old. The same study indicated 10 ways in which supermarkets could win their business:[22]

1. Provide clean rest rooms.
2. Use bulletin boards for information directed to this group.
3. Put family into basic vocabulary when directing ads to this group.
4. Have fun in store displays—that is, use balloons, costumes, figures of animals in store promotions.
5. Talk nutrition and health.
6. Keep up with school activities.
7. Know the language and fads of children.
8. Be a kitchen friend of the mothers by offering them recipes, and the like.
9. Keep ample stock of merchandise on hand.
10. Build a baby department.

The example of the young marrieds demonstrates how the supermarkets are attempting to capture a large share of the food trade of this market segment. In a similar manner other markets will have to be studied and analyzed so that they also may be properly served.

Retail Application. To see how an analysis of population might be useful, consider Andrea's Photo Service.

> Andrea is a young college graduate who enjoyed photography as a hobby. After graduation she opened her own studio to specialize in candid wedding snapshots. Before making the decision, she had gone to the city hall and obtained the number of wedding licenses issued in the past five years. She also copied the names and addresses of photographers who advertised this service from the yellow pages. From this information she calculated that there was one photographer for every 10,000 people, a number she believed to be inadequate. Andrea took a map of the city and placed a red pin to locate each of the present photographers. In this manner she chose a location that was under-served by a candid wedding photographer.

[22]"Consumer Dynamics Study, Young Marrieds," *Progressive Grocer* (April 1967).

Andrea purchased a listing of names of brides-to-be from a service that specialized in that type of listing.

Andrea then opened a shop and has been successful.

Incomes

Although people are crucial to a market, the money that they spend is of equal importance. Chapter 1 defined national income as the total of all income earned in the productive process, and it is of primary importance as a measure of the performance of the total economy. Income is important, but by *income* what we really mean is *buying power*. Many people who suffer temporary lapses in their income continue to have buying power because they are trusted to repay what they borrow during periods of temporary difficulty.

SUMMARY

Man is more than a physiological and psychological entity; he is also a social creature whose behavior patterns are conditioned by groups and family membership. Each of these factors interacts with the forces internal to each individual and causes a particular behavior to be manifested. Many individuals respond in the same manner, so generalizations can be useful.

Traditionally, consumer goods have been classified into three categories: convenience, shopping, and specialty goods. This type of classification helps to solve problems relating to branding, shelf position, and standardization. This analysis helps the retailer to understand the consumer through the products he or she buys and what expectations he or she brings to retail outlets.

All markets consist of people with needs and desires and the income or buying power to purchase the goods they prefer. Markets also include the people who are selling the goods and services. Modern retailing is concerned with understanding the forces that bring about an exchange of goods so that the seller makes a profit and the consumer receives maximum satisfaction. These desirable goals can be better achieved through the study of consumer behavior.

QUESTIONS FOR DISCUSSION

1. Describe the personality of a salesperson you might encounter in a store that caters to the lower social class; the middle social class; and the upper social class.
2. Cut out two or three advertisements of a retail store from your local newspaper and relate these ads to the store's image.
3. What is a boutique? Why have they become so popular with both retailers and consumers?
4. If you were a retailer of men's and boy's clothing and you thought it would be beneficial to seek advice from "opinion leaders," how and where would you find these people?

5. If you were a retailer specializing in fashions for college women, would it be useful to understand (1) the fashion cycle, (2) the trickle across theory in explaining the fashion cycle, and (3) the trickle down theory of explanations? Why?

6. If you were called in as a consultant by a local department store and you were asked to explain the relevance of convenience goods, specialty goods, and shopping goods to this store, what would you say?

7. What is a market? How may a local drugstore discover its market and use this knowledge to its advantage?

8. Other than examples given in the textbook, cite one or two implications for retailing today from these American cultural values:
   a. religion
   b. security
   c. theft
   d. achievement

9. Is there a distinct black consumer market? Defend your position.

10. Are people buying more goods on impulse these days? Explain.

5 THE STORE Where Retailing Takes Place

Central city retailers are fully aware of the rivalry brought by modern suburban shopping centers. In Kalamazoo, Miami Beach, Cologne, and many other cities, they have responded by converting city streets into shopping malls. In Minneapolis and Spokane, second-floor walkways have been built to connect important retailers; shoppers can walk from store to store for several blocks without getting out in the weather. And in Tokyo and Vancouver, underground shopping centers have been built, again avoiding the problem of noisy streets and automobile traffic.

In Berkeley and many other university towns, "street people" and other small merchants sell allegedly homemade jewelry, candles, and clothing from makeshift locations on Telegraph Avenue and other high traffic streets. Many of their expenses—rent, insurance, taxes, personnel—are low, but so is their sales volume.

In Paris, Galerie Lafayette and C. and A. department stores have both chosen locations across from the Gare Montparnasse, a railway station that serves a large number of French commuters. They have gone wherever the customers are likely to be. But Galerie Lafayette also operates a store in Belle Epine, one of Europe's largest shopping centers, just south of Paris; it has not forgotten the suburbanite. And on the Champs Elysees, Paris' most famous street, Bouchara vends yard goods. One would not normally expect to find sewing materials sold in such a high expense location, but European women still tend to sew at home more than do American women.

A major department store chain closed one of its outlets in a deteriorating section of San Francisco. It claimed that most of the kinds of people it was able to serve had moved to the suburbs, and the store was losing money. Critics argued that the chain had no "corporate conscience." They pointed out that the closing would compound the already serious problems of the area and would put several hundred people out of work; some of the employees were too young to retire but too old to move.

McDonald's Corporation has generally been successful at picking locations for its drive-in franchised and corporate-owned fast food restaurants. An important factor is that each outlet be located where automobile traffic is high for long periods throughout the day. This allows for the physical facilities to be used from early morning (Egg McMuffins) to late at night. The company has been much slower to open walk-in restaurants in office and shopping areas because pedestrian traffic drops off so sharply in the late afternoon hours. A McDonald outlet, designed to sell a large volume at low margins, generally cannot operate profitably under such circumstances.

These real life examples illustrate some of the problems—and some of the answers—concerning retail store locations. Although retailing may go on in places other than a store, the store symbolizes retailing. Not only is the store a symbol, but it also represents a considerable investment in land, buildings, and fixtures. Its basic function is to serve as the marketplace where shoppers and merchants meet to conduct business. However, it is the shopper who initiates the action by going to the store. A store's economic success depends, therefore, to a large extent on its location. We must examine the store in some detail if we are to understand retailing.

STORE LOCATIONS

A good location permits thc rctailer to develop all his merchandising plans at reasonable costs with the expectation of generating a profitable sales volume. The site must be easy for the shopper to reach and often must provide ample parking. Furthermore, the shopper must be offered a sufficient supply of merchandise, competitively priced, and attractively displayed.

Importance of Location

A good location is critical. Unless the store can be operated profitably, it will fail and must be closed. Success or failure is not, of course, solely due to location, for a store may fail because of poor fiscal management, lack of capital, changes in buying habits, economic depressions, technological changes, aggressive competition, or a combination of these or other factors. Table 5.1 shows the failure rate of retail business for specific types. It has been found that over 6 percent can be attributed to poor location.

A good location is not only important to the owner of the retail business, but in cases where the land and facilities are leased, it is important to property owners, too. Rents are highest where retail profits are high, and rents may be low if profits are low. Therefore, owners of land and buildings are anxious to lease their facilities to those who can utilize the resources in the most productive manner.

The general public also has a stake in the location of a store. Consumers expect retailers to locate and offer products and services at a minimum of inconvenience to customers. John Mertes confirms the importance of a site's accessibility to customers when he says: "Of all the location factors to consider, the site's accessibility to customers is the most important."[1]

Location—A Continuous Problem

Location is a continuous problem because of changing buying habits, changes in methods and types of transportation facilities, and changes in the social fabric of the community. A look at any large American city reveals the many changes that have taken place in recent years. This change is not limited to New York, Los Angeles, or Chicago, but is part of the trend wherein affluent people are moving

[1]John E. Mertes, "Store Location," *Small Business Administration Bulletin 116* (January 1964).

TABLE 5.1

Poor Location Is One of Many Reasons for the Failure of Some Retail Businesses

Retail Lines Ranked by Failure Rate
Year 1970

Line of Business	*Failure Rate Per 10,000 Operating Concerns*
Women's Ready-To-Wear	77
Furniture and Furnishings	74
Cameras and Photographic Supplies	67
Infant's and Children's Wear	57
Books and Stationery	57
Men's Wear	52
Appliances, Radio, and Television	45
Gifts	40
Sporting Goods	40
Bakeries	32
Automobiles	28
Auto Parts and Accessories	27
Eating and Drinking Places	27
Toys and Hobby Crafts	26
Farm Implements	25
Shoes	23
Drugs	21
Dry Goods and General Merchandise	21
Lumber and Building Materials	21
Jewelry	18
Hardware	16
Groceries, Meat, and Produce	15
Women's Accessories	14

Source: "Key Business Ratios," Dun & Bradstreet, Inc., Business Economics Department, New York, New York.

out of the core city to the suburbs. Dr. George Brown, Director of the Census, states that since 1960 central cities have grown in population by about one percent while suburban rings have increased their population by 28 percent.[2] One consequence of the growth in suburban population is that more retail sales are originating in suburban stores than from central city stores. The emergence of shopping centers and the decline of downtown as a consequence of the suburbanization process was discussed in Chapter 2.

LOCATION STRATEGY

The location question may be split into two parts. First, a decision must be made as to the city or community in which to locate. Second, the problem of the exact site within the city must be solved.

[2]"The 1970 Census," *Media Decisions* (July 1971), p. 77.

Choice of City

The following criteria are useful in determining city choice: population data, income data, state of competition, stability of the community, and traffic congestion.

Population Analysis. In choosing the city, an analysis of population is essential. Answers to the following questions are helpful.

1. What is the present population?
2. Is the population growing, decreasing, or static? What seems to be the trend?
3. What ages predominate?
4. What nationalities or races live in the site city, and in what proportion?
5. Is the population housed primarily in apartments or single family dwellings?
6. Does the city have a specific purpose for existing?
7. Is the city a suburban or satellite community?

Answers to the first question are easy to come by. Most cities, villages, and towns have reasonably accurate estimates of the current population. The census is taken every ten years, and many communities have a special census taken in between. At other times estimates are made by village and city officials after analyzing building permits, water service, telephone installations, and other pertinent data.

An analysis of a city's population statistics for a series of years can determine if the population is growing, declining, or static. In rapidly growing communities, the need for additional retailers is quite apparent. However, in communities where the population is declining there may be a net loss of retailers. It would be a mistake to locate in such a community unless special circumstances justify it.

Many people assume that all cities are populated with the same proportion of young marrieds, children, senior citizens, or teen-agers. Nothing is further from the truth. Some communities, such as Sun City, Arizona, were founded strictly for senior citizens, and an age limit is set to keep out younger adults. The needs of the older adults are different than those for young marrieds, and the retailing structure reflects this fact. Some suburban communities are inhabited chiefly by young marrieds with young families. It is quite obvious that retailers catering to the needs of the elderly would do better if they located in a senior citizen's city. In a similar manner, a college community may have a disproportionate number of young single adults, whose needs differ from those of other age groups.

Other cities and villages or sections of cities are populated by people whose national origin or race is similar—for example, San Francisco's Chinatown. Many large cities have communities which are Polish, Italian, German, Irish, or other nationality in origin. And many cities have large geographically concentrated black or other minority populations. Each ethnic or racial group is a subculture, which in part determines the type, kind, and number of retail establishments needed to cater to the wants of their particular group.

In some American communities the population is housed in single dwelling units, while in others multiple dwelling units predominate. In the latter case, great numbers of people live in one square block. For example, in some areas of New York City there are over 4,000 people in one block. Contrast this with a small town in Iowa where only ten families or less live in a single block. The needs obviously are dissimilar.

Some communities are organized around a single industry or some other major orientation. We have all read or known about cattle towns, mining communities, or steel towns. Rochester, Minnesota, the home of the famed Mayo Clinic, is medically oriented. People who travel there are generally seeking medical treatment, and consequently their needs would differ from those who visit Miami Beach, Fort Lauderdale, or Scottsdale. Communities that are close to national parks, such as Yellowstone, Glacier, or Grand Canyon, are filled with motels, souvenir shops, restaurants, and other stores catering primarily to tourists.

There are also communities that are satellites to larger cities. These communities often are simply places where the residents sleep; consequently, they may not support a large retailing complex. They are sometimes referred to as "bedroom communities."

Economic Analysis. Not only is it necessary to know something about the size and character of the population of the site city, but it is also necessary to know something about its wealth and income. Such questions as the following should be answered:

1. What is the total disposable income of the community?
2. What is the median family income?
3. How many families are in each income bracket?
4. In what social level are most of the residents?
5. Are there any industries in town? What kind and how many?
6. What is the usual unemployment rate?
7. How many families are buying their own homes?
8. Are there any natural resources in the area and are they exploited?
9. What percentage of married females are employed and in what capacity?
10. Are the heads of the households employed mainly as unskilled, skilled, or professional workers?

Answers to the above and similar questions go a long way in providing a profile of the community and the income earned by its residents. Inasmuch as retailers need profitable sales to survive, it is necessary to know as much as possible about the economic climate of the site city.

Not surprisingly, retail trade flourishes best in those communities where the employment rate and family income are high. It takes income to purchase the market basket of groceries and meats that sustains the family every day of the year. Income is needed to purchase the clothing that is desired by each household member. It takes income to purchase the refrigerators, stoves, furniture, and other accessories that turn a house into a home and to patronize the restaurants, theaters, cocktail lounges, bowling arenas, and other places of diversion and entertainment.

Hence, a retailer must inquire into the nature of family income when contemplating locating within a given city.

There are general buying power indexes available that are useful yardsticks to measure the purchasing power of any market. *Sales Management Survey of Buying Power* is the best known index, and it appears annually in *Sales Management* magazine. The index has a vast amount of information, including estimates of population in numbers and by households; estimates of retail sales in dollars classified by retail categories; and a breakdown of effective buying income in totals, per capita and per household. All of this information is available for cities, counties, and metropolitan areas. A sample page is shown in Figure 5.1. Furthermore, *Sales Management* data may be purchased on punched cards or tapes and may be tabulated in ways most suitable for the person purchasing the information. Since information is available for all markets, a comparison can be made of the buying power of one market vis-à-vis another.

Competition. The following questions should be answered by anyone who is considering opening a retail store:

1. What kind of stores are already located in the site city?
2. What is the condition of the physical plants of the existing stores?
3. Are most of the retail stores independently owned or members of a chain?
4. How close is the site city to other cities and towns?
5. Are there any regional or district shopping centers nearby?
6. Is the governmental structure in the community favorable for growth, or is there an antibusiness bias?

Stability of the Community. The potential retailer should consider the following:

1. Is the school system adequate for the community? What is its educational reputation?
2. Are the people proud of their community?
3. Is there adequate police and fire protection? What about insurance rates?
4. Are there organizations active in promoting well being, such as Rotary, Kiwanis, Elks, Chamber of Commerce, League of Women Voters?
5. Does the site city have its own newspaper and is it effective?

Traffic Congestion. The following questions should be carefully considered:

1. How many automobiles are registered in the community and what is the number of licensed drivers?
2. How much parking is available, both free and fee regulated?
3. What is the character, condition, amount, and types of streets, roads, and arterial higways in the site city?
4. How well does traffic flow in peak transportation periods?
5. Are there feasible plans to improve traffic flow in the near future?
6. Is public transportation available?

FIGURE 5.1

There are various sources of information regarding the population, income, retail sales, and merchandise line sales for a certain geographic area

DISTRICT OF COLUMBIA

POPULATION — SM ESTIMATES, 12/31/71

METRO AREA / County	Total (thousands)	% of U.S.A.	% White	% Male	% 0-5 Yrs.	% 6-11 Yrs.*	% 12-17 Yrs.	% 18-24 Yrs.	% 25-34 Yrs.	% 35-49 Yrs.	% 50-64 Yrs.	% 65 & Over	Households (thousands)	% Under 25 Yrs.	% 25-34 Yrs.	% 35-44 Yrs.	% 45-54 Yrs.	% 55-64 Yrs.	% 65 & Over
					Age Groups									Age of Household Head					
WASHINGTON	2,901.3	1.3982	74.9	48.4	10.5	11.6	11.5	13.8	16.0	18.2	12.5	5.9	915.1	9.7	24.9	20.7	20.1	14.1	10.5
District of Columbia	734.6	.3540	27.4	46.4	9.1	9.7	9.9	15.5	15.5	16.6	14.4	9.3	256.3	10.1	22.6	17.3	17.6	16.4	16.0
Montgomery, Md.	544.1	.2622	94.4	48.3	9.5	11.9	12.7	11.7	15.4	19.2	13.5	6.1	163.8	5.8	21.3	22.3	23.9	15.8	10.9
Prince Georges, - Md.	674.5	.3251	84.9	49.3	12.6	13.0	11.7	14.3	16.2	17.5	10.5	4.2	199.3	12.1	29.5	21.6	18.5	11.2	7.1
Alexandria, Va.	109.2	.0526	84.9	47.3	9.9	8.3	8.4	18.1	18.7	16.3	13.7	6.6	42.1	16.4	28.1	15.2	17.1	13.5	9.7
Arlington, Va.	176.1	.0849	92.5	47.1	7.8	7.3	8.1	17.0	16.8	17.7	17.5	7.8	70.7	12.0	23.2	15.0	19.8	17.8	12.2
Fairfax, Va.	479.5	.2311	95.7	50.1	10.5	13.4	13.9	11.7	15.6	21.0	10.9	3.0	133.9	7.2	24.5	26.9	25.2	11.4	4.8
Fairfax City, Va.	21.8	.0105	97.8	48.8	11.1	13.7	14.5	12.1	15.2	20.0	10.1	3.3	6.1	9.8	24.7	26.2	24.6	9.8	4.9
Falls Church, Va.	9.8	.0047	97.7	46.7	9.1	8.9	11.7	12.4	15.3	17.4	18.1	7.1	3.4	8.8	20.6	14.7	20.6	20.6	14.7
Loudoun, Va.	39.7	.0191	87.3	49.3	12.6	13.9	12.5	8.5	15.5	17.4	11.8	7.8	11.3	5.3	25.8	22.1	15.9	15.0	15.9
[1] Prince William, - Va.	112.0	.0540	93.7	51.4	14.8	15.9	12.4	12.7	19.7	15.9	6.0	2.6	28.2	10.3	36.9	27.3	13.8	7.1	4.6
TOTAL ABOVE AREAS	2,901.3	1.3982	74.9	48.4	10.5	11.6	11.5	13.8	16.0	18.2	12.5	5.9	915.1	9.7	24.9	20.7	20.1	14.1	10.5
STATE TOTALS	734.6	.3540	27.4	46.4	9.1	9.7	9.9	15.5	15.5	16.6	14.4	9.3	256.3	10.1	22.6	17.3	17.6	16.4	16.0

EFFECTIVE BUYING INCOME & CASH INCOME SM ESTIMATES, 1971

METRO AREA / County	Net E.B.I. ($000)	% of U.S.A.	Per Capita	Hsld. Median Income	Net Cash Income ($000)	$0-3,000 % Hslds.	$0-3,000 % Inc.	$3-5,000 % Hslds.	$3-5,000 % Inc.	$5-8,000 % Hslds.	$5-8,000 % Inc.	$8-10,000 % Hslds.	$8-10,000 % Inc.	$10-15,000 % Hslds.	$10-15,000 % Inc.	$15-25,000 % Hslds.	$15-25,000 % Inc.	Over $25,000 % Hslds.	Over $25,000 % Inc.
						Cash Income Breakdown													
WASHINGTON	13,749,528	1.8624	4,739	10,769	12,966,148	7.1	.7	6.7	1.9	17.6	7.9	14.6	9.0	25.8	22.4	20.4	28.4	7.8	29.7
District of Columbia	3,829,895	.5188	5,214	10,139	3,574,824	10.2	1.1	8.3	2.4	17.9	8.5	13.0	8.4	22.0	18.9	19.1	25.9	9.5	34.8
Montgomery, Md.	2,735,491	.3705	5,028	11,665	2,605,529	5.3	.5	5.2	1.3	15.6	5.8	14.7	7.4	27.8	21.5	22.1	29.1	9.3	34.4
Prince Georges, - Md.	2,556,663	.3463	3,790	9,441	2,413,717	5.9	.7	7.1	2.2	23.1	11.2	19.3	13.8	26.3	28.6	15.0	27.0	3.3	16.5
Alexandria, Va.	593,278	.0804	5,433	10,527	566,998	7.1	.8	7.7	2.3	18.1	9.0	14.4	9.6	25.7	22.9	19.8	27.8	7.2	27.6
Arlington, Va.	1,178,399	.1596	6,692	12,414	1,118,778	5.8	.5	5.3	1.4	14.0	6.0	12.0	6.8	26.8	20.3	25.6	30.7	10.5	34.3
Fairfax, Va.	2,254,829	.3054	4,702	12,920	2,128,797	4.1	.4	4.2	1.1	11.9	5.1	11.9	6.6	30.7	23.3	27.9	33.4	9.3	30.1
Fairfax City, Va.	102,929	.0139	4,722	13,262	97,608	3.7	.3	2.2	.6	10.0	4.3	12.9	7.2	32.5	24.5	30.3	35.9	8.4	27.2
Falls Church, Va.	58,200	.0079	5,937	13,010	55,645	4.6	.4	3.8	.9	11.1	4.6	12.2	6.8	30.4	22.4	27.4	31.7	10.5	33.2
Loudoun, Va.	109,905	.0149	2,768	6,442	102,982	22.4	3.6	16.1	7.1	22.7	16.0	12.4	12.1	13.5	17.6	8.1	16.7	4.8	26.9
Prince William, - Va.	329,939	.0447	2,946	8,594	301,270	10.2	1.4	10.6	4.1	24.3	15.1	16.6	13.8	21.5	24.1	13.0	23.0	3.8	18.5
TOTAL ABOVE AREAS	13,749,528	1.8624	4,739	10,769	12,966,148	7.1	.7	6.7	1.9	17.6	7.9	14.6	9.0	25.8	22.4	20.4	28.4	7.8	29.7
STATE TOTALS	3,829,895	.5188	5,214	10,139	3,574,824	10.2	1.1	8.3	2.4	17.9	8.5	13.0	8.4	22.0	18.9	19.1	25.9	9.5	34.8

RETAIL SALES — SM ESTIMATES, 1971

METRO AREA / County	Total Retail Sales ($000)	% of U.S.A.	Food: Total ($000)	Food: Supermarkets ($000)	Eating & Drink Places: Total ($000)	General Merchandise: Total ($000)	General Merchandise: Dept. Stores ($000)	Apparel: Total ($000)	Furn.-House.-Appl.: Total ($000)	Furn.-House.-Appl.: Furn.-Home Furnishings ($000)	Automotive: Total ($000)	Gas Station: Total ($000)	Lumber-Bldg.-Hdwre.: Total ($000)	Drug: Total ($000)	Buying Power Index
WASHINGTON	6,491,775	1.6536	1,329,011	1,189,364	502,830	1,300,705	999,023	346,051	279,476	180,071	1,200,867	390,998	173,799	328,647	1.7066
District of Columbia	1,962,271	.4998	291,067	232,039	240,370	357,941	251,270	139,595	108,942	68,015	250,678	89,326	34,773	118,548	.4800
Montgomery, Md.	1,275,741	.3250	260,487	237,249	61,862	298,934	241,312	64,900	59,503	38,916	261,843	71,560	41,453	46,824	.3351
Prince Georges, - Md.	1,410,193	.3592	342,196	313,617	89,544	293,387	210,480	61,395	34,734	21,720	295,091	94,435	34,118	69,101	.3458
Alexandria, Va.	291,094	.0741	45,795	41,756	12,577	90,450	82,212	18,686	8,388	5,202	70,488	13,847	5,254	10,757	.0730
Arlington, Va.	413,007	.1052	66,828	63,678	39,917	78,445	65,638	15,877	18,340	12,992	119,090	22,461	8,374	19,139	.1283
Fairfax, Va.	688,223	.1753	204,625	195,419	42,631	159,025	139,805	32,697	30,297	20,744	57,237	58,675	27,463	39,900	.2515
Fairfax City, Va.	138,412	.0353	30,718	29,627	4,781	2,782		2,292	6,775	4,388	62,174	10,066	3,281	6,834	.0196
Falls Church, Va.	63,983	.0163	14,250	13,699	1,329	1,405		2,145	4,082	2,644	30,773	3,400	2,362	2,142	.0098
Loudoun, Va.	60,357	.0154	18,144	15,469	2,261	2,494		1,612	1,332	863	10,142	6,289	6,788	3,852	.0159
Prince William, - Va.	188,494	.0480	54,901	46,811	7,558	15,842	8,306	6,852	7,083	4,587	43,351	20,939	9,933	11,550	.0476
TOTAL ABOVE AREAS	6,491,775	1.6536	1,329,011	1,189,364	502,830	1,300,705	999,023	346,051	279,476	180,071	1,200,867	390,998	173,799	328,647	1.7066
STATE TOTALS	1,962,271	.4998	291,067	232,039	240,370	357,941	251,270	139,595	108,942	68,015	250,678	89,326	34,773	118,548	.4800

MERCHANDISE LINE SALES, 1971

METRO AREA	Groceries, Other Foods ($000)	Cosmetics, Drugs, Health Needs, Cleaners ($000)	Womens', Girls' Clothing ($000)	Mens', Boys' Clothing ($000)	All Footwear ($000)	Major Appliances ($000)	Furn., Sleep Equip., Floor Coverings ($000)	Department Store Sales: Groceries, Other Foods ($000)	Department Store Sales: Cosmetics, Drugs, Health Needs, Cleaners ($000)	Department Store Sales: Womens', Girls' Clothing ($000)	Department Store Sales: Mens', Boys' Clothing ($000)	Department Store Sales: All Footwear ($000)	Department Store Sales: Major Appliances ($000)	Department Store Sales: Furn., Sleep Equip., Floor Coverings ($000)
WASHINGTON	1.246.421	240.196	467.408	220.720	136.327	207.737	246.687	30.970	29.971	261.744	106.895	40.960	80.921	69.932
TOTAL ABOVE AREA	1.246.421	240.196	467.408	220.720	136.327	207.737	246.687	30.970	29.971	261.744	106.895	40.960	80.921	69.932

1 Data received too late for inclusion in this issue indicates that population for Prince William County should be 120.2

Source: "Survey of Buying Power," *Sales Management*, July 10, 1972, C-26.

Choosing a Site within a City

Once the site city decision is made, the retailer must select a trading area within the city. Determining the trading area is significantly different for the retailer than for the manufacturer. A retailer is usually interested in a small area surrounding the store, while many manufacturers have trading areas that are nationwide or even worldwide in size.

Trading Area. What is a trading area? As we use the term, it is the area from which an individual store draws its customers. In some cases the trading area may encompass many square miles, such as is the case of huge downtown department stores in large cities. The trading area of a food supermarket is decidedly smaller. Robert Mueller, editor and publisher of *Progressive Grocer*, estimates that the typical food supermarket obtains its greatest share of sales from a two-mile trading radius.[3] Food stores in densely populated areas would have much smaller drawing power.

A regional shopping center draws customers from a wider area. As we learned in Chapter 2, one of the first shopping plazas to open in the Chicago area was Old Orchard. The *Chicago Tribune*'s Research Division, in its study of shopper mobility, stated that Old Orchard once had a trading area of 1500 square miles.[4] Old Orchard's trading area apparently was too large, for many additional regional centers have since been built. Most are located within a half hour's driving time of a million residents. Trading areas for regional shopping centers have been reduced, but they still cover at least 50 square miles. Inasmuch as today's shoppers are mobile, there is considerable overlapping of trading areas. In fact, most shoppers visit several shopping centers regularly and a few others occasionally. In like manner, trading areas of individual stores overlap those of other stores carrying similar goods.

Use of Mathematical Models to Determine Trading Areas. The type of store or shopping center is not the only factor affecting the size of the trading area. One must analyze population, competition, store image, and accessibility. (See Figure 5.2.) These factors are difficult to isolate, and even if they can be isolated, they must be converted into quantitative measures so that their relative importance may be determined.

Some people rely heavily on mathematical formulae to delineate the trading area. Reilly's Law was an early attempt to determine the breaking point where one city would attract shoppers over another. More recently, the mathematical

[3]Robert W. Mueller, "Food Retailing in the 1970s" an address given at the Annual Convention of the Supermarket Institute, Atlantic City, N.J., May 14, 1969, p. 17.

[4]*Chicago Tribune* Research Division, "How Chicago Shops—The Changing Retail Market," 1964, p. 34.

FIGURE 5.2

Highway accessibility is an important factor in selecting a shopping center store site; the construction of the Perimeter Highway in Atlanta, Georgia, led to the emergence of shopping center clusters, providing many choice store sites with excellent automobile accessibility

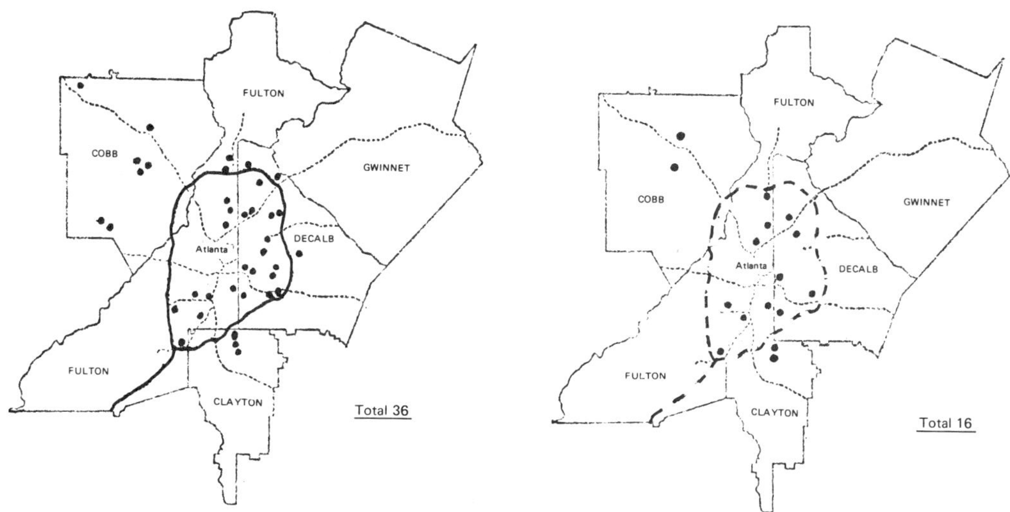

Source: Research and Marketing Dept., *Atlanta Journal-Constitution*, Atlanta, Georgia.

models have become highly sophisticated, and a person needs an excellent mathematical background to understand and to apply the formulae.[5]

Large retail organizations can afford skilled technicians who use computers as aids to site selection. Manuel D. Plotkin has described one such method in which credit accounts, optical scanners, and a computer are used to delineate an existing store's trading area.[6]

In Plotkin's example, customer characteristics are taken directly from the credit applications and coded on special cards. Data include such information as when the customer opened the account, whether a change of address has occurred, length of time a customer has lived in present home, age of customer, number of children and other dependents, source of income, whether or not the customer owns his or her home, and the store identification number. Next, an optical scanner reads the cards and transcribes the data on magnetic tapes. The data are then fed to a com-

[5]The student may wish to consult one of the following sources for a detailed explanation of a mathematical model: Russ W. Ritland, "New Methods of Estimating and Forecasting Retail Sales," *Journal of Retailing,* 39, no. 3 (Fall 1963); and William Appelbaum and Saul B. Cohen, "Trading Areas Networks and Problems of Store Saturation," *Journal of Retailing,* 37, no. 4 (Winter 1961–62), pp. 38–39.

[6]Manuel D. Plotkin, "The Use of Credit Accounts and Computers in Determining Store Trading Areas," in *New Directions in Marketing*, ed. Frederick E. Webster, Jr. (Chicago: American Marketing Association, 1965), pp. 271–82.

puter programmed to analyze this information. The computer provides a printout describing each store's trading area. The printout specifically identifies the primary trading area, the secondary trading area, and the tertiary (fringe) trading area. Sales penetration estimates for each segment of the trading area are then provided. This analysis is useful in determining the feasibility of expansion of retail facilities or relocating existing facilties. William Appelbaum and Saul B. Cohen are pioneers in this phase of site location theory.[7]

Systems Approach. Jac L. Goldstucker suggests a systems framework may be helpful in the location of retail outlets. Goldstucker says multiunit retailers set themselves the goal of "completing a geographical network of retail establishments in order to have full access to all appropriate markcts."[8] For example, in the case of a fast food chain, one must not have a marketing gap, that is, a market without a fast food outlet. The chain is complete only when all territories are served.

Goldstucker suggests a second locational goal is to choose a site that will give an acceptable rate of return on the investment and will at the same time complete the network (that is, satisfy the first goal). A third goal is the need for a retailer to establish his or her name and promote the store's image.

Given the three goals, the location problem is one of completing a system to serve the community as a whole. In Goldstucker's words:[9]

> If one takes as a reference point the community as a "total" system, then marketing is a subsystem of it, and retailing is a subsystem of marketing. It is appropriate to take the community as the reference point since it is the total system which ultimately must be served. As with all systems, the marketing subsystem must adjust in order to satisfy community needs; the retail subsystem must also make such an adjustment. The alternative is entropy. An example of a system that was non-adaptive and therefore entropic is the old general store.

Illustrative Case on Location. Assume that an individual is interested in opening a specialty shop in women's fashions; how would he or she choose the location? In this instance, let's say that Andrew Wilson has had experience in selling women's fashions, and that is the business he now wishes to pursue. Wilson believes that his style of retailing will be important to some segment of the population. In essence, he is seeking a "niche" in a vast industry. How does he go about making his decision? First of all, Wilson would have a good idea of his financial capabilities, so that he would not choose a location considerably beyond his means. This might rule out places such as Fifth Avenue in the fashionable section of New York City or the "magnificent mile" on North Michigan Avenue in Chicago. On the other hand, if he wishes to cater to upper middle class women, he would rule out lower income neighborhoods and their shopping districts.

[7]See William Applebaum and Saul B. Cohen, "The Dynamics of Store Trading Areas and Marketing Equilibrium," *Annals of the Association of American Geographers*, 51 (March 1961), pp. 73–101.

[8]Jac L. Goldstucker, "A Systems Framework for Retail Location," in *Science, Technology, and Marketing*, ed. Raymond M. Hass (Chicago: American Marketing Association, 1967).

[9]Ibid., p. 421.

A good starting point would be to make a profile of Wilson's expected customers, that is, the people who would most likely be interested in buying the type of fashions he plans to sell. After considerable thought, he comes up with this profile:

1. The women will be from the upper middle class.
2. They will represent families whose income is between $15,000 and $24,999 annually.
3. The male of the household probably will be a college graduate; the wife will have graduated or attended college.
4. The head of the household will be either a professional worker or employed in a managerial capacity.
5. The family will either own its own home or live in a luxury apartment.
6. If home owners, the house will have a market value of $50,000 to $65,000. If renters, they will pay a minimum of $325 in monthly rent.
7. The potential customer will be in the 34-to-49 age bracket.
8. Most families of the group who are likely to become customers will have children in high school and, in some cases, college.
9. The women will be fashion conscious and sufficiently socially or professionally active to require a good wardrobe. Furthermore, the customer will be knowledgeable about clothes.

Perhaps Wilson would jot down other characteristics his potential customers should have. He would continue his list until he believed that he had sufficient information to search for this type of customer.

If Wilson is acquainted with the general area, he may experience little difficulty in identifying the communities where such people reside. If he is unacquainted with the region, he might consult local realtors, chambers of commerce, census tracts, and newspaper advertisements on housing, or seek advice from friends.

Let's assume that Wilson makes a list of all the suburbs and central city locations where this kind of resident can be found. Because of the nature of central cities today, his list may contain mostly suburban locations. He might then drive to the area and investigate the nature of the homes and their environment. Assuming he locates several suburban areas where his type of customer lives, what might his next step be?

He could obtain a map of the area and locate all the shopping areas which are within the community or close-by. In particular, he would locate all the dress shops that handle the quality of merchandise that he intends to sell. These stores would be his competitors. He now may have to make a value judgment as to whether the area is "overstored" with dress shops or whether there appears to be an opportunity for an additional one. This value judgment may be based upon considerable investigation of the shopping areas, people counting, inspection of merchandise offered, and traffic counts. Retail trade associations often can advise a prospective entrepreneur about the average number of stores per thousand population.

Let's now assume that Wilson has decided on two suburban locations. In order to choose the exact site, he may decide that the proper action would be to buy out an existing store that caters to his type of consumer. On the other hand, he may decide to build his own store or to rent an empty one, or to become part of a new complex of stores being planned for a large regional shopping center on the outskirts of town.

If he builds his own store, he will be subject to the zoning regulations of the community. These should be consulted to determine whether or not a store of the type that he is planning is permitted. In some cases, the ordinances may have to be changed. In any case, he might find it to his advantage to locate in a community that has strong zoning regulations for all types of construction. This insures the protection of his investment while located in this community. Even if he should choose to locate in a planned shopping area, it would be advantageous to examine critically the zoning regulations.

Before picking out the exact site, Wilson will probably make a traffic analysis. One type is a pedestrian count. If the location is in an established shopping center, he can count the number of people passing by the potential site. A particular site might have a heavier traffic count than a second site, but the second site might have more people passing by who are prospective customers. What does this tell us? Simply that one must analyze pedestrians in terms of potential customers as well as in mere numbers. Even a simple count can be troublesome unless the counter has good instructions. If you are interested only in potential customers, you probably would not count children, men, service personnel, people hurrying to or from work, or others who were not actually shopping. Since Wilson is interested in women of a certain age group, those may be the only ones he will count.

Naturally, he would take into consideration such factors as the time the count was made, the day of the week, the month, and the season of the year. For example, Thursday, Friday, and Saturdays are normally heavier shopping days than Monday or Tuesday. Late afternoons might be a good time in terms of a large pedestrian traffic rather than early in the morning. The month of July usually is a poor shopping month for many retailers, while September, December, and May are excellent. Proper weight must be given to these factors before an evaluation of the traffic count is complete.

Another form of traffic analysis is an examination of the arterial streets and highways that bring shoppers to the site. If traffic is congested to the point that it is difficult to drive to and through the area, it may prove to be a poor location. Major advantages that newer shopping centers have over established street shopping areas are the parking facilities and the ease in reaching the site.

Once Wilson has selected a specific site that possesses the desired locational qualities, there are other factors that he, and any retailer in a similar situation, must consider.

THE FINANCIAL PLAN

Any retailer must concentrate on the desired financial plan once he or she has decided to establish a store. This problem is every bit as complex and important as is location. As a matter of fact, the most important single factor to be considered

after selecting the exact site is the *terms of occupancy*. That is to say, a decision must be made as to whether or not the store is to be owned outright or whether the site or building is to be leased. Each approach has advantages and limitations.

Ownership of the Store Site and Building

A major advantage of ownershp of the site and the buildings thereon is the independence that accrues to the owner of a business property. In particular, the store owner need not worry about the renewal of the lease at its expiration. The decision to continue the business on the site rests solely with the owner and not with an absentee landlord. You have perhaps seen signs on retailers' windows stating, "Lost our lease. Going out of business." Of course, simply losing a lease does not necessarily mean that the merchant goes out of business, because he or she may find another location that is equal or superior in every respect.

When a merchant owns the property and building, it may be altered or repaired at the owner's discretion, provided repairs are consonant with local building codes. When a building is leased, the terms of repair and alterations are spelled out; the merchant may not be able to carry out his or her own wishes.

Another advantage of site ownership is that any increase in its dollar value goes to the owner, in this case the retailer. It is also possible for the owner to lease a portion of the property to someone else, and the net profits of the merchant may be swelled by the rents earned in this way. Many a merchant who owns a building with space for other stores actually has become a landlord, as well as fulfilling the role of merchant in his or her own store. Department stores commonly rent space to independent merchants on a fixed monthly rental or percentage of sales basis. The leasee may operate an optical goods department, a jewelry department, or a photo department without the customer's awareness of the relationship. The leasee may use the store's advertising, credit department, personnel department, and delivery service, and as far as the customer can tell it is simply another part of the department store's operation.

The advantages of ownership can be summed up by stating that the owner has the independence to decide his or her own destiny and need not be subjected to a veto by a landlord.

Leases

A lease is a legal contract between at least two parties covering the conditions that will govern the use of the land and buildings by the renter. The rights and responsibilities of both owner and renter are spelled out in the lease. Any contract is a legal instrument drawn up to protect the rights of all parties according to the statutes of the state in which the contract is drawn. Therefore, it is imperative that a lawyer draw up the lease. Both contracting parties should be represented by attorneys, so that all terms and conditions are clearly understood; the rights, duties, and responsibilities of the tenant and landlord must be detailed so that any misunderstanding is minimized. It is difficult to generalize on the terms of a contract because each of the fifty states has statutes that differ significantly on specific terms.

Types of Leases. There are two types of leases: one requires a fixed payment of rent per month or per year; the other calls for a variable rent. An example of the first kind would be the merchant who rents a vacant store and agrees to pay a monthly rent of $500. This amount is fixed by the contract and cannot be increased or decreased during the life of the lease. The significant characteristic of this type of lease is that rental payments are fixed regardless of the sales volume. All increases in sales revenue accrue to the merchant, and the landlord does not share in the increase. On the other hand, this type of contract is disadvantageous to the retailer if sales in a particular month decline, for the rental payment would not be affected and the tenant would pay the same flat amount. Generally speaking, if the landlord expects a retail area to experience great sales growth, the flat payment contract would not be used, since the landlord would be denied any of the benefits due to the increased value of the property.

An example of the variable type is the percentage lease. This states that the renter will pay a stated percentage of net sales or profits as rent. In this lease there is no minimum or maximum dollar rent, although the landlord frequently inserts a provision that provides for a minimum guarantee. A percentage-type lease is desired by the landlord if the sales volume of a store is expected to rise because it permits the landlord to share in the increased valuation of the property. The landlord justifies a higher rent on the grounds that increased volume of sales are partly the result of increases or shifts in population, or greater incomes to the population, which result in larger sales (and profits) to the retailer. The percentage of sales arrangement gives some protection to the retailer in areas where there is a significant decline in sales volume. Sometimes these declines are due to factors that are beyond the retailer's control.

We stated that sometimes landlords specify a flat amount of rent as a minimum with an overall percentage of net sales. An example would be the lease that provides for a $16,000 annual rent or 5 percent of the net sales, whichever is the largest. Suppose that a store has net sales of $500,000; what would be the rent? Five percent of $500,000 equals $25,000; the rent would be $25,000. However, if the net sales had declined to $300,000 the rent would be $16,000, the guaranteed minimum, rather than 5 percent of the net sales, which in this case is $15,000.

Occasionally, contracts are written that specify both minimums and maximums. An example might be one that would state $16,000 annual rent as a minimum, or 5 percent of the net sales up to a maximum of $40,000 annually. In this case, sales that exceed $800,000 annually would not have an effect on the rent.

Other contracts specify differing rental percentages. For example, 5 percent of net sales of the first $100,000; 4 percent of the second $100,000; and 3 percent on all sales over the $200,000 volume.

The terms of the contract depend on the bargaining powers of the landlord and the tenant. If the landlord has an excellent site and there are several competitors bidding for it, the terms of the lease will probably favor the lessor. On the other hand, if the site is somewhat unattractive and there are no other bidders, the terms of the lease will favor the lessee.

It should be mentioned that the lease which is based on a percentage of net sales implies that the tenant does not falsify the records. Therefore, these terms are offered only to prospective merchants whose honesty is unquestioned and a suitable auditing mechanism is available.

Reasons for Leasing. Why do some merchants lease rather than own stores outright? There are several reasons. One important reason is the merchant's lack of capital to own the land and building, preferring to use his or her limited resources on inventory and day-to-day working expenses.

Yet, there are many large retailers who are strong financially, but still prefer to lease their buildings. They do so because they expect to receive a better return on investment (ROI) when funds are put into inventory rather than real estate.

Other merchants are forced to lease because a site is not for sale but may be leased. This merchant may have no alternative but to lease, especially if this is the best location and there are no other suitable substitutes.

Another important reason why some merchants lease the physical property is the unwillingness of the retailer to engage in the real estate business. He or she is then able to concentrate on the problems of merchandising and let someone else worry about property ownership. Also, some retailers think that ownership inhibits them from moving if that course of action is desirable. In a mobile society, this is an important consideration.

In the case of our mythical Mr. Wilson, after careful observation of all the financial plans and options, he is able to narrow his choice of location to one city and to a specific site within it. Then he chooses the financial plan that best suits his economic status and merchandising objectives. As you have seen, there are a great number of things an individual must consider in choosing both a site and a financial plan. Undoubtedly there are some who rely only on intuition to locate their retailing facilities. In all probability, their chances for success are far less than for Mr. Wilson.

THE STORE EXTERIOR

Once the site is determined and an appropriate financial plan is adopted, the retailer must give consideration to the physical building that will house the proposed retailing operation. There is little question that the outside physical appearance of the store is important to a prospective shopper. First, it identifies the kind of retailing taking place inside. Moreover, the outside appearance contributes to the store's image and does much to attract the kinds of customers the retailer desires. For example, the outside appearance may symbolize high fashion merchandise with corresponding high prices.

On the other hand, a store catering to shoppers with lower incomes projects an image of lower-priced merchandise. The merchandiser must exercise care here because families with modest incomes do not always buy the lowest priced item in each product category. In all cases the store's image should be one the store is attempting to project. It might be unfortunate if the shoppers perceived one image while the retailer thought his or her store projected a somewhat different image.

Nearly all people make instantaneous judgments regarding a store simply by inspecting the outside. This inspection includes the environment in which the building is located, the architecture of the building itself, and the type and character of the window displays. Potential customers always look for those cues which tell them that the store they are about to enter is "his or her type of store."

The very first impression a potential customer has of a store is gained from the store front itself. A store front should do the following: identify the store and attract its type of customers, invite the customer to come inside, and solidify the store's image.

Identifying the Store and Attracting Customers

The basic function of the store front is to attract people. Once they have been attracted, the store identifies itself in a generic way. That is to say, the shopper is able to determine whether it is a food store, a lingerie shop, a bakery, a drugstore, or whatever. It would be most disconcerting if a potential shopper could not identify the type of store as classified by the merchandise carried. Furthermore, the potential customer usually identifies the store as being a member of a chain or an independent. In most cases, chains use the same type of architecture for all their stores; therefore, the customer is able to identify the name of the store as well as its type. Large food chains such as A & P, Safeway, and Kroger are easily identified regardless of the city in which they are located. McDonald's drive-ins—whether corporate-owned or franchised—can be easily identified throughout the United States by their golden arches as can be seen in Figure 5.3. The store sign may help materially in the store identification process.

Inviting the Shopper into the Store

Ideally, the front of the store through its architecture, design, and use of window displays will invite the customer to come inside. In the case of very small stores, the window may be set at an angle toward the door; in effect, guiding the shopper to the door. Generally, he or she will be able to look inside the store and be further intrigued by what is seen. Display windows often play a key role in customer attraction.

A good display window does two things: (1) it shows off the merchandise, and (2) it invites the shopper to come inside. In showing off the merchandise, one must remember that the smaller the article to be displayed, the closer it must be brought to the customer. Consider a jeweler's window. You will find that the floor of the window is high so that the merchandise is near the shopper's eye level, and the window will probably be shallow—that is, the display area is near the window-shopper. On the other hand, a furniture store will have a window with a low floor, the display area will be broad, and the items on display will be some distance removed from the viewer so that the display can be better appreciated.

Some window displays have a back so that the person looking into the window cannot see into the store itself. This is called a *closed window*. Some windows are wide open so that the entire store in effect becomes a display. This is referred to as

FIGURE 5.3
The familiar "golden arches" of the McDonald's Corporation are a unique store identification sign

Source: Reprinted by permission of McDonald's Corporation, McDonald's Plaza, Oak Brook, Ill.

the *open display*. Some stores are partially open and partially closed. There is no absolute rule that dictates the type of window to use, so all types are found in most shopping districts. In more recent years, newer stores have favored the open display.

The store may also use marquees and awnings to protect window-shoppers from inclement weather. Some shops use infrared lamps or heated sidewalks to warm the shoppers on severely cold days, so that they can examine the contents displayed in the window at summertime temperatures, while remaining outside.

The entrance door should be easy to open, whether it opens automatically by an electric eye or by the customer's own power. The entrance should be free of hazards which could trip or slow the unwary shopper. And in many modern stores "air doors" are used. Not only do they impede shoppers the least, but the emission of heat in the winter and cool air in the summer is said to attract passersby.

Solidifying the Store Image

As discussed earlier, most stores provide clues to help the customer identify the type of image that the store wishes to project. An experienced shopper can generally classify a store as one catering to a specific social class simply by the aggregate effect created by the store front and the window display. Two cases illustrate this generalization.

Example One: Lisa's Shoe Salon. This shop features women's shoes that are of high fashion, with prices moderately high to expensive. The window display is a work of art with only a relatively small number of shoes on display. Other colorful artifacts are used in the window to create an aura of exclusivity and luxury. The prices on the shoes are in small numbers, if shown at all. The window is uncluttered, clean, and tastefully decorated. The shoes are intended to be sold to the more affluent woman who is sophisticated in taste. The shop features an open display, and one can see into the store clearly. Inside, the shopper notes the carpeting on the floor, the salon-type appearance, and the well-dressed shoppers being fitted for shoes. Even the salesmen fit into this expensive environment. The customers are from the upper-middle class to the lower-upper class.

Example Two: Community Store for Women. This store also features women's shoes. A shopper can tell immediately that the merchandise is low in price. Furthermore, the window is jammed with all types and styles of shoes. The price tags are displayed prominently, and feature large numbers. There is no attempt to create an artistic window; there are only shoes on display. There is no semblance of luxury or aura of exclusivity. Looking into the store itself, one can see a vast stock of shoes on shelves along the walls. They are not in a rear storage room as they would be in a luxury salon. Tables of shoes are indiscriminately placed throughout the store. The shoppers entering are price conscious, and there is little doubt that they are from the lower income groups.

THE STORE INTERIOR

Design and Facilities

Regardless of how attractive the store front might be, the interior is the heart of the store. Furthermore, it is the interior that ultimately determines whether the shopper will be satisfied or whether he or she will be disappointed and decide to shop elsewhere.

The interior of the store must permit the shopper to recognize instantly the store's atmosphere and the appeal that is being made. A small but expensive lingerie shop may stress its exclusivity, a ski shop may stress its appeal to young adults, a tobacco shop may appeal to men only. Whatever marketing strategy the store wishes to follow must be carried out by the decor of the store. The logical starting point for interior planning is to review the store's objectives in terms of types of customers to be attracted. The interior of a store may give an overall impression of dignity, prestige, and high prices, or it may convey low prices and large stocks. For example, in a dress shop catering to lower-income women, all merchandise may be displayed on racks. The shopper makes her selection, then goes to the dressing room for fitting. A woman from a higher-income class may select a store that is spaciously designed with carpeting on the floor and soft, comfortable chairs. Displays are in good taste, and dresses are not on racks. Rather the customer is taken to a fitting room, and the clerk brings dresses which she thinks the customer will like. The customer may ask for a specific salesperson who has served her before and who seemingly understands each customer's needs and tastes.

In laying out the interior of a store one must work around physical obstacles. The building that houses the store is the chief obstacle. Buildings are sometimes antiquated in terms of engineering; walls are often loadbearing, thus inhibiting their removal. Similarly, large pillars and columns often cannot be removed. If one has a shop in an older building, an interior display must be worked out that enhances the store image while utilizing those parts of the building that are too expensive to change. Architects and builders are skilled in renovating old buildings, and their services should be used.

Customer Safety and Comfort

Buildings must be engineered for the comfort and safety of the customer. Provisions must be made to combat fire and to permit the easy exit of customers in case of emergency. Almost all larger stores have automatic sprinkler systems that are activated by high temperatures. There should be plenty of exits, and all should be clearly marked.

Today almost every shop is air-conditioned for the comfort of shoppers. This may not be a severe problem for the small shop, but it does present quite an engineering problem for larger stores. Randhurst, the large, enclosed shopping center under one roof, which we discussed earlier, features a climate-control system that circulates 1,034,000 cubic feet of air per minute. A 72-degree temperature within the complex is maintained throughout the year regardless of outside conditions, and the system could heat or cool 1,500 homes at one time. Unless new forms of energy are discovered, architects may be obliged to forego some methods presently being used.

Lighting, Color, and Music

Most newer stores utilize color and lighting effects to enhance their marketing strategy. Lighting, of course, is necessary for illumination; but it often affects emotional responses, and hence, can be useful in putting the shopper into a favorable mood for responding to the goods being offered.

Color engineers are often employed to select hues that will be most effective. For example, shades of red are sometimes used to stimulate the appetite; hence, they are a favorite color for restaurants. Garden shops often use green as an aid to sell their merchandise. Gasoline stations utilize red and white to distinguish their stations. Pastel shades are used to decorate the walls of shops selling cosmetics, infant's wear, and ladies' lingerie. There is no doubt that colors enhance the appeal of some goods while the same colors might inhibit the appeal of others. Merchants are turning more and more to experts for help in this critical area. One large supermarket uses a tab of butter in a package of steak to help sell more meat. Apparently the yellow of the butter contrasted with the red of the beef provides a favorable color contrast which stimulates sales; another uses a sprig of parsley. Color psychology is becoming increasingly important as an aid in stimulating retail sales.

Music is also used to influence the moods of the shopper. In the very small shops FM radio may provide sufficient music. In larger stores, music is piped in by a service that provides soft, melodious, and familiar tunes. In general, the music must be unobtrusive and not intrude into a shopper's consciousness to the point that he or she cannot concentrate on the merchandise. It is claimed that the music can create the atmosphere which would be most helpful in setting the proper mood for shopping. In some supermarkets, the music is interrupted to announce special bargains of the day. The same technique is used in some discount stores. The music there is more strident in tone and sets the mood for that type of shopper. The music chosen must be the kind that hopefully is liked and appreciated by the type of customer to be served. Generally speaking, teen shops feature rock and similar music. Department stores use music that generally appeals to the mature shopper. Odors can also be purchased and wafted in the store or at the entrance. A tobacco shop dispenses the odor of pipe tobacco at its revolving door, a candy and nut shop blows the odor of chocolate out onto the street, and a used car retailer sprays all the automobiles in his inventory so they will smell as if they have new leather upholstery. It is said that the odor of freshly baked bread is about the only one that cannot be reproduced in a laboratory.

STORE LAYOUT

We have been discussing store interiors in general terms. A more basic question is: how does a particular store acquire its interior design in the first place? This is determined by the plans for the store layout. A *store layout* is the physical division of the store into selling and nonselling areas and the arrangement of the store's fixtures and equipment to insure a traffic flow pattern that effectively carries out the merchandising plan of the store.

Store layout recognizes four factors: (1) merchandise, (2) customers, (3) employees, and (4) store fixtures. The retailer arranges the fixtures and displays the merchandise so that the customer traffic flows through the store in a logical pattern. It is arranged, hopefully, to maximize profits while at the same time pleasing and safeguarding the customers.

Space Allocation Methods for Profitability

The type of retail outlet involved is the first consideration when determining the physical layout of a store. For example, the layout for a large department store occupying eight floors differs from the layout of a supermarket, a woman's dress shop, a bookstore, or some other form of retailing.

In laying out the selling area of a department store, one must first decide on the number of selling departments, or the types and classification of goods to be sold. Let us assume that the following decisions have been made: (1) women's coats, suits, and dresses, (2) teen-age girls' dresses, (3) children's clothing, (4) lingerie, (5) men's furnishings, (6) furniture, (7) housewares and appliances, (8) jewelry, (9) cosmetics, (10) gourmet foods, (11) hardware and paints, (12) stationery, (13) candy, and (14) draperies. Having decided on the broad category of goods, a further breakdown will have to be made. In order to illustrate, let us take the women's department. This grouping is broken down into the following categories: (1) cocktail dresses, (2) expensive dresses and suits, (3) coats, (4) skirts, sweaters, and other sportswear, (5) house dresses, (6) uniforms.

The physical size of each department will depend upon the size of the store and the relative importance of each department. If the store is confined to three selling floors of 50,000 square feet for each floor, one type of plan will emerge. On the other hand, if there are six floors of 50,000 square feet for each floor, a different plan results. Therefore, the scope of the operation largely determines the kinds and types of goods to be offered.

No one should underestimate the importance of profits in determining the space requirements of various departments. Increasing the sales volume, and ultimately the profits, is perhaps the most important factor in a store layout. There are two common methods of assigning space: (1) space productivity ratios, and (2) model stock planning.

Space Productivity Ratios. In the methodology involving space productivity ratios, the first requirement is to determine the percentage of total sales a given department will generate. That is to say, what percentage of total sales will each department contribute? In the case of a going business these ratios can be determined from internal records. Unfortunately, one of the factors that contributes to a department's sales record is its location in a store. High sales do not necessarily mean the product is popular, but may simply mean that it is being sold in a favorable (first floor, near the door, near an escalator) location. One cannot assume that if one department contributes five percent of total sales that it should occupy five percent of the total selling space. Some departments, such as furniture, draperies, and bedding, demand more physical space because of the sheer size of the goods. In these cases, the departments will be located in those parts of the store in which space is considered less valuable.

If an individual is opening a new store and has no prior experience in assigning space, he or she may consult such trade groups as National Retail Merchants Assocation. This group publishes information of this type classified by size of stores. It is also helpful to established retailers, who can compare their ratios with others like themselves.

All stores should compute the productivity of their various lines. Some stores use dollar sales per square foot of selling space, while others such as food stores will compute productivity on the basis of dollar volume per linear foot of shelf space. The important factor is the necessity of keeping records so that productivity can be measured. Everything else being equal, space is allocated on the basis of its ability to generate profits.

Chain stores formulate their own store plans in the central headquarters based on an analysis of expected sales and consumer behavior. Each store conforms to the model set up by centralized management.

Model Stock Planning. The model stock approach formalizes the desire of store management to stock merchandise that consumers want. The various styles, brands, sizes, varieties, and colors are listed and stocked in accordance with customer preferences. Price and profit considerations are also noted. The technique is related to merchandising and is discussed more completely in later chapters. Its inclusion at this time is solely to point out that store arrangement includes an analysis of sales potential and profits of the various departments.

Layout and Merchandising Strategy

The interior of the store is laid out not only to provide for the customers' comfort and convenience but also to move customers according to some merchandising strategy. For example, consider the multifloored department store. It is necessary to have stairways, elevators, and escalators, but their exact locations are to promote maximum circulation on the main floor. They should not be positioned so that a customer entering from the street would make a beeline for the elevator or escalator and ignore the first floor selling departments. Down escalators do not face exits. Many goods are of the impulse variety, and sales will be lost unless the customer sees them and has the opportunity to buy. One must also remember that the entrance to the other floors is by means of the stairway, escalator, or elevator. Therefore, aisles must be placed to encourage a good traffic pattern, one which maximizes the sales per square foot of selling space. Multistoried department stores have sometimes increased traffic throughout the store by constructing walkways from adjacent parking facilities to an upper level floor. For example, at Famous-Barr in Saint Louis, pedestrians enter the store on the first floor while those who come by car enter on the sixth floor. In this store—and in many others like it throughout the country—it can be argued that the sixth floor is just as valuable as the first floor.

The food supermarket is a good example of a store that allocates its space with a merchandising strategy in mind. The customer enters the store and then proceeds through a maze of aisles before arriving at the checkout counter. This is done deliberately to stimulate unplanned buying. For example, a shopper who intended to buy only a quart of milk is exposed to a variety of merchandise as he or she walks through the store to the dairy case and then to the checkout counter. The store management knows that in many cases the shopper purchases other items for which he or she had no previous plans to buy. Thus, the supermarket layout stimulates impulse (unplanned) buying. (See Figure 5.4.)

Traffic Pattern Studies

Traffic pattern studies are conducted by some retailers to determine the location of "hot" or "dead" areas within the store. *Hardware Retailer*, a trade journal, has conducted studies in various hardware stores to show the difference in travel patterns of male and female customers.[10] It was found that men tend to ignore housewares, gifts, and glassware. On the other hand, most women bypass power tools, hand tools, sporting goods, and such basic items as nuts and bolts, nails, and small

[10]See "Do You Know Who Your Customers Really Are?" *Hardware Retailer*, September 1966.

FIGURE 5.4

The layout of this supermarket requires the customer to travel the width of the store to reach the frozen meats and produce department

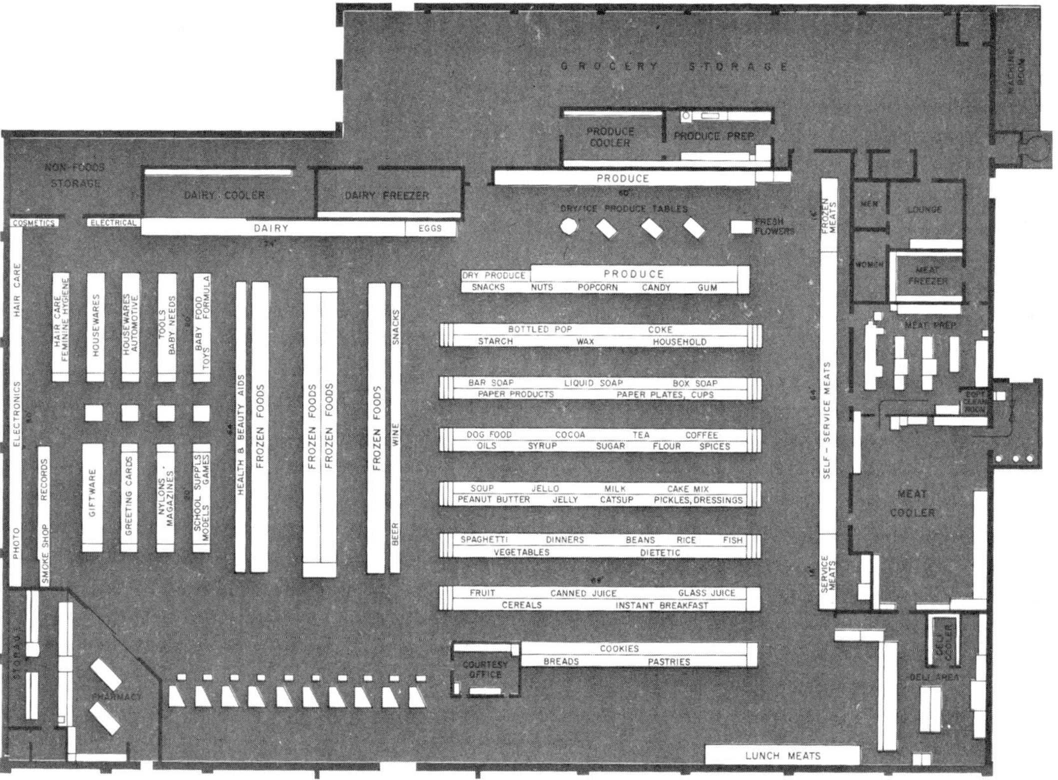

Source: Food Palace, Indianapolis, Indiana, as seen in *Progressive Grocer*, August 1971, p. 69.

tools. The ideal situation is to display the merchandise in such a way that both sexes have to walk throughout the store. *Hardware Retailer* found in its study that gondola ends are the most valuable display space in the store. Therefore, they have suggested that gondola ends be used to display high impulse items favorable to men and women.

Giftwares should neither be placed in a dominant position near the front of a store nor in some corner. If giftwares occupy too much space in front, men may be driven away to stores that have a more masculine appeal. On the other hand, if they are placed in a corner, men may never walk by them. This would result in lower sales, because men do buy the merchandise displayed in such departments. One solution is to place the gift department in the center of the store and arrange the aisles so that everyone is funneled in that direction. Just as hardware retailers are experimenting with traffic patterns, so are other retailers. Studies of this nature will increase as retailers attempt to make their displays more effective.

Customer Movement Considerations

A retailer must provide for the orderly movement of people throughout the store. In stores that utilize only one shopping floor, there is no need for mechanical means to move customers; in multifloor stores, elevators and escalators are usually provided.

Attention should be paid to making it easy and safe to move through store aisles. The store is laid out so that aisles are wide, well lighted, and safe. In supermarkets care should be taken that empty carts are not in the aisle impeding the flow of traffic or creating hazards for the shopper. Moreover, the aisles must be wide enough to accommodate the shopper and cart as he or she encounters other shoppers and their carts.

Main aisles in department stores should be wide enough to handle the major traffic flow, but they should not encourage customers to move through the store too rapidly. Side aisles should be spaced frequently enough to provide convenient places for customers to browse and yet not stop the major flow of traffic.

Even the positioning of counters with respect to the aisles is subject to careful planning. Some stores place their counters parallel to the main aisles, thus maximizing the display value of the counters. On the other hand, some stores think it is more effective if the counters are placed crosswise to the traffic.

Other stores, such as specialty shops, feature a free-flow floor plan. There are no discernible aisles, and customers are attracted to the various displays on the perimeter of the selling area.

Another factor involved in good traffic movement is the natural tendency of people to turn to the right after entering the store. This tendency could cause the left side of the store to have an insufficient traffic flow. In order to offset the tendency to turn right, a store might place a very attractive display of popular items on the left side. A red carpeting is also useful in guiding people in the direction the merchant wishes them to go. Store directories are useful tools in larger stores.

Planning for Nonselling Areas

The store must also provide a place where goods are brought into the store, marked, and kept in proximity to the appropriate selling departments. In the case of department stores this is a tremendous job and helps account for the large amount of space allocated to nonselling functions. Contrast the needs of a department store with a small dress shop operated by a proprietor and several employees. In the latter case, the merchandise must be delivered through the front door and brought to a back room where it is prepared for the selling floor and where it is kept as inventory. The larger the operation, the greater is the problem of control; expenses must be minimized, thus helping the store to make a profit.

If a store delivers its merchandise to the customer, provisions must be made for the handling of packages, wrappings, and delivery. Here again, the size of the store dictates the types and kinds of operations that are needed.

In the cases of men's suits and women's dresses, working rooms for seamstresses and tailors may have to be provided. For chain stores, the alteration department may be centralized in one location (assuming more than one store location within a city).

Trends in Merchandise Layout

A recent trend is to divide a store into several shops and to promote these separately. Gourmet food sections are frequently designed as a separate specialty shop, as can be seen in Figure 5.5. Jewel Foods speaks of its sausage shop, its bakery shop, and so on. Many department stores have divided their stores into boutiques.

There is a trend for many retailers to analyze their physical layouts so as to locate departments more scientifically. Intuition is not the best way to solve the problem of store layout. Retailers recognize the value of store space and the role of its proper utilization in the generation of profits. Thus, we see top management involvement in the store layout process, bearing in mind always that the paramount guide is customer convenience. With that should come greater sales and profits.

FIGURE 5.5

The gourmet food section of a supermarket can be designed as a separate specialty shop, having fixtures complementary to the high quality products on the shelves

Source: Handy Andy Stores, San Antonio, Texas. Reprinted by permission of *Telefood* Magazine.

SUMMARY

A retail store must have a good location if it is to be profitable. The first problem to be solved is to find the right community. Therefore the retailer must have a clear understanding of the type of customers he or she wishes to serve and then locate a store that is convenient for those people. Demographic studies revealing the characteristics of the people within a particular community are very helpful. Information about the wealth of the community and the amount of income of the typical househeld is needed.

Other factors impinge upon the location problem. These are traffic, competition, and stability of the community. There must be good traffic studies to point out patterns of traffic flow, points of possible congestion, and adequacy of parking facilities. The services offered by the community must be considered before a decision can be finalized.

A financial plan must be chosen that is advantageous to the retailer in carrying out his or her merchandising strategies. Sometimes it will be better to own the site and the building; at other times it will be beneficial to rent the facilities.

The retailer has to plan his or her facilities to attract the expected kind of customers. The store must be easily identified as to the type of merchandise carried and by the income class the owner wishes to attract. The internal layout of the store should be designed to move the customers easily through the store and to provide for their safety, well being, and comfort. Auxiliary services must be planned, such as telephones, water fountains, and rest rooms for both employees and customers. The retailer must provide space to carry out those nonselling functions that are required to implement the store's merchandising plan. The layout of a store should be attractive, convenient, and safe. Flow charts are a useful device to plan the location of types of merchandise that will be acceptable to all of the store's customers. The layout should never compromise on the safety of the customers. Their needs and wants should always dictate the layout that is selected.

QUESTIONS FOR DISCUSSION

1. Define store location. Indicate why the principal parts of your definition are important.
2. A retailer must consider demographic data in order to choose the right community in which to locate. Indicate the kind and type of information that would be helpful.
3. Why is an analysis of traffic and parking important in choosing the "good site?"
4. Contrast the advantages of ownership of a store site and its building with leasing the site and building.
5. Discuss the different types of commonly used leases. Indicate the circumstances when one would be superior to the other.

6. Give a good definition of store layout and cite examples from your own experience illustrating your definition.

7. Discuss the ways in which a store moves its customers through the store. Cite examples.

8. How do modern retailers attract their customers and invite them in the shop? In your answer include store architecture, window displays, and store arrangement.

9. How do modern retailers make use of color, lighting, and music? Give some examples from your own community.

10. Discuss as completely as possible the factors that determine store arrangement. Whom would you make responsible for a good store arrangement?

6 THE RETAIL ORGANIZATION

At Barney's, a large men's store in New York City, a salesman is permitted to help a customer choose an item from any department in the store's six floors of merchandise; no salesman need ever say, "Sorry, that's not my department." The store stocks over 60,000 men's suits and has over 200 tailors getting them ready for delivery. But in many other stores, departmental jurisdiction is very carefully defined and enforced. Unions often make sure that individuals don't do work they are not responsible for.

The president of a major midwestern food chain believes that store managers should have the responsibility for determining what will be sold in their outlets. Such a philosophy not only allows the manager to adjust to neighborhood circumstances, it also helps morale. But the president had to overrule a few managers who were stocking grapes and lettuce; all the stores in the chain were being boycotted by those who sympathized with striking farm workers.

At a small shoe store in Miami, the owner says, "I'm the buyer, personnel director, treasurer, promotion manager, and janitor. And everyone else who works here is my assistant." But in the headquarters of a large department store chain in Chicago, one man (and his staff) devotes his whole time to buying women's house slippers.

Shortly after World War I, Associated Merchandising Corporation was established by Lincoln Filene. One purpose of the organization was to buy goods in Europe on behalf of large American department stores that could not be represented by a full-time buyer. By using the organization's services, more than thirty American retailers have access to European output and have minimized their buying expenses. More recently, European clothing retailers can do their buying at trade shows in Frankfurt, Cologne, or Paris, and American manufacturers are increasingly represented. Through USATEX, a corporation that sells in Europe and Japan, American clothing manufacturers have permanent representation.

In one large southern department store, employees learn about new merchandise, economic trends affecting the country and the city, personnel policies, scores of the store's bowling team, upcoming promotional events, and "gossip" from the store's own newspaper. But important information also is discussed in regularly scheduled departmental meetings, posted on bulletin boards, and printed on slips enclosed in paycheck envelopes. Communication is taken very seriously by management. But the store's advertising department once ran a full page advertisement in each of the city's newspapers—only to learn later in the day that the merchandise being featured had not yet arrived from the supplier.

A retailer, as the above examples suggest, must face many important organizational issues. For retailing is no exception to the fact that all types of business activities need an organization to carry out their goals or objectives. The type of organizational structure selected by any particular retailer depends upon many factors. Some of these factors are: kinds of goods sold, magnitude of the sales in units or dollars, customer services performed, wishes of the major stockholders, amount of capital invested in the business, legal restraints imposed by various governmental bodies, location, quality of employees available, customs and traditions of the community where the business is located, and the desires of the customers.

This chapter focuses attention on those principles of management that create an effective organization. The principles apply equally whether the retailer is a department store, specialty shop, independent operator, or member of a chain. Special attention is given to those cases where largeness affects the principles of organization.

THE FUNCTIONS OF RETAIL MANAGEMENT

An organization may be defined as "a number of individuals systematically united for some end of work."[1] This definition does not explain *why* individuals organize themselves. Philip Kotler corrects this deficiency by describing organizations as:

> collections of interacting groups and individuals who seek to achieve something for themselves as well as for the company.[2]

We therefore define a retail organization as a collection of interacting groups or individuals who are united for the purpose of carrying out a merchandising plan in order to satisfy customer's needs, while the store itself earns a fair profit.

It must be stated categorically that the functions of retail management do not differ substantially from those of other business organizations. David J. Rachman concurs with this statement when he says:

> One should not get the impression that the functions of retail management are different from those of any other organization. Management performs the same functions whether for a manufacturing firm, utility, service organization, or military force.[3]

Therefore, the first step in any organization is to identify the function. For the retailers, these are: (1) determining the objectives, (2) planning, (3) organizing and coordinating, (4) assembling resources, (5) store operation, and (6) control. Let us look at each of these management functions in some detail.

[1]*New Collegiate Standard Dictionary* (New York: Funk and Wagnalls Company, 1957), p. 829.

[2]Philip Kotler, *Marketing Management: Analysis, Planning, and Control* (Englewood Cliffs, N.J.: Prentice-Hall, Inc., 1967), p. 132.

[3]David J. Rachman, *Retail Strategy and Structure: A Management Approach* (Englewood Cliffs, N.J.: Prentice-Hall, 1969), p. 19.

DETERMINING THE OBJECTIVES

Where are we headed? What are we supposed to do? The answers to these two questions go far toward determining the objectives for any retailer. Some people confuse objectives with motivations. This can be seen when these people are questioned about the objectives of a retail store and they respond by answering "to make money—that is, to make a profit." In our judgment objectives and motivations are not synonyms. The objective of any retailer is to offer merchandise or services to customers so that the customer will have his or her wants satisfied. The retailer does this with the hope (expectation) that the store will earn a fair profit. Let us take an example.

Hanson's Drugstore is located in a small suburb of Minneapolis. It is a typical drugstore, selling a variety of merchandise in addition to prescription drugs.

Question: What is the major objective of Hanson's Drugstore?

Answer: It is to service the needs of the customers by providing prescription and proprietary drugs, cosmetics, papers, magazines, sundries, candies and tobacco, and other similar goods. Hanson hopes to make a profit, but that is a reason or motivation for providing these goods which satisfy the needs of his customers.

Profits are as essential to retailers as they are to other types of business organizations. Profits, however, are not the goals or the objectives of the retailer.

Subobjectives

Ordinarily the major objective is divided into several subobjectives. In the case of retailing, answers must be sought to specific questions which may be conveniently classified into these groupings: product, customer, and other.

Product or merchandise questions

1. What goods will the retailer sell? Will they be drugs, meat, furniture, automobiles, clothing, or something else? Perhaps it will not sell goods, but rather offer a service. (A theater sells entertainment.)
2. What quality of merchandise will be stocked?
3. How completely will any one line of merchandise be stocked, and how many lines?

Customer questions

1. Who are the target customers? That is, are they men, women, teen-agers, children, entire families?
2. What is the socioeconomic class of target customers?
3. Do you intend to sell target customers by mail order, by locating a store in their neighborhood, or by calling at their homes?
4. What sales promotional techniques will you use to stimulate target customers to choose your organization?
5. What kinds of service will you offer target customers?

Other factors

1. What type of employees must you hire to staff your organization in order to carry out the store's objectives?
2. What are the plans for growth and expansion?
3. Are there any specific plans to carry out the store's mission?
4. What is the target rate of return on the capital invested in the business that the owners expect?

There has been no attempt to detail all the questions that might be asked. However, one can see that answers to questions of this type go far toward focusing attention on goals. Objectives must always be clearly stated, and put into writing. Then there is no confusion as to the mission of the particular store in question.

Let us examine Hanson's Drugstore to see how he answered the basic questions relating to his objective.

Product. Hanson's Drugstore, as the name implies, carries prescription drugs. However, as is the case with many other drugstores, Hanson's is not solely a prescription shop. It carries the usual line of proprietory drugs, cosmetics, papers and magazines, candies, tobacco, a limited line of toys, and some general merchandise.

Hanson has not made too many decisions regarding the quality of his merchandise, because in most cases the goods are standard and there is only one type available. All of Hanson's chemical supplies are purchased from the leading pharmaceutical houses, and he is able to fill all prescriptions brought to him. Papers, magazines, tobaccos, and candies are all standardized. He does carry a quality line of cosmetics. Hanson is not able to carry all brands and all products in equal depth. He limits his offerings of cosmetics, general merchandise, and toys to the leading competitive brands.

Customers. The customers of Hanson's Drugstore live in a two-mile radius of the store. His target customers are the entire family, although men and women are the major shoppers. Hanson's Drugstore is properly called a neighborhood store. He is located in an area of middle-class residents, most of his customers are white, Protestant, and of Scandanavian ancestry. The husbands are employed in semiskilled jobs and most wives do not work. Hanson places a full-page advertisement in the local newspaper every Friday.

Hanson's Drugstore employs five people including Hanson himself, who is also the pharmacist. Two of the other employees are women who work full time as clerks. He also employs two young men part time. The town is quite stable with respect to population growth and Hanson does not expect to grow; hence he has no plans for expansion. His income is regularly between $20,000 and $25,000 annually, and he thinks this is satisfactory.

PLANNING

Once the retailer's objectives are clearly spelled out, the next concern is planning. This means that one must identify the problems and decide on courses of action. There are numerous decisions to be made, some affecting the long-run behavior of the organization, others its short-run behavior. It must also be pointed out that an organization may have several alternative solutions to any one problem, and the decision maker must choose among alternatives. In order for a decision maker to make the right choice, he or she must have sufficient information relating to the problem. Furthermore, he or she must know something about the probabilities of various events occurring and the expected payoffs if alternative courses of action are followed. In any case, the identity of the decision maker is the first concern of planning.

Who Are the Decision Makers?

It is easy to identify the decision maker in a one-person operation, or even in a retail store that employs a dozen or more. But what about those organizations which have hundreds or even thousands of employees? What about chain stores or branch stores? Some people believe that decision making is restricted to only the top level executives. It is actually a fact that effective decision making must be made at all levels of management. There are several ways of dividing planning among the various levels: (1) by function, (2) by type of plan, and (3) by phase of operation.

Planning by Function. This type of planning is perhaps the easiest to accomplish. One simply assigns all advertising decisions to the advertising manager, the buying decisions to the buyer, the accounting decisions to the controller, the legal decisions to the legal counselor, and so on. In a department store, the merchandising manager may set the overall policy for the buying of merchandise, but the buyer of an individual department is responsible for the immediate decisions within the department. Whenever planning is divided by subjects, it is relatively easy to allocate the decision making to the various levels of management. Unfortunately, decisions often affect people in other areas or departments. Therefore, procedures must be set up to settle jurisdictional disputes and other conflicts within the total organization.

Planning by Type of Plan. Sometimes it is not practical to divide decision making by subjects. For example, a chain of food supermarkets might divide planning into that performed by general management, regional management, and store manager. The actual assignment of planning duties depends upon the degree of decentralization of management permitted. Guidelines are set up by a statement of policies, procedures, or reports. It is not uncommon for some retail chains to be highly centralized as to decision making. In these cases very few major decisions are made at the levels closest to the operations of the store. On the other hand, some retail organizations only formulate general guidelines and insist that the decisions be made at the level closest to actual operation.

Planning by Phase of Operation. Since planning is decision making, it consists of several component parts: (1) identifying the problems, (2) gathering facts and information, (3) formulating alternative courses of action, and (4) making and implementing the decision. In this type of planning, one group of individuals might be responsible for the identification of problems, another with obtaining information relevant to the problems, another will be given the responsibility of choosing solutions to the problems, while still another group may be responsible for implementing the decision. (See Figure 6.1.)

FIGURE 6.1
The planning process can be organized in three ways

THE PLANNING PROCESS

TASK DIVISION:

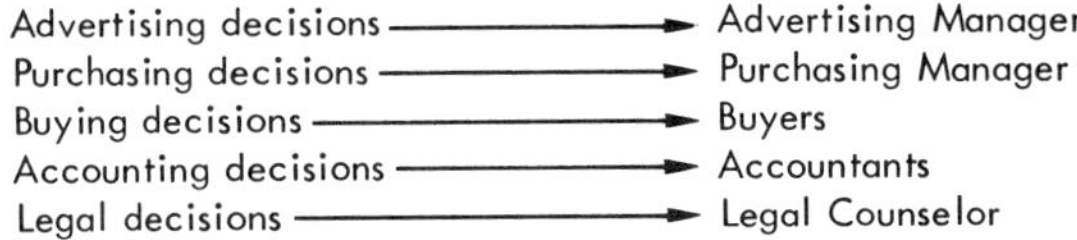

ORGANIZATIONAL PLAN DIVISION:

STAGE OF PLANNING DIVISION:

1. Identifying the problem
2. Gathering facts and information
3. Formulating alternative courses of action
4. Making and implementing the decision

Bayesian Statistics

Regardless of who is responsible for making a decision, or whether planning is determined by subject, type, or phase, the past decade or so has seen an increase in emphasis on scientific decision making. No longer is experience or intuition the only determinants for making a decision. Bayesian statistics have become a popular technique for improving the quality of decision making, although there are signs that its popularity is waning. Bayesian statistics is a methodology that quantifies information so that a choice may be made between alternative plans of action. It also provides a system to improve the probabilities of a given event occurring, and provides the mechanism to evaluate the cost of acquiring the additional information. Perhaps an example would clarify the technique.

Assume that a chain of hamburger stores wishes to determine the feasibility of opening a unit in a town in Georgia. The executives of the chain know from experiences in similar situations that there is a 70 percent probability that this unit will earn a $100,000 profit if it is located in this Georgia community. On the other hand, the executives estimate that there is a 30 percent probability that the hamburger unit will lose $20,000 if located at this site. What should they decide?

	Event 1	*Event 2*
Act 1 (open unit)	$100,000 (profit)	− $20,000 (loss)
Act 2 (do not open unit)	0	0

Since it has been determined that there is a 70 percent chance of Event 1 occurring and a 30 percent of Event 2 occurring, the information is processed as follows:

$$70\% \ (\$100{,}000) + 30\% \ (-\$20{,}000) = \text{Expected payoff of Act 1}$$
$$\$70{,}000 - \$6{,}000 = \$64{,}000 \ (\text{Expected payoff of Act 1})$$

The alternative is:

$$70\% \ (0) + 30\% \ (0) = 0 \ (\text{Expected payoff of Act 2})$$

Inasmuch as $64,000 exceeds 0, the decision maker should choose Act 1 (open the unit). The 70–30 percent probabilities are called personal probabilities because they are based on personal experiences in similar situations.

Suppose, however, that the executives possessed supernatural powers and had perfect information, what would be its value? It can be found by this procedure:

$$70\% \ (\$100{,}000) + 30\% \ (0) = \$70{,}000 \ (\text{Expected value})$$

That means, with perfect information no decision maker would elect the choice of opening the unit if it was certain that the unit would lose $20,000. Therefore, you would not open the unit 30 percent of the time; hence 30 percent (0).

If $64,000 is the expected value under conditions of uncertainty (previously computed), then use this formula:

$$\text{Expected value of perfect information} = \text{Expected value under certainty} - \text{Expected value under uncertainty}$$

In this example, EVPI = $70,000 − $64,000 = $6,000; and the value of perfect information is $6,000.

This sets up the dollar limit that the executives would pay to improve their probabilities. In other words, they would not pay more than $6,000 for additional information to improve the predictability for success of the venture.

Let us now assume that top management decides to improve the probability of making the correct decision. This involves purchasing more information and revising the probabilities. This is a highly technical process called posterior analysis. It is beyond the scope of this book to describe the process which is used to calculate the new posterior probabilities, but let us assume they are computed to be 90 percent—10 percent.[4]

In this case: 90 percent ($100,000) + 10 percent (−$20,000) = $90,000 − $2,000 = $88,000. If it costs $5,000 to obtain and process this information, the expected value of it would be $83,000. Since $83,000 is larger than $64,000, it would pay to obtain additional information.

The use of Bayesian statistics helps to make a decision by quantifying alternative solutions to a problem under conditions of uncertainty. The decision maker would act rationally and choose a solution that would offer the highest expected payoff.

The Strategy and Tactics of Planning

Strategy and tactics are usually used in military discussions, but there is no need to restrict these terms. Strategy is a plan to achieve a certain objective. Tactics are the means employed to achieve the objective. In military terms, strategy and tactics are made with competition in mind.

An example of the difference between strategy and tactics is L and T's Cafe Le Rouge. The proprietors of this French cuisine restaurant decided it would be good strategy to appeal to families whose annual incomes are between $15,000 and $24,999. In putting the strategy into operation, they will use tactics. The tactics include plans on advertising, promotion, decor, service, and quality of food. One tactic might be to use male waiters dressed in white ties and tails. Another tactic might be to purchase time on the local FM radio station and sponsor a program of symphonic music. Another tactic might be to feature dinner music for the restaurant patrons.

Generally speaking, only top level management is responsible for determining strategies, while middle and lower management may be responsible for tactics. In very small organizations, it is conceivable that the same individual is responsible for both strategy and tactics.

ORGANIZING AND COORDINATING

With respect to the activities performed, it does not matter whether a retailer is large or small. The activities the typical retailer engages in are: purchase of merchandise for resale, preparing the merchandise for sale, attracting customers, selling the merchandise, keeping the necessary accounting records, and evaluating the retailer's performance.

[4]For information explaining the calculation of posterior probabilities and preposterior analysis, see Paul E. Green and Donald S. Tull, *Research for Marketing Decisions*, 3rd ed. (Englewood Cliffs, N.J.: Prentice-Hall, Inc., 1975), chapter 1.

The distinguishing feature between the small and the large retailer is not the type of function performed, but rather the degree of specialization employed in carrying out the functions. (See Figure 6.2.) In the case of the smallest store, perhaps all the functions are performed by one individual. Let us assume that Barbara Hartman decides to open a small coin and stamp shop. Since this is to be a one-person operation, she will perform all the managerial functions, for she has no one to whom to delegate the duties.

FIGURE 6.2
This shoe department illustrates a high degree of specialization

Source: Brown Shoe Company and The Air Step Store, Murray, Utah.

As a retail store grows and acquires additional employees, there is a need to reassign the various functions of management, with the responsibility for carrying out a particular assignment charged to a specific individual. In very large retail organizations, the structure becomes complex and often cumbersome. The assignment of responsibility must be carried out with the organization's objectives clearly in mind.

Delegation of Authority and Fixing Responsibility

Whenever a store acquires employees, an assignment of duties must be made. This is true whether there is one employee or one thousand. An important principle to bear in mind is that responsibility cannot be placed on an individual unless authority has previously been delegated to him or her. It is not necessary for a person who is responsible for the performance of a specific duty actually to perform the task. Responsibility means that the one who is charged with the accomplishment of an assignment is accountable to a superior. In the case of nonperformance, the individual who is responsible must assume the blame and is accountable.

There are three inescapable features to delegation. These are: (1) assignment of duties, (2) granting of authority, and (3) obligation to complete the task.

Duties. In analyzing these three attributes, duties can be described in two ways:

1. First as a function. For example, Jack Flyer, a clerk in a retail store, may be assigned the duty of selling neckties. Ken Wilson, another employee, may be assigned the duty of sweeping the floors. A third employee, Henry Casper, might have the duty of recording sales in the proper accounting books.
2. Second in terms of the results that management wants to achieve. We may describe Jack Flyer's duty as the selling of $200 worth of ties in an 8-hour period. This method of describing duty is one that relates the task to productivity. From a managerial point of view, that is an obvious improvement.

Retail stores often assign sales goals to the department as a whole. The sales attained by a department on a specific day become the sales quota target one year later. For example, assume that a cosmetics department in a local department store had sales totaling $752.15 on April 6, 1975. An attempt is made to increase productivity by alerting all sales personnel to last year's sales, and hoping that the clerks will expend extra efforts to surpass last years' total. One obvious limitation to this theory is that dollar sales totals can rise without a concomitant increase in unit sales. In an inflationary period, this often is the case. A simple example will illustrate this point: 100 ties @ $3 each = $300 sales. Suppose prices increase 10 cents. Then 97 @ $3.10 = $300.70 sales. A decrease in sales of 3 units keeps the dollar sales almost constant.

Authority. Perhaps no aspect of management is so difficult to understand, and to put into practice, as the principle of delegating authority. Frequently, there is an attempt to oversimplify this principle and assume top level management has unlimited authority. In discussing this point, Newman, Summer, and Warren say:[5]

> No company president or plant manager can grant someone of lower rank the power to change the physical laws of the universe, the power to compel customers to sign orders or suppliers to sell raw materials, or the power to compel the enthusiastic cooperation of associates and subordinates. The rights that an administrator may transfer are more akin to authorization than they are to power.

There are other difficulties involved in the granting of authority other than limiting authority. One of these difficulties is the failure to make lines of authority clear. This may lead to a conflict between two or more individuals who believe a certain duty is their assignment. Much of the fuzziness may be eliminated by hav-

[5]William H. Newman, Charles E. Summer, and E. Kirby Warren, *The Process of Management*, 2nd ed. (Englewood Cliffs, N.J.: Prentice-Hall, Inc., 1967), p. 87.

ing good job descriptions, policy manuals, and statements of procedure. On the other hand, some organizations prefer to leave things fuzzy, and let tradition or custom dictate who has the authority. In the latter case, conflicts may not be avoided.

Obligations. Generally speaking, when an employee accepts a job, he or she assumes a moral obligation to carry out the assigned tasks. The employee is not free to carry out the duty or to reject the assignment as the spirit moves. Obligations reflect attitudes. If this is true, then it is necessary for management to do all in its power to make certain that the attitudes of subordinates are responsible. The morale of subordinates is related in part to the manner in which superiors relate to them.

No employee, regardless of rank or status in the organization, is free of obligations. An employee's attitude to the completion of an assigned task is shaped by the employee's own code of ethics, family background, and environmental and cultural influences. When an employer states that an employee is dependable, the employer is really saying that the individual is sensitive to his or her obligation, and that the employer can be reasonably certain the duty will be carried out.

Reasons for Poor Delegation

Retail proprietors in small organizations and top level executives in large organizations sometime fail to delegate authority properly. The principal reasons for this failure are:

1. Employers lack confidence in the ability of the subordinates, so they do the task themselves.
2. Executives lack competence and simply do not execute the principle of delegation.
3. There is a breakdown in the internal communications system, and responsible executives do not know what is taking place.
4. There is a lack of controls.
5. Some executives would rather do the job themselves than delegate it to someone else. Often this reflects a martyr complex.

On the other hand, subordinates may be unwilling to accept authority even if management is delegating it properly. The principal reasons are:

1. The employee lacks confidence in his or her own abilities.
2. The employee fears criticism by superiors if he or she makes a mistake.
3. The employee believes that the rewards are inadequate for assuming the responsibility.
4. It is easy for the employee to ask the boss to make the decision.

Organization Charts

An organization chart is a pictorial device used to show the functions of a business, the lines of authority, and the person responsible for carrying out specific assignments. It is a useful device to portray a clear picture of the retail organization.

Advantages of Organizational Charts. There are decided advantages to having an organizational chart. Some of the principal ones are:

1. There is a clear-cut statement of functions to be performed.
2. Each employee is assigned definite tasks, and thus responsibility is easily fixed.
3. Interrelationships among employees are clearly shown.
4. Specialization is clearly shown.
5. Delegation of routine duties is easier to accomplish.

One may conclude that whenever an organization can be charted, the store is likely to have:

1. Good morale and discipline.
2. Effective specialization.
3. Effective responsibility.

Small Store Organization. The appropriate organizational structure for any retail store is one that accomplishes all the retailer's objectives. In small stores this is quite easy to do, and the organizational structure is usually clearly understood by everyone within the organization. Unfortunately, a great number of small retailers do not use organizational charts to depict their structures. The reasons are a lack in understanding the basic fundamentals of organization, or the belief that organization charts are unnecessary in small businesses.

Let us examine some basic charts. First, Barbara Hartman's Coin Shop, a one-person organization.

Barbara Hartman's Coin Shop

Barbara Hartman—
Owner and Sole Employer

1. Buys all coins and stamps.
2. Performs all selling activities.
3. Writes all advertising copy.
4. Keeps all accounting records.
5. Analyzes and evalutes all activities.
6. Performs all maintenance.

Now suppose the coin shop grows, and Hartman employs four other individuals to assist her. The new organization chart might look something like Figure 6.3.

Retail stores may be organized by product line, functions, geographical limits, or a combination of them. Organization charts for each type are shown in Figures 6.4 and 6.5.

FIGURE 6.3
Chart for five-member organization

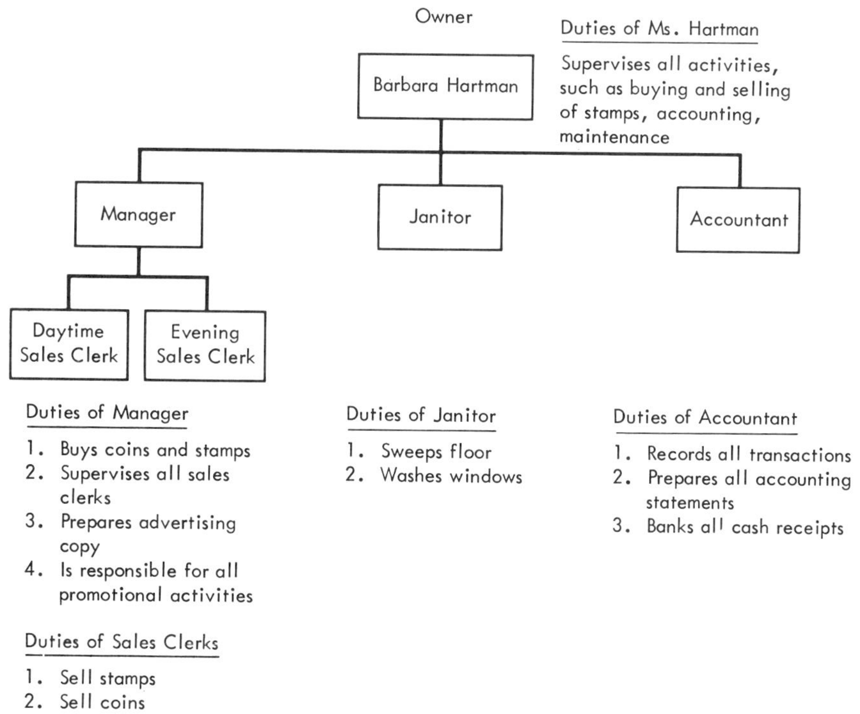

ASSEMBLING RESOURCES

Because this topic is vital to any organization, an entire chapter is devoted to personnel management. In Chapter 7 we discuss job descriptions, job analysis, hiring plans, and employee relations related to retailing. The purpose of mentioning assembly of resources here is simply to point out its place in the overall structure of the organization.

STORE OPERATION

The Behavioral Viewpoint

There is little doubt that people are the major resources of any organization and the most misunderstood. Throughout this chapter much of the discussion has centered around the formal organization. However, it is not the formal structure alone that determines the behavior of the employees. Behavior is determined

FIGURE 6.4
Retail stores may be organized in different ways

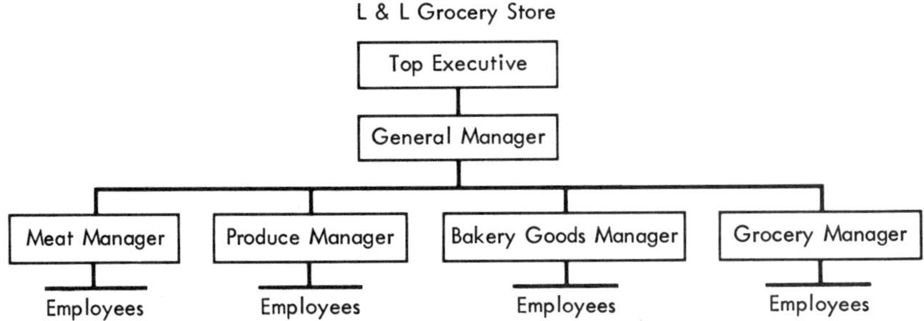

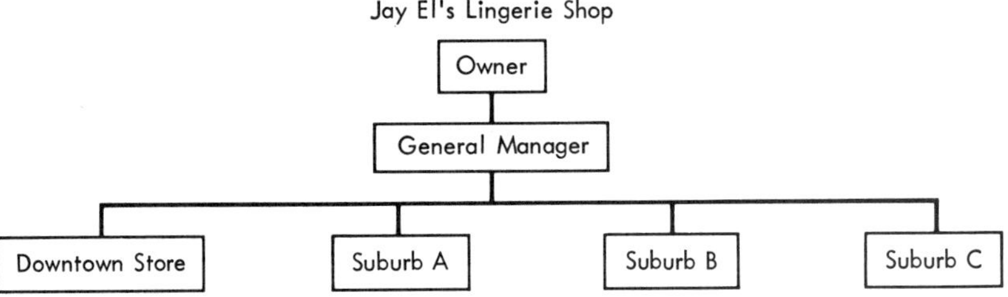

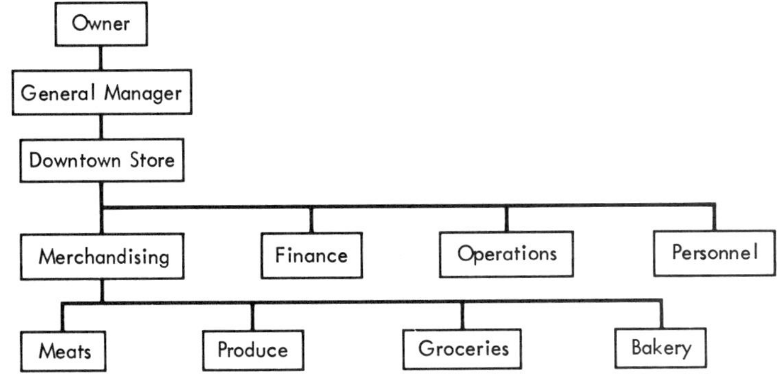

FIGURE 6.5
Complex retail store organization chart

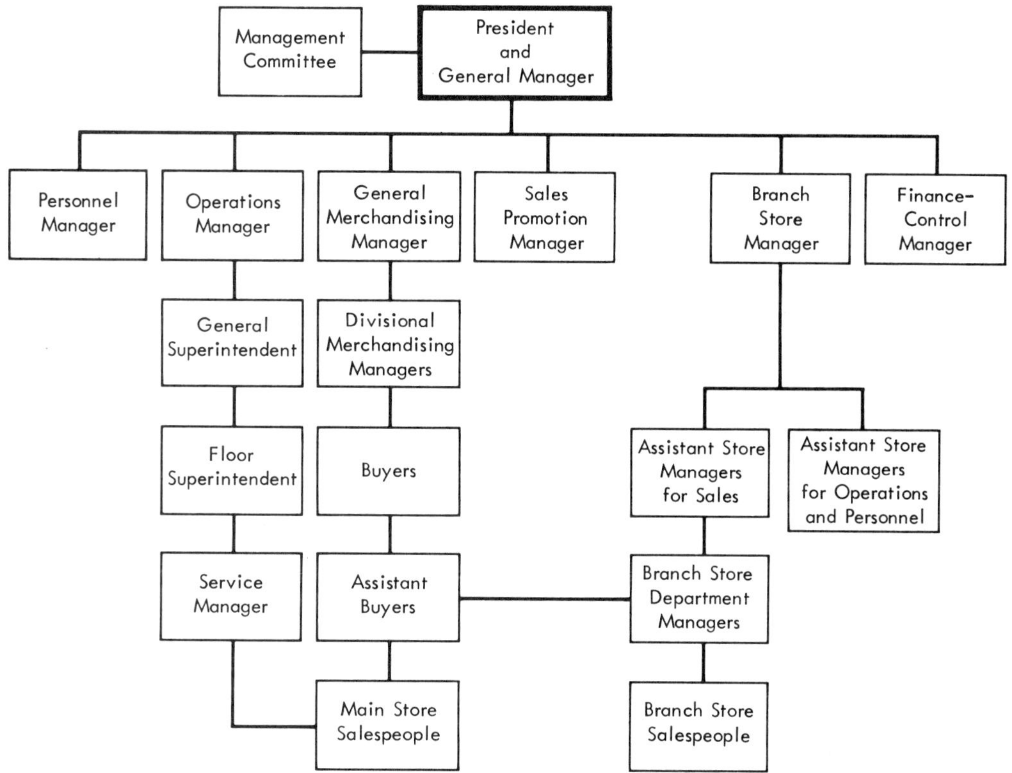

Source: "Organization in Multi-Unit Department and Specialty Stores," National Retail Merchants Association, New York, New York.

in part by such factors as culture, family background, educational level, personality, social class, and attitudes of opinion leaders and reference groups. People who work together develop a rapport which is manifested in their behavior. It is not surprising for an informal organization to develop whose interests are noncompany objectives.

The Clique

One of the worst types of informal organizations is the clique. This is a group whose membership is recruited from throughout the company. People join a clique because of common interests or because of a "cause" to which all jointly subscribe. The clique has been described as follows:[6]

[6]Newman, et al., *The Process of Management*, p. 187.

> In a business firm, a clique promotes its cause whenever it is relevant to the solution of a current problem, by being eager (or reluctant) to carry out plans that make the cause look good (or poor), and perhaps by rewarding the faithful.

One should not conclude that all cliques are bad per se. However, they do tend to disrupt company programs, especially in large organizations. The company can try to break a clique, but this is difficult and often unwise. The best solution is to try to have the clique's aims and goals harmonize with those of the formal organization. The retailer should always attempt to develop company loyalty and to minimize divisive effort.

Benefits from Informal Groups

Informal groups spring up in every type of work situation. Sometimes there may be as few as three people—occasionally considerably more. These are the people who eat lunch together, take their breaks together, or perhaps even socialize outside the working environment. Frequently, a strong bond of affection springs up among the members of these informal groups. Some of the benefits accruing to the organization because of the existence of these informal groups are:

1. Give workers a sense of belonging, thus increasing company morale.
2. Teach new workers company policy and procedure.
3. Aid in recruiting new employees who have distinct talents and skills.
4. Pressure individuals to conform to company standards.

It is obvious that people are social creatures and individuals seek out friends and companions everywhere. The company should always attempt to staff workers into the formal structure so that company objectives can be carried out in harmony.

COMMUNICATION

One of the essential attributes of a good organization is communication. This means that a retailer must develop a network of channels in order to communicate with customers, distributors, financial institutions, the government, the community in which he or she is located, suppliers, and employees. Each of these groups is composed of people with differing interests who cannot be reached by the same communication channels.

Factors Determining Effective Communication

Communication is composed of four elements: (1) the sender of the message, (2) the message itself, (3) the media through which the message is transmitted, and (4) the receiver of the message. A breakdown in any one of the elements may cause a communication problem. This chapter will limit the discussion of communication to the internal organization of the retail store. We are interested in the structure of the organization and the necessity of building the channels so that the organization can communicate with those inside and outside the store, and thus fulfill its mission. Communication is so commonplace that often too little thought is given to it. Consider this example:[7]

> Even a simple transaction such as answering an inquiry from a customer normally involves several chains of communication. A salesclerk must check with a stock clerk to find out whether enough inventory is on hand; to answer this question, the stock clerk probably has previously communicated with production and shipping people and has built up a record of current supplies. The sales order clerk will probably also check with the credit manager to determine whether the customer is entitled to credit.

One can clearly see that even a routine inquiry probably involves numerous people throughout the organization. (See Figure 6.6.) Therefore, it is essential to develop the proper communications network so that accurate answers can be obtained speedily. Traditionally, most organizations have relied on the chain of command for their main communication channels. That is, an employee expects to communicate with his or her superior, who in turn communicates with his or her superior, and so forth throughout the entire organization. There are some serious limitations to this single channel. These are:

1. The mass of detailed information that must be funneled through this channel is so great that it would overwhelm the system itself. Bottlenecks would be commonplace and the flow of essential information would be impaired.

FIGURE 6.6

Even a simple customer credit card check must go through a complex communications verification procedure

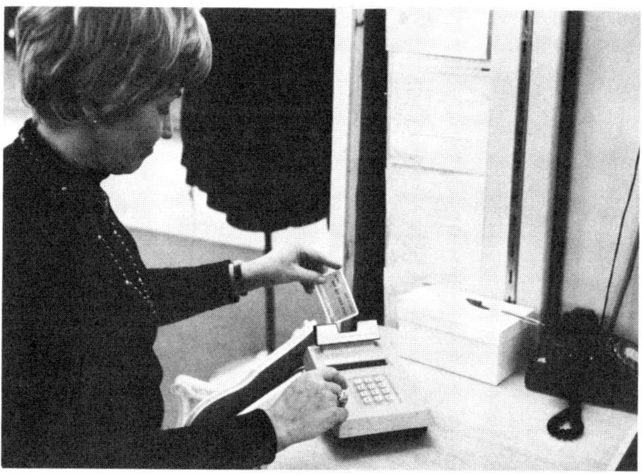

Source: *Chain Store Age, Executives' Edition*, March 1974.

[7]Ibid., p. 219.

2. The single command channel would contribute to "organizational distance." People are poor transmitters of messages, and when a message is relayed from person to person throughout a long channel, its accuracy decays rapidly. Most of us are familiar with the old party game where one person whispers a short message to the person on his or her right, who in turn whispers it to the next person, and so on through a chain. The last person then tells the message he or she received to the entire group. The result is usually hilarious because it does not resemble the original message. Accuracy has decayed from the original message because of organizational distance.
3. Another reason for inaccuracy is due to planned distortions of the message. A subordinate may tell the superior only what he or she wishes the superior to hear. The subordinate may be protecting him- or herself or someone else in the organization. In other words a protective screen will be set up to filter out information that someone wishes to withhold.

Therefore it is essential that large organizations use multiple channels of communication. In some cases this means doing away with the single command channel. Every supervisor maintains an open door and talks with anyone who has the information sought. In other words, "going through the channels" is scrapped. On the other hand, some experts maintain that this is unwise, since it will be difficult to hold anyone accountable for the performance of a task if proper channels are avoided.

However, whether or not the single command channel is eliminated, a company may do the following:

1. Develop and publish standard operating procedures for distribution of those who utilize the information.
2. Use the language that is best understood by those who are to use the information.
3. Cut down the organizational distance by placing the decision maker close to the center of operations.
4. Speed up the flow of communications by using liaison people, expeditors, sensing units, or special committees.
5. Use people to people oral contacts when these speed up communications and expedite decisions.

The Grapevine

The grapevine is any communications network within the organization that is not official. Every organization has a grapevine whether it wishes one or not. The grapevine is usually quite fast; messages generally go through it faster than they would through official channels. However, the messages also are often garbled, inaccurate, and distorted. The messages received through the grapevine are usually believed and often they can be the source of friction or embarrassment. Inasmuch as one cannot destroy the grapevine, it should be used to management's advantage. First of all, learn what the grapevine is reporting. If the message is inaccurate or false, the official network should correct the message or kill the rumor. Sometimes the grapevine can be used to transmit messages that the organization prefers not to be official. (See Figure 6.7.)

FIGURE 6.7

Information can be easily distorted when passing through the grapevine

In conclusion, one should carefully design a communications network that provides effective communication with maximum accuracy and a minimum of distortion. The network should make use of both written and oral approaches—whichever lends itself to be the most effective means of communication.

CONTROL

The purpose of control is to determine how closely the actual operations conform to established objectives. The control process always includes the following three elements:

1. Standards for performance.
2. Evaluation of the results.
3. Corrective action.

Standards of Performance

One cannot measure the performance of any activity unless there are some standards that are universally accepted by the people concerned. How can we tell if there is satisfactory performance? In the case of an individual baseball player—we can look at his batting average, his runs batted in total, or his fielding average. For example, a baseball player with a .300 batting average represents a high standard of batting prowess in the major leagues. A player who consistently bats higher than .300 is a superstar.

In the case of a retailer, net profits have been the traditional standard employed. Even this standard may be inadequate to describe a satisfactory performance. The accountant may substitute the following: net profit by item sold, net profit per square foot of selling space, or net profit per dollar of invested capital. (Chapter 16 discusses these standards and their computation.)

Other retailers use sales as the standard. They compare total sales in dollars or in units with those of other time periods. Frequently, the retailers express sales in terms of square feet of selling space, or by item, or by department, or some other way.

Control is most effective when results are related to an individual's performance. Sometimes the complexity of operations makes it difficult to relate results to an individual; therefore they must use group results. A retail food store may speak of its bakery sales, its produce sales, or its dollar volume in meats. In any case, some standard must be chosen as the first step in the control process.

Evaluation of Performance

The evaluation of a given performance is a difficult but necessary assignment. In our baseball example, we said that an individual's batting average could be used as a standard of performance. We also stated that a baseball batting average of .300 or higher would be considered quite good. To arrive at this judgment an evaluation had to take place. One method would be to array all the batting averages of all the players in a given year and count the number of players who bat higher than .300. If one did this, it would be obvious that only a few players each year reach this lofty plateau. Therefore, one could conclude that this average was very good.

In a similar manner one could take the dollar sales, or profits of a given retailer, and express them in one fashion or another. This standard could then be used to compare with similar performances in other time periods or by other retailers. In this way one could come to some evaluative conclusions. (Chapter 16 discusses this topic in detail.)

Corrective Action and Control Reports

The purpose of control reports is to call attention to actual performance results and to relate these results to some standard. Suppose that actual performance falls short of some suggested standard. The control report simply calls this deviation to the attention of the proper executives. Until corrective action is taken, nothing is really accomplished. Therefore a method must be set up either to (1) explain the deviations of the actual results from a standard, or (2) correct the deficiency. It should also be mentioned that if one examines a series of control reports arrayed in a time sequence, one can determine if a particular situation is improving or deteriorating. This type of information is also useful in determining the kind and type of corrective action that must be taken.

SUMMARY

All types of retailers need an organization to carry out their mission. The kind of organizational structure chosen depends upon many factors, but regardless of the size or complexity of the retailer, there are principles of management that make for effectiveness.

First there is a need to identify the retailing functions. These are: (1) determining objectives, (2) planning, (3) organizing and coordinating, (4) assembling resources, (5) operation, and (6) control.

The retailer first determines goals and objectives. These spell out in detail the mission of the organization. All of the objectives and subobjectives should be carefully thought out and put into writing so that everyone within the organization will be alert as to the directions the retailer intends to move and what will be offered to the customers.

Once the objectives are clearly spelled out, the retailer can turn attention to planning. There, he or she identifies the problems and decides on the action to be taken. This means the retailer must identify the decision makers and devise a plan to solve the problems inherent in the business. Decision making is never an easy undertaking, but the retailer must build into the organizational structure those devices that will aid in choosing between alternative courses of action.

All retailers, regardless of size, perform similar activities. These include: purchase of merchandise for resale, preparing the merchandise for sale, attracting customers, selling the merchandise, keeping the necessary records, and evaluating the entire operation. The organization must be structured so that authority may be delegated and responsibility fixed. Organization charts are helpful to show functions of a business, lines of authority, and the responsible office.

There are also informal organizations that are significant to the overall operation of a retailer. One of the worst types is the clique. Inasmuch as it is unlikely that it can be eliminated, management should try to have the clique's goals harmonize with those of the formal organization and to minimize divisive effort.

An essential attribute of any organization is a channel of communication that is effective. Good communication includes both oral and written approaches, single and multiple channels, and formal and informal methods of communicating. The emphasis is on information and a control over distortion.

Another ingredient to good organizational structure is control. Its purpose is to determine how closely the actual operations conform to established objectives. All control processes include standards of performance, an evaluative mechanism, and corrective action.

QUESTIONS FOR DISCUSSION

1. What is an objective? Why is it important to a retailer to state objectives?
2. Discuss the role of a decision maker in a small retail store, a large retail store, and a chain food store.
3. Discuss the general subject matter of delegating authority and fixing responsibility.
4. In your opinion what obligation does a retail employee have in carrying out assigned tasks?
5. Give the important reasons for failure to delegate authority properly.
6. What are the advantages to an organizational chart?
7. Suppose you worked for a large retail store and the president called you in to explain the theory of informal organization. What would you say?
8. What are the factors determining effective communication?
9. What is the "grapevine," and how would you make use of it?
10. The control process always includes these three elements: standards for performance, evaluative techniques, and corrective action. Discuss.

7 PERSONNEL MANAGEMENT

The president of a large New York specialty store "requested" that female salespeople adopt and wear a particular style dress that management believed would be fashionable. Many of the women believed they should be allowed to wear whatever they wanted; and besides that, a whole new wardrobe would be expensive. In this particular case, a confrontation was avoided when the local newspapers published the story, making the president look like an ogre to the public. The president soon "reinterpreted" his policy, and the saleswomen went back to wearing what they wanted.

Top management in a Detroit furniture store has had to determine which salesperson receives the commission on a sale that is originated by one salesperson but later completed by another. The problem arises when a salesperson spends much time with a customer who is on the verge of buying but wants to "look around" in other stores just to make sure. The customer returns later and quickly completes the sale with a different salesperson. The problem is not unique to Detroit or to furniture stores; it occurs anywhere there are salespeople working on commissions.

When a Chicago food retailer opened a giant store with an on-premise bakery, it was obliged to install shower facilities for the bakers. Baking is a hot job and the unions insisted that the men have the facilities for cleaning up before going home. Fortunately, those who are familiar with union contracts were permitted a voice in the store's construction.

Supervisors in one of America's largest mail-order houses regularly monitor the conversation exchanges between employees and customers who phone in orders. The company does so to show the employees how to speed up transactions and reduce mistakes, an entirely proper managerial goal. But the employees do not like what they call "snooping," arguing that it is unprofessional. They argue that the customer wouldn't like it either, if he or she knew about it. In those states where monitoring is legal, the retailer intends to continue the practice. But it is looking for a way to get its employees to see that it is a necessary part of the business.

In one particular week, the manager of a personnel department faced the following: a civil liberties group who queried him about a rumor that his department was about to initiate the use of a lie detector during hiring procedures (internal theft was reaching alarming proportions); a young salesman in the furniture department who came to work one morning wearing a single gold earring; a jurisdictional dispute between the stock people and the display people with regard to which group should put display cartons on a shelf; and a request from an employee with eight months' seniority that he be given a two-month maternity leave just before Christmas so he could help his wife with their new baby. Each of these four problems had to be resolved efficiently and legally. Furthermore, it was important that the employees who were involved should see that the method of resolving the dispute was fair.

These problems are just a few of the issues that face retail management or those involved in a store's personnel department. This chapter concerns the relationship of the retail manager to the people with whom he works, or whom some call "associates." Happily, Americans live in a society in which we are generally free to move among jobs, from location to location, and from employer to employer. Furthermore, we can collectively or individually press employers for what we believe are our "rights." Employers often have agreed with demands made by employees, sometimes with enthusiasm and sometimes reluctantly. As society undergoes more and more social changes in its institutions, the task of retail personnel management will become more demanding and challenging.

Today's retail manager is confronted by better educated and informed employees, who demand: (1) the opportunity to participate in the decision-making process, (2) greater rewards for their productive efforts, and (3) more participation of retailing institutions in community affairs. To complicate the management process, many retailers must negotiate with unions regarding wages, hours of employment, working conditions, and extent of fringe benefits to employees. The retailer must also negotiate under legal constraints imposed by some particular level of government. Much legislation has been enacted to prescribe the manner in which a retailer may operate his or her business, including relations with employees.

MANAGEMENT AND LEADERSHIP

Perhaps the most important function of management is to provide leadership. Dale Yoder believes that the major reason for the difficulty in providing effective leadership is the fact that workers insist they be given the right of self-management. He states:[1]

> They have their own ideas about working and make many decisions about when and where to work, whether to operate their own business or to work for others, and what they consider adequate and fair compensation for their contributions. Moreover, free workers change their minds in these questions, so that what they decided a year ago may not seem to them an appropriate answer today or tomorrow.

Retailing is in need of more effective leadership. This is evidenced by:

1. Deterioration in the quality of retail salesmanship.
2. Low employee morale.
3. High rate of retailer mortality.
4. High rate of employee turnover.
5. Difficulty of recruiting permanent employees.
6. Dishonest and unethical practices.

SOCIETY'S GOALS

Before examining those principles of management that relate singularly to the retail organization, it is necessary to point out that society imposes some rather

[1]Dale Yoder, *Personnel Management and Industrial Relations*, 5th ed. (Englewood Cliffs, N.J.: Prentice-Hall, Inc., 1962), p. 2.

stiff requirements upon all types of management. As a starter, the public demands full employment. Every individual, regardless of race, creed, sex, or nationality, who seeks employment should have a job permitting him or her to develop within the limitations of his or her abilities. Leading economists recognize that a large number of unemployed people represents a sizeable waste of manpower and is a situation that should not be tolerated. Unemployment is as detrimental to society as it is to an individual. Stable employment has become a national goal requiring the cooperation of everyone.

However, the worst economic slump since the 1930s began in 1974. Some experts in early 1975 predicted that the unemployment rate would reach 10 percent or more before it leveled off. New car sales for 1975 models were substantially lower than for the corresponding 1974 models for the same time periods. Consequently, thousands of auto workers were laid off or furloughed. Congress devoted a great deal of effort to solving this economic crisis; one result was a rebate on 1974 income taxes of up to $200 per family coupled with a lowering of 1975 income tax liabilities, both designed to inject more money into the system. A very large deficit was expected in the federal budget for the fiscal year starting in July 1975 as Congress passed legislation to stimulate the economy. Retailers of all kinds have experienced their own problems associated with the slump. However, the nation's retailers are expected to play a major role in employing a large share of the unemployed, thus contributing to the solution of the economic problem.

Society wants individuals to be employed in jobs in which race, religion, or sex is irrelevant to performance. Much of the civil rights movement since the 1950s has been concerned with the failure of business to employ the disadvantaged in productive jobs. Selective boycotts against retailers have been used, with some degree of success, to eliminate this type of discrimination.

Significance of Good Management for a Retailer

Good personnel management has tangible benefits for any organization. One such benefit for retailers is higher profits. Those who adhere to good principles of management will exercise their leadership roles more effectively, and therefore they will have larger net sales and in turn earn higher profits.

For permanent success a retailer must depend upon good customer relations. Customer impressions are based upon the shopper's contact with store personnel, whether the employees are salesclerks, delivery men, credit personnel, general management, or other employees.

It is likely that the main reason why a customer changes his or her patronage of a store is dissatisfaction with the store's employees. In today's marketplace, many stores stock about the same brands of merchandise, priced about the same; the difference is likely to be in the manners of the employees. One might say that the very survival of a store may depend on employees' attitudes. Management must try to choose its employees from among those who are most likely to encourage friendly customer relations.

PERSONNEL PROBLEMS OF RETAILERS

Inexperienced Workers

The retailing industry poses special problems for its manpower management. One problem, and a very important one, is the relatively large number of inexperienced employees who hold retailing jobs, often in rather sensitive customer areas. One need only walk through any shopping center and note the number of young salespeople. Not all young people are inexperienced, but retailers are the major employers of young people working on their first jobs. All of us are familiar with the stock boys or girls, carry-out boys, or baggers at the local supermarket. Notice the number of teenagers employed as checkers in the supermarket, or clerks in department stores, or carhops at drive-ins.

Part-time Employees

Not only are a great number of retail workers inexperienced, but many are working part time. Many young workers seek only part-time jobs near home; they can be accommodated by retailers who do not demand experience as a condition for employment. Most do not serve in an apprenticeship role since they are almost immediately productive, and very few accept a permanent job in retailing. Supermarket Institute estimated in 1968 that of its 820 thousand people employed in retail food operations, 350 thousand worked on a part-time basis. That is, 47 percent of the employees are part time. In 1975, 45 percent of the employees were part time, so there was no significant change in the seven year period. We may therefore conclude that the use of part-timers has stabilized.

Most supermarkets experience their greatest sales volume on Thursdays, Fridays, and Saturdays. *Progressive Grocer* estimates that the typical supermarket sells 76 percent of its volume on those three days. For this reason it is necessary to employ part-time help in order to staff the supermarket effectively.[2]

Variety of Jobs

All types of workers are needed to staff the variety of jobs within large retail stores. (See Figure 7.1.) A partial list of these are: salesclerks, bakers, butchers, stock boys, pharmacists, dieticians, nurses, cooks, waitresses, bartenders, beauty operators, travel counselors, service station attendants, garage mechanics, heating and air conditioning engineers, accountants, advertisers, and security workers. The need for good personnel management is obvious if people of varied skills are to be found and put to work in a retailing organization.

[2]"Part-timers Playing Increasingly Important Role," *Progressive Grocer*, 46, no. 4 (April 1967), p. 186.

FIGURE 7.1
Many jobs in retailing do not directly involve selling merchandise

Source: Safeway Stores Inc., Oakland, California.

Working Conditions

Working conditions are vastly different in the retailing industry when compared with the rest of the industrial world. There is a whole crop of problems peculiar to retailing. One relates to store hours. Retailers must cater to customer preferences; consequently shopping hours are long, frequently extending far into the night. Furthermore, most retailers are open on Saturdays, and a growing number maintain Sunday hours as well. Many of these hours are unpopular with regular workers of any age bracket, so part-time help is often recruited to staff the organization. There is little doubt that the personnel department is handicapped in obtaining full-time employees by the peculiarity of the retailing hours.

Low Wages

Another handicap is the fact that the prevailing average wage rate in retailing is low compared with other types of employment. For example, the United States Department of Labor reported the average weekly wage of a worker in wholesale and retail trade during December 1974 to be $122.08. It also reported for the same time period the average weekly wage for employees in the following industries:[3]

Mining	$227.22
Contract construction	260.15
Transportation and public utilities	$185.14

An examination of these weekly wages indicates the severity of the wage problem in the retail trade.

High Rate of Employee Turnover

The turnover rate among employees is especially high in retailing; the annual turnover may be as high as 50 percent. This means that one out of every two employees terminates employment each year. The reasons for the high turnover are due to all the factors which we have just discussed: inexperienced workers, temporary help, poor hours, low pay, better opportunities elsewhere, and low individual productivity. Retail personnel managers have a burden to recruit and select qualified personnel to fill the vacancies that occur with both regularity and frequency.

Appearance of Store Employees

In most business other than some offices, employees are not required to dress to please the general public; yet in retailing, because of the great emphasis placed on customer contact, considerable stress is placed on personal appearance and dress codes. For female employees, some stores specify the proper color and style of dress, the length of sleeves, sheerness of material, and length of hemline. Moreover they prescribe the amount of cosmetics the women may use. Male employees are required to maintain certain dress standards, perhaps requiring a necktie, white shirt, and suit coat. Ever since the early 1970s there has been considerable social

[3]*Employment and Earnings*, U.S. Dept. of Labor, Bureau of Labor Statistics, 21, no. 8 (February 1975), p. 105.

unrest regarding the relevance of dress codes and proper length of hair for males or females. The entire subject of what constitutes proper appearance can be troublesome to retailers, as it is to school officials and other segments of society. Neatness and good appearance are certainly still important for the typical retailing employee. The question is, "What is a good appearance?"

Seasonal Nature of Retail Trade

Another peculiarity of retailing is the seasonal nature of retail sales. In some stores, the Christmas trade may account for half of the year's total sales volume. Other peak periods coincide with Easter, Mother's Day, Father's Day, back-to-school, or other holidays. In some stores the entire summer season is one of reduced activity. The seasonality of sales presents problems of staffing during these peak periods—another headache for the personnel department.

PERSONNEL POLICIES

The retailer must be careful to formulate personnel policies that are compatible with the objectives of the organization. Policy on manpower represents only a part of the total policy, but it is an important one. Policies of any type flow from the objectives of the business and represent courses of action to be followed in order to achieve carefully defined goals. It is the manager's responsibility to develop and promulgate the policies appropriate to the situation.

Definition of Policy

Dale Yoder defines a policy as:[4] "a predetermined and accepted course of thought and action that is defined and established as a guide toward accepted goals and objectives." In essence policies are statements of intention. Retailing personnel policies are those that state the retailer's intention with respect to an individual employee or group of employees. For example, a retailer may have a policy of hiring no person under the age of 18.

Programs, Practices, and Procedures

It does little good to define a policy unless there are sufficient mechanics to carry it out. Programs, practices, and procedures are the ways in which policy is implemented. Yoder points out the difference among programs, practices, and procedures in this way:[5]

> Our firm may have adopted a policy of providing training for all employees as a means of preparing them for promotion. To implement this policy, we may have to develop a training *program*. That *program* may include specific job training for new employees, supervisory training for foremen and supervisors, and management development for members of the management group.

[4]Dale Yoder, *Personnel Management and Industrial Relations*, 6th ed. (Englewood Cliffs, N.J.: Prentice-Hall, Inc., 1970), p. 26.

[5]Ibid., p. 28.

In the supervisory training program, we may include role-playing as one of the many training *practices*. Again, it may be our *practice* to announce the availability of training courses in the spring and fall of each year. As a further step in the implementation of this policy, we may maintain specific *procedures* for enrollment or for maintaining an appropriate record of individual training.

Example

Policy: All employees must be trained.

Programs:

1. Training program for new retail clerks.
2. Training program for buyers.
3. Training program for supervisory personnel.
4. Training program for management development.

Practices:

1. Training sessions start twice a year.
2. Senior sales people are the trainers.
3. Role playing is used as a teaching tool.

Procedures: Training office maintains records of people who have been trained.

Significance of Policy

One might ask why it is necessary to emphasize policy, or whether it is essential to have a policy at all. Actually, most retailers have all types of policies, but all too frequently they are not explicit or well thought out. The major purpose of any policy is to obtain uniform decisions on problems that are alike, regardless of who makes the decision. It is foolhardy not to have a policy regarding problems which are sufficiently repetitive; one decision can then solve all these problems. One might add, policy sets the precedent upon which all future decisions may be made. Let us examine a rather simple policy in this example.

Suppose you have opened a boutique selling mod clothes to young women. You know from experience in similar ventures that many of your customers will make personal checks in payment for their purchases. In some cases the checks will be returned by the bank for insufficient funds. You, therefore, make the policy that a salesclerk may not accept a check of over $10 unless it is approved by the manager or yourself. Now whenever any of your five salesclerks accept checks, they know precisely what they must do.

Levels of Manpower Policy

In large retail organizations one can identify two distinct levels of manpower policy. First, there is the *general employment policy*. This type is an outgrowth of the total objectives of the organization and reflects the philosophy of management. General employment policy is determined by the major executives of the business. For example, a large retailer might define his employment policy as "progressive." He might interpret "progressive" to mean this organization would:

1. Inspire all employees to participate in the employment process.
2. Promote from within the organization.
3. Actively seek handicapped applicants.

The second type of manpower policy is *specific policy*. This is the way in which the general policy is put into operation. Specific policy affects individual workers in a particular situation. A retailer might have a general policy stating all employees must have their hours of work verified. The specific policy is that they punch a time clock when they begin and stop working.

Who Makes Employee Policy?

Most of the policies that relate to managing employees originate with one of the following: (1) government, (2) unions, (3) the employer. An illustration will be helpful in explaining each.

Illinois once had a state law limiting female employees to a maximum 8-hour workday. This limitation made it necessary for management to work out some arrangement if the store was open more than 8 hours. In this instance, the state government determined some of the working conditions for women employees. (The law has since been repealed.)

A union may further determine policy. An example is a union not permitting the sale of fresh meat in supermarkets after 6 p.m. In this instance, the fresh meat department is closed at 6 p.m., even though the store might continue to sell produce, dairy products, and groceries until its 9 p.m. closing.

Generally, most of the policies are determined by the employer. The following checklist would be helpful to any retailer who wishes to make a new policy or to revise old policies:

Checklist

1. The policy must be in writing.
2. It should be clear and understandable.
3. The policy should be consistent with public policy and/or society's goals.
4. The policy should be uniform throughout the organization.
5. The policy should be realistic.
6. It must represent management's philosophy.
7. The philosophy should be fair and just to all.
8. It should have some degree of permanence.

PERSONNEL ACTIVITIES

The kinds and types of personnel activities taking place in any retail organization depend upon such factors as: size of the retail organization, whether it is part of a chain or an individual unit, the philosophy of top management, and the quality of managerial competence. In most large retail organizations one will find policies, programs, practices, and procedures dealing with the following activities: planning and scheduling, selection of employees, placement activities, training and development, compensation plans, evaluation techniques, changes of status, and constraints.

Planning and Scheduling

Most retailers have to plan ahead so that their manpower needs will be taken into account. There are certain activities to be done: potential employees must first be found, go through a selection process, and be placed in a proper department. Later, training enters the picture. All of these activities require prior planning and an organization to carry it out effectively. The organization to carry out these functions is related to the size of the business. In small retail stores (10 or less employees) the owner or manager may carry out all the personnel activities when the need arises. However, as the organization grows in size and acquires more employees, the need for a separate personnel manager increases. In these cases a manager is appointed whose sole responsibility is to train the new employee in all the activities normally associated with the job. Perhaps at this stage of growth, the personnel officer needs only a single assistant.

Some retailers are large and employ hundreds and even thousands of employees. Furthermore these employees may be scattered throughout the fifty states and overseas. In these cases the personnel manager is probably a major officer of the company, and his or her activities are many and varied. Consider the size of the following retailers as an example: J C Penney—200,000 employees; Sears—440,000 employees; Macy's—40,000 employees; and W. T. Grant—85,000 employees.[6]

RECRUITMENT

Recruiting retail employees always involves the following: a job analysis, preparing job descriptions, planning manpower needs and developing skills needed to do the job, the conditions of the job, and the relationship of this job to other jobs. It is a formal way of recording the facts uncovered in the job study.

Job Description

The following formal written statement is a job description.

I. *Identification Data* — Code number *456*
Job title: Salesclerk — Department *16*
Date of analysis—Feb. 11, 1976 — Division *Men's*

II. *Job Summary*. Under the direct supervision of the section manager, clerk performs all selling duties, such as showing merchandise to a customer and writing the sales check. Furthermore, clerk must be able to use cash register, record credit sales, and maintain stock in a saleable condition.

[6] *Dun and Bradstreet Million Dollar Directory 1975*, Section I (New York: Dun & Bradstreet, Inc., 1974), pp. 1030, 1418, 1775, 2014.

III. *Work Performed (Job Content)*
Routine or daily duties.
1. Check merchandise to be sure it is neatly arranged.
2. Greet customers and assist them by showing merchandise.
3. Complete the sale by making out the proper type of sales check.
4. Record sales on cash register and make change for cash sales.
5. Give information to customers who seek it.

Occasional duties.
1. Help to bring merchandise from storage area to selling floor.
2. Prepare want slips.
3. Assist in taking annual inventory.

IV. *Minimum Job Requirements (Job Specification)*

Education	High school graduate
Experience	None
Abilities	Knowledge of arithmetic and basic writing skills
Supervisory responsibilities	None
Physical requirements	Much standing or walking, occasional lifting.

Planning Manpower Needs and Developing Supply Source

Karl Marx once promised that employers could pick from a vast army of unemployed, paying exploitative wages to the few who would be selected to work. Indeed, we do have rates of unemployment that sometimes are quite high, and retail workers generally are paid less than those employed in several other types of work. However, planning manpower needs and finding an ample source of workers are more difficult than Marx could have foreseen in the 19th century. In some instances, little planning or recruiting is necessary. For the simpler retailing tasks, store managers often need little more than a "help wanted" sign in the window or to go to their card file of people who recently have inquired about a job. Such approaches are common, but they do not assure the employer that he or she has exhaustively searched for the most suitable person for a particular job.

One large firm conducts a "manpower audit" each year in which it assesses its present position and its future needs. Based on its needs and historic information about previous employment efforts, it then has a rough estimate of the recruiting task that lays ahead. Although it does not divulge specific information, it is not difficult to reconstruct a hypothetical model of a firm's manpower planning. (See Example 1.) The firm forecasts that it will need 30 store managers three years from the present data. The store managers are those who began a training program three years before, working in the company's headquarters office and being rotated among departments in several different stores. Historic evidence is used to determine that if the firm wants 30 store managers three years hence, it probably will have to interview about 1,000 candidates. Every single element of the model is difficult to plug with a number since historic evidence may be unreliable. However, not to plan manpower needs is an unsatisfactory alternative. Large firms have such voracious manpower needs that such planning is essential. S. S. Kresge is one of the country's largest recruiters of college graduates, hiring about 1,700 in 1973 for its training program, which lasts about five years. In 1974 it had over 3,900 young men and women working in every position from stock person to assistant store manager. A few of the best were being trained at corporate headquarters.[7]

Example 1

1,000	Individuals seen in face-to-face interview situation.
−600	No further consideration given; either candidate or employer terminates relationship.
400	Candidates brought to regional or national office for further interviewing.
−200	No further consideration given; either candidate or employer terminates relationship.
200	Employment offers made.
−160	Candidates refuse offer.
40	Candidates accept offer; begin three-year training program.
− 10	Attrition rate in training program; includes terminations, diversion to other jobs in the company, deaths.
30	Number who complete three-year training program and become store managers.

Although every retailer would like to think that he or she has exhaustively sought out every possible candidate for a particular position before making the choice, the time and dollar cost of doing so would be prohibitive. Consequently, the retailer must look to those sources that hold the greatest promise of providing trainable human resources. The most common sources are newspaper advertisements, advertisements in college publications, university and college placement offices, high school counselors, professional placement services, the firm's own employees who may recommend their friends, other competing or noncompeting retailers or other types of businesses, and information provided by salesmen employed by suppliers. Some retailers limit their recruiting efforts because of an intuitive feeling that some of these sources are better than others. When a retailer says, "We recruit at small, liberal arts, denominational-type schools because these young people seem to accept our way of doing business," he or she has decided to risk missing a few candidates at large sectarian business schools. This *is* a risk, but business is full of such risks. A less frequent approach is to review the historic evidence of previously hired employees from each source, going back to those sources that have provided successful employees and dropping those that have not. Thus, if 80 percent of those hired from College A are still with the company after three years while only 30 percent from College B are still on the payroll, recruiters surely would want to raise questions about returning to College B.

[7]"Kresge's Discount Success," *New York Times* (April 7, 1974), Sec. 3, p. 1.

Selection of Employees

Whenever retailers possess adequate job descriptions and job specifications, they are ready to select employees from among the job applicants. The retailer is now able to match the applicant's characteristics and aptitudes against the job specifications. This matching of characteristics will be aided by devices such as application blanks, employment interviews, use of tests, and checking references.

The Application Blank. All retailers probably use some type of application blank. Through this technique, the retailer obtains vital information from the applicant, such as name, place of residence, age, education, work experiences, and personal references. Sometimes this information is sufficient to determine whether or not the applicant should be hired, particularly for jobs that are not complex and can be performed by individuals with little work experience or skills. In most cases more information is required. Applicants may have to indicate the kind of jobs they are seeking and why they think they have the requirements to fill them. Furthermore, they are likely to be asked to spell out plans for personal development. From the answers to these questions, the company is able to gain an insight into the character of the applicant, his or her ambitions and goals, and the manner in which the applicant communicates his or her ambitions.

The completed application blank is the first step in the selection process, and for some candidates it is the last. An advantage to this stage of the selection process is the discovery of some unqualified applicants. By an early identification of these people, the retailer stands to save the money that would otherwise be invested in them. They would not be hired.

If there are no openings at the time the application blank is completed, the retailer must decide whether the applicant should be interviewed for possible future employment. Good talent is difficult to find, and it is good practice to interview everyone whether there are openings or not. Completed application blanks should be filed away for future reference.

The Interview. The next step is the actual interview of the applicant. The length of the interview depends upon many factors. The interview will probably be brief in those cases where the job is easy to perform. Suppose the store manager of a large food supermarket needs an unskilled individual to bag the groceries as the checkout person totals the sales. In this case, the actual interview might take only a few minutes. On the other hand, if a large department store is seeking a young college graduate to become a management trainee, the interviews could involve a number of people and last several days. Furthermore, the applicant might be asked to take a battery of tests. The screening process could be lengthy and complex.

Interviews should be conducted in friendly surroundings. The interviewer must obtain the applicant's confidence so that the applicant is relaxed and free of tensions. Above all, the interview should be conducted in privacy in order that confidential information may be discussed freely. The entire interview should be well planned and conducted in a professional manner. The dignity of the applicant must never be put in jeopardy.

Tests. The use of psychological tests measuring the applicant's intellectual skills, aptitudes, and interests are less common than application blanks and interviews. Many retailing jobs require skills that cannot be verified except by psychological tests. If such tests are needed, competent people must be available to interpret the test results.

Many large stores require physical examinations of all new employees. This might be especially important in cases where retailers have company-sponsored pension and disability plans. Furthermore, physical examinations would uncover ailments that could handicap employees in carrying out their duties. For example, people selling clothes cannot be color blind, and food handlers must not have tuberculosis or other contagious diseases.

References. All references should be checked. Usually an applicant will include as a reference only those who will give good reports. To counter this, a telephone call to the reference is far superior than the written letter. More information can be obtained over the phone, and furthermore it offers an opportunity to question the reference. This is especially important when the reference is a previous employer. During the conversation it sometimes is helpful to ask the reference for the names of any other individuals who may know the candidate. In this way the interviewer may obtain opinions that are more forthright and not quite so biased to the candidates.

TRAINING

It is generally recognized that training programs are the primary responsibility of the retailers themselves. High schools, colleges, and adult extension programs may play a supplementary role, but little more than that.

Goals

Training is designed to accomplish the following goals:

1. Make an employee more effective—that is, improve his or her skills and productivity.
2. Increase the level of employee morale.
3. Ease the manager's job of supervision.
4. Strengthen the retailer's financial position by controlling labor expenses through lower turnover and higher productivity.

Benefits

Whenever training programs are effective everyone gains. First, the individual worker develops additional skills and sharpens the older skills so that he or she is a more effective worker. As a result, the worker enjoys the job more, productivity rises, and he or she is rewarded with higher earnings. Perhaps the most important gain is in the attitude of the employee. It is a human trait to want to do well in those activities in which one participates. Training helps the employee to gain confidence in his or her ability, and this is reflected in overall attitude and behavior toward the customers, the store itself, and fellow employees.

The store gains too inasmuch as better trained employees reduce labor costs and eventually increase profits. Furthermore satisfied employees are likely to stay on the job, so labor turnover will be reduced. There is less of a need to recruit new workers and costly training programs can be minimized.

Properly trained salesclerks will bring greater customer satisfaction and help to build patronage loyalty. This aids the retailer in the continuing battle to be better than the competition.

The nation also gains as employees become more skilled and more productive. Higher earnings help to raise national income and in turn bring in larger tax receipts, so that the country can finance some of its social responsibilities. Furthermore, satisfied workers reduce tensions and help to build more stable communities.

Types of Training

Small stores ordinarily subscribe to "on the job" training programs. In the worst situations these degenerate into what is popularly called "the sink or swim method." In this situation the new salesclerk is put on the job and told to sell. He or she learns simply by watching others, asking questions, or by trial and error. This method of training is simply not training at all and has nothing to recommend it. However, it is still being used in some retail operations.

Every employee is either trained, dismissed, or remains on the job untrained. Unfortunately, this training can be improper especially if the trainer is unqualified, unproductive, or both. The retailer must be certain that his employees are being trained correctly and by those who are able to impart good work habits.

Large retail organizations are most likely to have centralized training departments and use the most sophisticated techniques available. (See Figure 7.2, pp. 169-70.) Some of the better organized personnel departments use such visual training aids as closed circuit television, motion pictures, slides, and charts and graphs. They employ individuals to staff these departments who have teaching ability and are patient, tactful, and understanding in their roles. Obviously the money the retailer invests in the training department is returned in the skills imparted to the employees—resulting eventually in higher profits to the retailer.

Retailers who have centralized training departments may or may not engage in group training. This is most efficient, but it depends on the availability of sufficient trainees to form a class. Individual training is expensive but sometimes unavoidable.

Normally the centralized training divisions give only a minimum amount of training, for the major training thrust is left to the department itself. However, at Macy's, Marshall Field's, and other department stores the centralized training gives the new employees their first formal introduction to the stores. The training department interprets store policies, instructs all the new employees in store procedures, and disseminates information of interest to the general employee. If the new employee has been hired to work on the selling floor, instruction is given on

FIGURE 7.2

Experienced personnel instruct new employees in handling merchandise

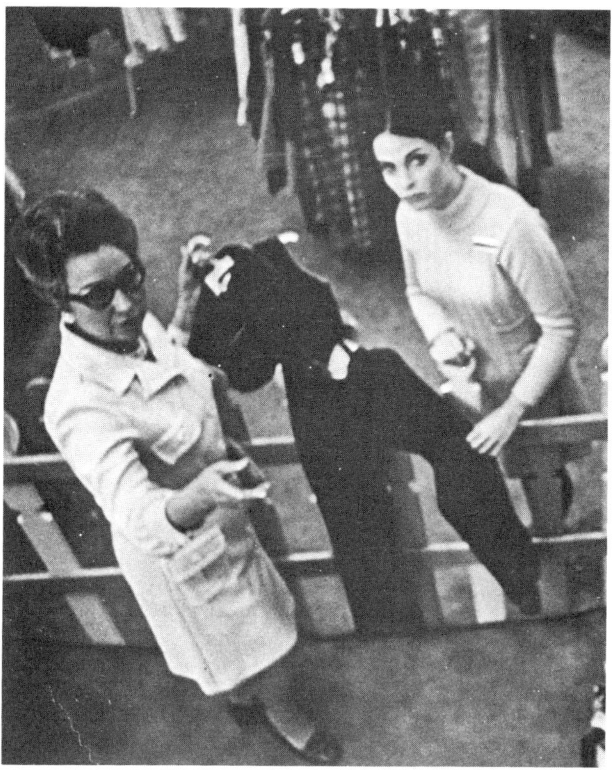

Source: Sears, Roebuck and Co., *1970 Annual Report*, pp. 6 and 7.

how to operate a cash register, how to write various sales checks, and the rudiments of how to sell. Furthermore, the training division offers periodic courses for groups such as section managers, assistant section managers, or floor managers. They coordinate training with all of the selling departments.

Retailers sometimes rely on the "sponsor" system to further train a salesperson after he or she has been initially trained by the centralized training staff. The sponsor is an experienced employee whose responsibility is to develop the skills of the trainee while the trainee performs on the job itself. The sponsor especially supervises the new employee in actual selling experience. Furthermore sponsors impart product knowledge to the clerks so that they will be more effective. The sponsor method of training differs from the "sink or swim" method in that a capable supervisor is on hand to advise, encourage, teach, correct, and instruct. The sponsor must have patience, tact, and understanding, as well as product and selling knowledge. A major limitation of this approach is that the sponsor may have developed bad habits and, in that case, is likely to pass them on to the trainee.

FIGURE 7.2 (cont.)

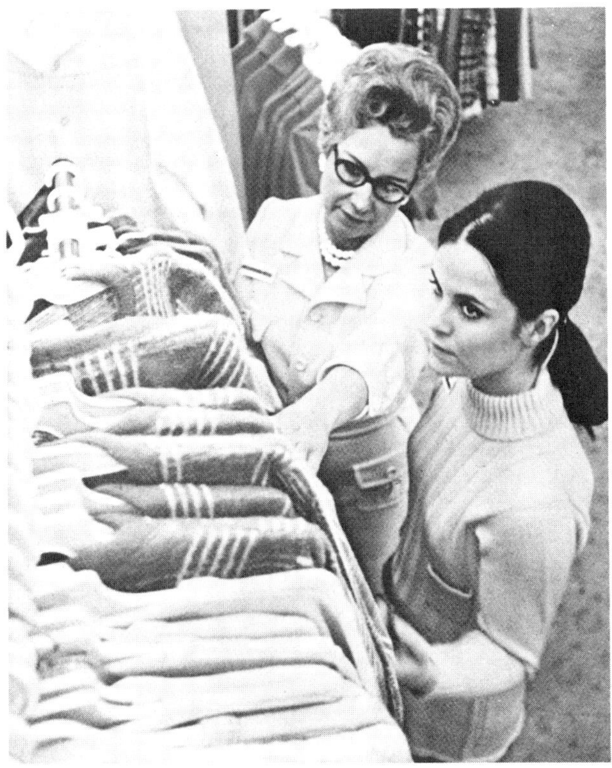

Continuous Training

All too often training is restricted to new employees. This is a mistake since regular employees easily slip into bad habits and need refresher courses to sharpen their morale or practices. (See Figure 7.3.) Formal training can be carried out in departmental meetings, through attendance at the centralized training department, or through self-improvement home studies. In the latter case programmed learning texts are ideal; however, the employee must be strongly motivated to complete a home study program. The subject matter of refresher courses, in the case of retail salespeople, would deal with the following topics:

1. Improving sales techniques.
2. Consumer behavior.
3. Store policy, programs, procedures, and practices.
4. Common errors.
5. Information on new products.
6. Helpful suggestions.

FIGURE 7.3

Management teams gather in workshops to sharpen skills as decision makers

Source: Sears, Roebuck and Co., *1970 Annual Report.*

Management Development Programs

Recruitment and training at the management level are crucial if the retailer is to obtain managerial talent for the future. Although forecasting is risky, managers who hope to be successful in future years should be educated in quantitative techniques requiring a sophisticated knowledge of mathematics, statistics, and accounting. He or she should be familiar with the computer. Furthermore, retailing is a business dealing with people, hence managers should be well trained in such behavior courses as anthropology, psychology, and sociology. The management development trainees will by necessity be college-educated, holding at least the bachelor's degree. On most campuses today major retailers compete for the talent being educated there.

An illustration of a management development program is the one used by W. T. Grant, a chain retailer who has some 85,000 employees. College graduates are recruited and then started out in a four-week general training session. This stage is one of indoctrination only. After the four-week session, employees are officially called management trainees. They then are given the responsibility for running a department. That means they are each responsible for the sales, layout, display, and customer service of the department assigned, although they are still supervised very carefully by superiors. After approximately one year, the successful trainee is promoted to division merchandise. At this stage trainees supervise several departments each. Assuming they make normal progress, the next step up is assistant store manager, and ultimately store manager. The entire process usually takes about seven years from the initial indoctrination to store manager. It is interesting to speculate on the role that a training program should play in forming an employee's ethical outlook. Perhaps no small part of Grant's economic difficulties of the mid-seventies was due to alleged mismanagement at the top level. Training—often with the use of case studies—can help illustrate the implications of certain decisions.

The Knowledge-Experience Gap

Retailing has lagged behind other segments of American business in the recruitment, training, and development of executive talent. In the past, retailing was dominated by family-oriented stores, and most of the managerial talent was supplied by family members. Today the family has been replaced by corporations, which are more impersonal and compete aggressively for talent.

The need for a management development program has become apparent because of a knowledge–experience gap. Graduates of colleges and universities come into retailing with sophisticated knowledge but little or no experience. On the other hand, present executives have the experience but not the latest knowledge of the newer graduates. This creates the knowledge-experience gap which must be bridged if retailing is to meet the challenges of today. A New York educator put the case this way:[8]

> the knowledge–experience gap will widen. A serious gap exists between today's new hiree, who is a recent MBA or college graduate, and his manager. The graduate's knowledge is current, but he lacks experience; the manager is experienced but his knowledge is not as current. Frustrations are built into this relationship for both the manager and the new hiree. This gap is self-perpetuating. By the time the graduate gains experience and subsequently becomes a manager, his knowledge is no longer current.

This knowledge-experience gap presents a challenge to training departments to strengthen the tools of the experienced manager while aiding the newer graduate to profit from the experience of the older manager. Basically, executive training must be essentially self-development.

Distributive Education

Distributive education is a government-sponsored program designed to help small to medium-sized retail stores. Congress passed the George-Barden Act in 1946 and the Vocational Act in 1963 in which federal money is made available to train retailing employees. The funds are allocated to the individual states based on population and require the states and local communities to participate in the funding. In general, high school students who are in distributive education take jobs with participating retail stores, and they work a minimum of 15 hours a week. Their classroom time in school is devoted to those subjects which are related to the work experience. The trainee is paid the prevailing wage by the retailer and the school gives the student educational credit. (See Figure 7.4.) Distributive education is also available for the high school graduate whether or not he or she is pursuing a formal education. More will be said about this program in Chapter 19 in our discussion of careers in retailing.

[8]Robert F. Vizza. "Marketing in the 1970's—Are You Ready to Meet Its New Challenges?" *Marketing Insights*, 3 (December 9, 1968), p. 9.

FIGURE 7.4

Retailing students learn some of the principles of fashion merchandising by setting up displays

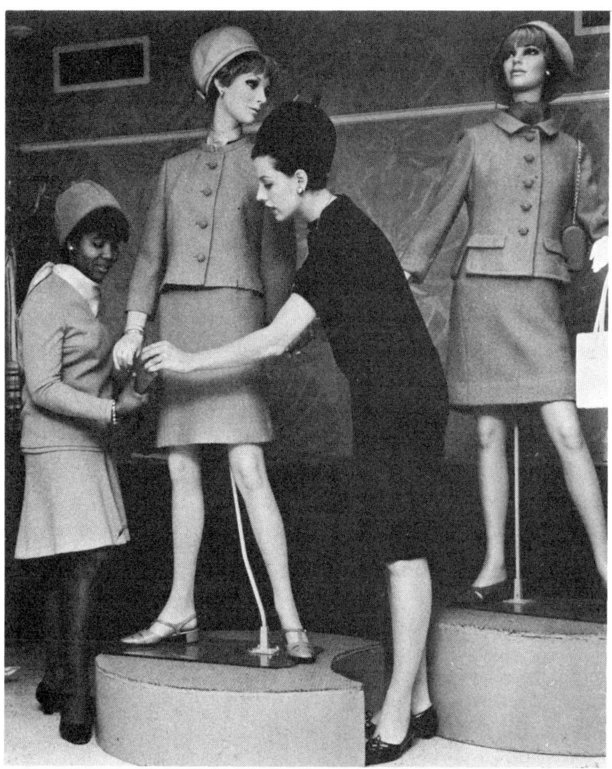

Source: Distributive Education Clubs of America, Falls Church, Virginia.

COMPENSATION

Another important managerial responsibility involves the creation and administration of an effective compensation plan. Perhaps nothing is the source of greater employee dissatisfaction than unfair or misunderstood compensation plans. Everyone will admit to the difficulty of creating a plan that pleases all; nevertheless, there are some elements that are common to an ideal plan.

Essentials of an Ideal Plan

The requirements for a good compensation plan are:

1. It should be simple—easy to understand and apply.
2. It should be easy to administer.
3. It should be fair to both employer and employee.
4. It should provide the incentives to increase productivity.
5. It should assure that earnings will be paid promptly and at regular intervals.

Common Types of Retail Compensation Plans

Most retail stores use one or more of the following types of compensation plans for their selling employees: (1) straight salary, (2) straight commission, (3) salary plus commission, and (4) quota-bonus.

Straight Salary. The straight salary is the easiest plan to understand and to administer. It is used by all types of retailers—large ones and small ones, independent and chain. This plan provides a fixed amount of salary for an employee for a specific time period. An example would be a retail clerk who is paid $120 for a 40-hour work week.

This plan is easy for the employee to understand, and since it provides a fixed amount of dollars for each payday, he or she is able to budget the salary accordingly. The employee does not feel pressured to increase productivity by using forceful selling techniques that customers might resent, as might be true under an incentive system. Furthermore, since the salary is fixed the employee is less likely to object if asked to do a nonselling task.

The employer finds the straight salary plan the simplest for bookkeeping procedures, and knows that employees on this plan can be moved among jobs in a store without the method of computing compensation being a factor. On the other hand, this plan has some serious limitations for the employer. The payment of compensation is very inflexible and may cause the wage-cost ratio[9] to get out of control. This is true when prices or sales are falling but salaries remain fixed. It is difficult to cut wages and salaries at any time, including recessions, when wages lag behind price reductions in other areas. Another major limitation to the straight salary method is that it does not provide additional incentives for employees to increase productivity.

Straight Commission. This plan provides a set rate of pay based on the dollar amount of goods an employee sells. Assume a retail salesperson works in the bedding department of a large department store and is paid a 5 percent commission. If a salesperson sells $1,500 of bedding in a particular week, his or her pay is 5 percent of $1,500, or $75. This amount would be reduced by the amount of commission that was paid earlier on merchandise that customers returned for credit.

This plan is easy for the employee to understand and earnings can be computed readily. In this plan, sales productivity is the only criterion used to determine earnings. Therefore the employee would resist being asked to perform nonselling functions. The chief advantage of this plan is that it offers an incentive for increasing sales and in turn individual earnings. On the other hand, if sales tail off for whatever reason, the employee's income is sharply reduced.

Perhaps one of the chief weaknesses of this plan is the resentment that might arise between employees or among customers. Salespeople on straight commission sometimes steal customers away from other salespeople. Occasionally this precipitates words on the selling floor between the rival salespeople, and the customer

[9] Wage-cost ratio is the percentage of gross margin consumed by wages.

is embarrassed. Another problem arises when a customer gives an indication that he or she is interested in a low-priced item or is "just looking"; the customer is ignored while the salesperson looks around for one who will purchase higher-priced merchandise. To counter this tendency, some retail shops use a call system to advantage. Here an official greeter meets customers and assigns them to a salesperson on a first-come, first-served basis. However, if a customer asks for a particular salesclerk, the request is granted.

Another weakness of the straight commission is the negative effect it has on store image. The salesperson is tempted to oversell since he or she is interested only in a large sales volume. This could increase the amount of returns, and in fact might damage repeat business.

The commissions that are paid salespeople should partially reflect management's selling goals. In many multiline departments commission rates may differ among products. Generally, those products that are easy to sell have a low rate while those that require genuine selling skill, or are more profitable to the store, have a higher rate. In one of America's largest warehouse-type furniture stores, management was obliged to realign its commission rates because it had been paying the same rate on all products, regardless of the profits to its stores. It had been paying its salespeople the same percentage of commission on low-margin "leader" merchandise, on which it made little profit, that it paid on high-margin merchandise that was difficult to sell. The retailer moved to a multirate commission system that was more complex, but it directed the salespeople's efforts toward more profitable products.

Occasionally the person who is paid only a straight commission is placed on a drawing account. This provides a fixed amount of money to be paid to the employee at regular intervals. The drawings are subtracted from the commissions earned at such times when a reconciliation is made.

The straight commission method is perhaps the least common of all the compensation plans. It is primarily used where the items sold have high prices, such as automobiles, major appliances, and furniture.

Salary Plus Commission. This very popular plan combines salary with a commission. The proportion that is salary and the proportion that is commission varies with the individual retailer. Frequently the salary is the major proportion and the commission the smaller part. There is no reason, if incentives are to be emphasized, that the salary may not be the lowest proportion of the earnings. Here is an example:

Peter Fredrickson, an employee of Deuce Hardware Store, is paid $90 in weekly salary, plus one-half percent commission on his net sales. Assume Fredrickson generated $1,200 in net sales the first week in April. What would he earn?

Salary	$90.00	
Commission	6.00	(.005 × $1,200 = $6.00)
Total earnings	$96.00	

The chief advantage of the salary plus commission plan is the compromise it provides between the straight salary and the commission plan. The employee can count on a fixed amount of income regardless of circumstances and at the same time can earn additional income through the commission feature. For the retailer the additional incentive should increase total sales.

Quota-Bonus. This is the most sophisticated of all the plans and also combines the advantage of the commission plan with the straight salary. The retailer must do three things:

1. Set a basic salary.
2. Determine a sales quota.
3. Set a commission rate on all sales beyond the quota.

Here is an example to demonstrate the manner of determining the earnings: Fredrickson of Deuce Hardware was put on the quota-bonus plan. His basic salary is set at $90. His quota is $1,800, and he is paid a bonus of $5 for each $100 of his sales over that amount.

Problem: How much will Fredrickson earn if his weekly sales are $2,197?

Solution:

Salary:	$ 90.00
Bonus: $2,197 − $1,800 = $397	
$397 ÷ $100 = 3.97	
3 × $5 = $15	15.00
Total income earned by Fredrickson:	$105.00

Note: In this unusual instance, Fredrickson was within $3 sales volume of earning another $5 bonus. If he had kept track of his weekly sales total, it would have paid him to purchase $3 of merchandise out of his own pocket.

The retailer first determines his basic salary in this plan by relating payroll expenses to net sales. In the Deuce Hardware example, let us assume that all payroll expenses are 5 percent of net sales. Then, since Fredrickson is given a $90 basic salary, his sales quota is $1,800. Any sales over the quota will be rewarded with a bonus. In our example it is $21.

This plan can be said to be both good and bad. First the salesclerk may find it a bit complicated. Furthermore, he might be in disagreement with both the quota and the commission rate. This is particularly true in periods of declining sales when the quota is hard to meet. On the other hand, if the employee believes the quota is too low, it will be very difficult to raise the quota. On the whole, however, it combines some of the best features of an ideal compensation plan.

Profit Sharing

A number of retailers have some form of profit sharing, although some plans are restricted to executives. Sears and Penney are examples of retailers who include all personnel in their profit sharing plans.[10] The details of profit sharing plans vary greatly, and it is beyond the scope of this book to discuss profit sharing in detail. However, a brief explanation of Sears' plan will explain the basic principles. This example is also useful in dramatizing the large amounts of profits that Sears shares with its employees.

Sears' Savings and Profit Sharing Pension Fund.[11] The Sears' savings and profit sharing fund was established in 1916. As of December 31, 1973, 227,225 eligible employees of Sears were participants in the fund. The assets of the fund grew to 2,965 million invested principally in Sears' common stock, 18.5 percent of the total common stock issued and outstanding.

Sears' employees contribute 5 percent of their income up to a maximum of $750 per year. That is, incomes up to $15,000 annually are subject to the 5 percent employee contribution. This ceiling keeps high salaried employees from obtaining a disproportionate share of the profits. Employees who make more than $15,000 annual income participate in a supplemental retirement plan which is not a part of profit sharing.

Sears contributes to the fund out of its consolidated net income, according to the following schedule:

Percentage	*"Consolidated Net Income" Range*
5	$250,000,000—299,999,999
6	300,000,000—349,999,999
7	350,000,000—399,999,999
8	400,000,000—449,999,999
9	450,000,000—499,999,999
10	500,000,000—599,999,999
11	600,000,000 or more.

Employees are classified into four groups according to length of service:

Group A—Employees with less than 5 years' service.
Group B—Employees with 5 to 10 years' service.
Group C—Members with 10 years' service or more, but excluding those who have 15 years of service and are over 50 years of age.
Group D—Members with 15 years of service and are over 50 years of age.

Sears prorates its contribution on the basis of the employee's classification. An employee in Group A has his or her annual deposit matched by Sears. Sears' contributions to Groups B, C, and D are on the basis of two, three, and four times the employee's contribution, respectively. That is, an employee in Group D who

[10]There were 145,000 associates on the payroll of Penney and its subsidiaries as of January 30, 1971. Full-time associates became eligible to participate in a retirement plan after 30 months of service. The plan combines a contributory pension fund and a deferred profit sharing fund.

[11]Information on Sears' savings and profit sharing pension fund was taken from three statements announcing the annual meeting of shareholders—dated April 15, 1969, April 6, 1970, and April 8, 1974.

deposited from his or her earnings $750 will have that account increased by $3,000 by Sears.

If a Sears employee withdraws from the fund and is in group B, C, or D, he or she receives the full value of the account. A group A employee who withdraws receives only his or her own deposits plus 5 percent interest (exception is death or permanent disability).

The fund is spectacular in rewarding its long-term employees. For example, one member of the fund has 4,963 shares of Sears stock and $56,213 in general investment. The employee has been a member of the fund since 1937. On June 18, 1975, Sears stock closed at $68⅜, so on that basis, the individual's account equaled a dollar value of $395,558. This share was based solely on earnings less than $15,000 since January 1, 1969, and less than $10,000 before January 1, 1969.

Executive Compensation

Plans to compensate executives are varied. The simplest is a straight salary, as it is in highly centralized chains where the store manager is doing a routine job. More common is the plan which pays the manager a salary and then a bonus, occasionally 10 to 15 percent of net profits. The exact terms of these plans vary from retailer to retailer. Often executives participate in stock option plans. Retail executives of large organizations may have total remunerations in six figures.

Fringe Benefits

Most retailers today include some fringe benefits in their compensation plans. The large chains and the department stores have more than do the smaller retail shops, which in some cases have very few fringe benefits. Some of the more common types of fringe benefits are:

1. Term life insurance.
2. Health and accident insurance.
3. Paid vacations.
4. Employee discounts.
5. Christmas bonus.
6. Pension plan.
7. Profit sharing.
8. Recreation facilities.
9. Disability insurance.
10. Sick leave.

EVALUATION OF EMPLOYEE PERFORMANCE

It is always necessary to evaluate the performance of the employees. The obvious reasons are to ascertain whether or not an employee should be promoted, receive a raise, be transferred to another department, or be released. The quality of the evaluation differs from one organization to another, but one can make several generalizations. Many small retailers have no formal evaluative techniques. The owner or manager makes a decision based on personal feelings. In some cases these intuitive judgments may be sound, but often they are faulty.

Those retail organizations who wish to be objective will use some type of yardstick in evaluating their personnel. The most popular yardstick for salespeople is net sales, as shown in the following example.

George Meyer of Little D's Dress Shop employs eight salespeople. He evaluates their work every six months. Part of the evaluation consists of comparing each person's net sales with a store average. Here is a comparison of Judy Grenke and the average.

	Net Sales Past Week	*Total Sales for 6 Months*	*Returned Sales for 6 Months*	*No. of Customer Complaints 6 Months*
Judy Grenke	$1,600	$45,000	$ 500	None
Average	1,150	30,000	1,000	Two

Using this technique, Meyer can easily rate each of his employees.

Larger stores often have a more comprehensive evaluation plan, and it is an important part of the services of the centralized personnel department. Some of the characteristics that are rated and noted on each employee's evaluation report are: attendance, personality, initiative, productivity, cooperation, store loyalty, personal appearance, knowledge of job, responsibility assumed, and reprimands. Several people are generally given the responsibility of evaluating any one employee in order to avoid bias.

Department stores often subscribe to a special service in which professional shoppers shop the store and make official reports on the strengths and weaknesses of the salesclerk being shopped. Frequently this technique is resented by the salesclerks on the grounds that it is unwarranted, and that the professional shopper attempts to provoke the clerk into making an error. There are times when these shoppers are rude, unbearable, and insulting, and they do precipitate a response from the salesclerk.

Effective evaluation techniques are helpful in making decisions on raises, promotions, transfers, or terminations. After every periodic evaluation, the employee should be called in by the superior for a conference. The purpose of the conference is to point out the strengths and weaknesses of an employee's performance. Furthermore, goals for improvement can be set. An evaluation is incomplete unless employee and superior can discuss all aspects of the job and the worker's relation to it. The superior also has the opportunity to praise the employee if it is deserved and to discuss the employee's future.

Terminations

Whenever an employee terminates services with a retail organization, an interview by a responsible representative of the personnel department should take place. This is known as the "exit" interview. The reasons why an employee elects to leave are useful in alerting management to any faults that may exist. Suppose

John Nick tells the personnel department that the real reason he is quitting is to get away from Leo Cole, his superior, who Nick claims is overbearing, rude, and short-tempered. Personnel has already noted that Cole's department has an unusually high labor turnover. However, no one has said anything detrimental about Cole before. Now a responsible executive might tactfully investigate the substance of the charge. Something can be done to rectify the situation if the charge is found to be true. In like manner all the reasons people give during exit interviews may be analyzed and acted on, if warranted.

CONSTRAINTS

Management is never free to make all decisions concerning the working conditions of its employees. Two principal external institutions which must be considered are government and unions. There are three levels of government which may regulate some aspect of employer-employee relations, although in labor relations, local governments are not as important as are federal and state governments.

Federal Legislation

In 1935 the federal government passed the National Labor Relations Act (commonly called the Wagner Act). This act gave the right to employees to form labor unions to bargain collectively for their wages and other working conditions. The act had far-reaching effects on the unionization of labor. Although the unionization of retail workers has been slow compared with other kinds of employees, the Wagner Act legalized union organizations. Other federal legislation has been passed to clarify issues and procedures. Two of the most notable are the Labor-Management Relations Act of 1947 (Taft-Hartley), and the Labor-Management Reporting and Disclosure Act of 1959.

Another type of federal law that affects all workers who engage in interstate trade is the Fair Labor Standards Act and all its amendments. This act establishes a minimum wage rate for a maximum of a 40-hour work week. At the present time a worker must be paid a minimum of $2.10 an hour. Retail stores were exempted from the provisions of this act until 1964. The effect of the amendment was to bring under federal control those retail workers who are employed in retail organizations whose sales total $250,000 or more annually. This limitation keeps the smallest retailers from control, but effectively brings in all the medium and large retailers.

The various civil rights laws that were passed in the 1960s also apply to most retailers (those with fewer than 25 employees are exempt). These acts make it illegal to discriminate against any employee because of sex, age, race, religion, or national origin with respect to hiring practices, compensation, and working conditions.

State Legislation

Although retail workers have the right to unionize, it is somewhat surprising to find that only about 10 percent of those eligible have chosen to do so. (See Figure

7.5.) This is in part due to the lack of attention given to this segment of business by strong union organizers, and by the jurisdictional disputes among rival unions. A more likely explanation for the lack of unionization is the lack of vocational commitment to retailing by the employees. This is due to the large number of female employees (a certain number will quit due to marriage), part-timers, and youngsters on their first jobs. Unionization succeeds best among those workers who are full-time employees and who have a lifelong commitment to a job. Those with a commitment have the zeal and enthusiasm to push for more benefits through unionization.

Some observations can be made about retail unions:

1. Some unions are strong, such as the Amalgamated Meat Cutters Union, the one to which butchers belong.
2. The eastern section of the United States is more unionized than the southern.
3. Chain store employees tend to be more unionized than independent store employees.
4. Department store employees are likely to be union members while specialty shop workers are not.
5. Unionism is growing among retail employees.

SUMMARY

The task of managing people in a free, democratic society is no easier for a retailer than it is for an industrialist. Leadership is the key to effective management, but it is difficult to apply in many segments of the retailing industry. One reason is the fact that retailing differs from other businesses. It uses a large number of inexperienced workers, many of whom are part-timers with no intention of seeking permanent employment in retailing. The working conditions within retailing differ. Retail stores must cater to customer's needs, so they are open nights, Saturdays, and sometimes on Sundays. The hours are unpopular among many prospective employees and contribute to the difficulty of recruiting permanent help. Furthermore, the wages or salaries paid to many retail employees are low when compared with factory or office workers.

Retailers, however, must formulate personnel policies, programs, practices, and procedures to carry out their assigned mission within the framework of the store's overall objectives. This will enable the organization to deal effectively with such activities as selection of employees, placement, training and development, establishing good compensation plans, and evaluating work habits.

Recruiting always involves making job descriptions and specifications, and then choosing from among the applicants those who have the qualifications that the retailer is seeking. The retailer is aided by such techniques as the application blank, the interview, and perhaps some kinds of testing.

Once an employee has been hired, it is often necessary to train him or her before he or she reports to work. The large retailers usually have a centralized training department that utilizes all the skills and tools of modern education. Training is a continuous process and should not be restricted to new employees. Developing

FIGURE 7.5

Union representatives discuss contract terms with members of the United Retail Workers

YOUR UNION CONTRACT:

WE BUILD
A STRONG
FRAMEWORK
TOGETHER!

Source: United Retail Workers Union, Westchester, Illinois.

talent at the executive level is becoming crucial because of the knowledge-experience gap. The training programs must provide the experienced employee with some of the newer tools, while at the same time aiding the newer employee to gain from the experience of the older.

Probably nothing is the source of greater employee dissatisfaction than a poor compensation plan. An ideal plan is one that is easily understood, easy to administer, and provides the incentive for an employee to increase earnings while reducing the labor expense cost to the retailer. Some of the more common wage plans are straight salary, straight commission, commission plus salary, and quota-bonus.

Retailers must also have a procedure for evaluating a worker's performance. This implies using a standard for rating each worker. The technique provides the information that a retailer may use in making salary adjustments, promotions, transfers, and terminations.

In conclusion it should be pointed out that management is never free to make all the decisions itself. Constraints are imposed by external forces, one of which is government. It has enacted legislation to regulate some aspects of the working conditions within the retailing industry. Another external force is the retail unions, although they have been relatively ineffective when compared with the impact of unionism in manufacturing.

QUESTIONS FOR DISCUSSION

1. How do society's goals affect retailers?
2. Retailing differs from other businesses. Discuss this difference in terms of personnel management.
3. Distinguish among the following: policy, program, practice, and procedure. Use an example to illustrate each.
4. What elements are necessary to good manpower policy for a small retailer and a large retailer?
5. Assume that you were called in by a large retailer as a consultant, and you were asked to set up a recruitment program. What would you include and why?
6. What goals may a retailer accomplish in setting up a carefully designed training program?
7. What is meant by the knowledge-experience gap, and how would you close it?
8. Good compensation plans are the responsibility of retailing management. Compare and contrast the typical plans one finds in retailing.
9. How important do you think incentive pay is to retailing employees? Does it have any disadvantages?
10. Discuss the reasons why it is necessary to have a program to evaluate a retail clerk's selling performance.

8 MERCHANDISING POLICIES

A supermarket operating in the downtown area of a major city carries a larger than ordinary assortment of collard greens, chitterlings, and convenience-type foods. It is attempting to cater to a large black population in the inner city and to working women who have little time to prepare dinner at the end of a long day.

A chain department store includes the weather report as part of its short-term market analysis. It operates in an area where weather conditions can differ substantially within a small geographic region. By anticipating the weather it can forecast a short-run demand for such products as snow shovels, umbrellas, and bad weather footwear, and can move such merchandise to the stores overnight by truck. The effort has been only moderately successful, but it is still trying.

A Japanese retailer that caters to teen-agers sews English language labels in his "California" brand clothing, even though it is made in Hong Kong. He believes that his customers respond more favorably to such labels. They probably know that the clothes are not really made in America.

A Kansas City department store divides its merchandise according to life style. The first floor, called "Earth," consists of leisure living merchandise such as sports equipment and informal clothing; the second floor, the "Elegance," features gracious living merchandise such as home furnishings and jewelry; and the third floor, called "Excitement," sells "now living" items such as astrological products and mod clothes.

Such names as Louis Roth, Geoffrey Beane, and Elsa Peretti are well known to those who are accustomed to buying the finest in men's clothes, women's clothes, and jewelry. These designers can be virtually certain that some of their popular designs will be copied by other suppliers—sometimes called "knock-off houses"—and sold at much lower prices. There is little the designers can do about others who steal their ideas except to try to impress retailers and customers with the fact that a copy is not an original. The retailer, if the ethical issues can be resolved, must decide whether the original or the copy will be most profitable.

The retail store exists basically to sell merchandise that satisfies its customers' wants and needs. As the above examples suggest, a retailer's merchandise policies can be varied and sometimes ingenious. The types and kinds of merchandise sold depend upon the wishes of the owner-management group, market opportunities, the state of competition, managerial objectives, and a host of other factors. In order to buy the right merchandise, the retailer must understand merchandising and must adopt sound merchandising policies.

MERCHANDISING—DEFINITIONS AND MEANINGS

Merchandising has been defined in many ways, so it is not surprising to find some confusion as to its meaning. One writer equates merchandising with retailing in the following definition:[1]

> Retail merchandising or retailing can be defined as the selling of goods in small quantities to the consumer.

A second definition of merchandising is . . . "the planning done by retailers to insure an assortment of merchandise balanced to customer demand and offering a profit potential."[2]

The second definition is an improvement over the first because it suggests that planning is at the very heart of effective merchandising. Furthermore the second definition relates merchandising to profits, an important consideration.

A widely accepted definition offered by the American Marketing Association says that merchandising is . . . "the planning involved in marketing the right merchandise, at the right place, at the right time, in the right quantities, and at the right price."[3]

In Chapter 7 we presented Dale Yoder's definition of policy as:[4]

> A policy is a predetermined and accepted course of thought and action that is defined and established as a guide toward accepted goals and objectives.

By combining the definition of policy with the American Marketing Association's definition of merchandising, we define merchandising policy as:

> *A predetermined course of thought and action to market the right merchandise, at the right place, at the right time, in the right quantities, and at the right price, so as to accomplish a retailer's general objectives and make a profit in the process.*

Interpreting Consumer Demand

Our definition of merchandising states the necessity for stocking the right merchandise. Therefore the first task of those involved in merchandising is to predict what the consumer will want, and then buy and stock the appropriate goods. Unfortunately, retailers may sometimes interpret consumer demand on the basis of intuition alone, and will fail to merchandise their goods successfully. Although in-

[1]Fred M. Jones, *Retail Merchandising* (Homewood, Ill.: Richard D. Irwin, Inc., 1957), p. 3.

[2]John M. Wingate and Elmer O. Schaller, *Techniques of Retail Merchandising* (Englewood Cliffs, N.J.: Prentice-Hall, Inc., 1956), p. 3.

[3]Committee on Definitions, *Marketing: A Glossary of Marketing Terms* (Chicago: American Marketing Association, 1960).

[4]Dale Yoder, *Personnel Management and Industrial Relations*, 5th ed. (Englewood Cliffs, N.J.: Prentice-Hall, Inc., 1962), p. 139.

tuition may often be useful, retailers who wish more reliable results seek help from four other important sources in interpreting consumer demand. These sources are: (1) the consumer, (2) other merchants, both competing and noncompeting, (3) salesmen, trade shows, and trade papers, and (4) internal records.

Information from Consumers. Since it is the consumer who makes the ultimate decision to buy or not to buy the offered merchandise, there is merit in beginning the search for information with the consumer. The more information a retailer has about customers, the better forecast he or she is likely to make with respect to consumer demand. Demographic questions are asked of shoppers to elicit answers relating to age, race, sex, occupation, place of employment, level of education, marital status, income, size of family, and family stage in the life cycle. To seek answers to demographic and other questions, it is necessary to interview a sample of representative shoppers. We shall not discuss in this chapter the technical aspects of surveying, because this material is covered in the chapter on marketing research for retailers. Marketing research is a specialized field, and it is a wise retailer who uses the services of those qualified to obtain meaningful answers. This is especially true if a retailer expects valid results to questions seeking information regarding consumer taste, standard of living, habits and customs, plans for future purchases, and opinions on the store's past merchandising performance.

Retailers sometimes obtain information from customers with little or no customer awareness, and at little cost to themselves.[5] One automobile retailer jots down the license number of any car that slows down when passing his dealership; he traces the number and immediately sends out a direct mail piece inviting the prospective customer to come in to get acquainted. A shoe retailer always asks for the name and telephone number of women who wear unusual size shoes on the pretense that it is for the store's mailing list. When shoes of her size are received, he calls her; she never knows that he is aware of her unusual feet—perhaps a sensitive issue—but she often is flattered by the attention. And one of America's largest retail food chains sponsors a permanent Consumer Advisory Council composed of housewives, students, educators, local government officials, minority leaders, and others, who furnish ideas about merchandising from a customer's point of view.

Information from Competing Stores. Every retailer must interpret consumer demand; therefore it is imperative to see how competing stores make their interpretations. A retailer may do this by:

1. Inspecting the window displays of competition.
2. Studying the stock of merchandise carried by competing stores.

[5]For a compendium of ingenious techniques used by researchers to get information (peanut vendors in Chicago baseball parks know to roast more peanuts in the late innings only if the score is close; police officers suspect that clean cars with dirty license plates or dirty cars with clean license plates may mean the cars are stolen; an automobile dealer knows the listening habits of his customers by checking the radio dial settings of cars brought in for repair), see Eugene Webb, Donald T. Campbell, Richard D. Schwartz, and Lee Sechrest, *Unobtrusive Measures: Nonreactive Research in the Social Sciences* (Chicago: Rand-McNally and Company, 1966).

3. Observing customers in the act of purchasing goods at other stores.
4. Analyzing the advertisements of competition.

Window displays are one clue as to how any particular retailer interprets consumer demand, as can be seen in Figure 8.1. One may find differences in kind and quality of goods featured, and finding answers to this difference may be helpful in understanding consumer demand. Furthermore the inspecting retailer may obtain suggestions previously overlooked.

A retailer should also tour his competition's store to observe merchandise carried and how it is displayed. He should be especially alert to spot differences in assortments, methods of selling, and price discrepancies. He should observe actual sales transactions, and be careful to note where the greatest sales activities are taking place. Once all this information is gathered, merchandising personnel should study and analyze the data and accept those ideas which are relevant to them. It does little good to gather and interpret data if subsequently the information is not used. A retailer must not inspect a competing store's merchandising efforts with the thought of making his retail store a carbon copy of the competitor's. To do so might lead to serious merchandising faults which otherwise could have been avoided. Indeed, the most successful merchandise strategy may consist of doing

FIGURE 8.1

Window displays are tangible evidence of how merchants interpret consumer demand

Source: Edison Brothers Stores, Inc., St. Louis, Missouri.

what most other retailers are *not* doing. Inspection is designed to spot the differences in merchandising, while analysis of those differences is useful in uncovering ideas which the retailer can use.

In small stores, the owner-manager may be the one who takes times to visit other similar nearby outlets. In large stores, however, comparison shopping is likely to be assigned to full-time shoppers who take notes and actually buy goods; the goods are taken to analysts who examine them for quality. Formal reports are prepared that go to the merchandise manager so that he or she will know what is being sold elsewhere and the circumstances under which the products are sold.

Retailers may also analyze the advertisements of their competitors for further clues in interpreting consumer demand. However, they should not assume that competitive messages reflect consumer demand correctly. It is simply one more tool to help assess the nature of consumer choice. There once was a time when small town retailers gave particular attention to the advertising of city retailers. They reasoned that new ideas took root first in the cities and later spread to outlying areas. Thus, the advertising of the city retailers was a forecasting tool. However, as travel and communication improved, small towns became more cosmopolitan, and the city retailer's advertisements meant less. Many still believe that the differential, although less than it once was, still exists, and retailers should continue to review the city newspapers very carefully.

Information from Noncompeting Stores. Information may also be obtained from noncompeting stores. A noncompeting retailer is defined here as one who is engaged in the same type of retailing, usually at the same level of sales, but is operating in a different market, usually located in a different city. Retailers often meet at conventions, shows, or buying trips and exchange information over coffee or at dinner. Good merchandising tips are thus exchanged in an informal atmosphere.

In many cases the information is acquired in a more formal and less haphazard manner. Independent resident buying offices are located in the principal cities where vendors display the goods that buyers purchase. These offices specialize in obtaining relevant information on such topics as fashion trends, new products, promotional ideas, and prices. Furthermore they give buying assistance to the retailer's buyer when he or she visits the city or for fill-in purchases between trips. Some of this assistance is locating merchandise in advance and making appointments with various vendors. Frequently they maintain offices and showrooms to facilitate the buyer's job while he or she is at the market. It is not unusual for a resident buyer to act on behalf of a merchandising manager in buying goods. Resident buyers also collect catalogs, bulletins, and special reports on information that is useful to the trade. This information could concern such things as products, economic forecasts, fashion news, or price bulletins.

Information from Vendors' Salesmen. Vendors' salesmen are excellent sources for information. As one would expect, they are technical experts on products they sell. Moreover they know effective ways to display the products. They have tips for their promotion, and they know how to merchandise them. Furthermore the vendors' salesmen have a fair understanding of supply and demand, and therefore they are able to predict the product's acceptability with the consumer with moderate success. However, vendors' salesmen are biased and they may present only favorable information in order to secure a sale. The buyer should probably take some of this information with the proverbial grain of salt. On the other hand, many salesmen are genuinely interested in helping the retailer, because it is in their best interests to do so. In any case a retailer's experience with various vendors and their salesmen is the best guide to the reliability of the data received.

Another useful source for information is the vendor's catalog. There the vendor has listed all product lines with their current prices. Inasmuch as the vendor must also interpret consumer demand, the retailer can gain an insight into the vendor's prediction of consumer demand before the retailer must make a commitment.

Trade Shows. Frequently manufacturers get together and present their merchandise in trade shows for the benefit of wholesalers and retailers. Such shows often are sponsored by the trade association to which the retailer belongs. A good example is the furniture show which is held at the Furniture Mart in Chicago twice a year. There the retailers may inspect the merchandise that the manufacturer thinks consumers will accept for the coming season. Retailers have ample time to visit with the vendor's representatives and obtain merchandising hints. Frequently the trade shows feature guest speakers who discuss topics relevant to the retailers' interests.

Trade Papers. There are many excellent trade journals reporting information and rumors useful to people in a particular kind of business. Examples are *Women's Wear Daily, Progressive Grocer, Skiing Trade News, College Store Executive*, and *American Druggist.* These journals present information on such topics as new products, merchandising tips, business indices and statistics, proposed legislation that would affect the industry, and feature articles of specific interest to their readers.

Internal Records. The store itself can provide considerable information to help predict consumer demand. Large retailers may have a merchandise control bureau to provide this information, while others rely on their accounting staffs. An example of one source of internal information is sales records. They classify sales by items, manufacturer, vendor, type of merchandise, size, color, or other meaningful factors. Data of this nature may be compared with similar data from other time periods. This information is helpful in identifying fast movers and slow movers. It also is helpful in identifying the vendors whose merchandise is selling well. In addition, information is obtained on styles that are selling, colors that are fashionable, and popular sizes. All of this information is useful in predicting trends for the next period.

Some retailers use a diary to supplement statistical data. Records are not likely to be misinterpreted if adequate diaries accompany the sales records. In these diaries comments may be made about successful sales promotions and their effects on sales. Comments may be made about unsuccessful sales promotions and the reasons for their failures. The diary may include suggestions for things that should have been done but were not. It may also include an analysis of markdowns, and a statement concerning the popularity of certain styles and colors. In short, a diary is useful in supplementing the raw statistical data contained in most records.

ASSORTMENT POLICIES

No retailer will stock every item produced or manufactured, although some retailers carry a wider assortment of goods than others, as can be seen in Figure 8.2. Therefore a potential retailer's first decision is to choose the class or classes of merchandise to be carried. The retailer must decide whether to stock meats, groceries, hardware, clothing, appliances, general merchandise, or their combination. Normally a retailer appeals to something less than a total market for a specific product. For example, a record shop may limit its assortment to please the musical taste of the teen-ager and/or young adult, and choose not to stock records appealing to older adults. Manufacturers frequently take a total market and divide it into several submarkets or segments. In our previous example, records are the total market. However, the record industry divides its output into classical, country and western,

FIGURE 8.2
This donut shop features 52 varieties in many shapes, sizes, and flavors

Source: Dunkin' Donuts of America, Inc., Schiller Park, Illinois.

rock, jazz, religious, and children's records. An individual retailer may decide to stock all categories or concentrate on one or more.

Most retailers respond to market segments in one way or another. In the case of ladies' dresses, one retailer may appeal to the petite woman and limit stock to sizes 10 or smaller. Another retailer of dresses might choose to appeal to tall girls, while still another might appeal to the women with ample figures. Department stores might stock an assortment designed to appeal to all types of women. When R. H. Macy Company of New York saw that it was missing much of the low-income market, it established "budget centers" in its existing stores. The centers featured lower-priced merchandise than customarily was sold in Macy's stores.[6] As the income levels of people living in urban areas change, astute merchandisers either change with them or move to locations nearer the customers they have served in the past. In other instances, retailers cater to different markets through entirely different types of outlets.

The merchandise which a retailer decides to carry and the store's location are closely related. In cities, people tend to live near other people of similar race, ethnic origin, or income level. Retailers who locate in a particular area must give much thought to merchandising for a specific group. Retailers who locate in a high-income area will merchandise their stock with this group in mind. On the other hand, retailers who locate in disadvantaged areas see their mission differently. Location is the prime manner in which a retailer indicates how he or she plans to respond to the market. The stock carried, the price structure, and the customers expected confirm this response.

Breadth and Depth Policies

Once a retailer has made the decision with respect to the segment or market to be served, policy must be set governing kind and type of merchandise to carry, the amount of investment in inventory, and the price lines that will be carried. Then there still remains the assortment problems of depth and breadth.

Depth refers to the number of brands or styles within a generic class. For example, a food store may decide to carry 15 different types of hair shampoo representing 5 brands and 3 sizes in each brand. On the other hand, another store may carry 30 types—10 brands and 3 sizes.

Breadth or width refers to the number of generic classes a store will carry. For example, a supermarket may stock in its health and beauty aids department such products as lipsticks, nail polish, eyeshadow, face powder, shampoo, hair rinses, and toothpastes. The more diverse the products stocked, the wider the assortment.

Merchandise assortment also has the dimension of consistency. This refers to the degree an assortment of merchandise is related in use. A retail shop stocking dresses, blouses, skirts, and hosiery has a consistent merchandise assortment. A sports store carrying equipment for baseball, tennis, fishing, skiing, and golf also has a consistent merchandise assortment. (See Figure 8.3.) A food store which adds a line of toys is following an inconsistent merchandise assortment policy. It should

[6]"Macy's Broadens Budget-Store Focus," *New York Times* (August 19, 1971), p. 49.

FIGURE 8.3
This ski shop features a consistent merchandise assortment policy

Source: *Black Enterprise* Magazine, December 17, 1971, p. 22. © *Black Enterprise* Magazine, 1971.

not be inferred that the word *inconsistent* is synonymous with bad, and *consistent* means good. Consistency merely refers to the degree in which the products are related in use. Many retailers quite successfully follow an inconsistent assortment policy.

Types of Breadth and Depth Policies. A retailer may follow any one of three assortment policies. These are: (1) narrow and deep, (2) broad and shallow, and (3) a compromise of the first two. An example might be helpful in understanding the differences.

Let us assume you are the buyer for a small dress shop catering to young misses. You have already made the decision on style and quantity and the fashion overtones for the dresses you are to have. Furthermore you have made the decision as to the price lines you are to stock. You have not decided on the number to order in each color and size. A research service, one in which you have confidence, has predicted the following preference for color in order of popularity: (1) lilac, (2) red, (3) orange, (4) green, and (5) yellow. The dresses come in all those colors and no others. You may also assume that your past sales records indicate a distribution of sales in the following sizes:

Size 10	18 percent
Size 12	24 "
Size 14	27 "
Size 16	15 "
Size 18	10 "
Size 20	6 "
Total	100 percent

If you could buy only 20 dresses, how would you make your merchandising assortment selection?

If you choose a *narrow and deep* assortment, you would limit your color selection to those that are predicted to become most popular; however, you would stock these colors in depth.

Sizes	Number of Dresses		Total
	Lilac	Red	
10	2	2	4
12	3	2	5
14	3	2	5
16	2	1	3
18	1	1	2
20	1	0	1
	12	8	20

The advantage of this policy is efficiency. Since there are only two colors, it is easy to control the inventory and to keep a running count of the stock. There would be less likelihood of markdowns because all merchandising efforts are concentrated on two colors and the likelihood of "stock outs" would be reduced. A disadvantage would be the lack of color selection for customers who preferred something other than lilac or red.

A *broad and shallow* policy is one making the assortment from all the colors; however, you would have very few dresses in each color category.

Sizes	Number of Dresses					Total
	Lilac	Red	Green	Orange	Yellow	
10	1	1	1	1	0	4
12	1	1	1	1	1	5
14	1	1	1	1	1	5
16	1	1	1	0	0	3
18	1	1	0	0	0	2
20	1	0	0	0	0	1
	6	5	4	3	2	20

The advantage of this policy is greater acceptance by the consumer, because she has a greater selection. However, the broad and shallow policy is usually considered more difficult to merchandise than the narrow and deep policy, and there would probably be a need to take more markdowns to clear the stock. This is because some colors and sizes would be less popular than others and would be difficult to sell. As the retailer stocks the marginally popular item, the difficulty of selling it increases.

In the *compromise* example, one might limit the sizes as well as the colors, and in this way you would obtain some depth as well as breadth.

	Number of Dresses				
Sizes	*Lilac*	*Red*	*Orange*	*Green*	*Total*
10	2	1	1	1	5
12	2	1	1	1	5
14	2	1	1	1	5
16	2	1	1	1	5
	8	4	4	4	20

The advantage of the compromise plan is that you obtain more depth as well as width by excluding both the less popular colors and sizes. The disadvantage is the exclusion of possible shoppers who have no choices offered to them. One now can see the advantage of appealing to a specific type of shopper. A dress shop catering to the petite figure can stock more variety by limiting its sizes to 10 and smaller.

Factors That Determine Breadth and Depth. There are some positive principles a buyer follows in limiting assortment. First, he or she must consider the amount of money to be invested in stock. The greater the investment, the larger the assortment can be. On the other hand, the less invested in inventory, the smaller the assortment must necessarily be. In our previous example, if the buyer is permitted to buy 40 dresses instead of 20, he or she could have a larger assortment both in breadth and depth.

Another factor is the customer. Americans are accustomed to free choice among many alternatives. This is true regardless of whether the shopper is seeking to buy a detergent, an automobile, a new suit, a dress, a color television set, or any other kind of product. Hence, the retailer must cater to customer demands and offer a wide assortment if regular patronage is expected. A buyer would perhaps limit the assortment within a product line by stocking only the most popular products. This would apply to the selection of brand, color, material, size, or any other characteristic that is deemed to be important.

A third factor has to do with the profitability of the total assortment. A buyer who wishes to broaden his or her assortment must consider the possibility that a new offering will reduce the sales of a second product. Let us look at an example.

Suppose a retailer selling dresses experiences these sales results in dresses categorized by price lines (not by size or color).

	Sales in Units for Month
Low price	400
Moderate price	300
Moderate to high price	200
Expensive	100
	1,000

The buyer is considering adding a second line of low-priced dresses and is warned by a superior to expect the following results:

	Sales in Units
New low-priced line	200
Old low-priced line	300
Moderate price	200
Moderate to high price	200
Expensive	100
	1,000

An analysis of the above prediction indicates that the new line would simply "pirate" sales away from the previous two lower-priced lines. The buyer would not add the new line if it was thought the above prediction would come to pass. On the other hand, the buyer might convince the superior of the merits of the buyer's own prediction, which looks like this:

	Sales in Units
New low-priced line	500
Old low-priced line	400
Moderate price	300
Moderate to high price	200
Expensive	100
	1,500

Growth Potential

In some instances, a retailer would add a new product to the assortment even though no significant increase in total sales was expected immediately. For example, a cosmetics department may add a new scent to its line of colognes even though the total dollar sales of colognes might temporarily remain constant. This would be true if the product was thought to have growth potential, or if the customers expect the store to carry new scents in colognes. Not to stock this particular item might identify the retailer as unprogressive by the customers. Frequently new products are promoted heavily on television, in magazines and newspapers. Retailers are virtually forced to stock these items if their customers come to their stores and wish to purchase them.

Competition

A retailer's assortment policy will also be dictated by the assortment offered the customer by other retailers of a similar nature. A wide assortment policy is an attempt to satisfy the customer's preference for one-stop shopping, but it inevitably means that the customer is obliged to undergo certain compromises. For example, few department stores are comparable with F. A. O. Schwartz, America's best-known toy store chain, because they know that they cannot stock the range of choice that a specialty store does. Rather they believe their competition to be other department stores.

The character of competition differs substantially between large cities and small towns. In the large city, a shoe store may sell only men's shoes, women's high fashion shoes, health shoes, or specialize in some other way. Its competition is not all other types of shoe stores; rather it is a fragment of the entire market and they must stock accordingly. In a small town with only one or two shoe stores, the retailer is likely to sell to the whole family and compares the store's offering with the store down the street or the next nearest one twenty miles away.

Discount houses frequently follow an assortment policy best described as mixed. They wish to appeal to a variety of tastes, so they carry a wide assortment of brands, colors, models, or sizes. On the other hand, their customers are likely to be price cognitive; so they do not stock a deep selection in all brands. Discount houses know that whenever price is a determining factor, customers will accept substitutes more readily. The discount house stocks popular items in some depth.

A retailer who has the necessary capital to dominate the market may choose to follow a policy of maximum assortment. This is likely to be a specialty store.

Business Cycle

The business cycle also plays an important role in determining the assortment policy. Generally when the economy is in an upswing, retailers are likely to broaden and deepen their assortments. On the other hand, they are likely to narrow assortments on the downward swing of the business cycle.

Seasonal Influences

The assortment policy is definitely related to the selling season for its products. This is especially true for those items with fashion overtones. As the season opens, the buyer will start with a wide and shallow assortment. This is due to the degree of uncertainty surrounding consumer acceptance. As the season progresses, the buyer observes those offerings which are popular with the shopper; consequently it is possible to narrow the lines but offer greater depth. After the season peaks, the buyer will begin to reduce the depth of any one line and limit the number of lines if possible. At the end of the selling season, the ideal state would be to have sold the entire stock. This is extremely unlikely, and the buyer will be satisfied if the leftovers are concentrated in the lower-priced lines.

Two principles concerning consumer demand are relevant to seasonal assortments. They are:

1. Customers who want high-priced goods will tend to buy them early in the season.
2. Customers are less discriminating as the season comes to a close, and they are willing to accept substitutes.

Rigidity of Demand

Demand rigidity is another important factor in determining the depth of an assortment. Rigidity of demand refers to the degree customers desire a specific product. A reader of the *New York Times*, who goes to a newspaper stand to purchase a copy of the paper, is unlikely to accept a substitute if no copies of the *Times* are on hand, but will more likely go to a different dealer and request a copy of the newspaper. Demand rigidity, therefore, refers to the willingness of a customer to accept a substitute.

A retailer may determine rigidity by examining specific characteristics of a product. A man who is purchasing a pair of shoes for himself will be rigid about the size. Regardless of how much he appreciates the style of a second pair of shoes, he will not purchase them if the size is wrong. There are many products like shoes where size is the rigid factor, and its style, color, price, or materials are the less rigid factors. Inventory is normally displayed on the selling floor according to the most rigid factor. A dress shop arranges dresses by sizes rather than by color, material, or some other criteria. A men's clothing store is likely to arrange shirts by neck size rather than by color, material, or price.

Retailers may also be obliged to stock those brands that customers expect to find and for which no substitute is acceptable. Such "brand loyal" buyers are contrasted with "brand switchers," who are willing to accept another brand because it is available, the price is lower, or for some other reason. Any one individual may be very loyal to, say, Arrow shirts but will accept any necktie if it is attractive. Or we may insist that only Maxwell House coffee be served in our home, but be indifferent about brands of ice cream. It is said that such food store products as soft drinks, gelatine, and soups have a high proportion of loyal users and a retailer's stock must reflect this loyalty.

In the low-income levels, customers tend to be rigid about price. A man who has decided to spend $1.50 on a tie may resist attempts to move him up to a more expensive one. On the other hand, he may accept a substitute color without any resistance if the price is right. As customers acquire more income, price becomes less rigid and other factors become more important. Experience will give each retailer the specific knowledge needed on this point.

Assortment policy is also a function of urgency. Customers generally expect a large assortment of merchandise at the beginning of a selling season, and therefore they will be more selective. Christmas shoppers who wait until Christmas Eve to shop are likely to accept substitutes more readily, and will not complain because of the poor assortment.

Merchandising Fashion Goods

Fashion goods are distinctive shopping goods purchased because of their current appeal. In Chapter 4 we discussed in some detail the nature of the fashion cycle and its four stages: distinctive, emulation, mass consumption, and declining.

We also mentioned the controversy as to whether the fashion cycle moved vertically or horizontally. Now we want to look at fashion merchandising in greater depth; the two theories purporting to explain the cycle are to be related to a proper merchandising policy. First we shall review the fashion theories discussed in Chapter 4.

Trickle Down Theory. Fashion experts traditionally believed fashions were adopted by taste makers who had a strong desire to be distinctive and sought to be first in trying out new styles. Couturiers and exclusive retail stores catered to this group. Eventually individuals in a lower social class would begin to emulate the taste makers in their choice of style, and the fashion entered its second stage. High quality department stores and specialty shops would begin to show the goods. Finally the people in the mass market would adopt the style, and the fashion would be at the height of its popularity. Mass-consumption stores would feature the current fashions, and one would see it everywhere. Eventually the mass market would tire of the style, consumers' attention would be drawn to a different style, and the fashion would have run its course. This explanation has been identified as the *trickle down theory*. Figure 8.4 illustrates this concept.

FIGURE 8.4
The trickle down theory

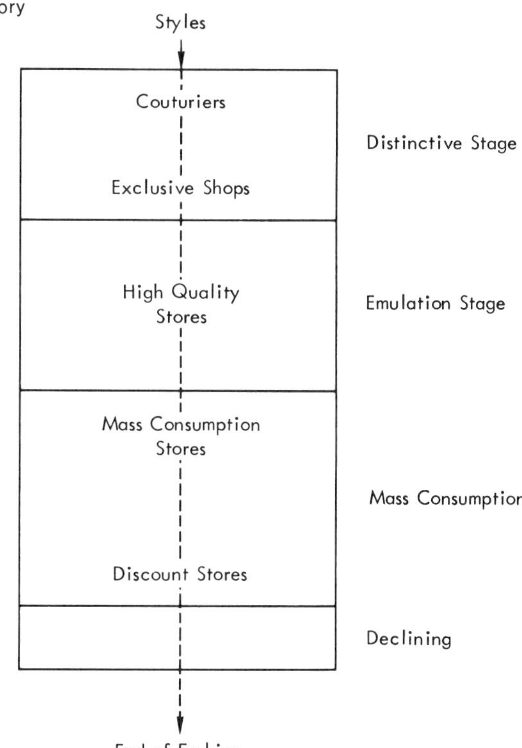

If one accepts this theory, it is relatively easy to formulate a merchandising policy with respect to fashion goods. The retailer would first identify the stage in which he or she wished to operate. This is a fundamental retailing decision and one that most retailers will have made prior to locating and opening a shop. Suppose a retailer operates a high quality store; then those styles would be stocked that appealed to the emulators. In this case, the retailer could look to the exclusive shops for clues indicating the next fashion. Presumably there would be sufficient lead time to buy those styles which seemed likely to become fashionable. In a similar manner, mass-consumption stores would look for clues in the high quality stores and make their plans accordingly.

Proprietors of the exclusive shops have the problem of supplying styles acceptable to their customers. They cannot look for clues elsewhere; therefore their intuitive judgments are very important. Twice a year leading couturiers present their styles in formal showings in the fashion capitals of the world, principally Paris, London, Rome, and New York.

Trickle Across Theory. It has been argued that the trickle down theory is no longer applicable.[7] These critics say that fashions emerge all at once and are adopted by people in all social classes simultaneously. This is known as the *trickle across* theory, illustrated in Figure 8.5.

FIGURE 8.5
The trickle across theory

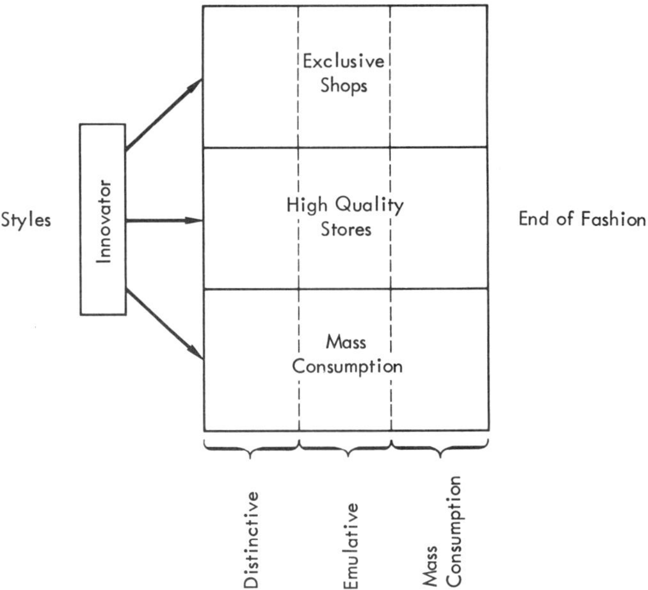

[7]Charles W. King, "Fashion Adoption: A Rebuttal of the 'Trickle Down' Theory," in *Toward Scientific Marketing*, Proceedings of the Winter Conference of the American Marketing Association, ed. Stephen A. Greyser (Boston, 1963), pp. 108–25.

This theory makes it far more difficult for a retailer to formulate a workable fashion policy. A retailer would still identify customers as to their social class, and would know whether or not the store would appeal to the mass market or a more exclusive audience. However, the retailer would have a difficult time choosing the styles to buy, because he or she could no longer look for clues in those stores that have a higher order in the hierarchy. A mass-consumption retailer could no longer expect to find buying clues by watching fashion trends in the high quality stores. The retailer would be forced to predict the acceptance of a particular style from his or her own expertise.

Another criticism is aimed at the concept "trickle." This word suggests a *slow* flow. Inasmuch as a fashion literally explodes among the public and is suggestive of speed, trickle is hardly the word to use; indeed, it is a high risk business. In any case it is difficult to predict which styles are to become fashionable in the volatile world of today.

Other Factors

Other factors are important in determining overall merchandising policies. A retailer must consider such things as (1) quality of merchandise, (2) standardization or exclusiveness, (3) continuity of product lines, and (4) taste of the consumer.

A retailer must decide on the quality of merchandise to carry, a problem to be faced before locating the store. In a sense, when the retailer considers the assortment problem, it amounts to a decision on the quality of merchandise to carry.

Policy must be set regarding the degree of standardization the retailer intends to employ. A retailer who wishes to carry a line of products that is essentially different from the competition will seek exclusivity, perhaps handling only those products that guarantee sole distributorship rights. Such items as Kuppenheimer men's clothing, Steuben glassware, or Rosenthal silver are sold through only a few carefully selected outlets in each area; the retailers carrying those goods have quasi-monopolies, at least for those particular brands. On the other hand, some retailers do not wish to be different from the competition. This will be reflected in the standardized character of their merchandise.

Continuity of product lines can be very important. Customers who buy silverware, china, or stemware expect retailers to stock their patterns long after they have made the initial purchase. Fine stores often guarantee brides that a pattern chosen in their store will always be available.

BRAND POLICY AND CONTROL

Every retailer must decide whether to be a re-seller of goods sold under a supplier's label or under the retailer's own name. The small retailer who decides to stock Del Monte canned peaches has relinquished several very important activities to the packer who owns and controls the brand name. (See Figure 8.6.) A & P, when it created the Eight O'Clock name for the coffee that it would feature, chose to burden itself with certain responsibilities that go along with brand ownership.[8]

FIGURE 8.6
This store features large displays of nationally known foods

Source: Chain Store Age/Supermarket Group, New York, New York.

Such a decision is not only being made by every retailer but also by every manufacturer and wholesaler in the country. Manufacturers may use part of their production capacity for goods that will be sold under their own labels, for which they assume the promoting and distributing responsibilities; with the rest of their capacity the manufacturer may act as an anonymous supplier to middlemen or even other manufacturers who will sell the same or a slightly modified product under a different label. It is quite possible that two labels sitting next to each other on the

[8]The terminology in this area is not clear. Such expressions as national brand, manufacturer's brand, private brand, distributor's brand, retailer's brand, and controlled brand probably mean different things to different people. National brands often mean the same as manufacturer's brands, and private brand often means the same as distributor's or retailer's brand. The implication is that a brand owned by a manufacturer is usually sold throughout the country, while a middleman's brand is generally sold regionally or locally. But such brand names as Allstate, owned by Sears, suggest the fallacy of such a view.

same shelf, and apparently in competition with each other, came from the same manufacturer. Hence we have the expression "the battle of the brands."

There are several advantages to a retailer who decides to assume responsibility for a brand. First, it is likely that a higher unit gross margin on products bearing such a label can be earned, usually because the cost of goods is less. The costs are less because the retailer has relieved the manufacturer of the responsibility and costs of certain vital finance and marketing functions. The manufacturer need not store goods in anticipation of a retailer's unpredictable needs or promote the goods, and delivery may be made in a single lot rather than in smaller lots over a long period of time. All of these expense savings can be passed along to the retailer. Second, ownership and control of a brand means that customers are loyal to the retailer rather than to the products sold. A manufacturer with a strong brand may choose to stop selling to a particular retailer, preferring to shift to a different retailer or sell through his own outlets. If the brand represents a significant part of the retailer's own business, the result can be disastrous. We have all heard of the "all the eggs in one basket" argument, and private branding lessens the likelihood that it will happen. Third, retailers sometimes believe that some customers are prone to buy national brands while others prefer private labels. If this is true, the retailer who sells both types has made an offering more attractive to a larger number of customers. Indeed, the very appearance of a wider choice—even to those who are strongly committed in one direction or the other—is an attraction toward a particular retailer. Finally, through private branding the retailer is less obliged to compete on the basis of price alone. If a men's clothing store is one of several in a city that sells Arrow shirts, it would normally be an unwise practice to sell at prices higher than those recommended by Cluett-Peabody, the manufacturer. However, if the merchandise is stocked and sold under the retailer's label, he may have a small degree of pricing flexibility.

The retailer who decides to engage in private labeling also faces several difficulties. A major one is finding and working with one or more suppliers who will consistently deliver the type, quality, and volume of merchandise to be sold. In some instances, manufacturers may be willing to furnish goods on an excess capacity basis, meaning that their regular customers take precedence over private label buyers. When there is ample capacity, this is no problem; but when a supplier has ample business, delivery may be somewhat slower. In other instances it is alleged that suppliers vary the quality of the product when it goes into private label merchandise more than for goods going out under their own labels; this allegation has face validity because the manufacturer's own name goes on one piece of merchandise and his reputation can be affected. A second problem is that if the retailer buys in the quantities often expected of a private labeler, expenses may be incurred that wipe out some of the gains from lower purchase costs. The retailer may pay extra for labeling or special packaging or may incur higher warehousing expenses because purchases are made in larger quantities direct from a manufacturer, and is likely to have more capital tied up in owning the larger inventory. One of the largest additional expenses is that of promoting the brand so that it will achieve customer acceptance. Well-accepted institutions such as Hudson's or Winn-Dixie may find ready acceptance for most of the products on which they place their own labels. However, other businesses may face a more skeptical set of customers, one that must be cultivated over a long period of time. Gaining market acceptance can be very costly. Many discount-type stores, even after many years in business, have been unsuccessful at selling brands that are little known because customers have no basis for judging quality. Such stores have been most successful at selling well-known manufacturer's brands in whom buyers have confidence. The cost of gaining buyer acceptance has been great.

A decision to engage in private branding through a cooperative or a voluntary group wholesaler can have important legal implications. During the 1940s a group of small supermarket chains formed Topco, a corporation intended to buy goods in quantity for its owner-members and distribute them under a variety of Topco-owned brand names. The 25 owner-members were licensed to operate in 33 states, but did not operate in each other's territories. Thus, each retail chain had a "controlled label" for about 1,000 different food and nonfood items in its own area. The cooperative was originally formed so that the small members could compete against the industry's giants, and it succeeded magnificently, selling over $2.3 billion of goods by the early 1970s. In 1972 the Supreme Court held that agreements not to compete in each other's territory unduly restrained trade and were illegal, rejecting Topco's argument that such an agreement was essential if it was to succeed against A & P, Safeway, National, and other large grocery chains.

Private labeling is a common practice in the food industry for many of the reasons already discussed. However, its use varies among types of businesses and products.[9] Large retailers are more likely to sell a part of their inventory under private label than are small retailers. But it is surprising that three-fourths of the country's largest retailers sell less than one-fourth of their food and grocery products under a private label; the manufacturer's hold on customer allegiance is strong. Perhaps it is also surprising that retailers who are affiliated with voluntary group wholesalers are more likely to sell under private labels than either unaffiliated retailers or members of a cooperative. Private label food products tend to be those sold in great volume (canned fruits and vegetables, dairy products, bakery goods, coffee, salad dressing, and mayonnaise are good examples) and those that are well established on the market. Products that are well established are particularly susceptible to private branding because generic acceptance has been established by manufacturer brands. Once consumer familiarity with a product has been gained, customers are more inclined to purchase on the basis of price; and a lower price is the major competitive weapon of the private brander.

THE ORGANIZATION STRUCTURE AND MERCHANDISING

All general policies are the responsibility of top management. In small retail organizations, it is the owner who is responsible for formulating merchandising

[9]Most of the material in this paragraph is synthesized from various parts of *Special Studies in Food Marketing*, Technical Study Number 10, National Commission on Food Marketing (June 1966).

policies; the owner may also be the one who carries out the policies. In large retail organizations, the responsibility also belongs to the top corporate executives, but they may delegate implementation to others. In either case, general policy is an outgrowth of the company's basic philosophy. Specific policy is the application of the general policy by the operating management. A greater understanding of merchandising is obtained by examining the organization structure of two very different types of retailer operation—the chain store and the department store.

Merchandising and the Chain Store

A chain is a multiunit retail operation under a common management. It could be a chain of food stores (Safeway or Kroger), a chain of variety stores (Woolworth or Kresge), or a chain of specialized stores (Pier 1 Imports). A chain may have very few outlets or it may have thousands of units. Many of our food supermarkets are members of a large chain. The largest is Safeway with 2,426 stores and sales over $8.1 billion in 1974.

Organizational Structure. The merchandising division of a chain is responsible for the functions of buying, pricing, and promotion of the merchandise stocked. Normally, the merchandising division is not responsible for personal selling, which is the responsibility of the operating division. Some chains manufacture most of the merchandise sold in their stores, and in these cases the merchandising function is much less complex; however, this is rare.

Figure 8.7 shows a typical organization chart for a chain's merchandising division. Note that the top executive is the director of merchandising, assisted by a promotion manager, a head buyer, and a merchandise control manager. Let us look at the duties and responsibilities of these individuals.

Director of Merchandising. The person chiefly responsible for the application of a chain's merchandising policy is the director of merchandising. He is

FIGURE 8.7

Typical organization chart for chain merchandising division

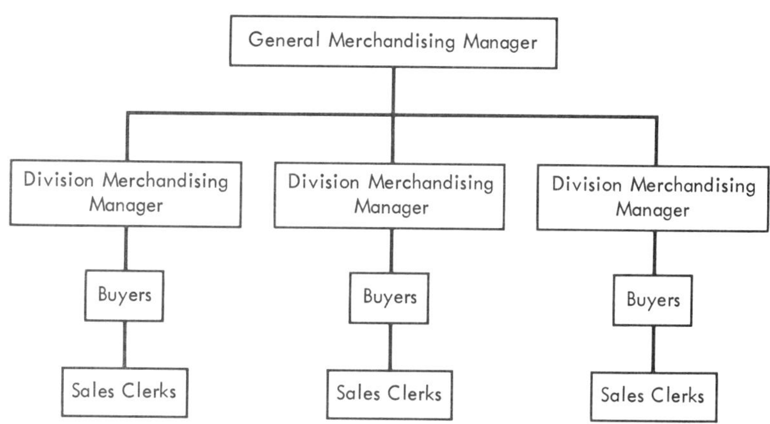

responsible for planning, selecting, and controlling the merchandise stocked, pricing it, and displaying and advertising it. He is not responsible for general merchandising policy, but is usually invited to participate in general policy discussions.

To clarify the authority of the director of merchandising, an example might be helpful. Suppose a food chain is contemplating the addition of a line of toys in all its stores. Assume this represents a change in major policy inasmuch as the chain has never sold toys. In this case, the administrative executives who have a higher position of authority than the director of merchandising make the decision. The director of merchandising probably attended many of the meetings where the change of policy permitting the addition of toys was discussed. His presence is desirable because his opinion is valuable; moreover he is responsible for the implementation of the new policy.

The director's responsibility for a decision to add or drop products is probably more important than it seems. One source estimates that new introductions have increased 300 percent in the past ten years, and there is every indication this trend will continue.[10] The same source stated supermarkets added an average of 903 products while dropping 691 in 1967. Indeed, by 1973 the typical supermarket carried 7,950 items compared with 6,600 ten years before.[11]

The director of merchandising holds considerable authority over prices. In most cases he has the authority to raise or lower prices in response to such forces as changes in supply costs or demand, competitive strategy, government legislation or pressure, or cyclical or seasonal forces.

The director of merchandising implements a retail store's general policy on promotion. He participates in conferences to determine the promotional budget and the plans for the promotional activities suggested by the merchandising plan. It is the merchandising director who chooses the lines of products to be promoted.

The Buyers. Authority to buy specific kinds of merchandise is delegated to buyers. In a food chain, one buyer specializes in dairy products, another in meats, a third buys produce, and still another has candies. An apparel chain has separate buyers for skirts and blouses, sports clothes, lingerie, and cocktail dresses.

In many chains a head buyer supervises all the buyers and coordinates their activities. In small chains the director of merchandising may act as head buyer.

The major function of a retail store is to sell merchandise; therefore the buyer must be certain the merchandise is salable and have the expertise to interpret consumer demand. It is difficult to predict consumer behavior and to stock the most salable merchandise; nevertheless this is the buyer's responsibility. Merchandise with a fashion overtone is an example of one of the most difficult products to buy; yet a buyer must make this decision in advance of consumer demand.

A buyer bears an important responsibility for purchasing those goods that are

[10]"Grocers Swayed by Test Market Data," *Marketing Insights,* 2, no. 8 (November 20, 1967), 7.

[11]"41st Annual Report," *Progressive Grocer* (April 1974), p. 136.

likely to generate an adequately maintained gross margin. The expression "Buy low, sell high," massively oversimplifies the buyer's problems, but it is not incorrect. It is important to note that much of the burden for the firm's profits rests with the buyer. Since the buyer must make the important buying decisions and must also decide on selling price, blame cannot easily be shifted to others when things do not go well. In short, by assuming the responsibility for both buying and selling, the buyer operates a "personal" profit center.

Merchandise Control Manager. Inasmuch as the buyer must purchase the right quantity, he or she must know what is in stock, what is on order, and what is in transit. The Merchandise Control Department furnishes all this vital information to the buyer. The control department is charged with the responsibility for maintaining all the records involving the physical movement of the merchandise. The merchandise control manager must supply the director of merchandising with all the statistics relating to fast moving items, slow movers, and level of inventory.

Promotion Manager. The promotion manager is responsible for the advertising and display of all merchandise. He or she has the expertise to devise a promotional strategy. However, it must be emphasized that the merchandising director is the one who ultimately decides to accept a certain plan.

Advertising Manager. An advertising manager has the technical knowledge on matters relating to advertising. For example, he or she arranges for newspaper space, chooses media, and prepares the materials used in advertisements.

Display Manager. The display manager, either alone in a small store or with the help of a staff in a large store or a chain retailer, has the job of planning and preparing in-store and window display materials. These plans must be compatible with those of the merchandising director and the promotion manager since those responsible for promotion rather obviously promote whatever the merchandising people have decided the store will sell. When a large department store decides to have a "British Fortnight" promotion or some other similar special event, collaboration is probably at its greatest. It means many buying trips to London, renting Beefeater's costumes for the doormen, displaying pictures of Windsor castle, having a double-decker bus parked in front, a "bobbie" walking through the selling floors, a rock combo from Manchester playing in the dining room, and many other things. In other instances, the display manager's job is more mundane. It may mean printing counter cards calling attention to a special price on selected merchandise or making sure that the front windows are cleaned every week.

Department Store Merchandising

Perhaps the most significant difference between the department store's merchandising organization and that of the chain is the location of the selling function. The Merchandising Division of the department store is responsible for both the buying and selling functions. A department is the key structural unit within the department store, and this unit is headed by the buyer who is responsible for buying the merchandise sold by the department. Furthermore it is the same individual, the buyer, who supervises the salesclerks. You will recall that the chain's merchandising division is not responsible for the personal selling function.

Figure 8.8 represents a typical organization chart for the merchandising division of a department store. Note that the key executive is the general merchandising manager, assisted by the division merchandise managers and buyers. We shall examine their duties more specifically.

FIGURE 8.8

Typical organization chart for department store

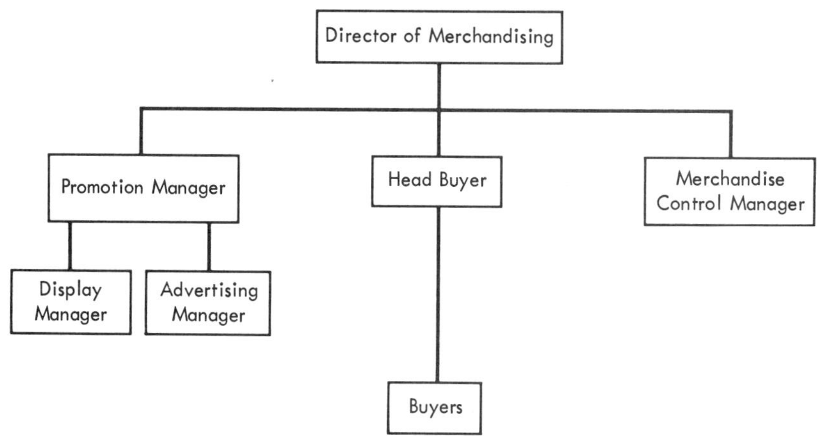

General Merchandising Manager. The general merchandising manager is responsible for the following activities: (1) maintaining a stock of salable merchandise, (2) planning the merchandising operation, (3) setting up a workable system of merchandise control, (4) promoting and selling the merchandise, and (5) analyzing environmental conditions.

The general merchandising manager is the key executive, the one who interprets consumer demand and sets the tone for all the merchandising activities that are to take place, including taking full responsibility for the preparation of both the merchandise and the expense budgets. Subordinates will carry out the plans, but it is the general merchandising manager who is ultimately held responsible for their success or failure. Immediate subordinates are the divisional merchandise managers.

Divisional Merchandising Manager. The volume of sales is usually so large that the general merchandising manager cannot handle the merchandising function alone. The responsibility is divided into smaller units, and each unit is headed by a divisional merchandising manager. For example, one divisional manager is responsible for home furnishings, another for women's apparel, another for men's apparel, and still another charged with the responsibility for the basement store.

Buyers. Buyers are key people in the department store at the operation level. The buyer must know all about the products that are bought and their marketability. Buyers interpret consumer demand and are responsible initially for satisfying consumer wants. Buyers are assisted by various types of reports, such as the "want slip." This is a memo prepared by the salesclerks requesting merchandise not in stock. Obviously, if a buyer has sufficient requests to stock a particular good, he or she will seriously consider doing so. Some of the other reports examined by the buyer are sophisticated analytical documents prepared by the control department.

Furthermore the buyer attends conventions, visits the market, talks with vendors, reads trade magazines, and analyzes financial reports on the state of the economy. All of these are helpful in interpreting consumer demand and aiding in making the decisions as to what and how much to buy. In summary, the buyer utilizes whatever resources are available which will contribute to increased technical knowledge.

Buyers are responsible for physically taking control of the merchandise, seeing that it is marked with the proper price tags, and having a source of inventory close to the selling floor. It is a buyer's responsibility to arrange the merchandise on the selling floor attractively. Buyers are also responsible for the selling function. The buyer must supervise all the salesclerks in the department, taking the responsibility for their activities while they are on the selling floor. The salespeople actually sell the merchandise, so the buyer must see to it that they are properly motivated. The salespeople are the ones who come face to face with the customers, and they often benefit from motivation and instruction.

Separation of Buying and Selling. There are many who believe that buyers should not be responsible for the implementation of both buying and selling functions. Two of the principal arguments advanced are:

1. Buyers have no selling ability, and therefore they play down this function.
2. Buyers fail to supervise salespeople properly.

Buyers, it is alleged, constantly downgrade the selling function. Perhaps this fault can be expected if buyers truly believe they are buying the right merchandise and pricing it right, and the merchandise is available in right quantities at the right time. To the extent that this is true, the shopper will need the assistance of those on the selling floor only for the purposes of showing the merchandise, ringing up the sale, and wrapping the product. However, there is an old saying, "Goods well bought are half sold." Assuming this is true, there is a need for good salesmanship to complete the sale.

Buyers are sometimes criticized because of their absence from the selling floor, and consequently they cannot supervise the salesclerks personally. Inadequate supervision may result in customer dissatisfaction. A dissatisfied customer may not return to a store, and this could be disastrous if it occurs frequently.

The buyer is also responsible for the implementation of all the promotional activities affecting his or her department. Buyers select items to be promoted and cooperate with the promotion department in whatever way they can. The buyer requisitions newspaper space, window display space, and special display materials to be used on the selling floor.

SUMMARY

A retailer must purchase the right merchandise, in the right quantities, and offer it for sale at the right place, at the right time, and at the right price. To do this a retailer must do considerable planning and establish guidelines that are easy to follow. The responsibility for making general merchandising policy belongs to the planners, while its implementation is handled by a merchandising division. Chain stores structure their merchandising divisions much differently than do department stores. The major difference is in the responsibility for the selling function. Chain stores do not include the selling function within the merchandising division, while department stores do.

Good merchandising policies come from an interpretation of consumer demand. Retailers receive their input of information by surveying their customers, inspecting other stores, going to the market, attending trade shows, reading catalogs, bulletins, and papers, and listening to vendors' suggestions. Diaries should accompany the records so that misinterpretation will be held to a minimum.

All retailers must determine a brand policy. Shall they carry their own brands or shall it be a national brand? The factors that help them make these decisions are the protection afforded by having one's own brand, gross margins, customer preference, and the added costs of buying, physical handling, and promotion.

Merchandise assortment policies depend upon many factors. First, a retailer may limit appeal to a fraction of the total market, thereby engaging in market segmentation. There are many things a retailer must consider in determining the breadth and depth of stock. Some of these factors are amount of capital available to invest in inventory, growth potential of new products, consistency of the merchandise, state of competition, cyclical and seasonal influences, and the rigidity of demand.

Policy with respect to fashion goods is extremely important. There have been two major theories used to explain the fashion cycle. The trickle down theory permits retailers lower in the hierarchy of the industry to look for clues that are helpful in predicting fashions. However, others point out that in today's world products explode simultaneously among all social groups (the trickle across theory), making it extremely difficult to predict with any accuracy which styles will become fashionable.

Chain stores are organized in such a way that the buying function is performed by a central office group of highly skilled individuals. Determining the merchandise to be stocked, seeking out suitable suppliers, and negotiating are performed for all the company's stores at one time, thus relieving the individual store managers of what would otherwise be a difficult and time-consuming task. Thus, the buying and personal selling functions are widely separated. Critics of this approach believe that the two functions are not properly separable, a view often reflected by the organization structures used in department stores. Department managers usually are responsible both for buying the type and amount of goods that they believe they can sell and for supervising the day-to-day activities of those on the selling floor.

QUESTIONS FOR DISCUSSION

1. Define merchandising policy, and discuss the problem of responsibility for its planning, execution, and change.
2. Do you think the buying and selling functions should be separated? Why or why not?
3. How may customers be helpful to buyers in their interpretation of consumer demand?
4. What importance are competitors to the overall understanding of consumer demand for a retailer?
5. How is market segmentation related to merchandising policy?
6. Breadth and depth are important factors to an assortment policy. What is meant by these terms?
7. Give the principal factors that aid a retailer in choosing a specific assortment policy.
8. Distinguish between a consistent and an inconsistent merchandise assortment policy. Give some examples.
9. Demand rigidity is an important factor in determining the depth of an assortment. What is meant by this concept?
10. Why is the merchandising of fashion goods so difficult for modern retailers?

9 MERCHANDISE MANAGEMENT

A record store manager in Raleigh, North Carolina, knows that he cannot sell to everyone's tastes, but he also notes that his largely young clientele seem to be scattered across the income spectrum. He watches very carefully to make sure that he has an ample selection of records that will sell at $3.88, $4.88, and $5.88. He keeps a careful count of his stock by price.

Bucherer's, a jewelry retailer operating mostly in Switzerland, has no trouble keeping track of its most expensive merchandise. Each item has a specific place on a particular tray, and every space is filled. When an item is sold, another takes its place. The physical count is constant. This is a common inventory control practice.

Departmental buyers at the Famous-Barr store in the Saint Claire Square Shopping Center near Saint Louis, Missouri, know that they must buy and merchandise with middle- and upper-income customers in mind. "Famous" has long been successful at selling to this particular market segment in the area. But it faces considerable peripheral competition from a Venture discount department store directly across the highway, not more than 200 yards away. Customers apparently enjoy comparing the values between the Famous-Barr and the Venture stores. The fight for customer patronage is particularly interesting since both stores, although operating independently, are owned by the May Company.

The manager of a women's dress department for a Houston department store visits the new Dallas fashion center with a specific dollar amount that he is permitted to spend. This amount is known as his "open to buy" position, meaning the unobligated balance of his purchasing budget for the period immediately ahead.

Harrods, one of London's best known retailers, claims, 'Omnia, Omnibus, Ubique," or "Everything for everybody, everywhere." Although it is like many large firms in that it caters to a wide market, it does not, in fact, quite live up to its motto.

These are some of the problems retailers face, and the sometimes strange ways they resolve them. For they must be resolved if retailers are to be successful.

Several keys are required to open the door to successful retailing. One is the retailer's ability to satisfy the product needs and wants of a changeable consumer. Goods generally are purchased in anticipation of demand, and sales are made from a stock of goods held in reserve. An ideal state is one where the retailer has always stocked the right goods in the proper assortments so as to satisfy all consumers' needs. In this utopia there would be no leftovers and no need to worry about running out of stock. Unfortunately, retailing is not a utopia; it is necessary for retailers to manage their merchandise offerings so as to please and satisfy their customers through the utilization of their investment capital with the maximum efficiency.

A retailer must supervise the stock of merchandise carefully if he or she expects to maximize sales. A small retailer may have little trouble in solving the problem of inventory management because he or she is able to devote close personal attention to it. Since the inventory is limited, the retailer can tell if the stock is moving more slowly than anticipated and if the total assortment is out of balance. Visual inspection may be a satisfactory tool for a small retailer (see Figure 9.1), but it is most unsatisfactory for the merchant with a large and complex stock of goods. The large retailer must initiate and maintain a number of written records on the state of the merchandising effort. These records and their use are the heart of merchandise management.

FIGURE 9.1

Keeping jewelry trays filled allows customers to have a wider range of merchandise from which to select

Source: Persin & Robbin Jewelers, Arlington Heights, Illinois.

MERCHANDISE CONTROL

The purpose of merchandise control is to achieve retailers' objectives by satisfying their customers' wants. By responding to customer wants, the retailer expects to earn a fair and just profit. Merchandise planning and control enables a retailer to avoid the twin perils of either being over- or understocked. The consequences of having too little merchandise are rather obvious—the profit that would have been earned is lost. But if the customer does not return to the store, a stream of future revenue is also lost. When the retailer loses not just a single sale because of understocking but also loses a customer, the cost is substantial. Given this threat it is easy to overreact by overstocking. But there are five major ways in which the cost of overstocking can eat away at profits: (1) the explicit or implicit interest charges on the value of the goods held in inventory; (2) the cost of either owning (an implicit cost) or renting (an explicit cost) space in which to store the goods; (3) higher real estate taxes that accompany higher investment; (4) the cost of insuring the goods and (5) the greater likelihood of pilferage and theft, obsolescence, and physical damage. It is often said that the total cost of store goods is *at least* 25 percent of the value of the merchandise. Therefore the retailer who increases inventory investment from $100,000 to $150,000 in order to accommodate customer demand is paying $12,500 each year for the privilege of doing so.

There are two major merchandise control methods. (Traditional methods of merchandise control are being supplemented by more sophisticated ways of obtaining and processing data, which will be discussed in Chapter 17, devoted to these new methods and the computer.) *Dollar control* emphasizes the value of merchandise, while the *unit control* emphasizes the physical stock. Suppose we examine the inventory of a retailer who sells women's dresses. The retailer could state the value of her inventory in dollars by reporting her inventory on December 31, 1975, as worth $10,500. If during the course of the year, the retailer manages her stock by controlling the number of dollars invested in dresses, she would be following a dollar control system. On the other hand, if the retailer's inventory report states her inventory as 100 blue dresses, 100 green dresses, 75 white dresses, and so on, she would be following a unit control system. It is not unusual for some retailers to employ both methods of control at the same time. Let us examine each of these inventory control methods in greater detail.

Dollar Control

A retailer who employs a dollar control method of inventory management has the option of using either a perpetual inventory system or a periodic inventory system. Regardless of the system used, all the records are kept in retail prices and not at invoice cost. We shall illustrate both systems by example.

Perpetual Inventory System. Rod's Tie Store sells only neckties in three price lines: $3, $5, and $10. On February 1, 1975 Rod had the following stock on hand:

100 ties priced at $3	value $ 300
200 ties priced at $5	value $1,000
200 ties priced at $10	value $2,000
Total value of inventory	$3,300

During February, Rod purchased $6,000 in new merchandise and sold $5,000 worth of ties.

In the perpetual inventory system, records are kept on the following: (1) dollar value of the stock on hand at the beginning of a period; (2) dollar value of goods purchased; and (3) dollar sales made during the accounting period. When these records are available, it is possible to estimate the dollar value of the inventory without actually computing it. Let us look at the data from Rod's Tie Store to illustrate this point.

Beginning Inventory (February 1)	$3,300
Add goods purchased in February	+ 6,000
Total value of ties available to be sold in February	$9,300
Subtract ties sold in February	− 5,000
Estimated Inventory on Hand (February 28)	$4,300

The inventory value derived in this way is an estimate, but it is used to compute net profit. At least once a year the retailer actually counts stock and compares the actual value with the estimated value. This would give a retailer a measurement of the stock shortage. In our example, suppose Rod actually counted all his ties which were unsold on February 28, 1975. He would then multiply the number of ties by their price and thus obtain a dollar value of his inventory. Assume this is $3,900. Rod would then compare the actual value of the physical inventory ($3,900) with his estimate ($4,300). Rod now knows he is short $400 in ties. This fact causes him to look for reasons why. Perhaps some of the ties were shoplifted, or perhaps he miscounted his physical inventory. On the other hand, his records of markdowns or employee discounts may not be accurate. Rod will take steps to identify the causes of the shortages and institute measures to reduce them in the future.

An important advantage of the perpetual inventory system is that it permits the retailer to compute net profit without actually counting inventory.[1] Retailers like to compute the net profit frequently because it is the best single way for evaluating performance. A retailer could compute net profit without using the perpetual inventory system; however, he or she must then count physical inventory. A physical count of the inventory is time-consuming and costly. Wages must be paid out to those who count the stock, and this could be a sizeable expenditure. For this reason a retailer usually counts inventory only once a year. At other times he or she estimates the inventory via the perpetual inventory system.

Periodic Inventory System. The periodic inventory system differs from the perpetual inventory system in several respects. First, a physical count of the inventory is always made. Second, a retailer need not have statistical data on sales in order to compute net profit. *Do not misunderstand*: A retailer *always* keeps ac-

[1]The computation of net profit will be explained in Chapter 16.

counting records on dollar sales. However, these sales records may not be available when the retailer wishes to compute net profit. Morever the sales records may be kept for the store as a whole, but the retailer wishes to compute the net profit of a department for which sales figures are not kept. The periodic inventory system permits the retailer to estimate sales. Records are specifically kept for purchases, markdowns, and the value of the beginning inventory. All of these records are kept in retail prices. In this system, a retailer also estimates stock shortages. Once again let us examine Rod's Tie Shop to illustrate this system. Rod had the following inventory on hand on February 1, 1975:

100 ties priced at $3	value $ 300
200 ties priced at $5	value $1,000
200 ties priced at $10	value $2,000
Total value of inventory (February 1, 1975)	$3,300

Rod purchased $6,000 in merchandise in February. In the periodic inventory system, sales records are not available at this time, so we do not know the dollar value of sales; however, we can derive it from the data available. Rod physically counts his inventory at the end of February, and it is $4,000. Assume further that Rod estimates his stock shortage to be $300. The data is processed as follows:

Beginning inventory February 1, 1975	$3,300
Purchases in February	6,000
Total value of the ties available for sale	$9,300
Less ending inventory (by actual count)	4,000
Estimated sales plus stock shortage	$5,300
Less stock shortage (estimate)	300
Estimated sales	$5,000

It is now possible to utilize the sales estimate and compute net profit. A retailer may do this as often as he or she thinks necessary; however, many retailers compute it only semiannually. The reason is the difficulty and expense associated with taking a physical inventory.

Unit Control

A retailer may elect to keep his records in physical units rather than in dollars. If he does this, he would be following the unit control system. Just as in the dollar control system, the two basic methods for unit control are the perpetual inventory system and the periodic inventory system. Once again let us examine each of these systems through the example of Rod's Tie Store.

Perpetual Inventory System. On February 1, 1975 Rod had the following inventory on hand.

100 ties priced at $ 3
200 ties priced at $ 5
200 ties priced at $10
500 ties on hand

During the month of February, Rod purchases 1,100 ties and puts them into stock to sell at the following prices:

500 ties at $ 3
300 ties at $ 5
300 ties at $10

Rod keeps a daily log of his sales. Every time a tie is sold, the clerk enters this fact in a sales book. Inasmuch as there are only three price lines, it is not difficult to do this. However, if there were hundreds of items all with varying prices, it would be a major task to keep track of sales by this technique. But all sales are rung up on the cash register, so Rod knows his total dollar sales each day.

At the end of February 1975 Rod examines his sales book and notes the following:

400 ties sold at $ 3	$1,200
200 ties sold at $ 5	1,000
280 ties sold at $10	2,800
880 ties sold	$5,000

All the information is processed as follows:

	$3	*$5*	*$10*
Beginning inventory (February 1)	100 ties	200 ties	200 ties
Purchases	500	300	300
Total ties available for sale	600	500	500
Less sales (from sales log)	400	200	280
Total ties on hand (February 28, 1975)	200	300	220

Just as in the dollar control method, the derived inventory on hand at the end of the month is an estimate. If Rod wishes to compute his stock shortage, he now physically counts his inventory. The difference between the physical count and the estimate is the shortage. Shortage, as we have said before, is the reduction in inventory not accountable by sales. A retailer needs to know the extent of shortages before taking corrective measures. Whenever shortages are excessive the retailer institutes those measures he or she thinks will curb them. On the other hand, if the shortages are few, the retailer has the satisfaction of knowing the safeguards are working.

The perpetual inventory system in units is best used by retailers whose stock is relatively large in terms of the physical size of the item itself. Retailers of shoes, appliances, and dresses often use this system. For example, in a dress shop part of the price tag may contain information on the color of the dress, style, price, type, and manufacturer. All of this information can be extremely helpful to the retailer in analyzing sales. (See Figure 9.2.)

The perpetual inventory system in units is difficult to use for those stores which sell goods that are physically small. For example, a drugstore would find this system cumbersome.

Periodic Inventory System. In this system, the retailer must derive the net sales figure to compute net profit. To do this, the retailer counts physical inventory. Let us once again use Rod's Tie Store.

As in the other examples, the February 1 inventory is:

100	ties priced at $ 3
200	ties priced at $ 5
200	ties priced at $10
500	ties

During the month of February, Rod adds to his stock the following purchases:

500	ties priced at $ 3
300	ties priced at $ 5
300	ties priced at $10
1,100	

At the end of February, Rod counts the inventory still unsold and obtains these results:

170	ties on hand priced at $ 3
280	ties on hand priced at $ 5
209	ties on hand priced at $10
659	ties on hand

FIGURE 9.2

Tags placed on garments help retailers to maintain control

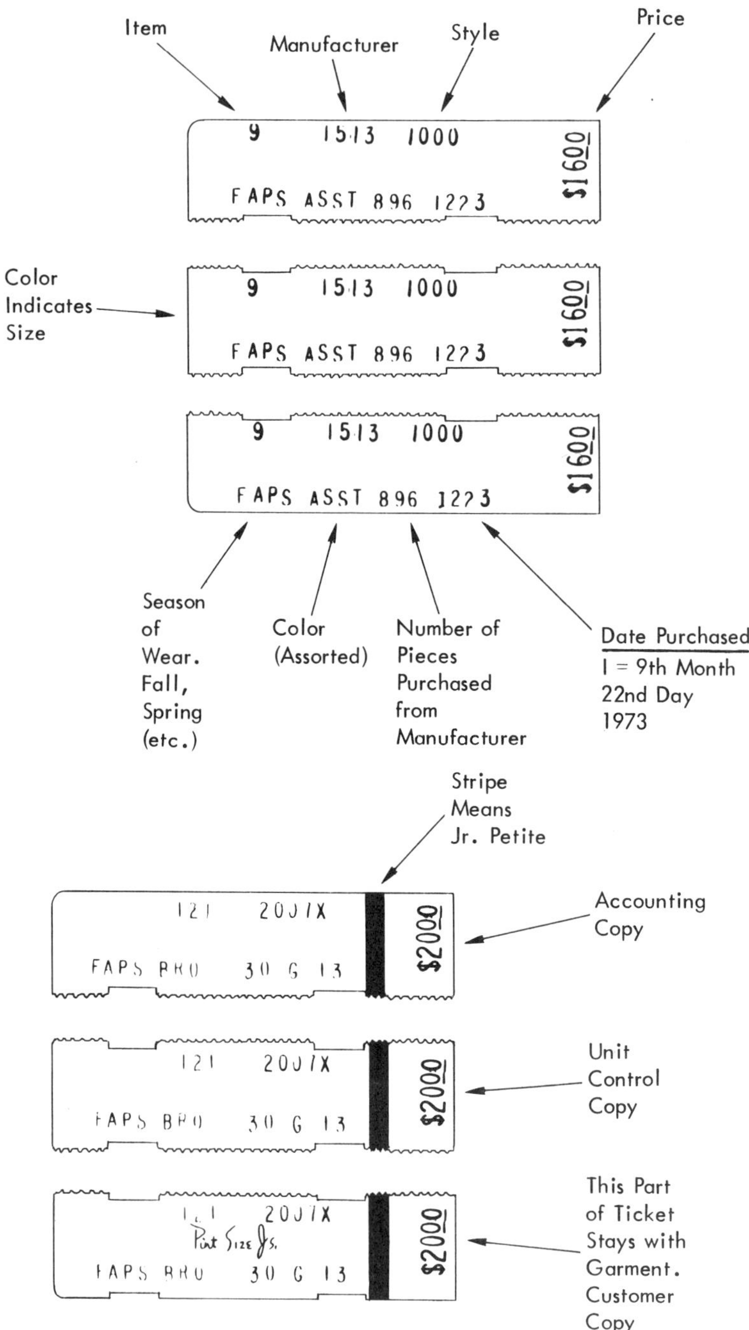

Source: Pint Size Juniors, Chicago, Illinois.

It is now possible for Rod to derive his sales. For example:

	$3	$5	$10
Inventory, February 1, 1975	100 ties	200 ties	200 ties
Purchases	500	300	300
Total ties available to be sold	600	500	500
Less ending inventory (by physical count)	170	280	209
Reductions in stock	430	220	291

Value of reductions:	
430 ties at $ 3 =	$1,290
220 ties at $ 5 =	1,100
291 ties at $10 =	2,910
Estimated sales plus shortage	$5,300

Rod now knows that his stock has been reduced by $5,300. Most of this is sales; however, some of the reduction is due to pilferage or a failure to record markdowns. Suppose Rod estimates, from his previous experiences, that shortages are $300. He now computes his sales.

Values of reductions to stock	$5,300
Less estimate of shortage	300
Estimate of sales	$5,000

Rod now can compute his net profit.

Advantage of Unit Control. It appears that a unit control system is more cumbersome than a dollar control system, so a good question to ask is why a retailer should use unit control. The answer is that the unit control system identifies the physical items sold and those that are not. This helps a buyer to decide on the items to reorder and to promote, and those to markdown. All in all, unit control permits a better interpretation of consumer demand. For the retailer handling fashion merchandise, this additional information allows him or her to manage this volatile merchandise more effectively. (See Figure 9.3.)

All of the essential information is made available to the buyer by the use of daily reports. These reports record unit sales by price lines, styles, color, brand, size, or vendor. Fast sellers and slow movers can be easily identified. Let us once again visit Rod's Tie Shop, which is using the perpetual inventory system in units. One day's report supplied the following information:

1.	sold 150 ties at $ 3	$450
	sold 50 ties at $ 5	$250
	sold 25 ties at $10	$250
	225 ties—total sales	$950

FIGURE 9.3

Color control helps sell panty hose and facilitate inventory control

Source: Safeway Stores, Inc., Oakland, California.

2. All of the \$5 and \$10 ties were the 4″ width.
   Of the \$3 ties, 100 were the 4″ width and 50 were the 3″ width.
3. Rod carries ties of 5 manufacturers (vendors). The following are the sales results classified by vendors:

Vendor A
- 50 ties at \$ 3
- 20 ties at \$ 5
- 10 ties at \$10
- 80 ties sold

Vendor B
- 3 ties at \$ 3
- 0 ties at \$ 5
- 0 ties at \$10
- 3 ties sold

Vendor C
75 ties at \$ 3
20 ties at \$ 5
15 ties at \$10
110 ties sold
Vendor D
12 ties at \$ 3
8 ties at \$ 5
0 ties at \$10
20 ties sold
Vendor E
10 ties at \$ 3
2 ties at \$ 5
0 ties at \$10
12 ties sold

Rod knows immediately his sales by price lines, vendors, and tie width. In this example, Rod notes that his \$3 ties are the largest sellers. Furthermore he notes that of the 225 ties sold, all but 50 were the 4″ width. This fact indicates the wider style tie continues to be fashionable, and that Rod should continue buying this style and reduce orders of the 3″ width. Rod also notes the ties purchased from Vendors A and C are the most popular with his customers. He makes a note to discontinue buying ties from Vendors B and E because their ties sell poorly in his store. Rod made this decision after reviewing his sales reports for the past months—all of which showed ties purchased from Vendors B and E sold poorly. Last, Rod decides to promote his \$10 ties by means of a special advertising campaign in order to stimulate sales since they generate a higher margin than do the others.

Departmental Control

We have illustrated two major methods of merchandising control—dollar control and unit control. In each of these methods, the retailer may elect to use the perpetual inventory system or the periodic inventory system of control. Small retailers are likely to keep these records for the store as a whole and not attempt to provide records for smaller divisions within the store. On the other hand, retailers whose total sales volume is rather large and whose physical stock is complex keep their stock manageable either by departmentalizing or classifying the merchandise or both.

Departmental control begins by subdividing the organization structurally into departments. For example one retailer might divide the store into the following departments: toys, infant's wear, children's clothes, ladies' apparel, men's furnishings. Each department is responsible for managing its own merchandise; therefore department records are maintained on sales, returned sales, gross margin, markdowns, markups, physical inventory, and purchases. Given all this information, the department can determine its profitability and the success of its merchandising efforts. For example, Rod's Tie Shop could be a single department in a large department store. The data would be processed exactly the same as we have illustrated.

The limitation of departmental control is its failure to disclose weaknesses within the department itself. That is to say, the department as a whole could be profitable but several problems could exist. In order to help disclose hidden weaknesses within the department, related types of merchandise are grouped together and records are maintained for them. It is as if the retailer created subdepartments within the department. Some of the factors used to classify goods for the purpose of control are sales volume, similarity of markup, stock turnover, customer buying habits, and seasonal activity.

Grouping by Similar Markups. One approach to merchandise control is to group merchandise items together if they have similar markups. One never places goods with low markups into the same classification as goods with high markups. To do so would make it impossible to arrive at a reasonable conclusion concerning the items being controlled.

Markup refers to the difference between the selling price and the cost of merchandise. It is expressed either in dollars or as a percentage. For example, if the selling price of an article is $16 and its invoice cost is $10, the markup is $6, 37 percent of selling price, and 60 percent of cost.

Slow Movers and Fast Movers. Just as a retailer groups merchandise with similar markups together, he or she might also group slow-moving items with other slow movers and fast movers with other fast movers. We must emphasize this grouping is for inventory control (via records) and does not mean that the physical items are actually grouped together on the selling floor.

Customer Buying Habits. Another method of classifying goods is to examine customer buying habits. Some products are tied together in customers' minds because of their use, such as shirts and ties, slips and bras, shoes and socks, or gloves and purses.

Seasonality of Goods. The seasonality of goods is a possible way of classification. It is not desirable to include goods that are sold in different selling seasons in the same classification. For example, summer suits are not likely to be classified with overcoats. To do so would restrict a retailer's ability to manage the stock effectively.

Recapitulation. Regardless of the criteria used, a merchandiser can subdivide the records within a department so as to measure the profitability of a line of merchandise, a class of merchandise, or a group of lines. Small retailers may simply use an inventory control system for their whole store. A moderately large retailer may set up an inventory control system for each department within the store. Very large retailers may have an inventory control system for classes of merchandise within the department. The actual operation of the inventory control system is the same whether for the store as a whole, for a department, or for a class of goods.

Other Unit Control Systems. There are other types of physical unit control systems. In some departments it is impossible to establish a unit control system, so the control is maintained through the stock room. In these cases, the selling department requisitions its stock from the storeroom (where records are kept), and the storeroom treats the requisition as if it were a sale. The stock room can utilize either the perpetual inventory system or the periodic system in a manner previously described. This is called a reserve stock control system.

Another unit control system is by means of a tickler file. In this instance, a periodic inventory is always used, but the department does not take a physical count of all its merchandise at the same time. Each day a different item is counted. The tickler system simply identifies the item to be counted.

Still another system is a checklist in which the items on the list are checked out against a model stock. Actually this is little better than a visual system and has little merit.

A fourth type is the warehouse system. This is useful when the items being controlled are very large, such as refrigerators, television sets, or washers and dryers. Customers select choices from among samples on the department's selling floor; however, the actual unit delivered comes from the warehouse. In this case the control system will be at the warehouse. In every other respect it will be similar to the major systems previously described.

THE MERCHANDISE BUDGET

There should be a balance between the stock on hand and the actual sales; this requires a retailer to plan his or her entire merchandising operation. One tool that assists the merchandise planner is the merchandise budget. One definition of the merchandise budget is:

> A forecast of specified merchandise activities for a definite period of time. It usually involves setting down on paper the desired results (plan) for a specified period and the appropriate methods by which these results will be accomplished.[2]

A second definition is as follows:

> The merchandise budget is the device commonly used to incorporate forecasts in actual plans, set attainable standards, schedule buying on a time basis, and provide a basis for judging progress and evaluating results.[3]

An examination of these definitions reveals several key words—forecast, merchandising plans, standards for buying, and evaluation. All budgets are based on estimates of future activity. A homemaker who keeps a household budget actually is attempting to forecast expenditures within the limitation of the family's income. A retailer uses a budget to forecast sales either in dollars or units or both. Merchandise plans refers to the need to purchase and maintain a stock of inventory

[2]Delbert J. Duncan and Charles F. Phillips, *Retailing Principles and Methods*, 6th ed. (Homewood, Ill.: Richard D. Irwin, Inc., 1963), p. 377.

[3]Pearce C. Kelley and Norris B. Brisco, *Retailing: Basic Principles*, 3rd ed. (Englewood Cliffs, N.J.: Prentice-Hall, Inc., 1957), p. 326.

balanced to achieve maximum sales from the opportunities presented. Standards for buying refer to the need for supervision of the entire buying function. Evaluation is the final step, one in which the forecast is compared with actual results; therefore a judgement may be made about the efficiency of the entire operation.

Purpose of a Budget

A budget is a plan for the future; a merchandising budget forces a retailer and the buyers to look ahead and chart a course for all merchandising activities. This should:

1. assist the buyer in purchasing his or her entire stock of merchandise;
2. help the retailer adjust his or her inventories to meet actual sales requirements;
3. aid the retailer in planning advertising, promotions, and sales events;
4. help management evaluate the performance of all merchandising personnel;
5. aid the financial planners.

Requirements for a Budget

First, a merchandise budget should always be prepared in advance of the selling season. Inasmuch as there are a considerable number of meetings to be held on the subject, because there are a number of people involved and because there are a number of factors to be considered, the planning sessions begin several months in advance of the selling season. As an illustration, consider those stores having only two selling seasons: the spring season—February 1 through July 31—and the fall season—August 1 through January 31. In this illustration the budget planning should start no later than December 1 for the spring season and June 1 for the fall season.

Second, a budget should be simple. The budget is a plan that management expects to follow, so it must be written in language that is easy to understand and follow. Regardless of how well a merchandise budget is prepared, it is useless if those who use it do not understand it.

Third, a good merchandise budget should involve people. All merchandising personnel should play a role in its preparation because they are more likely to carry out a plan if they have a hand in its planning. There are some buyers who do not see the value of planning ahead, or are fearful that the budget will be used to their disadvantage. In these cases the merchandising executives must correct the misapprehension and educate the buyers in the merits of the budget.

Fourth, the specific budget should be prepared for a relatively short period of time. It is difficult to forecast under the most favorable conditions; therefore one should not complicate the budget planning by choosing a time period far into the future. A six-month planning period is maximum. Long-range forecasts have their place, but not in a merchandise budget where emphasis is on the retailer's exact buying plans.

Fifth, a budget should be flexible. All merchandise budgets are plans and estimates of merchandising events predicted to occur in the immediate future. Conditions may change and alterations in the plans must be made. A budget should never be so rigid that change is impossible.

STEPS OF A MERCHANDISE BUDGET

There are five major steps in any merchandise budget. These are:

1. Estimating future sales.
2. Planning the stock.
3. Planning reductions.
4. Planning purchases.
5. Planning the gross margin.

Estimating Future Sales

Estimating future sales is the starting point in the preparation of a merchandise budget. The estimate may be made in dollars, in physical units, or both. A retailer begins the estimate for next season's sales by examining last year's sales statistics, and then making a determination as to what adjustments, if any, must be made There are many factors to consider in the adjustment process; some are external to the company while others are internal. External factors are the general economic conditions within the nation, population trends, state of competition, and such conditions as war or peace, labor unrest, civil strife, or some other unusual occurrence.

Economic Health. All forecasts for sales must consider the economic health of the nation. In prosperous times the normal expectation is that sales will rise, but they will not increase at the same rate for all retailers. In the absence of any other criteria, a sales growth equivalent to the expected increase in gross national product is probably a safe initial assumption.

Inflation is another factor which should be considered. Everything else being equal, a 6 percent increase in prices because of inflationary influences will increase dollar sales on the average by the identical percentage. Unit sales in this case will not increase. On the other hand, a reduction in the overall price level could cause the budget planners to adjust their sales forecast downward. Consumers are said to become apprehensive during recessions and postpone purchases of many goods, especially "big ticket" items such as autos, television sets, washers and dryers, or luxury goods of any category. Retailers who sell goods with an inelastic demand, such as food, are usually less affected by economic fluctuations than are those who sell goods with an elastic demand, such as autos, although the rapid rise in food prices in recent years (see Figure 9.4) has caused drastic revisions in consumers' eating habits.

Planners also must consider both the fiscal and monetary policies of the government. Fiscal policies are always concerned with the incomes and expenditures of the federal government; therefore tax increases or decreases are as important as changes in welfare payments or social security outlays. A higher income tax levy is designed to reduce spending; consequently a retailer may experience a reduction in sales. On the other hand, a tax decrease, an increase in social security payments, or an increase in welfare payments are all designed to increase the capacity of the householders to spend more. A retailer naturally considers the likelihood of an increase in sales.

FIGURE 9.4
Double digit inflation in 1974 helped to cause meat prices to soar

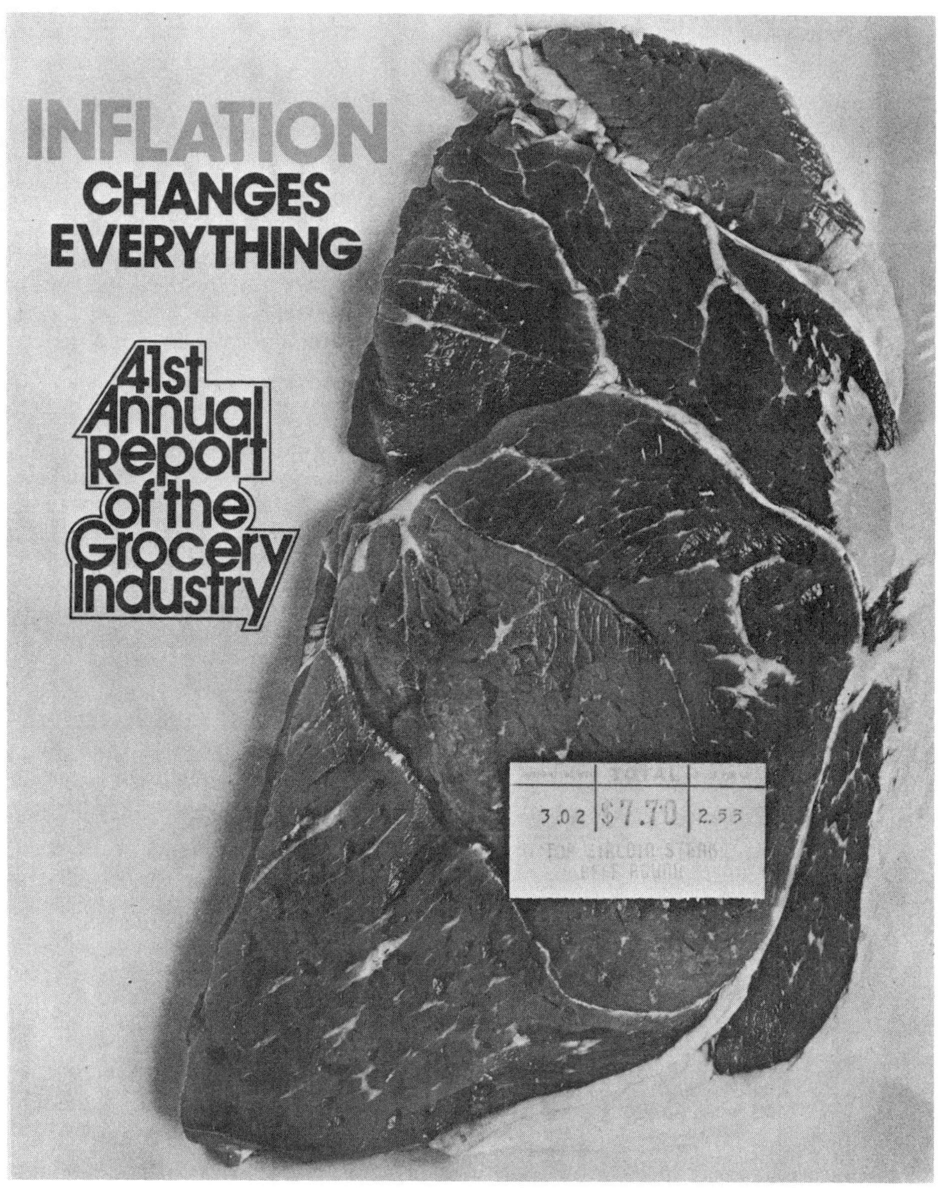

Source: "41st Annual Report," *Progressive Grocer*, April 1974, cover.

Monetary policy reflects changes in the level of the stock of money. Whenever the demand for money is larger than the supply, banks and other lending institutions increase the interest rates, and a "tight" money market ensues. In this case, postponement of purchases is a distinct possibility, and the retailer will adjust the sales forecast downward.

Population. Sales forecasts are also dependent upon changes in population, not so much in the national aggregate but in the areas in which the retailer operates. There are both quantitative and qualitative factors to be considered. A retailer who is located in a trading area experiencing a dramatic increase in construction of new housing units is usually justified in expecting an increase in sales. On the other hand, a retailer may plan for reduced sales if the trading area is losing population in significant numbers.

Population shifts can also be important. Young adults (high spenders) could move out of a trading area and leave behind other couples whose spending habits are substantially different. Moreover the cultural background of a trading area is important as an indicator of the tastes of the people and the kind of goods they wish to buy.

State of Competition. Any forecast of sales must take into account the nature of competition. One retailer may suddenly be exposed to the competition of a large regional shopping complex. Another retailer may see competition pulling out and abandoning the territory and customers. Other retailers may change their assortment policies and become competitors. Therefore it is essential for a budget planner to take into account the merchandising plans of competitors in order to forecast his or her own sales accurately.

Other External Factors. Other factors must be considered if they appear relevant to sales. For example, during World War II, shortages of many types of goods developed, and retailers experienced a major shift in consumer purchases. When the war ended, pent-up demand and large amounts of liquid consumer funds generated a burst of consumer spending. Forecasting and budgeting were extremely difficult at that time. However, during the Korean and Viet Nam wars, there were very few noticeable shortages of consumer goods.

Labor unrest could be a factor, especially in those communities where one industry dominates the employment picture. If workers strike for an extended time, retail sales are always seriously affected. Labor peace would have the opposite effect. Strikes of public transportation workers or newspaper employees historically have always had an impact on retail sales. Where customers (and employees) have had difficulty traveling to a shopping area or where they cannot read about new products for sale, sales have suffered.

Merchants who sell fashion goods have a particularly difficult time when one style appears to be faltering and another style has not been fully accepted. In this twilight zone, many people may postpone their purchases until they see what direction the fashion is taking. The majority will often base their decisions on that of the fashion leaders in their peer groups.

Internal Factors. Retailers must consider their own merchandising plans before completing predictions of next season's sales. They may have plans to increase assortment or number of product lines. On the other hand, they may plan to limit assortment or reduce product lines. Perhaps a retailer is planning on increasing the physical plant or opening a second unit. In any case, a retailer must consider all of his or her plans for the effect they may have on sales volume.

Beating Last Year's Figures. Some retailers estimate their sales by using the technique of beating last season's sales. A retailer occasionally makes a fetish of this technique. One small merchant controlled the date on his cash register, and in this way always beat last year's sales records and achieved his quota. For example, if on April 23, 1975, his sales were $903.49, and one year later he had $879.70, the merchant would simply continue to count sales into the next day until they exceeded the desired quota. At one time his cash register date was four days behind the calendar date. But this merchant always felt self-satisfied because he made his daily quota.

Planning the Stock

After a retailer has estimated sales for the next season, he or she must plan to have merchandise on hand to meet both sales expectations and inventory requirements. There are four basic methods used to help with this problem. They are (1) the basic stock method, (2) the percentage variation method, (3) the week's supply method, and (4) the stock-sales ratio.[4]

Basic Stock Method. Retailers always carry more goods in stock than they believe they will sell during a particular period. This gives them flexibility and reduces the chances of being out of stock if sales are higher than the retailer anticipated. It is also necessary to keep a larger stock of inventory on hand than planned sales indicate because of the lag in receiving replacement goods after they are ordered. This cushion of goods is called the basic stock.

In the basic stock method, the merchant simply adds planned sales to basic stock and thus obtains the amount of merchandise that should be on hand. This is done each month of the selling season. A formula to compute the basic stock is:

$$\text{Basic stock} = \text{Average stock for season} - \text{Average monthly sales}$$

To illustrate this plan, consider the following data taken from Madeleine's House of Fashion.

Selling Season—6 months beginning August 1.
Planned Stock Turnover—4.

[4]For a more detailed explanation of the four methods of planning stock, see John W. Wingate and Elmer O. Schaller, *Techniques of Retail Merchandising*, 2nd ed. (Englewood Cliffs, N.J.: Prentice-Hall, Inc., 1965), pp. 376–88.

Planned Sales:

August	$10,000
September	15,000
October	20,000
November	25,000
December	35,000
January	15,000
Total	$120,000

The average monthly sales are: $120,000 ÷ 6 = $20,000

The average stock is $\dfrac{\text{sales}}{\text{turnover}} = \dfrac{120,000}{4} = \$30,000$

Basic stock = $30,000 − 20,000 = $10,000

In August Madeleine has planned sales of $10,000, so she must have on hand inventory for these sales plus the reservoir (basic stock). In this example, Madeleine stocks $20,000 of merchandise on August 1. On September 1, she has $25,000 on hand. The following table shows the data for all months within the selling season:

Stock on Hand	*Planned Sales*	*Basic Stock*	*Total Stock on Hand*
August 1	$10,000	$10,000	$20,000
September 1	15,000	10,000	25,000
October 1	20,000	10,000	30,000
November 1	25,000	10,000	35,000
December 1	35,000	10,000	45,000
January 1	15,000	10,000	25,000

Assume Madeleine has just opened her store on August 1. She buys $20,000 worth of merchandise to cover her anticipated sales for August of $10,000 and the $10,000 invested in basic stock (reservoir). For September 1 Madeleine needs a stock of $25,000, but since she already has on hand $10,000 at the end of August, she will buy only $15,000 in merchandise. Each month's stock will be determined in exactly the same manner. In the event that the actual sales depart from the planned sales—and they almost certainly will—an adjusting step must be taken. For example:

Stock on hand August 1	$20,000
Actual August sales	$11,000
Stock on hand August 31	9,000
Stock needed for September 1	25,000
Buyer will purchase (not $15,000)	$16,000

Percentage Variation Method. The percentage variation method is recommended when the stock turnover is more than six times a year. In this method, it is theorized that the actual stock on hand in any month should vary from the average stock planned only half as much as the percentage change in actual sales varies from the average sales expected. This appears to be complicated, and an example might be helpful. Assume the following information concerning Madeleine's House of Fashion.

Planned sales for the season	$120,000
Length of season	6 months
Planned sales for October	20,000
Planned turnover	8 times

Then, planned average monthly stock = 120,000 or $15,000.

Suppose the October sales of Madeleine's Shop are running 50 percent higher than planned. How much larger should Madeleine's stock be increased so as to insure not being out of stock?

According to this plan, since sales are $30,000 (50 percent increase over $20,000), stock should be increased one-half of 50 percent or 25 percent over average monthly stock. In this case, 25 percent of $15,000 is $3,750; therefore the monthly stock would be raised to $18,750. Madeleine would have $18,750 worth of merchandise on hand at the first of the month.

Week's Supply Method. The third method of determining the amount of stock to have on hand is to plan sales on a weekly basis. The stock on hand should be an amount that is equivalent to several weeks' sales. Suppose an annual turnover of 10 is desired, and assume planned sales for the year are $120,000. A single week's sales would average out as $2,308 (120,000 / 52). An annual turnover of 10 is equivalent to 5.2 weeks. Therefore the inventory would be set as 5.2 ($2,308) or $12,000. This method assumes that the same turnover can be maintained throughout the selling season—such an assumption often is unwarranted. Inasmuch as the stock carried is in direct proportion to the sales, the retailer is likely to stock too much merchandise in peak selling periods and not have sufficient stock in dull sales periods.

Stock-sales Ratio. The fourth method of estimating the amount of stock to be carried is the stock-sales ratio. From experience, a retailer knows that he or she must maintain a certain ratio of goods on hand to sales generated. For example, suppose this is two, meaning that if the retailer plans for $10,000 sales volume he or she must have 2 (10,000), or $20,000, of merchandise on hand. The chief limitation to this method is the availability of proven stock-sales ratios. A merchant selling a variety of kinds of merchandise would need dependable stock-sales ratios for each kind of merchandise. If these ratios are available, the method is satisfactory for determining the stock to be carried.

Planning Reductions

When preparing the merchandise budget, allowances must be made for changes in the value of the stock due to reduction other than sales. These reductions are markdowns, discounts (generally employee), and stock shortages. A markdown occurs whenever the selling price of an item is reduced to a lower one. Markdowns always affect the dollar value of the stock. One example illustrating this is as follows: Stock on hand: 1,000 items priced at $1.00 = $1,000 total value. Assume that the entire stock is reduced to $.90 each. Then stock on hand is 1,000 items priced at $.90 = $900. $1,000 − 900 = $100 (the reduction in value because of markdowns).[5]

Causes of Markdowns. Markdowns are inevitable and are taken for the following reasons: buying errors, declining price levels, clearance of soiled merchandise, reaction to competition, and special events. Selling errors also can contribute to markdowns.

No buyer willfully buys the wrong merchandise; however, buyers are human and can make mistakes. They may have misinterpreted consumer demand and bought too much merchandise. In other cases they may actually buy the wrong item, especially if it is merchandise with strong fashion overtones. Perhaps they overstocked in the wrong size or wrong color patterns. In all of these cases the buyer may be forced to reduce the initial selling price to sell the merchandise, particularly toward the end of a selling season.

Occasionally the buyer may overprice the merchandise, and the result is lagging sales. In order to correct this situation, a markdown must be taken. Sometimes a series of markdowns are taken before merchandise is finally sold. In some years, economic conditions force a downward movement in prices. Whenever this occurs, markdowns must be taken by all retailers.

Merchandise often becomes soiled or shopworn and therefore cannot be sold at its initial price. Therefore the merchandise is marked down in order to sell it. At other times, a buyer thinks it good retail strategy to cut prices to stimulate sales. This may or may not be in response to competition. Merchandise that is subject to annual model changeover is particularly subject to markdowns whenever the new models are put on sale.

Selling errors also lead to markdowns. Clerks who do poor selling jobs contribute to markdowns. Poor salesmanship can lead to increased customer returns, and eventually markdowns. In other cases merchandise may not be displayed effectively, and eventually markdowns must be made to move the merchandise.

[5]It is absolutely necessary to keep a record of markdowns. This problem is discussed in Chapter 16.

The planners of the merchandise budget realize that markdowns are inevitable, so they must be considered in the planning phase. One advantage of including them in planning is to make everyone concerned sharply aware of their importance. Buyers should be so conscious of them that they try to minimize buying errors. Furthermore, a buyer who supervises the selling department should be encouraged to minimize the selling errors that lead to markdowns.

Other reductions are discounts and stock shortages. Employees in many retail stores are offered opportunities to purchase merchandise at a discount. Discounts must be recorded so as to account for stock reductions properly. (Chapter 16 discusses the consequence of disregarding employee discounts.)

Stock shortages are the reductions in the stock for unaccountable reasons. Primarily, goods may be shoplifted by customers or pilfered by employees. Moreover, fragile merchandise may be broken and no records kept of the fact. Stock shortages are generally estimated through experience. They may vary anywhere from 1 to 3 percent of sales depending upon store security.

Planning Purchases

The fourth major step in the preparation of the budget is to plan the purchases so as to have on hand the stock necessary for sales, basic stock, and reductions. The computation of purchases is relatively easy, as the following formula illustrates.

$$\text{Planned purchases} = \text{Planned ending inventory} + \text{Planned sales} + \text{Planned reductions} - \text{Beginning inventory.}$$

For example, budget planners for Laura's Dress Shop have made the following estimates for the season:

Planned sales	\$50,000
Opening inventory	21,500
Planned reductions	5,200
Planned ending inventory	22,000

What are the planned purchases? Substituting in the formula,

$$\text{Planned purchases} = \$22{,}000 + 50{,}000 + 5{,}200 - 21{,}500 = \$55{,}700$$

Open-to-buy. In the above example, we determined by a formula the need to purchase \$55,700 worth of merchandise. This planned purchase is a unit's "open-to-buy" position. The buyer does not purchase all the merchandise that may be needed during the period because he or she may be unsure of what will sell well and because he or she wants to minimize the amount of capital tied up in inventory. This balance is maintained by employing one of the four basic methods of stock planning: basic stock method, percentage variation method, week's supply method, or stock-sales ratio method.

For some people, open-to-buy is a little difficult to compute after the selling season has begun. However, a little practice is all that is necessary. Consider Laura's Dress Shop and the following information:

Actual sales	$21,000
Goods purchased but not delivered	5,000
Goods purchased and delivered	31,000
Actual reductions	1,000
All other data is the same as before.	

In order to determine the open-to-buy, the data is processed in a logical way. First, determine how much merchandise is needed, then compute how much of this merchandise is already available. The difference between them is the open-to-buy.

Look at our example of Laura's Dress Shop and the additional information given. First, we shall compute the amount of merchandise needed for this period. We have already determined that the planned ending inventory is $22,000, so we start with that. Next, we add the remaining sales that we expect. This is determined by taking the planned sales of $50,000 and subtracting the sales already experienced for this period. Thus, $50,000 − 21,000 or $29,000. Then we add the reductions to that total. We planned for $5,200 reductions and have already experienced $1,000 of reductions, so the dollar value of remaining reductions is $4,200.

Therefore:

Amount of Merchandise Needed

Ending inventory	$22,000
Remaining sales expected	29,000
Remaining planned reductions	4,200
Needed	55,200

Now let us look at the merchandise available. We started the period with an inventory of $21,500. During the period we purchased $31,000 in merchandise and it has already been delivered. We also purchased $5,000 in merchandise that has not been delivered. Thus, during the period we have had available $21,500 of beginning inventory and $36,000 of purchases, or a total of $57,500 in merchandise. We have already experienced $21,000 in sales and $1,000 in reductions, so we still have $35,500 available in merchandise. Inasmuch as we need $55,200 and have $35,500 available, we are open-to-buy $19,700 in merchandise. This can be summarized as follows:

Beginning inventory	$21,500
Purchased and delivered	31,000
Purchased but not delivered	5,000
Total	$57,500
Less sales for this period	21,000
	$36,500
Less reductions taken	1,000
Available	$35,500
Needed	55,200
Open-to-buy	$19,700

If the amount of goods on hand had exceeded the amount needed, the store would have been in an "overbought" position. Purchase control is always necessary to insure that the stocks on hand are in line with the plans. Open-to-buy reports are sent to the merchandise managers as well as the buyers, so that everyone concerned knows exactly what the buyer is ordering and whether the budget permits it. It should be apparent that all buyers' orders must be approved by a merchandise manager in order to maintain control.

Open-to-buy is computed at retail prices, but the actual purchases are made at cost. Therefore it is necessary to convert the retail open-to-buy to cost figures. If the margin is 40 percent, cost is 100 percent −40 percent, or 60 percent. In the last example, $19,700 open-to-buy at retail becomes .60 (19,700) = $11,820 at cost.

Planning the Gross Margin

The last requirement for planning the merchandise budget is the gross margin. This is the difference between the selling price and the cost of the stock. The planner must recognize that the initial selling price may not hold up, and markdowns will have to be taken. Furthermore, prices will have to be set high enough to yield income to cover such reductions as pilferage, employee discounts, or breakage. The retailer knows from experience or observation of similar units the gross margin percentage he or she hopes to realize. For example, a supermarket may set its gross margin at 20 percent, a department store may use 40 percent, a specialty shop, 45 percent. The gross margin is important because it is the revenue that covers all store expenses and hopefully yields a profit.

Budget Adjustments. It is hoped that the actual operating results conform closely with the planned budget figures. All excessive variances must be analyzed and appropriate action taken. Some of the reasons the actual operating results differ from the planned budget are: (1) haphazard planning, (2) conservative or liberal planning, and (3) factors beyond the control of a planner.

Haphazard planning occurs when insufficient time goes into the preparation of the budget, or if wishful thinking is substituted for judgment and research. Conservative planning occurs when the planned budget figures are chosen to insure the success of the actual results. Planning of this type is not planning at all but a device to make the actual figures look good.

Sometimes events occur which are beyond the control of the merchandise department. Actual sales may fall because of strikes, price decline, or government action of one kind or another. A variance of this kind has to be accepted.

Sophisticated Management Control Systems

The traditional methods of merchandise control are being supplemented by more sophisticated ways of obtaining and processing data (see Figure 9.5). Retailers are becoming involved in an electronic revolution. We think this subject matter is so important, Chapter 17 has been devoted to it and the computer. It is in that chapter that more sophisticated management control systems are discussed.

FIGURE 9.5
The computer is a great help in controlling merchandise

Source: Sears, Roebuck and Co., Chicago, Illinois.

SUMMARY

A retailer purchases his or her stock of merchandise in anticipation of consumer demand. Stock must be purchased in sufficient quantities so as not to run out of stock and hence lose sales. On the other hand, a retailer cannot overbuy and keep excessive merchandise on hand. Merchandise control is designed to maintain the proper balance between inventory and sales, and to effect greater sales from a given stock of merchandise.

Merchandise may be controlled either in dollars or in units, or both. Dollar control emphasizes the value of merchandise while unit control emphasizes the physical stock. Regardless of which system is chosen, the retailer must decide whether or not it is necessary to subdivide the entire store's merchandising performance. If so, the usual way is to have departmental control. Even departmental records can be further broken down.

Regardless of whether the retailer uses dollar control or unit control, a choice must be made between the perpetual inventory system or the periodic inventory system. Each has its advantages and limitations; however, the purpose is to measure the profitability of the store as a whole and its various departments.

The unit control method has certain distinct advantages for the merchandising department that are not possible with dollar control. It is helpful to the retailer both as a buying and selling tool.

Another control tool aiding the retailer is the merchandise budget. This is a plan for the future, and it forces the retailer to chart a course indicating all merchandising activity for the next selling season.

The preparation of a merchandise budget begins with an estimate for sales. The planners consider many criteria, some external to the store, others internal. Examples of external factors are the trend of population growth, the economic health of the nation, and the intensity of competition. Internal factors refer to the retailer's own plans that could affect sales. Examples are adding a new assortment of merchandise, eliminating a department, or perhaps adding a whole new store in a suburban location.

Next, a retailer plans stock. The purpose of this stage of the planning is to decide on the investment to be maintained in inventory. There are four methods commonly used. A third step in a merchandise budget preparation is to plan the reductions to the inventory other than sales. These reductions are markdowns, shortages, and employee discounts.

Once the first three steps are completed, the purchase plan can be easily determined. This gives rise to the open-to-buy concept, which is the dollar amount in the budget which the buyer has available to spend for additional merchandise. The last requirement in the preparation of the merchandise budget is the planned gross margin.

Only after the season has ended can a final determination be made as to the quality of the merchandising effort. A significant variance in the actual performance from the planned performance must be analyzed and appropriate action taken.

QUESTIONS FOR DISCUSSION

1. What is merchandise control and how does it help a retailer?
2. Why is it necessary to take a physical count of the inventory at least once a year if a retailer employs the perpetual inventory system?

3. What advantages does a unit control system have over dollar control?
4. Assume that you are the decision maker for a retail store. What inventory control system would you adopt and why?
5. What is a merchandise budget and how does it help with merchandise control?
6. Discuss the requirements for the preparation of a merchandise budget?
7. One of the key elements in a merchandise budget is the estimate of future sales. Discuss the factors the planner takes into consideration for making this estimate.
8. Why do markdowns occur? What measures may a buyer take to minimize them?
9. What is meant by the term "open-to-buy"? Discuss its usefulness to the merchandise manager.
10. What are some of the major reasons that actual operating results differ from those planned in the merchandise budget?

10 BUYING POLICIES AND ACTIVITIES

A neighborhood hardware store manager has joined a cooperative buying program in which he and other noncompeting hardware stores can purchase their needs in such volume that they usually earn important concessions from their suppliers. For the greatest success he must agree with the buying committee's recommendations. However, some of the products they recommend are not well accepted in his neighborhood. He must decide what compromises he is willing to make in order to remain a part of the group.

A retail food chain knows that it wants to add ladies' pantyhose to its merchandise line. It must decide whether to buy L'Eggs from a specialty jobber or a less well-known brand from another wholesaler from whom it buys other goods. The L'Eggs brand is well known, but the chain's aggregate monthly purchases from the wholesaler qualify it for a substantial volume discount.

A dress shop owner in North Carolina travels to New York City twice a year to visit various suppliers on Seventh Avenue. She does most of her buying at that time, placing additional orders by telephone as the season moves along. But she also retains the part-time assistance of a resident buyer in the city; the buyer keeps her informed on what is happening in fashion, knows where similar merchandise can be purchased at lower cost, and generally is an effective troubleshooter.

An appliance retailer is disturbed that the distributor from whom he has been buying has begun to sell more and more to the final consumer: in short, the wholesaler is rapidly becoming a retailer and thus competing with his own customer. He can afford to do so because he has been receiving the functional discount that a wholesaler expects to receive, obtaining the goods at a much lower cost than the retailer. A realignment of prices—or a switch of suppliers—may be in order.

One view is that a retailer is the purchasing agent for his or her customers. Although this is not quite true, the retailer certainly faces the tasks of seeking out suppliers who will offer merchandise that is acceptable to the store's clientele and negotiating for its purchase. As the above examples suggest, this is not a simple task. The examples hint at the conflict that often arises between retailer and suppliers, the variety of suppliers that the retailer may deal with, and the difficulty of certain pricing decisions that must be made. This chapter deals with these and other issues that relate to how the retailer acts as a buyer for the customer.

In some cases initial contact is made by the retailer. More frequently this task is performed by the manufacturer or wholesaler. Once contact is established and the goods involved seem suited to the needs of the retailer and customers, the retailer enters into active negotiations on such matters as price, terms of sale, delivery dates, and promotional aids. There are times when the retailer negotiates as the dominant power; on the other hand, some retailers are in submissive roles. The relative bargining power is dependent upon "who needs whom." A manufacturer with a strong brand name can usually choose retailers if effective marketing strategy calls for the selective approach. On the other hand, strong retailers, such as Rich's in Atlanta, Hudson's in Detroit, and Field's in Chicago, provide such important outlets in key markets that the manufacturer is in a weaker bargaining position. In many instances retailers and their suppliers collaborate for very long periods, dividing the aggregate of functions to be performed into parts so that each institution specializes in whatever it is best at doing. The various institutions—usually manufacturer, wholesaler, and retailer, along with the consumer—make up a marketing channel.

THE MARKETING CHANNEL

A marketing channel is the path through which title to goods flows between producer and consumer. It begins when the goods are formed or processed, and it ends when the goods are either consumed or again change form. Those who take title to the goods are generally the manufacturers, wholesalers, jobbers, export merchants, retailers, and the consumer. Others, such as insurance companies, trucking firms, banks, manufacturers' representatives, and public warehouses, perform essential marketing functions, but usually do not take title—and the risk that goes with ownership—to the goods; consequently they are sometimes called "facilitating middlemen."

In a highly developed economy such as the United States, retailers have a rather wide choice with respect to membership in a channel. The role that a retailer is to play often is a conscious and important decision because it is one that may last for a long time. Retailers are seldom free to flit from one system to another without cost and inconvenience. There are a variety of channels for consumer goods; the major ones are shown in Figure 10.1. The retailer plays a role in the two most important channels where merchandise is purchased either from the manufacturer or from a wholesaler (or jobber).

Over a long period of time, efficient channels will tend to develop and inefficient channels will decay. This occurs because business people continually are exploring more profitable ways to get more goods to customers at lower cost. This exploration includes the way in which the necessary marketing functions will be divided among possible channel members. In some instances, the answer is that the channel will be a very long one. For example, a gift shop manager may buy Sarna bells from a wholesaler, but the goods may have passed from a small manufacturer in India to an Indian wholesaler, and then on through an export house in Bombay to an import house in New York before being purchased by the wholesaler. This may be a very efficient channel, meaning that no other combination could move the bells

FIGURE 10.1
Typical marketing channels

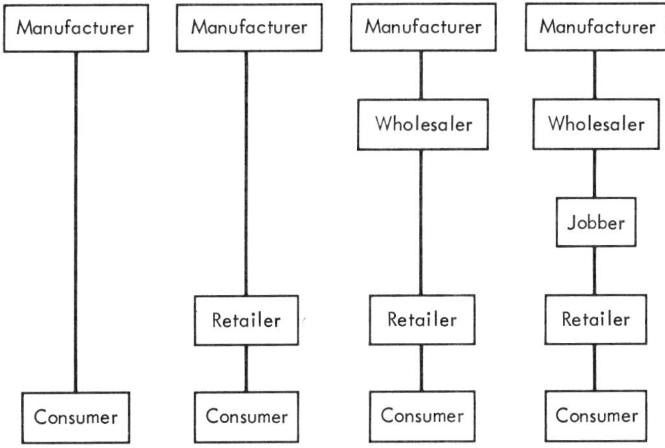

at a lower cost. In other instances, the channel will be very short. A Terre Haute, Indiana, custom shirt manufacturer sells direct to consumers by mail order. The customer picks the fabric and style from a catalog, measures himself, and sends the order and his money directly to the factory. The manufacturer and the customer have absorbed many functions normally performed by the retailer. Although this is an unusual channel in the United States, it seems to pass the market test, the best test for determining which institutions grow and which ones languish or die.

One explanation for the presence of business institutions is that as markets grow, specialization becomes economically possible.[1] Activities that a business would otherwise have to perform for itself can be "spun off" to others who can perform the activity more efficiently. If it were not for resident buyers, retailers in the Midwest would either have to make more buying trips to the city or leave the activity undone. The size of the American market is so great that a specialized buyer can represent many small retailers and do so quite efficiently; hence, another institution is born. Indeed, the role of retailers can be explained by the fact that they can perform functions that the consumer cannot perform for him- or herself nearly as well.

In short, most manufacturers cannot perform the marketing functions as effectively as specialists such as wholesalers and retailers. These middlemen have the expertise and experience to perform their roles more efficiently than can manufacturers. Whenever this is the case, the channel is likely to be longer and include retailers and wholesalers. The choice of the proper channel then is related to the

[1]George Stigler, "The Division of Labor Is Limited by the Extent of the Market," *Journal of Political Economy* (June 1951), pp. 185–93.

cost of performing channel tasks. Philip Kotler substantiates this conclusion when he says:[2]

> The issue of who should perform various channel tasks is largely one of relative efficiency and effectiveness. To the extent that specialist intermediaries achieve economies through their scale of operation and their know-how, the producer can gain through transferring some of the channel functions to their charge.

A large retailer may be in the dominant role as the following illustrates.[3]

> Sears provides the example of a retailer who not only controls the channels for many products which pass through it but even is responsible for bringing into existence some manufacturing firms to fill gaps in its assortment. The development of dominant retailers reflects the existence of economies of scale and assortments in distribution exceeding those in production.

We are not concerned with the problem of channel conflict as such; our concern is with the criteria that determines the choice of a specific supplier.

Classification of Middlemen

Nearly everyone understands the function of a manufacturer, but the functions of wholesaling middlemen are probably unclear. There are two classes of wholesaling middlemen: (1) those who take title to the goods, known as merchant wholesalers, and (2) those who do not take title, known as agents. There are many ways to classify merchant wholesalers, but perhaps the most meaningful is to classify them by the services they perform. Generally speaking, merchant wholesalers can be divided into two kinds: full service wholesalers and limited function wholesalers. (See Figure 10.2.)

Full Service Wholesalers. Full service wholesalers are the largest in terms of number, the volume of goods they sell, the number of people they employ, and in most other ways. These wholesalers perform a variety of marketing functions. First, they anticipate their customers' needs by predicting consumer demand. Based on their assessment of consumer demand, service wholesalers provide the assortment of goods from which their customers (retailers) make their selections. Then these wholesalers send out their salesmen to tell retailers about the wholesalers' stocks of goods and to solicit their business. Service wholesalers deliver their merchandise to the retailers' places of business, and normally they extend credit. Service wholesalers frequently help retailers by providing technical assistance, selling aids, and promotional material. Not every service wholesaler provides all of these services, but they do provide most of them.

Full service wholesalers may handle general merchandise, a single line of mer-

[2]Philip Kotler, *Marketing Management: Analysis, Planning, and Control* (Englewood Cliffs, N.J.: Prentice-Hall, Inc., 1967), p. 391.

[3]Ibid., p. 392.

FIGURE 10.2
Classification of middlemen

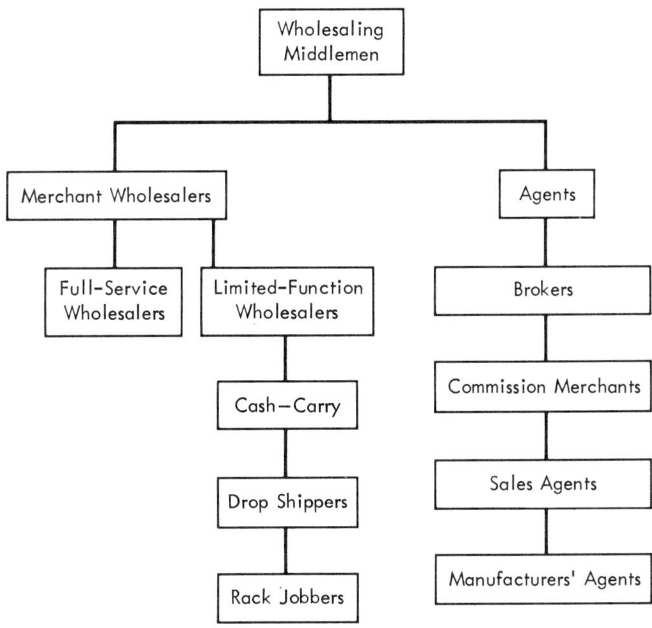

chandise, or confine themselves to a single specialty. General wholesalers carry a broad assortment of staple, nonperishable products. This assortment includes hardware, electrical supplies, furniture, drugs, cosmetics, auto equipment, and even farm supplies. Because the general wholesaler carries a broad line, a variety of different kinds of retail stores can be served. Among the general wholesaler's customers are drugstores, hardware stores, general stores, small department stores, and appliance shops.

Single line wholesalers restrict their assortments to a narrower range. The assortment will not be nearly as broad as that of the general wholesaler. For example, a food wholesaler may limit the line to dry groceries only, to meats, or fresh fruits and vegetables. Other single line wholesalers may specialize in hardware, or in drugs, or some other limited category of merchandise.

A specialty wholesaler may confine the offerings to a single product. For example, a food wholesaler may limit assortment solely to frozen foods, to health foods, or to any other narrow line of foods.

Limited Function Wholesalers. The second major classification of wholesalers is limited function wholesalers. In contrast to service wholesalers, they provide only some of the marketing functions. Examples of wholesalers who limit their functions are cash-carry wholesalers—as the name implies, they do not extend credit to customers nor do they deliver goods to customers. As one might expect, cash-carry wholesalers sell goods at lower prices and consequently are patronized by small retailers.

Drop shippers never take possession of the merchandise sold. These middlemen are important in such product lines as lumber, limestone, sand, and gravel. Moreover they are common in cases of bulky products such as furniture. For example, a drop shipper sells a shipment of beds to a local furniture store. The drop shipper directs the furniture manufacturer to ship the beds to the retailer named by the drop shipper. In this case the drop shipper is billed by the manufacturer, and in turn the drop shipper collects from the retailer. The importance of the drop shipper is in the control of shipping costs. That is to say, it is less costly to load bulky goods on a carrier and ship them to the retailer than to ship them to the drop shipper first, and then reload and ship to the retailer. Therefore the drop shipper provides only selling services and consequently operates on a lower margin. The retailer pays less for the merchandise than would normally be the case.

Rack Jobber. A rack jobber is important to supermarkets for the delivery of such nonfood items as cosmetics, health aids, toiletries, housewares, and hardware. Supermarkets are reluctant to purchase such items directly from the producer because it involves the purchase of many kinds of items in relatively small quantities. The supermarkets make space available to rack jobbers who stock the supermarkets' shelves with nonfood items. The rack jobber retains title to the merchandise while it is on display in the supermarket, and therefore is responsible for its replenishment and its freshness as is illustrated in Figure 10.3. Generally the rack jobber checks the merchandise weekly, and collects from the retailer for the merchandise sold during the previous week. The rack jobber gives the retailer a large enough margin, so it does not pay for the retailer personally to buy and stock these items. Any one store might be serviced by several rack jobbers, because each rack jobber restricts services to one line of products. As the volume of nonfood items sold in supermarkets increases, the position of rack jobbers is sometimes threatened. Whenever retailers find it to their advantage to buy direct, they are likely to do so. However, rack jobbers are still important.

Agents. Agents are those middlemen who do not take title to the goods they sell. In this category are brokers, commission merchants, sales agents, and manufacturer's agents. Most agents are very important in the services they perform on behalf of manufacturers. However, they are not so important for retailers. An exception is the food broker. These agents sell directly to large retailers who perform their own wholesaling. Food brokers have considerable expertise in the products they represent, and often assist food stores in setting up displays so that their products may be merchandised more effectively. It is the food broker's responsibility to see that the products represented are being purchased and offered to the consumers attractively and effectively.

FIGURE 10.3

Rack jobbers are responsible for stocking displays with their products

Source: L'EGGS Products, Inc., Winston-Salem, North Carolina.

SOURCES OF SUPPLY

We have briefly examined the cast that mans the trade channels, and now we turn to the problem of choosing the proper supplier. Inasmuch as retailers purchase many types of products in a variety of assortments, it is normal for them to buy from a number of sources. Some are manufacturers, while others are wholesalers or agents. Even chains who buy most of their needs directly from manufacturers occasionally use wholesaling middlemen. There are three primary sources for a retailer to obtain an assortment of merchandise: (1) manufacture his or her own merchandise; (2) buy direct from a manufacturer; or (3) buy from a wholesaling middleman.

The Retailer as Manufacturer

Only the very largest stores or chains can contemplate manufacturing some of the goods they sell. In fact, some large retailers find it advantageous to own factories and thus control the physical merchandise from its manufacture to its sale to the ultimate consumer. This process is known as *vertical integration.*

Small stores have little choice but to purchase all of their merchandise from outside sources. However, most merchants regardless of size prefer to engage in retailing activities rather than spend their capital and energy in manufacturing. Perhaps the major reasons that retailers do not do more manufacturing are:

1. Retailers are reluctant to invest capital in manufacturing assets when they could use the same capital for more effective merchandising.
2. Retailers believe their merchandising capabilities are limited if they must restrict their assortment to goods they manufacture.
3. Ownership of manufacturing facilities may invite federal investigation for possible violation of antitrust laws.
4. Most retailers are simply not interested in manufacturing and all the problems associated with the production of goods.

Buying Directly from a Manufacturer

The key decision for most retailers is whether or not to purchase their assortments directly from the manufacturer or through wholesaling middlemen. In some cases, the retailer has no choice, as when the manufacturer through his own policies does not sell directly to retailers. In these instances, the retailer must go to the wholesaler if this particular brand is to be stocked. On the other hand, a manufacturer may not use wholesaling middlemen. In these cases, the retailer must buy stock directly from the manufacturer.

In general, fashion goods and specialty goods are purchased directly from the manufacturer, while convenience goods are sold by both producers and wholesalers. Fashion goods must be sold quickly because of their vulnerability to the whims of consumer taste. It is simply too risky to move fashion goods through long and slow channels. Because of the rapidity of obsolescence, fashion goods are produced as close to the selling season as possible. Neither the manufacturer nor the retailer is willing to assume the risk of a shift in consumer taste by storing large stocks of inventory. The risk of style obsolescence is minimized when retailers buy their assortments of fashion merchandise directly from manufacturers.

Perishability is not restricted to goods with fashion overtones. Foods such as milk, bakery goods, sea food, and fresh meats are physically perishable. Consequently these products are purchased in relatively small quantities at frequent intervals, and often directly from the producers.

Manufacturers often find their retailing customers concentrated in large markets. Whenever this is the case, there are strong reasons why the manufacturers choose to sell their output directly to the retailers. A channel that is appropriate for selling in thinly populated areas (Wyoming, Montana, Idaho) often is not proper, where a denser population (New York, Massachusetts, New Jersey) can support a more intense selling effort.

Buying from a Wholesaler

A retailer may choose to buy from a wholesaler. This is certainly true for those retailers who buy small quantities at frequent intervals, often called hand-to-mouth buying. Retailers who choose to buy small quantities may be doing so because they can spend their budgets on a wider assortment. Even large retailers buy small quantities occasionally, and when they do so, they turn to the wholesaler. This is especially true if the goods have low unit value.

Some retailers place their largest order directly with the manufacturer, using a wholesaler to supplement their line or to fill in stock if sales exceed expectations. Wholesalers are also very important in cases of emergency, and when retailers need additional stock quickly.

Wholesalers are particularly helpful to small independent retailers. The competitive squeeze has been especially harsh upon small retailers, who are at a disadvantage in making their stores as attractive as their large competitors. They suffer in terms of store arrangement, management of inventory, and efficiency in advertising. But perhaps the greatest disadvantage of small retailers is their weak buying power compared with that of large competitors. This is important because small retailers need to price their merchandise competitively. Help has come to the small retailers through group action.

Voluntary and Cooperative Chains

Independent retailers have improved their competitive position vis-à-vis chain competition by forming groups for the purpose of securing buying, merchandising, and promotional advantages. One such group is the voluntary chain, a retail group organized and sponsored by a wholesaler for the express purpose of making a common cause against integrated competitors. The retailers who join the voluntary chain purchase their merchandise from the wholesaler, and because of the large quantities involved, obtain a pricing advantage that would not be available if they acted alone. This buying advantage permits the independent supermarkets who are members of the group to price their merchandise at a lower level than would otherwise be the case. Therefore they are more competitive with the giant chains such as National Tea, A & P, Safeway, and Kroger. Members of a voluntary chain use a common store front and promotional aids, obtain advice from capable consultants, and receive other merchandise assistance. Independent Grocers Alliance, Ben Franklin variety stores, True Value Hardware, and Western Auto stores are independent retailers who are affiliated with a voluntary wholesaler. (See Figure 10.4.)

Another type of joint action involving independent retailers and wholesalers is organized by retailers who establish their own wholesaling facility. The basic purpose of the cooperative chain is to obtain buying advantages so that they may price their goods more competitively. As in the case of voluntary chains, they may use common store fronts, share promotional aids, exchange store information, hold

FIGURE 10.4
IGA stores are examples of stores affiliated with a voluntary chain

Source: Independent Grocers' Alliance Distributing Co., Chicago, Illinois.

conventions, and employ specialists to educate the members. An example is Certified Grocer.

In the case of the voluntary chain and the cooperative chain, the basic motive is to permit member retailers to buy their assortment of merchandise at lower prices so that they in turn can price their own stocks at lower prices.

Statistical data indicate cooperative wholesalers have reduced their margins to a lower level than voluntary wholesalers, largely because cooperatives do not engage in as many marketing activities as do voluntaries. Table 10.1 shows this information. Table 10.2 shows the number and type of grocery wholesalers and the 1973 sales volume.

Key Resources

Once a retailer has decided whether to buy direct from a manufacturer or from wholesaling middlemen, he or she must now choose which manufacturer or wholesaler from whom to buy stock. Those selected will be key resources. In choosing key resources, retailers consider the nature of the product, its profitability, the reputation of the resource, availability of the vendor, and reputation of the brand.

Nature of the Product. The first consideration by a retailer in selecting a key resource is the nature of the product. Food retailers will choose food distributors,

TABLE 10.1
Margins in Grocery Wholesaling*

	All Wholesalers	*Voluntary Wholesalers*	*Cooperative Wholesalers*	*Unaffiliated Wholesalers*
1974	6.6%	6.6%	5.6%	8.0%
1973	6.4	6.4	5.5	7.6
1972	6.1	6.4	5.6	7.6
1971	6.1	6.5	5.6	7.5
1970	6.2	6.4	5.7	8.1
1969	6.1	5.9	5.7	7.7
1968	5.8	5.7	5.6	7.3
1967	5.7	5.5	5.5	7.1
1966	5.6	5.4	5.3	7.0
1964	5.5	5.4	5.3	7.0
1962	5.4	5.4	5.3	6.7
1960	5.6	5.7	5.5	7.1

*Average margin on total sales.
Source: "41st Annual Report of the Grocery Industry," *Progressive Grocer* (April 1974), p. 154, and "42nd Annual Report of the Grocery Industry," *Progressive Grocer* (April 1975), p. 137.

drugstores will choose drug suppliers, and furniture stores will choose furniture suppliers. However, in any category of products suppliers may only be alike in that they handle the same generic product. For example, furniture is furniture, but there may be a world of difference in style, design, material, and quality. A retailer will narrow the choice of furniture suppliers to those who sell the style, design, and quality his or her customers prefer. Let us look at an example.

Warren Meyer operates his own furniture store, and he specializes in Early American furniture. Consequently, Meyer is interested only in those furniture manufacturers who sell this particular style. Furthermore, Meyer handles only lines that are moderately priced. Therefore he limits his selection of suppliers to those who sell Early American furniture in the moderate price range.

Just as a furniture retailer limits selection by style, design, material, or price, so do retailers who sell men's clothing, ladies' apparel, or something else. A retailer is likely to have many choices among resources who handle the exact product wanted, and in those cases the retailer will select the supplier based on other criteria.

Profitability. One such criterion is the profitability of the merchandise. Everything else being equal, a retailer will choose a vendor whose products are the most profitable to resell. To a casual observer it may appear that all sources will sell equally profitable goods, but such is not the case. One vendor may have larger discounts, longer selling terms, lower freight charges, or a more liberal credit policy. All of these factors could affect the profit that a retailer may earn. To choose a rather simple example, one supplier may be located physically closer to the retailer than another supplier, and so the lower freight charges of the first supplier is the

TABLE 10.2
Statistical Data—Wholesale Grocery Firms (1974)

	Number of Establishments
Total firms	1,485
Voluntary wholesalers	347
Cooperative wholesalers	141
Unaffiliated wholesalers	997
	Sales (in billions of dollars)
Voluntary wholesalers	$20.8
Cooperative wholesalers	12.3
Unaffiliated wholesalers	9.1
Total	$42.2

Source: "42nd Annual Report of the Grocery Industry," *Progressive Grocer* (April 1975), p. 135.

determining factor in the choice. In another section of this chapter, all the factors which affect the ultimate price paid by the retailer are discussed.

Reputation of the Resource. Not all vendors have the same reputation for good service, prompt adjustment of complaints, quality merchandise, and fast delivery. In some cases, a vendor may be unethical and should be dropped. It is important for a retailer to choose a resource who will provide quality products, dependable service, and a competitive price, because shifting suppliers can be a costly and time-consuming task.

Availability of the Vendor. Some vendors, through selective and exclusive arrangements, limit their retail outlets to a favored few. If a retailer is not a party to one of these arrangements, the vendor is simply not available. Whether or not a retailer would benefit from an exclusive arrangement is another question.

Reputation of the Brand. A retailer may also consider the popularity of the brands. Some manufacturers spend a great deal of time and money to advertise their brands and to build strong consumer acceptance. It is somewhat obvious that popular brands are usually salable and in the best interests of the retailers to stock them. However, there often is an inverse correlation between a brand's reputation and the gross margin it generates. Those who control popular brand names know that they need not "pay" the retailer quite so much—payment taking the form of gross margin—to stock their brands.

Other Criteria. A retailer may choose one supplier over another for additional reasons. One vendor may offer financial assistance while another will not. Some may offer assistance in advertising, promotional aids, or sales force training, while others limit their assistance in these vital areas. Almost any advantage accruing to a specific retailer is reason enough for selecting one supplier over another. It may be simply a matter of one vendor and staff being more friendly than another.

Making Initial Contact

Once a retailer has decided to use manufacturers or wholesalers or a combination of them as key resources, there still remains the problem of making contact. This contact may be made by salesmen, through buying offices, by telephone and mail or, visiting the market.

Salesmen. The traditional method of making contact is through the visits of the vendors' salesmen. Although this method may not be as popular as it once was, it is still quite important. A retailer should have a standing rule to see all salesmen who call, for these people are the representatives of the suppliers and they possess a great amount of useful information. They are knowledgeable about the products they sell, they understand market conditions, and they are usually aware of new trends and developments. Frequently they can give retailers valuable tips with respect to advertising and promotional aids. Indeed, many buyers have the patience to talk with every salesman who calls, even though they are quite sure they will not buy; they hope they will learn from him. Needless to say, the salesman is likely to be helpful to those who show him respect and courtesy.

Buying Offices. Some cities in the United States have earned a reputation as a major central market. Among these are New York, Chicago, St. Louis, Dallas, Atlanta, Los Angeles, and San Francisco. Occasionally, a small city such as High Point, North Carolina, is an important central market. High Point is the furniture capital of the United States, and most furniture buyers are present when High Point presents its furniture shows. New York City is the largest of the central markets and the largest wholesaler market for fashion goods. Because of its size and importance, many kinds of resident buying offices are located there.

Perhaps the best way of classifying resident buying offices is to say that some are store owned and others are independent. The large stores located outside New York City frequently set up an office in New York for the express purpose of aiding their buying staff. These official representatives make all the arrangements for the buyer when he or she comes to New York, or they can narrow the selection to a manageable level, or they actually may place orders. They serve in whatever capacity the retailer wishes, for they are the "eyes and ears" of the retailer at the market. Almost all of the chain merchandising stores as well as large independent department stores maintain resident buying offices in New York. This includes such large retailers as Sears, Montgomery Ward, and Penney.

Other resident buying offices are independently owned. They operate under contracts signed by the retailers, who pay an annual fee to have an independent buying office represent them at the market. Small retailers usually cannot afford a continuing relationship with a resident buyer, so they utilize a merchandise broker to represent them in a given transaction.

Regardless of the form and type of buying office, all perform certain services that are beneficial to the retailers. They are always in the central markets, so they know what goods are available and where, what prices are being asked and whether or not they are fair, which supplier is likely to have the best merchandise for a particular retailer, and what direction fashion seems to be moving. Moreover the buying offices aid the retailer in the central market by taking him or her to the various vendors and by furnishing space, stenographic, and secretarial services during the retailer's short buying trip. The resident buying offices also are in contact with the buyers when they are not in the central market.

Group buying should also be mentioned here. This is simply joint purchasing and involves noncompeting stores. In other words, independent retailers merge their buying so as to realize various advantages. Foremost among their hopes is the expectation of buying merchandise at a lower cost than if they were to act independently. A major reason that a group can obtain a lower price is because of the economies realized by the seller in processing a large order. These economies might be either in selling, transporting, or production costs. Because the seller has lower costs, some of those lower costs are passed on to retailers in the form of lower prices.

Another reason why group buying is advantageous is the alleged improvement in the judgment of the decision maker while placing an order. It is argued that a group of knowledgeable buyers buying jointly will make a better decision than any one of the group might do acting independently.

A third reason why group buying is advantageous is the attention given the group by the manufacturer or supplier. A group is likely to place a large order; therefore the supplier is apt to respond to the order by being more attentive to its needs. That could mean more prompt deliveries, merchandise tailored to special needs, or faster adjustment of claims. This could give a competitive advantage to the group.

Telephone and Mail. The telephone and mail are used primarily when a retailer wishes to reorder. It is likely that the telephone is used when speed is important or in cases of emergency. A retailer may have heard about a particular resource, and may telephone the resource for additional information or perhaps to invite a salesman to call.

Visiting the Market. Many buyers go to the market to make their purchases. This is common in the case of fashion merchandise such as men's clothing, women's apparel, sports clothes, shoes, and home furnishings. Whenever a trip to the market is contemplated, the buyer should plan the trip carefully. Buyers should know how much they are open-to-buy, whom they intend to see, and how much time they intend to spend at the market. Visits to the market should be timed to coincide with formal presentations of the goods by the manufacturers.

ANALYSIS OF PRICE TERMS

Negotiations

Before a retailer completes a purchase with a vendor, the price must be negotiated. The "true" price paid depends upon the terms of sale, an expression which includes discounts and liability for transportation costs. A retailer may have to choose between two identical list prices but differing terms of sale. In determining choice, the retailer examines the framework of prices as well as the price level of the merchandise.

Price level refers to the actual price listed or quoted. If we go into a sporting goods store and inspect a tennis racket whose tag indicates a price of $12.95, we are considering its price level. However, a retailer may be quoted the list price of tennis balls as being $12 a dozen. The quotation of price is subject to discounts, datings, and shipping terms, which would alter the true price that the retailer pays. If that is the case, we speak of the framework of prices. Retailers are always concerned with the terms of trade in making a choice between two prices quoted by competing vendors. This section gives the reader an insight into the various terms of sale, or in other words an insight into the confusing world of price quotations.

Negotiations must be made under harmonious conditions if both parties to a negotiation are to be satisfied. It is no surprise to find examples of negotiators who have had friendly relations with one another for many years. This does not mean that the bargaining is soft, for successful negotiators are expected to bargain from positions of strength and to seek the most favorable terms they can obtain. But it does mean that each party, whether the manufacturer, the distributor, or the retailer, must be honest, friendly, and forthright, and above all each must respect one another if longevity of the buyer-seller relationship is to be expected.

To be good negotiators, buyers must be knowledgeable and have access to information that is helpful in the negotiation process. They gain this information from previous purchases, conversations with other vendors, attendance at trade shows, through reading newspaper articles, trade journals, and catalogs. Experience is a good teacher, and successful buyers (retailers) soon learn from the methodology of acquiring useful and valid information.

To negotiate properly, a retailer must be familiar with discounts, shipping terms, and datings to make sense out of price terms. Usually a manufacturer quotes a list price, from which certain discounts are permitted. There are a number of discounts, but the common ones are functional, quantity, seasonal, promotional, and cash.

Functional Discount

A functional discount, also called a trade discount, is one given by a manufacturer to a wholesaler or a retailer for the performance of some service for the manufacturer. Inasmuch as discounts are given for the performance of a service on behalf of a manufacturer, the size of the discount varies depending upon the quantity and quality of the service performed. Suppose a retailer is offered an item at the list price of $150 less a 40 percent trade discount. The retailer then pays $90 for the item ($150 − $60), and the $60 is the amount of the functional discount.

Manufacturers may offer functional discounts of various sizes to different kinds of retailers. The manufacturers justify the variance because of the savings they realize in the performance of their marketing functions. Assume a buyer for a chain of 1,000 hardware stores is offered an item carrying a 50 percent discount from a list price of $100. On the other hand, an independent hardware retailer is offered the same item at a 40 percent discount from a list price of $100. The manufacturer argues that it takes only one salesman to obtain an order of several thousand units from the chain. He further argues that it takes one salesman and just as much time to sell three units to the independent retailer. Therefore the selling cost is much less per unit for the chain's order, and the manufacturer recognizes this fact by giving a larger discount to the chain buyer.

Chain of Discounts. Functional discounts sometimes are expressed as a chain of discounts. A product may be priced at $100 less 40, 30, and 10 percent. If this is the price quoted to a retailer, he or she would pay $37.80 for the item. This is computed as follows:

Dollars	*Discount*
$100.00	
− 40.00	40% = (40% of $100) = $40.00
60.00	
− 18.00	30% = (30% of $60) = $18.00
42.00	
− 4.20	10% = (10% of $42) = $ 4.20
$37.80	

The important point in figuring a chain of discounts is that each successive discount is figured on the remainder figure rather than on the original list price; a chain discount of 40 percent, 30 percent, and 10 percent is *not* the same as a discount of 80 percent.

The key reason for a chain of discounts is that it permits a manufacturer to list the products in a catalog at the list price with a series of different discounts. This permits the seller to offer the item to different buyers at a different point in the chain. For example: a manufacturer lists an item in the catalog at $100, less 40, 30, and 10 percent. This means that the manufacturer recognizes three different sets of customers who might buy the product, each of whom earns a different discount because each performs a different function. A wholesaler might receive the entire chain of discounts, meaning that he would pay only $37.80 for the product. A jobber would be entitled to a list price less 40 percent and 30 percent, paying $42 for the goods. A retailer, taking the 40 percent earned discount, would pay $60 for the product, and would resell it to customers for $100. Note that if the product moves through the longest possible channel—from manufacturer, through wholesaler, jobber, and retailer, to the final customer—the discount that the retailer receives from the supplier is supposed to reflect the retailer's cost of doing business and give him or her a profit on the transaction.

Another reason for the development of a chain of discounts is that it makes price changes much easier. For example, the original terms may have been $100 less 40 percent. Suppose a recession forces a decline of prices. Rather than reduce the list price of $100, the manufacturer may simply add a second discount. Whenever prices advance at a later date, the manufacturer removes the discount. Market changes could also alter the structure of discounts. That is, if a competitor of the manufacturer lowers the price, the manufacturer could respond by adding another discount to the chain rather than by changing the list price and rendering the catalog obsolete. Price sheets that supplement a catalog can be changed frequently and at much less expense than to change an entire catalog.

Legality of Functional Discounts. The Robinson-Patman Act, passed in 1936 in the depths of the depression, attempts to limit the circumstances under which a seller can offer goods to different buyers at different prices. However, since the act does not specifically mention the functional discount, its legal status has always been somewhat uncertain. In interpreting the Robinson-Patman Act, the courts have been reluctant to require manufacturers to prove that functional discounts are related to the performance of marketing services. In fact the silence of the courts gives tacit approval to the functional discount. E. T. Grether writes:[4]

> Although the absence of specific reference to functional discounts did leave an important gap in the Robinson-Patman Act, silence in this instance is generally assumed to reflect approval.

Much of the dilemma relating to functional discounts and the Robinson-Patman Act is due to the structure and relationship of the various institutions within the marketing channel. Many manufacturers have dual distribution systems, meaning that they distribute their product through their own wholly owned outlets and at the same time distribute their products through independent wholesalers and retailers. The courts evidently believe these conflicting channel relationships are too complex to be solved by a narrow interpretation outlawing the functional discount. Therefore the Federal Trade Commission and the courts have taken the position that as long as various trade discounts are offered to buyers of the same class, the discounts are legal.

Quantity Discounts

Quantity discounts are a second defense available to the seller who is accused of discriminatory pricing. As the name implies, this is a reduction in price accorded

[4]E. T. Grether, *Marketing and Public Policy* (Englewood Cliffs, N.J.: Prentice-Hall, Inc., 1966), p. 66.

to those who buy in large quantities. This common practice is predicated on the economic fact that large orders produce lower unit costs for the manufacturer. Lower unit costs may be the result of savings in manufacturing, selling, or delivery. To the extent that a large order permits a manufacturer to achieve lower production costs, a lower price may be offered to the large buyer through the mechanism of a quantity discount, but the magnitude of the discount is limited to no more than the provable cost savings that are involved.

Suppose a retailer of ties is offered the following set of price terms:

1 dozen to 3 dozen ties—$24 a dozen
4 dozen to 10 dozen ties—$20 a dozen
11 dozen to 25 dozen ties—$18 a dozen

The lower quoted prices may be justified because of the lower selling costs involved when 4 dozen or more ties are purchased. It may also be justified because of lower packaging, delivery, and billing costs. Moreover the manufacturer may save on production costs as well, although this is unlikely.

Quantity discounts are sometimes cumulative in nature, that is a retailer obtains a discount if the total purchase exceeds a predetermined volume. These discounts encourage a buyer to concentrate purchases with a single manufacturer. Again, cumulative discounts are justified because a manufacturer claims the order lowers costs. The manufacturer then may pass on this savings in cost through the mechanism of a discount.

Legality of Quantity Discounts. The quantity discount is clearly influenced by the Robinson-Patman Act. This act makes it illegal to offer a quantity discount that is not solidly based on differences in costs of manufacture, selling costs, or delivery costs as the direct result of the larger order. Furthermore, the burden of proof rests on the seller of the merchandise to substantiate the quantity discounts. The Federal Trade Commission needs to show only that a quantity discount schedule exists. The manufacturer then must prove the discount schedule is based on cost differentials. The purpose of the act is to prevent one buyer from securing an unfair competitive advantage over another simply for buying in larger quantities.

There remains considerable confusion as to the interpretation and effect of the Robinson-Patman Act. Some critics point out that the economy is not more competitive because of the law. In fact they suggest the act keeps prices higher than they would normally be because it lessens tough (ruthless?) price competition. Furthermore, small retailers, whom the act was intended to protect, report very little advantage. Nearly everyone agrees that the law is controversial and is the subject of misunderstanding and misinterpretation.

Seasonal Discounts

Seasonal discounts can be earned by retailers for ordering merchandise in the "off season." That is to say, retailers may be given a seasonal discount if they order and receive Christmas merchandise for early summer delivery rather than the customary late summer or early fall delivery. Inasmuch as the retailer receives the merchandise at an earlier than normal date, the retailer should be aware of additional costs. He or she must store the merchandise in costly warehousing space; the investment capital is tied up in inventory for a longer period; and the risks inherent in ownership must be borne, such as market shifts, spoilage, shrinkage, and fire. Unless the seasonal discount is larger than the extra costs incurred, it will not pay the retailer to accept the seasonal discount.

It is easy to see the advantages accruing to the manufacturer when offering a seasonal discount. First, the manufacturer is able to schedule operations over a long period of time and avoid the pitfall of interrupted manufacture. It is to the manufacturer's advantage to operate his plant the entire year at a stable level of production rather than to operate at peak production part of the time and be closed at other periods. For one thing, the same number of employees can be maintained throughout the year, rather than to have a skeleton staff and recruit extra help for the peak periods. Manufacturers also reduce storage costs if they sell their merchandise early. Furthermore, seasonal discounts permit the manufacturer to minimize the risk of an adverse price change. After merchandise has been sold it is the responsibility of the buyer to bear the risk of all price movements.

The Robinson-Patman Act does not disallow the seasonal discount. It is permissible provided comparable buyers are offered the same discount for similar periods.

Promotional Discounts

Retailers often perform advertising or promotional services for a manufacturer. A retailer may advertise one of the manufacturer's brands in the local newspaper or on television, or may build an island display in the store or feature the manufacturer's product in one of the windows. If the retailer does this, he or she is performing part of the advertising function for the manufacturer and is given an advertising discount. It is clear that both the retailer and the manufacturer gain when merchandise is promoted. A promotional discount is simply a monetary acknowledgement of the value of a given bit of advertising or promotion.

Legal Status of Promotional Discounts. This discount also comes under the Robinson-Patman Act. A supplier may not offer promotional service to one retailer without offering similar allowances to all others on proportionally equal terms. The portion of the Robinson-Patman Act that alludes to promotional allowances has been particularly difficult to interpret. However, it seems to mean that if a supplier gives a 3 percent discount to a buyer of $100,000 worth of merchandise as a promotional allowance, 3 percent must be offered to the buyer of a $1,000 merchandise shipment. Likewise a 5-cent per case allowance must be given to those who purchase 100,000 cases or 1,000 cases. The courts have interpreted this to mean equal percentages to all retailers, or equal dollar allowances on a unit basis.

Cash Discounts

The cash discount is frequently thought of as a prompt paying discount. A vendor permits a reduction in the amount to be paid if it is paid prior to the date due.

A common cash discount is one written as 2/10, n/30. Assume the date of the invoice is October 22 and the amount is $100. How do we interpret the discount?

1. First, the customer has 10 days to take advantage of the discount; in this case, the latest date for the discount is November 1 (nine days left in October plus one in November).
2. If the invoice is not paid within the discount period, the retailer has an additional 20 days to pay the full price. In the example, $100 must be paid by November 21.
3. If the retailer pays the invoice within the prescribed 10 day limit, he or she is entitled to a 2 percent cash discount. In this example, $100 − $2 = $98.

The 2 percent cash discount does not seem like much until it is translated into its equivalent annual interest rate. A retailer who neglects to take advantage of a discount in a 2/10, n/30 situation actually is paying the equivalent of a 36 percent per year interest rate for using the supplier's capital for 20 days.[5]

Although the cash discount is a common one and is intended to encourage early payment, there are other cash discount practices that encourage delayed payment. Some of the more common cash discount quotations are:

1. E. O. M. (End of month)
2. M. O. M. (Middle of month)
3. R. O. G. (Receipt of goods)
4. Extra
5. Anticipation

E. O. M. (End of Month) Datings. Suppose a retailer purchases merchandise with an invoice price of $680.90, dated March 7, 1975, and bearing terms of 6/10 E. O. M. A 6 percent cash discount will be allowed provided the retailer remits the balance within the prescribed time period. E. O. M. datings assume the invoice is dated at the end of the month, and so the retailer has 10 additional days to take advantage of the discount. In this example, the invoice is dated March 7, so the assumption is that it is equivalent to March 31. We now take the 10 days, and the last date for the 6 percent cash discount is April 10.

Invoices dated on the 25th of the month or later customarily are treated as if dated on the first of the next month. Suppose we consider an invoice of $700 and it is dated March 26, 1975 with terms of 6/10 E. O. M. In this case, the invoice date is assumed to be April 1, since the actual date is after March 25. Since the date is April 1, we go to the end of that month before beginning our count of 10 days. Thus, this retailer has until May 10 to take advantage of the 6 percent cash discount of $42.

[5]To determine the true annual interest, calculate the number of days that the retailer is using the supplier's capital. In this case, it is 20 days. Divide the 20 into a 360-day year, which gives the number of time periods in a business year. In this case there would be 18. Multiply the 18 by the 2 percent cost of capital to obtain the true annual interest rate.

It is always to the retailer's advantage to plan purchases at the end of the month so they are dated the 25th or later. Let us examine two examples:

Example 1: $700 invoice dated March 24, 6 percent E. O. M.
Discount period expires April 10.
Example 2: $700 invoice dated March 25, 6 percent E. O. M.
Discount period expires May 10.

One can see that the retailer in Example 2 has the use of the $700 for 30 days longer than the retailer in Example 1. This can be converted to a 72 percent equivalent interest rate (6 percent for one month = 72 percent for 12 months).

M. O. M. (Middle of Month) Datings. In this dating, all invoices dated from the last of the month through the 15th of the month must be paid by the 25th of the month in order to take advantage of the 10-day discount period. All invoices dated from the 16th of the month through the end of the month must be paid by the 10th of the next month in order to take advantage of the cash discount. Here are some examples:

Assume in all cases an invoice of $700 with 6/10 M. O. M. datings.

Invoice Date	*Final Date to Take Cash Discount*
March 1	March 25
March 9	March 25
March 14	March 25
March 15	March 25
March 16	April 10
March 18	April 10
March 25	April 10
March 30	April 10
March 31	April 10

R. O. G. (Receipt of Goods) Datings. Some retailers receive terms with R. O. G. datings. That means the retailer does not have to pay the invoice until after receiving the goods. Consider this example:

A retailer purchases $1,000 worth of merchandise on June 21, 1975 with terms of 2/10, n/30, R. O. G. Suppose the merchandise is not received until September 5. The retailer would then remit $980 by September 15 to take advantage of the discount, or $1,000 by October 5.

The advantage of this dating is that the retailer does not pay for the merchandise until after receiving it.

Extra Datings. Some retailers receive terms allowing extra time to take advantage of the cash discount. Consider the following:

2/10, 60x, n90—invoice dated February 11.

Normally the cash discount must be taken by February 21, but the retailer is given 60 extra days to take advantage of the discount period. In this case, if payment is received by April 22, the retailer can take the discount. This is computed as follows:

Original invoice date February 11.
10-day discount period February 21.

February	7 days	→ "FREE" Days
March	31 days	
April	22 days	
Total	60 days	

Last date for discount April 22.

Extra datings are given to encourage purchasing in advance of the normal buying season; the practice bears on relationship to prompt payment.

Anticipation. Anticipation permits a retailer to pay the invoice in advance of the last date of the discount period and be rewarded with a further price reduction. A supplier who offers anticipation offers a lower selling price to the retailer. Let us look at an example:

A retailer purchases merchandise worth $1,000 dated March 27, with terms of 6/10 E. O. M. with 6 percent anticipation allowed.

With this dating, the cash discount may be taken through May 10. However, if the invoice is paid prior to May 10, the retailer would be entitled to a 6 percent interest for the number of days the invoice was prepaid. In this case, if the bill is paid on April 10, the retailer would be entitled to 30 days of anticipation. This is computed as follows:

$$30/360 \times 6\% \text{ or } ½ \text{ of } 1\%.$$

On April 10, the retailer would first deduct the 6 percent cash discount: that is, 6 percent (1,000) or $1,000 − 60 = $940. On the $940, the retailer is entitled to one-half of 1 percent anticipation. So, .005 ($940) = $935.30. The retailer would remit $935.30 if the invoice was paid on April 10.

Whenever computing anticipation, a retailer must remember:

1. to deduct cash discount before taking anticipation;
2. anticipation is allowed for the number of days in which the discount is paid in advance;
3. anticipation is assumed to be 6 percent unless stated otherwise.

Shipping Terms

Shipping terms are also important in considering the price offers of respective vendors. They are important because they specify whether the seller or the buyer will pay the freight charges and who is obligated to file claims in case the merchandise is damaged or lost in transit. F. O. B. (free on board) origin is the most common of all the shipping terms. At the time the supplier delivers the merchandise to the carrier, title passes to the retailer, and the retailer is liable for the payment of the freight charge or for making adjustment claims.

A more favorable shipping term for a retailer is F. O. B. destination. In this instance the seller of the merchandise pays the freight to the point of destination, which may be the retailer's warehouse. Title does not pass until the merchandise reaches its destination. Therefore the seller (supplier) is responsible for filing a claim against the carrier in case the merchandise is damaged in transit.

There are other shipping terms that are occasionally used. In most cases they merely alter the liability of one party or the other. An example is F. O. B. origin, freight allowed. In this case, the seller of the merchandise agrees to be liable for the freight charges, so in that respect, it is as advantageous for the retailer as F. O. B. destination. However, title passes to the retailer at the point of origin; therefore if anything happens to the goods in transit, the retailer files the claim.

In other cases, freight costs are paid to the shipper when the goods are placed on board. The actual liability can be assumed by either the seller or the retailer, or perhaps shared by both. In any case the retailer is interested in two things: (1) the terms which give the lowest freight charges, and (2) who is responsible for filing a claim in case the goods are damaged in transit. The actual terms are the result of negotiations between the seller of the goods and the retailer.

Additional Terms. There are times when retailers take physical possession of merchandise without taking title. The major advantages to retailers are that they have no obligation to pay for the merchandise until it is sold and they do not bear the risks that are inherent in ownership. One of the principal methods available to retailers is buying on consignment, in which a supplier sends merchandise to a retailer but does not transfer its title. Because the supplier is the owner, the supplier normally sets the selling price and makes the decision on whether it should be sold for cash or credit. The retailer remits the proceeds after the goods are sold, but first the retailer deducts a commission for the role played. In this instance, the retailer is only the agent for the supplier. The advantages to the retailer of consignment buying are (1) no investment by the retailer in inventory, (2) no risk for the retailer in case the goods cannot be sold, and (3) the retailer earns an income for selling services at a minimum of investment risk.

Sometimes a retailer has goods shipped with an option to buy. This is known as buying on approval. The title to the goods remains with the seller until such time as the retailer agrees to purchase them. However, the retailer must secure title to the goods before selling them to customers. The advantage of this method of buying is the right of inspecting the merchandise at the retailer's place of business before actually completing the transfer of title. Furthermore, it enables the retailer to postpone buying the merchandise until after the goods are in his or her possession.

A retailer who buys on memorandum assumes title to the merchandise as he or she would in normal cases. However, the retailer has the right to return for full credit any merchandise that cannot be sold. In this case, the retailer need not worry about the risk of stocking unsalable merchandise. This method of buying is more common when the merchandise is expensive, such as furs and jewelry.

The Robinson-Patman Act and the Retailer

Earlier we discussed the purpose of the Robinson-Patman Act and indicated that it often severely limits the freedom of business people in pricing practices. The major sections of the act apply to those who supply the retailer. In most instances, if a retailer is involved in price discrimination, he or she is on the receiving end. If the retailer is less powerful than the supplier, there often is little the retailer can do about it except to turn to alternate suppliers or counteract the supplier's power through joint buying.

There is only one section of the Robinson-Patman Act that applies to the buyer rather than the seller, but it is a very important section to retailers. Section 2 (f) declares that it is unlawful for a buyer "knowingly to induce or receive a discrimination in price" that is illegal. This part of the act has been roundly criticized because it exposes the strong retailer to the risk of bargaining too hard for the lowest possible price. The Robinson-Patman Act more than any other has been criticized for protecting competitors rather than protecting competition. Critics argue that competition—and thus the consumer—is best protected when business buyers are free to drive the hardest possible bargains in negotiations with their suppliers.

Buyers cannot easily avoid problems by shrugging their shoulders and saying, "we didn't know we were pushing for a discriminatorily low price," because the term "knowingly" in Section 2 (f) is generally interpreted as meaning either "knows" or "has an obligation to know." In one celebrated case, a Portland, Oregon, operator of 13 supermarkets was held to have illegally obtained promotional allowances from his suppliers. More specifically, he collected $350 from each supplier of products that would be featured in a book of coupons available to shoppers. Each page contained a coupon that entitled the customer to buy the featured product at a reduced price. The fact that the retailer had substantial market power was sufficient for the court to decide that enough pressure was exerted on the suppliers so that Section 2 (f) was violated.[6]

RECEIVING THE MERCHANDISE

The buying process is not completed until the goods are in the store and made ready for sale. At that point a number of things must be done. First, physical provisions must be made to receive the merchandise, which must be inspected for damage, and checked against the buying order to ascertain the accuracy of the shipment. If everything is correct, the merchandise is marked and moved to a storage area near the selling floor. The accounting department is notified of the receipt of the merchandise, and the invoice is paid.

The extent of the physical space needed to accomplish the receipt of the mer-

[6]*Fred Meyer, Inc., F.T.C.* (U.S. Supreme Court, 1968).

chandise varies with the size of the store. Some small stores receive all the merchandise through the front door, while in other cases elaborate loading docks are available.

Checking the Merchandise

The first thing one must do when the merchandise arrives is to check its physical condition. Sometimes this can be done without opening the shipment, but in other cases the actual packages have to be opened. The retailer should always notify the carrier if the merchandise arrives damaged because it may be necessary to file formal claim charges; whenever possible, the notice should be given to the shipper's employee before he leaves the receiving dock. If the title to the merchandise remains with the supplier, the supplier should be notified in order to file the claim against the carrier. Other things to do before the carrier leaves are: (1) make certain the merchandise is the same as described on the bill, (2) inspect the freight charges, (3) sign the carrier's receipt, and (4) mark the shipment with a receiving number.

The second major step is to open the merchandise and check to see if it is the quantity ordered. There are two principal ways to do this: (1) the direct check, and (2) the blind check. The direct check is to take the buying order, which lists all the items ordered, and check each off as it is counted. The advantage of this method is that any discrepancy can be quickly noted and steps immediately taken to correct the error. However, this is a time-consuming practice, and thus a costly one. The blind check is simply one in which merchandise is listed as to type but no quantities are noted. The inspector must physically count the items and record them; the count is then compared with the number that was ordered. This eliminates the danger of a superficial check as in the case of a direct check. The blind check is the best method of maintaining control of the merchandise and the invoices that account for it.

The quality of the merchandise is the responsibility of the buyer, and he or she assumes this responsibility whenever it is feasible for the buyer to check the merchandise.

Marking the Merchandise

The merchandise is then marked. This means that it is ticketed with a tag showing the price and other information. In the case of food products, the price is written on the merchandise itself. Marking the price on the merchandise has these advantages:

1. Customers expect to see price tags on merchandise because it aids them in making their selections.
2. It helps the salesperson who needs to know the price of an item if he or she wishes to complete the sale.
3. It aids the department in taking physical inventory.
4. It is useful information for determining the profitability of the department.

The ticket usually carries more information than just price. It may include the date in which it was put into stock, the name of the department, the source from whom it was purchased, and its style, size, and color. Almost any kind of useful information is included on the ticket.

With the goods on the selling floor, the buying process has ended.

SUMMARY

Once the retailer has decided upon the magnitude and composition of the merchandise budget and has made critical decisions concerning the width and depth of his or her assortment, the merchandise must be bought. It is normal for a retailer to buy from several suppliers, which become key resources, even though this usually increases the retailer's buying expenses.

Retailers may obtain their stock by manufacturing it themselves. However, most retailers are reluctant to do so because they lack interest in manufacturing; they lack manufacturing know-how; they have too little capital for such a venture; or they believe their capital would be more productive if invested in retailing facilities and inventory.

Most retailers purchase their assortment from others—usually manufacturers or wholesalers—because of the perishability of the product, the easy availability of the supplier, the need for quick delivery, and the quantity of goods to be ordered.

Retailers make initial contact with suppliers by mail, telephone, through salesmen's calls, through visits to the market, or through buying organizations. Each has its advantages, and the individual retailer makes contact with his or her resources in the way most appropriate to his or her operation.

Before retailers complete their purchases, they negotiate price and other terms of trade. It is here that datings, discounts, and other terms of trade become important. A retailer must understand the structure of prices to compare those offered by competing vendors.

The principal types of discounts are functional, quantity, seasonal, and cash. The setting of discounts is limited by the Robinson-Patman Act to insure that price discrimination may occur under limited circumstances.

Transportation costs are also important to the retailer. In some cases the vendor pays the freight charges, and in other instances it is the responsibility of the retailer. Moreover the shipping terms indicate the time that title passes to the retailer. This is important in cases where the goods are damaged or lost in transit, because the person holding title to the goods is the one who initiates complaints and possible legal action.

The buying process is not completed until the goods are in the store and ready for sale. They must be checked as they are received to ascertain the accuracy of the shipment and the condition of the merchandise. They are then marked or ticketed with tags indicating price and other desirable information. It is at this point that the buying process has ended.

QUESTIONS FOR DISCUSSION

1. What is a channel of distribution, and what kinds of middlemen are found in the channel?
2. How does a rack jobber help a retailer?
3. How may wholesalers aid small retailers? Do you think their aid has been effective?
4. Why are fashion goods generally purchased direct from their manufacturers?
5. What is a voluntary cooperative chain? Discuss the role of the wholesaler in this venture.
6. Discuss the general topic of making contact with the marketplace. That is, how does a retailer get into the negotiating stage with a supplier?
7. What does the Robinson-Patman Act say about functional discounts, and how have the courts interpreted these discounts?
8. Discuss the legality of quantity discounts under the Robinson-Patman Act.
9. Discuss the general topic of shipping terms and indicate why these terms are important to a buyer.
10. What are the advantages and limitations of the direct check and the blind check in receiving merchandise?

11 PRICING POLICIES AND PRACTICES

A Weight Watchers outlet in Philadelphia carefully abided by the pricing guidelines of its supplier, even though the manager believes that he could have earned a higher profit by charging higher prices on such things as membership fees, class tuition, scales, and other products. The owner argued that local conditions would have permitted higher prices than were allowed by Weight Watchers International, the supplier. The Philadelphia company sued International for $15 million damages because the latter "contracted, combined, and conspired in restraint of trade and commerce among the several states in violation of Section One of the Sherman Act."

Only a year before the energy shortage of 1973, a Westland, Michigan, retailer cut the price of gasoline to 6.9¢ a gallon in an attempt to keep the price a penny a gallon below a rival's price. The "war" stopped only when the local police began ticketing motorists who were blocking the streets while waiting in line to fill their tanks.

In every state except Ohio, some sort of law has prevented retail druggists from advertising or promoting pharmaceuticals on the basis of price. In some instances listing or advertising the price of specific prescriptions is illegal, and in other states using such expressions as "discount" or "cut-rate" is prohibited. In some states—Florida, New Jersey, and Illinois are examples—the laws have been challenged with varying results. Such laws profoundly affect a retailer's pricing practices and are only remotely related to supply and demand.

A stationery store manager purchases pen and pencil sets for $5 and marks them to be sold at $10, suspecting that he will sell very few at such a high price. A few days later he re-marks them to be sold at $7.50, and posts a "Formerly $10" sign over them. The Federal Trade Commission's "Guides Against Deceptive Pricing" defines such behavior as deceptive because the bargain would not be a genuine one.

Retail food chains in almost every major city have had to decide whether prices should be uniform throughout their operating areas or should respond to neighborhood circumstances. Residents in low-income areas have been particularly sensitive to this issue and have sometimes argued that the prices they must pay are higher because they lack the mobility of those living in upper-income areas. The top managers in such chains have had to decide how much freedom they will give their managers; if they enforce a uniform pricing system, much of the basis for evaluating the store manager's ability to operate profitably has been lost.

One of the most important functions a retailer performs is to determine the prices that customers must pay for the goods and services they buy from him or her. The above examples suggest just how complicated this activity can be. The retailer must devote considerable time to interpreting those forces that will affect the prices of products, an activity that is vastly more complex than it may appear. It is true that prices have a lot to do with where supply and demand curves intersect, but the place of the intersection is not a "given" to the retailer. Retailers must attempt to discern what would happen to profits if they were to ask various prices for their products—surely not an easy task. Thus, it is more correct to say that retailers "administer" prices rather than "set" them; those forces over which they have little or no control establish prices while the retailer's task is to bring out the meaning of those forces.

The problem of arriving at the selling price for products and services cannot be dismissed with, "Oh, it's just a simple matter of supply and demand." While supply and demand are powerful determinants of price that cannot be ignored, they are neither simple to interpret nor are they the only variables that affect a retailer's pricing system.

DETERMINING GENERAL POLICY

Retailers generally set an overall policy governing the strategy they intend to follow in setting specific prices. This overall policy is also known as the general price policy. The major factors that determine a retailer's overall price policy are the target customers, the state of competition, and special circumstances.

The Target Customer and Income

When target customers are selected, the retailer has to a large extent determined the course of his or her general pricing strategy. A major characteristic distinguishing shoppers from each other is family income. Retailers are aware of this, and direct their merchandising activities to appeal to low-income receivers, moderate-income receivers, or high-income receivers. Seldom does a retailer appeal to all income levels at the same time, except in smaller towns where the limited size of the market does not permit more than one store.

Merchants directing attention to low-income customers in all probability feature low-priced goods. On the other hand, merchants who cater to the upper-income level feature merchandise of high quality, and it is necessarily high priced. The retailer responds to the market segment being served by pricing the merchandise appropriately.

Income is not the only variable in the buying decision, although it perhaps is the major force in determining any individual's standard of living. Consumer behavior is complex, and the role of the consumer is dependent upon such other factors as family influences, culture, reference groups, personality, attitudes, and motivations. Because of the complexity of consumer behavior, retailing is more of an art than a science. Nowhere is this more in evidence than in price determination.

Competition

Another factor influencing a store's overall price policy is the state of competition existing for a particular store. A retailer who appeals to the upper five percent of all income receivers clearly is not in competition with retailers who are appealing to customers of the lower five percent. However, each retailer who has identified the target customer faces other retailers who are appealing to the same customer. These retailers are competitors.

Retailers who direct their merchandising attention to the same category of customers are likely to have the same attitude on various pricing strategies. Rival stores tend to have similar prices, although they are not necessarily equal. Some retailers offer more services such as credit, delivery, and return privileges. These extra services are reflected in higher prices in those stores who offer them.

Special Circumstances

Special circumstances may also generate an effect on a store's overall price level. For example, some housewives willingly pay a premium price for foods when they are purchased late at night, on Sundays, or holidays. The convenience food store does a lively business during those hours that most supermarkets are closed. In this case, a higher overall price policy reflects the convenience of odd-hour shopping.

A retailer who enjoys a near-monopolistic position is one whose prices are likely to be higher than under competitive conditions. An example is the theaters that charge high prices for popcorn because they have no competition. Patrons who attend the theaters do have the alternative of bringing their own popcorn with them—an alternative seldom followed. Or those who buy gas, oil, or other automotive needs on a turnpike may have to pay slightly more than at other outlets simply because the retailer has a quasi-monopoly location.

Even though pockets of monopoly do exist here and there, most retailers have fierce competition and their prices reflect this fact. A characteristic of the American economy is the many alternatives available to each shopper to obtain the goods which are satisfying, particularly at the retail level. Most retailers realize the options a shopper generally has to purchase identical merchandise. This fact is considered by a retailer in setting prices. Also, the federal government helps to keep the retailing industry competitive through the enforcement of antitrust laws.

PRICING GOALS

One of the first decisions must be just how large a role price will play in a retailer's competitive arsenal. There are many instances in which price decisions are rather easy to make or are made by others in the marketing channel. Decision making with respect to price may be unimportant when (1) legally binding price decisions made by the supplier can be imposed on the retailer, (2) consumers hold strong expectations about the "proper" price of a product and are intolerant of any substantial deviations, (3) suppliers have suggested a price at which their products can be resold at a profit and the retailer has no reason to believe otherwise, (4) price is an unimportant element in the marketing mix to the customer whose allegiance would not be significantly affected by a price reduction, and (5) a price increase would not be followed by other retailers but a price cut would instantly be matched, and thus its impact would be neutralized. In these cases, the retailer may elect to use price only as a passive competitive weapon. Location, quality of product, service to the customer, delivery, and other elements of the marketing mix assume much more importance in determining customer patronage.

On the other hand, aggressive retailers may elect not to follow the leadership of either suppliers or other retailers; they may choose to decide about prices themselves rather than to relinquish the task to others. It should be noted that the decision to be active or passive with respect to pricing is a conscious decision. Those retailers that decide to be price leaders may be expected to turn increasingly to more sophisticated tools in the future. As we learn more about such things as forecasting demand, probability theory, modeling competitive reaction to price changes, fixed cost allocation, and inventory cost reduction, we can expect each retailer to give more attention to his or her own pricing problems and less attention to following blindly the practices of other retailers. Larger retailers already do so.

In those firms where management has decided to pursue an aggressive pricing policy, the major goals that influence pricing practices are:

1. Profit maximization.
2. Target return.
3. Nonprofit goals.

Profit Maximization

This is a worthy goal, but it is difficult for a retailer to know when it has been achieved. Economic theory tells us that an entrepreneur expends money until it matches dollar revenue. That point in a business where marginal cost equals marginal revenue is the most profitable of all possible points. The firm that is maximizing its profits actually has made a very large number of maximizing-type decisions. In a department store it means that top management has allocated exactly the right floor space among the various departments, that the advertising manager not only has been accorded the "right" budget but has spent it properly among the media, that the fur department manager has the right types of fur coats in inventory and has hired neither too many nor too few salespeople, and that everything else has been done exactly right. No institution is so perfect, of course, but this does not lessen the value of profit maximizing as a goal. As retailers experiment more with the way cost expenditures affect output, greater efficiency is achieved and profit maximization is more likely.

Target Returns

There are three types of target returns: (1) target returns on investment (ROI), (2) target returns on sales, and (3) profit stability. Some retailers specify a definite return on investment. Sears, Roebuck and Company has stipulated a desire for a return of 10 to 15 percent on its investment after taxes. On the other hand, many retailers specify a need to earn a profit expressed as a percentage of sales.

Nonprofit Goals

Still other retailers follow nonprofit objectives. These retailers are more interested in expansion, obtaining a certain share of the market, or in preserving the status quo. Retailers sometimes are empire builders and enjoy expanding their sales to "box car" figures even though profits lag behind.

PRICING METHODS

Every retailer must take in enough revenue to cover both the cost of merchandise sold and the expense involved in selling the goods. In the long run, the penalty for not generating sufficient revenue is failure. This simple statement about the relationship of revenue to costs does not mean, however, that costs can never exceed income for short time periods or that cost must be less than price on every item in the retailer's line. Indeed, there are times when total sales revenue may fall below aggregate store costs for weeks or even months at a time—general business conditions slump and so do retail sales; excavation takes place in front of a store and diverts pedestrian traffic; a heavy snowfall paralyzes the transit system; a seasonal lull depresses sales in a tourist town during the few weeks between the end of the winter vacationers and the first of the summer visitors; and many other factors may temporarily affect a retailer's revenue. There also are situations in which, sometimes even in the long run, the retailer cannot expect to sell specific items at prices that cover all costs—a retail druggist offers a well-known brand of toothpaste at a discounted price; a food store operator sells turkeys at cost or below at Thanksgiving time because others are doing so and housewives are watching the price-per-pound very carefully; and other examples suggest that not every item must return a profit to the retailer. So we return to the maxim: In the long run, the retailer must generate enough sales volume to cover the cost of goods sold, expenses, and sufficient profit to stay in business.

Retailers use two important techniques in setting specific prices. One is the percentage markup method and the other is the dollar margin method.

Percentage Markup Method

A *markup* is the amount a retailer adds to the invoice cost of merchandise to cover operating expenses, overhead, and profit. Markup is usually expressed as a percentage. Let us look at an example:

June Tee is a retailer of ladies' apparel, and she purchases 500 dresses of assorted fabric, color, style, and size for $15 each. She adds a markup to her invoice cost to cover such expenses as salaries, rent, light, telephone, advertising, and maintenance. Let us assume an extra $10 will cover all of Tee's expenses and afford her a modest profit. To summarize:

Invoice cost of merchandise	$15
Markup to cover expenses and profit	10
Selling price	$25

The markup may be expressed either in dollars or as a percentage of cost or selling price. In this example, it is either $10 or 40 percent $\left(\frac{\$10}{\$25}\right)$. We could say that Tee has added a 40 percent markup on selling price to cover her operating expenses and to yield a modest profit.

The Uniform Percentage Markup. A very popular pricing practice is the uniform percentage markup method, one in which a retailer seeks to achieve an *average markup* of 25 percent, 40 percent, or some other percentage. How does a retailer choose the uniform percentage markup? Normally the retailer examines past accounting records, assuming that historic profits have been satisfactory. Suppose these records indicate a 32 percent operating cost and a 4 percent net profit. In this case, the retailer might decide to choose a 36 percent markup and apply it to all items of the store's merchandise. However, the retailer would soon realize the mistake because a factor must be added to cover such retail reductions as shoplifting, price reductions, employee discounts, and shrinkage. (Shrinkage is a common retailing term which means that a product carried in stock diminishes in quantity. It covers such losses as breakage, spillage, and evaporation.) To determine the proper percentage to apply initially, the retailer would use the following formula:

$$\text{Initial markup} = \frac{\text{Maintained markup} + \text{Retail reductions}}{100\% + \text{Retail reductions}}$$

In our example, the retailer wishes to have a maintained markup of 36 percent (32 percent to cover expenses plus 4 percent profit). Suppose retail reductions are estimated to be 4 percent. Therefore:

$$\text{Initial markup} = \frac{36\% + 4\%}{100\% + 4\%} = \frac{40\%}{104\%} = 38.4\%$$

A retailer who uses a 38.4 percent initial markup would achieve a 36 percent maintained markup. Remember that the maintained markup is the gross margin on retail sales.

Other retailers may examine their records and decide on 20, 30, 40, or 50 percent, or some other higher or lower percentage, as their maintained markups. It is, however, not determined intuitively, but rather from experience as determined by examinations of the accounting records.

Even though a retailer decides to use a single (uniform) markup percentage (say 38.4), this percentage cannot be used on every item priced. Instead the retailer strives to maintain an average markup percentage of a given level. In any type of store, a retailer finds each item sold has its own markup. For example, *Progressive Grocer* states that a typical supermarket has a gross margin of 20.93 percent.[1] Yet the same supermarket has a different margin for soups and detergents (approximately 10 percent) and candies, gums, and nuts (25 percent). As a matter of fact, almost every product category in the supermarket has a different gross margin. Therefore a retailer cannot take a single percentage of gross margin and apply it to all products. What is true for the supermarket is not quite true for the department store because most of the latter's markups tend to be more nearly alike. However, even with the department store there is variation.

In other words, it is unlikely for any retailer to apply a single markup percentage to each and every item stocked. The major reasons are: (1) demand for all products is not identical, (2) competition affects the margin through the prices that must be set, (3) some goods require a higher margin to cover their costs because they require more handling, more warehousing, or more salesmanship. However, a retailer does attempt to have an average markup of a given percentage.

To illustrate, let us assume that a large supermarket operator wishes to earn a 19 percent gross margin, and to achieve it he intends to price every item he carries at invoice cost plus 19 percent markup on retail. He would soon find in the competitive world of food retailing that his prices on some items are higher than his competitors. Therefore he might sell only a few of those items. For example, if most supermarket retailers receive a 10 percent margin on detergents, how can any one retailer expect 19 percent? In other cases the supermarket retailer may be selling some items at a lower price than his competitors if he follows a single uniform markup of 19 percent. Housewares are an example. As we stated, a merchant cannot usually follow a single markup policy for each item stocked, but can strive for an average markup percentage of a given magnitude.

Alternatives to Single Markup Percentage. An alternative to a single markup policy is to classify merchandise into groups and use a different markup for each group. For example, a food market operator may divide total stock into the following: meat, produce, dairy, bakery, frozen foods, grocery, and household supplies. A single percentage markup might be used for each product group. This is unlikely because of the variance of factors involved within each product category. For example, the supermarket operator could break down household supplies into cleaning compounds, cleaning equipment, waxes and polishes, disinfectants, deodorizers, and shoe polishes. Each of these subcategories might have a different gross margin. Eventually, the retailer could subdivide the subcategories into smaller units and set a different markup for each one. Under household supplies, the cleaning compound subcategory could be further subdivided into scouring powders, window cleaners, bowl cleaners, drain cleaners, rug cleaners, dry cleaners, oven cleaners, metal polishes. If one carried this practice to its extreme, a retailer would be following an individual item percentage pricing policy. Some retailers such as supermarkets and discount houses do precisely this. The theory behind the policy is that a retailer maximizes over-

[1] "41st Annual Report of the Grocery Industry," *Progressive Grocer* (April 1974), p. 128.

all profit if each item sold is contributing its maximum gross margin. This is best achieved if each item's price is considered individually rather than to assume an average markup to cover a wide selection of merchandise. Furthermore, some items can be priced at cost or near it so as to build traffic.

Advantages of Percentage Markup Method. Retailers who advocate the use of the percentage markup method say it has the following advantages:

1. It is simple to understand, which makes it appealing and popular. This is especially true if a uniform percentage is used.
2. Retailers are accustomed to expressing their sales and expenses in percentage. The percentage markup policy is an extension of this, and therefore acceptable to retailers.
3. There is a common assumption that expenses vary directly with the retail price of merchandise. That means dollar expenses increase as the price of merchandise increases. The percentage markup policy automatically accommodates variations in expenses according to this principle. As an illustration, suppose a retailer applies a 40 percent markup on two goods. One is priced to sell at $10 and the other at $1. The first good provides $4 to cover expenses, while the lower-priced good has but 40¢; presumably the former incurs ten times as much expense as does the latter.
4. Some retailers believe the percentage markup policy aids them in their negotiations with suppliers. There is an implication that prices at the retail level are difficult to adjust. Therefore the retailer argues that the supplier should offer merchandise at a price enabling the retailer to maintain a customary markup percentage.
5. Some retailers believe the percentage markup policy can be justified because it is widely accepted as a fair basis for pricing. The retailer sets prices using a percentage rate that covers the retailer's expenses and a modest profit, both of which the general public usually accepts as necessary for a continuing business. During periods of rising prices, the retailer should not be blamed for the higher retail prices, it is argued, because the retailer maintains the same percentage rate of markup; the retailer is not exploiting the consumer when raising prices.

Limitations of Percentage Method. A serious limitation to the percentage markup policy is the fact that it encourages retailers to believe percentages are somehow virtuous in themselves. It embodies the suggestion that it is the price level that generates the profit. The department store has always supported and popularized the uniform markup percentage method. Inasmuch as department stores offer many services to their customers, the cost of maintaining them is covered by the markup. This preoccupation with the markup percentage price policy assumes that services attract customers more than do low prices, an assumption that is not borne out by the policies followed by mass merchandisers.

Mass Merchandisers and the Percentage Method. Mass merchandisers have certain common characteristics that identify them. First, they are hard buyers in that they must buy merchandise at the lowest possible cost in order to price it low. (This does not imply that mass merchandisers are more astute buyers than other retailers, only that mass merchandisers have to be cost conscious to an *n*th degree because as retailers they seek to price their merchandise at a low level.) Furthermore they usually limit their stock to fast-moving items, and thus they limit the number of markdowns they must take. The mass merchandiser strives for the lowest possible cost ratios by reducing some customer services, and in some instances eliminating them completely. Many mass merchandisers sell their stock for cash only, and except for consumer durables (refrigerators, washers, dryers, television sets) require the customer to carry home purchases, thus reducing both the financing and delivery functions and the costs they incur. The mass merchandiser does not rely on expensive fixtures, nor are the customers pampered with an abundance of sales help. On the contrary, the customer tends to wait on him- or herself, uses inexpensive fitting rooms, and is willing to take merchandise off pipe racks.

Because of hard buying policies and tight control over expenses, a mass merchandiser of consumer durables may operate within a markup range of 20 to 30 percent, in contrast to the 35 to 40 percent range of more traditional appliance retailers. The point to be made here about mass merchandisers is that services don't necessarily attract customers, as some retailers claim, more than low prices. However, there *are* customers who like services and are willing to pay for them through higher prices.

Markup Computations. A discussion of the percentage method is incomplete unless the "nitty-gritty" of markup computations is explained. There are two ways of computing the markup percentage:

1. One method is to express the dollar markup as a percentage of the cost of the merchandise. Assume the invoice cost of a dress is $15, and a dollar margin of $10 is added to the invoice cost to determine the selling price. Then:

$$\frac{\$10 \text{ (Dollar margin)}}{\$15 \text{ (Invoice cost)}} = 66\tfrac{2}{3} \text{ percent}$$

   This is identified as the markup on cost.

2. The second method expresses the dollar markup as a percentage of the selling price. In our example:

$$\frac{\$10 \text{ (Dollar margin)}}{\$25 \text{ (Selling price)}} = 40 \text{ percent}$$

   This method is customarily called a markup on retail and is the method most retailers use in expressing their markups. The reasons for this are discussed in Chapter 16 when the retail method of accounting is explained.

Changing Markups from Cost to Retail and Vice Versa. Markups can be converted from a markup on cost to a markup on retail without distorting the essential information. In the example we have used, the markup on cost of 66⅔ percent is equivalent to a 40 percent markup on retail. Both methods will yield the same dollar markups. However, one must apply the markup on cost to the cost of the merchandise, while the markup on retail is applied to the retail price. To demonstrate:

\$15.00	Cost of merchandise	\$25.00	Selling price
x .66⅔	Markup on cost	x .40	Markup on retail
\$10.00	Dollar markup	\$10.00	Dollar markup

There is a procedure for changing the markup percentage expressed either on cost or selling price to the other. The following two formulas are used.

1. $$\frac{\text{Markup on retail}}{100\% - \text{Markup on retail}} = \text{Markup on cost}$$

2. $$\frac{\text{Markup on cost}}{100\% + \text{Markup on cost}} = \text{Markup on retail}$$

Suppose that we wish to convert a 25 percent markup on retail to its corresponding markup on cost. We would use formula 1.

$$\frac{\text{Markup on retail}}{100\% - \text{Markup on retail}} = \text{Markup on cost}$$

Substituting,

$$\text{Markup on cost} = \frac{25\%}{100\% - 25\%} = \frac{25\%}{75\%} = 1/3 = 33\tfrac{1}{3}\%$$

Therefore, a 25% markup on retail = 33⅓% markup on cost.

Next, assume we wish to convert a 100 percent markup on cost to its equivalent markup on retail. Therefore, we use formula 2.

$$\frac{\text{Markup on cost}}{100\% + \text{Markup on cost}} = \text{Markup on retail}$$

Substituting

$$\text{Markup on retail} = \frac{100\%}{100\% + 100\%} = \frac{100}{200} = 1/2 = 50\%$$

A 100% markup on cost = a 50% markup on retail.

Table 11.1 shows equivalent markups on cost for a number of markups on retail.

Reason for Conversion. Generally speaking the need to convert arises when the retailer marks his or her price on the merchandise. Suppose a toy retailer re-

TABLE 11.1
Equivalent Markups

Markup on Retail	Markup on Cost
5 %	5.3%
10	11.1
15	17.7
16.6	20.0
20	25
23	30
25	33.3
28.5	40.0
30	42.8
33.3	50.0
35	53.9
40	66.6
45	81.8
50	100
60	150

ceives a shipment of dolls, and the merchant wishes to price them and put them out for sale. Let us assume the retailer desires a 40 percent markup on retail for a particular doll. That markup yields a price that is competitive with other retailers selling a similar item. Furthermore, this price gives sufficient margin to cover the costs of handling the item, and it yields a profit. Assume the invoice cost of the doll is \$8.90. In order to determine the desired dollar markup, the retailer must convert the 40 percent markup on retail to its corresponding markup on cost. In this example, it would be 66⅔ percent. The retailer now can compute the dollar markup and then determine the selling price.

$$\$8.90\ (66\tfrac{2}{3}\%) = \$5.93 \text{ markup}$$

then

$$\$8.90 + \$5.93 = \$14.83 \text{ selling price}$$

A selling price of \$14.83 gives the retailer the 40 percent markup on retail. You may wish to verify this by dividing the \$5.93 by \$14.83. In practice, it is not generally necessary to do the arithmetic to convert a desired markup on retail to its equivalent markup on cost since retailers usually have access to tables that provide such information. (Table 11.1 is an example.) Nonetheless, it is important to know how such tables are derived.

The Dollar Margin Method

An alternative to the percentage price policy is the dollar margin method of pricing. In this method the dollar markup for each item or for a group of items is determined after estimating the volume of sales a retailer is likely to experience at a corresponding schedule of prices. To illustrate this method of price determination, consider the following price schedule.

Sample Price	*Estimated Volume*
$5.00	100 items
4.75	150 items
4.50	200 items
4.25	250 items
4.00	300 items

If we assume the item under consideration has an invoice cost of $3, we can determine its profitability at all price levels.

Price	*Estimated Volume*	*Total Revenue*	*Total Invoice Cost*	*Gross Margin*
$5.00	100	$500	$300	$200
4.75	150	712.50	450	262.50
4.50	200	900	600	300
4.25	250	1,062.50	750	312.50
4.00	300	1,200	900	300

For this example, the retailer would select the $4.25 price because at that price level the largest total gross margin would be obtained. It is irrelevant that the percentage of markup is lower at $4.25 than it is for the following prices: $5.00, $4.75, and $4.50. Note that the retailer would not select the lower price of $4 either, because the increase in total revenue does not assure an increase in total gross margin. All of this assumes that other expenses would be the same, regardless of the number of units sold.

Retailers who follow the dollar margin price policy are not concerned with the theory that each item offered for sale must be profitable. These retailers recognize the fact that a specific item may be unprofitable from an accounting point of view. The item may be used as a traffic builder, with the profits being made on other items. Even though an item is unprofitable, it may be essential in the store's overall operation. Perhaps it can be likened to the blocker on a football team whose skill enables the running back to score the winning touchdown. The leading practitioners of the dollar margin price policy method are supermarkets and discount houses. Generally speaking, retailers who use the dollar gross margin method are oriented to high turnovers and volume selling.

PRICING STRATEGIES

Regardless of whether a retailer uses the percentage markup policy or the dollar margin method, he or she may employ common strategies and tactics. These pricing strategies are leader pricing, bait and switch pricing, odd prices, multiple unit pricing, price lining, one-price policy, and variable pricing. Let us examine each more closely.

Leader Pricing

A leader pricing strategy is one in which the retailer sells key items in the line at less than their usual margins, in the hope that customers who are attracted by the low price will purchase other products that carry a higher margin. For the practice to succeed, the products selected must be those that customers quickly recognize as a bargain. For example, an item that is customarily priced at $1 may be recognized as a bargain if it is priced at 79¢. Normally the products chosen for a price leadership role are convenience goods that are purchased frequently, since customers are more likely to be alert to their customary price.

There are two kinds of leader prices. First, there are those products priced lower than their cost. These are called "loss leaders," and their name clearly defines their nature. A second type of leader pricing is the one used to price goods below their customary prices but higher than their costs. The second yields a small profit but one that is less than normal for such an item. E. T. Grether points out that loss leader selling is a promotional technique employed by retailers who sell many different kinds of products.[2] It is designed to bring in customers who will also buy other merchandise priced at normal markups. Grether also states that loss leader pricing hits sharply at those competitors who sell a single product or at best have narrow assortments. National brands are frequently featured as loss leaders because they build store traffic, and customers are more aware of their "normal" price.

Criticism of Loss Leader Pricing. Many people have criticized loss leader pricing on the grounds that it is an unfair trade practice and that the intent is to destroy competition. The validity of this criticism has been accepted by at least thirty states that have passed statutes limiting the price cutting freedom of retailers. The intent of these laws is to prevent what some argue is unfair price competition by setting a floor below which a retailer may not lower prices. The exact nature of the laws varies among the states, but generally they are of two sorts. In some states a retailer may not sell at less than unit invoice costs; in other states cost is defined as invoice cost plus a small markup (generally between 4 and 12 percent) to cover expenses. Some states permit exceptions to the unfair trade laws by allowing more extensive

[2]E. T. Grether, *Marketing and Public Policy* (Englewood Cliffs, N.J.: Prentice-Hall, Inc., 1966), p. 74.

price cuts if goods are priced to meet the legal prices of another retailer or to sell damaged or aged merchandise, even though the new price is below costs.

Bait and Switch Pricing

"Bait and switch" is a form of pricing that is ethically and morally wrong. Bait pricing, as the name implies, is to attract customers into a store by advertising an item at a very low bargain price. When the customer comes into the store, the advertised merchandise either is not available or the salesclerk convinces the customer that a much better substitute is available. For example, an appliance store may advertise a branded refrigerator at a price well below its normal market price. When the customer seeks to purchase the item, he or she is informed that this brand of refrigerator is sold out or does not meet the standards attributed to it by its advertising. The customer who has accepted the "bait" will then have his or her attention switched to another brand at a considerably higher price and margin. It is hoped that the customer will purchase the substitute merchandise.

In most cases, the bait pricers have no intention of selling any item that is bait priced. Of course, this practice is outright deception. Customers who spot bait pricing tactics should report them immediately to their local Better Business Bureau, a group seeking to raise the standards of practice in the industry, or to the Federal Trade Commission, which also seeks to eliminate such deceptive practices.

Odd Prices

Another common retailer practice is to select odd prices at which to sell products. Such amounts as 66¢, 88¢, 99¢, or even $69.99 are consciously picked more often than one would normally expect. Indeed, the number "9" is used more often by some retailers for the ending digit than any other number. (See Figure 11.1.) In one food retailer's newspaper advertisement, 32 of the 51 items ended with a 9. Among the explanations for the "9" phenomenon is that it attracts the attention of the customer—probably untrue if the practice is widespread; customers perceive a $1.99 price to be substantially lower than a $2 price; it forces the salesperson to use the cash register to obtain change, thus lessening the likelihood of theft; and it has the historic explanation that the amount of the sale plus the state tax added up to an exact amount. (There was a time when state retailer occupation sales taxes were commonly one percent, so a price of 99¢ plus tax made an even dollar sale. This explanation, of course, encourages the salesperson *not* to use a cash register.)

Multiple Unit Pricing

A retailer's version of the quantity discount is multiple unit pricing. That is, a retailer sells one item at a particular price, but if customers purchase two units, they obtain a lower unit price. For example, a 16-ounce can of cranberry sauce is priced at 29¢, or two cans for 57¢. American customers are conditioned to expect lower prices if they purchase in large quantities. Thus, a retailer may stimulate sales through this method of pricing. Supermarkets use multiple unit pricing to

FIGURE 11.1

Prices for items usually end in odd numbers—most often nine

Source: *Chain Store Age, Executives' Edition.*

a marked degree, especially for their canned goods, frozen foods, and bottled foods. Whenever supermarket operators use this method of pricing, they experience a decline in the percentage of gross margin, but have a larger sales volume, and to them this is the significant factor. Presumably the costs will remain the same, and volume selling increases net profit. (See Figure 11.2.)

Price Lining

Many retailers practice price lining. A store may appeal to one general segment of the market that has substantially the same price preference. The retailer then selects three price ranges for its merchandise which is attractive to that group. To illustrate, a retailer of men's shoes sells his entire stock at the following prices: $14.99, $17.99, and $19.99. No shoes are sold at any other prices. There are definite advantages to price lining for both the customer and the retailer. The customer is helped because the confusion of many price alternatives is avoided. Moreover salesclerks tend to answer fewer questions regarding the quality of merchandise

FIGURE 11.2
One of the first one-cent sales was held in 1918 by Schlegal Drugstore in Davenport, Iowa

Source: Rexall Drug Company, St. Louis, Missouri.

when there are noticeable price differences. And salespeople are aided because they do not have to learn the prices of many lines, thus speeding purchase transactions. For the retailer, the most important advantage is the simplification of the buying process. That is, the retailer can select merchandise that fits into the chosen price lines and reject all other merchandise. It is important to note that the usual buying practice is reversed by the retailer who practices price line merchandising. In a sense, he or she is engaged in inverted pricing, meaning that the retailer identifies the retail prices at which to sell the merchandise and then seeks out suppliers whose wholesale prices are low enough to allow profitable sales at the chosen retail prices. If the retailer sells women's dresses price lined at $29.95 and must have a one-third markup on selling price, a supplier must sell dresses to the retailer for $20. This places a very strict limit on the number of suppliers with whom the retailer must deal. Note that the retailer does *not* go on a buying trip in which he or she indiscriminately talks with suppliers who have merchandise at various prices to sell. To the price lining retailer, the costs of the goods sold does not determine selling price; rather, the retail selling price determines what will be purchased.

Those who engage in price lining face certain difficulties. The principal one is the gap it leaves in the price alternatives to the customer. This is only a disadvantage when the lines are improperly chosen by the retailer. Effective price lining does not allow such large gaps in the lines that cause customers to be dissatisfied.

Another problem is the price lining policy of a competitor. It is difficult to maintain a price line if a competitor establishes a lower price line, and if customers perceive the merchandise as being of identical quality.

A third difficulty is in maintaining price lines during periods of rising costs. One solution is to eliminate the lowest price line and add another line at the top level.

One-Price Policy

Most Americans are accustomed to entering a store and purchasing the merchandise at the price marked on it. A one-price policy means that a product is priced the same for any and all who seek to buy the item at a particular time. (See Figure 11.3.) Consequently, the retailer and the customer never bargain over the price. The retailer makes the price decision determination before the customer arrives on the scene, and if the price is wrong the retailer suffers the consequences of poor judgment. The major advantage of a one-price policy is that it vastly speeds

FIGURE 11.3

Tags, placed conspicuously on the sleeve of each garment, state the price for anyone who wishes to buy the article

Source: Pint Size Jrs., Chicago, Illinois.

up the transaction, since only the customer must decide whether or not to complete the sale. Even before the customer entered the store, the retailer decided to sell the goods at a specific price. A one-price policy also permits goods to be marketed through largely nonpersonal means that are less costly than salespeople. Self-service stores, vending machines, and sales through catalogs would be impossible if the price of each item was subject to negotiation between seller and buyer. Finally, there is the alleged advantage that a one-price policy reduces any possible postsales dissonance that might affect a customer's willingness to make future purchases. It can be argued that some customers are unwilling to buy a product where the price varies because they are afraid that others may be obtaining a lower price. (This is debatable; it also can be argued that some customers enjoy haggling over price and their "victory" over the retailer.) The major limitation of a one-price policy is that it does not permit the retailer to discriminate among customers on the basis of their willingness to pay for the product. Consequently, retailers in certain types of retailing tend not to practice it. Those who sell automobiles, furs, or artwork are examples, but there are instances in almost every type of retailing where the listed price is the point where bargaining begins.

Variable Pricing

The opposite of the one-price policy is variable pricing. Discount houses have frequently practiced a variable price policy, but as their volume expands and they strive for "legitimacy," they move toward a one-price policy. (See Figure 11.4.) In variable pricing, the best bargainer obtains the lowest price. A few years ago a group of students were assigned to study the pricing structure of a discount store selling consumer durables. Their assignment was to find out if the quoted prices on the tickets were the actual selling prices, and if not, how much the prices could be driven down through bargaining. One enterprising student took his girl friend to the store and they posed as husband and wife, seeking to purchase several major items. They bargained intensively, and the salesman wrote his last quotation on his business card; the young people left the store on the pretense that they had to talk it over. The student then sent his parents to bargain for the identical merchandise from the same salesman. For each item, the older couple succeeded in obtaining a lower quoted price.

There is evidence that some customers enjoy bargaining for a lower price. In fact, haggling is part of the folklore of auto buying. Some critics have accused auto dealers of raising their initial prices—called price packing in the industry—in order to permit greater price concessions to the customers in the negotiation process. For this reason Congress enacted the Automobile Information Disclosure Act in 1958. This act requires the dealer to have a sticker on the window of each new car stating the list price of the automobile and the list price of each of the accessories that is priced separately. The act does not preclude an individual from bargaining with a dealer as to the ultimate selling price. It is quite normal for a customer to visit several dealers and compare the "deals" that can be obtained for the identical car and

FIGURE 11.4

Not all retailers who advertise discount prices follow a variable policy; these prices are not subject to bargaining

Source: *Chain Store Age, Executives' Edition.*

accessories. It is not surprising for the net price (after allowance for trade-in) to vary considerably.[3]

A variable price policy has serious economic implications for both the customer and the retailer. The practice of bargaining to determine the selling price might increase the labor cost to the retailer. This is obvious because the haggling process would take the time of the retailer or employees to engage the customer in bargaining over prices. The increase in labor cost would raise the price of the merchandise, and the customer would end up with fewer goods to satisfy his or her needs. Imagine the turmoil, confusion, and long lines at the checkout counter in a supermarket if each customer bargained with the checker over the price of every item purchased.

It is probably safe to conclude that price haggling is more likely to occur in the sale of those items for which a salesperson is needed, where the number of customers seen each day is relatively few, initial gross margins are high, and the item is infrequently purchased. Salespeople for products that meet these criteria are frequently idle for long periods of time as they await their next customers, and so they

[3]See Allen Jung, "Price Policies and Discounts in the Medium and High Priced Car Market," *Journal of Business* (October 1960), pp. 343–44.

feel they have the time to negotiate. Labor costs do not rise if these conditions are met. On the other hand, merchandise presold through mass communications media cannot be the subject of price negotiations without abandoning the self-service principle, thus increasing labor costs and ultimately prices.

Suggested Price Policy

Frequently manufacturers determine the retail price, even though they have relinquished title to the goods and would seem to have little concern for the price at which goods are sold to the final user. There are several ways they do this, and perhaps the most common method is to print the price on the package itself. The next time you are in a supermarket, discount store, variety store, or specialty shop count the items on sale that carry the price as part of the printed matter on the package itself. The manufacturers reinforce the suggested price by quoting it on their radio and television commercials or by including it as part of their advertising messages in the printed matter.

One reason that manufacturers suggest the retail price is to provide a guideline to the retailer. Many retailers appreciate this service because it shifts a "nasty job" to the manufacturer, and permits them to devote their time to other retailing activities. Furthermore, these retailers assume that the manufacturer can do a better job in pricing. One must not assume, however, that the suggested price line is obligatory. Retailers generally feel free to reduce the price below the suggested one, but seldom do they raise it. Sometimes the suggested price is a fair traded price, and the retailer must use it. This subject is discussed in another section of this chapter.

Shoppers also are said to favor a suggested price because it helps them to decide on the value of the merchandise. For some types of merchandise the quality is hidden from view, so retail price acts as a surrogate of quality. Where the customer assumes there is a reasonably close relationship between price and quality, he or she may welcome the manufacturer's statement of the price—and thus the quality—of the goods offered. If the price-quality relationship is to be sustained by the manufacturer over a long period, so that repeat patronage is assured, the customer must be satisfied, or he or she will not buy the product again. One clothing manufacturer, for example, sells men's suits under one label for about $140 to $150 and another label for $170 to $190. The only difference, salesmen point out, is the quality of the tailoring under the lining, which cannot be discerned by shoppers. The manufacturer and retailers have built a very successful business based on this difference which is important to some of their buyers.

The price-quality relationship has been studied under laboratory conditions in which other elements of the marketing mix can be controlled. In one such study, a group of women were asked to judge such factors as quality, durability, looks, and fragrance for paired carpeting, cologne, stockings, sweaters, and a chair. A piece of shag and a piece of plush carpeting were shown to a respondent, one with a fictitious high price tag and the other with a fictitious low price tag. The shopper was asked to evaluate the two. The other four types of products were similarly paired, and an evaluation was made. Even when the price tags were reversed and the high-priced product became a low-priced product and was shown to a different group of shoppers, the results were the same: the high-priced product was perceived to have superior traits to the low-priced product, again confirming that price and quality are closely related.[4]

Buyers also may use a manufacturer's suggested price as a basis for their negotiations with retailers who they suspect may offer them a discount. The listed price acts as a standard for comparing the size of the discount offered by rival retailers. However, it is important that the product be identical among retailers if the comparison is to be a fair one. Consumers sometimes have been deluded into thinking that the size of the discount rather than a product's quality should be the basis for choice. There have been instances in which retailers have purchased products for re-sale with fictitiously high price tags from collaborating suppliers so that apparently high discounts could be given. For example, a men's clothing store would buy men's hose premarked by the manufacturer at $1.50, so that the retailer, leaving the manufacturer's price on the package, could re-mark them at 88¢ and still make a profit. The manufacturer would have been willing to mark the socks at any price requested by the retailer, both of them understanding that the consumer would be duped into believing that the hosiery was really worth the higher price. Such practices are illegal but not unknown.

PRICE SENSITIVITY

There is much doubt among marketing people as to the importance that price plays in determining customer patronage. At the one extreme it can be argued that even modest price differences among products will result in a substantial switch of consumer allegiance to the lower-priced product. Advocates of this position tend to side with those who believe that there are traces of pure or perfect competition in our society. At the other extreme it can also be argued that price is an important element in the marketing mix, but it may be less important than the consumer's perception of the product's quality, the ease with which the product is made available, his or her understanding of how it fits into personal life style, and other factors that affect purchasing decisions. Those who take the second position point to the increasing income and wealth of those who make up the market, the difficulty of obtaining accurate and complete information about products, and the importance of saving time in a busy society as indications that customers give little attention to prices among rival sellers; in short, the prospect of saving a few pennies or even dollars is not worth the trouble. Probably neither view is entirely correct. Rather, it may be that the American public is scattered throughout the price sensitivity spectrum. No doubt people's awareness of price differences varies among types of products at different times in their lives and under different buying circumstances, and may be related to such demographic or behavioral traits as income, education, sex, marital status, number of children, self-confidence, and leadership abilities.

[4]Benson P. Shapiro, "Price Reliance: Existence and Sources," *Journal of Marketing Research* (August 1973), p. 286.

Information about customers' price sensitivity is essential for the successful retailer if he or she expects to engage in pricing decisions other than a simplistic "follow the leader" strategy. The retailer must rather obviously know something about the shape of the demand curve for his or her products to maximize profits. This is difficult for the limited-line retailer, and even more complex for the retailer who must price several thousand items. Much field research has been done on this issue and it is useful to review a small portion of it.

In a research study that a grocery chain called "The Price Is Right," shoppers showed vast differences in their abilities to state the price at which the product was displayed and sold in the stores.[5] The firm took sixty high-volume products and asked the respondents how much they would expect to pay for each product. About half of those interviewed were able to come within five percent of the actual price on such products as a six-pack of Coca-Cola, cigarettes, tomato soup, and applesauce, while few were able to come close to the actual price for cake mix, minute rice, Saran wrap, or Nestle's Quick. The important matter is that customers generally have limited abilities to know specific prices; however, they use their awareness of certain "key" items in a store to infer high or low prices to other items. Astute retailers are known to fix low margins to those key items whose "right" prices are known to housewives, while earning higher margins on fringe products.

Even though there is much similarity among gasolines, one study, completed before the oil crisis, indicated that it was sold for as little as 26¢ a gallon and as much as 35¢ a gallon in the same city, a price difference that could easily be observed from the posted price on the pump and sometimes from signs in front of the station. Although automobile owners generally are aware that there are price differences among stations, not all of the business gravitated to the low-priced stations. Furthermore, the use of signs announcing prices tended to increase during price wars, even among those stations that had not cut prices as drastically as had others. This would suggest that station managers believe that buyers are more sensitive to price during gas wars than when prices are normal.[6] (See Figure 11.5.)

The National Commission on Food Marketing—a special temporary task force set up to study the production and sales of food products—learned that a high proportion of shoppers tended to choose the lower-priced commodity when given a choice in food stores. More specifically, 50 percent of the respondents to a questionnaire agreed with the statement, "I usually look for the lowest possible price when I shop." The most common choice where a price difference existed was between manufacturer-owned and retailer-owned brands. The latter generally are slightly less expensive and were bought by about half the customers. Presumably these customers either did not believe that the slightly higher price of the manufacturers' label indicated higher quality or were unwilling to pay for it.[7] (See Figure 11.6.)

[5]"How Much Do Customers Know About Retail Prices?" *Progressive Grocer* (February 1964), p. 104.

[6]Neil M. Ford, Urban B. Ozanne, and Gilbert A. Churchill, Jr., "The Impact of Price Fluctuations on Three Elements of Gasoline Retailing," *Journal of Retailing* (Spring 1971), p. 36.

[7]"Special Studies in Food Marketing," Technical Study Number 10, National Commission on Food Marketing (June 1966), p. 82.

FIGURE 11.5

Gasoline price wars vanished in 1974 as the energy crisis focused attention on the shortage of gasoline

Source: Union Oil Company of California, Palatine, Illinois.

Unit Pricing

Some time ago critics complained that supermarket shoppers could not intelligently compare prices of similar products because of the variance in container sizes. Some argued that some type of common denominator should be used to help the shopper determine the lowest price among the choices. The result was an in-

FIGURE 11.6

Delicatessens and supermarkets use a system of tagging to show the customer that she is not being overcharged

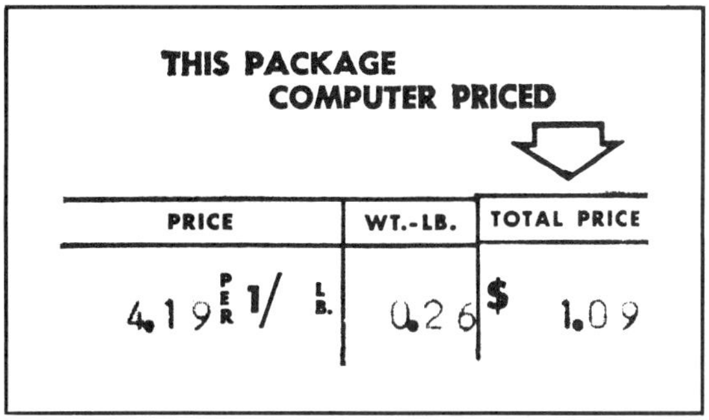

THIS PACKAGE COMPUTER PRICED

PRICE	WT.-LB.	TOTAL PRICE
4.19 PER 1/ LB.	0.26	$ 1.09

crease in unit pricing, voluntary in most instances but obligatory in certain states or cities. One early advocate of unit pricing was Jewel Food Company, which termed the practice "compar-a-buy." Jewel concluded that homemakers were sensitive to prices but were unable to calculate the lowest price when products of different units of measure were offered for sale. For example, consider the problem of calculating the lowest price among the four following products:

Hunt's Tomato Juice	13½	ounce can	10¢
Libby's Tomato Juice	18	ounce bottle	28¢
Cherry Valley Tomato Juice	46	ounce bottle	28¢
Stokely's Tomato Juice	46	ounce can	49¢

When a shelf label states the price per quart, a new and possibly useful piece of buying information is available to the customer. Jewel's shelf labels indicate that the four products are 24¢, 32¢, 19¢, and 26¢ a quart respectively; if price is the only factor—and it seldom is—the Cherry Valley would be the best value for the customer, even though at first glance it might not have seemed so. It has been pointed out that unit pricing permits the customer to buy the package size that allows the lowest price for a particular brand—the 18-ounce versus the 30-ounce bottle of Libby's Tomato Juice; to buy the package size that allows the lowest price for a particular type of product without regard for a brand—Hunt's or Stokely's; to buy the package size that allows the lowest price among types of products that are roughly substitute products—tomato juice or orange juice.[8] Business critics have pointed out that unit pricing centers undue attention on price, the implication being that the lowest-priced product is the best buy; the differing qualities among the products undergo no such scrutiny. There are additional administrative problems that add to a firm's costs. The retailer must solve such questions as printing thousands of labels that must be changed every time prices change, supervising the stocking of the merchandise so that merchandise and shelf label match, printing and attaching labels that are readable yet small enough to accommodate even the smallest item, and—for the interstate retailer—abiding by the various state laws.[9]

Weber's Law and Price Sensitivity

Weber's Law, which was originally introduced in Chapter 3, is so important to the discussion of price sensitivity that it is being repeated here. Weber's Law was developed in 1934 to provide a theoretical framework for measuring the intensity of a stimulus. Marketing people have found it useful in providing insight into shoppers' sensitivity to price change. The law can be written as follows:

[8]Hans R. Isakson and Alex R. Maurizi, "The Consumer Economics of Unit Pricing," *Journal of Marketing Research* (August 1973), p. 277.

[9]Kent B. Munroe and Peter G. LaPlaca, "What Are the Benefits of Unit Pricing?" *Journal of Marketing* (July 1972), p. 16.

$$K = \frac{\triangle I}{I}$$

where:

K is a constant over all stimuli,
$\triangle$ is the smallest increment of change in intensity which is noticeable to the observer, and
I is the intensity of a stimulus.

This formula has served as the basis for many of those who have investigated the magnitude of a price change that would be necessary in order for the observer to be aware of the change. The equation states that the threshold at which the observer perceives a price change is a function of the price at the time the change in price takes place. Meyers and Reynolds suggest the meaning of Weber's Law in the following:

> Weber's Law is illustrated rather well by consumer response to pricing. An increase of $200 in the price of an American compact car would certainly be perceived as being much greater than the same $200 increase in the price of a Cadillac or a Continental. Weber's Law is also the psychological underpinning of the retail practice of marking down items (i.e., lowering the original price, as during a sale) on a percentage rather than an absolute basis. The higher the original price, the greater is the dollar amount of markdown required to produce an adequate customer response.[10]

There is much to be learned about how customers perceive prices, but the following two retail practices seem to be compatible with Weber's Law:

1. Markdowns and discounts often are promoted in percentage terms off original price rather than in absolute dollars, because the size of the discount may seem greater. A retailer's sign that proclaims "End of Season Sale—25 percent off!" on $20 dresses probably has more impact than "$20 Dresses, Prices Slashed to $15!"—even though they are the same.
2. If markdowns or discounts are to be perceived as important to the consumer, the dollar amount must be more for the more expensive products. If Weber's Law is valid, the dollar amount of the discount should be proportionate to the price of the product.

There is much controversy about the circumstances under which Weber's Law is operable. Indeed, one writer states, "There is still no valid test of the applicability of Weber's Law to pricing."[11] Nonetheless, it is still widely acted upon, even by those who have never heard of Weber and do not know what he said.

[10] James H. Meyers and William H. Reynolds, *Consumer Behavior and Marketing Management* (Boston, Mass.: Houghton Mifflin Co., 1967), p. 13.

[11] Kent B. Monroe, "Buyers' Subjective Perceptions of Price," *Journal of Marketing Research* (February 1973), p. 76.

The Law of Demand and Price Elasticity

Both economic theory and common sense tell us that buyers purchase more of a particular good at a lower price than at a higher price in a given market at a given time. We are so sure of this market phenomenon that we call it a "law"—the law of demand. In its simplest form the law says that a seller will move more of a product at, say, $90 than at $100, although it does not tell us how much more. The two major exceptions to the law that are of interest to marketing people are where the price-quality relationship is operable or where there is an element of "snob appeal" to the higher price. In some instances, a price may be so low that people mistrust the worthiness of any product that is sold for so little—as we have indicated earlier, price may be taken as evidence of quality. In other cases—and there are not many—people take pride in paying a high price for a product because it affords them a certain standing with their peers who know about such things as prices. A Chicago restaurant blatantly appealed to snobbism when its waiters were directed to give male diners a menu containing regular prices and female diners menus containing fictitious prices that were double the regular prices—every man could look like a big sport, presumably without ever being discovered. And at Christmas, one can see liquor advertising in which the high price is the central feature of the advertisement. In short, high price can sometimes be a positive attribute, if everyone knows the price is high, and it symbolizes, presumably, ability to pay. But these are exceptions to the law of demand.

Elasticity

Elasticity is the response of a buyer to a change in price. Economists identify three types of price elasticity: elastic, inelastic, and unitary. Demand is said to be elastic, if as the price of a good goes down, buyers increase their purchases so much that total sales revenue increases. The converse, of course, is also true for goods with elastic demands. That is, if the price of a good is increased, buyers decrease their purchases of the good, causing total sales revenue to decline. Most goods sold in the marketplace have elastic demands. Consequently, when retailers lower their prices, they expect to sell a larger quantity and thus have higher revenues. On the other hand, if they raise the price, sales fall off and total revenues decline.

Demand is inelastic, if as the price of the good increases, the sales volume falls off very little, and the result is an increase in total sales revenue. If a good has an inelastic demand, consumers are less sensitive to an increase in price. Usually goods for which there are no substitutes (or poor ones) have inelastic demands. Table salt is a good example. Whenever the price of salt is increased, there is little chance of volume falling off, and most certainly total sales revenue will increase. Another example is the public transportation fare. An increase in the fare usually results in total revenue increasing, and only a small drop in passengers carried.

The third type of price elasticity is called unitary elasticity. In this case, if price is lowered, sales increase; however, total sales revenue remains constant. The increase of revenue from the newly tapped customers exactly offsets the decrease of average revenue generated by each unit sold.

The importance of elasticity in the real world of prices cannot be overstated. For example, most basic farm products have inelastic demand curves. This means that if farmers have bumper crops, the increase in total output causes farm prices to fall, so the result to the farmer is lower farm income. On the other hand, if farm output declines through crop control measures or natural disasters, the inelasticity of the demand causes farm prices to rise, and the result is higher farm income. (See Figure 11.7.)

Food at the local supermarket also tends to have relatively inelastic demands. However, customers can make substitutions in products they purchase, thus they have a degree of control over their responses to prices. For example, if the price of beef rises but the price of chicken remains constant, the shopper may switch from beef to chicken. However, if the shopper is a beef eater and accepts no substitute, for that person the demand for beef is relatively inelastic.

With the advent of television some years ago, movie theater owners experienced a serious decline in patronage. As a consequence, they raised ticket prices, only to have a further decline in both revenue and patronage. The reason, of course, is the

FIGURE 11.7

Milk prices rose rapidly in 1973–74, but consumption remained stable, demonstrating the inelasticity of the demand for milk

Source: Tony Kelly, Consolidated Foods Corporation, Chicago, Illinois.

TABLE 11.2
Principal Differences Between Elastic and Inelastic Demand

Elastic Demand	*Inelastic Demand*
1. Want for the good is urgent.	1. Want for the good is not urgent.
2. Substitutes are available.	2. Substitutes either are not available or are poor.
3. Expenditure for the product is significant.	3. Expenditure for the product is usually small.
4. The good has multiple uses.	4. Good is usually wanted jointly with some other complementary good.
5. Typical examples are autos, refrigerators, clothes, and shoes.	5. Typical examples are matches, salt, and fares on public transportation.

elastic demand for movies. Table 11.2 shows the principal differences between goods with elastic and inelastic demands. Retailers must take into consideration the elasticity of demand when they price merchandise.

RESALE PRICE MAINTENANCE

For one class of products—those that manufacturers elect to "fair trade"—retailers have little decision-making power with respect to price. During America's Great Depression that began in 1929, manufacturers became concerned that some of their products on which they had spent so much promotional money were being discounted from the price consumers had learned to pay. They feared that the price cutting would permanently detract from the perceived value they had built into their products over the years. Small retailers, particularly druggists, also feared the price competition that rapidly arose at that time, and clamored for legislative aid. In response to the pressure, in 1931 the California State Legislature enacted legislation that would permit the manufacturer to enter into a contract with the retailer to dictate the price at which products would be sold by the retailer to the consumer; in 1933 the legislation was amended to include all those resellers who knew about the contract but were not a party to it, a provision that came to be called the "nonsigners" clause. Other states followed with similar legislation, and by the time Delaware passed a Fair Trade Law in 1941, 45 states allowed the brand owner to determine retail prices. Since such laws were clearly contrary to America's public policy position toward competition, the country's antitrust legislation had to be amended if the state laws were to apply to interstate commercial transactions. Congress enacted the Miller-Tydings amendment to the Sherman Act in 1937, which meant that the prices on goods sold across state lines could legally be dictated to by the manufacturer long after he had relinquished title to them. In short, it legalized price fixing.

The second important piece of federal legislation was passed shortly after a

Supreme Court decision that made most of the state legislation inoperable. Schwegmann Brothers Food Stores, a large New Orleans retailer, had been selling Calvert liquor products at less than the price listed by the brand name owner (Calverts), arguing that the retailer had never signed a fair trade contract and thus was not bound by Louisiana law to sell at Calvert-dictated prices. The legal issue concerned whether or not those who had never signed a fair trade contract were bound by the nonsigner provision of the state laws. The issue was fought through the courts, and the United States Supreme Court held that they were not; the Miller-Tydings legislation did not legalize the nonsigners clause.[12] Since the court ruling would virtually have destroyed fair trading, Congress was pressured to "do something." In 1952 it passed the McGuire Act, which would include the nonsigner provision. There have been many additional Congressional efforts to strengthen fair trade practices in the United States, but the Miller-Tydings and McGuire laws are the only two that have been enacted.

Fair trade laws continue to play an important role in the pricing of certain products, but they have become much less important in recent years. Nebraska repealed its legislation in 1959, and a decline in their importance began. Repeal in other states or unfavorable court decisions have lessened their importance since that time. In fact legislation was introduced to Congress in 1975 by Senator Edward Brooke of Massachusetts to repeal the Federal Antitrust laws that permit state fair trade laws. This would make the state laws unenforceable. Although many of the states patterned their laws after the initial California legislation, one must look at each state for the details of the laws. Among the differences are such factors as whether damaged or deteriorated goods are exempted from the law, whether fair-traded goods can be sold at lower prices when combined with nonfair-traded goods, whether trading stamps can be given on such goods, whether nonprofit sellers are covered, and whether suitable penalties can be assessed against violators. All in all, price maintenance laws have represented a real quagmire for chain retailers that operate across state boundaries.

The rationale for price maintenance laws is difficult to understand today, since we are so long removed from the Great Depression. But it was a fearful time in America, when many had begun to lose confidence that free competition was all it was cracked up to be. There were cries to "do something," and state legislators responded with what many believe was poor legislation, some of which remains with us today. The legislation seems to be based on three major fears: (1) manufacturers had spent untold millions of dollars building up their brand names and marks over the years and were entitled to protect their investments. Customers were accustomed to paying an amount determined by the manufacturer, and that amount represented the "value" of the product. If a product was sold at many different prices, confusion would result, and the goodwill built up over the years would be lost; (2) the price cutting would take place in the large retail outlets, small retailers would be unable to compete, and there would be a tendency toward monopoly at the retail level as

[12] *Schwegmann Brothers* v. *Calvert Distillers Corporation*, 341 U.S. 384, 1951.

the smaller retailers went out of business. This argument is moderately appealing, and became particularly attractive to legislators when they compared the number of small businessman voters with the number of large businessman voters; and (3) many argued that without such laws many retailers would engage in the unfair practice of featuring well-known products at discounted prices only to switch the customer to other products once he or she had entered the store. Baiting and switching was a more common tactic at that time, and many argued that it would be minimized if the retailer could be assured a high margin on well-known goods. With a high margin assured by fair trade laws, there would be no reason for a retailer to attempt to switch a customer to a different product.

Fair trade laws have been roundly criticized by those who believe that America's public policy position should emphasize competition as its controlling feature. Fortunately, relatively few goods—some say less than ten percent—ever were sold under the various states' price maintenance laws. Furthermore, both the courts and the legislatures have been unkind to such legislation; probably fewer than twenty states have workable price maintenance laws today. They represent an exemption from our country's antitrust position and an attempt to protect competitors rather than competition.

SUMMARY

One of the most difficult assignments a retailer faces is to determine price policies. First, a retailer chooses general price policy and then within this framework chooses the specific price policies to follow to aid merchandising efforts.

A traditional method for determining the price of each individual item is to add a predetermined markup to the invoice cost of the merchandise. Retailers customarily express this markup as a percentage. It is usually calculated as a markup on retail, but can be easily converted into a markup on cost.

Some retailers use a single markup percentage for all their stock while others follow a multiple percentage system. Department stores have championed the percentage markup policy. They say it is easy to understand, automatically accommodates variations in expenses, and can be defended on social grounds.

An alternative to the percentage markup price policy is the dollar margin method. This policy is advocated by the mass merchandisers who price their merchandise to maximize their turnover, and thus increase total profits. This concept is not based on the assumption that each item must be profitable; it may be kept in the line if it builds traffic and stimulates customers to buy other goods. Dollar margin retailers may use leadership price policies as a strategy to increase sales. One such stratagem is to price a particular item below cost so as to attract shoppers. Some states have enacted unfair practice acts to control this type of policy.

A subject of increasing interest relates to the price sensitivity of the shopper. Most research is inconclusive but does indicate that customers react to some prices or price changes more than others. Weber's Law is a useful explanation of the sensitivity of a shopper to a price change. Markdowns are taken on a relative basis rather than in absolute dollar terms because the awareness factor is present.

Retailers often use odd prices, particularly those that end in "9." The principal reason for using odd prices as a strategy is the belief that customers perceive odd prices as a substantial reduction.

Other kinds of price policies that retailers follow are the one-price policy, the variable price policy, or a suggested price. Since the middle of the 19th century, the one-price policy has been traditional in the United States; every shopper is offered the merchandise at the same price. A few large ticket items such as automobiles lend themselves to variable pricing.

Some retailers abide by agreements to maintain prices determined by a manufacturer. These agreements are in response to state fair trade laws, an outgrowth of depression years. Today, there is a noticeable decline in the advocates for fair trading.

Most retailers have definite pricing goals and objectives. Some retailers assume an aggressive stance with respect to prices and they assume a price leadership role. Others are content to be followers and simply meet competition. The principal objectives that influence pricing practices are target return, profit maximization, or nonprofit goals.

QUESTIONS FOR DISCUSSION

1. Discuss the factors determining a retailer's general price policy.
2. Change the following markups on retail to markups on cost: 25%, 20%, 40%, 50%. Change the following markups on cost to markups on retail: 66⅔%, 100%, 33⅓%, 25%.
3. Give the advantages and disadvantages of the percentage method of determining prices.
4. Explain as fully as possible the strategy of dollar margin price policy.
5. What is leadership pricing? How is it implemented and what steps have been taken to control it?
6. Discuss the entire subject of price awareness and price sensitivity. Give examples to supplement your discussion.
7. Compare and contrast the one-price policy with a variable price policy.
8. What is meant by price lining? State its advantages and limitations.
9. What are fair trade laws? How important are they today?
10. What is meant by the following:
    a. pricing to obtain a target return?
    b. pricing in order to maximize profits?
    c. pricing in order to achieve nonprofit goals?

12 RETAIL PROMOTIONAL POLICIES

The Maison Blanche department store on Canal Street in New Orleans dresses its window mannequins in the costumes that will be worn by paraders during Mardi Gras week. Thousands of people will see the lavishly dressed models while waiting for one of the approximately 54 parades that take place during the last few days before Ash Wednesday.

A Tokyo radio and television dealer floats a helium-filled balloon several hundred feet over his shop and attaches announcements to the balloon's cable that tell the name of the store and the nature of its business. Balloons are much more popular as an advertising medium in various parts of Asia than in the United States.

A high-volume liquor store owner in Saint Louis agrees to allow a representative of Four Roses whiskey enough space on a busy Saturday afternoon for a "tasting" session. Passersby are permitted a taste of Four Roses in hopes that they will switch from whatever they have been drinking.

A variety store manager in Sacramento puts together a "Back to School" promotion every August. He is careful to coordinate his inventory, window display, inside display, and newspaper advertising so that each centers attention on the clothing and utensils that youngsters will need at school. Other store managers throughout the country are using the same event as the focal point for their merchandising and promotional efforts.

A travel agent in Lima, Peru, projects colored slides of various travel resorts onto the white wall of a nearby building every night. His business is located in an affluent neighborhood where there are many pedestrians, and he reasons that a few of them may have their interest in travel excited and will ask him to arrange their vacations or business travel.

When Neiman-Marcus decided to have a show of French couture, it sent its buyers to Paris to select merchandise that would be shown. But in addition to bringing the suits and dresses from Europe, it brought French models from Paris to Dallas in order to give the show the right tone. Local events such as art exhibitions and concerts were coordinated with the Neiman-Marcus effort.

These are just a few of the ways in which retailers draw attention to their stores and their products. For once the merchandise is in the store, stocked and priced, retailers must attract customers inside in order to sell them the products. A retailer's promotional effort can range from the spectacular to the routine. This chapter and the three following deal with how a retailer attempts to attract buyers to the store. This chapter centers on the store's promotional efforts.

PROMOTION IN RETAILING

All human activity is described in specialized patois by the people engaged in various endeavors. Business has its own nomenclature, as does retailing, and full understanding of business and retailing processes requires that the neophyte know what the practitioner means by the terms used. One troublesome term is *promotion*.

McCarthy includes promotion, along with product, price, and place, in his list of the four major variables with which the marketer works.[1] He defines the term in very simple language as communication between seller and buyer.[2] Thus, at the heart of promotion is communication. When any marketing venture is viewed as a total system, it contains three principal subsystems: product, distribution, and communication.[3] The communication subsystem "includes the intake of information, or marketing research, as well as the two primary forms of information output—personal selling and advertising."[4] These two vital forces, along with such helpers as public relations, publicity, and sales promotion, are the motivators that lead to retail purchases. Without them, retailers would rarely make many sales in our modern world of mass production, and their enterprises would soon fail for lack of adequate business. This chapter concentrates on the impersonal forms of marketing communication as they operate between the retailer and potential customers. In the main these impersonal techniques, sometimes described as "mass selling," are used by retailers to attract potential customers to the retail outlet, where it is anticipated that the products displayed, along with the salespeople's persuasions (as explained in Chapter 13), will lead to the consummation of sales. Advertising is usually the most important form of nonpersonal promotion in the retailer's communication or promotional mix.

RETAIL ADVERTISING

It hardly seems necessary to explain what advertising is. Everyone knows what advertising is; we see it every day in newspapers and magazines, on roadside signs, buses, and taxis. We hear advertising on the radio and see and hear it on television. Advertising, as retailing, is all pervasive in our society.

One estimate of the number of advertisements to which the typical consumer is exposed daily is 1,500. Obviously most of these messages are hardly noticed. Each consumer responds to only a fraction of the total advertisements directed to him or her. An important reason for these wasted attempts at communications is that many advertisers do not really understand what advertising is all about.

[1]E. Jerome McCarthy, *Basic Marketing*, 5th ed. (Homewood, Ill.: Richard D. Irwin, Inc., 1975), p. 75.

[2]Ibid., p. 386.

[3]This discussion based on John S. Wright, Daniel S. Warner, and Willis Winter, Jr., *Advertising*, 3rd ed. (New York: McGraw-Hill Book Co., 1971), p. 184.

[4]Ibid., p. 184.

Advertising Defined[5]

The most widely accepted definition of advertising is devised by the American Marketing Association, which recommends the following:[6]

> Advertising is any paid form of nonpersonal presentation and promotion of ideas, goods, or services by an identified sponsor.

Four parts of this definition are worth close scrutiny because they are designed to help distinguish advertising from other activities with which it is often confused.

Paid Form. This phrase is intended to distinguish advertising from publicity. When a company or a product or a service is mentioned favorably in a magazine or newspaper article, the item is presumed to provide information or entertainment for the readers. This is publicity. Whether the favorable comment appears in printed media or on a radio or television program, no payment is made by the organization that benefits. Advertising, on the other hand, is usually—although not always —published or broadcast because time or space has been purchased to tell the advertiser's story. Each has its place in the promotional activities of an organization.

Nonpersonal Presentation. When a personal or face-to-face presentation is made, the process is called *personal selling.* While advertising is a complement to or a substitute for personal selling, it is done in a nonpersonal manner through intermediaries—or media—such as newspapers, magazines, radio, television. There is a close relationship between advertising and personal selling, but they are two very different activities.

Ideas, Goods, or Services. Advertising is not concerned exclusively with the promotion of tangible goods. Services offered by banks, insurance companies, airlines, railroads, resorts, and laundries are advertised just as aggressively as are automobiles, canned corn, or beer. (See Figure 12.1.) And while the objective of most advertising is to help sell goods or services to prospective customers, an increasingly important use of advertising is related, not to marketing processes, but to public service goals. Advertising has become recognized as an effective force in helping to prevent forest fires, promote traffic safety, fight pollution, increase educational facilities, secure blood donations, conserve raw materials, gain acceptance for polio immunization, and in advancing a host of other ideas that are social rather than commercial.

The Identified Sponsor. When the source of an idea is unknown, it is difficult for the receiver to evaluate the merit of the idea. So the "identified sponsor" is useful in distinguishing between advertising and what is, or has been, a popular concept of propaganda. Propaganda attempts to present opinions and ideas with the

[5]This discussion based on Wright, et al., *Advertising*, pp. 3–12.

[6]*Marketing Definitions*, by Ralph S. Alexander and the Committee on Definitions of the American Marketing Association, copyright 1960, p. 9.

FIGURE 12.1
Newspaper advertisements often represent a variety of goods and services

Source: Herald Newspapers, May 10–May 16, p. 3, a division of Paddock Publications, Inc., Arlington Heights, Illinois.

objective of influencing attitudes and actions. So does advertising. But to many people, the word *propaganda* carries a connotation of distortion, deception, and hidden manipulation, because the propagandist may remain anonymous. Within this popular concept, publicity can be a form of propaganda. Advertising, on the other hand, discloses or identifies the source of the opinions and ideas it presents.

In 1973 about $11 billion was spent on local advertising compared with about $14 billion spent on national advertising, and much local advertising is retail advertising. Moreover, of $3.8 billion spent in 1973 for newspaper advertising, over $2 billion was spent by retailers.[7] In other words, $1 out of every $2 spent on news-

[7] *1975 The U.S. Fact Book, The American Almanac, The Statistical Abstract of the U.S.* (New York: Grosset & Dunlap, 1975), pp. 771–72.

TABLE 12.1

Newspaper Advertising Expenditures for 64 Cities
(in millions of dollars)

Year	*Total*	*Retail*	*Automotive*	*Classified*	*Financial*	*General*
1973	$3,786	$2,044	$100	$1,024	$139	$479
1972	3,497	1,925	98	881	115	478
1971	3,208	1,807	101	752	103	445
1970	3,120	1,759	93	724	117	426

Source: *1975 The U.S. Fact Book, The American Almanac, The Statistical Abstract of the U.S.* (New York: Grosset & Dunlap, 1975), p. 773.

paper advertising is spent by retailers (see Table 12.1). According to *Advertising Age*, Sears, Roebuck and Co. is the nation's second largest national advertiser (Procter and Gamble is first), spending at least $215 million in 1972. In addition, *Advertising Age* estimates that individual Sears stores also invested a total of $250 million in newspapers, local TV and local radio, direct mail, and outdoor advertising. Altogether, Sears spent perhaps $447 million in advertising.[8] Table 12.2 lists the ten top retailers and their 1973 advertising budgets.

TABLE 12.2

The Top Ten Retail Advertisers for 1973

	Sales	*Advertising*
1. Sears, Roebuck & Co.	$12,306,279,000	$447,000,000
2. J C Penney	6,243,557,000	127,300,000
3. S. S. Kresge Co.	4,633,233,000	130,011,000
4. Montgomery Ward	4,077,415,000	113,000,000
5. F. W. Woolworth	3,722,107,000	105,500,000
6. Federated Dept. Stores	2,962,057,000	109,500,000
7. W. T. Grant	1,849,802,000	58,850,000
8. Allied Stores	1,598,301,000	58,000,000
9. May Dept. Stores	1,554,641,000	57,500,000
10. McCrory Corp.	1,424,018,000	25,000,000

Source: *Advertising Age* (September 30, 1974), p. 30.

The importance of advertising is further suggested by the fact that for many retailers, advertising is the enterprise's second largest expense, second only to salaries. For others it is the third largest, following salaries and occupancy expenses.

Retail Advertising Policy

Retail advertising is distinctively different from the advertising of nationally branded and distributed products. In essence, national advertising is attempting to

[8] *Advertising Age* (August 24, 1974), p. 176.

sell one type, or a limited line, of products in many stores. The retail advertiser, regardless of size, is attempting to sell a number of different products in one or a limited number of stores. The retailer's advertising is always a "local" effort, regardless of how widespread the geographic location of the stores, because the retailer must always attempt to attract customers to the particular location to shop for the goods and services advertised. He or she must compete with other retailers in the same market area on a local basis. The retailer must sell customers on the entire "package" of goods and services offered, including quality and variety of goods to choose from, convenience, credit, pleasant surroundings, and many other factors comprising a particular retailer's image to customers.

Two Types of Retail Advertising

Just as the image of the store determines the type of customer attracted, it also determines the types of advertising used. Good retail advertising reflects the character of the store presenting it and that of the potential customers it addresses. All types of retail advertising can be grouped into two broad classifications—*institutional* and *promotional.*

Institutional advertising is an attempt to sell the prestige of the store as a good place to shop for any merchandise it handles. Promotional advertising presents specific merchandise for sale and attempts to build customer traffic in the store, usually during a specific period of time. It seeks immediate sales, whereas institutional advertising seeks business over a longer time period.

Every type of merchandise carried by a retailer goes through a particular life cycle, or as it is sometimes called, a fashion cycle. The position of any item of merchandise in its fashion cycle has a direct influence on the type of advertising used. When merchandise is first available to the public, it is in its *introductory* stage. Probably few shoppers know much about it or try it during this stage. If the merchandise becomes better known and accepted by a larger number of customers, it will enter the *acceptance* stage. Later, if improvements are not made in the product to meet competition, it will likely enter into the stages of *maturity, decline*, and eventually *abandonment.*

Charles Edwards and Russell Brown in *Retail Advertising and Sales Promotion* refer to this cycle as the "merchandise acceptance curve," shown in Figure 12.2. In accordance with a product's location on the acceptance curve, a retailer will vary the advertising. In the introductory stage, the retailer will likely rely heavily on institutional (prestige) advertising. During the acceptance stage, when sales of the product rise most rapidly, retailers may use a mix of prestige and promotional (basically price) advertising. In the latter stages of the product's life cycle, the retailer may rely almost exclusively on promotional advertising to move the remaining inventory from shelves and make room for the introduction of new merchandise.

The Advertising Plan

Most progressive retailers realize the need for a thoughtfully conceived and administered advertising plan, sometimes known as a sales promotion plan or a

FIGURE 12.2
Merchandise acceptance curve

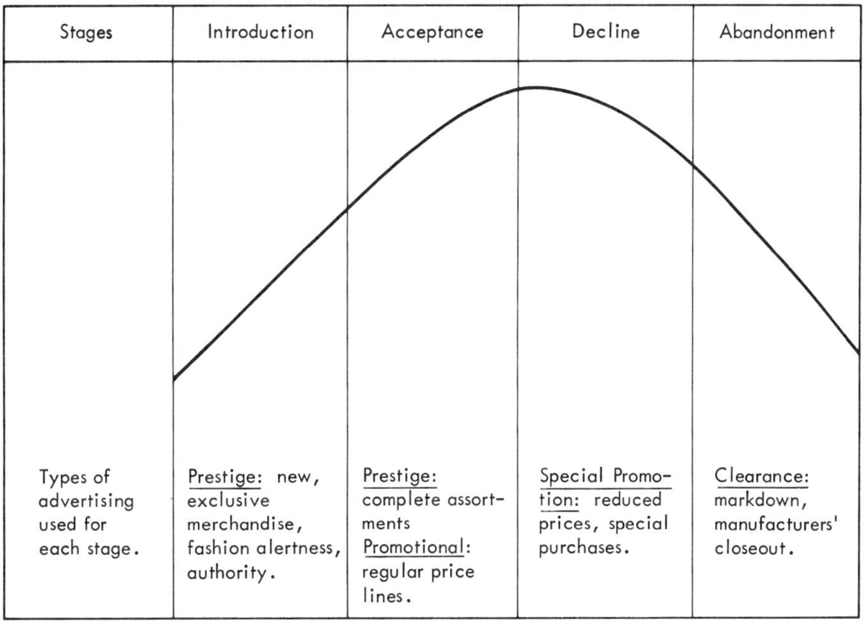

Stages	Introduction	Acceptance	Decline	Abandonment
Types of advertising used for each stage.	Prestige: new, exclusive merchandise, fashion alertness, authority.	Prestige: complete assortments Promotional: regular price lines.	Special Promotion: reduced prices, special purchases.	Clearance: markdown, manufacturers' closeout.

Source: Charles M. Edwards, Jr., and Russell A. Brown, *Retail Advertising and Sales Promotion*, 3rd ed. (Englewood Cliffs, N.J.: Prentice-Hall, Inc., 1959), p. 167. © 1959 by Prentice-Hall, Inc.

sales plan. The advertisers of nationally or internationally distributed products may refer to it as an advertising campaign, but they all loosely refer to the same type of planning.

Edwards and Brown define a retail advertising plan as:

> A forecast for a season (6 months), a quarter (3 months or 13 weeks), a month, or a week, of the advertising that the store intends to employ in order to attract business. The advertising plan is part of the entire publicity budget including all types of sales promotional activities, such as displays, special events, and other promotional techniques. Usually the two are formulated concurrently. Generally, this plan outlines the dates on which advertisements are to be run, the departments and articles to be advertised, the estimated sales of the advertised merchandise, the media to be employed, the amount of space to be used in each medium, the cost of the space to be utilized, both in dollars and as a percentage of sales.[9]

The formulation of the advertising plan involves seven basic areas, or planning steps, for the retailer:

[9]Charles M. Edwards, Jr., and Russell A. Brown, *Retail Advertising and Sales Promotion*, 3rd ed. (Englewood Cliffs, N.J.: Prentice-Hall, Inc., 1959), pp. 129–30.

1. An analysis of the marketing situation.
2. The determination of advertising objectives.
3. Advertising budgeting and control.
4. The selection of advertising media.
5. The creation of the advertising message or copy.
6. The coordination of advertising with other promotional and selling methods.
7. Evaluation of the results.

These planning stages are not necessarily decided in the sequence shown here. For example, the nature of the advertising message may cause a change in the selection of the advertising media. The decision to use one medium rather than another may cause adjustments in the advertising budget. Actually several of these planning steps are usually being considered simultaneously. However, the analysis of the market situation and determination of advertising objectives must precede the other five steps.

Setting the Advertising Budget

In setting a retail advertising budget, there are many different approaches. One method of setting an advertising budget may be more adaptable than another for a particular retailer. Certain approaches, such as the task method of budget allocation, have distinct advantages over the others, but all have their shortcomings. Regardless of the method used, setting the proper advertising budget is a difficult task for any retailer and requires skill and experience, but by observing certain ground rules the retailer can avoid many of the pitfalls.

Probably the most important rule is always to consider advertising *not merely as a cost*, but as an *investment*. Just as the costs of rent, salaries, and merchandise are investments, so are advertising expenditures. During a period of retrenchment, when the economy as a whole is lagging, advertising expenditures are usually cut drastically. Inasmuch as a depression lowers the income and spending of the whole market, it is usually advisable that retailers curtail advertising expenditures. Nevertheless, expenditures for advertising and other publicity for a retailer should *not* be reduced in direct proportion to the reduction in sales volume. Advertising and other sales promotion techniques are needed most when consumers are less willing to spend, and competition intensifies. Advertising appropriations during such periods, while smaller in dollars, should usually represent a higher percentage of total sales. Indeed, the management at Filenes, said to be the world's largest specialty store, was one of the first to advertise more during a business turndown. The large Boston firm has long practiced an inverse advertising cost/sales revenue relationship.

Over the years many different methods of determining the advertising budget have been developed. While the task method remains popular and seems to be the most satisfactory, other methods are still used. Perhaps the oldest method of determining the advertising budget is simply by allocating a set percentage of the sales volume figure. This figure is usually based either on an industry average or on what the company has spent in the past. The major shortcoming of the percentage-of-sales method is that it fails to recognize the specific needs of the individual retailer and his or her special competitive situation.

The what-can-be-afforded-method of setting the advertising budget is used by a great many otherwise sophisticated retailers. "We will spend what we can afford on advertising" may seem to be a sound philosophy, but under this method the advertising budget is usually left to the whim of management and the general business psychology of the moment. The size of the advertising budget is simply a matter of chance.

Retailers who use the competitors expenditure method generally have adopted either one of two points of view. Some retailers attempt to match competitors' advertising expenditures, while others try to spend more than competitors. Neither approach is sound, however, as no two competitors' advertising needs are quite the same. This competitive follow-or-beat-the-leader philosophy is similar to the one that entangles automobile service stations in periodic gasoline price wars. The net effect is usually less profits for everyone.

Most budget methods have one fault in common: advertising is not treated as a vehicle for achieving stated business objectives. The advertising task is given very little thought. The task method, often called the objective method, seems to be the answer to using advertising to smooth the functioning of the marketing process. Three steps are taken to implement the task method: (1) *Set the objectives of the advertising program.* Some sellers use advertising primarily as a means of getting sales leads and arousing interest among consumers. Others want to achieve a certain level of store traffic and sales during particular periods. Still others want to establish or maintain store prestige and help guarantee a specified flow of sales year round. (2) *Determine the type and amount of advertising required to achieve the goals specified.* This second step is the truly difficult part of the task method. A high level of advertising and business expertise is usually required to accomplish this step with any efficiency. Many retail firms utilize the expertise of professional advertising agencies or business consultants when the volume of sales at stake is high enough to warrant it. (3) *Determine the overall cost of the advertising program.* This is a fairly mechanical operation. Once the cost figure is reached, however, the retailer must decide if the firm is financially able to make this investment. The significant difference between the task and other methods is that the task method "builds up" while others merely "break down" the budget.

The American Newspaper Publishers Association (ANPA), through its Bureau of Advertising, has developed sound procedures similar to the task method for setting retail advertising budgets. Although the motive behind the plan is to convince retailers to advertise in newspapers, the basic plan can be used by most retailers for allocating the advertising budget to all media. The ANPA approach involves the following four steps:

1. *Set a sales goal*, usually in terms of the previous year's sales figures broken down by department on a monthly basis. These figures are then adjusted for changing conditions, such as store expansion, increased population, higher incomes, greater employment, competitive activity, and other factors.

2. *Decide how much advertising will be required to accomplish this goal.* As in step two of the task method, experience is the critical factor in determining the amount and type of advertising required.
3. *Decide what to promote.* This decision is basically an allocation problem of how much of the budget should be allocated to each department, if the store is departmentalized, and further to individual products. To implement this step of the ANPA approach, the retailer must be able to predict with some accuracy what his other customers will want item by item each month. In this way each department and merchandise item receives advertising funds according to its sales opportunities.
4. *Schedule the advertisements day-by-day.* The final step is primarily timing and is involved more with the advertising plan than determining the advertising budget. In order to facilitate the correct timing of advertisements, ANPA has developed a monthly work sheet.

Every retailer should attempt to develop a step-by-step advertising planning procedure which will permit him or her to devise an advertising budget tailored to help meet sales goals.

Selecting the Advertising Media

As a retailer grows larger and extends the store's area of market influence, it is progressively more difficult to have personal contact with customers. With this loss of personal contact and communication, the retailer must find an effective go-between to transmit the selling messages to his or her growing community of customers. When the retailer purchases advertising space or time, he or she is attempting to bridge this gap and communicate the selling message to present and potential customers effectively and economically.

The objective of media selection, then, is to deliver effective advertising messages to the greatest number of prospects at the lowest possible cost. However, no one medium can be considered better than all others. Too many variables affect the ability of any medium to communicate a particular advertising most effectively. Few retail advertisers rely on only one medium.

The greater part of almost any advertising budget must go toward paying the costs of space or time in the media. Yet, many retailers are so impatient to see the results of their advertising that they often select a medium without adequate evaluation in relation to specific selling problems, the desired target audience, and the message itself. Advertisers annually waste large sums of money in media that are unproductive for their particular selling needs.

If retailers are to plan complete, well-balanced advertising programs, they must carefully weigh the merits of all of the advertising media available. Compounding the problem of selecting the best media is the large number from which the retailer may choose. A retail advertiser should maintain a list of available media. A sample list might look something like this.[10]

[10]This list is a modification of the one in Edwards and Brown, *Retail Advertising*, p. 320.

A. Periodical advertising media:
   1. Newspapers
      a. Metropolitan (daily)
      b. Suburban (weekly and daily)
   2. Shopping publications:
      a. merchant-owned
      b. independent
   3. Miscellaneous periodicals:
      a. local and community publications
      b. college and school publications
      c. directories (including phone directory Yellow Pages)
      d. theater programs
      e. national magazines

B. Direct advertising media:
   1. Direct mail:
      a. letters
      b. envelope enclosures:
         stuffers
         folders
      c. circulars
      d. postcards and mailing cards
      e. self-mailing folders
      f. broadsides
      g. booklets and catalogs
   2. Miscellaneous direct media:
      a. dodgers, handbills, circulars
      b. prints of advertisements
      c. package inserts
      d. wrapping supplies, merchandise labels
      e. gift novelties
      f. telegrams
      g. special delivery letters
      h. store publications
   3. Telephone

C. Sign (or transit) advertising media:
   1. Outdoor signs:
      a. posters
      b. painted bulletins
      c. electric signs
   2. Cards:
      a. car cards
      b. station posters
      c. bus cards
   3. Miscellaneous signs:
      a. taxicab signs
      b. truck signs and posters
      c. theater curtains, slides
      d. movie shorts
      e. street banners
      f. sky writing
      g. kites and balloons

D. Broadcast advertising media:
   1. Radio
      a. direct or live broadcasts
      b. electrical transcriptions (tapes)
   2. Television
      a. direct or live broadcasts
      b. videotape broadcasts
   3. Miscellaneous broadcast advertising media
      a. portable loudspeaker systems

Add to this list a number of internal media to reach the customer in the store, and the retailer has a formidable array of sales promotional vehicles from which to choose. The problem lies in understanding the characteristics of each and making the right selection.

Publication Media

This group of printed media refers mainly to newspapers and magazines. They deliver the advertiser's message to measurable groups of readers in a package consisting of other advertisements combined with news, entertainment, or similar noncommercial content. The audience for the advertiser's message is preselected for him or her by the circulations of the media. In fact, most of the retailer's decision deals with selecting the media whose audiences match the prospective markets the retailer hopes to reach.

In addition to the distinction between those newspapers that provide broad coverage within a particular community and those with regional or national circulation, newspapers are generally classified by two other methods. One is according to page size or format, the other according to the frequency of publication and the characteristics of the local markets they serve.

In terms of format and page size, newspapers are generally classified as standard or tabloid. Traditionally the standard newspaper size is approximately 21 inches deep and 8 columns wide, with each column about 2 inches in width. In practice, however, the actual size may vary greatly, and the standard size newspaper varies a great deal among publishers. Basically, standard simply means a large size page. Tabloid newspapers are approximately half the standard size, or 5 columns wide by 14 inches deep, but there is also a great deal of variation. This variation often causes real problems for advertisers who wish to run the same advertising message in several different newspapers.

Because the cost of newsprint skyrocketed in 1974 and 1975, many newspapers are contemplating reducing the width of their newspapers to 13¾ inches. This necessitates a change from 8 columns to 6. The length of the newspaper will remain unchanged. In early 1975 the *Los Angeles Times* and the *Miami Herald* started using this new format. Some newspapers contemplate using a 6 column format for both news and display advertising, while others will go to a 6 column format for news but retain the 8 column format for advertising.

By frequency of publication, newspapers fall into two broad groups, dailies and weeklies. However, dailies may be published four, five, six, or seven days a week, and weeklies may be published once or even three times a week. Daily papers may further be broken down as community dailies[11] or metropolitan dailies. Metropolitan dailies often reach homes or families far beyond the city limits or even beyond retail trading zones. Community dailies, on the other hand, have little circulation beyond the local trading zone, although geographically this might be quite extensive.

Weekly newspapers are even more localized in circulation and editorial appeal. Their content is largely local and personal news of the communities they serve, and within these communities they may enjoy a more thorough and careful reading and a longer life than either the metropolitan or small town daily. However, the cost per reader in weekly newspapers is higher than dailies, and weekly circulation is usually small and not verified by independent audits. Also many weekly newspapers are either voluntary pay or free to the readers (that is, there is no price charged for delivery).

The advertising department of a typical daily newspaper usually consists of three subdepartments. One handles only classified advertising, which is placed in a special section of the paper and arranged by specific product and service classifications. Classified advertising is an important source of revenue for newspapers, but display advertising is of greater interest to retailers. Display advertising offers a variety of layout designs, space sizes, and type, and may be placed throughout the paper. (See Figure 12.3.)

Two of the three subdepartments are concerned with display advertising. One department handles advertising by national or regional advertisers. The other handles advertising by retailers and other local advertisers. For retailers without the services of professional advertising agencies or their own advertising departments, most newspapers offer assistance with layout design and preparation of advertising materials.

The rate structure of almost all newspapers offers different rates to national and local retail advertisers. The local rate is frequently lower and allows no commission to advertising agencies. The basic unit of space for local advertising is the "column inch," an area one column wide and one inch deep. In the *Atlanta Journal*, for example, the standard black-and-white rate for local advertisers is $18.20 per column inch. However, by volume discounts, the local retail advertiser can trim as much as 40 percent from the standard rate. Another basic unit often used to measure newspaper advertising space is the "agate line." There are 14 agate lines to the column inch. Any rates quoted per line can easily be converted to the rate per column by multiplying the line rate by 14.

The basic rates quoted by newspapers are generally the "run-of-paper" (ROP) advertising rates, meaning that the retailer cannot specify the position in the paper he or she wishes the advertisements to have. Preferred position on the page or in

[11]The *Arlington Heights Herald* (Illinois) is an example of a community daily published Monday through Saturday. *The Chicago Tribune* is an example of a metropolitan daily published every day.

FIGURE 12.3
Many food chains make use of display advertisements featuring coupons

Source: Paddock Publications, Inc., Arlington Heights, Illinois.

special sections usually requires an additional charge of from 5 to 20 percent above the base rate. Also, the base rate is for advertisements printed in black ink only. The addition of color in newspaper advertisements necessitates an extra charge, which may vary from 15 to 50 percent above the base rate, depending on the number of colors used.

Newspapers, principally because of their local nature, have accounted for the majority of retail advertising expenditures. In 1973 newspapers carried \$6.5 billion in local advertising, compared with \$2.3 billion in local radio and local television advertising combined.[12] Although the broadcast media appeared to be headed for

[12] *1975 The U.S. Fact Book*, p. 772.

spectacular gains in dollars of retail advertising in the 1970s, newspapers still account for about 76 percent of the total spent on retail advertising. Retailers' increased expenditures in broadcast advertising seldom seem to be accompanied by cuts in their expenditures for newspaper advertising.

Magazines offer the advertiser advantages which in many respects are opposites of those offered by newspapers. The newspaper appeals to all kinds of people within a community; the magazine appeals to particular kinds of people often in many different communities. Also, the life of a newspaper advertisement is usually less than 24 hours, while a magazine advertisement may produce results for a week, month, or even longer. The printing quality of newspapers is usually limited, while magazines usually offer much finer reproduction which helps lend a quality image to certain types of merchandise and stores. The basic unit of sale in magazine advertising is the page.

Although magazines have traditionally been considered a medium only for advertisers with national distribution, many magazines now offer regional, sectional, or even state and metropolitan editions. *National Geographic* magazine, for example, offers local and regional advertisers the opportunity to advertise in any one or a combination of 50 states and several metropolitan areas. A black and white, full page advertisement in the Chicago edition of *National Geographic* would cost $1,890, which is considerably lower than the $24,100 cost of the same advertisement nationally. The flexibility of regional, state, and metropolitan editions is made possible by special regional printing plants. The only basic difference between one regional edition and another is its advertising.

Broadcast Media

Printed media depend upon the ability of the reader to see and read advertising messages in order to understand them. For radio, only the ability to hear is mandatory; even the illiterate person can be reached by this medium. One advantage often claimed for radio advertising is that messages received through the ear are less impersonal than those read in newspapers or magazines.

Advertising messages on television are able to attract through both sight and sound. But it does not merely combine the appeals of printed media and radio, for it has the additional impact advantage of motion. Since television advertising permits motion, it is often used when demonstration is important in making a sales point. Some of the special advantages of personal selling are found in many television commercials.

In the broadcast media the rate structure is based on the hour and the minute. Programs are sold to sponsors for periods of time which are portions of an hour. Spot announcement time is usually sold for periods which are fractions of a minute. Announcements of 10, 20, and 30 seconds are most frequent in television, while those of one minute are dominant in radio. The national-local split rate structure in newspaper advertising is less common in broadcast advertising, with most stations tending toward the single rate structure typical of magazines.

Frequency and volume discounts are usually given to advertisers by both radio and television stations, just as in newspaper advertising. Special rates are charged for advertising messages to be broadcast in preferred time positions. Broadcast rates vary greatly depending upon how large an audience the radio or television station has during any particular time period during the day.

In broadcasting, a careful distinction is made between the terms *circulation* and *coverage*. Circulation is the number of actual listeners or viewers, while the coverage of a broadcasting station is its potential audience. In essence, the coverage of a radio or television station is that geographical area where the station signal can normally be received.

Advertisers using the broadcast media can purchase time for advertising messages in three basic ways: network, spot, and local. Both spot and network advertising purchases are normally made by national advertisers. However, retail advertisers with regional markets also use spot advertising, which refers to non-network purchases of announcements on a group of selected radio or television stations. Most retail advertisers purchase local broadcast time directly from the station. According to figures in *Radio/Television Age* magazine, local television billing grew at a faster pace than spot or network in 1969.[13] In the first quarter of 1970, retail advertisers' rising interest in television continued, with a reported 51 percent increase in retail investments. Radio people are also pleased by retailer interest in television as a break with retail's traditional loyalty to newspaper advertising.[14]

Local broadcast advertising accounted for 20 percent of the total expenditure by local advertisers in 1973, according to the McCann-Ericson Index. Radio with $1,175 million leads slightly with 10 percent of the total; local television accounted for 9.6 percent, or $1,085 million.[15]

Woolworth, although traditionally relying almost exclusively on newspaper advertising, is one of a number of retailers who have begun using television extensively. In mid-1970 Woolworth launched an all-out campaign in 38 markets with the results showing excellent consumer response. Woolworth was able to key each commercial to a major merchandise promotion each month. The messages were light and informative, showed the wide variety of merchandise available, and added significantly to Woolworth's efforts to upgrade its image. And F. and P. Lazarus and Company, one of the Federated's chains of department stores operating in Columbus, Ohio, produces its own television commercials. It even sells the commercials to its suppliers who can use the advertising in other market areas.

Position Media

Position advertising media differ from most other forms of advertising in that the prospect goes to the advertising message rather than the message going to the prospect as in publication, broadcast, and direct mail advertising. That is, the message is placed where prospects will be exposed to the advertiser's story as they

[13]"Local TV: With department stores setting pace. . . ," *Television/Radio Age* (January 26, 1970), p. 27.

[14]"Radio Report," *Television/Radio Age* (September 21, 1970), p. 17.

[15]*1975 The U.S. Fact Book*, p. 772.

go about their normal activities. The word *position* is applied to this type of advertising because the strategy involved consists in physically placing the message in the correct place or position, usually along heavily traveled pedestrian and vehicular traffic routes.

The major categories of position media are outdoor advertising, nonstandardized signs, and transportation advertising. (Point-of-purchase advertising, another important category of position advertising, will be covered later in the chapter under in-store promotions.) A source of some confusion is very often the distinction between outdoor advertising and nonstandardized sign advertising. The key to the difference between these two is the word *nonstandardized.*

Outdoor Advertising. Outdoor advertising accounts for only about two percent of the total amount spent by national and local advertisers. The other two types of position media are of such relative unimportance that they are lumped in the miscellaneous category. Although position media are only a small percentage of total advertising dollars spent by local and national advertisers combined, it is reasonable to surmise that they are a more important factor to local retail advertisers alone.

Among position media the dominant subtype is outdoor advertising. However, not all advertising that appears out of doors falls into this classification. The most common term used to refer to outdoor advertising media is the billboard. But not all the billboards on the streets and highways are included in the technical definition of outdoor advertising. Only those which meet certain standards set by the Outdoor Advertising Association of America are so classified. The standards deal with size, design, and method of construction of billboards, which are called either posters or painted bulletins. Roadside and on-premise devices which are not standardized are in turn called "signs" by the industry.

The most commonly encountered billboard is the poster. Approximately three-fourths of the national outdoor sales volume is realized by this form. Most posters today are 24-sheet posters. They measure 104 inches high and 234 inches long, and are framed by a border that remains permanently part of the structure. Although the term *24-sheet poster* still refers to billboards of this size, modern printing techniques permit the typical poster to be prepared from only 10 separate sheets. Each of these sheets is individually pasted to the billboard to make the complete advertising message.

Several variations of this normal poster size have been added by the outdoor advertising industry to meet new needs. The 30-sheet poster was developed to give 25 percent more space to reach more effectively modern, faster flowing auto traffic. Two other minor variations are the 6-sheet and 3-sheet poster for use in congested areas or to reach pedestrian traffic. Posters may also be illuminated or regular (non-illuminated), depending on the volume of night traffic in an area.

The second major form of outdoor advertising is the painted display. Instead of being printed on sheets of paper, the message is painted. The cost is generally higher for painted displays, and they usually remain in an area for a relatively long period of time. However, copy parts on section facings making up a painted bulletin may be moved (rotated) from one bulletin location to another. Variations of the painted bulletin are the three-dimensional painted bulletin and the moving, or multivision, bulletin. Electric spectacular signs are another type of outdoor advertising, and the costs associated with these spectaculars are usually high.

Outdoor advertising is usually sold in monthly periods. One board is the minimum an advertiser can purchase, although the individual poster is seldom sold as a single unit. Instead, the basic selling package is called a 100 showing. Theoretically, a 100 showing is a particular combination of posters which will insure that 100 percent of the people in the market will see the advertiser's message in a 30-day period.

Nonstandardized Signs. Nonstandardized signs are basically all those advertising signs which fall outside of the standards set by the outdoor advertising industry. These signs fall basically into two groups: roadside signs and on-premise signs. Due to legal restrictions and faster speed of automobile traffic, the number of new roadside signs has been on the decline. Most retailers use on-premise signs to tell consumers of their existence and their products and services.

The growth of shopping centers with huge open-air malls has prompted the development of a hybrid form of position media which tastefully combines art displays with commercial messages. The People's Gallery program created by Metromedia has developed what it calls the "triosk." As the name implies, each triosk is a three-sided display. Each is seven feet high and supported by a sculptured base. The unique feature of this medium is that one facing is devoted entirely to the display of noncommercial fine art.

Transportation Advertising. Transportation advertising is the third major type of position media. Transit advertising, as it is also called, is similar in function and method of industry operation to standardized outdoor advertising. About 70 percent of the money spent on transit advertising is for car cards, which appear in the overhead racks of buses, subways, and trains. Another major type, traveling displays, appears on the sides of buses and streetcars and is really a hybrid between car cards and the outdoor poster. Station posters are a third type included in the classification of transportation advertising. Ads are placed in bus, train, and air terminals to reach travelers on the move.

Direct Advertising

Direct advertising, principally direct mail advertising, offers the retail advertiser the advantage of delivering a message to a particular target market with little or no waste circulation. No other medium can offer the advertiser both the geographic and the qualitative selectivity possible with direct advertising. Letters are perhaps the most widely used form of all direct advertising, but other commonly used forms are leaflets, folders, broadsides, booklets, brochures, catalogs, and company publications. The variety of shapes, sizes, and formats of direct mail advertising material is limited only by the ingenuity of the advertiser, the budget, and postal regulations.

First and third class mail account for all direct mail advertising, except for occasional specialties or samples sent by parcel post. The advertiser's choice between first and third class mail must be determined by a number of factors—particularly the product and the firm image the retailer wishes to portray. First class is faster and enjoys more prestige, but is more costly. Third class is more economical, but it is slower, less impressive, and likely to get less attention.

Both the quantity and the quality of direct mail circulation are determined by the mailing list the advertiser uses. Ideally, a mailing list should include only those people who are bonafide customers or potential customers of the retailer's establishment. Names must be spelled correctly and addresses kept up to date to make the direct mail effort effective. Retailers who have charge account customers or maintain similar lists have an excellent nucleus for a direct mail list.

Many other specialty forms of advertising media are available to the retail advertiser—too many to cover here individually. But many of these media can be used very effectively by the retailer. They include calendars, novelties, gifts, exhibits, film advertising in local movie theaters, advertising in directories such as the classified phone directory, and many more.

CREATION OF ADVERTISING

Most retail advertising is local in nature, primarily offering information about the products a merchant has for sale. The advertisement describes the products, states their prices, gives the name and location of the store, and states whether the goods may also be purchased by telephone or mail. In short, retail advertisements are ways of giving simple, direct, and specific information to potential customers. Moreover, most retail advertisements are shown at somewhat regular intervals as part of a continuous series in which retailers present their products.

Acceptance of Retail Advertising

Retail advertising is well accepted by the general public, and in fact is a key part of most newspapers from the reader's point of view. A very recent survey showed that advertising ranked seventh out of 24 selected features in overall interest, outranking national sports news, feature stories, editorials, and stock market reports. In the same study, the respondents were asked to state what newspaper features should be retained if a paper shortage dictated that some features would be dropped. From a list of 34 features, food advertising was chosen by 87.7 percent of the readers. Only national news, state news, and local news received higher ratings. This survey confirmed the fact that readers accept retail advertisements readily and, in fact, advertisers' messages are read avidly for news of new products, items on sale, price changes, and other useful information.

Use of Illustrations

Retail advertising can easily become trite and dull when the emphasis is on giving information. Yet it need not be dull; in fact, each advertisement should be distinctive in order to stand out from similar advertisements placed by competitors. Illustrations and layout design are as important to retail advertisements as they are to other advertisements. It is said that a picture is worth a thousand words, and good retail advertisements use pictures effectively. Retailers who rely on catalogs to sell their merchandise by mail know the value of illustrative materials; Sears' and Ward's catalogs are still highly desired by American families.

Store Personality

Inasmuch as all retail advertising gives clues about a store's image as well as information about the products and services for sale, it is important for a retailer to choose the layout design, illustrations, and copy that reinforce the image that he wishes to project. The layout of a retail advertisement is the most important symbol of a store's personality. For example, a store whose major appeal is price and whose customers are from the lower income groups is likely to have an advertisement that is crowded with items for sale. On the other hand, a prestige store whose customers are from the upper income groups may use advertisements that feature considerable white space with an absence of clutter.

Who Creates the Retailers' Advertisements?

Large stores, including department stores, food chains, and variety chains, frequently have their own advertising departments and hence create their own advertising. Manufacturers often give smaller stores illustrations to use in their advertisements, and in some cases, small retailers design their own advertisements without help from anyone. Newspapers, too, help small retailers through suggestions by their salespeople when they solicit the retailers' advertising business.

In summary, then, retailers use advertisements primarily to attract customers to their stores and thus build traffic. Rarely does retail advertising seek to create a favorable impression about a single product as is usually the case with national advertising. For this reason, there is a good deal of sameness that characterizes retail advertising.

COORDINATING AND EVALUATING ADVERTISING

Developing a retail advertising program is a complex process, and there are many factors that must be considered and controlled. Research usually backdrops these activities, and ideally provisions are made for the evaluation of the advertising in order that future efforts may be improved. Every step along the advertising planning route should be closely scrutinized to see that advertising expenditures yield the highest possible returns. Effective coordination of advertising with other retail activities, however, often is overlooked. Also, the evaluation of retail advertising is frequently inadequate to pinpoint problem areas, to correct past mistakes, and to set objectives to present and future advertising.

Common Mistakes by Retail Advertisers

Professor John O. Whitney of the Harvard Business School notes the uncertainty and diversity of opinion among retailers about the proper use of their advertising expenditures. He says:

> Unfortunately, one of the few things retailers seem to agree on—privately but generally—is that there is too much waste in their advertising; however, they find themselves in the position of John Wanamaker, who reportedly said, "I know that half of my advertising is wasted, but the problem is I don't know which half."[16]

Most of the common mistakes made by retail advertisers can be overcome by basic planning, setting realistic objectives for advertising, coordinating the execution of advertising with other retail activities, and then properly evaluating the results. Of course, this sounds much easier to do than it really is, but an understanding of some common problems is a step in the right direction.

One basic mistake committed by retail advertisers is the poor allocation of the advertising budget. Often, rules of thumb are used in setting the budget instead of the real needs in the competitive market situation. Many retailers begin a heavy thrust of advertising only after their competition has pushed them into it. The only objective of such advertising is a hazy notion that it will hopefully blunt the competitor's advertising. Another area of significant waste is the proportional allocation of advertising dollars to departments based on past departmental sales. This practice overlooks the sales potential of certain departments and often does not enhance the overall image of the entire store.

Another common misuse of advertising by retailers is to advertise low-priced, "hot" items merely to inflate weekly sales volume and store traffic figures. This practice often results in prices being set too low to cover all the retailer's expenses. The retailer has created what may look like prosperity, but it is essentially a profitless prosperity. It may even damage the overall personality of the store.

In many cases, retailers also fail to realize the dual effects which their advertising has on sales. One effect is short term and can be evaluated by weekly sales volume, the number of items sold, and customer traffic. The other effect is long range; yet, many retailers measure advertising effectiveness only in the short run. Whitney points out that foods chains, department stores, and general merchandise discounters are not the only organizations that have fallen into the trap of evaluating advertising solely in the short term. He continues:[17]

> Banks and savings and loan associations, which at one time enjoyed a rate advantage over other savings instruments, often advertised their interest and dividend rates to the exclusion of other customer benefits. However, those financial institutions which emphasized their full range of services in many instances fared better

[16]John O. Whitney, "Better Results from Retail Advertising," *Harvard Business Review* (May-June 1970), p. 111.

[17]Ibid., p. 113.

> than their competitors. . . . It is understandable, in the fiercely competitive retail world, that performance measurement is an imperative management function.
>
> Nevertheless, it is paradoxical that the very tools intended to measure and improve performance so limit advertising's potential that they contribute to the very waste they are intended to reduce.

Another similar oversight by retail advertisers is their failure to recognize the value of advertising as a management tool. There are at least two audiences for all retail advertising. One is the store's customers, the other its employees. Much of the good effects of advertising are lost if employees are unaware of what is being advertised. Astute merchandisers take steps to make sure that salespeople are familiar with the store's advertising each day, including the products that are featured, their prices, and where they are stocked and sold. Such steps include posting the ads in the employee locker rooms, describing the goods in the employee newsletter, announcements on the store's public address system, and through the daily meeting with the department heads.

One example of the beneficial effects of advertising on employees is a campaign by Trans World Airlines, which used its advertising to reward employees directly while at the same time encouraging better service. A 1969 TWA campaign, built around a $1 million bonus to employees for good service, motivated employees directly and gave potential passengers a tangible reason to believe that they would receive better service on TWA.

DISPLAY POLICIES

Sales promotion in the retail store has been the subject of a wide divergence of opinion in recent years. Some have defined retail sales promotion as merchandising; others have applied the term to special sales events or publicity stunts, such as fashion shows, classes, and prize contests. Actually sales promotion can refer to an almost infinite list of activities which contribute directly or indirectly to sales. However, this section will deal exclusively with the most important subarea of in-store sales promotion, specifically merchandising and display policies. Other promotional techniques are covered in the following section.

Most of the activities which are grouped under the general heading of merchandising are really point-of-purchase sales promotion, often called point-of-purchase advertising. When the consumer arrives in the retail trading area, the "moment of truth" has arrived. Probably the consumer has been attracted to the retailer's store by some phase of this advertising. However, once in the store, the consumer still must be convinced to purchase the retailer's merchandise. Through point-of-purchase advertising the retailer has one final chance to direct the consumer's attention to specific goods and services and to convince him or her to buy the goods in *that* store. In addition, the retailer may, through appealing displays, influence the consumer to make unplanned purchases by reminding him or her of additional needs and wants.

Point-of-purchase advertising has been defined as: "Promotional materials situated in, on, or immediately adjacent to retail distribution points, designed to build traffic for the retailer, register advertising impressions, redirect in-store traffic, and actually sell merchandise."[18] The variety of point-of-purchase promotional materials is virtually endless. The types we will discuss in this section include window displays, special interior displays, wall displays, display cards, and merchandise racks and cases.

Window Displays

In certain types of retailing, store location is extremely important. One basis for selecting a location may be that a sizable volume of traffic passes the spot. If this is the case, and the type of merchandise is such that it would attract the attention of hurrying passersby, then the retailer could probably use window display to great advantage.

Window displays for such merchants are intended to slow down the pace of the passing consumer long enough to persuade him or her to come into the store and look further. Thus, the display must be striking since it is the face that the store presents to the public. Window displays are an important part of the store image in the consumer's mind. All retailers should give serious thought to what they have in their windows. Displays should be imaginative, changed frequently, and topical. (See Figure 12.4.)

FIGURE 12.4
An attractive window display in a mall setting can be used to advantage

Source: Edison Brothers Stores, St. Louis, Missouri.

[18]William W. Mee, "How Point-of-Purchase Is More Efficient as an Advertising and Sales Medium," *Media/Scope* (September 1963), pp. 55–56.

Interior Displays

The use of displays within the store can have the same effect as window displays by attracting consumers to particular departments or sections. Interior displays often are as appealing and as large as window displays. Nearly every type of interior display can be classified as either an assortment display, a theme display, or an ensemble display.[19]

Assortment displays, as the name indicates, show a complete range of a particular kind of merchandise, including styles, colors, materials, and prices. From the shopper's point of view this type of display is perhaps the most helpful. Advantages for the retailer are that assortment displays can be used to impress shoppers with the variety and completeness of the stock, and they enable shoppers to make selections quickly. (See Figure 12.5.)

FIGURE 12.5
Food stores use assortment displays to induce buying

Source: Keebler Company, Elmhurst, Illinois.

[19]For a further discussion of various types of interior display, see Edwards and Brown, *Retail Advertising and Sales Promotion.*

Theme displays are built around a selling theme such as "National Clean-up, Fix-up, Paint-up Week," or "Harvest Week." The variety of theme, or idea, displays is as limitless as the imagination of the display manager. The important point in theme display is to select an idea that will kindle the interest of consumers and supply them with a valid reason for making a purchase. Theme displays do not necessarily have to be elaborate, but they should develop one selling idea in a dramatic way.

Ensemble displays are those in which related merchandise is combined to provide a complete display effect. Ensemble displays may promote children's swings and other toys by showing an entire playground setup, or they may promote the sale of a living room suite by depicting an entire room setting, including a rug, furniture, lamps, and draperies. Even though an ensemble display may be promoting a number of items, as a general rule only one central item should be featured. (See Figure 12.6.)

FIGURE 12.6
An ensemble display promotes the sale of merchandise

Source: Pint Size Jrs., Chicago, Illinois.

Wall Displays

In addition to the major types of interior displays already mentioned, wall displays can also be used effectively to attract consumers' attention and promote particular merchandise. Poster-like ads promoting particular brands of merchandise may be affixed to the walls of the store. Many displays of this type are available directly from product manufacturers. Soft drink manufacturers have been eager to make available window and wall displays to retailers upon request. Often displays of this type have a powerful impact in directing consumers to particular types and brands of merchandise carried by a retailer. (See Figure 12.7.)

FIGURE 12.7
Merchandise itself is frequently used as part of a wall display

Source: Pint Size Jrs., Chicago, Illinois.

Display Cards

A considerable amount of point-of-purchase promotion is placed on various sizes and shapes of cardboard. The cards may vary from life-size cutout models which stand on the selling floor to reproductions of a magazine advertisement. These display cards may be used in window displays, as counter top cards, or in any type of in-store display. They perform the function of silent salesclerks and often provide information about special offers, prices, and merchandise.

Merchandise Racks and Cases

A very effective point-of-purchase device is the rack or case. Not only is the consumer presented with a message about the product, but he or she sees the merchandise itself. A good example of this form of promotion is the candy rack designed by Life Savers. This rack presents the merchant's collection of candy in a case that fits near the cash register where impulse buying is highest. Merchandise racks for bigger items are placed on the floor instead of on the counter. Greeting card companies place such cases in retail outlets; cards are displayed attractively and a reserve supply stock is stored below.

Other Promotional Techniques

Trading stamps are more of a mechanism for obtaining consumer loyalty than they are quick action stimuli for increased sales. These devices are merely a small premium to reward customers for purchasing merchandise from a particular retailer. The stamps are accumulated until a sufficient quantity can be exchanged for premiums of some value.

Since the prime purpose of trading stamps is to promote store loyalty, they should be promoted aggressively by the retailer. They should not be distributed grudgingly to customers. Every customer must be encouraged to save the retailer's brand of stamp if customer loyalty is to be built by this method of sales promotion.

Historically, as many as 80 percent of American families have participated in one or more stamp plans, and the number of stores involved has been as high as 260,000. However, more recent indicators show that the appeal of trading stamps is waning In fact, sales of trading stamps dropped 15 percent in 1973, primarily because gasoline stations no longer needed to give trading stamps to promote sales. The loss of gasoline stations was serious for trading stamp companies because they accounted for 25 percent of the stamp business. Prior to the oil crisis, the stamp industry had suffered a major blow when food chains, such as A & P, dropped stamps in favor of discount prices.[20]

One gas station in California satisfied both stamp and nonstamp saving customers by dividing its pumps into two sections. One offered trading stamps, the other lower prices. Stamp customers received eight times the normal amount of stamps with each purchase. Customers who didn't want stamps received a ten-cent discount on each gallon of gasoline. The station manager claims stamp and nonstamp customers were divided about half and half.[21]

Contests have been a valuable sales promotional device for many retailers. However, care and planning should be exercised in selecting an appropriate type of

[20]"Energy Shortage Buffets Trading Stamps," *New York Times*, April 27, 1974, p. 39.

[21]"Buyer's Choice: Stamp or Savings," *Business Week* (February 7, 1970), p. 106. But note that in 1975 gasoline stations did not need to promote the sales of gasoline because of the energy crunch; thus stamp plans were abandoned.

contest. Inappropriate contests can damage the public image of a firm. The public furor of past years over games sponsored by oil companies and national manufacturers, and their methods of awarding prizes, have caused many consumers to become skeptical of all such contests.

There are two fundamental kinds of contests: contests of skill and contests of chance, or semilotteries. When skill is involved, customers are asked to do something which is judged, and prizes are awarded for superior performances. Customers may be asked to knit, cook, make a dress, compose a limerick, draw a picture, or think up a slogan. In one midwestern town, a local bank has sponsored a doll making contest for years. Hundreds of entries, many of them elaborate, are received each year from all over the state and are exhibited in the bank's branches to attract bank patrons and visitors.

When the chance, or so-called sweepstakes, approach is used, customers' names are pooled and the winner's name is selected at random. More entries are likely with this method. Entrants are usually required to come to the retailer's place of business to register. Very often gifts of merchandise are given in addition to, or instead of, cash prizes.

Retailers sometimes give free goods of various types to induce customers to buy specified merchandise during designated periods. These "premiums" may take many different forms, and the retailer may occasionally make a small additional charge to help cover the expense of the extra merchandise. The premiums usually have some relationship to the merchandise being promoted for sale. For example, a sporting goods store may give away a ticket to the local skating rink with each pair of skates. Provided premiums are chosen with consideration for the likes and dislikes of possible customers, they can be potent sales stimulants.

Giving consumers samples of merchandise can be a valuable sales aid because it affords them the opportunity to see for themselves how the merchandise actually works. For nondurable goods, samples allow customers to get their hands on the good, or a specimen of it, and prospects are often turned into customers. It would be unrealistic to give customers samples of expensive durable goods, such as televisions and washing machines, but free trial offers or in-store demonstrations can often accomplish the same thing.

One of the main objectives of a retailer's publicity division is to "humanize" the store's image to its customers. There are many ways to achieve this reputation. Special instructions of classes have been used with great success by many retailers to enhance their images. Classes are primarily noncommercial and do not attempt to sell merchandise directly.

F. and R. Lazarus, for example, recognized the yearning of preteen girls to overcome their awkward years. They conduct a charm school to teach young girls good grooming, graceful walking, and care of the skin and hair. No fee is charged and no merchandise is shown. The benefit for the retailer is the establishment of the company as one that cares about its customers beyond strictly making a profit. Many retailers offer similar classes for their employees.

Special departments can perform a similar function, as in the case of Rike Kumler of Dayton, Ohio, which sets up a Tykes' Shop at Christmas. This special shop is a secret spot where the tiniest tot can choose gifts in complete privacy. The entrance is three feet high, and the only persons admitted are those who can walk through standing up. No item costs more than a dollar, and the company keeps emergency piles of pennies inside to make up the difference between the tiny shopper's cash-on-hand and the actual retail price.[22]

JOINT PROMOTIONS

Joint retail promotions fall into two broad categories: horizontal cooperative promotion in which a group of retailers cooperate, and vertical cooperative promotion in which a national advertiser pays all or part of the expense of the promotional featuring his or her product.[23] Both categories are usually lumped under the term cooperative, or co-op, advertising, although a wide variety of promotional techniques may be used. The object of horizontal promotion is to obtain greater impact than any one retailer could generate from the same expenditure not used cooperatively. The object of vertical promotion for the national advertiser is to identify the product directly with the local retailer, while for the retailer the purpose is to supplement his or her own promotional budget.

There are two types of horizontal cooperation among retailers. One is the affiliation of merchants in the same type of business through a voluntary chain or other cooperative group for the purpose of jointly promoting specific goods and services. Examples would be the advertising of voluntarily affiliated independent grocers, such as the Independent Grocers Alliance (IGA) in the Midwest. By pooling their efforts, these independent retailers can compete effectively with the giant corporate chains. Suppliers often financially support the advertising of these retail cooperatives, making the promotional both horizontal and vertical.

A second type of horizontal promotion is that of retailers selling different lines of merchandise who cooperatively sponsor promotions for a shopping center or other business district. These promotions are generally in the form of sales such as Washington's Birthday sales, sidewalk sales, midnight sales, and so on. The object is to generate greater customer interest than any one store could hope to accomplish alone.

Co-op advertising generally refers to the practice by a manufacturer or other supplier of reimbursing the retailer for part or all of the advertising expense in promoting the manufacturer's product. It is not uncommon for the manufacturer to pay 50 percent or more of the retailer's advertising expense for particular promotions. In addition, the manufacturer may furnish the retailer with newspaper mats, radio and television copy, tapes, films, and other advertising material that might otherwise be prohibitively expensive for the individual retailer to produce.

The main advantages of co-op advertising to the retailer are that the advertising

[22]Harriet Wilinsky, *Careers and Opportunities in Retailing* (New York: E.P. Dutton and Co., Inc., 1970), p. 103.

[23]William R. Davidson and Alton F. Doody, *Retailing Management* (New York: Ronald Press, 1966), Chapter 7.

budget can be stretched and that professionally prepared advertising materials are available, which add to the image of the store. The major advantages for the manufacturer or supplier are that he attaches a local identity to the product, and that he may take advantage of cheaper local advertising rates (principally in newspapers). Allowances available to the retailer for co-op advertising are usually calculated from a specified percentage of sales by the manufacturer to the retailer. These commonly range from one to five percent. Most co-op advertising traditionally has been placed in newspapers, but radio and television are receiving a good deal more co-op advertising dollars.[24]

Although the emphasis has been on co-op advertising expenditures, allowances are also made for other sales promotional events. These may include payment for interior or window displays using the manufacturer's product, incentives for salespeople, demonstrators, free goods, and many other promotional devices.

In many consumer goods industries there are substantially more cooperative funds available to retailers than can be used, so suppliers generally encourage retailers to participate in their plan. However, cooperative promotional plans frequently have been abused, particularly by those suppliers who have favored larger customers. The Robinson-Patman Act—best known for limiting the circumstances under which sellers can sell to competing buyers at different prices—rather carefully lays out the rights of a retailer with regard to promotional allowances. Since promotional expenditures are so important to many retailers, it behooves the retailer to know what demands can be made of the supplier under Sections 2(d) and 2(e). Section 2(d) applies to those circumstances where the seller pays the buyer (retailer) to perform promotional services, while Section 2(e) is applicable when the seller performs the task but it affects the businesses of his or her buyers. Both sections require that the seller accord to competing customers promotional allowances on proportionally equal terms with regard to goods of like grade or quality.

The retailer has four major rights under the law as it is interpreted by the Federal Trade Commission:[25]

1. The right to insist that payments and services be provided on a proportionately equal basis. A dress manufacturer who grants a $1 allowance to retailers who buy 10 dozen dresses and $1.50 to those who buy more is violating the law. Such quantity discounts are not on promotionally equal terms. The small retailer who buys only 10 dozen dresses is entitled to the same allowance per unit as the large buyer, although the large retailer will obviously earn a larger aggregate allowance than the small buyer.
2. The right to participate in an alternate plan provided by the supplier where the basic plan is not feasible. The manufacturer cannot legally insist that all cooperative money be spent on television advertising, knowing that only the largest resellers would be able to implement such a promotional program. This was a particularly difficult problem for the cosmetics manufacturer for many years, who believed that in-store demonstrators were the most efficient way

[24]"Advertising in a New Co-op Era," *Merchandising Week* (January 12, 1970), p. 18.

[25]*Guides for Advertising Allowances and Other Merchandising Payments and Services,* as amended August 4, 1972, Federal Trade Commission, Washington, D.C.

to sell their products. Such an expensive program was not warranted in smaller stores where traffic was light, so manufacturers were obliged to put together an alternate plan in order to conform to the law.

3. The right to be fully informed about exact terms of the plan. Most manufacturers who have substantial cooperative plans have a mechanism to assure that all who qualify for the plan know about its existence and how it operates. A small retailer who buys through a wholesaler has as much right to know the details of a cooperative plan as does the larger retailer who buys directly from the manufacturer. And the manufacturer is obliged either to make sure that wholesalers inform the small retailers or he must use the wholesaler's customer list to make sure the information gets through the marketing channel.
4. The right to know that all resellers who receive allowances are policed equally with respect to their use. Suppliers who furnish promotional allowances frequently establish procedures for assuring compliance with the conditions spelled out in the basic plan. Cooperative plans have a long and unhappy history of instances in which a manufacturer paid for advertisements that were never run; retailers are known to have insisted that an advertisement was run and demanded payment. Valued customers often were not challenged, so the effect was one of a price discount rather than a promotional allowance.

SUMMARY

Promotion is the communication between a seller and a buyer. It encompasses both personal selling and advertising—both of which are vital to a retailer. Frequently, advertising is confused with other activities such as propaganda and publicity. However there are four characteristics that identify advertising: (1) it is paid for by an advertiser, (2) it is a nonpersonal presentation, (3) it is used to sell ideas and services as well as goods, and (4) it has an identifiable sponsor.

Retail advertising differs from national advertising because the retailer is trying to attract customers to a particular store or to a limited number of stores. It is essentially local in nature. On the other hand, the national advertiser is trying to sell a product or a group of products over a wide geographic area—usually including many stores. Retailers use institutional advertising to sell the store itself, and they use promotional advertising to sell specific merchandise for a specified period of time.

Retailers should use thoughtfully conceived advertising plans if they wish to obtain the most value for their advertising dollars. A plan must include all of the following:

1. An analysis of the marketing situation which they face.
2. A statement including all of their advertising objectives.
3. Alternative methods of budgeting the advertising dollars.
4. Selection of the media in which to place their advertising.
5. Creation of the advertising message.
6. Coordinating the advertising with other selling methods.
7. Evaluation of results.

Many retailers find their advertising is not as effective as they had hoped. This may be due to their own mistakes. Some of the common mistakes retailers make are: (1) allocating their budget funds unwisely, (2) advertising low-priced, "hot" items in order to inflate store volume and store traffic figures, (3) using only advertising for short-term effects, (4) not using advertising as a management tool, and (5) lacking coordination with other selling methods.

Retailers also employ sales promotional activities within the store itself. These include window displays, wall displays, and interior arrangements. Throughout the store, point-of-purchase promotional advertising may also be used.

Retailers often act cooperatively with other retailers in advertising. Sometimes the retailer has the help of a national advertiser who pays all or part of the promotional expense. The purpose is twofold: (1) to obtain a greater impact than a retailer could obtain alone, and (2) to enable the retailer to supplement his or her own promotional budget. The Robinson-Patman Act is an important statute which carefully lays out the rights of a retailer with regard to promotional allowances. In the past, cooperative promotional plans have been abused, particularly by some suppliers who favor large customers. Therefore it is important for the retailer to know what demands can be made from suppliers and what his or her rights are.

QUESTIONS FOR DISCUSSION

1. How does advertising differ from publicity, from propaganda, from promotion?
2. Discuss briefly the two broad classifications of retail advertising.
3. What are the major component parts of an advertising plan?
4. Identify and describe the different methods of determining the advertising budget.
5. What advertising services do newspapers perform for retailers?
6. Evaluate broadcast media and print media from a large retailer's point of view, then contrast it to the views of a small retailer.
7. When and how should a retailer use direct mail advertising?
8. Discuss the most common mistakes made by retail advertisers.
9. What is meant by point-of-purchase advertising?
10. What is the prime reason retailers use trading stamps? Do you think the use of trading stamps is declining in your community?

13 PERSONAL SELLING

The direct marketing division of Jewel Companies continues to send its salesmen out to call on household customers, just as it has since 1899 when they sold only tea. They now sell over 350 grocery items, all of which are carried on their trucks and sold at a higher price than in Jewel's retail stores. The customers are willing to pay the premium, usually because it either saves them time or they are unable to get to the store regularly. The salesmen are not responsible for generating new business—someone else does that—and have known some of their customers for many years. The division is declining in importance but still does about four percent of Jewel's total sales.

A salesman in a San Francisco art gallery who is also part owner of the business learns that a West German businessman is interested in seeing a Joan Miró that the gallery has acquired. Knowing that a personal presentation will be more effective, the salesman takes a polar flight to Germany with the Miró and several others under his arm. He does not sell the other works, but the Miró is sold for $65,000 and the businessman returns to San Francisco four days after he left. (The painting had been displayed in the gallery for over a year at $44,000.)

Every summer about 8,000 young people spend three months calling on homes in the South to sell Bibles, dictionaries, cookbooks, and home medical reference books for the Southwestern Company, a subsidiary of the Los Angeles Times Mirror Company. Unlike the man from Jewel, who covers a developed route, the "Bible salesmen," as they are sometimes called, must make "cold turkey" calls, usually considered one of the most demanding kinds of selling. The salespeople (many are women) are told to arise at 6:15 so the first call can be made at 7:59, review the sales talk that has been memorized word-for-word, play a fast record to get ready for the day, do not take time to read the morning newspaper, carry a sandwich so that no time need be taken for lunch, and stop working at 9:00 p.m. For all this, the salespeople often earn enough to return to college, and probably learn an incalculable amount about people and good work habits.

An attractive young woman is employed by a cosmetics manufacturer to demonstrate the firm's products to women patrons of various retail stores. She helps women with their makeup problems and suggests how the brand she represents may solve them. She is paid by the manufacturer and only works in those stores that are willing to give her high-traffic space for demonstrations. (Other promotional allowances are offered smaller stores, where a demonstrator would be uneconomical, in order not to run afoul of the Robinson-Patman Act.) She is sometimes called a "hidden demonstrator."

Retail selling often conjures up the notion of "clerking" at the nearest variety or drugstore, a position that many would prefer to avoid. But, as the above examples demonstrate, there is an almost unlimited variety of retail selling positions, and many can be interesting, satisfying, and financially rewarding.

Retailers are naturally concerned with selling merchandise, the inference being that there generally is some sort of salesperson-to-customer relationship. Noteworthy exceptions to the person-to-person contact are retail sales made by mail and through vending machines. Self-service stores also minimize personal salesmanship. However, personal selling—the focal point of this chapter—still plays a vital role in the marketing of many types of goods and services. Indeed, for many customers, the salesperson is the only contact with a firm, a fact that can bode well or ill for the company and its attempt to repeat patronage.

It would be false to suggest that retail selling is usually as rewarding as has been suggested by the above examples. In many retail situations, the salesperson's job is physically demanding. In the course of a day's work the salesperson may have spent at least eight hours standing, walking, stooping, and bending, while trying to be pleasant. This physical effort is hard on the feet, legs, and back, so it is not surprising that many retail salespeople are exhausted at the end of a day. Moreover the job can be mentally tiring as well, because of its monotonous nature. However, some individuals believe that the retail selling job is mentally stimulating because of the opportunities to mix with people and to interact with them. Unfortunately, the interaction is not only brief but is considered too elementary by some and does not provide the personal satisfactions many might hope for. Customers are sometimes demanding and discourteous. This can also contribute to a salesperson's feeling of exhaustion.

IS PERSONAL SELLING OBSOLETE?

It is commonly thought that retail salesmanship is outdated because of modern merchandising techniques. This position is taken most frequently by mass merchandisers who think an "order taker" is all that is necessary. Mass merchandisers contend that goods are sold by informative packaging and advertising, word of mouth communication, and conspicuous displays. Consequently, a retailer only needs a clerk to answer routine questions, to complete the financial transaction, and to wrap or bag the merchandise. Personal salesmanship is simply unnecessary at the retail level—so they say.

The self-service food store is perhaps the best example of a retail shop that minimizes personal salesmanship. These stores need employees to stock shelves, check out the orders, and to assist customers in other minor ways. Most customer questions arise in connection with meat or produce; therefore employees in those departments are most apt to be involved in personal salesmanship techniques. However, even the meat department often is self-service and customer contact is minimized. It can be safely said that the self-service food store makes only a limited use of creative selling, as is shown in Figure 13.1.

Another example of a type of retailer that minimizes personal salesmanship is the variety store. Customers simply walk through the various departments and

FIGURE 13.1

Personal selling is minimized in a self-service food store

Source: Tony Kelly, Consolidated Foods Corporation, Chicago, Illinois.

select merchandise that appeals to them, then take their selections to a check-out station where the goods are wrapped and they make their payments. Employees are available on the selling floor to assist customers who need help. Even the standard department store sometimes utilizes self-selection whenever possible. Greeting cards, books, records, tapes, and some soft lines are examples of goods that are selected by customers with a minimum of creative salesmanship.

CREATIVE SELLING

Creative selling is blending intelligence, sensitivity, imagination, and salesmanship techniques into a combination that insures the maximum amount of sales success. (See Figure 13.2.) A number of people do not believe that creative selling is possible in retailing today. A typical comment is the following:

> The activity of face-to-face selling in a retail store has little resemblance to the activity as performed at the manufacturer and wholesaler levels in the channel. The basis of retail selling is the provision of product information and order taking. In many cases even these aspects of selling tasks are poorly performed, for creative selling at retail is almost a lost art.[1]

[1]James F. Engel, Hugh G. Wales, and Martin B. Warshaw, *Promotional Strategy*, rev. ed. (Homewood, Ill.: Richard D. Irwin, Inc., 1971), p. 485.

FIGURE 13.2
Creative selling may be important in persuading a prospective bride to choose a wedding ring

Source: Persin and Robbin Jewelers, Arlington Heights, Illinois.

Creative selling is lacking because of the nature of the job, customer behavior, and the economics of retailing. Store sales personnel are required to do other things as well as sell. For example, they usually do such housekeeping chores as stocking shelves, straightening out merchandise, bringing stock from storage, and keeping records. These activities often prevent the salesperson from devoting full attention to salesmanship.

Another major reason for the lack of creative selling at retail is the arrival of customers in groups rather than as individuals. That is, customers do not come into the store at regularly spaced intervals. It often is either feast or famine; therefore the salespeople are either very busy and cannot take care of each customer properly, or there are few customers and the clerk is completely nonproductive.

Furthermore, because of the low level of productivity, the wage level of the average retail clerk is also low, and this usually results in the employment of individuals who lack the skills that would give them other employment opportunities.

Barriers to Creative Selling

Bad habits are perhaps one of the greatest barriers to creative selling, and bad habits may be either physical or mental. Physical habits of salespeople surface in their general demeanor, the ways in which they greet and talk to customers, and in their conduct and deportment while on duty. Let's look at a few examples of poor salespeople; perhaps you have encountered some of them in your shopping experiences.

Talkative Tess. Tess is a nonstop talker, and all she needs is an audience. Fortunately for her, the store's customers are a ready-made audience, and she loves to give them her ideas, opinions, and personal gossip. Unfortunately, Tess is a poor listener and does not give the customer equal time. Moreover she forgets why the customers are there in the first place. As a consequence, many shoppers are bored or they are driven away—sometimes never to return. Tess is directly responsible for both lost sales and lost customers.

Friendly Florence. Florence is a friendly, outgoing person who calls her customers "honey," "sweetheart," or "dear." It makes little difference to Florence that many people are turned off by salespeople who use endearing names. Florence is also directly responsible for lost sales and lost customers.

Sloppy Sue. Sue works in the ladies' dress department and she can be spotted very easily. She is the one whose slip hangs a full inch below her hemline. Notice how all those chic, sophisticated, and well-dressed customers avoid her.

Teena Teen-ager. Teena is a high school student who works part time—usually evenings and weekends. Teena thinks the store is a groovy place to entertain her friends. You can usually find her in the center of a group of young people. Teena believes that if you ignore customers they eventually go away. This permits Teena to concentrate on her social activities and catch up with the latest teen gossip.

Freddy Flirt. Freddy is the young man who is partial to pretty girls, and he selects them for customers regardless of whether others have waited a longer time to be served. Freddy thinks he is the store charmer, and he uses his talents to sell himself rather than the merchandise. Sometimes Freddy entertains Teena Teenager, and consequently both ignore their customers.

Temperamental Tom. Tom has a terrible temper especially when things do not go his way. Tom believes in the principle that he is always right and the customer is always wrong, especially when he is involved in a dispute with one. Whenever a customer offers an objection that Tom cannot answer, he loses his temper, and the store loses a sale and a customer.

Commission Charlie. Charlie is paid by commissions on what he sells; consequently he feels justified in looking after his own interests. Charlie will drop one customer to approach a second shopper if it appears that the second is a better prospect for him to earn a larger commission. And in some instances he tries to wait on two or even three customers at one time. Charlie also takes customers away from other clerks in spite of its embarrassing effect on the clerk and the customer. Charlie maximizes his own earnings and believes that this is in the best interest of the store.

Irritable Ina. Ina is easily irritated, and customers are usually the source of her annoyance. Ina thinks many customers are too demanding, and for this reason they need to be put down. She dislikes providing extra service for customers, and she avoids those who seek any kind of special aid. For Ina any transaction is troublesome if it is out of the ordinary, and this makes her irritable. Customers avoid Ina, and sometimes they shop elsewhere to be certain they will definitely avoid Ina and her sharp tongue.

The cast of characters one meets in a retail store as salespeople include more than just the above eight. However, they illustrate some whose personal habits interfere with creative salesmanship. All sales personnel should be open-minded, flexible, sensitive, alert, friendly, and customer oriented. They should also realize that they are, first of all, employees of the store, and their major function is to sell merchandise. Good hiring practices and continuous training programs can result in the individual who makes customers and friends for the store.

The Problem Customer

The problem customer constitutes a challenge to the skills and patience of the salesperson. People are not always friendly when they are shopping—some are downright intolerable. Shopping disappointments may temporarily turn a usually pleasant person into a disagreeable one. Some shoppers apparently believe that the customer is always right and should be treated that way, some begrudge the time that must be "wasted" while shopping, some believe they cannot trust the salesperson and must be on guard, while still others use the opportunity to bolster their egos by putting the salesperson in "his (or her) place." Unfortunately, some customers use a shopping opportunity to do and say anything regardless of the conflict and animosity it creates in the store among store personnel. It is difficult for a salesperson to be tolerant, considerate, and patient when the customer is ill mannered or disrespectful. Some of the criticism directed at salesclerks is the result of abrasive customers who have upset the salesperson so much that he or she cannot cope with the situation. Retailing jobs are often filled by people whose talents, experience, and education are such that they cannot respond adequately to problem customers. However, there are always problem customers, and the solution is to hire and train personnel who are most likely to be able to cope with them in a friendly but firm fashion.

ELEMENTS OF PERSONAL SALESMANSHIP

Personal Salesmanship Is Essential

Although affected by self-service retailing, personal salesmanship is still a major part of the retailing mix of many stores. This is especially true when the product sold is technical or complex and the customer needs instruction in its use, application, limitations, or operation. Examples of such products are cameras, stereo equipment, motors, sports equipment, and household appliances. Personal salesmanship is also important in those retail stores where the customer seeks the advice and counsel of a knowledgeable person. Often this advice and counsel is important for those people buying furniture, draperies, paints and wallpaper, hardware and tools, men's suits and coats, ladies' dresses, lingerie, foundation garments, musical instruments, jewelry, cosmetics, and much more. (See Figure 13.3.) Finally, personal salesmanship is important where the final effective selling price is subject to negotiation. Retailers sometimes discriminate among customers by charging some more than others. Whether or not to offer a discount, the size of the discount, credit terms, whether or not there is a delivery charge, and the value of any trade-in have an impact on the effective retail price and cannot be dealt with unless a salesperson is present.

FIGURE 13.3

Personal salesemanship is necessary in shops featuring fashion merchandise

Source: Pint Size Jrs., Chicago, Illinois.

Personal Salespeople Are Specialists

Salespeople are specialists who are employed principally to persuade customers to buy the goods that the store stocks. For some, the word *persuasion* has negative connotations. These critics contend that persuasion is the art of selling merchandise to people who do not want it and, indeed, have little need for it. It is also contended that salespeople tend to encourage customers to discard useful products so that they may be sold new merchandise. However, persuasion is more realistically viewed as an interpersonal activity by which customers are changed from uninformed shoppers searching for a product to contented buyers of a product that fits certain needs. A salesclerk is also essential to point out the various advantages and limitations of competitive brands so that the customer can make an intelligent decision among alternatives.

Common Characteristics of Personal Salesmanship

Whether or not a salesperson is employed by a manufacturer, a wholesaler, jobber, retailer, or financial or service institution, there are certain distinguishing characteristics common to all. All types of salespeople do the following: (1) seek out customers, (2) determine customer needs, (3) help customers to make appropriate decisions, and (4) close sales.

Seeking Out Customers. A retail salesclerk's task in identifying potential customers varies with the nature of the goods sold, the kind, size, and ownership of the store, and the various selling strategies and tactics the store uses. However, the store salesperson usually has less difficulty in seeking out potential customers than do other types of salespeople. This is because shoppers come into a store environment, a practice that is in sharp contrast to industrial and wholesaler's salesmen, who leave the company environment to call on customers at their places of business.

The alert retail salesperson need not be entirely passive with respect to finding buyers. There are two important ways in which a skilled salesperson can increase sales, thus earning higher salaries or commissions and generating more profits for the employer. First, he or she must be sufficiently observing and sensitive to distinguish those who seem prone to purchase from those who are simply browsing, particularly during busy hours when there is too little time to deal with everyone adequately. This is exceedingly difficult, and some department managers would argue that browsers can be turned into customers by genuinely effective salespeople —a moot point. In many instances the customer virtually declares that either he or she wants to be left alone or needs help ("No, just killing time, thanks" versus "Yes, I'd like to see a beige sweater, size 42, preferably V-neck"). Salespeople may have certain decision rules that they abide by, some of which may be only roughly accurate. One automobile salesman indicates that he spends little time showing new automobiles to those driving cars more than six years old because "When we get down to talking monthly payments, it dawns on them they just can't afford it." A woman in a high fashion woman's specialty store says, "I take my lunch hour from 12:00 to 1:00, since that's when the secretaries who eat lunch at their desks have an extra thirty minutes to look around. And I don't want to be off the selling floor when some of my regular customers who can afford our merchandise are likely to stop by." Neither salesperson would argue that their decision rules are flawless, but only that they are crude devices for allocating effort when time is a scarce resource.

The second way in which an efficient salesperson can generate sales is to devote some ot his or her time to bringing customers into the store who would otherwise not come in. A men's outerwear salesman in Chicago sends postcards in mid-December to previous customers reminding them that his store's post-Christmas sales start December 26, and that he'll be there early that day to help them with their needs. A saleswoman in a designer dress shop always mentions to women who are about to leave her store—either with or without a purchase—that a new shipment of merchandise is expected very shortly. She says, "It never hurts to whet their curiosity and to let them know that the inventory is always changing. Then, too, they're more likely to come back to me than one of the other women since they believe that I want to help them, which I do." An automobile salesman regularly goes back into the repair shop to talk with car owners waiting for repairs to be finished. It is an ideal time, he argues, to plant the idea that maybe trading up to a new or newer car would be a good idea. And all kinds of salespeople review the marriage and birth sections of their local newspapers for sales prospects, believing that such events indicate a significant change in people's needs. Such practices can be useful, but require that salespeople be sensitive to the needs of customers. In addition, they also must often spend time organizing and maintaining the system. If time is valuable, the practice is not without its cost.

Determining Customer Needs. The second essential task of a salesperson is to identify the customer's needs. In some elementary retail sales situations, the tasks of identifying customer needs are quite simple. A town parade can serve as an example. At the parade were several balloon vendors. They simply walked through the crowds shouting "Balloons!" They were quickly surrounded by customers, usually small children, who held up coins to the vendors—all the while the children agonized over decisions as to whether the balloons should be red, yellow, blue, orange, green, or some other color. In such a case a salesperson has an easy job in identifying a customer need and selling the product to satisfy the need.

Usually, when selections offered are few in number, and where the customer has definite ideas as to what he or she wants, the task of identifying needs is rather easy. In a great many cases the customer simply announces to the salesclerk what is wanted. Examples are customers purchasing cigarettes, gum, candy, film, newspapers, magazines, and similar products. Even restaurants featuring limited menus make the task of identifying customer needs an easy matter. (See Figure 13.4.) Most convenience goods are of this type, and very little personal salesmanship is needed to sell them.

However, when a retailer offers a multiplicity of products, brands, price lines and sizes, the task of determining customer needs is more difficult. Consider the salesclerk in a hosiery department of a large urban store. Hosiery comes in many sizes, styles, colors, brands, fibers, and price lines. The salesclerk must be prepared to give prospective customers considerable information and guidance. This is not to deny the fact that some women will ask for a specific brand, size, color, and price line. When this occurs, the salesperson's task of identifying the customer's need is simplified. However, it is likely that the hosiery clerk has a more difficult assignment in determining the specific customer need then has the balloon vendor, the cigarette clerk, or the order taker at the hamburger stand.

FIGURE 13.4

Colonel Sanders offers only a limited menu in the familiar fried chicken outlet

Source: Davis Food Service, Inc., Atlanta, Georgia.

In other selling situations, the retail salesperson's job in assisting the customer to make a purchase decision is still more complex. It includes "sizing-up the customer," that is, observing such facts as sex, approximate age, dress, overall appearance, and general behavior. Much of this must be absorbed in the few seconds it takes for the customer to approach the salesperson. Let us assume that a customer has just entered a small dress shop and approaches the only saleswoman on duty. The saleswoman will probably prepare herself mentally to show one style dress if the approaching shopper is an 18- to 21-year-old young woman, but quite another style dress if the approaching shopper is a woman of about 60. Moreover a customer who is well groomed and tastefully dressed may elicit one kind of salesperson response, while a sloppy, ill-dressed shopper elicits a different response. Nevertheless, first impressions are often ill conceived and faulty; therefore sales personnel must be trained to be alert for signs that will be valid and trustworthy.

Generally, the best way to appraise the customer is to wait for some sort of customer commitment. The customer may ask to see a specific product and brand. The salesperson should bring the specified merchandise and be prepared to answer questions concerning it. In cases where the requested item is out of stock, the salesperson should suggest a substitute, and at the same time indicate when the out-of-stock item will be available. Many sales are lost by salesclerks who fail to suggest alternatives if the requested item is not available.

During the entire transaction, customer comments are particularly helpful. They indicate the progress that the salesperson is making to complete the sale. Furthermore, the comments are clues to the tastes or preferences of the shopper. Some people speak out directly and it is easy for the clerk to determine their needs and to complete the sale. On the other hand, some customers are timid and some are mistrustful of the salesperson, while still others may not articulate their desires adequately. In these cases the salesperson has a more difficult time eliciting information that can be used to help the customer. Shoppers occasionally are accompanied by a member of the family or a friend—often called "influentials"—and these people have to be sold as well as the person initiating the sales contact. Some people are impulsive by nature and buy the first item suggested. Other shoppers are more deliberate and must be shown many items before they decide on one selection. Here again, the good salesperson learns the best way to handle various situations and is adaptive to each as it arises.

In other buying and selling situations the customers have a decided lack of technical knowledge about a product, and consequently they are uncertain as to what their needs are. However, the customers are aware of a problem or difficulty, even though they are not always willing to confess their need for information. One spring a man noticed his ornamental plum tree showed signs of disease, so he went to a local garden store for advice. The owner of the store was able to identify the disease from the description of the symptoms, and he prescribed a product that successfully treated the tree. Many of us have problems of one kind or another which we take to a retailer for a solution. Furthermore, in many instances the retailers have products to solve the problem.

Helping the Customer Make a Decision. In suggesting that one of the principal duties of a retail salesperson is to help the customer make a decision or selection, there is an implication that the salesperson has adequate product knowledge. For example, most people know very little about jewelry, so they rely on the jeweler for information and guidance. A jeweler must be able to explain why one diamond is more costly than another, and then assist the customer in obtaining the greatest value for the money he or she wishes to spend. An old cliché states that a man who doesn't know diamonds should know his jeweler. This statement may be extended to include almost all kinds and types of specialty goods.

Product knowledge implies that a salesclerk should know how the product he or she sells is used or how it functions and operates. Furthermore, the salesperson should know the product's advantages and limitations in solving typical problems. The salesperson must be able to point out the differences in quality if several price alternatives are available. Where necessary, the salesclerk must instruct the customer in the proper care and maintenance of the product. In addition the salesclerk must know who manufactures the product and the kinds of materials used in its manufacture. The salesperson must also be aware of any guarantees and assure the customer of the integrity of the company producing it. In short, the salesperson must know all about the product he or she sells and how it is used.

How does the retail clerk obtain the required product information? This varies with the store and the quality of the store management. Occasionally the retail salesclerk obtains all product information through his or her own initiative. The resourceful clerk seeks out knowledgeable people and questions them about the products. He or she also reads and digests books, pamphlets, and technical bulletins, and listens to customers who are familiar with the product and its use. He or she also learns from personal mistakes.

However, a retail store that leaves the teaching job solely to a clerk's own initiative is itself making a mistake. It is management's function to teach its employees, and this function cannot be delegated to the employee. On the other hand, retailers should provide the climate to encourage employees to strive for self-improvement. Those who do improve themselves should be rewarded by a salary increase or a promotion, or perhaps both.

Another way that a store salesclerk become knowledgeable about the merchandise he or she sells is through the efforts of the manufacturer, the wholesaler, or both. This may be accomplished by literature written expressly for this purpose, or through trade shows featuring the merchandise of the various manufacturers. In some cases, the manufacturers send their own representatives to the retailer's store for the sole purpose of instructing and training the sales personnel in their product's use. However, in the final analysis it is the management of the retail store itself which must assume the responsibility for training the store personnel. In large stores, training departments are a necessity, as we discussed in Chapter 7.

Let us follow a professor into a clothing store to see how a good suit salesman helps the customer make a selection.

Clerk: Good-morning. May I help you?

Professor: Good-morning. I'd like to see some suits. I wear a size 40 regular.

Clerk: Would you step over to the other side of the room, please? (Clerk directs the professor to that section of the store where size 40 suits are displayed on racks, takes one off the hanger, and offers it to the customer.)

Professor: I'll put it on, but I can tell you now that I don't care for the color.

Clerk: (as the professor tries on the coat) Did you have a particular color or pattern in mind?

Professor: No particular color, although I dislike brown. (Customer looks into mirror and agrees that the size 40 coat fits very well.)

Clerk: Please look through that rack of size 40s and see if there's a color that appeals to you.

Professor: Here's one I like very much. What is the price?

Clerk: (assists customer into the coat of the suit selected) All suits on this rack were originally priced at $149.95, but they are marked down to $124.95 for this week only.

Professor: The price is right and I like the suit, but I'd like to look at some others before I decide.

Clerk: You look very good in this grey color, but try on as many as you like. This suit should be very comfortable, but you might want to keep in mind that it's a looser weave and probably won't hold a crease as long as a tighter knit.

Professor: Thanks. (He then tries on four additional coats before going back to his original choice.) I'll take the grey suit, I think.

Clerk: I think you'll be happy with that choice. Notice the lapels and the cut of the garment. It's very fashionable and one of our best-selling styles. Why not try on the entire suit?

Professor: Thank you, I will.

Clerk: The dressing room is in the corner. In the meantime, I'll call the tailor. (Professor nods his head. The tailor is called, and when the customer returns, the suit and trousers are marked for alteration. The clerk then fills out the sales check and completes the transaction. After suggesting shirts, ties, and other accessories, the clerk bids the professor good-bye.)

A customer must always be shown the merchandise requested if it is in stock. This is true even though the salesclerk believes another product might serve the customer better. However, in the latter case the salesclerk should bring the second product as well as the one requested by the customer. Then he or she can point out the advantages of the suggested product over the requested one. Some merchants reject the idea that the salesperson should attempt to change the customer's mind. They argue convincingly that a salesclerk's job is to sell as much merchandise in a given time period as possible, and time should not be taken to resell the customer on another item. This criticism is most valid when the department is busy and other customers are waiting to be served. However, the ultimate purpose of all sales is to satisfy a need, and if the salesperson thinks the customer will experience greater satisfaction with another product, then he or she should take the time to point out the superiority of the second product. A store's training program should devote time to handling this situation.

There are three important rules to be applied while showing merchandise to a customer. They are: (1) show only a few articles at a time, (2) put the merchandise into the customer's hands, and (3) demonstrate the product.

A salesclerk must never overwhelm the customer by showing too much merchandise at one time. To do so only hinders the decision-making sequence. A good rule is to show only three articles at one time. Whenever the customer rejects one or two of the articles, the salesperson can add one or two new selections, thus keeping the total being inspected at three. For example, suppose a customer enters a men's shirt department First, the salesman ascertains the desired shirt size and asks if the customer has a preference in color or style. Whether the customer has expressed a preference or not, the salesclerk shows only three shirts at one time. The shirts could represent different prices or different color patterns. In any case they should be selected to heighten the contrast and help the customer to come to a decision. Whenever the customer rejects one shirt, it should be replaced by another until the choice is narrowed to one price line, one style, and eventually one shirt.

Whenever feasible, the merchandise is placed in the customer's hands or on his or her person. This is the reason a suit salesman attempts to get the customer into a coat as soon as possible. This is also the reason a saleswoman has a customer try on a dress. In the case of sports equipment, the customer who is buying golf clubs is encouraged to take a practice swing. A customer who is involved physically with the merchandise being shown has his or her interest strengthened. Tactile sense is very important in developing interest. (See Figure 13.5, pp. 348-49.)

Some products must be demonstrated if they are to be sold. The salesclerk who is selling appliances such as refrigerators, freezers, stoves, dishwashers, washing machines, and television sets knows that he must explain all the knobs, buttons, and gadgets that operate the appliances. The auto salesman encourages a prospect to drive the new car at some time during the selling process. A properly demonstrated product aids the customer to make the ultimate decision.

The experienced salesperson anticipates customer objections and consequently attempts to answer them before they are raised. However, not all objections can be anticipated regardless of the experience of the salesperson; therefore there are always objections that require answers. The salesperson should assume that all objections are honest reasons why the customer does not wish to buy the product. Frequently when the objections are countered, the shopper is sold and the sale is consummated.

A more difficult objection to answer is the one that is never articulated by the customer. Sometimes the shopper hides the real objection to a product while stating one that is easily answered. In this case the salesperson must find the real objection and counter it. An experienced salesperson is likely to be more adept at finding hidden objections and offering positive counter arguments. Good training is helpful in preparing sales personnel in this problem area.

All salespeople should adhere to the following rules in meeting objections: (1) assume that the customer's objections are legitimate and honest; (2) anticipate objections and counter them before they are raised by the customer; (3) never argue with the customer, but be firm in countering objections; (4) do not belittle a competitor or his products; (5) be friendly, tactful, and persuasive; and (6) ask for help if you cannot counter an objection due to a lack of information. Creative salespeople follow these rules implicitly.

Closing the Sale. Some of a salesperson's best skills must be brought out when it is time to complete a sales transaction. The relationship between a customer and a salesperson may have proceeded rather smoothly until it is time for the customer to make a decision. The salesperson can subtly "force" a decision from one who is unwilling to decide without help. The salesperson who helps a customer in this way must be sure that the decision is in the best interests of the customer, meaning that he or she will have no postpurchase regrets about having bought the product.

The salesperson who learns effective closing techniques is likely to sell more merchandise than others who leave the final decision entirely to the customer. First, the salesperson's conversion rate is likely to be higher, meaning he or she will turn more "lookers" into "buyers." There is little doubt that it is easier for a customer to walk away from a transaction than to complete it, particularly if there is any linger-

FIGURE 13.5

A necessary step in the selling process is successfully encouraging the customer to try on the merchandise

Source: Persin and Robbin Jewelers, Arlington Heights, Illinois.

ing doubt about the product's merits, even when the doubt can only be dissipated through use. Effective salespeople should be able to help customers over such hurdles. Second, the salesperson who has learned effective closing techniques will spend less time with each customer, and thus can meet more customers each work day, a strategy that surely increases an individual's sales results. There is the rather obvious danger, of course, that the customer will feel the pressure to complete the transaction and that ill feeling will be created toward the store and the salesperson. Skilled salespeople sense the pace at which a customer can be led toward the completion of a sale and do not abuse the closing techniques they have learned.

The techniques for closing a sale are both physical and verbal. Again, they often are so skillfully used that observers—including the customer—are unaware that anything is happening unless they are particularly looking for it. Physical maneuvers to close the sale would include putting obviously unwanted merchandise out of the customer's sight so that selection becomes easier, taking out an order book and

FIGURE 13.5 (cont.)

perhaps beginning to write up the sale, bringing out the box or bag in which the customer will carry the merchandise out of the store, or even starting to wrap it. Verbal moves toward closing a sale would include such statements or questions as, "That sofa is certainly going to add something to your living room," "Will that be cash or charge?" "Have you decided on the blue or the grey?" "We can deliver in your neighborhood either Thursday or Friday. Which do you prefer?" Note that the questions afford the customer the opportunity of making a decision to buy ("I'll charge it") without having to articulate the decision in specific terms ("Yes, I'll take it"). And in every instance there is the implication that the customer is going to make a purchase, the only real issue being one of narrowing down the choice.

There are certain important administrative duties that the salesperson sometimes must perform during the closing process. Generally, the salesperson must either write out the sales check, or ring the sale through the cash register, or both, or process the customer's charge sale through a charge plate. It also means that the goods are wrapped, packaged, or boxed, and made ready for the customer to take along. In cases where the goods are to be delivered, the salesperson must be certain that the sales check shows the correct address and that all the information is legible.

The salesperson always suggests related merchandise while finishing up the sale of the initial product. A shoe salesman suggests to his women customers such related items as handbags, purses, and hosiery. Trite and self-defeating expressions such as "nothing else, is there?" must be avoided. Many customers appreciate a salesperson who suggests other articles that might interest them. Perhaps the customer's attention can be called to articles that are specially priced or will soon be out of stock because of their seasonality In any case, suggestion selling is part of the after-sale.

When the customer is about to depart, the salesperson says good-bye in a friendly tone. The customer is thanked for the business and invited to come back. One such method is, "Thank you for shopping at Jones; come back again soon." The statement "Have a good day" is often used. However, it isn't the words as much as it is the quality of the message and the tone of voice of the one saying it. Be oneself is the best advice on the subject. Say a good-bye with feeling; a half-hearted expression often is worse than none at all.

TRAINING THE SALESPERSON

Training Increases Productivity

Nearly everyone admits that training a salesperson is worthwhile, yet many retailers do not put their hearts into it. In some cases, it is difficult to get people released from their jobs to attend training classes. On this point, Ann Karlsson, training director for Allied Stores, says:

> Can training increase productivity? This question may seem unnecessary since everyone generally agrees that training is a good thing. And yet, it often requires considerable persuasion to get a department manager to release his people to attend a training class.[2]

Perhaps it is easy to adopt a cynical attitude toward training sales personnel, because it is difficult to prove that the increase in productivity pays for the cost of the training. (See Figure 13.6.)

In a study conducted by Allied Stores, two groups of 15 salespeople were selected. The people of each group were matched on such factors as length of employment, kinds of departments represented, and the same mixture of rated salespeople, categorized as good or poor. In short, each group of 15 people was as alike as it was humanly possible to make them. One group was designated the control group and the other the experimental group. The experimental group of 15 salespersons was given four hours of classroom training in principles of salesmanship. The training was accomplished in half-hour sessions held once each week for eight weeks. The control group received no training.

Here are some of the results:[3]

[2]Ann Karlsson, "Does Retail Training Pay?" *Training in Business and Industry* (February 1969), p. 25.

[3]Ibid., pp. 26–27.

FIGURE 13.6
A training class in sales techniques can be helpful to the sales staff

Source: Sears, Roebuck and Co., *1970 Annual Report*, p. 6.

	Control Group	*Trained Group*
Average hourly rate of sales increases	28.1%	104.2%
Departmental increase	26.1%	59.4%

Interpretation. The control group increased its average hourly rate of sales by 28.1 percent, while those in the same selling departments who were not part of the experiment increased their hourly sales by 26.1 percent. The difference in productivity of 2 percent does not appear to be statistically significant. On the other hand, the 15 salespersons in the training group increased their hourly sales on the average by 104.2 percent, while those other members of their department who were not involved in the experiment averaged an increase of 59.4 percent. This is a substantial difference of 44.8 percent (104.2 − 59.4 percent). Furthermore, when the trained group is compared with the control group, the difference is 104.2 percent versus 28.1 percent, or 76.1 percent. The trained group also registered an average net increase in sales 60.5 percent larger than the store as a whole (that is, 104.2 percent for the trained group as compared with 43.7 percent for the store as a whole).

The increase in sales as shown by the trained group may be due to what is called "the Hawthorne effect." That is, the salespeople were told that they were part of the experiment, and consequently they may have tried harder and responded by being more productive. No doubt the control group was also aware of the test and may have responded in some way that was not observed by the researcher.

The cost of the training was calculated to be $1,208, and the net gain in sales for the entire training period was approximately $20,000. A still more accurate measure of the value of training would be to relate it to net profit, but such data are much more difficult to sift out. Those who attempt to evaluate sales training often limit their analysis to the effect it has on net sales.

One interesting question which the study raises is whether it is more profitable to train the good salesclerk or the weak one:

> We don't know yet whether it is more profitable to train the weak salesman, the average, or the good one. Department managers inevitably send their lowest producers to training classes in salesmanship, but this may not be the person the stores find more profitable to train. If you can double the sales productivity of either the best salesman in a department or the worst, it is obviously more advantageous to train the one who seems to need it least.[4]

However, the Allied Stores experiment did indicate that it was more profitable to train salespeople in the "big ticket" departments. For example, a saleswoman in the notions department increased her hourly sales by 448.8 percent, but her net hourly increase in dollars was only $8.26. On the other hand, a furniture salesman, after training, increased his hourly sales by only 110.2 percent (as contrasted to 448.8 percent) but his dollar increase was $60.99, over seven times larger than the woman in notions.[5]

The Allied Stores experiment suggests the beneficial effects of at least a rudimentary form of training on sales performance. However, one should not base a conclusion on a one-shot experiment. Nevertheless it tends to validate the hypothesis that training increases the productivity of the sales staff.

More effort and time is being devoted to training than ever before, including the use of sophisticated mathematical models. Michael Toye has constructed a training design algorithm formulated to solve the format of a good training program.[6] An algorithm is a procedure for solving a problem and relating decisions to each other as well as specifying the decisions to be made. The purpose for mentioning algorithms at this time is to make the point that training of retail sales personnel is being subjected to mathematical models, a far cry from the intuitive judgments of the past. The use of algorithms is still minimal but if it proves successful in one training program it will be widely copied in others. Sophisticated methodologies to improve training are not substitutes for good retail management, but rather another tool to implement a training policy so as to provide more productive retail workers.

[4]Ibid., p. 27.

[5]Ibid., p. 27.

[6]Michael Toye, "Training Design, al' go-rithm," *Training in Business and Industry* (October 1970), pp. 36–37.

Other Purposes of Training

Much of the time in training programs is devoted to matters other than increasing the trainees' effectiveness in personal selling. Indeed, in many formal training programs for new employees salesmanship may be relegated to a minor role because many of the trainees have not been employed to work on the selling floor. Those who have been hired to work in the advertising department, inventory control, or window display may have only a passing interest in salesmanship, but largely for reasons of economy will participate in the same training program as sales floor personnel. So, formal training programs often have the following objectives:

1. To promulgate and explain the company's philosophy and objectives.
2. To build loyalty to the firm—and thus, presumably, reduce employee turnover and dissatisfaction.
3. To introduce upper echelon management people to lower level personnel so that the way the organization works will be better understood.
4. To identify prospective managerial talent more quickly, on the basis of success in the training program.
5. To explain or thwart misunderstandings or rumors about such things as changes in the economy and how they will affect the firm, changes in rival retailers' practices, the firm's competitive position, and any other events that might affect the employees' morale and effectiveness.

Each of the above objectives is important, so it is no surprise that there often is little time remaining in which those working on the selling floor can be taught how to become better salespeople.

Objections to Training

Although most retailers have some form of training for employees—either a formal program or on-the-job training—there are a number of reasons why it does not generate more interest than it does. First, a formal training program operated by a training department within the firm or by outside specialists can be expensive, and many executives doubt that sales productivity will increase enough to warrant the cost. Explicit costs may be small where trainers are recruited from the various departments in a firm, no special facilities are required, and no expensive equipment or training materials are used. But in other cases, training departments may have substantial budgets that are sure to bring doubts about their worth.

Second, another type of cost is the explicit expense of having employees sit through training programs while being paid, or the implicit expense of the effect on their morale if they must attend training sessions on their own time.

Third, some would argue that it is easier and less expensive to pirate trained personnel from other retailers rather than to incur the expense of one's own program. And a corollary thought is that there is little point in spending large sums of money on a training program only to find that one's own "graduates" soon take positions with competitors.

Fourth, the thought that salesmanship cannot be taught in a formal training program still seems to persist among some retailers. Those who believe this would argue that such personal traits as intuition, sensitivity, and hard work are the keys to sales success, and that such characteristics are not learned in a classroom.

Finally, some believe that training may be important but should largely consist of learning by observing rather than in a formal training program. On-the-job training generally means that the new salesperson is expected to watch how more experienced and successful salespeople handle the various situations that arise. Proponents of this sort of training would argue that learning by doing is more effective, more realistic, and less costly.

EVALUATING SALESMANSHIP

All retail sales personnel should have their performances evaluated periodically if the store's management is to determine whether or not a specific individual is an effective and profitable salesperson. All too often sales personnel are rated intuitively or not rated at all. The following four-step program suggests an approach to evaluation and control of a salesperson's selling efforts: (1) the development of performance standards, (2) the measurement of actual performance, (3) a comparison of actual performance with the standard, and (4) the implementation of corrective action.

Development of Performance Standards

Management must spend considerable time establishing sales standards for its selling personnel for both business and moral reasons. The standards that are determined will be used as a partial basis for deriving the employee's paycheck, for deciding who is well suited for promotion to higher positions in the store or who should be terminated, for informally deciding on "status" within the firm, and for many other purposes. The determination of standards is too important to the business and to the employees not to be taken seriously.

One of the simplest approaches is to use a salesperson's record for the same period a year earlier, making adjustments for changes in economic conditions or inflation or moving holidays. Thus, if a salesperson sold $1,200 of merchandise during the second week of January during a particular year, his or her "quota" would be about $1,200 for the second week of January the following year. If nationally available data indicates that retail sales are down three percent from the previous year and if the week contains no moving holiday (Easter is a moving holiday) that would affect sales, the salesperson's quota would be $1,144 in "real" dollars.

A major assumption—and flaw—in such an approach is that the salesperson is performing satisfactorily during the base period. Unfortunately, such assumptions are widely made ("Let's beat last year's figures!") but often are unwarranted because no one knows whether the sales effort made during the base period was good, mediocre, or downright bad.

A second approach, particularly in a large firm, is to use the experience of the entire sales force to determine standards. This essentially means that each salesperson's quota will be determined by comparing it with everyone else's in a comparable position. It would be patently unfair to ask someone working in cosmetics to sell as much as someone in appliances. However, it is not unreasonable to insist that a new salesperson in cosmetics sell as much merchandise as new salespeople usually do in the firm's other stores. Again, in order to be fair the manager must look for reasons why a firm's base data may not be useful in a particular situation.

A third approach is a modification of the second, and usually is more useful to a small firm. It consists of using the data generated by the firm's trade association in lieu of the firm's own information. One of the principal activities of trade associations is to gather and exchange useful information from its members. Careful study of such data can sometimes tell management what it can expect of its salespeople.

Standards can sometimes be established that will lead to higher sales volume for the salesperson but are not, in themselves, dollar oriented. When properly established, however, they will surely lead to greater sales productivity. Management would do well to consider them. For example:

> A home delivery, fruit juice retailer insists that each route sales delivery man make three "cold turkey" calls a day in order to add new customers to the route. The conversion rate is just about enough to replace those who drop the service and increase the size of the route at a modest rate.
>
> A shoe store manager periodically audits the number of invoice lines on the sales checks written in his store. He believes each salesperson's checks should contain 1.3 lines, meaning that about every third buyer has bought a second item. The 1.3 rule encourages salespeople to suggest hosiery, shoe trees, polish, and other high margin items that might otherwise be sold only infrequently.
>
> A men's specialty store insists that every time a new suit is sold the salesman must show the customer a new tie that would complement the suit's style and colors.
>
> An automobile dealer compels each of his salesmen to place "would you takes" under the windshield wipers of 10 cars on the street each day. A "would you take" is a card suggesting an amount an old car might be worth (approximately the Blue Book price) when used as a trade-in on a new car. The dealer's assumption is that at least a portion of those who see the card will have their curiosity aroused and will stop in. And some will buy.

Measurement of Actual Performance

After developing an acceptable performance standard, the retail store then measures the actual dollar sales achieved by each salesperson. Some stores go much further and use a sophisticated distribution cost analysis to compute the gross margin and net profit contributed by each salesperson. In the process, expenses are broken down and assigned to each individual. This methodology is used to rate the effectiveness of each salesperson to his or her department and to measure the amount of net profit each one earns for the department. New computer techniques make the mechanics of this type of evaluation much easier to accomplish. (This procedure is explained in Chapter 17, which is devoted exclusively to computers and their application to retailing.)

Comparison of Actual Performance with Standards

The purpose of having standards is to have a value that can be used for comparison purposes. Usually salespeople become more efficient when they know they are subject to regular periodic evaluations. Most people strive to attain good records when they know they are being rated and evaluated. Many managers believe that a competitive spirit should be encouraged because it stimulates productivity and promotes efficiency.

A comparison of actual performance with the standard also plays a major role in personnel guidance. It provides the evidence so that a diagnosis can pinpoint the strengths and weaknesses of the salesperson being rated. This diagnosis is essential before corrective action can be taken.

A good evaluation program generally boosts the morale of employees, especially if they know that all salespersons are being rated fairly and equally and with justice. This is reflected in the attitudes that salespeople display to their customers, superiors, and fellow employees.

Implementation of Corrective Action

Diagnosis reveals the areas where corrective action must be taken. It must be remembered, however, that a good salesperson is not evaluated solely by the sales volume generated on the net profit resulting from the sales. This is especially true if the salespeople have limited control over their sales volume. The diagnosis is made in a merit rating plan in which five factors are judged: (1) job knowledge, (2) management of the job, (3) sales results, (4) customer relations, and (5) personal characteristics and habits. Strengths and deficiencies in any of these five categories can be used to determine whether future training is indicated, the salesperson is to be commended and rewarded, shifted to another type of job in the firm, or if separation is the best action to take.

Who Does the Rating?

The rating should be performed by the employee's immediate superior, and the results reviewed by higher management. This is necessary to insure that the rating form has been properly filled out and that the rater has done a fair and objective job. Specifically, the rater must not let personal bias enter into judgment. A retail salesperson should be rated at least once annually. More frequent ratings are to be discouraged because of the expense involved and the fact that ratings are only duplicated and thus lose their meaning to those being evaluated.

Review

Once the ratings are made and approved, they should be discussed in a personal interview with the person being rated. In this interview the strengths and weaknesses of the salesperson are discussed. It is essential that the interview be completely frank but held privately so that on one else can listen. The employee should be complimented on areas of strength and be given sound advice as to how to overcome any weaknesses. Continued good ratings should be rewarded by a salary increase or promotion, or both. In any case such a salesperson should be commended and praised. On the other hand, a poor performer who has had consistently poor ratings should be dismissed if it is thought that further training or experience would not be worthwhile.

Case Example. Robert J. Paul and Robert W. Bell conducted a survey to determine if there was a statistically significant difference in the time utilization patterns of high-dollar sales volume salespeople as contrasted with low-dollar sales volume people?[7]

In their evaluation of retail sales personnel, Paul and Bell considered such factors as: (1) selling time, (2) time doing stockwork, (3) idle time, (4) time absent from selling floor although on the job, and (5) time spent doing miscellaneous activities. The following measures were made: (1) sales volume in dollars for each salesperson, (2) a rating of the tempo at which each salesperson worked, (3) a determination of permissible time out for personal needs, and (4) a review of each salesperson's personal data.

Paul and Bell concluded:

1. There is a statistically significant difference in the activity patterns of high-dollar volume salespeople and low-dollar volume sales personnel. Specifically, high-volume salespeople work harder at selling, that is, they spend more time in actual selling activities.
2. The high-volume salespeople also used a higher percentage of their work time in doing stock work than did low-volume salespersons.
3. The high-volume salespeople worked at a faster pace or tempo than did low-volume salespeople.
4. Sales personnel who produced the lowest volume were absent from the selling floor a greater length of time than high-volume salespeople.
5. The low-volume salespeople were most productive when the high-volume salespeople were off the selling floor.
6. The high-volume sales producers were usually older, better educated, and more experienced than low-volume salespeople.
7. There was no correlation found between dollar volume as a measure of productivity and personal evaluation data. Apparently the reason for this is the fact that there is no way to measure such factors as sincerity, courtesy, or care for customers.

Studies such as this are useful in providing insight into the behavior patterns of retail personnel, especially with reference to sales productivity. Each retail store should make its own evaluation and determine for itself what characteristics good

[7]See Robert J. Paul and Robert W. Bell, "Evaluating the Retail Salesman," *Journal of Retailing*, 44, no. 2 (Summer 1968), pp. 17–76.

salespeople possess as contrasted with poor salespeople. A determination can then be made as to whether training can be helpful or whether changes must be made in hiring policies and procedures. It is good business to evaluate retail employees if the store is to operate more efficiently. This is just as true for stores with only a few employees as it is for those who employ hundreds and even thousands.

SUMMARY

Personal selling is important today in many types of retail operations, even though many merchants who use mass-merchandising techniques do not agree. Creative selling is less common in retailing today because of the acceptance of the self-service concept, the nonavailability of qualified personnel, and the economics of retailing. The low level of productivity at the retail level sets a low wage ceiling and therefore attracts workers who are generally less capable and talented than industrial salespeople.

All sales personnel perform four functions: (1) seeking out customers, (2) determining customer needs, (3) helping a customer to make a decision, and (4) closing the sale.

Retail salespeople need not leave their stores to seek out customers because the store attracts its own clientele. In this respect it differs from industry, where salespeople must seek out customers. One of the most essential sales tasks is to identify customer needs. In some respects this is quite easy since the customers announce their needs to a salesperson. On the other hand, some customer needs are quite nebulous, and the salesperson must use considerable skill in finding the need and fitting the product to the need. Usually when the retailer offers a multiplicity of products, brands, and sizes, the task of determining needs is more difficult.

All salespeople must have sufficient product knowledge if they are to help the customer make a selection. Sales personnel obtain this product knowledge from their own resourcefulness, through training, and by experience. In any case it is the store management's job to see that their sales staff is knowledgeable about its merchandise. Good training in all aspects of salesmanship increases the productivity of the sales personnel.

Closing a sale is a natural phenomenon that occurs almost automatically if the entire sales presentation has been handled effectively. Proper closing means filling out the sales check correctly, suggesting other merchandise, and bidding the customer good-bye.

All retail sales personnel should have their performances evaluated periodically. This is accomplished in four steps: (1) setting standards, (2) measuring actual performance, (3) comparison with the standard, and (4) taking corrective action. The rating should be performed by the salesperson's immediate superior and then reviewed by higher management. The actual rating is discussed privately with the salesperson concerned and proper action taken.

QUESTIONS FOR DISCUSSION

1. Under what retailing conditions is personal selling obsolete?
2. In your opinion what is the difference between a well-trained order taker and a retail salesperson?
3. From your own experience describe three retail sales types who you think practiced creative salesmanship.
4. What kinds of people are problem customers and how would you handle them if you were the salesperson on duty?
5. Under what condition is personal salesmanship an essential part of the retailing mix?
6. One of the most essential sales tasks is to identify customer needs. Discuss.
7. In your opinion do you think retail management should train the good salesperson or the poor one? Why?
8. Do you think a retail salesperson should sell a substitute product to a customer if in the salesperson's opinion it is better than the product requested?
9. Answering objections is an important part of the selling process. How would you go about finding hidden objections if you were the salesperson?
10. Do you think retail sales personnel should have their sales performances evaluated? If so, what are the major parts of your evaluation?

14 CUSTOMER SERVICE POLICIES

An art gallery in New York City takes paintings to a prospective customer's home and hangs a painting where it will best complement the customer's other furnishings. It offers a five-year guarantee on its artworks, meaning that the customer can return the art any time in the five years after purchase and the price paid will be applied to any other art in the gallery. Needless to say, the gallery sells very expensive art.

Restaurants in several major cities offer their diners transportation to and from major sports events. The customer is spared parking charges at the athletic arena and the aggravation of driving through traffic. There is usually no extra charge for the transportation.

For its most important visitors, a luxury hotel in Colorado will redecorate a room in the favorite color of the guest, emboss the guest's name on its stationery, and maintain a regular supply of fruit, flowers, or candy in the room during the guest's stay.

A lumberyard in Chicago sets aside Saturday mornings as "home fix-up" day, a time when it willingly sells building materials in small quantities and keeps a consultant on hand to give advice to homeowners on how to make home repairs. Lumberyards have never been too happy with such small orders, believing that they cost more than they are worth. Saturday at this lumberyard has turned into a moderately profitable operation.

Customer services are an important part of retailing throughout the world because they can so powerfully affect customer patronage. Indeed, when the products and prices among retailers are not strongly differentiated, rivalry quickly is reduced to whichever retailer can offer the service mixture that is most appropriate for a particular market segment. As the above illustrations suggest, the services offered by retailers vary from those that most would agree are "sensible" to those that merely appeal to vanity.

Although these are interesting examples of attempts to cater to either the real or whimsical needs of the customer, merchandisers in more recent years have openly questioned the philosophy and practice of granting large numbers of costly services to their customers; and in many instances they have actively curtailed services and openly announced the fact through advertisements. The reduction of services has been converted to a positive selling tool since it infers that a retailer is pursuing a policy of low prices.

Changes in the nature of services that marketers have offered customers have been carefully studied, and contrary to what might be expected in an opulent country such as the United States, some kinds of services offered by retailers have been reduced over the years. In other instances, services to the customer have increased, while in still other cases activities that once were performed by retailers have been shifted to other functionaries. Harold Barger[1] has studied the changes over the years and concludes the following:

Activity	*The Change Involved*
Home trial and return privileges are	Greatly improved, the "customer is right" idea more widely accepted.
The store's physical surroundings are	Greatly improved, much more pleasant places to shop and buy.
Packaging is	Improved, but responsibility has been shifted upward in the channel, no longer performed by the retailer.
Credit is	More widely available, but shifted to outside financial organizations, less often the responsibility of the retailer.
Delivery is	Not much changed.

Barger's study covered the time period 1869 to 1950 and suggests the way in which manufacturers, middlemen, and consumers have continually redefined the roles they have wanted to play in a marketing channel. There is no doubt that the assessment will continue, and that retailers will continue to accept new functional responsibilities; shift traditional responsibilities upward to their suppliers, downward to their customers, or laterally to specialists; and increase or decrease the place of such services in their marketing mix.

The preferences that customers have for services are highly personal and must be viewed by the retailer as a given. Some shoppers want to be pampered with just about every conceivable type of service and are more than willing to pay for such services in higher prices.[2] On the other hand, some shoppers are willing to forego services to purchase merchandise at lower prices. There are retailers who cater to each group, and it is naive to assert that one set of retailers is right and the other wrong. A retailer is right if he or she provides only those services the customers want, but foolish to provide services customers do not want or need.

CUSTOMER SERVICES

At this point it might be wise to have a workable definition of services. Ronald Gist believes the entire subject of retail services has inherent ambiguities and needs to be clarified. He thinks there is some confusion between retailing services such

[1]Harold Barger, *Distribution's Place in the American Economy Since 1869* (Princeton University Press: National Bureau of Economic Research, General Series, No. 58, 1955), p. 36.

[2]The reader must be wary of the simple statement that "more retailer services bring higher prices." If the additional services generate more business for a particular retailer, so that the retailer's fixed costs are more efficiently utilized, average costs can decline and the retailer may elect to lower prices.

as renting automobiles or garden equipment, and such services as credit, delivery, or wrapping. Gist says:[3]

> It is never clear, for example, whether the term "retail services" refers to (a) the type of service that often attends the rule of physical merchandise (e.g., wrapping), (b) the type of services that are sold without merchandise (e.g., appliance repair and professional "service"), or (c) services that involve rental or lease agreements (e.g., automobile rental, lawn and garden tool rental).

Fred Jones describes retail services this way:[4]

> In a broad sense all activities of a store are services since all store activities are directed to having the right merchandise at the right place in the right quantity at the right price and the right time. To the extent that a store performs this service efficiently, it is economically justifiable. The services that are discussed here, however, are certain activities that facilitate the performance of the basic service or principle of retailing.

David Rachman says:[5]

> Services are nonprice devices used to help the retailer differentiate his offerings in order to achieve higher sales and thereby maintain a certain segment of the market.

All of the above definitions and clarifications are useful because they help to focus attention on those nonprice activities that are necessary to carry out the basic retailing function. Our definition is:

> *Services are all those nonprice activities undertaken by a retailer to assist him or her in carrying out the mission to achieve the twin objectives of customer satisfaction and higher sales volume.*

Typical Services

Perhaps the best way to explain retail service is to present a list that anyone can identify when visiting retail stores. Table 14.1 is a version of such a list. There is no attempt to include each and every service available, but the list is representative. It is difficult to find many stores who offer all the services on the list, and finding a retailer who offered none would be impossible.

Classification of Services

There are probably many ways in which services may be classified. One method is shown in Table 14.1. Services are grouped into three types: prepurchase, postpurchase, and ancillary. The first two classifications identify the period of time when

[3]Ronald E. Gist, *Retailing: Concepts and Decisions* (New York: John Wiley & Sons, Inc., 1968), p. 430.

[4]Fred M. Jones, *Retail Merchandising* (Homewood, Ill.: Richard D. Irwin, Inc., 1957), p. 580.

[5]David J. Rachman, *Retail Strategy and Structure: A Management Approach* (Englewood Cliffs, N.J.: Prentice-Hall, Inc., 1969), p. 207.

TABLE 14.1
Typical Retail Service

	Prepurchase Services		*Postpurchase Services*		*Ancillary Services*
1.	Accepting telephone orders	1.	Delivery	1.	Check cashing
2.	Accepting mail orders (or purchases)	2.	Regular wrapping or bagging	2.	General information
3.	Advertising	3.	Gift wrapping	3.	Free parking
4.	Window display	4.	Adjustments	4.	Restaurants
5.	Interior display	5.	Returns	5.	Repairs
6.	Fitting rooms	6.	Alterations	6.	Interior decorating
7.	Shopping hours	7.	Tailoring	7.	Credit
8.	Fashion shows	8.	Installations	8.	Rest rooms
9.	Trade-ins	9.	Engraving	9.	Baby attendant service
		10.	C. O. D. Delivery		

the retailing services are performed, that is, before or after the customer buys the merchandise. The ancillary grouping is not directly related to the time of purchase, but it is important nonetheless. For example, advertising, wrapping, and delivery are related directly to the merchandise. Furthermore, advertising is a service performed before the actual purchase, while wrapping and delivery are postpurchase services. On the other hand, check cashing, restaurants, and parking are important but not product related.

The weakness of the classification system in Table 14.1 is that nothing is said about the importance of the retailing service offered. For that reason, we suggest a second classification, again using three groups—essential, expected, and optional.

Essential Services. Essential services are basic, and the retailer must provide them. This category usually includes parking areas, maintaining store hours, having salespersonnel on hand, advertising, display, wrapping and/or bagging, and adjustments These services are called essential because nearly every one of a retailer's customers uses them. However, this list of essential services is *not* universal throughout the world of retailing. For example, some retailers do not provide parking facilities for their customers, yet they do a lively business. In other cases, the city designates streets to be used by patrons for parking. The point is that any one retailer knows which services are absolutely basic to the store's operation. Such retailing services are classified as essential. (See Figure 14.1).

Expected Services. Some services are expected by many of a store's patrons in addition to those on the essential list, and often the deciding factor is the type of merchandise stocked. For example, most persons who buy a washing machine, dryer, or some other large appliance expect it to be delivered. Therefore appliance dealers generally add this service to their list, because it is helpful to many of their customers. We did not classify delivery service as essential, because some customers prefer to provide their own delivery. The appliance dealer may also add credit to

FIGURE 14.1

Ample free parking is an essential service supplied by most supermarkets

Source: Independent Grocers' Alliance Distributing Co., Chicago, Illinois.

this list of services because many customers need to finance their purchases.[6] It is not included as essential because it is not universally used by all customers, inasmuch as some prefer to pay cash.

Let us examine another type of retailer—one who sells apparel. In the case of men's clothing, the retailer generally provides free alteration service, and it is essential that he provides dressing rooms. A store that also sells neckties, shirts, socks, and shoes to men in addition to suits, slacks, and coats is a different matter. In this instance, some customers who are purchasing shoes or ties need not use either alteration or dressing rooms. For that reason, the alteration service is classified as expected. The distinction is in the percentage of a retailer's customers who use the service. If the percentage is close to 100 percent, we classify it as expected.

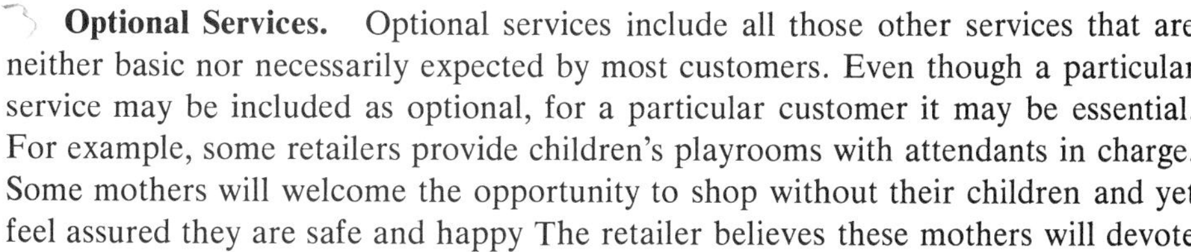

Optional Services. Optional services include all those other services that are neither basic nor necessarily expected by most customers. Even though a particular service may be included as optional, for a particular customer it may be essential. For example, some retailers provide children's playrooms with attendants in charge. Some mothers will welcome the opportunity to shop without their children and yet feel assured they are safe and happy The retailer believes these mothers will devote

[6]It should be noted that retailers often hold very different views about the reasons for extending credit. To some it is a strategy for attracting customers to their stores. But to others, the finance charges can be quite profitable. Indeed, a few retailers have abused the financing of goods so that finance charges are the major source of their profits.

their full attention to shopping, and so expects to obtain more sales than might be the case if the mother were accompanied by the children. (See Figures 14.2 and 14.3.) For other mothers, a children's playroom is a service they can do without, and they never avail themselves of the opportunity to use it.

Each retailer must analyze his or her own situation before adding a service. Optional services are seldom used by most shoppers; therefore great care must be exercised in their selection.

FIGURE 14.2

A leading Minneapolis department store provides this kiddie care corner

Source: Dayton Hudson Corporation, Minneapolis, Minnesota.

DETERMINANTS FOR SERVICE

Service is part of a retailer's strategy to attract and hold customers. Consequently, a retailer decides on a given set of services only after considering such factors as: the type of merchandise handled, competition, type of operation, location, and financial strength.

FIGURE 14.3

These tots enjoy the elephant slide while their mothers shop at their leisure

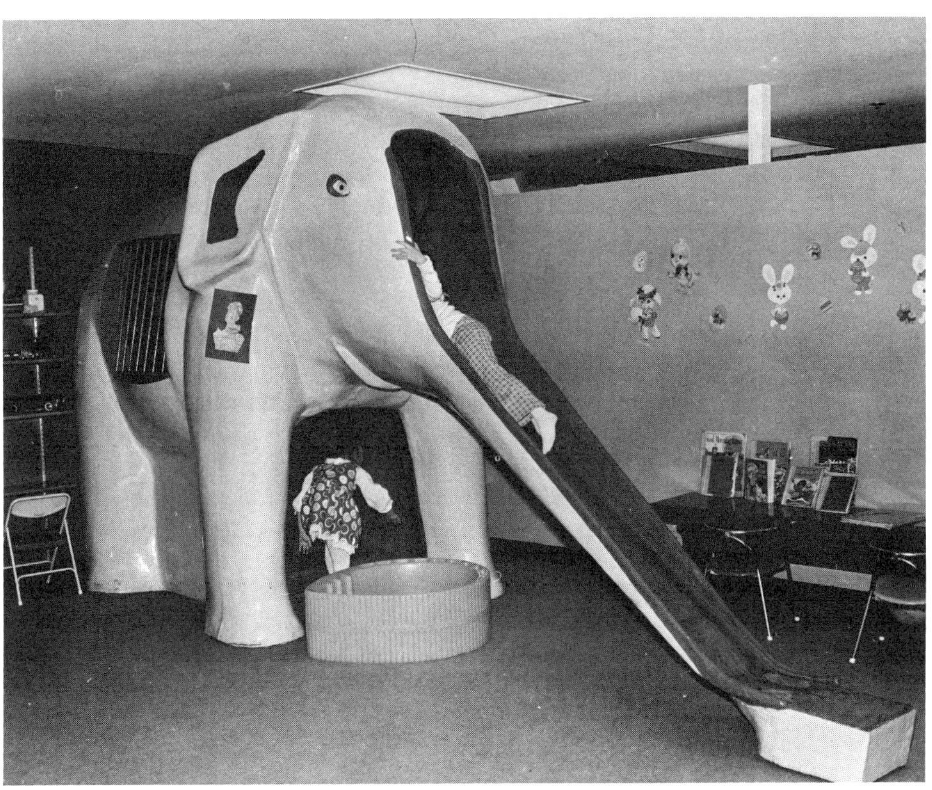

Source: Dayton Hudson Corporation, Minneapolis, Minnesota.

Type of Merchandise Handled

To a large extent, the kinds of retailing services to be offered by a particular retailer is determined by the type of merchandise carried. For example, a food supermarket provides free parking, convenient store hours, advertising and display, and free check cashing service (for those who are qualified and registered). A gasoline service station provides free air for tires, battery testing, and windshield cleaning. Some stations provide towing service for customers and free car washing privileges. Full service department stores furnish most of the services listed in Table 14.1 for they add a great number of services to attract and hold a variety of customers. Appliance dealers add credit and delivery service to the basic services of parking, convenient hours, advertising, and display. This list of examples is almost endless; the point is that the kinds of merchandise handled is a prime determinant for the services that the retailer offers.

Competition

A second determinant for retailing services is competition. Essentially all competition is divided into two general classes—price and nonprice. We have already pointed out that retailers who compete on the basis of price usually believe in the philosophy of obtaining a large sales volume through low prices. Therefore in order to reduce their margins on each item, they restrict services to essential ones. However, a mass merchandiser must provide as many services as other mass merchandisers provide; otherwise he would lose customers to competitors.

Nonprice competition is important for a great number of retailers. These merchants attempt to differentiate their stores from those of competitors by providing a service not performed by others. However, it is difficult for a retailer to remain unique because competitors will soon add the same service if it has customer appeal.

Professor McNair's wheel of retailing hypothesis claims new retailers enter the industry with a minimum of services because they seek to acquire a price advantage over the established retail stores. These newer stores gradually add services which increase their costs, and soon they begin to lose their price advantage. The stores ultimately mature into high-priced shops offering a maximum of service. The wheel of retailing continues to turn, and the retailers ultimately lay themselves open to the competition of aggressive newcomers who feature low prices and a minimum of service.

Type of Operation

This factor is closely associated with the type of merchandise carried and the state of competition. A retailer who identifies with the mass merchandisers will provide fewer services. Furthermore, if he or she has a low quality discount enterprise, the offerings may be entirely different from a store that sells higher quality goods. There is a spectrum of alternative possibilities, and the retailer usually matches his or her operation with others of the same type and size. The retailer who can identify his or her type of operation may choose to provide essentially the same services as rival retailers.

Location

Location may also be an important determinant of services offered. For example, stores in shopping centers need not furnish parking facilities since they are provided by the shopping center for the benefit of all the tenants. On the other hand, retailers located on city streets may find parking their greatest problem. Lack of parking has driven many customers away from one retailer into the store of a competitor who has ample parking. Location is also important in identifying the class of the retailers and the affluence of their customers. Some locations are elegant, and shops must provide many optional services to pamper the type of customer who shops there. The so-called Magnificent Mile on Michigan Avenue in Chicago is an example.

Frequently, retailers locate in shopping centers where the center provides the location and maintains the landscaping for each tenant for a fee. An example is Bullock's, which set up a 45-acre fashion square in Santa Ana, California, to include I. Magnin and 35 other tenants, and space for 3,500 cars. In reporting on this story, *Business Week* said:[7]

> A quality atmosphere for quality goods means to Arnett good landscaping. The Santa Ana square has over 400 trees, including 45 olive trees at $450 each, and an oleander hedge at the entrance.
>
> Tenants pay about $1,000 a month rent for the average 2,500 square foot shop, and a small percentage of their sales for painstaking maintenance.

Financial Strength

Financial resources are another determinant, because many of the services the retailer may consider offering the customer can be very costly. It takes more than good intentions and desire to provide a delivery system, fitting rooms, restaurants, free parking, or a number of other services. Customer services that require a considerable investment generally are offered only by those who are financially capable. There are, however, exceptions. Pop and Mom stores are low on financial resources; yet many grant credit to their customers because it is their differentiating characteristic. Pop and Mom stores may also offer services where the costs are hidden rather than explicit. Longer store hours or the use of a high-school-age boy for delivery are seemingly low-cost services that may appeal to customers. However, if opportunity costs are identified, the costs of such services may be very high.

Responsibility for Decisions on Store Services

Like any other major store activity, policies relating to services are the responsibility of the owners and top level management. Once retailers state their objectives, they have gone a considerable distance in determining the services they must perform. Once the policies are formulated, it is within the jurisdiction of the operating management to implement them. Moreover the degree of formal policy making that takes place is a function of the size of the retail store, what its competitors are doing, expectations of customers, and social pressures.

For the owner-operated retail store, the need for a policy on service is every bit as important and necessary as it is for a larger corporation. However, in the one-person retail store decisions are based on experience and customers' needs. The retailers need not necessarily consult with anyone else.

Ethics of Service

Retailers are sometimes accused of adding services not wanted by customers because they believe this will increase their profits. These critics allege that a larger margin is added than is necessary to cover the cost of the services the retailers

[7]"Prestige Store Grows Without Losing Gloss," *Business Week* (April 9, 1966), p. 62.

perform; in short, they add a markup to the actual cost of the services provided. To the extent this is true, it permits a retailer to earn excess profits. However, this allegation is difficult to prove.

Other critics allege that retailers who earn high profits are embarrassed by them. It is said that these embarrassed retailers add more customer services to placate their consciences. This allegation is even more difficult to prove than the first because it involves motivations.

It is likely that retailers are neither more nor less ethical than other people. That is to say, retailers—like people in other occupations—can be found all across the ethics spectrum. Profit is one of the more conspicuous incentives that motivates most business people. Some merchants believe aggressive price competition is the way to maximize profits. Other retailers believe service competition is the best means. Each kind of competitive strategy is usually ethical. It is inappropriate to label the pricing strategy either more or less ethical than a service strategy. Retailers of all types hope to maximize profits.

TYPICAL SERVICES

It would be impractical to describe every retailing service; however, there are some that are more widely offered than others. Furthermore, these services have special problems associated with them that merit explanation.

Delivery Service

Many retailers provide delivery services. The three major types of delivery systems are: (1) store owned, (2) independently owned, and (3) parcel post and express.

Store-Owned. Many retailers own their own delivery systems, and the majority are small independent merchants. For these small retailers, a panel truck, a station wagon, or even the retailer's personal automobile is sufficient. Frequently a small retailer leases equipment or pays mileage to an employee who furnishes the car. One only needs to read the classified advertisements that say "must have own car" to see how common the practice is.

A few retailers have well-organized formal systems. Marshall Field in Chicago is an example. Such retailers enjoy distinct advantages by owning or at least operating their own delivery systems. One advantage is the prestige a store gains, or believes it gains, by using its own fleet of trucks. Generally the store's name is painted in large letters on the side of each truck, and this makes it identifiable as it is driven throughout the store's trading area.

Perhaps the major advantage of ownership of a delivery system is the control the retailer can exercise over the delivery schedule. Furthermore, all delivery personnel are store employees and subject to the rules and procedures of the store. This permits the retailer to furnish a high quality service, and reduce to manageable proportions one source of customer complaints.

The chief disadvantage of ownership of a delivery system is its initial cost and the expense of operating a well-organized one. Only the more affluent of the retailers can afford a high investment in a fleet of trucks. Many retailers not only minimize their investments but avoid maintenance problems by leasing their operating fleets. A second disadvantage is one of efficiency. That is, if a store has sufficient trucks to meet peak load requirements, the equipment is only partially used at other times. It is costly for both the retailer and ultimately the customers to have capital tied up in idle trucks.

Even without idle trucks, there may be inefficiencies. This would be true for the retailer who provides delivery service over a wide area. In this case, the driver and the truck may be utilizing most of the time traveling to deliver relatively few purchases. This is expensive in terms of wages paid the driver and in terms of truck expense. To counter this type of inefficiency, some retailers cooperatively own and operate a delivery system. Deliveries can then be concentrated for each route. In this way both the driver's productivity and that of the truck are increased, and diseconomies kept to a minimum.

Independently Owned. Because of the great expense involved in delivery, many retailers use companies that are organized solely for the purpose of providing delivery service. An example is United Parcel Service (see Figure 14.4). Its trucks deliver parcels throughout the United States. Companies like United Parcel provide all the necessary equipment, personnel, and warehousing to do the complete delivery job. The procedure is for the delivery company to pick up packages at the retail store according to an agreed schedule. The packages are taken to a centralized warehouse where they are grouped with parcels collected from other retailers. The packages are sorted by routes and delivered according to a fixed schedule. These independent delivery companies assume responsibility for lost merchandise. They usually make C.O.D. deliveries and pick up merchandise that customers wish to return. A retailer is charged on the basis of size, weight, and number of items to be delivered.

The advantage to the retailer is that no investment has to be made in equipment and warehouses. Furthermore, the entire operation is in the hands of another company and the retail store is able to devote its time to merchandising goods. Of course, the store gives up some degree of flexibility and sacrifices control over an important aspect of retailing.

Parcel Post and Express. Parcel post and express services are important to most retailers. For example, large retailers who have their own equipment regularly use parcel post to deliver small purchases to customers living outside their delivery area. In fact, parcel post permits retailers to set up personal delivery only in areas where their customers are concentrated in large numbers. In this way, parcel post helps retailers to utilize their drivers and equipment more efficiently.

Mail order retailers, both large and small, are particularly dependent upon parcel post, railway, and air express. This includes such large retailers as Montgomery Ward and Sears, as well as the countless smaller mail-order specialists and

FIGURE 14.4

United Parcel Service is the delivery arm for hundreds of retail department stores throughout the nation

other retailers who solicit mail-order business through newspapers, Sunday supplements, or direct mail.

Parcel post service was established by the post office in 1912. It is given considerable credit for increasing the sales volume of mail-order companies. However, the post office imposes limitations on the size, weight, and perishability of the parcels it handles. For this reason, express companies are important. Inasmuch as they are private companies, they can set their own conditions to meet the need. REA is the most important of the express companies.

Delivery Problems. There are several major problems associated with delivery service. One of the most troublesome is that customers are eager to have their merchandise delivered as quickly as possible; therefore they may complain bitterly if it is not delivered on the day it has been promised. Some customers are so irked at delays that they cancel the order or refuse the merchandise when it does arrive. Retailers are understandably anxious to fulfill all promised deliveries on schedule.

Delivery problems often arise for which no one is to be blamed but which require good judgment to correct. An example is the customer who is not at home when the merchandise is delivered. In these cases, a decision has to be made. Should the merchandise be left at the front door, with a neighbor, or returned to the warehouse and another attempt at delivery be made on a different day? All of these proposed solutions have limitations. Goods left at the door may be stolen. Some neighbors may not wish the responsibility for accepting merchandise. And returning the goods to the warehouse is costly because it may take many attempts before a successful delivery can be made.

Most retailers have a delivery policy to attempt delivery as many times as is necessary to put the goods in the customer's hands. However, some retailers make only one attempt, often leaving a notice in the mail box asking for further instructions regarding delivery. This policy seems both wise and prudent.

Another reason for poor delivery service is a poorly written sales check. One cannot expect a parcel to be delivered if the address is illegible. A store must continually remind salesclerks to print the name and address of each customer and to add any instruction which simplifies delivery.

Free Delivery? Another important decision is whether or not the delivery service should be free. In a real sense, no delivery service is free, because the price of the merchandise must reflect the cost of delivery. Whenever delivery is "free" everyone who is a customer of the store pays for the service. Therefore some retailers subscribe to the philosophy that only those customers who use the delivery service should pay for it. These retailers make separate charges for delivery, and the burden of payment falls directly on those customers who use it.

A few customers take advantage of retailers who offer free delivery service. They have everything delivered regardless of size and value. In order to discourage this type of customer, some retailers restrict deliveries to merchandise of a given value. For example, a retailer may have a policy not to deliver merchandise valued at less than $5. (See Figure 14.5.)

Retailers encourage shoppers to take merchandise home with them rather than have the store deliver it. Signs are posted reminding customers that goods taken home are available for immediate use. This practice apparently works well in suburban stores, for it is not unusual to see suburbanites carrying large parcels to their cars. Frequently retailers furnish shopping carts to aid the customer in this activity. Salespersons can be extremely valuable in persuading customers to carry their own purchases. (See Figure 14.6.)

Merchandise Returns

Merchandise is sometimes returned for any of a number of reasons: faulty goods, employee errors, or customer mistakes. Most stores, therefore, have a merchandise return policy. It may be a policy in which all sales are final and no merchandise is permitted to be returned for any reason. On the other hand, a retailer may have a policy so liberal that no time limit is imposed on customers with respect to returns. A great number of retailers have a policy some place between these two extremes. A five-day return period is quite popular. Rich's Department Stores,

FIGURE 14.5
A delivery boy can still be found in some communities

Source: *Family Weekly* Magazine.

based in Atlanta, practice a very liberal policy concerning returned goods, as do some other stores. It takes back merchandise with which the customer is not satisfied even when the customer cannot furnish a sales slip. The returned merchandise may not have been purchased at Rich's, and in a few instances customers have been known to return goods carrying a competing retailer's private label.

Faulty Goods. One of the major reasons that merchandise is returned is because it is below standard, is broken, or has some flaws. This usually has nothing

FIGURE 14.6

Many stores stress that goods taken home by the customer are available for immediate use

Source: *Family Weekly* Magazine.

to do with the integrity of the retailer or the manufacturer. Fragile merchandise is sometimes broken regardless of the precautions taken to protect it. Parts sometimes are missing in goods that are packaged at the factory. Merchandise may carry the wrong sizes and labels. Colors sometimes fade in the first washing even though they are guaranteed to be colorfast. Minor defects are detected when merchandise is inspected closely at home. For all of these reasons, and others like them, merchandise is returned. Defective goods is a valid reason for having a return policy, and it is a rare retailer who will not make an adjustment under these circumstances. Returns are also made because of buying errors, but this is a merchandising problem and is discussed in those chapters relating to it.

Employee Errors. Occasionally merchandise is returned because of store error. For example, merchandise may not be gift wrapped even though this service was requested. This error may anger the customer so much that he or she returns the merchandise. Perhaps the delivery of some item has been delayed unreasonably so that the customer no longer wishes the merchandise after it is delivered. Overselling is another reason for returned merchandise. Some clerks encourage customers to purchase beyond their needs; the goods are sent back after the customer becomes aware of it. Some clerks actually encourage customers to take home merchandise and try it out in the comfort of their homes, an entirely proper suggestion when properly used. However, this merchandise is sometimes returned, either because the customer upon more careful thought decides the goods do not fit his or her needs or he or she did not want to argue with an aggressive salesperson while in the store.

Stores that take telephone orders sometimes substitute merchandise if the requested article is out of stock, so it is often returned. Perhaps the clerk makes an error in filling a telephone order. The result again is returned merchandise.

Customer Mistakes. Frequently the customer is at fault but cannot be openly blamed for creating the problem or denied a solution to it. Some customers overbuy, and they do not realize it until they are home and have had time for more careful reflection on their needs. The result is returned merchandise. In some cases, the customer insists on buying the wrong size in spite of salesperson resistance. These goods are also sent back. Customers seldom openly admit to these faults, making the adjustment problem difficult.

Returned Merchandise Must Be Controlled. For whatever reasons that merchandise is returned, the retailer must seek to minimize the volume of returns. Returns are costly in several ways. First, it costs the retailer some of his or her margin. Returned merchandise, if it is resalable, sometimes must be marked down in price. Second, a mechanism must be created to accept returns, including adjusting the customer's charge account or issuing a credit memo or cash; verifying the departmental origin of the goods and the purchase price; preparing the goods for resale if possible; and perhaps even picking up the goods at the customer's home. Finally, a way must be found to resell or otherwise to dispose of the returned merchandise. The problem is easy when the goods have not been damaged, but merchandise often cannot be sold as new if it has been unfolded, tried on, scratched, or otherwise changed. Such goods may be physically segregated for quick sale, wholesaled out to other retailers, or given to charity. But whatever the solution, it is expensive.

The store must acknowledge that returns are a part of retailing and accept the responsibility. It should be easy for a customer to come to the store and make a complaint or return merchandise. The store personnel should be sympathetic listeners and not irritate the customers through rudeness or impolite accusations. Adjustment decisions should be made promptly, and every attempt must be made to make reasonable adjustments.

In order to reduce returns, a store can do the following:

1. Train store personnel, particularly salespeople, to perform their functions more efficiently.
2. Supervise store personnel so that they make fewer errors.
3. Schedule delivery services so that they will be met.
4. Eliminate merchandise which is chronically faulty.
5. Do not oversell.
6. Encourage customers not to overbuy.

Adjustments—Decentralized and Centralized. Customers may wish to complain about poor delivery service, minor defects in merchandise, poor performance of appliances purchased in the store, or any one of a variety of other problems. The retailer must "adjust" some store service to one that is acceptable to the customer. There are two major types of adjustment systems—decentralized and centralized.

In the decentralized system, customers go directly to the department where they originally purchased the goods and discuss their problems with one of the salespeople. The department manager is charged with the responsibility for making an adjustment and must make the final decision; however, he or she may delegate the decision to others in the department if he or she has confidence in their judgment.

The decentralized system has several disadvantages. First, the salesperson may be reluctant to make the adjustment, especially if he or she is on commission. Furthermore, the salesperson may not want to devote time to adjustment activities, since he or she often is judged on the basis of sales volume rather than helping to resolve disputes. From the retailer's point of view, decentralized adjustments take salespeople from selling activities and tie up personnel in work for which they are not trained.

The major advantage accrues to the customers. They have no difficulty locating the department to lodge their complaints, and furthermore, on an even exchange they can obtain new merchandise immediately.

A centralized department, on the other hand, is staffed with personnel who are selected and trained for adjustment problems. These workers are less likely to be biased, and they can make prompt settlements after a respectful and courteous hearing. All the records associated with complaints can be maintained at a central point, handy in case they are needed.

A centralized department is only feasible when the store has sufficient returned sales to justify the high expenses for running it.

Wrapping

American customers are quite pampered as shoppers, and perhaps this is most apparent in the area of wrapping and packaging. The task of wrapping differs among types of stores. In a supermarket the checker simply puts all the purchases into bags. In department stores and specialty shops, special boxes and bags are used. In most cases, the wrapping material is distinctive and helps to identify the store. There are four kinds of wrapping services: (1) salesperson, (2) department, (3) central, and (4) gift.

Salesperson Wrap. Usually in small stores the salesperson is responsible for the wrapping. Sometimes this service is nothing more than placing the merchandise into a bag and handing it to a customer. For special events such as Christmas, Easter, or Mother's Day, the clerk is expected to use special boxes and to gift wrap the package. This special wrapping service is also generally expected by customers when they purchase birthday presents, anniversary or other gifts.

The advantages of salesperson wrap are:

1. It gives fast service to the customer.
2. It helps to promote goodwill for the store.
3. Salespeople and customers are in continual contact, and this may lead to extra sales.

The main disadvantage to wrapping by the salesperson is the loss of time in performing their selling functions. Under normal circumstances this may not be too serious, but at the Christmas season it is difficult to keep up with both the selling and wrapping functions. Another disadvantage is the lack of ability by many salespersons to gift wrap a package artistically, and they resent being asked to do so. However, good selling talent is harder to find than wrapping talent, and salespeople should not be expected to excel in both.

Department Wrap. Some stores are much too busy to tie their salespersons to the wrapping function, so an employee is hired within the department to act as cashier and wrapper. The advantages to this system are that the salespeople are relieved of the burden of wrapping, and the customer can obtain a well-wrapped package by a specialist. The salesperson often takes time to hand the wrapped package to the customer and solicits goodwill for further purchases.

Central Wrap. Some large retailers provide central wrapping stations throughout the store. The volume of business has to be substantial to keep these employees busy.

Gift Wrapping. Some stores have special gift wrapping departments. They provide two types of service: (1) regular gift wrapping free of charge, and (2) special gift wrapping at a fee. In the latter case, the packages are wrapped artistically; there is a conspicuous difference between the two services.

Store Hours

Sunday Openings.[8] In response to customer demand, many retailers provide shopping opportunities seven days a week. This is most noticeable in regional shopping centers that serve suburban areas, but it also occurs in small towns where customers cannot easily complete their shopping during the week. Many of the downtown stores remain closed on Sundays because of the scarcity of shoppers. Not all retailers, even where there is sufficient traffic and there are no so-called Blue Laws against it, have decided on Sunday openings, but enough have so that almost any type of product may be purchased somewhere on Sunday.

The popularity of Sunday openings may be attributed to the following:

1. Public attitude toward Sunday retailing is favorable.
2. Working women need the extra time to complete their shopping.
3. Sunday shopping is a pleasant experience that includes the whole family.
4. Blue laws are less effective than in earlier years.
5. More families are engaged in do-it-yourself projects and they need to obtain supplies that have not been anticipated.
6. It is a convenience, and this is reason enough.

Retailers have mixed reactions to Sunday openings. For some, it presents an opportunity to increase sales volume and to add to profits. For others, it is a defensive move in response to competition, especially the competition of mass merchandisers. To the group who respond defensively, Sunday hours may not be profitable but prevent a loss of sales to a competitor.

Sunday openings have created new problems and compounded old ones. For example, retailers find it difficult to staff their stores with sufficient numbers of salespeople. Supervisory personnel are also in short supply. Self-service, or some other form of self-help, is being used to a greater degree. In other stores where the help of a salesperson is essential, customers often must be patient and wait until they can be helped.

Sunday openings have increased direct store expenses for many. In some cases store traffic has been quite modest, and the extra sales have not offset the rise in incremental costs.

Blue Laws. Some states and local governments have laws prohibiting retail stores from operating on Sundays. These are called Blue Laws and usually they are defended on religious grounds. That is, Sundays are set aside for worship in most Christian denominations, and retail stores should not provide an attractive alternative. The effect of Blue Laws is to reduce time competition. In recent years, the

[8]The energy crisis of the mid-1970s may have an adverse effect on Sunday openings. In 1974 most gas stations were closed on Sundays, so that auto travel was curtailed. The effects on retail sales are still uncertain, with some stations open and some not. Congress has not spelled out a definitive energy policy and so the uncertainty remains.

trend has been to rescind Blue Laws if they have proved to be unenforceable. Retailers more commonly decide on their own hours.

Store Hours Other Than Sundays. Many retailers are keeping their stores open evenings as well as on Sundays. One reason is the pressure of consumer demand. Another, and perhaps more important, reason is that selected retailers have recognized changed living patterns or consumer life styles, and offer late hours as a means of getting customers. In other words there was a *latent* need, and innovative retailers recognized it and provided the new shopping hours. The retailers who keep the longest hours are probably the convenience food markets, often open from 7 a.m. to midnight. Many traditional retailers responded to the challenge of the convenience outlets and extended their operating hours until 9 or 9.30 p.m. The extended hours are a convenience to the shopper and a recognition of a changed life style.

Self-Service

Whenever one mentions self-service retailing, it is easy to picture a homemaker pushing a shopping cart through a food supermarket. We see her selecting items from well-stocked shelves as she winds her way through the store. She pauses and inspects the merchandise. Sometimes she selects two items and compares them, finally putting one in the cart and the other back on the shelf. Eventually, our shopper reaches the check-out counter; and she meets the first employee who assists her directly. Self-service is a way of life at the supermarket.

History. Self-service originated as early as 1912. One of the early pioneers was Clarence Saunders, who opened the first self-service Piggly-Wiggly store that year in Memphis, Tennessee. California merchants also pioneered in this development. John Hartford of the A & P experimented in 1912 with stores that dropped delivery service and extended no credit. However, the stores did not offer self-service.

Rom Markin gives this explanation for the early success of self-service:[9]

> Self-service was regarded early as the ultimate in retail grocery store arrangement and operation. And an important lesson was soon learned by proponents and users of this new system: The American shopper is a highly impulsive creature. If she is given the opportunity to browse and look over attractive assortments, emotional influences frequently take over and average sales begin to go up. One early report stated that average sales per transaction went up from $0.72 to $1.60, and labor costs dropped considerably after changing from clerk help to self-service merchandising.

Since the end of World War II, self-service has spread from the supermarket to many other types of retailing.

[9]Rom J. Markin, *The Supermarket: An Analysis of Growth, Development, and Change* (Pullman, Wash.: Bureau of Economic and Business Research, Washington State University, 1963), p. 9.

Reasons for Popularity. One reason for the popularity of self-service is that customers find it convenient. For one thing it permits a shopper to inspect the merchandise closely, even to the point of picking up the item. In this inspection a customer may compare prices and quality, and if he or she chooses, even squeeze the merchandise. For many items, customers implicitly believe they are the best judges. Perhaps these decisions are arrived at intuitively, but nevertheless customers believe them to be sound.

Because of their food supermarket experience, customers have approved the extension of the self-service principle to other types of retailing. In essence, the food supermarket has taught many shoppers to prefer self-service.

Retailers have welcomed the self-service principle because of its alleged beneficial effect on the wage cost. Moreover employees have been difficult to recruit for menial jobs in retail stores; therefore the customer's acceptance of self-service is a boon to the retailer. Many retailers offer some version of quick service, simplified selling, or self-service.

Characteristics Necessary for Self-Service. Self-service eliminates personal selling in many cases and minimizes the need for it in others. Some kinds of goods can be sold through impersonal promotional efforts and can be effectively distributed through self-service outlets. In part this is accomplished by descriptive labeling or other instructional materials on the package. Such labeling should anticipate the customer's questions about such matters as how the product is to be used, its quality, its longevity, the quantity contained in the package, and any other issues that may be important to the buyer. Successful self-service is also likely to occur where advertising can replace personal selling. Indeed, advertising has been used increasingly to explain a new product's characteristics, where in earlier years the salesperson would have been the source of the customer's information. Self-service retailing has made few inroads in distributing those products where personal attention and explanation continue to be important.

Items sold in self-service stores tend to be those purchased at frequent intervals. The customer's initial purchase of a product may be made with much care and only after investigating alternate products and weighing their merits. But satisfaction with a product leads to routine repurchase, a buying trait particularly conducive to self-service. The shorter the interval between purchases of a product, the less is the likelihood that the customer must again think through a particular purchase.

It is difficult to generalize about what goods can be sold through self-service outlets and what goods must be marketed by personal attention; exceptions are rampant. However, other than most food products, goods which have the necessary characteristics for successful self-service are proprietary drugs, cosmetics, hardware, greeting cards, records, books, and stationery. Personal selling continues to play an important role in marketing men's suits and overcoats, women's furs, fine art, furniture, carpeting, and automobiles. Even within a particular store, some items can be sold with a minimum of assistance, while customers may need help with others. Men may often prefer to select their own ties, underwear, shirts, and socks, but need help in choosing suits, jackets, and overcoats. And many women may be willing to select their own blouses, sweaters, or handbags, but want assistance in purchasing dresses, suits, or shoes.

Not Everyone Wants Self-Service. Simply because a good possesses all the characteristics necessary for self-service is no reason to assume it will be sold that way. Not everyone wants self-service. There are many shoppers who value personal selling more than any other type of service. Prestige stores cater to this kind of customer.

There are also customers who think the modern world is too impersonal. These people are driven, with almost righteous fervor, to seek stores that employ salespeople and maximize personal contact. These individuals believe so much in this principle that they will put themselves to some inconvenience to find stores that meet these needs. Gregory P. Stone calls such customers "personalizing consumers." They are likely to make such statements as, "People in smaller stores greet you cordially when you come in," "The customer doesn't mean anything to the clerk in the big chain stores," or "I feel at home in the small stores."[10]

Expansion of Retail Services

Not all supermarkets are expanding retail services. Early in 1970 the Red Owl Stores closed customer service departments in 12 of its chain supermarkets. This department was used by customers to cash both personal and paychecks, to purchase money orders, and to pay utility bills. The chain claims it has reduced bad check losses, saved on employee wages, and added more space to merchandise its goods by eliminating the service center.[11]

Department stores have been identified as advocates of service, while discount houses (mass merchandisers) are advocates of limited services. Today, many of the traditional stores are entering low-margin retailing with new stores, although they are careful to separate the stores by name from the parent organization. Table 14.2 lists some of the important ones.

Some department stores have added a new service—the preparation of income tax returns. For those who are engaged in service competition, this is another step in servicing customers for all their needs, including the task of preparing a tax return. (Perhaps this is not strictly a service since the store does charge the customer for preparing the return.)

Shopping Centers

Shopping centers have become the focal point for many unusual retailing services; in fact, the *Wall Street Journal* said in 1969 that they were becoming the focus of suburban life.[12] By 1975 regional shopping centers were accepted by the public

[10]Gregory P. Stone, "City Shoppers and Urban Identification: Observations on the Social Psychology of City Life," *American Journal of Sociology* (July 1954), p. 36.

[11]"Red Owl Drops Service Units: No Ill Effects," *Marketing Insights*, 4, no. 14 (February 2, 1970), p. 6.

[12]"Meet at the Mall," *Wall Street Journal* (February 20, 1969), p. 1.

TABLE 14.2

Mass Merchandise Outlets Classified by Department or Variety Store Ownership

Parent Company	*Subsidiary*
Kresge	K Mart
Dayton's	Target Stores
J C Penney	Treasury
Woolworth	Woolco
Federated Department Stores	Gold Circle
	Gold Triangle
Allied Department Stores	Almart
	Hunter
May Company	Venture

Source: *Grey Matter*, Grey Advertising, Inc., 15, no. 4 (July 1969), pp. 2–3.

as a place to see art exhibits, hear rock concerts, or even to hear a symphony orchestra perform. Some shopping centers have ice rinks, a legitimate theater, ballet, and much more.

Push-button Retailing

E. B. Weiss reported in 1969 that a new store may revolutionize retailing in the 1970s and 1980s.[13] In the robot store (being tested in Europe) a customer simply walks through a store which displays only samples on its shelves. The customer takes a punched card for each item selected, and turns in the punched cards at the checkout counter where they are processed, and her order is filled and assembled.

In Atlanta, Georgia, a bantam-type food store is incorporated into a gas station operation. A driver pulls into the gas station and parks near a selection board with appropriate push buttons. The selection board has an intercom, so one push button can be used for a product such as cigarettes. The customer simply tells the attendant the brand name desired. The mini-store has about 75 to 100 items plus cigarettes—all fast movers. Hopefully, the customer also gets gas while he or she push-button shops.

Catalog Sales

An increasingly popular method of retailing is catalog sales; consumers view merchandise in a showroom and then order their choices from a catalog, as shown in Figure 14.7. An advantage of this method of retailing is the elimination of the expense of maintaining a sales staff, thereby allowing goods to be sold at lower prices.

[13]See E. B. Weiss, "The Bread Basket System: Pushbutton Innovation in Retailing," *Marketing Insights*, 3, no. 2 (January 6, 1969), pp. 8–9.

FIGURE 14.7

A customer can often conveniently call a catalog sales center located in the store to place an order

Source: J. C. Penney Co., New York, New York.

SUMMARY

Customer services will always distinguish American retailing, although some retailers stress them more than others. Customer services are all the nonprice activities employed by a retailer or an association of retailers to supplement merchandising activities. Some of these services are basic and the retailer must provide them whether willingly or not. Other services are not universal to all retailers, but are basic to one type. For example, retailers selling clothing must usually provide fitting rooms and alterations. A third category of services is optional, and retailers add them when they believe the services will aid in securing patronage.

For any individual retailer, the determinants for a given set of services are: (1) the type of merchandise handled, (2) competition, (3) financial capability, (4) type of operation, and (5) location.

Some argue that service competition is unethical. It is alleged that retailers use services as a cover-up for the high margins they use in pricing merchandise. That is, they are somewhat embarrassed by the excess profits earned and they compensate by adding various services. Other critics assert that retailers often add to price a margin larger than necessary to cover the cost of these services. Still others make no effort to judge the behavior of retailers, believing that the marketplace will decide what the customer is or is not willing to pay for.

Self-service has become a way of life for many retailers since 1912 when Clarence Saunders opened his first self-service Piggly Wiggly in Memphis, Tennessee. Inasmuch as self-service eliminates personal selling, goods often must be sold through advertising or by packaging that explains the product's qualities. Consumers often are willing to perform some of the services themselves in order to obtain lower prices.

There is a trend for many retailers to expand services, although there is some curtailment by mass merchandisers and a few supermarket operators. However, the most important trend in more recent years has been the increase in services performed for tenant retailers by shopping centers. In fact, some have become the focal point of all social activities. Push-button retailing is making an appearance, and some predict it is the store of the future.

QUESTIONS FOR DISCUSSION

1. Retail services may be classified into three major categories. What are they and do you think this classification system is useful?
2. Service is part of a retailer's strategy to attract and hold customers. Discuss the factors which help the retailer to decide on a given set of services to be offered.
3. Discuss self-service from the following points of view: (1) its history, (2) reasons for its popularity, (3) necessary characteristics, (4) prognosis for its future.
4. Discuss pro or con the following statement: "Service competition should be strictly governed because it is unethical and permits retailers to earn an unfair profit."
5. What are the major advantages and limitations of a store-owned delivery system?
6. Discuss the nature of delivery problems and some of the ways in which they can be overcome.
7. Do you think it is possible for any retailer to eliminate all merchandise returns? Why or why not?
8. What are the advantages of salesperson wrap, department wrap, and central wrap?
9. How would you account for the popularity of Sunday openings?
10. Do you think the regional shopping center has become the focus of social life for the suburbanite? Explain.

15 CONSUMER CREDIT POLICIES

For many years a small retail druggist avoided extending credit to his customers because of various costs involved. However, he recently entered into an agreement with a bank in which he would honor the bank's credit card, forwarding the invoice of the customer's purchases for discounting. So, on a $5 prescription sold through a bank credit card, he receives $4.80 from the bank and has none of the worries of investigating the customer's credit worthiness, collecting debts, or writing off bad accounts. The bank worries about those things and he worries about running a drugstore.

A newly married couple purchases $1,200 worth of furniture, agreeing to pay for it in 12 equal monthly installments. They are aware that they must pay more than they would for a cash purchase (it is spelled out very clearly in their purchase contract), but they also know that they lack the willpower to save $1,200 cash. Hence, they view installment buying as a "forced" saving technique.

A major department store chain opens a store in a newly developed suburb and is anxious to get residents to open credit accounts. It contracts with an account solicitation firm that specializes in getting qualified prospective customers to fill out credit applications and return them to the store. The firm has had much experience in identifying likely credit customers and knows a great deal about how to contact them so that they are likely to apply for credit.

An appliance retailer in the central city sells shoddy products to his customers on legal credit terms. He promptly factors out the credit paper to a specialized financial institution. When a dissatisfied customer returns to the store, the manager takes an "I can't help you" stance. The financial institution does not like to get involved in the dispute and insists on being paid. Indeed, the "holder in due course doctrine" requires that the payments continue even though the product has stopped working. State laws are changing, but this charlatan is getting very rich.

An expressway driver calls the nearest automotive service station and explains that he has just had a tire go flat and needs a new one. He is far from home and somewhat short of cash, so he must use his gasoline credit card. He doesn't normally buy such things as tires on credit ("If you can't pay cash for things for the car, then you shouldn't drive"), but this is an emergency. To this particular individual, credit is for large expenditure items (houses, boats, automobiles) and for emergencies. He is a prudent man and keeps his credit cards for just such purposes.

These illustrations suggest some of the common and not so common uses and abuses of credit. Since about the mid-1960s consumer credit has almost exploded in the extent of its use, creating both opportunities and problems for businesspeople and customers alike.

These stories suggest the importance of credit to both the retailer and the consumer. Credit permits the shopper to purchase merchandise in the present and to pay for it in the future. The user of credit is willing to pay what may be a substantial interest charge for this privilege. There is little doubt that its advantage for many retailers is an increase in sales. However, there is some element of risk. Fortunately, the risk is manageable if the lender exercises proper caution.

CHARACTERISTICS OF CREDIT

Credit has three identifiable characteristics: (1) risk, (2) time, and (3) limited acceptance.

Element of Risk

A merchant who sells goods on credit permits the shopper to take possession of the goods with the expectation that the retailer is to receive something of value in payment for the goods at a later date. The risk is simply whether or not the customer will pay for the goods. Actually the aggregate risk is relatively small.

This performance is attained because most lenders follow proved methods for granting credit. They must carefully identify the customers to whom credit should be made available and tailor the terms to the individual's personal and financial characteristics. Each credit applicant is evaluated on what is called the three Cs of credit: character, capacity, and capital.

Character refers to the maturity and responsibility of the person seeking credit; it is the willingness of the debtor to pay his or her obligations. The assessment of character is probably the most important element of the three Cs. A person's character is generally determined by a credit manager, perhaps through a personal interview, by an analysis of the application for credit, and also by contacting outside references. A person builds his or her credit character every time a credit obligation is met. This track record can usually be determined rather easily by a retailer, and is the single best source for estimating an individual's credit worthiness. Credit bureaus are operated either privately or cooperatively by a group of retailers, building up intensive files on all the credit activities of customers who charge merchandise with any retailers willing to furnish information about their charge account customers. This credit history is very useful in judging the character of any credit applicant. Furthermore, credit information is exchanged between credit bureaus located anywhere in the United States.

Capacity refers to the earning power of the credit applicant. A person has capacity if his or her earnings are high enough to permit him or her to charge merchandise and to pay for it out of future earnings. The credit department is responsible for determining the *line of credit* allowable to any one applicant. There are no hard and fast rules to determine the amount of credit that an individual can assume responsibly. A rule of thumb suggests that installment payments should never exceed 10 percent of an individual's take-home pay. For example, a man with a \$500 monthly take-home pay can afford \$50 a month in installment debt payments.

Capital refers to the tangible assets an applicant owns. Everything else being equal, someone with a high net worth is a better risk than an individual with a low net worth. This is indicative that the person concerned has been sufficiently thrifty to accumulate assets. Furthermore, tangible assets may sometimes be seized for nonpayment of a contractual debt.

Time Element

A second characteristic of credit is the time element. This means that there is a lapse between the time a customer takes possession of the purchases and when they are paid for. The retailer permits the customer to take possession before payment, because the retailer is reasonably assured that the customer will keep the promise to pay. The length of repayment time, which we will discuss later, helps to identify different types of consumer credit.

Limited Acceptance

A third characteristic of credit is its limited acceptance in contrast with cash money, which has general acceptance. Money is very flexible, for it enables a shopper to purchase and take possession of goods from any retailer who offers the goods for sale. On the other hand, credit may only be used in those retail outlets that recognize a shopper's credit privilege.

ADVANTAGES OF CREDIT

To the Retailers

Credit is a strategy to increase sales. It accomplishes this in several ways. For one thing, credit tends to stimulate installment buying. Credit buyers are generally less price conscious than cash shoppers. Because of their lower sensitivity to prices, credit buyers purchase goods carrying higher price tags. This fact has been observed by retailers for a long time. The premise has been retested and related to the social class to which the shopper belonged. Evidence indicates that the lower social classes use more installment credit, and consequently buy more expensive merchandise. The report said:[1]

> In large part, these findings confirm the previous contention that installment users are buying "big ticket" items and are using credit cards as a financing device. The fact that convenience users' balances are significantly less than the installment users' lends additional support to our interpretation.
>
> The consumers who buy furniture, TV sets, or stereophonic phonographs at terms of "a dollar down, a dollar a week" are prepared to pay the interest charges. These cardholders are not concerned with "how much?" Rather they ask the merchant, "how much per month?"

[1]H. Lee Mathews and John W. Slocum, Jr., "Social Class and Commercial Bank Credit Card Usage," *Journal of Marketing*, 33, no. 1 (January 1969), p. 77.

Consumer credit also stimulates a greater amount of impulse buying. This may occur at either the customer's home or in the store. For example, two homemakers may be equally stimulated by a retailer's advertisement as they read the morning newspaper and drink a second cup of coffee. One woman, who has credit privileges with the retailer, may react to the ad by telephoning immediately to place her order. The other woman, without credit privileges, although equally stimulated, makes only a mental note to buy the item the next time she shops at that particular store. Unfortunately, time may erode her impulse to buy the item, and the sale may never be consummated.

While in the retailer's store, a shopper with a charge card is more likely to give in to an impulse and buy the items wanted. Consequently, credit enhances a shopper's buying power, and most shoppers act accordingly. This fact is well recognized by most of the nation's largest retailers. There are exceptions, however. E. B. Weiss, writing in *Advertising Age*, is highly critical of Woolworth's for abandoning its experiment with credit.[2] Weiss states that the shopping public demands credit and a wise retailer offers it. To substantiate his argument, Weiss points to J C Penney and Sears. In 1973 $2.2 billion of Penney's sales and 52 percent of Sears' sales were credit sales.[3] Furthermore, Weiss says that Kresge, McCrory, Grant, Newberry, Kress, and Neisner all offer credit.

It is alleged that credit tends to promote store loyalty. Robert Entenberg cites studies indicating that charge accounts increase customer buying ratios in a particular store from 1 to 1 to 3.8 to 1.[4] It is believed that a credit customer concentrates purchases in stores where he or she has credit. This is true even though a customer may be shopping with cash.

A retailer obtains another advantage when credit is offered. The roster of charge customers is an effective mailing list. Announcements and promotional information are sent to this select group as "stuffers" in monthly billing statements, and generally result in additional retail sales to a group who already are customers.

To the Customers

Credit is also advantageous for the customer. Perhaps the most important advantage is the increase in current buying power. A customer need not finance a purchase out of current income or savings. Merchandise can be purchased immediately and paid for out of future earnings. The availability of credit allows American families to be impatient. It permits them to have goods and services in the present rather than wait until sometime in the future, after they have saved enough to finance the purchase. For young families who are setting up new households, this impatience is particularly acute. These families must purchase expensive items such as furniture and appliances at a time when their incomes are low but their needs

[2]E. B. Weiss, "Will Woolworth Become Variety's No. 2?" *Advertising Age* (January 13, 1969), pp. 64–66.

[3]*1973 Annual Report of Sears* and *1973 Annual Report of Penney's*. Both reports issued in 1974.

[4]Robert D. Entenberg, *Effective Retail and Market Distribution* (Cleveland and New York: The World Publishing Co., 1966), p. 432.

are great. Credit helps them to bridge the gap between present needs and future earnings.

Another advantage of retail credit to the consumer is convenience. The shopper can buy all his or her purchases on credit and once a month send checks to the appropriate retailers or financial institutions. H. Lee Mathews and John W. Slocum, Jr., in their study on social class and credit card usage, point out that the upper social classes use their credit more as a convenience than as supplementary buying power. Lower social classes rely less on the convenience factor and are more impulsive buyers. They say:[5] "On the other hand, the upper classes have a greater tendency than the lower classes toward convenience use. This result supports the theory for deferred gratification. That is, while upper classes would not use credit for installment purposes, there is no reason they could not use it for convenience."

Another advantage accruing to the charge customer is the advance notice about sales sent to this group. Frequently they are permitted to purchase sale merchandise a day or two prior to a general announcement. This allows the charge customer to have greater selectivity in choice of sale merchandise.

A further advantage for the customer is the ease of returning merchandise. Every credit sale is recorded and it is easy to identify goods even though the sales ticket is missing. Moreover, it is thought that retailers tend to cater more to charge customers than cash customers when merchandise is being returned.

GROWTH OF CONSUMER CREDIT

Statistical data supply much evidence to show the growth of consumer credit. Table 15.1 indicates this growth. For example, in 1939 total consumer debt was $7.2 billion. By December of 1974, total consumer debt had increased to $190.1 billion. One major area of rapid growth is installment credit, both relatively and absolutely. In 1939 installment credit totaled $4.5 billion, or 62.3 percent of the total consumer credit outstanding. By the end of 1974, installment credit had risen to $156.1 billion, and it represented 82.1 percent of the total retail credit.

Table 15.2 shows disposable personal income, total consumer debt, and the percentage of consumer debt to disposable personal income. One can see that consumer debt has grown from 9.9 percent of disposable personal income to 19.4 percent from 1941 to 1975—a sizable growth.

Table 15.3 provides a comparison of the percentage of installment credit extensions to disposable personal income. These data are frequently used to show the rate of growth of consumer credit. This ratio during the 1960s fluctuated around 15 percent, although in 1973 it had risen to 16.1 percent. By the end of 1974 it dropped slightly to 15.9 percent.

TYPES OF RETAIL CREDIT

Basically there are only two types of consumer credit: installment and noninstallment. Retailers, banks and other financial institutions, and other groups are

[5]Mathews and Slocum, *Journal of Marketing*, p. 73.

TABLE 15.1

Consumer Credit (in millions of dollars)

	Total Credit		Installment Credit		Noninstallment Credit	
1939	$ 7,222	100%	$ 4,503	62.3%	$ 2,719	37.7%
1941	9,172	100	6,085	66.3	3,087	33.7
1945	5,665	100	2,462	43.5	3,203	56.5
1950	21,471	100	14,703	68.3	6,768	31.7
1955	38,830	100	28,906	74.5	9,924	25.5
1960	56,141	100	42,968	76.4	13,173	23.6
1964	80,268	100	62,692	78.1	17,576	21.9
1965	89,883	100	70,893	78.9	18,990	21.1
1966	96,239	100	76,245	79.3	19,994	20.7
1967	100,783	100	79,428	78.8	21,355	21.2
1968	110,770	100	87,745	79.2	23,025	20.8
1969	121,146	100	97,105	80.1	24,041	19.9
1970	127,163	100	102,064	80.3	25,099	19.7
1971	138,394	100	111,295	80.2	27,099	19.8
1972	157,564	100	127,332	80.8	30,232	19.2
1973	180,486	100	147,437	81.6	33,049	18.4
1974	190,121	100	156,124	82.1	33,997	17.9

Source: *Federal Reserve Bulletins* (December 1973), A54 and (February 1975), A47.

TABLE 15.2

Total Consumer Credit Related to Disposable Personal Income (in billions of dollars)

	Disposable Personal Income	Total Consumer Debt	Percentage of Debt to Income
1941	$ 92.7	$ 9.2	9.9%
1950	206.9	21.5	10.3
1962	385.3	63.2	16.4
1963	404.6	70.5	17.4
1964	438.1	80.3	18.3
1965	473.2	89.8	19.1
1966	511.9	96.2	18.7
1968	591.0	110.7	18.7
1969	634.4	121.1	19.0
1970	691.7	127.1	18.4
1971	746.4	138.4	18.5
1972	802.5	157.6	19.7
1973	903.7	180.5	19.6
1974	979.7	190.1	19.4

Source: *Federal Reserve Bulletins* (June 1970), A54 and (February 1975), A47 and A57.

TABLE 15.3

Relation of Installment Credit Extension to Disposable Personal Income (in billions of dollars)

	Disposable Personal Income	*Installment Credit Extension*	*Percentage of Installment Credit Extensions to Disposable Personal Income*
1962	$385.3	$ 55.2	14.3%
1963	404.6	61.3	15.1
1964	438.1	70.7	16.0
1965	473.2	70.9	15.0
1966	511.9	76.2	14.8
1967	546.5	79.4	14.5
1968	591.0	87.7	14.8
1969	634.4	97.1	15.3
1970	691.7	102.1	14.7
1971	746.4	111.2	14.8
1972	802.5	127.3	16.0
1973	903.7	147.4	16.1
1974	979.7	156.1	15.9

Source: *Federal Reserve Bulletin* (February 1975), A47 and A57.

important in both categories. However, since the middle of the 1960s the nation's commercial banks have extended their importance in consumer credit with the issuance of bank credit cards. Oil companies and travel and entertainment groups are also involved in the use of credit cards. Retailers favor three basic types of credit: (1) open account, (2) installment credit, and (3) a combination called revolving credit.

Open Account

In the open account, a customer enters into an arrangement with a retailer to purchase and take possession of merchandise and to pay for it at a later date, usually within 30 days. All goods purchased within the immediately preceding time period are billed on the same statement. Large retailers have so many charge customers that the billing dates are staggered. For example, customers whose last names begin with the letter L may be billed for all purchases made prior to the 18th of the month. Customers whose last names begin with the initial T may be billed as of the 22nd. The billing date is shown on each statement.

Another characteristic of the open account is that it is free of all interest and service charges. Furthermore, the customer is unlikely to make a down payment or to pledge tangible property as security. Retail outlets offer charge account privileges to those who have the character, capacity, and capital to fulfill their responsibilities. Table 15.4, in particular the column headed charge accounts/retail outlets, indicates that retail outlets granted $8.0 billion in noninstallment credit in 1974, an amount equal to 23.6 percent of all noninstallment credit outstanding.

TABLE 15.4

Noninstallment Credit Outstanding
(in millions of dollars)

		Single Payment		*Charge Accounts*		
	Total	*Commercial Banks*	*Other*	*Retail Outlets*	*Credit Cards**	*Service Credit*
1939	$ 2,719	$ 625	$ 162	$1,414		$ 518
1941	3.087	693	152	1,645		597
1945	3,203	674	72	1,612		845
1950	6,768	1,576	245	3,291	$ 76	1,580
1955	9,924	2,635	367	4,579	216	2,127
1960	13,173	3,884	623	4,893	436	3,337
1964	17,576	5,950	924	5,587	608	4,507
1965	18,990	6,690	981	5,724	706	4,889
1966	19,994	6,946	1,026	5,812	874	5,336
1967	21,355	7,478	1,080	6,041	1,029	5,727
1968	23,025	8,374	1,158	5,966	1,227	6,300
1969	24,041	8,553	1,194	5,936	1,437	6,921
1970	25,099	8,469	1,206	6,163	1,805	7,456
1971	27,099	9,316	1,269	6,397	1,953	8,164
1972	30,232	10,857	1,399	7,055	1,947	8,974
1973	33,049	11,753	1,488	7,783	2,046	9,979
1974	33,997	11,500	1,479	8,012	2,122	10,884

*Service stations and miscellaneous credit card accounts and home heating oil accounts. Bank credit card accounts are included in estimates of installment credit outstanding.
Source: *Federal Reserve Bulletin* (February 1975), A47.

Installment Credit

Installment credit differs from open accounts in several ways. One difference is in the opportunity to spread payments over a long period of time. For example, a store may permit a customer to pay for a $120 purchase in 12 equal installments. Sometimes a down payment is required, and the customer is asked to pay finance charges or a service fee. According to the Truth-in-Lending Act, the retailer *must* disclose the charges at its "true" annual percentage rate. (See Figure 15.1.) Frequently the retailer uses a conditional sales contract to secure the purchase. This contract withholds the legal passage of title until the entire purchase price is paid. Failure to pay for the merchandise permits the retailer to repossess the goods. An example to illustrate installment credit follows.

Deborah Ray purchases a Haynes Flute at the Smith Music Store. The flute is priced at $415 and the sales tax amounts to $14.60. Ray is required to make a down payment of $110 and she is charged a service fee of $60. She has 24 months to remit $369.60 in 24 installments of $15.40 each. Deborah Ray signed the conditional sales contract agreeing to all the above terms. To summarize:

Flute (price)	$415.00	
Sales tax	14.60	
Total selling price	$429.60	Terms: 24 installments of $15.40
Less down payment	110.00	
Balance owed	$309.60	
Service fee	60.00	
Total due	$369.60	

Table 15.5 shows the amount of installment credit held by retailers for selective years. Total credit granted by retailer has increased from $1.4 billion in 1939 to $19.5 billion in 1974.

FIGURE 15.1

Atlantic-Richfield Company complies with the Truth-in-Lending Act by stating its retail charge agreement for merchandise paid in installments

Enjoy this porcelain-on-carbon steel cookware in your home

FREE for 10 days

MAIL THIS FREE TRIAL OFFER CARD TODAY

Yes ... please send ☐ (quantity) 14-piece West Bend Cookware set(s) which will be mine to use for 10 days without obligation. If I am not completely satisfied at the end of this period, I may return it and owe nothing. Or you may charge my ARCO credit card account in the manner indicated below.

CHECK ONE

☐ **MONTHLY PAYMENT.** 12 monthly payments of $7.95* each (which includes 46¢ per month for shipping and handling). Total Amount $95.40*

☐ **SINGLE PAYMENT.** Bill me one time for $89.88* (plus $5.52 shipping and handling.)

*State and local taxes, if any, are additional

8128

NO FINANCE CHARGE if payments are made when due.

RETAIL CHARGE AGREEMENT

I agree to pay the amount as checked plus **FINANCE CHARGES** (determined by applying the periodic rates shown below to unpaid billed amounts less payments, credits and unpaid **FINANCE CHARGES**) imposed on amounts not paid within 25 days from closing date of statement.

The monthly periodic rate is 1-1/2% on amounts of $500 or less and 1% on amounts over $500. **ANNUAL PERCENTAGE RATE 18%** and **12%** respectively in all states except as follows (the periodic rate is shown first; the **ANNUAL PERCENTAGE RATE** is shown in parentheses). N.Y. and VT. 0.62% (7.5%); MD., MINN. and W.VA. 0.66% (8%); ARK., DEL., Iowa and N.D. 0.75% (9%); MO. 0.75% (9%) on amounts over $500; S.D., TEX. and OREG. 0.83% (10%); CONN., KAN., WASH. and WISC. 1% (12%); PA. 1.25% (15%). Rate shall in no event exceed that which is permitted by law.

Payments for this purchase are due as billed. Entire outstanding balance may be declared immediately due and payable upon default in payment. These terms apply to this purchase, all subsequent purchases (until terms are changed) but only to charges made with credit cards issued by Atlantic Richfield Company, P.O. Box 100002, Atlanta, Georgia 30348.

Offer expires June 30, 1974

Notice to Buyer: Do not sign this before you read it or if it contains blank spaces. You are entitled to a copy (see enclosed brochure). Keep it to protect your legal rights. You have the right to pay in advance the full amount due.

Signature ✓

ORDER MUST BE SIGNED BY CARDHOLDER

Please print your street address if label carries only a P.O. box number

For fastest service fill in your ARCO credit card number below.

10905

Source: Atlantic-Richfield Company—Products Division, Philadelphia, Pennsylvania.

Revolving Credit

In this plan the retailer sets up a line of credit for the customer, and the customer may purchase merchandise up to this dollar limit at any time. The credit is always open, provided the limit has not been exceeded. A payment chart indicates

TABLE 15.5
Installment Credit Held by Retailers
(in billions of dollars)

	Total	*Auto Retailers*	*Other Retail Outlets*
1939	1.4	.123	1.3
1941	1.6	.188	1.4
1945	.7	.028	.658
1950	2.9	.287	2.6
1955	4.5	.487	4.0
1960	6.3	.359	5.9
1964	8.8	.329	8.4
1965	9.8	.315	9.4
1966	10.8	.277	10.5
1967	11.5	.287	11.2
1968	12.0	.281	11.7
1969	13.1	.250	12.9
1970	13.9	.218	13.7
1971	14.1	.226	13.9
1972	15.0	.261	15.7
1973	18.1	.299	17.8
1974	19.5	.286	19.2

Source: *Federal Reserve Bulletin* (February 1975), A48.

the amount due each month. To see how it operates, consider the minimum payment schedule of Jackie's Boutique:

Unpaid Balance	*Monthly Payment*
$10–60	$10
61–90	15
91–120	20
121–150	25
151–180	30
181–210	35
211–240	40
241–270	45
271–300	50

Suppose that a customer purchases $300 worth of merchandise from Jackie's Boutique, the maximum line extended to her. Looking at the payment schedule, one can see that $50 is the amount due at the end of the first month. Assuming no further purchases, the customer would pay $45 the second month, $35 the third month, $30 the fourth month, and so on until the balance is ended. However, the customer need not wait until the original purchase is paid in full. She can purchase more goods provided the limit to her line of credit is not exceeded. Suppose our customer in this example had reduced her payments to $205. She could purchase additional merchandise valued at $95. If she did, her new payment would again be $50.

Revolving credit accounts are typically assessed a finance charge of 1½ percent per month (corresponding to an annual rate of 18 percent). Customers are advised of this, pursuant to the requirements of the Truth-in-Lending Act. Revolving credit has grown in importance in more recent years. Many retailers automatically grant revolving credit to a customer whenever the customer's credit application is approved. It is up to the customer to decide whether or not to use the credit as an open account or as a revolving credit. Let us look at an example.

Sarah Hale opens a charge account with People's Department Store. She buys $45 worth of merchandise the first month, and she receives her first statement saying that she has the option of paying the bill in full and not being charged a service fee, or making a monthly payment of $10. If she chooses to pay in installments, the store will charge her 1½ percent per month on the unpaid balance. Mrs. Hale may use her credit either as an open account or as a revolving charge. In this example, she pays the entire $45, and consequently pays no interest (finance) fee.

CREDIT CARDS

Credit used to be merely an arrangement between a retailer and a customer. Retail credit consisted of open accounts, installment credit, or revolving credit. Today credit cards of all types are important; by the end of 1973, 65 million Americans had bank credit cards, and 11,000 of the country's banks now offer them. On December 31, 1973, bank credit card debts outstanding were $5.6 billion. At the end of 1973, the travel and entertainment credit card debt was $1.8 billion; oil company credit card debt was also $1.8 billion; and retail store credit card debt was $6.5 billion. All in all, the use of credit cards is of tremendous importance to retailing in the mid-1970s. In fact, it was reported that the police department in Cannon Beach, Oregon, began accepting BankAmericard for bail up to $500.[6]

History of Credit Cards

Credit cards are not a new idea; they have been in use since at least the 1920s. Oil companies were among the early pioneers in issuing credit cards. A cardholder purchased gasoline, oil, and other auto products at any of the oil company's service stations throughout its trading area. The oil company billed its customers monthly, and the entire statement was due and payable after its receipt. Oil companies extend some revolving credit, although most oil company charges remain essentially a convenience and are treated as open accounts.

[6]John H. Allan, "As Prices Soar, BankAmericard Use Jumps," *New York Times* (April 22, 1974), pp. 57–58.

After World War II, travel and entertainment cards were introduced by three major competitors. Diner's Club is the oldest, founded in 1950. By the end of 1974 its membership approximated two million cardholders. American Express made its entry in 1958 and quickly emerged as the leader. It is estimated that three million American Express Credit Cards are outstanding. Carte Blanche is the smallest of the three[7] with a membership estimated to be 650,000 people. These three firms offer what are considered "prestige" cards and charge cardholders for the privilege of using them. (See Figure 15.2.)

FIGURE 15.2
Sample of a credit card issued by Diners Club

Source: Diners Club, New York, New York.

Bank Card History

Banks entered the credit card business in the 1950s; however, it was not until 1966 that real growth began. In 1974 BankAmericard sales increased 29 percent over 1973 to $7.8 billion, and at the end of 1974 $3.9 billion of that was still outstanding. At the same time Master Charge had $8.6 billion in sales and at the end of 1974 it had a $4.8 billion balance.[8]

BankAmericard and Master Charge are the two major bank credit card systems in operation. The Bank of America was a pioneer in the use of credit cards; because of its success in California it began franchising the right to disburse its cards to other banks outside of California. By the end of 1969, it was reputed to have had 25 million cardholders. By the end of 1973, National BankAmericard, Inc., had 26 million cardholders, indicating the rate of increase had slowed somewhat.[9]

The Interbank Card Association is the licensor for Master Charge. It was organized in 1967 by Wells Fargo and three other banks with an announced goal

[7]Andrew F. Brimmer, "Statement to Congress," *Federal Reserve Bulletin* (June 1970), p. 500.

[8]"The Recession Catches up with Credit Cards," *Business Week* (February 17, 1975), p. 47.

[9]Ibid., p. 47.

of competing with BankAmericard. Master Charge has grown explosively since then and is now larger than BankAmericard. On December 31, 1973, it had 31.3 million cardholders and by the end of 1974 that number had risen to 34 million. (See Figure 15.3).

FIGURE 15.3
Master Charge has over 34 million cardholders

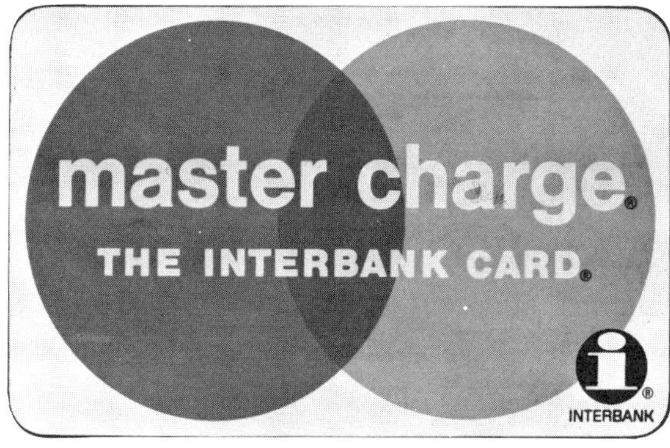

Source: Master Charge Department, American National Bank and Trust Company of Chicago, Illinois.

By 1975, however, the country's economic slump had begun to affect bank credit cards adversely. BankAmericard reported that its delinquency rate had increased from 4.3 percent to 5.0 percent. Master Charge reported that its delinquency rate had risen to 5.4 percent—up from 4.5 percent. As a result, both these systems vowed to make it more difficult to obtain cards and to watch balances owed by cardholders more carefully, threatening to suspend cards of delinquent members.[10]

BANK CARD PROCEDURES

Bank card procedures are illustrated in Figure 15.4.

In step (1) the cardholder selects merchandise from a participating merchant, using the bank credit in payment for the purchase. The salesclerk checks the validity of the card, and then fills out a special bank credit sales slip. After the customer signs the sales slip, he or she takes the merchandise along. In step (2) the merchant deposits with the bank all the sales slips issued during the day. The bank deducts a previously negotiated charge, called a discount rate, from the merchant's deposit, and puts the balance into the merchant's checking account. In step (3) the bank sends a monthly statement to the cardholder. Step (4) the cardholder remits payment to the bank.

An example may clarify the procedure.

Kim White has two bank credit cards issued by two different banks in his community. One is Master Charge and the other is BankAmericard. White has a

[10]Ibid., p. 47.

FIGURE 15.4
Bank card procedures

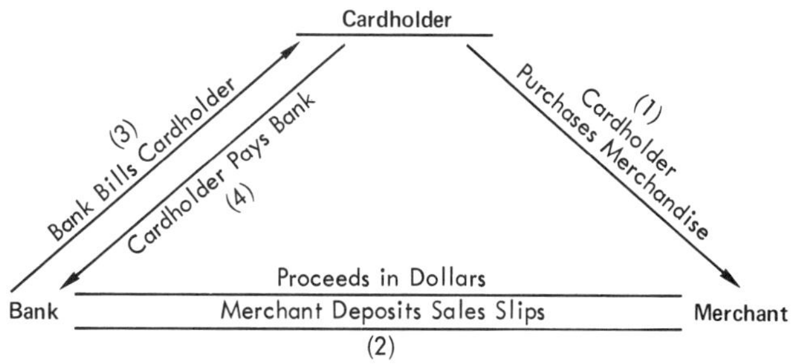

$400 credit limit for each card. He has not used either one, so he has an open credit balance of $400 with each.

On Saturday, June 27, 1975, White goes to Bill's Hardware Store to purchase a rotary lawn mower. He notices a Master Charge decal on the window. After selecting the merchandise White presents his Master Charge credit card in payment of the $94.15 purchase.

The salesperson accepts the card and checks the date to see that it is current. The salesperson also checks a revoked card list to make certain that White's card is valid. Because White's purchase was for an amount higher than the allowable credit for any one purchase (usually $25), the salesperson calls an authorization center for approval of the credit. Within seconds, the authorization center approves the purchase of the lawnmower for the amount of $94.15. The salesperson then prepares a special sales slip describing the merchandise purchased, its price, the sales tax, and the date. The sales slip is imprinted with White's account number as well as the hardware store's identification number. White signs the sales slip, receives his copy of it, and takes the merchandise home.

At the end of day, Bill Walters, proprietor of Bill's Hardware Store, assembles all the sales slips that he has filled for customers using Master Charge that day. Walters lists each slip by dollar amount on the face of a special envelope issued by his bank for that purpose. Let us assume that Bill Walters has five sales slips, including the one signed by Kim White. He lists these separately on the envelope as follows:

	Sales Slip	
Kim White	#1	$ 94.15
Judy Green	#2	10.30
Nora Black	#3	42.70
Joseph Brown	#4	30.15
Maureen Blue	#5	12.16
	Total	189.46

On the face of the envelope, he uses a section to summarize the transactions. His envelopes will contain the following information:

5 sales slips	$189.46
Less credit slips	0
Net sales	$189.46
Less 4% discount	7.58
Net proceeds	$181.88

Also on the envelope, Walters adds the following information in appropriate spaces: name of depositing bank, American Banking Association, number of bank, deposit date, merchant's name and account number, and the bank checking account number. Inside the envelope, Walters will include the originals of the five sales slips.

The bank, upon receipt of the deposit envelope, adds to Walters' checking account the net proceeds, in this case $181.88. Approximately one month later, the bank sends a statement to White.

Assuming White has made no other purchase, he would have the option of paying the entire $94.15 (thus avoiding all finance charges) or remitting a minimum of $10. White notices that his bank statement clearly states that he will be charged 1½ percent a month on his unpaid balance (annual rate equals 18 percent).

Advantages of Bank Credit Cards to Cardholders

The major advantage accruing to the cardholder is the instantaneous credit with all the merchants and banks who participate in the plan. Master Charge claims to have 700,000 merchants in their plan: therefore a Master Charge cardholder has credit in any of these 700,000 retail outlets for a total equal to his or her line of credit. In our example, Kim White could purchase merchandise on credit at any of the 700,000 outlets, but his total purchases in all stores combined could not exceed $400.

A cardholder may have several bank credit cards, each with its own line of credit. That is, an individual may have a BankAmericard with a line of credit of $400 and a Master Charge for $500. Lines of credit may be increased if the bank credit cardholder applies and it is approved. Most cards have a line of credit between $300 and $500.

There are several bank groups that are cooperatively affiliated with Master Charge, and an individual could have a credit card in each. For example, in Chicago, Town and Country bank plan and Charge It both joined the Master Charge plan in 1969. Cardholders of Town and Country and Charge It now are issued Master Charge cards. Therefore it is possible for an individual to hold two or more Master Charge cards at the same time, each with its own line of credit.

Cardholders have another major advantage. They may obtain a cash advance up to the limit of their line of credit from any participating bank. They then can spend the proceeds in any way they choose. If a cardholder accepts a cash advance, interest accrues immediately on a daily basis.

Merchant Advantages

Bank credit plans are also advantageous to the participating merchants. First, the participating retailer need not operate a credit department, thereby avoiding all the expenses customarily involved with credit. More specifically, the retailer avoids the cost of investigating the credit worthiness of prospective charge account customers, has no loss on delinquent accounts, no labor expenses in staffing a credit office, and has significantly reduced the need for capital that would be tied up in accounts receivable.

Previously we mentioned the discount rate which merchants are assessed when they deposit sales slips. This rate is determined at the time they sign an agreement to participate. Some large retail chains are able to negotiate a low discount rate—occasionally as low as 2 percent—because rival bank groups compete for their patronage. Most merchants settle for a 3 to 4 percent discount, and there are cases when the discount rate is 6 percent. However, 4 percent is probably the discount rate for most retailers.

A retailer with a credit department compares the cost of that operation with the discount rate offered in a bank plan. If the bank plan offers the lowest cost, it seems reasonable that the retailer would switch. For many small merchants, the cost of operating their own credit departments averages 6 to 7 percent of net sales. These merchants are eager to join a bank plan at a 4 percent discount rate. For them, the bank credit plan is distinctly advantageous.

Another advantage of the bank credit plan for merchants is the avoidance of tying up capital in accounts receivable. Each day the retailer simply deposits the sales slips with the bank, and the cash proceeds are deposited to his or her account for immediate use. This liquidity is a major advantage of bank credit card plans.

Large Retailers and Bank Credit Plans

Department stores and other large retailers are reluctant to subscribe to a bank credit card plan, thus eliminating their own credit department. Their reasoning is quite sound. One of the functions of a credit plan is to gain a group of loyal customers, and customers tend to shop those stores where they have credit. Bank card plans to give the shopper flexibility in that the holder may shop a wide variety of stores. However, a large department store attempts to hold its own share of customers by honoring only its own credit card. It does not want to be party to a plan that permits a sharing of its customers with other retailers. For this reason, large retailers generally oppose any credit plans but their own.

Travel and Entertainment Cards vis-à-vis Bank Cards

The impact of bank credit cards on the major travel and entertainment cards—Diner's Club, American Express, Carte Blanche—is difficult to assess. However, there are some major differences which operate to the disadvantage of these prestige cards. Each travel and entertainment cardholder must pay an annual fee to obtain the card (currently $20.00 for American Express, for example). The holders of bank credit cards do not pay a fee, and to this extent bank cards are free.

Travel and entertainment cardholders do not have the option of paying their statements in installments. Holders of these cards must pay the entire statement in full or become delinquent. However, American Express has a plan that circumvents this deficiency: a cardholder establishes a line of credit with his or her bank in conjunction with the American Express Company, in which case the bank's name appears on the credit card. An individual may charge any amount with affiliated merchants, restaurants, and the like, as long as the aggregate total charged does not exceed the line of credit. The cardholder is billed monthly by American Express with the option of paying the bill in full or completing an executive credit activator, which in effect is a draft drawn on his or her bank. The bank then makes an installment loan to the cardholder. Because the cardholder can convert the monthly charge to an installment payment plan, these American Express cards are competitive with bank credit cards. In the case of American Express, the cards are called Executive cards and are gold in color to distinguish them from their regular cards.

Merchants also see some differences between bank cards and travel and entertainment cards. One difference is the discount rate. One source indicates that bank cards average out at 4 percent while travel and entertainment cards average out at a 7 percent discount.[11] To illustrate the difference:

Merchant A on the bank plan presents $500 of sales slips to his bank for discounting at 4 percent. His net cash proceeds equal $480.

Merchant B on the travel and entertainment plan presents $500 of sales checks to the plan headquarters and is assessed a 7 percent discount rate. Her net cash proceeds equal $465.

Merchant B is at a clear economic disadvantage over Merchant A.

A more important difference is in the collection of the proceeds. A participating merchant under the bank plan deposits sales slips and receives an instantaneous collection of proceeds. Merchants under the travel and entertainment plans must mail their sales slips to the company issuing the credit card. It takes approximately a week for the merchant to obtain the proceeds.

Oil Company Credit Cards

Oil companies accounted for $1.8 billion of the consumer debt outstanding as of December 31, 1973. Initially, a cardholder was permitted to charge gasoline, oil, and related products on a 30-day charge. Now arrangements may be made at any participating station to purchase major items such as tires, batteries, and repairs on the installment plan. The credit card holder must exercise this option at the time of purchase. Assuming an individual chooses to buy tires on a six-month deferred payment plan, the monthly bill will include all current charges plus the installment on the tires.

Oil companies use their card lists to sell various items by mail. For example,

[11]"The Santa Claus that Makes You Pay," *Business Week* (December 20, 1969), p. 79.

Mobil Oil once offered its credit customers an opportunity to buy a set of luggage, the customer having the option of paying for the merchandise in full or in 12 equal installments. In either case, the customer is billed on the regular statement. Customers who purchase the luggage on the installment plan are charged an interest or a finance fee. Other items offered by the oil company's merchandising department are radios, cameras, blenders, and tape recorders. Most major oil companies have a merchandise center that is responsible for selecting merchandise to sell to their cardholders. Inasmuch as their offerings are restricted to a few items, their impact on the retailing world is uncertain.

Credit Cards and Cash Discounts

In 1974 a suit was brought against American Express by Consumers' Union, who charged that the former was violating anti-trust laws by not allowing merchant members to give a cash discount. Consumers' Union claims that merchants who honor credit cards pay a service fee ranging from 2 to 6 percent, depending upon the merchant's volume and his type of business. Consumers' Union also alleges that merchants who accept credit cards take into consideration the service fee when they set prices. Therefore, it follows that those customers who pay cash subsidize those who use credit cards. Later in the year, American Express, in an out-of-court settlement, notified those who honored American Express cards that cash discounts are not prohibited. Consumers' Union is now bringing suit against other card-issuing companies, including BankAmericard and Master Charge.[12]

Some people argue that no cash discount should be given to those who pay cash because honoring credit cards is merely one of many services that retailers give. Thus, if a retailer provides restrooms for the benefit of his customers, he should not be obligated to give a cash discount to those who do not use them. Since acceptance of credit cards is a service, why should a retailer give a cash discount to those who do not use them? American Express also argues that if cash discounts are given, these discounts should be formalized and such offers be posted in conspicuous places. Never should cash discounts be the subject of bargaining.

In all fairness, Consumers' Union is not arguing that cash discounts be mandatory, but that the credit card company should not prohibit the granting of discounts in its agreement with participating merchants. Much publicity has been generated over the issue, but at this time very little negative effect has been incurred by the major card companies.[13]

RECENT LEGISLATION AFFECTING CREDIT

Congress passed the Depository Institutions Act in 1974, legislation—long overdue—outlawing credit discrimination based on marital status or sex. This legislation

[12]Leonard Weiner, "Pay Cash, Pay Less, CU Argues," *Chicago Tribune* (September 15, 1974), Section 2, p. 13.

[13]Ibid., p. 13.

was the result of complaints by women who had been denied credit in spite of the fact that they had good incomes and good credit histories. Single women frequently were denied bank loans or were given smaller amounts than single men with similar financial backgrounds. Under this law, the Federal Reserve Board must develop the regulations to enforce the act. However, the Federal Trade Commission will enforce retail store credit, the Federal Deposit Insurance Corporation will supervise bank credit, and the Securities Exchange Commission will keep watch over stock transactions.[14]

CONSUMER PROTECTION

Truth-in-Lending

On July 1, 1969, the Federal Consumer Credit Protection Act became effective. It is commonly called the Truth-in-Lending Act.

The purpose of the act is to aid consumers when shopping for credit terms by requiring a uniform method for stating credit. All lenders must state their credit terms either in annual percentage terms or the dollar equivalent. Prior to the enactment of this law, banks frequently quoted their rates in terms of dollars per $100 borrowed. The banks would either use an add-on or a discount method to arrive at the proceeds borrowed. In the add-on method, the bank would lend $100 but would require the borrower to repay $105. In the discount method, the borrower would receive $95 but repay $100. The true rate of interest would be 9.2 or 9.5 percent, depending on the method of lending, and not 5 percent as many people believed.

Computing True Rate of Interest. Let us take an example. Suppose Larry Dee borrowed $1,200 at the bank for one year at the rate of $5 per $100. This means he would have to pay $60 in interest, and assuming the add-on method would repay $1,260. Dee would, of course, receive only $1,200, and he would have the use of the entire $1,200 for only one month if he repaid his loan in 12 equal installments. He would have the use of $1,100 for two months, $1,000 for three months, $900 for four months, and so on until the last $100 would be used for the entire 12 months. On the average, Dee would use $640 for the entire year. Therefore the true interest would be based on the $650, and that equals 9.2 percent.

An easier way to compute the true rate of interest is with his formula.

$$\text{True rate of interest} = \frac{2MI}{P(N+1)}$$

where

M = Number of payments per year.
I = Interest charges in dollars.

[14]"Women's Equal Credit Approved by Senate," *Chicago Tribune* (October 12, 1974), Section 1, p. 5.

P = Amount of actual dollars borrowed.
N = Total number of payments.

Going back to our example, we substitute:

$$\text{True rate of interest} = \frac{2(12)\ (\$60)}{1{,}200\ (12+1)} = \frac{1{,}440}{15{,}600} = 9.2\%$$

Using the same example and assuming the discount method, we compute the interest as follows:

$$\text{True rate of interest} = \frac{2(12)\ (60)}{1{,}140\ \ (13)} = \frac{1{,}440}{14{,}820} = 9.7\%$$

$1,200 − $60 (interest) = $1,140 (proceeds of loan)

Applying the Truth-in-Lending Law. The Truth-in-Lending Act applies to all bank loans, including the bank credit card and revolving credit accounts. It also applies to credit purchases from retailers. In short, the law applies to all credit transactions whether one borrows cash, charges a purchase, or finances a suit of clothes, an appliance, or an automobile. Finance charges must be stated as an annual percentage rate. It is common for finance charges to be quoted as 1½ percent per month, which is the equivalent of an 18 percent annual rate.

The purpose of the law is to inform the credit customer of the rate rather than to regulate either rates or terms. The American Bankers Association made this statement in a prepared leaflet which was sent out to bank customers.[15]

> Its intent is to foster the informed use of credit by consumers. The law makes it mandatory that the lender or merchant provide complete information to you. Once you have this information, it is up to you to make a responsible decision. Informed shoppers will find it much easier to make comparisons between different credit sources.

Regulation of Credit Extension

One of the most vocal complaints in the 1970s was associated with the issuance of unsolicited credit cards. Initially, most banks mailed their cards to people who had not requested them. The banks have claimed that they exercised reasonable restraint in creating their lists of names for approved credit. Some banks apparently were too liberal in mailing credit cards, while others used discretion. Andrew Brimmer, in his report to Congress, stated that the Federal Reserve Bank found the majority of banks were selective. Furthermore, Brimmer stated that the number of complaints were small in relation to the number of cards issued.[16] Congress, however, thought the complaint serious enough to require legislation. Accordingly Sen-

[15]"Truth-in-Lending," a statement prepared by American Bankers Association for general distribution.

[16]Andrew F. Brimmer, *Federal Reserve Bulletin* (November 1967), pp. 1886–87.

ate Bill 721 was introduced to restrict the issuance of credit cards. On March 13, 1970, Senate Bill 721 was reported out of the Banking and Currency Committee. The law states its purpose as:[17]

> A bill to safeguard the customer by requiring standards of care in the issuance of unsolicited credit cards, and by limiting the liability of consumers for the unauthorized use of credit cards, and for other purposes.

In 1970, the Federal Trade Commission issued an order which prohibited the mailing of unsolicited credit cards to anyone in the United States.

Consumer Awareness of Credit Cards

Because of the furor raised over the issuance of unsolicited credit cards and the lack of information available at the time, the Board of Governors of the Federal Reserve Board authorized a survey of consumer awareness regarding bank credit cards.[18] The survey used a sample of 5,137 respondents and it reflected attitudes prevailing as of June 1969. The survey was released the following June. In part, it disclosed the following facts: (1) the higher the level of education the greater percentage of bank credit card ownership; (2) the higher the level of income, the greater the percentage of bank credit card ownership. Table 15.6 has the complete data. Looking at the data, we note that of the respondents with a grade school education or less, 13.3 percent owned bank credit cards. Of those who graduated from college, 40.1 percent owned bank credit cards. Likewise, of those whose annual incomes were $3,000 or less, 10.2 percent had bank credit cards. Of those whose annual incomes exceeded $15,000, 43.6 percent had bank credit cards. The implication is that bank credit cards were selectively issued to those families who seemed likely to use credit wisely. Nothing was said about the usage of bank credit cards as a convenience or as revolving credit.

In 1970 another survey, conducted among 2,567 families, attempted to find out if there was any relationship between the use of credit cards and the level of income of those who used them. The survey clearly showed that as the income level increases, the use of credit cards in general increases. Furthermore, this was true of all kinds of credit cards. For example, of those who earned less than $3,000, only 17 percent used credit cards of any kind; 8 percent used gasoline credit cards; 16 percent used bank credit cards; 9 percent used travel and entertainment cards; and 11 percent used retail store credit cards. On the other hand, those who earned over $25,000 used credit cards extensively: 81 percent used credit cards of any kind; 67 percent—gasoline; 37 percent—bank; 40 percent—travel and entertainment; and 61 percent—retail store.[19]

[17]From a reproduction of Senate Bill 721 as amended February 26, 1970, and distributed by Interbank Card Association, New York, March 13, 1970.

[18]Brimmer, *Federal Reserve Bulletin* (June 1970).

[19]*1975 The U.S. Fact Book, The American Almanac* (New York: Grosset & Dunlap, 1975), p. 461.

TABLE 15.6

Ownership of Bank Credit Cards, June 1969*
(By Income and Educational Level)

Income Level	*Percentage with Bank Cards*
Less than $3,000	10.2
3,000–4,999	16.3
5,000–7,999	21.4
8,000–9,999	28.7
10,000–14,999	33.7
Over 15,000	43.6

Educational Level	*Percentage with Bank Cards*
Grade school or less	13.3
Some high school	20.5
Graduated high school	27.3
Some college	31.5
Graduated college	40.1
Advanced work in college	39.7

*Data taken from a survey of 5,137 respondents reflecting ownership of bank cards as of June 1969.
Source: *Federal Reserve Bulletin* (June 1970), p. 503.

Unfortunately, studies of this type are not done as frequently as is necessary, so the data may be questioned. However, it is likely that there has been little change since the 1969 and 1970 studies were made.

RETAIL INSTALLMENT CONTRACTS

It is customary for retailers who grant installment credit to use contracts to formalize the sale of merchandise and to fix legal responsibility in case of nonperformance. There are four kinds of contracts: the conditional sales contract, the chattel mortgage, the bailment lease, and general credit contracts.

Conditional Sales Contract

Perhaps the most popular type of contract is the conditional sales contract. To explain it, let us use an example. Suppose Ed and Marge Stein purchased a $500 color television set, and they signed a conditional sales contract. The Steins would have the set delivered to their home but also would begin making regular monthly installment payments to the creditor according to the terms of their contract.

The retailer has the authority to repossess the set if the Steins do not pay the installments. This is possible because the title that gives evidence of ownership does not pass to the buyer until all payments are made. Even if the set is repossessed and sold to a second buyer, the Steins' legal obligation has not ended. The proceeds from the second sale will be applied to the balance owed by the Steins, but if it is not sufficient the Steins are liable for the difference. This type of contract is used mainly in the sale of durable merchandise such as automobiles, appliances, and television sets, which have resale value. For clothing and perishables, the conditional sales contract is not suitable.

Chattel Mortgage

In this type of contract, the title of ownership passes immediately to the buyer of the merchandise. However, the merchandise is immediately mortgaged to secure the credit, and the merchant is the mortgage holder. Again, if the buyer does not fulfill the contract, the merchandise may be repossessed and sold.

Bailment Lease

In this contract, the merchandise is technically rented to the buyer, and the rent is paid in installments. Whenever an agreed upon number of rental payments are made, the title is given to the buyer on the payment of a nominal fee, sometimes as little as a dollar.

General Credit Contracts

This type of contract gives no right of repossession to the merchant; however, the merchant may sue the buyer. The general credit contract is popular because the right of repossession is less of an advantage than one might think. For one thing, there are many kinds of goods that have little resale value if repossessed. Clothing is an example. Furthermore, it is costly to repossess the merchandise and resell to someone else. A better alternative is to be careful in granting credit, so as to minimize delinquent accounts. In some cases, merchants find it advantageous to liberalize the terms of repayment for those in difficulty. In this way they may assure themselves of eventual payment.

Some merchants use wage assignments to secure the credit. In these cases, a default permits the retailer to garnishee the wages of the debtor. This attachment of the debtor's salary is disliked by the employers as well as the debtor, and it grows less and less popular. Nevertheless, many merchants have their customers sign wage assignments as security.

COLLECTIONS

No discussion of credit policies is complete without mentioning collection procedures for delinquent accounts. Remember that delinquency can be reduced by careful screening of credit applicants. For those merchants who screen their applicants carefully, collection may not be troublesome. For those who pride themselves on their liberal credit policies, collection may be more difficult. Many retailers—

particularly the smaller ones—now can avoid the headache of collection by joining a bank credit plan and letting the bank worry.

However, for those who do maintain their own credit departments, collection is part of their responsibility. Most individuals do not become delinquent purposely, and they do intend to pay for their merchandise. Sometimes it only takes a reminder that their statement is overdue. In other instances, more stringent measures are needed, such as a strong letter urging payment or a telephone call. Usually these measures are sufficient. However, there are a few hard-core delinquents. For these people, a decision must be made to sue or to turn the account over to a collection agency. Frequently, the account is too small to bother with, and it is simply written off as a bad debt. Most retailers attempt to collect the overdue accounts before it is too late.

There are advantages to early collection of customer accounts. The more apparent ones are: (1) less capital tied up in delinquent accounts, (2) less direct expense for salaries of employees in the credit department, and (3) more favorable relations with customers. Good customer relations is the aim of most retailers, and all store policies are directed toward this objective. However, if a retailer permits a delinquent account to go uncollected, it is almost certain that hard feelings will develop, and the result is a lost customer and lost sales. On the other hand, a prompt collection plan may save the customer and insure future sales.

MEASURING CREDIT DEPARTMENT EFFECTIVENESS

All retailers desire to know whether or not their credit departments are functioning effectively. One way to measure effectiveness is the number of credit applications processed in a month's time, and the percentage of credit applications approved. Every store has attrition in its customers, and these must be replaced if the store wishes to maintain the status quo. Furthermore, if the store expects to expand its credit sales, new accounts must be continually added.

Retailers should also be aware of the status of their delinquent accounts. The accountant furnishes a report called "aging the receivables." This report shows the extent to which accounts are current or delinquent.

For example, the accounting department shows all the outstanding balances of its customer accounts in a schedule somewhat similar to the following:

Customer Balances Owed	*Dollar Amount*
Not due	$10,200
0 to 30 days overdue	2,400
30 to 60 days overdue	1,100
60 days to 6 months overdue	510
More than 6 months overdue	950
Total	$15,160

Each "aging of receivables" report can be compared with other monthly reports to determine the trend of delinquent accounts. From an analysis of successive reports, an evaluation can be made of both the credit department and the collection process. These reports can also be compared with similar reports of other retailers.

The credit department can also furnish the amount of delinquent accounts charged off to bad debts. This report is also useful in evaluating credit sales. For example, if delinquent accounts are excessive of credit privileges, steps must be taken to be more selective.

The credit department must also be evaluated on the basis of its cost of operation. Here again a comparison of its cost can be made with other time periods and other credit departments.

SUMMARY

Credit is among the strategies a retailer uses to increase sales volume. This strategy faces the risk that the shopper may not pay for the merchandise. However, the risk is limited to an acceptable level if the correct selection procedure is used. First, one examines the character of the individual seeking credit in order to ascertain whether or not the credit seeker has the maturity and responsibility to assume a debt. Second, the investigator checks the capacity of the credit applicant to pay for charged merchandise. Third, the credit investigator checks on the capital (amount of tangible assets) owned by the credit applicant.

Credit can be wisely used. For the retailer credit usually means increased sales. Studies confirm that credit buyers purchase more expensive merchandise than do cash buyers. Moreover credit stimulates a greater amount of impulse buying. Retailers also believe it promotes store loyalty. The most important advantage for the credit shopper is the ability to buy merchandise in the present and pay for it in the future. Other shoppers use credit as a convenience factor.

Consumer credit has grown rapidly in the 1970s. One of the best measures of credit growth is to relate credit extensions to disposable personal income. During the 1960s this measure increased from 14 to 16½ percent.

Basically there are two kinds of credit—installment and noninstallment. A popular form of installment is revolving credit. A customer is granted a line of credit and may purchase merchandise at any time provided the line of credit is not exceeded. A payment charge indicates the amount due each month. This payment includes a service fee based on the amount of the unpaid balance due.

Credit cards have become increasingly important. The Federal Reserve Board estimates there are 600 million unexpired credit cards outstanding. That is approximately three cards for each man, woman, and child in the United States. Credit cards are issued by banks, travel and entertainment groups, oil companies, and retailers. The rapid expansion of bank credit cards was the most important credit story of the 1960s. Approximately 60 million cards are in circulation today. Most commercial banks belong either to Bank Americard or Master Charge.

Bank credit cards are advantageous to consumers, retailers, and banks. For the consumer, a bank card is the guarantee of credit at thousands of retailers across the country. Moreover the consumer can obtain a cash advance at thousands of banks. Customers, of course, may not exceed their line of credit, and they are charged finance fees on their unpaid balances if they pay in installments. Small retailers find bank credit cards attractive because it permits them to engage in credit sales without sacrificing liquidity or assuming the costs or risks of credit extension. Banks believe it is a logical extension of their services, and it permits them to earn a larger income.

Travel and entertainment cards are a form of open account credit. Diner's Club and American Express are the two most important companies in this category.

Oil companies are very important in the credit card business. Although they extend both revolving and noninstallment credit, they are not as important as banks in the overall credit picture. They have also become involved in merchandising items such as photographic equipment, radios, and luggage to their credit customers.

The federal government has become increasingly involved in legislation affecting credit, most notably with the Truth-in-Lending Act. This law requires all lenders to state their credit terms explicitly in annual interest rates so that credit users can be better informed of their options and alternatives.

Retailers who sell merchandise on the installment plan protect themselves through four different kinds of contracts: conditional sales, chattel mortgage, bailment lease, and general credit. Only the general credit contract does not employ the goods themselves as security behind the credit. However, it is becoming more important because repossession and the resale of merchandise are often costly, time-consuming, and impractical.

Credit policies must include good collection procedures. Inasmuch as delinquency will occur, the credit department must take steps to minimize its occurrence, and to collect an account as promptly as possible. Hard-core delinquents should either be turned over to a collection agency or written off as bad debts.

QUESTIONS FOR DISCUSSION

1. Credit has three identifiable characteristics: risk, time, and limited acceptance. Discuss these and use examples to illustrate.
2. How does credit increase sales?
3. Discuss the general topic of growth in consumer credit. In your answer:
   a. Show the statistical data that are relevant.
   b. Discuss types of retail credit and their relevance.
4. What are the advantages of bank credit cards:
   a. for the consumer?
   b. for the retailer?
   c. for the banks?
5. Compare bank credit cards with travel and entertainment card.
6. Explain revolving credit and its importance in the overall credit picture.

7. What is the purpose of the Truth-in-Lending Act? Do you think it has been successful in accomplishing its purpose?

8. Compare the following: conditional sales contract, chattel mortgage, bailment lease, and general credit contract.

9. How would you evaluate the performance of a credit department of a retail store?

10. Do you think bank credit cards are the first step in a cashless society? Why?

16 ACCOUNTING CONTROLS

The manager of the restaurant in a Minneapolis department store is paid a year-end bonus for profits earned in his department. But restaurants in department stores are almost never profitable because they must serve food and drinks at competitive prices, are usually inconveniently located, and seldom serve more than one meal (lunch) each day. The restaurant manager knows enough about cost accounting to argue that the simple allocation of rent expense based on square feet of floor space used is unfair because he is located on one of the less valuable upper floors. He also argues that his department "contributes to overhead," although it does not earn a net profit. His job and his bonus depend on making these arguments believable.

When Kresge stores changed to a discount type retail operation, each store manager had to re-orient his thinking about his store's goals. Each manager knows that he is expected to turn his inventory over eight times a year even though the industry average is only six, he is expected to attain a return on the store's investment (ROI) of twenty-five percent each year, and that no more than forty percent of his funds should be invested in inventory. If he is a good manager, he watches these and several other key figures very carefully.

A small retail druggist does not want to bother with record keeping, so he (and many others in his position) hires McKesson and Robbins Drug Company to keep track of their products in his store. This service costs him $5,000 a year. They furnish him with a monthly computerized report on profit margins, a quarterly report on shelf space use, and recommendations on how it can be used more effectively. He also receives an electronic ordering terminal that is connected to a McKesson warehouse; physical distribution is speeded up, so the amount of inventory he keeps on hand is substantially reduced. He has not eliminated the need for record keeping since McKesson's service applies only to their products.

The owner of a paint and wallpaper store read in a September issue of *Dun's* that owners of other paint, glass, and wallpaper stores experienced a 3.2 percent "net profits on net sales" rate during the previous year. He believes that he earned a 3.8 percent ratio. His initial reaction is a pleasing one, but he quickly realizes that either the input data may be different between the sample and his own store or that there may be a localized explanation for the difference. Indeed, it may even mean that his prices are higher than in other stores and that he is losing business to his rival retailers. And his total profits may be less than they should be.

As you can see, those who are involved in retailing at just about any level must understand the rudiments of accounting. While they may not be responsible for maintaining the firm's financial records, they often will be asked to furnish information or must take action based on their interpretation of records that others have given them.

The above incidents suggest the range of record keeping and conceptual problems that retailers may face. Indeed, it may seem that reasons for keeping accounting records are so obvious it is not necessary to state them. In fairly recent years, federal income tax laws have alerted taxpayers to the need for keeping adequate personal records to verify and support their income tax statements. However, even if all income tax laws were repealed, the need for keeping accounting records would still be necessary. These are the major reasons:

1. The profitability of past operations can be determined.
2. Current operations may be evaluated more effectively.
3. Information is provided for internal and external comparisons.
4. Financial information is available to obtain credit from banks and vendors.
5. Information required by various government units is on hand.
6. The retailer is able to compute the value of inventory at any time without taking an actual count.

FINANCIAL STATEMENTS

The Income Statement

The most important statement a retailer prepares is the income statement, or, as it is also called, the operating statement. This statement summarizes the revenue earned and expenses incurred by the retailer over a period of time. The difference between revenue and expenses is the profit or loss. Table 16.1 shows a simplified income statement. Note that the important elements are (1) sales, (2) cost of goods sold, (3) operating expenses, and (4) profit or loss.

TABLE 16.1
Shirley's High Fashion Boutique: Statement of Income for the Period July 1, 1976, through December 31, 1976

Gross sales		$105,000
Less: Returned sales and allowances		2,000
Net sales		$103,000
Less: Cost of goods sold		60,000
Gross margin		$ 43,000
Less:		
Selling expenses	$20,000	
General expenses	10,000	30,000
Net operating profit		$13,000

Gross Sales. The merchant keeps records by posting all cash and credit sales in a sales ledger. At the end of a given time period, he or she totals these accounts and thus has available the information called gross sales. In other words, gross sales are simply the total of all sales made by the merchant whether or not the sales are for cash or credit. In the case of Shirley's High Fashion Boutique, total sales for the period July 1, 1976, to December 31, 1976, were $105,000.

Returns and Allowances. Returns and allowances are reductions from total sales because of merchandise returns to the retailer by some customers, or because the retailer made some financial adjustment to a customer due to defective or otherwise unsatisfactory merchandise. Let us again look at Shirley's Boutique for the explanation of the $2,000 deduction for sales returns and allowances.

> One of Shirley's charge customers returned a dress that she had purchased and charged. She claimed that her husband disliked it. The sales price was $50, and Shirley gave her credit. It is a returned sale.
>
> Another of Shirley's customers brought in a dress she had purchased on July 6. Her complaint was that the material had a slight flaw. The customer liked the dress, and since there was no other available in her size, she accepted a $2 adjustment allowance and kept the dress.
>
> Still another customer is given a refund for the difference between what she paid for a pair of shoes and the price at which the identical shoes are sold in a boutique in a nearby town.

During the six-month period between July 1, 1976, and December 31, 1976, other customers came back to the store with similar complaints. Altogether Shirley's Boutique made adjustments totaling $2,000. When the $2,000 is subtracted from the gross sales, the result is net sales.

Cost of Goods Sold. The cost of goods sold is the delivered dollar cost of the goods represented by the net sales; it is the price the retailer has to pay suppliers for the merchandise sold to customers. Table 16.2 illustrates the way the cost of goods sold is computed.

The concept is rather easy to understand, but the calculation of the cost of goods sold might appear complex to the student with little or no accounting knowledge. The retailer's accountant knows the dollar value of the inventory still on hand at the beginning of the accounting period, either from a recent physical

TABLE 16.2

Shirley's High Fashion Boutique:
Computation of Cost of Goods Sold
for the Period July 1, 1976, through December 31, 1976

Opening inventory (July 1) at cost	$22,500
Net purchases at cost	61,000
Freight in	1,500
Total cost of goods handled	$85,000
Less: Inventory on hand December 31 at cost	25,000
Cost of goods sold	60,000

count or from continuing records. In our example, Shirley's Boutique had on hand $22,500 of unsold merchandise on July 1, 1976; this was her opening inventory. During the six-month period, Shirley purchased $61,000 of new merchandise. It also cost $1,500 in freight charges to get the merchandise to her store. Altogether her store had (available for sale in the six-month period) $85,000 of merchandise (cost value). This does not mean that this much merchandise was ever available at any one time; rather it was the aggregate amount available for sale. At the end of the accounting period—that is, on December 31—she still had $25,000 in merchandise she had not sold. This was her closing inventory, and her opening inventory on January 1, 1977. Therefore, Shirley's Boutique sold merchandise that had cost $60,000 ($85,000 − $25,000).

Gross Margin. Gross margin is simply the difference between the dollar figure of the retailer's sales and the cost of the merchandise sold. It was once known as gross profit, but this terminology led many people to confuse it with true profit. Therefore, gross margin is more commonly used. Gross margin represents the amount available to cover all expenses and afford the owner a profit.

Operating Expenses. The retailer has other costs besides the amount paid for the merchandise sold, for example, rent expenses if the store is leased. Most certainly there are such expenses as wages and salaries (including the retailer's own), heat, light, gas, and telephone, and probably advertising, postage, stationery, and delivery expenses. The accountant totals all the expenses that the retailer incurs during the accounting period. These are classified as selling and general expenses. (More will be said about these expenses and their control later in this chapter.)

Net Profit. Net profit is the difference between gross margin and all operating expenses. If gross margin is larger than expenses, the retailer has a net profit, but if the expenses exceed the gross margin, the retailer has a loss. In our example, Shirley's High Fashion Boutique has a net profit of $13,000.

Significance of Income Statement

We are interested at this point only in how the information included on the income statement can be beneficial to the retailer. The statement is important for two major reasons: (1) it is the principal document used to determine the income tax liability of the retailer, and (2) it is the principal statement the retailer uses to evaluate merchandising performance with respect to objectives or goals.

The Income Statement and the Tax Authorities

The income statement is especially important to both federal and state tax collectors. This document discloses the magnitude of the profit or loss, and hence, it becomes the basis that determines tax liability. In the case of state sales tax, the income statement determines the basis for that particular liability. Tax authorities do not accept the income statement blindly; the retailer must be prepared to validate all the expenses, costs, and revenues that are used in the preparation of this statement.

The Income Statement as an Evaluation Tool

Earlier we pointed out the four major components of the income statement—sales revenue, cost of goods sold, expenses, and net profit. The retailer uses the income statement to compare his or her operating results with others within the industry, as well as relating the data to personal goals and objectives. Let us examine sales revenue as it is presented in Table 16.3.

TABLE 16.3

Ken's Other Store: Income Statement For the Period January 1, 1976, through December 31, 1976

Gross sales	$102,000
Less: Returned sales and allowances	2,000
Net sales	100,000

Evaluating Gross Sales. First, Ken examines the magnitude of the dollar gross sales. Are they satisfactory? How do they compare with his expectations or last year's sales? How do they compare with other retailers of similar size in his industry? In determining his expectations, he can start with the previous year's gross sales and add to it an increase based on an expected growth rate. Some retailers assume a growth rate equal to that of the retailing industry as a whole. Other retailers think their growth rates should equal that of the average retailer engaged in a similar type of retailing. Others may choose as a standard rate of growth a figure equal to the rate of increase in the gross national product of the nation. Regardless of how the retailer estimates rate of growth, he or she can compare sales increases for any time period with the chosen standard and make a conclusion as to his or her own performance. This sales performance is stated in dollars and percentages.

Except in the most elementary retailing business, the retailer shows sales by departments or by lines of merchandise. Sales are computed in a variety of ways, such as volume of sales per square foot of selling space, volume of sales per employee, or volume of sales per salesclerk. These specific ways of measuring sales permit the retailer to make tests on the efficiency of his or her operation. Normally, the retailer compares results with similar results of past years. Obviously, if the comparison shows disappointing results, the retailer seeks a logical explanation for the shortcomings. Trade associations or groups of retailers engaged in similar trades publish information useful to individual retailers. Table 16.4 shows information of this kind.

The point is that each retailer should compare sales with such standards as (1)

TABLE 16.4
Sales Gains by Type of Retailer, 1972 vs. 1971

All U.S. retail stores	9.6%
Grocery stores	7.7
Eating, drinking places	8.6
Drugstores	6.2
Auto group	12.0
Apparel stores	5.3
Furniture, appliances	15.0

Source: "40th Annual Report of the Grocery Industry," *Progressive Grocer* (April 1973), p. 96.

his or her own expectations, (2) experience in past accounting periods, and (3) those published by reliable sources. After such comparisons are made, the retailer is in a position to judge his or her sales performance.

Evaluating Returned Sales and Allowances. Earlier we discussed the concept of returned sales and allowances. For one reason or another customers sometimes return purchases and are given full refunds. At other times they are given rebates in the form of an allowance. Returned sales and allowances often reflect retailing errors. Let us examine some of the more common ones.

1. *Inappropriate merchandise.* If the merchandise proves to be substantially different than the customer expected when it was originally purchased, it is likely to be returned. Regardless of price, goods should always meet the standards of their class of merchandise; otherwise the customers may return the merchandise. In addition to the loss of sales, the store might experience considerable customer ill will.
2. *Salesperson oversell.* Some salespeople make impossible claims for merchandise, so that customers are certain to be dissatisfied when the product is used. Perhaps more serious are those who permit customers to take home several items with the tacit understanding that they can further narrow their choice in the comfort of their homes and then bring back those items they do not buy. For example, a customer may be encouraged to purchase several dresses, take them home, show them to her husband, and then select the one she intends to keep, finally returning the others. The returned merchandise is frequently spotted or dirty so that it no longer can be sold at its original price and will have to be marked down if it is to sell at all. Salespeople who sell on commissions often are guilty of overselling their merchandise. A retailer should have a written policy governing the quantity of merchandise a customer may take home for a trial.
3. *Salesperson undersell.* The manager must also be alert to the possibility that too few goods are returned for refund or credit. There are a few stores where returns are not permitted, but these are exceptions. In most instances, retailers would prefer that dissatisfied customers bring back purchases so that adjustments can be made. Where too few goods are returned (again, in comparison with similar stores), the retailer must ask why. A common answer is that sales-

people are too cautious in their selling tactics toward undecided customers. A sensitive salesperson knows when to make a positive statement such as, "Perhaps you'd like to try on the dress at home tonight before you make a final decision. I'm sure you'll like it, but if not you certainly can bring it back." Such sales comments directed at on-the-fence customers often increase sales dramatically and may be worth the risk of a higher rate of returns and adjustments. When too few goods are returned it may be because too few salespeople are making such comments.

4. *Customers are also at fault.* Many customers think they have an inalienable right to over-purchase merchandise, take it home for a trial period, and then return those items they really don't want. One shopper habitually purchases three or four pairs of shoes, knowing that she intends to keep only one pair. In order to discourage this type of customer, some retailers have a policy that all sales are final. Whenever this is the policy, the retailer must be certain that the customers are fully aware of it as they make their selections. Most retailers are not willing to go to the extreme of making all sales final because they want their customers to know that they stand behind all the merchandise they sell. Marshall Field's has earned a reputation by following a policy that the customer is always right. The store will always take merchandise back if the customer is dissatisfied. Most retailers want their customers to be completely satisfied even though it increases the amount of returned goods and the privilege often is abused.

Evaluating the Net Operating Profit. Net operating profit, as we have seen earlier, is the result of the relationship between sales revenue, cost of goods sold, and all operating expenses. It is repeated in Table 16.5 in simplified form.

It is impossible to conclude by examining the income statement whether or not profits are adequate. Furthermore, it is impossible to judge whether they are meaningful with respect to the store's expectations or objectives. Some years ago Wingate and Schaller made the following observation about profits:

> The profit figure takes on signifiance only as it is related to some other factor. This factor may be (1) the profit of a previous year; (2) the sales; (3) the merchandise investment made to earn the profit; (4) the net worth, which is the owner's equity

TABLE 16.5

Ken's Other Store: Income Statement For the Period January 1, 1976, to December 31, 1976

Gross sales	$122,000
Less: Returned sales and allowances	2,000
Net sales	$120,000
Less: Cost of goods sold	70,000
Gross margin	$ 50,000
Less: Operating expenses	20,000
Net operating profit	$ 30,000

in the business; (5) the number of transactions realized; (6) the space occupied in order to earn the profit; and (7) the number of shares of corporate stock to which the profit is to be allocated.[1]

This observation is equally true today. Consequently, it would be beneficial to readers if we illustrate some techniques for making the profit figures meaningful.

1. *Relating net operating profits to last year's figures.* Assume a 1976 profit of $30,000 and a 1975 profit of $20,000.

1976 net operating profit	$30,000
1975 net operating profit	20,000
Difference	$10,000

Conclusions:

a. The magnitude of the dollar increase is $10,000

b. $\frac{\text{Difference of \$10,000}}{\text{1973 profit of \$20,000}} = 50\%$

The store increased its profits by 50 percent.

2. *Net operating profits relative to net sales.* Suppose that net sales are $200,000 and the retailer earned $30,000 net profit. Then

$$\frac{\text{Net profits}}{\text{Sales}} = \frac{\$\ 30,000}{\$200,000} = 15\%$$

Conclusion: Every $100 of net sales results in $15 of net operating profit, at least while the store's sales remain at about $200,000.

3. *Net operating profit relative to merchandise investment.* Assume that the retailer's inventory averaged $70,000 throughout the year. Assume also that net operating profit is $30,000. Then

$$\frac{\text{Net operating profit}}{\text{Merchandise investment}} = \frac{\$30,000}{\$70,000} = 42\%$$

Conclusion: The retailer earns slightly over 42 percent on the investment in merchandise inventory.

4. *Net operating profit relative to net worth.* Assume that the owner's equity in the business equals $300,000 and net operating profit equals $30,000. Then

$$\frac{\text{Net operating profit}}{\text{Owner's equity}} = \frac{\$\ 30,000}{\$300,000} = 10\%$$

Conclusion: The net operating profits are 10 percent of the owner's investment in the business; the owner earns $10 for every $100 invested.

[1]John W. Wingate and Elmer O. Schaller, *Techniques of Retail Merchandising*, 2nd ed. (Englewood Cliffs, N.J.: Prentice-Hall, Inc., 1956), p. 75.

5. *Net operating profit relative to transactions.* Assume that the store had 3,000 separate sales transactions and the net operating profit equals $30,000. Then

$$\frac{\text{Net operating profit}}{\text{Transactions}} = \frac{\$30,000}{3,000} = \$10$$

6. *Net operating profit relative to space occupied.* Suppose that a store occupies a building containing 60,000 square feet of space, of which 40,000 square feet is selling space and a $30,000 net operating profit is earned.
   a. $\frac{\$30,000}{60,000} = \$.50$ per square foot of building space
   b. $\frac{\$30,000}{40,000} = \$.75$ per square foot of selling space
7. *Net operating profit relative to capital stock investment.* Assume that a retail store has 1,000 shares of common stock outstanding and the store earns $10,000 of net operating profit. Then

$$\frac{\text{Net operating profit}}{\text{Shares outstanding}} = \frac{\$10,000}{1,000} = \$10$$

   Conclusion: The store earns $10 of net operating profit for every share of stock outstanding.

The computations of these ratios are not ends in themselves. Retailers must compare them with appropriate standards so that a judgment may be made concerning the efficiency and the profitability of the business. These standards are both internal and external. The retailer would compare his or her current operating results with those of other years—this would be the internal analysis. Likewise, the retailer would compare results with similar operating results of other retailers doing a similar volume of business. The external standards are provided by trade associations and journals, United States Department of Commerce, and other reputable sources.

Stock Turnover

Stock turnover is another important technique that measures the efficiency of the retailer's operation. Specifically, the rate of turnover measures the length of time merchandise is carried as inventory before it is sold. Stock turnover may be computed in annual terms, monthly figures, or in days; however, it is usually stated as the number of stock turns per year. For example, a stock turnover of six indicates that it takes two months to turn the stock (sell it) one time. Actually, it is quite easy to make this computation. The information comes directly from the income statement.

Computing Rate of Stock Turnover. There are three principal methods of computing the rate of stock turnover. They are:

1. $\frac{\text{Net sales}}{\text{Average inventory at retail}}$

2. $\dfrac{\text{Cost of goods sold}}{\text{Average inventory at cost}}$

3. $\dfrac{\text{Sales in units}}{\text{Average inventory in units}}$

Illustration. Assume all of the following:

Net sales	$100,000
Cost of goods sold	60,000
Opening inventory—at cost	15,000
Closing inventory—at cost	9,000
Opening inventory—at retail	25,000
Closing inventory—at retail	15,000
Unit sales	20,000 items
Opening inventory	5,000 units
Closing inventory	3,000 units

In each of the examples for computing turnover the first step is to compute the average inventory. This is done by adding the inventory at the beginning of the period to the inventory at the end of the period and dividing by two. When inventory is carried at retail figures, the following methodology is normally used.

Opening inventory at retail	$25,000
Closing inventory at retail	15,000
Total Inventory	$40,000

$$\frac{\$40{,}000}{2} = \$20{,}000\text{—the average inventory at retail}$$

If inventory is carried on the books at cost, one would simply add the cost value of the opening and ending inventories and divide by two. Looking back to the figures in our illustrations, the opening inventory at cost is $15,000 and the ending inventory is $9,000; therefore the average inventory at cost is $12,000.

Some retailers may carry inventory in terms of physical units rather than dollars. Thus from the data in the illustration, average inventory in units is 4,000 units (5,000 units + 3,000 units = 8,000 ÷ 2 = 4,000 units). The next step, after computing the average inventory, is to divide it into net sales, cost of the goods sold, or into unit sales. Thus, if the average inventory at retail equals $20,000 and net sales are $100,000, the turnover is 5.

If, however, the average inventory at cost is $12,000, you must divide it into cost of the goods sold ($60,000), and the turnover is 5.

You could compute turnover if all information was stated in physical units.

Thus, if 20,000 equals unit sales, and 4,000 units is the average inventory, then the turnover is 20,000 divided by 4,000, or 5.

These three methods are summarized as follows:

1. $\text{Turnover} = \dfrac{\text{Net sales}}{\text{Average inventory at retail}} = \dfrac{\$100{,}000}{\$\ 20{,}000} = 5$

2. $\text{Turnover} = \dfrac{\text{Cost of goods sold}}{\text{Average inventory at cost}} = \dfrac{\$60{,}000}{\$12{,}000} = 5$

3. $\text{Turnover} = \dfrac{\text{Unit sales}}{\text{Average inventory in units}} = \dfrac{20{,}000 \text{ units}}{4{,}000 \text{ units}} = 5$

One must clearly understand that the solution would be the same regardless of which of the three methods is used to compute the rate of turnover, as long as the data relates to the June inventories.

Interpreting Rate of Turnover. As we said earlier, the turnover rate is usually expressed in annual terms. In the preceding example, the turnover of five means the average stock of merchandise was turned over five times in a year. Viewed from a different perspective, it took 2.4 months (12 ÷ 5 = 2.4) to sell the average stock of merchandise on hand. The turnover could also be expressed in days, although it is not common to do so. In our example, 360 ÷ 5 = 74 days. It took 74 days to sell the merchandise on hand. The turnover rate is important because it indicates the efficiency of selling the merchant's investment in inventory.

Advantages of Increasing Turnover. It is usually advantageous to increase the rate of turnover. Among the principal advantages are:

1. It permits a more efficient use of the capital investment in merchandise inventory. To illustrate, assume that a retailer has an annual turnover of 5 and annual sales of $30,000. Then $\dfrac{\$30{,}000}{5} = \$6{,}000$, the capital needed in inventory. However, suppose the turnover rate could be increased to 6 through better selling or more careful inventory management; then $\dfrac{\$30{,}000}{6} = \$5{,}000$, the amount needed to generate the same $30,000 in sales. The savings of $1,000 in inventory investment means the retailer can use it in some other way.
2. Markdowns are fewer if the goods remain in stock a shorter period of time. The inventory will have a shorter period to become shopworn, and in the case of fashion merchandise, it will have a greater chance of being sold before the fashions change. The merchandise is fresh, and thus easier to sell.
3. Wherever the turnover rate is increased, other expenses such as insurance and interest costs often are reduced.
4. Generally speaking, if the turnover rate is increased, markdowns are reduced, and there are savings in expenses, the retailer will experience larger net operating profits.

Limitations of Increasing Rate of Turnover. The greatest disadvantage to increasing the rate of turnover is that it can become an end by itself. There is no purpose for increasing the turnover rate unless it results in higher net profits. To illustrate: suppose a retailer reduced all prices below costs. This probably would result in a significant sales increase and hence a higher turnover rate. Nevertheless, since all the prices were below cost, the result would be large operating losses.

Another possibility that could occur if the turnover rate is overemphasized would be an incomplete stock of merchandise available for sale. If a store is out of merchandise, some sales will be lost. One cannot complete a sale if adequate merchandise is not on hand. Many customers are not willing to wait until the merchant replenishes stock. A customer usually has the alternative of going to a competitor who does have the merchandise on hand. Whenever a merchant fails to carry sufficient stock, there is the risk of losing goodwill and future sales. A store must carry sufficient inventory so that sales may be made on all opportunities that are presented to the store. This means that the retailer must carry slower moving items, even though it results in a lower turnover rate.

In spite of the inherent dangers of emphasizing a rapid turnover rate, some retailers engage in hand-to-mouth buying, meaning they buy in small quantities but frequently. This succeeds in increasing the turnover rate, but at the expense of higher buying costs, usually through the loss of quantity discounts and higher delivery expenses. The total effect may be lower operating profits.

Achieving a Higher Turnover Rate without Decreasing Profits. A merchant may logically pursue a goal of achieving the maximum efficiency in his or her investment in inventory. In order to do this and achieve the proper turnover rate, the retailer must re-examine periodically (1) the efficiency of buying methods; (2) the pricing policies followed; (3) the efficiency of the sales staff; and (4) the presence of an adequate stock control system.

1. *Buying weaknesses. The store buyer must purchase merchandise that will sell.* He or she cannot afford to make too many buying mistakes, for the result will be an increase in stock of inventory, an increase in markdowns, and a poor turnover ratio.
2. *Pricing mistakes.* The store must price its merchandise so that it will sell, and yet the price must be large enough to cover the costs of the merchandise and all expenses incurred in selling the goods. Obviously, the merchant must use good judgment in taking markdowns as well as pricing the goods properly when they are first offered for sale.
3. *Selling faults.* In order to have a higher turnover rate, the retailer must increase sales. One way to do this is to employ qualified personnel who will emphasize selling. Even though the buyer purchases salable merchandise, and the price is right, sales may be lost due to inept salespeople. Selling faults would also include poor displays, poor advertising and sales promotions, and a general lack of good selling techniques.
4. *Stock control.* A merchant should have a good control system. He or she then will know the total amount of goods on hand, which ones are fast movers, which are slow movers, and where problems are developing. The computer will be of great benefit to the larger retailers in this regard. Intelligent use of the computer can easily increase the efficiency of merchandise control.

The Statement of Financial Condition

The statement of financial condition, or the balance sheet as it is sometimes called, is very important to the retailer. This statement shows the condition of the business at a particular time. Specifically, it identifies and quantifies all the assets and then shows the equity of the creditors and the owners in the business. Table 16.6 is an example of a simplified statement of financial condition.

In its simplest form, a statement of financial condition is quite easy to understand. Assets are all those things of value which the business owns. These include such tangible assets as cash, accounts receivable, equipment, real estate, and buildings. It would also include prepaid expenses and even intangible items such as goodwill. All the assets are listed on the left side in an order prescribed by most practicing accountants.

The business also has indebtedness. Those debts which the business owes to creditors are called liabilities. Some of the more common ones are accounts payable, notes payable, or mortgages payable. All of the liabilities are owed to those outside the business.

The business also has an obligation to its proprietors. This obligation is called proprietorship, owner's equity, or simply net worth. Each of these terms is used, but they all have identical meanings.

To summarize, all the things of value the business owns are called assets. The rights to these assets are called equities, and they include creditors' equities, which are liabilities, and owner's equity, which is proprietorship or net worth. In the simplified example of Table 16.6, Scarlett's Draperies owns $10,500 in assets, which includes cash, accounts receivable, inventory, and equipment. The business is indebted to creditors for $2,500, while Scarlett, the owner, has an equity of $8,000.

The Proprietorship Equation. The proprietorship equation is the relationship of the three major components of a balance sheet. More specifically, it is

$$\text{Assets} = \text{Liabilities} + \text{Owner's Equity}$$

TABLE 16.6
Scarlett's Draperies: Statement of Financial Condition, December 31, 1976

Assets		*Liabilities and Equity*	
Cash	$ 2,500	Accounts payable	$ 1,000
Accounts receivable	1,000	Notes payable	1,500
Inventory	2,000	Total liabilities	$ 2,500
Store fixtures	3,000	Net worth:	
Delivery equipment	2,000	Owner's equity	8,000
Total assets	$10,500	Total liabilities and equity	$10,500

This equation illustrates the fundamental point that the statement must always be in balance; hence the name—balance sheet.

Purpose of a Balance Sheet. The fundamental purpose of the statement of financial condition (balance sheet) is to show: (1) how many dollars in capital are invested in the business; (2) how this capital is distributed into various kinds of assets; (3) how much of the capital has been invested by the creditors; (4) the nature of the liabilities; and (5) the amount of capital invested by the owner or owners.

Making the Balance Sheet Meaningful. The proprietor will certainly compare each statement of financial condition with similar statements from past years. This will permit him or her to assess changes that have occurred since the last time, and to seek reasons for these differences. Just as in the case of data taken from the income statement, standards must be introduced so that comparisons are meaningful. Some of these standards are:

1. Balance sheets of prior accounting periods.
2. Ratio analysis.
3. Standards prescribed by outside authorities.

A retailer might also compare the balance sheet with similar evidence published by trade associations, trade journals, or government bureaus.

Ratio Analysis. All types of businesses compute ratios from information that is presented in a statement of financial condition. Some of these ratios have become so widespread in their use that rule-of-thumb standards have developed. An example would be the current ratio, which is supposed to be 2 to 1. A ratio of 2 to 1 may or may not be satisfactory for any given business. It depends upon the type and level of business activity, its current situation, and its objectives and goals. The purpose of introducing the concept of 2 to 1 is simply to illustrate a ratio that has become so standardized that it is assumed to be somewhat of a law.

Common Ratios. Let us examine some of the more common ratios and how they are computed.

$$1.\quad \text{Current ratio} = \frac{\text{Current assets}}{\text{Current liabilities}}$$

In the case of Scarlett's Draperies (Table 16.6), it would be computed as follows:

$$\text{Current assets} = \text{cash} + \text{inventory} + \text{accounts receivable} = \$5{,}500$$

$$\text{Current liabilities} = \text{accounts payable} + \text{notes payable} + \$2{,}500$$

$$\text{Current ratio} = \frac{= \$5{,}500}{= \$2{,}500} = 2.2$$

Interpretation: The business has $2.20 in assets which are quickly converted to cash to pay each $1 of liabilities that is payable immediately. A ratio of 2 to 1 is said to be desirable because it permits the assets to shrink to half their value before there is any danger that the firm cannot pay its current liabilities.

$$2.\quad \text{Acid test ratio} = \frac{\text{Quick assets}}{\text{Current liabilities}}$$

Quick assets are defined as those current assets which may be quickly converted to cash. These generally include cash and the accounts receivable, but exclude inventory because it cannot usually be liquidated quickly. It is said that a 1 to 1 ratio is good. In the case of Scarlett's Draperies:

$$\text{Acid test ratio} = \frac{\$3{,}500}{\$2{,}500} = 7 \text{ to } 5 = 1.4$$

$$3.\quad \frac{\text{Net income}}{\text{Owner's equity}} = \text{Rate of return on capital or capital ratio}$$

This particular ratio is useful because it shows the ratio of return (ROR) the retailer is earning on personal capital investment.

To illustrate, assume that in the case of Scarlett's Draperies, Scarlett earned $2,000 in net income in 1976. Then:

$$\frac{\text{Net income}}{\text{Owner's equity}} = \frac{\$2{,}000}{\$8{,}000} = 25 \text{ percent}$$

This ratio states that for every $4 that Scarlett has invested in the business, she earned $1 as net operating income in 1976.

$$4.\quad \frac{\text{Sales per year}}{\text{Cash at end of year}} = \text{Turnover of cash or cash accumulation}$$

This ratio gives the approximate number of times the cash balance was received and paid out. When this ratio is compared with similar ratios of other years, it gives some indication of the amount of cash being accumulated. Cash should never be accumulated in amounts that are in excess of those required for financing current operations.

EXPENSE CONTROL

Every business must incur expenses while it is in operation; two basic managerial responsibilities are to plan the firm's financial expenditures and to make sure that actual outlays conform with the plan. The first thing a retailer does is to compare expenses with those of previous periods, or with expenses of other retailers engaged in the same type of retailing—that is, as a percent of sales. As an illustration, a food retailer might wish to compare his own operating expenses with those shown in Table 16.7.

Many people believe that expense control always means reducing the amount

TABLE 16.7
Composite Chain Store Operating Expenses as a Percent of Sales, (1972–73)

Payroll	11.57
Supplies	.93
Utilities	.79
Communications	.08
Travel	.10
Services purchased	1.36
Promotional activties	1.07
Professional services	.07
Donations	.01
Insurance	.68
Taxes and licenses (except on income)	.91
Property rentals	1.42
Equipment rentals	.13
Depreciation and amortization	.81
Repairs	.65
Unclassified	.76
Interest	.65
Credits and allowances	(−.63)
Total	21.36%

Source: "41st Annual Report of the Grocery Industry," *Progressive Grocer* (April 1974), p. 108.

of expenses. This may not be true. For example, a retailer may find that if he or she increases advertising expenses, sales will increase so much that overall profit increases. That is to say, other expenses might not increase proportionately, so that profits are maximized even though dollar advertising expenses are increased. If a retailer wishes to control expenses, there are four things he or she must do: (1) identify all expenses; (2) classify expenses by one system or another; (3) measure the expenses; and (4) compare expenses to an appropriate standard.

Identification of Expenses

The retailer's accountant normally identifies and classifies expenses. Table 16.7 shows the identification of chain store expenses. Some of the larger expenses for retailers are payroll, rental costs, depreciation, advertising and promotion, taxes and licenses, supplies, and utilities.

Classification and Measuring of Expenses

There are four systems in common use that classify expenses. They are natural, functional, expense centers, and production unit accounting. As the retailer enters the dollar amounts into these various systems, he or she is measuring the expenses.

Natural Expense Classification. According to this system, expenses are classified by items. For example, wages and salaries are expenses common to all retailing businesses. Therefore all wages and salaries are classified as payroll expenses. It makes no difference as to the function of these expenses or where they are incurred —executive salaries would be treated no differently than wages paid to salespersons or delivery men or maintenance men. All wages and salaries are payroll expenses in the natural system of expense classification. Other examples of natural expenses are rent, advertising, supplies, insurance, depreciation, interest, and donations.

Various trade associations, such as the National Retail Merchants Association, National Retail Furniture Association, or National Retail Hardware Association, publish standard classification systems that are most helpful to stores of their type. The advantage to a retailer is that he or she can compare and evaluate performance with other retailers who sell similar goods at the same volume.

Functional Expense Classification. Large stores are more likely to classify expenses on the basis of function of activity to be performed, since such an approach gives a better understanding of costs. Expenses that would be recorded under a natural account are recorded here under an account that suggests a major store function such as selling, buying, or store management. Thus, a retailer's monthly payroll, normally a natural account, would be recorded under selling (the salespeople's salaries, salaries in the advertising department), under buying (salaries of the departmental buyers, the resident buyer in New York City), and under store management (salaries of the security officers, window display artists, night cleaning crew). Travel expenses, also a natural account, would appear under selling (when salespeople visit suppliers' factories to acquire new information about products), under buying (air tickets and living expenses when buyers visit the market), and under store management (the chief financial officer attends a seminar dealing with sale and lease-back of business property).

Expense Center Accounting. Weaknesses in the natural and functional expense classification systems—at least as far as large stores are concerned—have led the National Retail Merchants Association to devise expense center accounting. The Association has discerned 20 major areas into which expenses can fall, each of which can be further divided into functional expenses. The 20 centers defined by the Controller's Congress of the Association is quite similar to 17 accounts that fall under the functional system. The advantage of this system is that those who "keep the books" in department stores generally follow an identical system. Indeed, the chief accountant for a department store in Omaha could move to a similar job in Sacramento, and the adjustment would be rather easy. More important than the accountant's mobility, however, is that the store manager can compare his or her own store's experience with Association data to learn where the store may be having trouble. Deviations from industry norms often are entirely explainable and proper, but they are often one of the first places a manager looks when analyzing financial data.

Production Unit Accounting. This is a still different approach to analysis of costs within a store, with particular attention to labor productivity. The major ingredients of this system are (1) the amount of work to be done, generally expressed in "units," (2) the rate at which the work should be done, called "productivity," and (3) the labor costs of performing that particular task. Assume, for example, that the billing department has 1,000 units of work to do each day, and that it has taken 1,000 hours to do the work. The productivity of the department is 1.0 (divide the 1,000 by 1,000), which, let us further assume, is approximately average for this type of work when compared with similar departments in other stores. If the average hourly pay for those working in the department is $3, we know that labor cost per work unit is $3 and total labor costs are $3,000 (1,000 hours × $3). If such data are kept over time, the analyst can observe whether deviations from the norm are due to changes in productivity or pay rate. In this instance, the norm may be either the analyst's own historical experience or the experience of other retailers.

Expense Distribution by Departments. The expense allocation systems we have discussed up to this point are based either on the operation of the total store or by expense centers. However, many stores operate their departments as profit centers. A profit center is a unit (cosmetics department, designer dresses, sleepwear) in which revenue generated by that unit is matched with the costs it incurs so that the profit or loss of the unit can be known. The advantages of such information are: (1) it shows management the greatest trouble areas, so that action can sometimes be taken, (2) it motivates people within the department to greater efforts because they know that their results are being measured, (3) it serves as a factual basis for making unpopular decisions (closing down an unprofitable department, dropping a product that generates high commissions to the salespeople). The two methods in common use are the net profit plan and the contribution plan.

Net profit plan. Those who advocate the net profit plan believe it is important to allocate all of the revenue generated by the firm to the departments from which it comes and to allocate all costs to the departments that incur them. It is a rather easy matter to identify the origin of revenue by department, since it consists of little more than maintaining a record of sales by department. However, the allocation to individual departments of all the costs that a firm generates is more difficult. The two types of costs that accountants must allocate are direct and indirect (or joint) expenses. Direct costs are those incurred entirely within a particular unit of operation. For example, salaries paid to the salesclerks who work only in the housewares department are a direct expense of that department. Rental expenses also can be allocated to each income generating department generally on the basis of the amount of space used and its location within a store. Advertising media costs can be allocated usually on the basis of the amount of broadcast time or print space used. Indirect costs are those for which no indisputable basis for allocation exists. Corporate level executive salaries are an example. Such executives as the president, treasurer, or vice president for public relations perform services for all the departments. If the accountant elects to allocate all expenses to revenue generating departments, a reasonable way must be found to allocate all expenses to revenue generating departments and a reasonable way must be found to allocate the pay these executives earn. One popular way is to allocate the total in proportion to the share that each department generates of aggregate store sales. Thus, if the housewares department generates 12 percent of the firm's total sales, it must bear 12 percent of the executive salary burden. Such an approach has two major faults: (1) the amount charged may bear no relationship to the "true cost" of the activity; the top executives in the firm may have spent far more or less than 12 percent of their time dealing with the housewares department, and (2) as more and more accounts are allocated on the basis of sales, each department's profits increasingly correspond to its share of total sales. (It may be useful to think what would happen if *all* expenses were allocated according to sales generated; if so, then a department that sold 15 percent of the store's merchandise would create 15 percent of the store's profits, and so on. The resulting profit and loss statement for each department would be pure fiction.) Unfortunately, the net profit plan demands that all expenses be allocated; yet there is no universally acceptable basis for allocating some of the indirect expenses.

Contribution plan. This approach—sometimes called the contribution margin plan—is to allocate only the direct expenses to revenue-generating departments. Adherents believe that there is so much dispute over the basis for allocating indirect expenses that the effort is futile. So the profitability of a department is determined by the amount of money each department contributes to the firm's overhead.

There are several advantages to the contribution approach:

1. Attention is focused on all those costs that are controllable by the department manager, who is not charged for expenses outside his or her managerial jurisdiction.
2. It is perceived as a fair and just method by those whose performance is being judged.
3. It is easy to understand and simple to administer.

However, there are disadvantages:

1. It is argued that selling departments will assume that the service of nonselling functions are free, and the services will be used unnecessarily.
2. There is a temptation to permit a department to operate because "it contributes to overhead," even though a wiser move might be to eliminate it. Losing operations do not stand out so sharply when using the contribution margin approach as they do when a department's net profit or loss is determined.

An important conceptual error often creeps into the analysis of a department's profitability when the analyst uses direct and escapable (sometimes called avoidable) costs interchangeably. They are not the same. Let us illustrate the distinction. Suppose that the Gourmet Foods department of a store has generated $2,500 in sales during a particular month, and $2,000 of expenses can be directly attributed to its operations. Furthermore an additional $1,000 overhead has been allocated to the department. The department is contributing $500 to the store's overhead (and thus

Gourmet Foods Department: Profit Statement

Net sales	$2,500
Direct expenses	$2,000
Indirect expenses	1,000
Contribution to overhead	500
Net profit (loss)	$ (500)

by one definition it is profitable), but it is incurring a net loss of $500 (by a different definition of profit). An argument can be made that even though the department is incurring a loss of $500, it should be allowed to continue operations because it bears $1,000 of indirect expenses that presumably will not diminish.

Now let us change the assumptions slightly. Suppose that the department's direct expenses are $2,700, so that it makes no contribution to the firm's overhead. Furthermore, suppose that $600 of the direct expenses are salaries paid to long-time employees to whom management feels a moral obligation to retain on the payroll. These expenses are direct but inescapable; if the department were eliminated because it does not contribute to the firm's overhead, these particular expenses would continue and would be shifted to other departments in the store. The moral of the story is that elimination of a losing department does not necessarily increase a store's profits.

Comparing Expenses to an Appropriate Standard

Regardless of what system is used to identify and measure expenses, the retailer must make a comparison with an appropriate standard. This means he should compare the figures in his current period with those of previous years and, if possible, with those of a similar retailer who uses the same system. It is the comparison of his performance with an appropriate standard that enables the retailer to recognize any problems and to take any corrective actions necessary.

RETAIL ACCOUNTING

Cost Method

Nearly all retailers used the cost method of accounting until early in this century. That is, they showed their inventories at cost, their purchases at cost, and all their operating expenses at cost. A price tag showing the sales price, item, color, vendor, and other important information was placed on each item the retailer sold. The cost of the item was also included on the price tag; however, the cost figure was in code. The philosophy underlying the cost method is to price merchandise for sale substantially above costs, so that the retailer is assured of a profit. Since each item has both the selling price and its cost on the selling ticket, the retailer can see at a glance the gross margin on the item. Therefore the most important disadvantage of the cost system is the unwarranted attention paid to cost.

Another disadvantage of the cost method is the inability of the retailer to know whether he or she is making a net profit each month. In order to determine net profit, the retailer first must calculate the cost of goods sold. In order to arrive at the total cost of goods sold, the retailer must know the dollar value of the inventory on hand at the end of each month. One way of ascertaining this amount is to take a physical inventory and count each item and record its cost value. In the case of very small stores, this is probably done without too much difficulty. In the case of large department stores with a great amount of inventory, it is simply not feasible to count the merchandise more frequently than once a year because of the time and costs involved. Therefore if the merchant does not know the value of the inventory at the end of each month, the cost of goods sold cannot be calculated and net profits cannot be determined. For this reason, a merchant using the cost method cannot direct merchandising activities intelligently.

A further disadvantage to the cost method is the inability to account for stock shortages, because the merchant has no idea what the dollar value of the inventory is until it is counted physically. After it is counted and the dollar cost value determined, there is no dollar total that the retailer can compare it with; hence, it is impossible to determine the dollar value of shortages. This, of course, prevents the merchant from evaluating stock shortage in order to take appropriate action.

Valuation of Inventory—Cost or Market

Many accountants value inventory at cost or present market value, whichever is lower. This is very burdensome for the merchant employing the cost system. Inasmuch as it is necessary to obtain a true dollar valuation of the inventory, the merchant using the cost system is forced to take a physical inventory. Each item inventoried has a price ticket on which the cost of the item is entered in code.[2] The cost must then be analyzed to determine if the present replacement price is lower or higher than the original cost. If it is higher, then the original cost of the item is used. On the other hand, if the present market price is lower, then it must be used in determining the value of this item. Each item in the inventory must be similarly valued in order to arrive at the true value of the inventory in accordance with the rule "cost or market, whichever is lower." Let us look at an example to explain this principle.

Lisa of Lisa's Shoe Salon is taking a physical inventory. The first pair of shoes she is inventorying has recorded in code its cost, which is $19.50. Lisa determines that the same pair of shoes today would cost her $20.25 to purchase from her resource. Since the original cost is $19.50 and the replacement cost is $20.25, according to the rule of cost or market whichever is lower, the first pair of shoes is valued at $19.50.

[2]To preserve secrecy, the cost often is in code. A popular code is to assign letters to each number, zero through nine. Thus, when a customer sees $99.95/XRAA on a price tag it means that the retail price is $99.95 and the merchant paid $65.00 for the merchandise since in this particular store X = 6, R = 5, and A = 0.

The second pair of shoes was purchased for $22.75. However, she is able to replace them today for $21. In this case, the shoes would be valued at $21, the present replacement price, because it is lower than the original cost.

Assuming that Lisa has 1,000 pairs of shoes in stock, she would have to analyze each pair to determine whether the original cost or replacement price is lower. This is a very burdensome job, and it is a serious disadvantage to the cost system.

Retail Method of Accounting

Prior to 1920, some merchants began using procedures that required all records to be kept at retail figures. However, it was not until the Internal Revenue Service approved this newer method of inventory valuation that it gained wide popularity. Today most retailers accept this method of accounting, although a small number still cling to the cost method.

Necessary Records. In order for a merchant to install the retail method of inventory valuation, he or she needs to keep additional records. These are (1) purchase journal, (2) sales journal, (3) price change journal, and (4) stock ledger.

In the *purchase journal* both the retail value and the cost value of each item purchased from the various vendors are recorded. Any transportation charges paid by the store to obtain the goods that they sell is also recorded. This is known as freight-in or transportation-in. The *sales journal* records all sales that take place, whether cash, charge, or C.O.D.

The *price change journal* is a written record of all the changes that take place in the selling prices of the merchandise before it is sold. Sometimes goods are reduced in price as in a sale. This is called a markdown, and it is recorded. Perhaps less often goods are priced higher than their original selling price. This is a markup. Any and all changes in the price of the goods for sale are recorded in this journal.

The *stock ledger* keeps track of all the data contained in the sales journal, the purchase journal, and the price change journal. This enables the merchant to compute the book value of the inventory more frequently than once or twice a year.

All of these records are kept for the store as a whole; however, a retailer may wish to keep the records by departments so that he or she may determine the profitability of each department. In this case, each department has a purchase journal, a sales journal, a price change journal, and a stock ledger. Moreover a retailer could keep these same records for lines of merchandise.

Changing Retail Value of Inventory Cost. Inasmuch as all figures in the retail method are kept in retail, it is necessary to change the value of the closing inventory from retail to cost; otherwise, it would be impossible to compute cost of goods sold. To see how this is done, assume that at the end of the period (December 31, 1975), a physical count of the inventory is made and the retail value of the inventory is $100,000. Since all price tickets on the merchandise are retail prices, there is no way the cost value of the inventory can be obtained from the tickets themselves. However, the stock ledger has the information, thus the accountant can come up with data that enable him to average out the costs. Table 16.8 calculates the

TABLE 16.8
Calculation of Cost Percentage Ratio, December 31, 1975

	Cost	*Retail*
Opening inventory (January 1, 1975)	$60,000	$ 90,000
Net purchases	20,000	30,000
Total merchandise available	$80,000	$120,000

$$\text{Cost percentage ratio} = \frac{\text{Total merchandise available at cost}}{\text{Total merchandise available at retail}}$$

$$= \frac{80,000}{120,000} = 66\tfrac{2}{3}\%\ \text{percent}$$

cost percentage ratio, a step necessary to determine the average cost of the merchandise stocked.

The accountant uses the cost percentage ratio to compute the cost value of the closing inventory. In our example, the cost percentage ratio is 66⅔ percent and the value of the closing inventory (by physical count) is $100,000. The accountant simply multiplies the closing inventory ($100,000) by the cost percentage ratio of 66⅔ percent. Therefore the cost value of the closing inventory is $66,667.

The closing value of the inventory is automatically the valuation of the opening inventory for the next period. In our example, on January 1, 1976, the retail valuation of the opening inventory is now $100,000 and its cost value is $66,667.

Illustration—Bernice's Boutique. In order to demonstrate the methodology of computing net profit, we present data from Bernice's Boutique. Her records disclose the following for the month of January, 1975.

Net sales	$16,700
January 1 inventory at cost	10,000
January 1 inventory at retail	16,000
January purchases at cost	5,000
January purchases at retail	9,000
Markdowns	500
Shortages	300
Operating expenses	4,100

Bernice's accountant would first compute the cost percentage ratio. Table 16.9 shows this calculation.

Now assume that the book value of the inventory on hand January 31, 1975, equals $7,500 at retail. Therefore, the cost value of the inventory on hand January 31, 1975, is 60 percent ($7,500) = $4,500.

TABLE 16.9
Bernice's Boutique: Calculation of Cost Percentage Ratio, January 31, 1975

	Cost	*Retail*
Opening inventory January 1	$10,000	$16,000
Add January purchases	5,000	9,000
Total merchandise available	$15,000	$25,000

$$\text{Cost percentage ratio} = \frac{\text{Total merchandise available at cost}}{\text{Total merchandise available at retail}}$$

$$= \frac{15{,}000}{25{,}000} = 60 \text{ percent}$$

Bernice's accountant is now able to calculate the cost of goods sold and net profit. Tables 16.10 and 16.11 illustrate the computations.

TABLE 16.10
Bernice's Boutique: Calculation of Cost of Goods Sold, January 31, 1975

January 1 inventory at cost (See Table 16.9)	$10,000
Add purchases at cost (See Table 16.9)	5,000
Total merchandise available at cost	15,000
Less closing inventory at cost (See page 437)	4,500
Cost of goods sold	$10,500

TABLE 16.11
Bernice's Boutique: Calculation of Net Profit, January 31, 1975

Sales (from sales journal)	$16,700
Less: Cost of goods sold (Table 16.10)	10,500
Gross margin	6,200
Less: Operating expenses	4,100
Net profit	$ 2,100

Earlier we stated the value of the closing inventory to be $7,500. We did this in order to minimize the confusion in computing net profit. Now we shall show how this book value of the inventory was determined.

Net sales (from sales journal)	$16,700
Add markdowns (from price change journal)	500
Add shortages (estimate from past experience)	300
Total retail reductions in inventory	$17,500

Since Table 16.9 shows the derivation of total merchandise available, we note this to be $25,000. Therefore:

Goods available for sale	$25,000
Less: Retail reductions in inventory	17,500
Retail value of ending inventory	$ 7,500

Cost value is retail value multiplied by cost percentage ratio or .60 ($7,500) = $4,500.

In this example, it is not necessary to take a physical inventory in order to compute the net profit because sufficient information is available to determine the book value of the inventory. For purposes of computing the net profit, the ending value of the inventory (book value) is assumed to be the same as if it had been physically counted.

In Chapter 9, we first mentioned the necessity of actually taking a physical inventory at least once a year. This is a most important point to remember. Once the retailer takes a physical count of the inventory, a comparison with book value can be made. If the two disagree, the retailer has either a stock shortage or overage. Normally, the merchant has a stock shortage because the actual inventory is reduced due to such factors as pilferage, shrinkage, or breakage. Another reason for shortages is the lack of proper record keeping. Two areas of record keeping that are sometimes neglected are employee discounts and markdowns. Until these two types of records are kept accurately, the true nature of shortages may never be known.

Employee Discounts. Employees are traditionally given discounts on merchandise they purchase for themselves. Records must be meticulously kept showing the total of these discounts. Let us illustrate the reason why with an example.

Assume a stock of $10 retail prices and that the following events took place.

1. Customers purchased merchandise valued at $5 in retail prices.
2. An employee bought merchandise with a price tag of $2. The employee received a 20 percent discount, so the clerk rang up sales of $1.60 ($2 less 40¢).

Problem: What is the dollar value at retail of the goods still available to be sold?

Example 1: Not keeping track of employee discounts:

	Retail
Goods available for sale	$10.00
Less: Sales to customers	5.00
	5.00
Less: Sales to employees	1.60
Goods left to sell	$ 3.40

Suppose you now take a physical inventory and determine that the unsold stock is valued at $3 at retail. What happened to the 40¢ (difference between $3.40 and $3)? No one will be able to tell you—at least not from the records.

Example 2: Keeping track of employee discounts:

		Retail
Goods available for sale		$10.00
Less: Retail reductions		
Customers' sales	$5.00	
Employees' sales	1.60	
Employees' discount	.40	
Total		7.00
Goods left to sell		$ 3.00

A physical count of the merchandise left to sell will agree perfectly with the book value of the total.

Markdowns. Markdowns are also another way of reducing the retail valuation. Nearly everyone is aware that merchants reduce the prices of goods they offer when the goods cannot be sold at their original prices. Unless markdowns are recorded, the store will have no idea what happened to some of the merchandise that was available for sale. It may erroneously be decided that the merchandise was pilfered. Let us look at a simplified example.

Assume: (1) there were avaailable for sale 25 items priced at $1 each, for a total of $25 at retail; (2) that 10 items were sold at $1, and 10 items were sold at 90¢ after the manager reduced the price in a storewide sale.

Example 1: Not keeping track of markdowns:

Sales	10 at $1.00	$10.00
	10 at .90	9.00
		$19.00
Goods available for sale		$25.00 at retail
Less: Sales		19.00
Inventory remaining at retail		$ 6.00

A physical check of the inventory determines that there were only five items left. Five times the price of $1 gives a value at retail of $5. Where is the missing item? Some might think it has been pilfered. In a simple example such as this, someone would realize that they lost 10¢ on each of 10 items sold in a sale—and this accounts for the missing $1. However, in the case of sales of thousands of items and many markdowns, who is likely to remember? Therefore:

Example 2: Keeping track of markdowns:

			Retail
Goods available for sale			$25.00
Less: Sales	10 at $1.00	$10.00	
	10 at .90	9.00	
		$19.00	
Add markdowns 10 at .10		1.00	
Total reductions			20.00
Inventory on hand at retail			$ 5.00

A physical check of the inventory would confirm this total.

Critique of the Retail Method of Inventory Valuation. Perhaps the most important advantage of the retail method is the orientation of the retailer. Because records are kept on markups and markdowns, the retailer is forced to think about the salability of the merchandise. The result may be prompt markdowns on items that cannot be sold at the original price.

A second advantage is the establishment of a comparative standard so that stock shortages can be determined. The retail method permits a retailer to estimate the value of the ending inventory. Then when the retailer actually takes a physical count of the inventory, there is a standard to which it can be compared. This comparison enables the retailer to determine actual stock shortage. Furthermore, the actual taking of a physical inventory is easier under the retail method, since a retailer is not concerned with costs. That is, the retailer need not decode costs from price tickets or obtain cost figures from other sources when tickets are missing or mutilated. By the retail method, only the physical count of the item and the selling price are needed to compute the valuation.

A third advantage to the retail method is that the retailer may compute net profit without taking a physical inventory. This can be done as frequently as the retailer thinks necessary. If profits are unsatisfactory, steps may be taken to correct the situation.

The retail method enables the book value of the inventory to be determined at any time without benefit of a physical count. This is useful for insurance purposes if the inventory is lost in a fire. Furthermore the merchant can keep the proper insurance on the inventory. Therefore, he or she will neither be overinsured or underinsured. This helps to control insurance expenses and adds to profit.

The retail method encourages a conservative estimate of the value of the ending inventory. That is to say, the retail method gives a lower dollar value to the ending inventory; consequently, cost of goods sold becomes larger. The result is lower gross margin and, in turn, lower net profits. The reason is in the computation of the cost percentage ratio. A conservative inventory valuation occurs whether the store takes markdowns because of a declining market or if it has additional markups due to a rising market. A retailer will then pay less income taxes under the retail method than if the cost method of inventory valuation is used. Incidentally, the retail method is accepted by the Internal Revenue Service as a method for computing income tax liability.

The most serious limitation to the retail method is that it is a method of averaging costs. Therefore it may not be the best way to determine the most accurate cost value of the ending inventory. This is because the retailer purchases merchandise with different markups, and they affect the cost percentage ratio.

Other disadvantages to the retail method are greater bookkeeping expenses and the need for more supervisory personnel. This is because records must be kept on many more accounts, and close supervision is needed to insure accuracy.

Merchandise Management Accounting

The objective of merchandise management accounting is to determine costs for individual items in a more satisfactory manner, thus de-emphasizing the aggregative approach to merchandising. It is believed that the retail method overemphasizes storewide or department gross margins, and hence little attention is paid to the gross margin produced by a single item. Critics also point out that the expenses are applied on a departmental basis, and hence the profit-making ability for any one item is lost among the totals.

The merchandise management accountants would group products together whose variable costs are similar. That is to say, some items do not take a great deal of selling effort to effect a sale. An example might be cigarettes. On the other hand, another item might take considerable selling effort. Thus, departments would be set up that grouped products together on the basis of item selling expense. Here is an example:

Item A—priced to sell at $1

Very little advertising and sales effort needed to sell it. Analysis indicates that 15¢ will cover these expenses. Assume the product has a cost of 60¢.

Sales price	$1.00
Invoice cost	.60
Gross margin	.40
Selling cost	.15
Difference	$ .25

The 25¢ will cover overhead expenses and net profit. Assume that overhead costs are 20¢—net profit will be 5¢.

Item B—priced to sell at $1

Again assume an invoice cost of 60¢. In this case, assume that selling expenses are twice those of Item A; thus:

Selling price	$1.00
Invoice cost	.60
Gross margin	.40
Selling cost	.30
Difference	$ .10

If this item is assigned a similar overhead cost of 20¢, it will show a loss of 10¢. Merchandise management accounting de-emphasizes the concept of percentage gross margin and focuses attention on the dollar amount of profit that remains for a single item after all the variable costs have been covered. Furthermore, merchandise management accounting has the advantage of developing patterns of expenses associated with different items. Inasmuch as expenses are classified either as fixed relative to selling price of the item, or variable relative to the selling price, the retailer can do a better job of controlling the variable expenses. It is believed that focusing attention on the net profit contributed by each item is the best way of maximizing the store's profits.

There are two major criticisms of merchandise management accounting. First, it fails to show the influence of stock turnover in the system. In other words, the volume of goods sold plays an important role in determining a store's profit; yet this fact plays no part in merchandise management accounting.

Merchandise management accounting classifies expenses into those varying with selling price. This introduces an inconsistency as to their accuracy. For example, expenses such as warehousing or delivery costs can be determined to the penny and allocated to the individual item that is sold. However, those expenses, such as advertising or personal selling, which may vary with selling price can only be approximated as they are allocated to the individual item. This seems to be inconsistent.

A third, and minor, criticism is that when a certain pattern of expenses becomes customary, there may be a tendency to continue its usage, even though a particular pattern or particular method of allocating variable expenses may be outmoded.

The fundamental purpose of merchandise management accounting is to concentrate retail management on the proper price for each individual item. Therefore, if the merchandiser can allocate correctly all the expenses incurred by the item, the price of the item could be fixed so that total dollar profit could be maximized. This, of course, would avoid pricing based on the average gross margin percentage. Its principal failures are to evaluate stock turnover properly and the effect it has on profitability.

SUMMARY

Retailers keep accurate accounting records for two major reasons: (1) to determine whether or not they are operating profitably, and (2) to supply management with data that guide them in future operations. The accountant assembles information in two principal statements that highlight important facts. The income statement is a form used to summarize sales income, cost of goods sold, and operating expenses. These items are arranged so that net operating profits or losses may be easily ascertained. Information in the income statement is processed into dollar totals, percentages, and ratios. This permits a comparison to be made with similar statements of past periods or with such standards as those published by trade journals, trade associations, or government sources.

The statement of financial condition and how it is used by the retailer as an evaluative tool was explained. In this context we discussed the significance of the current ratio, acid test ratio, capital ratio, and cash turnovers.

A major emphasis in this chapter is expense control. From the viewpoint of the store as a whole, the merits of such plans as natural expense classification, functional expense classification, expense center accounting, and production unit accounting were explored. The strengths and weaknesses of the net profit plan and the contribution plan with respect to departments were also discussed.

Finally, the retail method of accounting was explained. Its principal advantages are: (1) profits or losses can be determined at any time without taking a physical inventory, (2) shortages may easily be determined, and (3) attention is properly focused on the customer and not the cost. The chief disadvantage is that it is a method of averaging costs. Merchandise management accounting was introduced. Its chief advantage is to focus attention on the individual item and that item's contribution to the profit of the store. Unfortunately, this method does not take into account stock turnover, so its usefulness is problematical.

Merchandisers will continue to pursue the objective of finding the perfect accounting system. However, it is doubtful if a system will be developed that will be useful for each class and type of retailer. In other words, accounting systems must be tailored to an individual's needs while generating data that permit outside evaluation consistent with an individual retailer's objectives and goals.

QUESTIONS FOR DISCUSSION

1. What is an income statement and how can a retailer use it as an evaluative tool?
2. "Returned sales and allowances often reflect buying errors." What is meant by this statement?
3. What is the fundamental purpose of a statement of financial condition, and how may a retailer use it as a management tool?

4. Why is it essential to control expenses? If one wishes to control expenses, what four things must be done?

5. Explain the natural and the functional systems of expense classification, giving the advantages and limitations of each.

6. Compare and contrast the net profit and contribution plans of distributing expenses by departments.

7. Explain why a retailer must take a physical inventory to determine profit or loss if he or she is on the cost method.

8. Why does the retail method of accounting aid in controlling stock shortages?

9. Does the retail method of accounting have any major shortcomings? If so, what are they?

10. What is the objective of merchandise management accounting? What is its principal limitation?

17 THE COMPUTER IN RETAILING

A salesman in a shoe department in a major department store in Saint Louis takes a punched card out of a shoe box immediately after selling the shoes. The card was inserted in the box by the shoe manufacturer. It will be returned by the retailer to the manufacturer and represents a reorder of the identical merchandise. The same information is stored in the retailer's computer and represents goods on order.

A large Chicago food chain prints a coded number on each item it sells in its stores. At the checkout counter the checker punches the coded number into the register. The register searches the memory of the store's computer to which it is linked to learn the price of the product. The computer feeds the price back to the register for computing the customer's bill. The customer will know the price of the item by looking at the sign above the bin in which the merchandise is stored. The store can now quickly and inexpensively change the price of any item in the store by changing the price on the storage bin and the price stored in the computer. However, many shoppers object to the system. They want to see the price marked on the merchandise and have asked city government to take action. The retailer has a real problem.

A furniture store has a complicated compensation system for its salespeople. It pays a small base salary to each employee, a commission that varies among products, and gives "spiffs" for aging products that have been slow to move. However, with the use of a computer, paychecks are rather easily determined. In addition—one mark of an efficient compensation system—the computer prints out for each salesperson the exact origin of each dollar. The salesperson no longer needs to wonder if the amount is correct or why this month's paycheck is larger or smaller than last month's.

A Los Angeles automobile dealer doesn't have the automobile ordered by a customer and knows that it will take several weeks to have one built to the buyer's specifications. So he enters an "order" into the computer operated by Los Angeles dealers. The computer keeps in its memory system a list and description of all the new cars held in stock by cooperating dealers. If a dealer in the area has an automobile that matches the first dealer's needs, the car is wholesaled out from one dealer to the other. Instead of waiting several weeks, the customer has the car in a day or two.

The age of the computer is upon us. Computers are highly sophisticated types of capital goods that are especially efficient in recording and processing information. Moreover they are very helpful in problem solving and consequently are an aid to a retailer in decision making. Whether or not a retailer should use a computer depends in part on the costs associated with computers, and if the information generated by the computer will be worth the costs.

The above sketches suggest some of the varied ways in which retailers use computers in planning and record-keeping operations. There is much misinformation concerning the computer and its application. Until facts are separated from fantasy, the involvement of some retailers with the computer will remain minimal. Fortunately many retailers already utilize the computer and we have considerable information about their successes and failures. From these reports will come the information that may accelerate the utilization of this tool for retailing problems. A new breed of retail managers who are sufficiently sophisticated to cope with the computer is developing.

In this chapter we shall avoid much of the technical information associated with operating procedures of the computer. Instead of discussing engineering technicalities or comparing the engineering performance of one model to another, we will concentrate instead on the benefits that a retailer derives from the use of a computer. Where necessary, computer terms and technicalities will be explained.

COMPUTER HISTORY[1]

The history of computers is rather brief, beginning in the 1940s. World War II necessitated the maintenance of records of millions of servicemen and their dependents, as well as much other information on war-related matters. It became apparent that a machine had to be developed to process the vast amount of information being generated. The development of radar and electronics indicated that the scientific knowledge and technical capabilities existed to create such a machine. Late in the war (1944) Professor Howard Aiken of Harvard University designed the Mark I computer. Punched cards were used to feed input data into the machine. Then electromechanical devices processed the data, and the results were produced on punched cards. Subsequently Aiken designed the Mark II, III, and IV computers. All of these designs were built by IBM Corporation.

Two other computer pioneers were John W. Mauchly of the University of Pennsylvania and J. Presper Eckert. These men experimented with their version of the computer at the same time Aiken was designing his model. Mauchly and Eckert designed and built the ENIAC (Electronic Numerical Integer and Calculator). Their model also used punched cards for both input and output. However, they introduced the vacuum tube as the basic electronic component for storing data. This technological improvement permitted the ENIAC to multiply 300 times faster than any other equipment then available. Mauchly and Eckert founded their own company to produce this computer, but the company was soon acquired by Sperry Rand Corporation, who subsequently designed and built the famous UNIVAC.

ENIAC and Aiken's Mark IV are credited with being the first successful digital computers. A digital computer is one whose numbers are represented in discrete rather than continuous form.

[1]This section on computer history is based on material presented by Nathan Berkowitz and Robertson Munro, Jr., *Automatic Data Processing and Management* (Belmont, Calif.: Dickenson Publications Co., Inc., 1969), chap. 7.

Another computer of the 1940s was EDVAC (Electronic Discrete Automatic Computer). This computer utilized the unique principle of storing instructions within it so the concept of programming was born. John Von Neumann wrote the first program in May, 1945. A program is the set of instructions given to the computer to solve a problem.

Beginning with the 1950s the history of computers is spoken of in generations. The first generation computers were produced commercially in the early 1950s, and their distinguishing characteristic is the vacuum tube. The second generation computers replaced the vacuum tubes with transistors, and they utilized printed circuitry. This technological advance made the second generation computers much faster than the first generation models in assimilating and processing data. The third generation's (1970s) distinguishing features are the small transistors and diodes. The third generation computer is both flexible and versatile. It can handle both input and output devices simultaneously. It can use punched cards, paper tape, magnetic tape, magnetic disks, or their combination.

The distinguishing feature of present computers is their great speed in assimilating, processing, and printing information. In 1950 IBM introduced the Selective Sequence Electronic Calculator. This particular computer was put to work on a problem for the Atomic Energy Commission (AEC), a problem requiring nine million mathematical operations! The SSEC came up with an answer in 150 hours. The same problem, without the computer, would have required 1,500 man-years to solve. Although the SSEC was fast for its time, computer technology soon produced computers that were even faster. The slowest IBM computer of the third generation is twice as fast as any second generation computer. More startling is the fact that the fastest of the third generation computers is 50 times faster than the slowest computer of the third generation. These third generation computers are so fast that they measure internal speed in billionths of a second.

Third generation computers are married to various communication systems, so they are more valuable than any previous generation of computers. For example, American Telephone and Telegraph Company uses equipment to link a dataphone with two computers, one at each end of the line. It is reported that speeds up to 500,000 words per minute have been transmitted. With this equipment, all kinds of documents can be sent from one place to another in a very short time. This is important for businesses with units in many different geographical locations.

DATA PROCESSING

Data processing is a term commonly associated with the computer. However, it need not be restricted to computers. For example, data processing is performed by a student adding a column of numbers on the blackboard. Data processing is simply assembling and processing data in a logical fashion to obtain a result. Two authors of a textbook on data processing confirm this definition when they say:[2]

[2]Ibid., p. 2.

What, then, is data processing? It is a planned operation on facts (data) in a series of logical steps to achieve a desired result (information). This definition could apply to the most archaic information system using the goose quill pen, as well as to a modern information system using high-speed computers.

There are at least three important types of data processing systems: punched card data processing, electronic data processing, and integrated data processing. Punched card data processing is an information system that uses punched card equipment. Electronic data processing uses computers in its system to analyze the data. Integrated data processing is a system in which data are recorded manually on some medium which can be read and processed by a machine. An example is a cash register operated by a checker at the supermarket recording the purchases of a shopper on a special tape that is read by a scanning device into the computer. (See Figure 17.1.)

Automatic data processing is best defined as follows:[3]

> Automatic data processing is an integrated systematic network of people and equipment (mechanical, electrical, and/or electronic) combined to process data.

FIGURE 17.1

An early model scanner records purchases into a computer cash register

Source: U.S. Department of Agriculture, Agriculture Research Service, Hyattsville, Maryland.

[3]Ibid., p. 2.

In other words, automatic data processing is a broader concept than electronic data processing. It assumes computers and people are merged into a system to process information.

Tools of Automatic Data Processing

Inasmuch as computers are extremely efficient in processing data, we shall briefly examine the four tools accounting for its effectiveness. These tools are: (1) input hardware, (2) computer hardware, (3) software, and (4) an integrated system.

Input Hardware. A computer system starts with a device or devices capable of reading information (facts) into the processing unit. Berkowitz and Munro have likened these devices to the human senses. They say:[4]

> Machine communication can be likened in some ways to human communication. The media and devices that provide input and output in a computer system resemble human senses; optical scanning equipment "sees," audial telephone sending and receiving units "hear" and emit sounds; keyboard equipment responds to touch.

Input hardware are those items of physical equipment that obtain the information to be processed by the computer. An example is the optical scanner. This is a device which reads data from an originating source and then transcribes it on punched cards or magnetic tape, so that the information can be fed into the computer. Again the example is the special cash register being used as part of a computer system to facilitate the processing of information. This cash register uses a special optical font to print stylized characters on a tape which can be read by the computer. Later in this chapter we will discuss this type of cash register and how it is useful to retailers.

Computer Hardware. Computer hardware is the actual physical equipment associated with the word *computer*. It includes all the mechanical, electrical, or electronic devices used. In short, it is the entire battery of machines including the input hardware, the processing unit, and the output unit. The control center of the entire system is the central processing unit (CPU), commonly referred to as the "brain." Its components are the arithmetic-logical unit, the control section, the storage unit, and the console. These are the parts performing the mathematical functions of adding, subtracting, multiplying, and dividing. Moreover this part of the system makes the decisions built into the system, manipulates the data, and stores the information. The console is the "face" of the processing unit, and it has the external controls.

Software. Software is the term given to the programs and routines associated with a computer. A program is the set of instructions telling the computer what to do. A programmer is the person who writes the set of instructions (or program). Programs are written in special kinds of languages, and there are three basic types:

[4]Ibid., p. 114.

(1) actual machine language, (2) assembler language, and (3) problem-oriented languages.[5]

The *actual machine language* is the only language the computer understands, for it is the one built into the computer by the manufacturer. For this reason machine language is unique to each computer. It is the language that operates the complicated electrical circuitry making possible the processing of data and ultimately giving the results.

Assembler languages are coded computer procedures designed by the manufacturer to speed up the work of assigning locations of data within the computer. However, processing of the data cannot take place until the computer is given its instruction in machine language. The manufacturer provides the program to translate the symbolic assembly languages into computer machine languages. Examples are IBM's "Auto-Coder" and Minneapolis Honeywell's "Easy Coder."

The third kind of language is called *problem-oriented*. The development of this kind of language has made it possible to operate computers independently of manufacturers, for these languages can be used by all brands of computers. The most common problem-oriented languages are COBAL, FORTRAN, and Basic.

COBAL means Common Business Oriented Language, and as the name implies it is used chiefly for business problems. The purpose of COBAL is to have a universal programming language acceptable on any computer regardless of manufacturer. However, this language must be translated into machine language in order for the computer to function. Most manufacturers of computers have developed programs to speed the translations; therefore COBAL is very popular for business applications.

FORTRAN means Formula Translation, and it is the language used primarily by mathematicians and scientists. This language also must be translated into machine language before the computer can operate. The manufacturer provides the program to make the translation.

Basic is a computer language developed under National Science Foundation funding. It uses English language symbols and is generally considered easy to learn and simple to apply. For this reason it is a good language for beginners. The Computer Sciences Corporation uses Basic as its language in its Computer Time-Sharing Service call Infonet.[6] The subscribers use standard, typewriter-like keyboard terminals to transmit instructions to a computer. The language used is Basic because of its simplicity.

It is not always essential that a program be especially written for the contemplated operations. There are standard software packages available to perform various instructions.

Software is alleged to be the bottleneck to rapid computer applications. George

[5]Ibid., p. 258.

[6]From a brochure put out by Computer Sciences Corporation describing its Information Network Division, copyright 1969.

J. Berkwitt believes industry is uptight about software. Commenting on the importance of software to the entire computer process, he says:[7]

> But the fact is that even the latest third generation monsters, with their mammoth problem-solving potential, are by no means omniscient, nor, for that matter, are they in any sense self-sufficient. All of them require elaborate and costly preparation, the most sophisticated computer in the world is no more than a mechanical idiot. The name of the game, in short, is software.

Software is a bottleneck because of the lack of qualified personnel who are capable of programming. Software is far more expensive than hardware because it involves high-priced labor, e.g., those involved in coding and programming. Moreover, in the beginning there were not sufficient numbers of people who had the technical knowledge to write programs. In the 1970s more and more students began studying computer science and thus the software bottleneck is starting to dissolve. In 1971, almost 2,400 students earned bachelor's degrees in computer science and systems analysis; almost 1,600 earned master's degrees; and 128 earned doctorates.[8] As these people enter the job market, computer applications are becoming more commonplace.

Many complaints against the computer are actually complaints due to the software. In fact, some people assert that computer hardware has been oversold because adequate standardized programs are not available. In these instances the computer gathers dust because computer customers are not prepared to do their own programming. However, there are signs that manufacturers of hardware and software are combining their talents to produce a workable system. National Cash Register (NCR) is a good example, and we shall discuss their system in another portion of this chapter.

The big news in 1975 was not the technological improvement in hardware and software, but rather the lack of consumer acceptance of scanning-equipped checkout systems in supermarkets. William E. Olsen, president of IGA, said recently:[9]

> Consumer acceptance so far has been less than enthusiastic, and our own industry is largely to blame. You may have read about the reaction in Maryland, where consumer groups passed out leaflets opposing scanning-equipped checkstands in a corporate chain store. They said they don't like the idea of having no prices on individual items. When a chain store spokesman emphasized the substantial savings that can be expected from such a nonpricing system, they were not appeased. Their reaction was understandable; the savings are for the retail store and not for the customer.

[7]George J. Berkwitt, "Uptight in Software," *Marketing Insights*, 3, no. 13 (January 13, 1969), p. 12.

[8]*1975 The U.S. Fact Book,The American Almanac, and The Statistical Abstract of the U.S.* (New York: Grosset & Dunlap, 1975), p. 139.

[9]"The President's Page," *Grocergram* (March 1975), p. 11.

Later in this chapter, we shall explain the Universal Product Code, which is the heart of the controversy.

Integrated System. An integrated system is the fourth tool of a computer operation. Any system is the organization of parts into an entity. Our interest is a management system tailored for retailers. An integrated system for a retailer will coordinate people, books of original information, and the computer into a meaningful system. An integrated system for a retailer will plan, direct, evaluate, coordinate, and control the entire operation in an economic manner.

REASONS TO AUTOMATE

Why automate? There are good reasons why retailers are turning to automatic data processing systems for help. First, it improves decision making by providing information rapidly and in large quantities. For example, a typical third generation computer can read 1,000 cards and punch 300 cards every minute. Better decision making is a worthwhile goal because of its favorable effect on revenue, costs, and profit. The computer improves decision making by improving the accuracy and quality of information as well as by providing an increased quantity. Specifically, a computer system helps a retailer in the following areas: accounting, inventory management, merchandising, and location analysis.

Accounting

One of the earliest applications of the computer by retailers was in billing charge customers. It is rather easy to store into the computer all the information relative to a customer's account, including name, address, telephone number, and current balance. Every day the computer can be fed new data indicating new charges and payments. Delinquent accounts can be easily identified at any time, so the retailer is able to take appropriate action quickly.

The computer is also useful in payroll accounting. All the information necessary to compute the payroll can be handled by the computer. For large retailers with many employees this can be a saving in both time and money.

Inventory Management[10]

Inventory decisions are very important to retailers. Inventories are carried so that sales may be made continuously without running out of stock. Inventory decisions are of two kinds: (1) when to order and (2) how much to order. One approach is for a retailer to re-order merchandise whenever the stock falls to a predetermined level. This level is called an order point. The determination of the order point depends upon three things: (1) the lead time, (2) the usage rate, and (3) service standard. Suppose it always takes exactly 15 days after an order is placed to

[10]For a more complete discussion, see Philip Kotler, *Marketing Management: Analysis, Planning, and Control* (Englewood Cliffs, N.J.: Prentice-Hall, Inc., 1967), p. 434.

obtain delivery and have it available on the selling floor. Assume further that the retailer sells 10 units a day. Then the order point would be 150 units if the retailer is never to run out of stock. In this example the lead time is 15 days and the usage rate is 10 days. The service standard is the percentage of sales to be filled from inventory while waiting for the new order to be delivered. A 100 percent service rate means that the inventory is just exhausted as the new order arrives to replenish the stock.

Large retailers must manage inventories for thousands of items. The cost of maintaining a system to manage this amount of inventory is costly both in time and dollars. The amount of work entailed in an inventory management system is staggering. Philip Kotler describes it this way:[11]

> Take the question of order point. To implement the previous theory a perpetual unit control system is required. The inventory status of all items in the product line has to be updated daily so that it can be determined when an order point is reached. Each day's beginning quantity on hand must be corrected by new stock arrivals, and existing stock sales require a considerable amount of posting because of the large number of different items sold and received daily.

Because of the great amount of work associated with a perpetual unit system, large retailers make some arbitrary decisions. They select only important items for perpetual unit control. The level of all other items is checked only periodically. Therefore the chances of having the stock of some items below the order point are quite high. This usually results in a frantic emergency order, or an out of stock situation. This may be critical because of the lost sales, and perhaps lost customers who go elsewhere.

The computer is a particularly appropriate tool to manage inventory and to avoid this type of critical situation. The retailer who uses the computer will feed into its memory all the data regarding the current inventory position. This will be done for each item so that the computer can be programmed with the order points of each rather than for a select few. For example, a supermarket stocking 8,000 separate items will program the computer with 8,000 order points. Each day the computer is fed the proper input information with regard to sales and orders to stock received. The computer will prepare a daily report on items that have reached their order points. In fact, the computer can write the orders, and in this way out of stock will be minimized, if not eliminated.

Merchandising

An automatic data processing system is also an aid to the retailer in merchandising activities. For example, a computer can provide daily information of the following kinds: sales by departments or by classification of goods, or both; comparative sales figures for any period specified; trend of this year's sales; identification of both fast movers and slow movers; and much more.

[11]Ibid., p. 439.

The newest types of cash registers are part of an automatic merchandising control system. These cash registers are equipped with many special keys so that it is possible to record information other than the retail price of the item. For example, one key may be the classification of the item, another key its material or composition, a third key its manufacturer, and still other keys to identify such factors as color, size, brand, or name of vendor. The salesperson will punch keys for the item's price and indicate whether the transaction is cash or charge. All of this data is recorded on optical tape. The tape is later read by an optical scanner, and the information is read into the computer processing unit along with similar information taken from all the other cash registers. Shortly after, all the people who could use the processed information will have it. This would include the accounting department, the inventory control department, individual department heads (buyers), and top merchandising executives.

An advantage to this system would be the return of the buyer to the selling floor to become reacquainted with the customer. Without the computer to help, the buyer is often too busy counting stock to know what the customers want. Automatic data processing will inform everyone concerned with the status of what is selling and what isn't. The buyer will then be able to make the appropriate merchandising decision, such as whether to reorder more stock or to mark down goods that are not selling.

National Cash Register Example.[12] National Cash Register Company uses a systems approach to sell its computers and cash registers. Systems selling is essentially a "marketing plan under which an organization offers its prospects a fully developed methodology for using a product to the greatest advantage rather than offering simply the product itself."[13] In other words systems selling is one in which software and hardware are combined in a coordinated fashion, along with the proper people, so that the computer will truly be operational in a meaningful sense. National Cash Register's system is tailor-made to help small and medium-sized retailers. (See Figure 17.2.)

Input hardware includes optical scanners, cash registers, and adding machines. This equipment captures information and puts it on magnetic tape that is read into the computer for processing. The computer then issues its output report. For example, the computer provides three different kinds of inventory reports: direct cost, total cost, and retail. The retailer chooses the report that best fits his or her accounting system. To illustrate, suppose a merchant uses the retail method of accounting. In this case, the basic inventory management report will provide 12 columns of information. Specifically, the report identifies for each type of goods its dollar sales volume, the percentage of sales of this good to total sales, the gross margin of the item in dollars, the maintained margin in percentage, the number of months' stock in hand, additions to inventory at cost, additions to inventory at retail, dollar markdowns at retail, ending dollar value of the inventory at retail, end-

[12]This section is based on "NCR: Ringing the Bell with System Selling," *Marketing Insights*, 2, no. 29 (May 13, 1968), pp. 15–18.

[13]Ibid., p. 15.

FIGURE 17.2
A salesgirl feeds information into an NCR systems cash register

Source: National Cash Register Company, Dayton, Ohio, as seen in *Business Week*, April 10, 1971.

ing dollar value of the inventory at cost, and the percentage of total inventory represented by each type of good. All of this information is available by kind of merchandise, by departments, and for the store as a whole.

The advantage of this report is in the answers the retailer receives to many basic questions. For example, the retailer is able to determine inventory investment in dollars by kind of good as well as for the total inventory. This information is available daily. The retailer can identify both fast movers and slow movers and take appropriate action. The retailer will know the identity of the following: goods producing the greatest profit margins, the turnover ratios of each good, and the goods taking highest markdowns.

If the retailer wants a completely integrated system, NCR will mail statements to all charge customers, age the receivables, and identify by name, address, and telephone numbers the delinquent accounts.

Location

In Chapter 5 we discussed the computer as an aid to site location. Specifically, we mentioned Plotkin's model for identifying primary, secondary, and tertiary areas. The computer is able to estimate the amount of sales penetration the retailer enjoys in each segment of the trading area. Then the retailer is able to make a judgment on the feasibility of expanding present facilities on the present site or relocating the business to another area. Much of the procedure is highly mathematical and beyond the scope of this book to explain.

Special Problem Solving

The computer is important also to a problem solver because of its speed in making calculations. It takes only minutes to make calculations which once took people weeks or even months to make. On this point, Kotler says:[14]

> Management's efficiency in information processing and problem solving has been tremendously enhanced by the recent development of high-speed electronic computers. The speed of these machines has enabled problems to be solved in minutes which had formerly taken several men days or weeks of calculations. The calculating power of these machines has enabled users to achieve a depth of analysis formerly beyond their reach. Properly utilized, these machines cannot fail to extend the capacity of executives to make more and better decisions.

In more recent years marketing has been paying a great deal of attention to model construction, particularly as an aid in solving nonroutine marketing problems. A model is a construction, applying theory, designed to explain a particular problem.

Models have become especially important in selecting sites, predicting the demand of a good, forecasting sales, and in allocating scarce resources. Models can be classified in two general ways: (1) according to purpose and (2) according to technique. In the first category are descriptive and decision models. Examples of a descriptive model are the "black box" and other behavioral models.

"Black box" models are those linking together two or more variables, but nothing is said about the elements that relate the variables to each other. In this model, the inputs and outputs are known, but the contents of the box are unknown; hence the name. Behavioral models attempt to explain the relationship between the variables rather than to ignore it.

Decision models are either heuristic or those dealing with optimization. Heuristic models are used whenever computational methods are unavailable, but good "rules of thumb" are available to help in intuitive judgments. Chester Wasson describes heuristics aptly as follows:[15]

> Heuristic programming offers promising possibilities as a really cheap substitute for extensive practical trial-and-error in many business decision situations for which we have no very satisfactory mathematical models capable of yielding optimum solutions.

[14]Kotler, *Marketing Management* p. 241.

[15]Chester R. Wasson, *Understanding Quantitative Analysis* (New York: Appleton-Century-Crofts, 1969), p. 218.

Optimization models, in contrast to heuristics, have mathematical models available to the decision maker, who chooses the one which yields the optimum answer. The computer is useful in decision models because it can process millions of computations in a relatively short period of time, so that it is possible to simulate many conditions and take into account many variables simultaneously. Both optimization and heuristic models are useful for the retailer in solving location problems.

Five other models are important to retailers: allocation, game theory, waiting line, brand switching, and simulation. All of these models are mainly quantitative and use sophisticated mathematical procedures to calculate their results. The allocation model could be used by the retailer to allocate advertising dollars among competing media to achieve optimum results. Game theory is useful in investigating the results a retailer could expect by following a certain course of action while competitors followed another. Waiting line models are especially important to retailers who have customers waiting in line for service. As an illustration of the waiting line model, consider the supermarket that experiences a lineup at the checkout counters. In this instance, would it be worthwhile for a supermarket to open checkout stations and reduce the lines, or should the retailer accept the lines, with the implied threat that he would lose some of his customers to other stores. The waiting line model (also called queueing model) will give the answer.

Simulation models are extremely complex for they use techniques where ordinary mathematical solutions are not practical. They are especially useful to large retailers who are attempting to locate warehouses in the best sites possible.

The purpose of model construction is to identify all the elements and their relationship in a given problem. When a computer is used, it permits the investigator to manipulate the data and to interpret vague assumptions and relationships quantitatively. It is well to remember that it is the model and not the computer that is the most important breakthrough. Kotler says:[16]

> It is important to emphasize that it is the mathematical model, not the computer, which represents the breakthrough in each case. However, many of the models require such complicated and extensive calculations that they would be fruitless without the high-speed calculating power of the computers.

To summarize, retailers can use computers whenever retailing processes are so complicated that they cannot be solved by ordinary mathematical deduction. Because the computer eases the burden of calculation, it can be programmed with complex mathematical formulae, and through quantitative models help to solve the problems associated with brand switching, queueing, allocation of resources, optimizing profits, and solving the problems of logistics.

Perhaps the promise of the computer in solving complex problems through various models was too optimistic in the late 1960s, for M. S. Moyer makes these observations about management science in retailing:[17]

[16]Kotler, *Marketing Management*, p. 243.

[17]M. S. Moyer, "Management Science in Retailing," *Journal of Marketing*, 36, no. 1 (January 1972), p. 9.

> Retailers who would like to employ operations research techniques should understand that successful applications are fewer in retailing than in other areas of marketing, and much fewer than in industry as a whole. . . .
>
> For example, store location and product line decisions—both critical to merchants—have been largely unimproved by management scientists. Conversely, media models and routing techniques—both interesting to operations researchers—have been irrelevant to retailers.

COMPUTER APPLICATIONS

One of the best ways to understand the importance of the computer to retailers is to look at examples. Those presented are by no means exclusive, but they are representative of different kinds of retail operations.

Supermarket

Supermarkets are installing computers at checkout stations. The supermarket checker totals up the customer's order by punching code numbers on a terminal keyboard. When the computer receives the code number, it prints the price on a receipt tape.

A most interesting experiment is the automatic checkout. Each product has a code number which is read by an optical scanner. For each customer, the register prints a tape giving specific details of each item purchased. For example, one item could be Heinz Catsup, 12 oz., 69¢. Each item purchased will be similarly listed, and finally the entire order will be totaled. For the first time, the customer has a detailed register tape. (See Figure 17.3.)

An important advantage of connecting the computer with equipment being used at the checkout station is the up-to-date information it provides about a firm's inventory position. The computer has a record of the movement of all items both in the store and warehouse. Chain headquarters also has the information. Whenever inventories fall to a predetermined level (order point), the computer automatically reorders the stock. Inventory management of this nature helps to solve the out-of-stock problem, and it permits a more efficient use of storage space. Furthermore it increases the inventory turnover rate and thus has a favorable effect on net profits.

A computer at the checkout station has another beneficial effect. Because the scanner reads the price of each item, it virtually eliminates the undercharge. Inasmuch as supermarket profit margins are very small (1 to 2 percent), the accuracy in printing the actual price can be very important.

The supermarket checkout cannot possibly use the computerized checkout system without the proper labeling of all products sold in the supermarket. Consequently, the Universal Product Code (UPC) was adopted by the food industry in 1973 for this purpose. The UPC is an inch-square symbol that is composed of 12 sets of vertical lines and 11 numerals. The first number and line in the UPC symbol identifies the product; e.g., 0 is used for grocery items and 3 for drugs. The next

FIGURE 17.3

A sample checkout receipt issued by an electronic checkout system

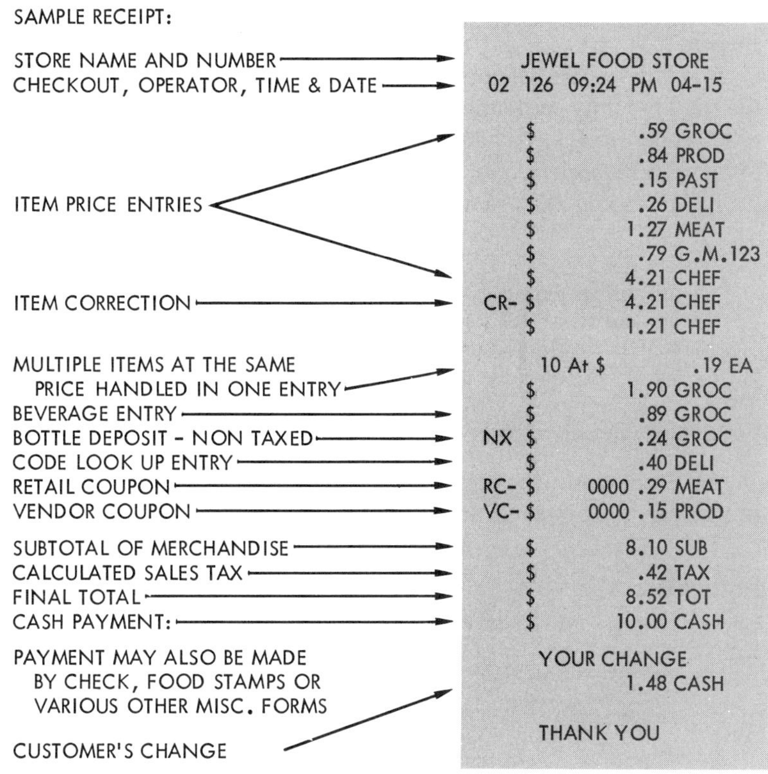

Source: Jewel Food Stores, Melrose Park, Illinois.

five lines and numbers identify the manufacturer, and the next five lines and numbers represent the product. The last line is a mathematical formula to validate the computer's accuracy. As of 1975 about 60 percent of all food items sold in supermarkets had this symbol.

Ellen Soeteber explains how the system works:[18]

> The vertical lines are "read" by a laser scanner built into the base of a checkout stand. As the symbol passes over the scanner, an in-store computer picks up the laser reading and translates back to the checkout register the package's brand, product, and store price—in a hundredth of a second.

Meanwhile as the customer is being checked out, the name and price of the item is flashed on a display panel, and simultaneously it is printed out on the receipt tape.

[18]This section is based on a recent newspaper article by Ellen Soeteber, "Computer Checkout Brings out Beefs," *Chicago Tribune* (March 2, 1975), Section 1, p. 3.

The advantages of this automatic system to the food retailer are acknowledged to be outstanding. For example, it should increase merchandising efficiencies in ordering, controlling inventory, and cutting losses due to theft and waste. In general, it should lower food costs. Almost certainly it will make the food retailer more efficient.

As of mid-1975 there were about 25 stores in the United States and Canada that had the fully computerized checkout system. It is forecast that by 1980 almost 8,000 supermarkets will be using it. Supermarkets are anxious to adopt the system because of its projected efficiencies and its potential positive effect on store profits. Earl J. Barbin of IGA says:[19]

> The projected economic benefits of electronic scanning at the retail level are truly significant: increased sales up to 10 percent because of faster customer throughput, 45 percent increased productivity per checkstand, and increased efficiencies by 75 percent due to considerable error reduction. Very significant is the projected net saving of 1.0 percent to 1.5 percent of a store's gross weekly sales.

Problems with Supermarket Shoppers

National consumer organizations are alarmed at the prospect of widespread use of the scanning systems and in 1975 started protesting vigorously. They feared that

FIGURE 17.4
Butchers often use digital computing scales

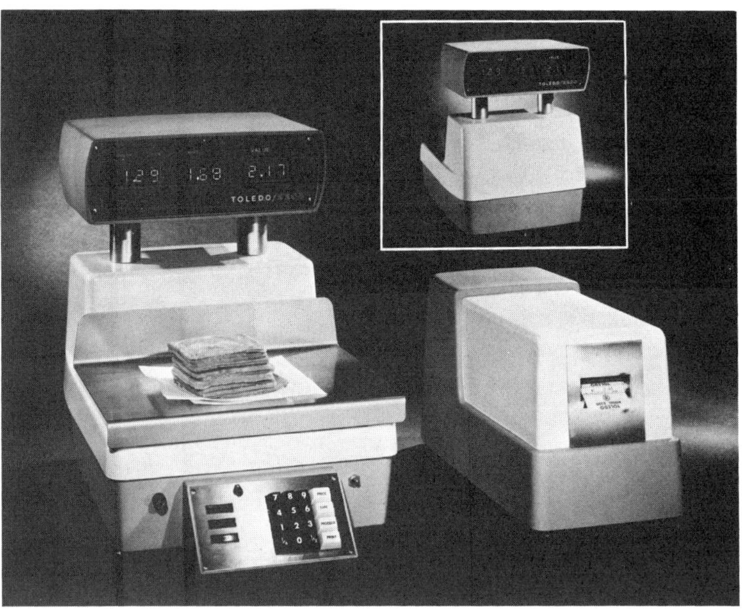

Source: Toledo Scale, Toledo, Ohio.

[19]Earl J. Barbin, "Revolution," *Grocergram* (March 1975), p. 14.

UPC will eliminate the practice of stamping prices on items, thus inhibiting the shopper from comparing the prices of items on varying dates. Furthermore, consumer protestors fear that if any efficiencies are realized, the retailer will not pass the savings along to the customers in the form of lower prices. Grocery clerks' unions are also afraid that the new system will cost some of their members their jobs.

Protests by some consumer groups were so vigorous in Illinois in 1975 that legislation was introduced to require item pricing on food products.[20] In the meantime, many chains are watching very closely the experiences of those who are already embarked on the program. It is hoped by the innovators of the system that consumers will accept the new system, pointing out that they will obtain a detailed sales receipt and they can read the prices of the items on the shelves as they shop, both of which will make comparing prices easier. (See Figures 17.4 and 17.5.)

FIGURE 17.5

The automatic label printer is used in conjunction with the computing scale

Source: Toledo Scale, Toledo, Ohio.

[20]Soeteber, *Chicago Tribune*, Section 1, p. 3.

Mail Order

An example of a computer application to a mail-order business is furnished by a German firm that conducts a $350,000,000 sales volume from a single warehouse.[21] The interesting fact about this business is that it is done almost automatically with the aid of a computer.

The process begins when goods are delivered to the mail-order house by its suppliers. With the exception of large appliances and certain other hard goods, goods are delivered in small standardized cartons. Upon their arrival at the warehouse, the incoming inventory is placed in any available six-foot square area. All shipments are registered by a computer, which assigns space based on availability of space and not class of merchandise. For example, toys may be assigned one space, shirts may be in the adjacent space, and children's clothes may be next to that.

When the goods arrive at the warehouse, they are picked up by the computer on its inventory control. The initial recording is tentative until a sample of the shipment is taken by the inspection department; if the sample is accepted, the new stock can be added permanently to the inventory. Incidentally, the inspection must be superior inasmuch as only one percent of all merchandise shipped out to customers is returned. For comparative purposes, 10 percent is the United States experience.

The order picking bins are located on the second and third floors of the warehouse. Each bin contains two cartons of merchandise. One carton is for order filling and the other is its replacement. After the first box is emptied and removed, the second box slides into place, and in so doing trips a relay switch which informs the computer of this information. The computer then dispatches a new reserve carton from the warehouse via an overhead monorail conveyor.

Assume that a customer sends in an order. First the order is keypunched into the computer. Next the computer prepares individual packing tickets for all items in the order and arranges the tickets in the proper sequence for easy assembling. The actual process of selecting the items in the order is a complex mechanical-electronic process—one in which the bins move. Ultimately the items are delivered to the packaging department where they are packed. It is at this point that the first human comes in contact with the goods. He packs the order and sends it on its way. This complicated mechanical-electronic computer procedure can process two million items in an eight-hour day.

If an item is out of stock, the computer selects four substitutes, and the responsible buyer at the mail-order house chooses one of the four to ship to the customer. Frequently the substitute merchandise has a higher value than the merchandise originally ordered. However, the customer only pays the price of the merchandise originally requested. Utilizing this substitution process, 99.8 percent of all orders received are shipped within one day of the order's receipt.

[21]Emanuel K. Fruman, "The Automated Way to Mail-Order Merchandising Profits," *Marketing Insights*, 3, no. 15 (January 27, 1969), p. 17.

The computer is in charge of managing the inventory. It keeps up-to-the-minute records of approximately 4,000 items at all times. It is easy to reorder, since the level of all stock is known at all times.

Woodward and Lothrop

In Washington, D.C., Woodward and Lothrop has one of the most sophisticated electronic data processing systems in department stores. As long ago as January 1966, with the help of IBM they laid out a model computer-oriented department store.[22] All standard cash registers were replaced with consoles.

The salesperson enters each sale on the keyboard, recording such information as (1) identification of the item, (2) selling department number, (3) amount of sale, and (4) identification of the salesperson. The tapes are read by optical scanners and transferred onto magnetic tapes so as to be assimilated into the computer. Each day all the executives and buyers have a detailed report of the previous day's sales broken down by department, subdepartment, and buyer. Every week the system reports on the relationship of inventory to sales.

Montgomery Ward[23]

Another application of the computer for department stores is Montgomery Ward. In 1970 Montgomery Ward opened what was then the nation's largest computer-operated store in Rockford, Illinois. (See Figure 17.6.) Ward claimed

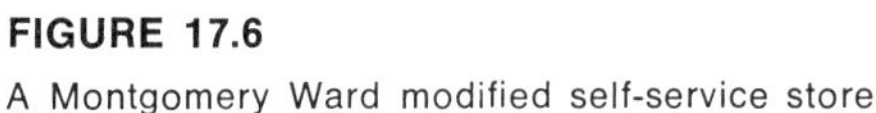

FIGURE 17.6
A Montgomery Ward modified self-service store

Source: Montgomery Ward, Chicago, Illinois.

[22]"Where the Computers Care, Too," *Business Week* (March 13, 1966), pp. 140–46.
[23]From a release by Public Relations Department, Montgomery Ward, Rockford, Illinois, November 17, 1970.

that 50 percent of the goods sold in the store would be merchandised by computer. Specifically the computer is responsible for the following activities:

1. Create seasonal merchandise plans.
2. Write all purchase orders and reorders.
3. Note color, size, and style trends.
4. Handle all customer accounts, record keeping, and billing.

In order to obtain a greater understanding of the computer's application, let us note what happens when a customer purchases a gallon of green latex enamel paint.

At the checkout station the salesperson examines the sales ticket attached to the can of paint. The salesperson notes the numerical codes on the sales ticket and enters the code numbers on a 5300-style National Cash Register. There are code numbers for: (1) the identification of the item (latex enamel paint), (2) its color (green), (3) size of item (one gallon), (4) price ($5.99), (5) selling department (75), and (6) whether the transaction is cash or charge. In the case of a charge sale, the clerk inserts the customer's credit card in a special receptacle on the register, and the information is imprinted on a paper tape. All the other information (code numbers) is imprinted on the paper tape also.

At the end of the day, the paper tape from the register is sent to a processing center in Chicago. There the tape is run through an optical scanner, and all the information is transferred to a magnetic tape. The data on the magnetic tape are next read into the computer. At this point the data are divided into two kinds: (1) credit information and (2) merchandising information. The credit information is extracted from the magnetic tape by the computer and sent to central credit for billing purposes. Information useful to the auditing department is sent to the auditors. Most merchandise information is sent to Merriam, Kansas. However, fashion merchandise information is sent to New York City.

As an illustration, the information regarding the green latex paint, sold by Department 75 of the Rockford, Illinois store, is sent by wire to Merriam, Kansas. The computer center in Kansas accumulates all the information in merchandise sent to it. Every two weeks a computer run is made to determine reorder needs. Inasmuch as the computer is programmed with data indicating the size of inventory of all merchandise stocked by type of goods, the computer can keep track of all inventory. In the case of the green enamel paint, the sale is noted by the computer and the sale of one gallon is subtracted from the inventory. Whenever the supply of green enamel paint reaches a predetermined level, the computer automatically reorders. The resource ships the new order of green enamel paint to the Rockford store, and the computer automatically records it.

Ward claims the computer system: (1) maintains a better balanced stock and minimizes out-of-stock situations, (2) increases turnover rate, and (3) increases the net profit of the store.

Another advantage of the computerized store is the elimination of nonselling efforts by store personnel. Therefore more time may be devoted to the store's major function—selling merchandise. As an example, consider the Rockford store where 70 percent of the store's overall area is selling area. Furthermore, since payroll, credit, and sales audits are performed outside the store, the people who usually perform these tasks are not needed at the store. For this reason the Rockford store needs only 225 employees. That is 120 fewer employees than the 345 people needed in a comparable noncomputerized store. Moreover, the employee on hand can concentrate on the selling function.

A surprising fact is that Ward operates its fashion departments in the Rockford store without department managers. The floor staff is headed by a department merchandiser who is sales trained and sales oriented. The computer is charged with the responsibility for ordering and reordering merchandise.

THE LAG IN COMPUTER ACCEPTANCE

In spite of its capabilities, there appears to be a lag in accepting the computer. The reasons for this lag are usually fear, mistrust, cost, or misuse. These reasons were pointed out in the late 1960s but unfortunately they are still true today.

Fear and Mistrust

Some retailers do not incorporate the computer into their operations because they are apprehensive and fearful. They do not know the technicalities associated with automatic data processing, and they fear they cannot learn. Consequently they cling to old methods until they are forced to make changes. People dislike feeling obsolete, yet the computer encourages this belief. A number of fearful retailers are simply overwhelmed with the quantity of information generated by computers, and they panic. On this point *Grey Matter says:*[24]

> Some people are quickly overwhelmed by numbers, such people in management are frustrated when the swollen current of information leaves them far behind. They have come to the conclusion that *too much* information too fast may be worse than too little and they let the stream go by.

A more subtle reason for the lag in computer applications by the retailers is mistrust. More specifically, it is the mistrust in a machine acting like a human being. *Grey Matter* also comments on this point. It says:[25]

> Retailing has always been an eyeball-to-eyeball business. It is therefore understandable why so many top executives in retailing today still look at the computer as a *monster* which will "dehumanize" our society in general and *retail business* in particular; it will stifle imagination and transform retailing into a robot operation without any emotional or aesthetic value.

[24]"Computer Lag in Retailing," *Grey Matter*, Grey Advertising, Inc., 13, no. 3 (May 1967), p. 2.

[25]Ibid., p. 2.

Cost

A second reason for the lag in computer application is its cost. However, cost is a relative concept and must be associated with other concepts in order to be meaningful. For example, a retailer who focuses attention on the dollar cost of computer hardware and its cost of operation without considering its impact on revenue is doing him- or herself a disservice. The computer may or may not be too costly. It will take an expert to assess this fact. It is probably true that small and medium-sized retailers cannot afford their own equipment. Perhaps they can afford the services of data processing companies. The point is simply that some retailers dismiss computer application on the grounds that it is costly, without obtaining the facts. For example, in 1975 to install a fully computerized checkout system it cost approximately $125,000 for a store with 10 checkout stations. This is about twice what it cost for a conventional checkout station. However for a large supermarket whose annual sales are $3 million or more, the savings can be as much as $35,000 a year. At this level of savings it would only take two years to recover the additional costs.[26]

Misuse

Another serious criticism of the computer is that it has been misused. In the early days there was an attempt to think of the computer as a new type of accounting machine. Therefore it is not surprising that controllers were put in charge of computer purchase and installation. For this reason computer application began with billing and simply recorded accounting transactions. It also was used to simplify payroll accounting. But it was not used as an aid in merchandising until more recent years.

Criticism of the Computer

Some early critics believed that the computer has dehumanized retail management and perhaps chilled their relations with their customers. One such critic is E. B. Weiss. He comments on the dehumanizing process this way:[27]

> I contend that the abuse of the computer in mass retailing is leading many large retailers into precisely the frosty, dehumanized stance that typified banks and bankers years ago. (It is odd that the computer is pressing banks to accelerate their trend toward a more human customer relationship while, at retail, the computer is being permitted to pressure retailing into a remote detached, uninterested pose toward its customers on a scale never even approached by banks in their more austere days).

Many people in the 1970s would agree with Weiss on this matter. Weiss further charges that retailers who use computers to forecast variations in consumer demand

[26]Soeteber, *Chicago Tribune* (March 2, 1975), Section 1, p. 3.

[27]E. B. Weiss, " 'Dat Ole Davil': The Retail Computer," *Advertising Age* (May 27, 1968), p. 62.

are doing so incorrectly.[28] He says that the computer is interpreting demand in an arbitrary fashion, basing its decisions, in a cold-blooded fashion, on very rigid statistics. Consequently the customer is finding: (1) stocks are poorly balanced, (2) out-of-stock is more common, (3) inventory is not based on present customer desires, but last season's sales, (4) items are discontinued arbitrarily, (5) new products are mishandled, and (6) new fashions are followed more cautiously.

A more serious charge is one claiming that the customer is always wrong when he or she complains to store executives. For example, charge account statements (prepared by the computer) are sometimes in error, and to get them corrected is a frustrating experience. Adjustments of any kind are an aggravation.

Weiss believes that younger people will be less tolerant of the arbitrary behavior of retail executives. He says:[29]

> But I am positive that even new generations, who have been brought up in an era in which "the shopper is always right" has been changed to the "shopper is always wrong," will not accept this state of affairs with docility; the younger generations in particular will rebel; they are not so easily pushed around.

People are still the heart of retailing, and once executives understand the limitations of a computer, there will be less complaints such as those registered by Weiss. Woodward and Lothrop look upon the computer as an opportunity to delegate the tedious work to computers and free their salespeople to carry out the store's tradition of service.

SUMMARY

Computers are efficient recorders, processors, and storers of information and facts. They are also becoming more important to the retailer as an aid to decision making. Computer history is quite brief, since the first computers were designed and built in the 1940s. We are now in the third generation of computers. They are distinguished by their great speed in absorbing data, calculating answers, and printing results.

Automatic data processing is an integrated system of people, equipment, and computers designed to process information and data into meaningful results. There are four tools needed: (1) input hardware, (2) software, (3) computer hardware, and (4) an integrated system.

Retailers have good reasons to turn to automatic data processing systems for help. The chief advantage is in the improvement of decision making. This is made possible because of the great amounts of information that can be processed in a short period of time. The computer not only provides a great quantity of information but improves the quality of decision making.

Specifically, a computer system helps a retailer in locating stores, delineating trading areas, managing the inventory, making merchandising decisions, and as an

[28]Ibid., p. 62.
[29]Ibid., p. 64.

aid to the customer. In more recent years the marketer has formulated various models to help solve special kinds of problems. The computer makes it possible to use the models as a technique because they can perform the burden of mathematical computations. The retailer is likely to find the following models useful: allocation, game theory, waiting line, brand switching, and simulation.

The use of computers is best understood through the study of their application in various situations. The computer is being used at the checkout stations of supermarkets where its chief advantage is the management of inventory. A mail-order house in Germany proves that automated retailing is a reality today. A Washington, D.C., department store was a pioneer in the use of a completely integrated system. It believes the computer frees its people to serve the customers in a better way.

In spite of its advantages, the computer is not being used by everyone. Some of the reasons are mistrust, fear, and cost. A new breed of managers has been appearing who are educated in the use of the computer. These people have been bringing the retailing industry rapidly into the computer age.

Some people are highly critical of the computer. One such critic is E. B. Weiss. He charges that retail executives make arbitrary decisions on old data which results in deteriorating customer relations. This is likely to change as the retailing industry works the bugs out of its computer systems and reestablishes its roles in the retailing process.

QUESTIONS FOR DISCUSSION

1. Better decision making is a worthwhile goal because of its favorable effect on costs, revenues, and profits. How does the computer improve decision making?
2. Discuss the role of the computer in inventory management.
3. How is an integrated electronic data processing system helpful to a retailer in merchandising activities?
4. Do you think the computer is a help or a hindrance at the checkout station of the supermarket?
5. Woodward and Lothrop believe the computer is able to profile its customers by keeping track of family purchases electronically. Comment on the implication of this.
6. Do you think the computer will eliminate the out-of-stock problem? Comment.
7. There appears to be a lag in accepting the computer by some retailers. Why?
8. E. B. Weiss claims that computers have caused retailers to make some rather arbitrary decisions in merchandising. Show whether you agree or disagree.
9. Assume that you are the chief executive of a large department store with sales of $100,000,000 annually and 6,000 employees. How would you use the computer?
10. Comment on whether the computer has been a boon or a curse to the retailing industry.

18 MARKETING RESEARCH FOR RETAILERS

A shopping center developer flies his private jet over a half dozen possible business sites in four different states in a single day. He looks for housing density, housing quality, major highway arteries and traffic patterns, rivers or railroads that impede traffic, schools, and rival shopping centers. He quickly eliminates most sites through casual observation. But a few are subjected to further study, using every piece of published information about the area that can be found.

The owner of a small restaurant in a large city observes how the area in which he operates has rather quickly changed from a "family" to a "singles" neighborhood. He knows that such a change will affect his operating hours, menu, decor, promotion, and probably other aspects of his business. Since he suspects he needs more information and that other retailers on his street face a similar problem, he proposes "some sort of study" be undertaken by his street's retail association.

An automobile dealer in Chicago instructs his mechanics to turn on the radio of each car being repaired and note the station to which it is tuned. Since he wants to reach his regular customers, he has decided to spend most of his advertising budget on the two or three most popular stations.

A hardware retailer in a medium-sized town has operated rather successfully over the years but now is thinking about the impact that a proposed thruway will have on his business. The highway will make the next town, a larger one, more accessible. The retailer and his wife recently have been taking a "Sunday drive" to other nearby towns to assess their likely attraction to his long-time customers. His research approach is casual and inexpensive, and he may be learning something.

A women's specialty store in a large city hires a marketing research firm to investigate the impact of its customers' movement both to and from the suburbs. The store caters to only a small fraction of the city's population and can afford few mistakes. The movement away from the city may have been arrested and some believe that it may even have reversed. It is vital that the firm have this information, which it can buy from a research firm. The store's management believes that the purchased information is more reliable and may cost less than if management had attempted to undertake the study itself.

A food store operator audits his cash register tapes quite frequently, and notices that the average tape is higher before lunch than after and is higher when the female shopper is accompanied by a male. Perhaps this is attributable to the prelunch hunger drive in the first case and the less concern that male food shoppers are said to have for prices in the second instance. Although such findings are interesting, the retailer has not yet found a way to make these results useful.

Research is an inquiry into the facts which will either aid in the solution of, or will anticipate, a problem. This means an investigation should be objective, systematic, and complete. The researcher may be guided by the principle that all information is to be assembled, analyzed, and interpreted for the purpose of offering a solution to the problem under study. Marketing research came of age following World War II, and excellent techniques are employed today in solving a variety of marketing problems. However, the application of marketing research principles and techniques to the solution of purely retailing problems has not been employed as widely as one would wish. A lack of understanding by retailers is partly responsible for this condition.

Marketing research studies can vary in their intent, sophistication, and methodology. The above examples only hint at the range of activities that can be called marketing research.

All retailers are seeking answers to their operational problems. Some are asking questions relating to the identification of their customers. This implies more than their names. Perhaps they wish to know where their customers live, their sex and ages, their incomes, and above all their tastes and desires. They want answers early enough so that meaningful decisions can be made. Marketing research is one tool—certainly not the only one—that can aid the retailer. The merchant who learns to employ research techniques will stock the right merchandise at the right time and in the proper quantities. He or she will be rewarded by continued patronage of customers, and will probably do so profitably.

SCIENTIFIC METHOD

In order to make research objective, a clear understanding of the scientific method is essential. Some would argue that science is merely an extension of common sense. However, one writer suggests that there are at least five differences. They are: (1) the scientist constructs a theoretical model to be tested for internal validity, (2) a hypothesis to explain the relationship of the data to be tested is formulated, (3) controls are employed to measure the changes of a single variable within the problem context, (4) the scientist seeks out all the relationships that he or she wishes to study, and (5) all metaphysical data are ruled out.[1]

STEPS IN MARKETING RESEARCH

The market researcher should use the following steps while employing the scientific method of inquiry.

1. Define the problem.
2. State the objectives of the research in writing.
3. Formulate the hypothesis to be tested.

[1]Fred N. Kerlinger, *Foundations of Behavioral Research* (New York: Holt, Rinehart, and Winston, 1964), pp. 4–6.

4. Check all available secondary sources for data that explain the variable or variables under study.
5. Define the limits of the universe to be studied.
6. Set up all necessary controls.
7. Determine the kind and size of the sample.
8. Gather the information.
9. Process the information into meaningful tables, charts, and analysis.
10. Test the hypothesis for external and internal validity.
11. Employ all the statistical tools that will explain the relationship under study.
12. Prepare the presentation.
13. Make all the necessary decisions relevant to the problem context.
14. Make predictions based on the research.

Some of these steps are discussed below.

The Problem and Objectives

All inquiry begins with a definition of the problem and a written statement of the objectives. It is not surprising to find merchants seeking answers when they are unaware of the problems. For example, in a situation where retail sales are declining, a group of retailers may be seeking ways to improve parking facilities—without first ascertaining the real cause of the sales decline. The probable causes could be faulty merchandising, inadequate advertising, poor management, or a combination of these, rather than a lack of parking facilities. One must understand the nature of the problem and all the probable causes before undertaking corrective measures. Consider the following example.

> Debbie has a dress shop catering to young women 18 to 30. Her shop is located on the main street of a rather well-to-do suburb. The lack of free parking facilities is the subject of considerable merchant complaints at every Chamber of Commerce meeting.
>
> Debbie has been in business for ten years at the same location. She actively manages the shop herself and is assisted by three clerks. She has a successful business —but she is alarmed over the decline of sales (10 percent in the last year). She attributes the decline to a lack of free parking for her customers; therefore she has joined four other merchants in providing free off-street parking. Sales continued to decline, so she called in a marketing consultant. He tested various hypotheses that he thought were responsible, and finally recommended an increase in her advertising budget and a change in newspapers that carried her ads. He flatly stated that parking had not been her problem. In the past two months her sales have increased 15 percent (after seasonal adjustment), and she is confident that her problem is solved.

The Hypothesis

Once there is a clear understanding of the problem and a written statement of the objectives, the research generally formulates a hypothesis to be tested. It is often necessary to conduct an exploratory study to state the proper hypotheses. Working hypotheses for a retailer—statements that he or she is trying to prove or disprove—might include: (1) that those who respond favorably to offers made by direct mail are measurably different from those who do not respond to such offers, (2) that there is a strong correlation between a customer's income and the art that he or she purchases for the home, or (3) that those who shop on Saturdays are more responsive to special deals (they are "deal prone") than those who shop early in the week.

Check Available Sources

The retailer may elect to use his or her own internal records, or might choose to go outside his or her business to gather information about potential customers. In any case a thorough search of all secondary sources is essential. A vast store of information is available in government reports and documents, magazines and trade journals, reports of trade associations and foundations, Ph.D. theses and academic monographs and reports, and independent research data. One should assemble all the pertinent information available so that it may be read, analyzed, and related to the problem. The researcher must *always* be aware that secondary information is *dated*, and hence may have only limited usefulness. Perhaps never before has so much information been available, and never before has it become obsolete so quickly. Since many decisions are based on old data, is it any wonder that the decisions are faulty?

One must also be on the lookout for biased information. Many articles, reports, and documents are written by those who have vested interests in particular solutions. However, if one is able to use secondary data, the savings in money and time could be appreciable. This might insure an early solution to the problem.

OBTAINING PRIMARY INFORMATION

Questionnaires

Unfortunately, solutions to many problems are not readily available in the nation's libraries, and the researcher is forced to go to the primary source. A popular method of obtaining information is by means of questionnaires. Usually the questionnaires are highly structured and the interviewer seeks only information that the respondent is able and willing to furnish. Information occasionally is sought that is of a confidential nature; then the researcher uses indirect means of obtaining the required answers.

Nearly everyone has been the subject of an interview, and therefore believes that he or she has some expertise on the art of questionnaire construction. The truth is that questionnaires are difficult to design, and a great deal of creativity and experience are needed to word the questions properly. As we mentioned earlier, one of the most popular questionnaires is highly structured. This type permits only a few predetermined answers to be selected. For these questionnaires, yes and no or multiple choice answers are commonly used. There is no attempt to disguise the questions, and a direct answer is expected. In extreme cases, a free choice answer is the only practical solution. This permits the respondent to answer as subjectively as he or she wishes. Obviously, the free choice answer is difficult to tabulate and to evaluate.

Figure 18.1 demonstrates some of the principles of questionnaire construction. Note that most of the questions are direct and that the answers are easily tabulated.

Rules for Questionnaire Construction. It is difficult for a beginner to create a good questionnaire; therefore we have formulated a set of rules that should be helpful.

1. *Use simple words—ones that the respondent understands.* The author of a questionnaire must always bear in mind that the words used must have the same meaning to everyone, and above all they should not be so difficult that the respondent is uncertain of their meaning. Generally, a pretest of the questionnaire will uncover words that violate this rule. It is much better to err on the side of simplicity than to include words that will lead to misunderstanding.
2. *Ask for data that the respondent can remember.* Most people are delighted to supply answers to questions if they can recall the facts. For example, assume that a researcher is anxious to find out the number of pizzas that are consumed at home by the households of Dodge City. The researcher might ask: "How many pizzas did your family consume at home last year?" Since it would be an unusual respondent who could answer such a question correctly, it would be much better to break down the question into several parts:
   a. Does your household eat pizzas?
      Yes ______ No ______ Don't know ______
   b. Were these pizzas consumed at home?
      Yes ______ No ______ Don't know ______
   c. If yes, how frequently do you have pizza?
      1. once a week ______
      2. twice a week ______
      3. 3 to 5 times weekly ______
      4. once every two weeks ______
      5. once a month ______
      6. other ______
      7. don't know ______
3. *Avoid generalizations.* Questions should ask for specific information. This permits the researcher to use the specific data that is collected to formulate his or her own generalizations. One example of a question that violates this rule is: Do you prefer branded merchandise over nonbranded? The reason this question violates the rule of overgeneralizing is that the respondent may prefer some branded products and also prefer some nonbranded goods. He or she would find it difficult to answer the question. It will be necessary for the interviewer to ask specific questions regarding the respondent's preferences from a category of goods—and then the interviewer can judge whether or not the respondent prefers branded merchandise.
4. *Avoid technical words or terms that the respondent does not understand.* Consider this question:

   Do you like or dislike "add-on" credit terms?
   Like ______ Dislike ______

   It is self-evident that most respondents would have difficulty answering this

FIGURE 18.1

Example of a marketing questionnaire

Questionnaire # ______ Interviewer # ______
Census tract ______ Date ______
Type ______ Started interview ______
Ended interview ______

How do you do. I am Shirley Hanson of the Wilson-Gardner Research Company. We are conducting a survey to determine your preferences in Christmas trees. Your household has been selected to participate, and your response will help determine the preferences of all households in our city.

Name ______ Phone ______
Address ______ Sex ______

1. How many persons are there in your household? (Include yourself, all adults, and children.) ______

2. How many adults are there in your household? (Include yourself and all others 18 years or over.) ______

3. Are there any children under 18 years in your household?
   Yes ______ No ______ How many? ______

4. Do you celebrate Christmas in your household?
   Yes ______ No ______
   (If yes go on to other questions.)

5. Do you set up and decorate a Christmas tree in your household?
   Yes ______ No ______

6. What type of Christmas tree is it?
   Live ______ Artificial ______

7. If live, what kind is it?

   a. spruce ____
   b. balsam ____
   c. Scotch pine ____
   d. other ____
   e. don't know ____

8. If artificial, what type is it?

   a. aluminum ____
   b. green ____
   c. flocked ____
   d. other ____
   e. don't know ____

9. Who buys the Christmas tree for your household?

   a. head of household ____
   b. wife ____
   c. son ____
   d. daughter ____
   e. other ____
   f. don't know ____

10. Would you please look at this card and tell me the number of the age group you and your spouse are in?

	18-24	25-34	35-49	50-64	65 and over	will not tell
Husband	____	____	____	____	____	____
Wife	____	____	____	____	____	____

Thank you very much for your time. Your cooperation has been most helpful.

question since many do not know about "add-on" credit. The danger is that technical words might be so familiar to the researcher that they creep into the questionnaire almost unnoticed. The pretest should eliminate almost all questions of this type.

5. *Avoid complex sentences that are involved and difficult.* This is good advice in all types of writing, and *it is essential* in questionnaire construction that *complexity be avoided.*
6. *Eliminate all leading questions.* Most researchers do attempt to eliminate all bias in their questions, but nevertheless they sometimes lead a respondent to a predetermined answer. Consider this question:

   When you last shopped in a large retail store, was it Bullocks?
   Yes ______ No ______ Don't know ______

   This question will have more respondents shopping at Bullocks than probably did. A better question would be:

   In what large stores have you recently shopped? ______
7. *Omit questions that raise personal bias or prejudice.*
8. *All questions should provide for conditional answers.*
9. *The questions should be made as easy to answer as possible.*
10. *The questions should be arranged in a logical sequence.*

Once the questionnaire has been designed, it should always be pretested to be certain that the questions are understood and the respondent has answered them properly. It is not unusual to revise the questionnaire once or twice after weaknesses have been highlighted by a pretest.

Types of Interviews

The information that the questionnaire is designed to gather may be obtained by telephone interview, mailed questionnaire, personal interview, or by direct observation. There are advantages and limitations to each type, and the researcher must weigh their relative strengths and weaknesses before choosing the type most suitable for his or her purposes. In general, the researcher must consider such facts as amount of money for the study and the technical know-how of the research team. For example, if there is very little money budgeted for the project, personal interviews would be unsuitable. On the other hand, if there is sufficient money and time available, and it is important to do some probing for answers, the personal interview is the choice. The most important advantages and limitations are as follows:

Telephone Interview.

Advantages

1. A fast way to contact a respondent. One may complete a call to someone who is normally difficult to interview—for example, a physician.
2. Generally less costly than either the mail or personal survey.
3. Easiest of all to administer.
4. One may complete a great number of interviews in a short period of time.

Limitations

1. The interview must be completed in a very short period.
2. One never knows for certain who is being interviewed.

3. Many calls may never be completed because the person called hangs up on the interviewer.
4. People without telephones, those with unlisted numbers, or those who live in apartment hotels served through a switchboard, cannot be included in the sample.
5. No way to supplement the information that is being gathered by observing the respondent in his or her environment.
6. Respondents are said to be increasingly skeptical about the intentions of the interviewer, and therefore reluctant to cooperate.

Mailed Questionnaire.

Advantages

1. No bias introduced into the data by the interviewer.
2. Respondents have sufficient time to think over answers and record more accurate information.
3. One may contact individuals who may not be at home either for telephone interviews or personal calls.
4. Fewer administrative problems than encountered in the personal interview.
5. Sample can include everyone selected because just about all people have mailing addresses.

Limitations

1. One has no control over the interview, and therefore the interviewer cannot supplement the data collected by observing the respondent and environment.
2. It is uncertain that the desired person is the one who fills out the questionnaire.
3. Returns are often slow and incomplete.
4. Difficult to test the statistical reliability of the sample.
5. Good mailing lists are hard to obtain.
6. This method of gathering information is quite inflexible and the questions cannot be changed to fit the respondent. The answers are determined by a set of unalterable written questions.

Personal Interview (see Figure 18.2)

Advantages

1. Permits the greatest amount of flexibility. The interviewer may reword questions so as to maximize the respondent's understanding.
2. Questionnaire usually can be longer than either the telephone- or mail-type.
3. Interviewer may supplement the information gathered on the questionnaire by also recording socioeconomic data that is observable.
4. Sample is more likely to be statistically reliable.
5. Interviewer is certain that the person giving the information is the one that should.

Limitations

1. May be considerable interview bias.
2. Problem of call back exists if the respondent is not home.
3. Many people refuse to be interviewed under any condition by strangers. (This is especially and increasingly true of women at home being interviewed by men; women, therefore, as indicated in Figure 18.3, are the better choice for interviewers.)
4. Considerable costs attached to this method of interviewing.

FIGURE 18.2
A woman is being interviewed at home

Source: Mid-America Marketing Research Company, Chicago, Illinois.

5. Often takes considerable time to complete the study.
6. Considerable administrative problems with their burden of costs.

Direct Observation. Another method of obtaining information is to observe the respondent in the act of buying a product. Generally the customer is not aware that he or she is being observed; consequently no attempt at an interview will be made. The advantage of this method is quite obvious—the customer is being him- or herself, and there is little doubt about preferences or behavior.

Most retailers claim that they observe their customers, and those that do actually profit by this research. Unfortunately, there is usually very little attempt to formalize these studies by employing a scientific method; consequently there is little certainty about the significance of the results.

Some retailers use the observation method of gathering information to establish the identity of the shopping area that surrounds their stores. They do this by recording the numbers of car license plates parked nearby, and then they identify owners and addresses from lists that state governments make available. It is almost certain that the boundaries of the shopping area can be determined in this way. Therefore it is surprising to find retailers who cannot identify, even if in a vague way, the residential area from which they draw customers.

Mechanical and Electrical Counters

Mechanical means of obtaining information are available, such as traffic counters, hidden cameras, and recorders that are mounted on television sets to record viewing habits. There are "eye" cameras to photograph the movements of a shoppers's eyes as he or she walks through the aisles of the local supermarket.

All of the mechanical devices have the advantage of providing permanent rec-

FIGURE 18.3

Women are better interviewers than men for many reasons

Source: Mid-America Marketing Research Company, Chicago, Illinois.

ords of the information gathered. Often they have the additional advantage of providing detailed information that could not be obtained in any other way. Football fans have been thrilled to watch a replay of an exciting touchdown run on video tape. In a similar manner a replay of a customer's shopping habits can be exciting to the retail researcher.

The hidden camera is an excellent example of a device that provides a valid record of a shopper's behavior, but some people object to these cameras on moral grounds. Critics believe it to be unethical to film a shopper without permission. If the shopper's permission is obtained, it is then uncertain that his or her behavior is normal. Each retailer who uses hidden cameras must question his or her own conscience on the ethics involved.

Experimental Studies

In recent years there has been an attempt to determine cause and effect relationships. Experimental studies are organized in such a way that the data collected are relevant to a given cause and effect problem. One noted writer on principles of marketing research defines experimentation in this way:[2]

[2]Harper W. Boyd, Jr., and Ralph Westfall, *Marketing Research: Text and Cases* (Homewood, Ill.: Richard D. Irwin, Inc., 1956), pp. 78–80.

Experimentation, then, can be said to be the collection of data in such a way as to permit clear and unconfused conclusions as to the correctness of a hypothesis which involves cause and effect relationships.

By using this method, the researcher first formulates a hypothesis, then sets up all the controls that are necessary for its objective testing. Many of these designs are quite complex and involve some expertise in mathematics; hence they are unsuitable for use by the average retailer. One of the simplest and best is the "after only with control group" design. Let us look at an example.

Assume that a retailer has two supermarkets in the same city—both catering to the same types of people. Assume that in one (the experimental store) he sets up a special island of tomato juice in a conspicuous location. In the other (the control store) he does not set up a special location for the tomato juice, but keeps it on his shelves at the regular site. Next assume that tomato juice is singled out as an item to be shown in the store's weekly food advertisement, and the owner is attempting to ascertain the value of locating the tomato juice in a special location. The researcher at the end of the test period measures the sales of tomato juice in the control store and the experimental store. The difference between the sales would represent the effect of locating a special island of tomato juice.

Experimental research has not been used in marketing to any major degree. Perhaps the major reason for its limited use is that few marketing research people consider themselves sufficiently knowledgeable to employ this technique. However, as the demand to examine causal relationships increases, this method will be used more frequently.

Attitude and Opinion Polls

Nearly everyone has encountered the public opinion polls that seek to identify the average American's attitude on vital issues of the day or preference for candidates seeking political office. (See Figure 18.4.) The technique of identifying opinions and attitudes has been borrowed from social scientists and been converted to marketing research. What is the distinction between "attitude" and "opinion"? Green and Tull clarify them in this way:[3]

> Attitude and opinion have frequently been differentiated in psychological and sociological investigations. A commonly drawn distinction has been to view an "attitude" as a predisposition to act in a certain way and an "opinion" as a verbalization of the attitude. Thus, a statement by the respondent that he prefers viewing color to black and white television would be an opinion expressing (one aspect of) the respondent's attitude toward color television.
>
> When used to predict actions that the respondent will take, this distinction between "attitude" and "opinion" becomes blurred. Since the major purpose of attitude-opinion research in marketing is to predict behavior, this differentiation is, at best, of limited usefulness.

[3]Paul E. Green and Donald S. Tull, *Research for Marketing Decisions* (Englewood Cliffs, N.J.: Prentice-Hall, Inc., 3rd ed. 1975), p. 115.

FIGURE 18.4
Shopping centers are favorite locations to obtain opinions and attitudes

Source: Mid-America Marketing Research Company, Chicago, Illinois.

CONSUMER BEHAVIOR

Considerable activity takes place today regarding consumer behavior, as we discussed in some detail in Chapters 3 and 4.

Motivation Research

Whenever one begins to analyze people's behavior and questions the motives involved, additional techniques and procedures are used. The term that was popularly used in the 1950s to explain this type of inquiry was *motivation research*. The marketing literature of the 1950s is filled with case studies of this approach. In essence, motivation research employs some of the tools of the psychologist and the sociologist to obtain information which will help to understand the behavior of the consumer. Some of these tools are word association tests, sentence completion tests, the third person technique, and thematic apperception tests.

Word Association Tests. In the word association test, a series of words are given to a respondent one word at a time. The subject responds by giving the first word that comes to mind. After the test has been finished, the researcher is able to analyze the data in some meaningful manner. Perhaps it will reveal the consumer's true attitude toward a product or service.

FIGURE 18.5
Word association example

Write the name of the first brand that comes to your mind as I give the product category. For example, if the product is razor blades, you might respond by stating "Schick."

Product	Brand
1. Razor blades	1. Schick
2. Laundry detergent	2. ________
3. Rice	3. ________
4. Butter	4. ________
5. Toothpaste	5. ________
6. Lipstick	6. ________
7. Aspirin	7. ________
8. Hair spray	8. ________
9. Mouthwash	9. ________
10. Eye shadow	10. ________

A word association test seeking to identify the brand preferences of a sample of consumers for a limited number of products could be the example in Figure 18.5. This could be the basis for the retailer who wishes to allocate the best shelf position to the brands most desired by the customers.

Sentence Completion Tests. Closely related to the word association test is the technique of asking respondents to complete sentences. The respondent is handed a list of incomplete sentences, and is asked to complete each one with the first thoughts that come to mind. Again the idea behind this technique is the hope that information explaining consumer attitudes will be revealed. Normally the persons that are asked to complete the sentences are timed to make certain that their first thoughts are those used. Figure 18.6 shows a sample of this technique.

FIGURE 18.6
Sentence completion example

1. A woman who wears a mini-skirt at the office is ________.
2. Low calorie cola drinks are purchased primarily by ________.
3. Mother likes seat belts in her car because ________.
4. People who purchase foreign automobiles are ________.
5. The woman who colors her hair is ________.
6. Men who wear beards are ________.
7. Winter vacations in Florida are ________.
8. Boutiques are shopped by ________.
9. Discount stores are shopped primarily by ________.
10. Ski shops are found ________.

Third Person Technique. Another device is to ask a respondent to write a paragraph or two analyzing a certain situation that has been carefully explained. It is believed that the respondent will reveal considerable information regarding his or her own attitudes and opinions. For example, a man is seated alone in a very sophisticated restaurant eating a rare steak. He is dressed in work clothes and is bearded. All other patrons are expensively and conventionally attired. The respondent is asked to comment on the personality of this diner and give an opinion on why he chose this restaurant—especially since he seems to be out of place.

Thematic Apperception Tests. The thematic apperception tests (TAT) use cartoons or pictures showing subjects in various situations. The respondents are asked to tell a story about the picture by assuming the role of the shopper. An example would be the illustrations in Figure 18.7 which show a shopper at the dairy case examining margarine and butter. If a sample of housewives were shown these cartoons and asked to reproduce the thoughts in the mind of the shopper, it is a good bet that each respondent would reveal her own thoughts and attitudes toward butter and margarine.

It should be pointed out that all of these techniques require special skills in interpretation of responses. Boyd and Westfall say:[4]

FIGURE 18.7
Thematic Apperception Test example

[4]Boyd and Westfall, *Marketing Research*, p. 518.

> Results from such tests are difficult to interpret. Their meaning tends to be interpreted in terms of the hypotheses of the researcher. A "fact" is only relevant when it is related to other "facts" and interpreted within the framework of psychological theory. The scoring of TAT results in a complicated procedure. It has to be elaborate if subtle relationships are to be uncovered. Also, even persons disciplined in psychology and TAT work often disagree in their interpretations. Thus, such test devices cannot always be considered conclusive in themselves.

The subject of unstructured questions should also mention the depth interview. This technique, as might be expected, has been borrowed from the clinical phychologists. In essence, the interviewer probes the respondent's mind to obtain answers to explain behavior, or attitude, or underlying bias to a product or service. One can see that here also great skill is needed in the probing process and the analytical summary.

Obtaining Confidential Information

Information is often of a confidential nature, and respondents are reluctant to answer questions on age, income, or political and religious affiliations. Fortunately there are techniques which can aid the researcher in this area. One method that has proved successful is to hand the respondent a card such as the one illustrated in Figure 18.8. The respondent is asked to give the letter corresponding to the category in which his or her income falls. For example, the respondent may say "D." This indicates that his or her income falls between $8,000 and $9,900. The success of this technique is due to the fact that people hesitate to verbalize their incomes, but do not mind identifying income if an appropriate method is offered.

FIGURE 18.8
Illustration of a card with suggested incomes

	Card Three	*Household Income*
A	Under $3,000	
B	$3,000–$4,900	
C	$5,000–$7,900	
D	$8,000–$9,900	
E	$10,000–$14,999	
F	$15,000 and over	

ERRORS IN GATHERING INFORMATION

A researcher is always interested in obtaining accurate information from the respondents. However, any attempt to obtain information directly is subject to three major sources of error. They are response error, nonresponse error, and sampling error. The latter is the most difficult to understand.

Response Error

Response error occurs when the information recorded by the interviewer differs from the true value of the subject under discussion. For example:

Interviewer: How many miles do you get per gallon of gasoline?
Respondent: I would estimate 18.

Assume that the respondent is a woman who does not drive a car, and she has no idea at all as to the right answer. She responds with 18 simply because she wishes to give an answer and not appear stupid in the eyes of the interviewer. The recorded answer (assuming it is wrong) is a response error.

Suppose that the respondent is a man who is knowledgeable about his auto's mileage per gallon. However, for personal reasons (such as wanting his car to seem better than it is) he chooses to give the wrong answer. This would also be a response error.

Response errors result from the unwillingness or the inability of respondents to give the right answers. Generally, the reasons that people give inaccurate responses are perceived loss of prestige, invasion of privacy, or a personality clash with the interviewer. Rarely is the reason simply dishonesty. Other times the respondent wishes to be helpful and tries to give the information that he or she thinks will please the interviewer, even though this information may be erroneous, exaggerated, or simply untrue. Consider this example:

A young woman who dislikes classical music has just purchased a gift album of Beethoven and is approached by an interviewer.

Interviewer: Do you like Beethoven's music?
Respondent: Yes, very much.
Interviewer: Did you purchase the album for your own collection?
Respondent: Yes.

In this example, the respondent may fear a loss of prestige if she answers truthfully. This information-gathering problem is called a response error.

Nonresponse Error

A nonresponse error occurs when an individual is chosen to be included in a sample, but for a variety of reasons is never contacted. Assume that the local Ford dealer is contacting a sample of 50 people who purchased new cars at the agency within the last two years. Dave Coffelt is one of the people to be contacted. During the time of the interviews, Coffelt is away from home on business, and thus is never interviewed. This would be a nonresponse error because no one knows what his answers might have been. Some marketing research practitioners are convinced that people who refuse to be interviewed, or who are seldom home to be interviewed, differ in many ways from those who are successfully contacted. Unfortunately, it is virtually impossible to compensate for the nonresponse error because the direction of the error is unknown.

Sampling

One cannot interview every single person in a given market, nor is it necessary. A good sample will yield reliable information. Therefore it is necessary to understand sampling procedures and techniques. At this point a few definitions are helpful.

1. *Universe*—frequently called the population. It is the whole and includes all the characteristics of whatever is measured.
2. *Sample*—part of the whole.
3. *Random Sample*—a sample which is representative of the universe from which it has been taken. It is without bias; it has the same characteristics as the universe, and they are distributed in the same proportion.
4. *Representative Sample*—a sample which allegedly has the same characteristics as the universe. This may or may not be true. Most samples claim to be representative.
5. *Parameter*—a true measure of the universe.
6. *Statistic*—an estimate of a parameter.

What Is a Universe Mean? It is often necessary to measure or evaluate the characteristics of a given universe. A large chain of food stores might wish to know the average amount of income that a typical household spends on food weekly. One way to obtain this average would be to interview the head of every household and record the weekly expenditure. If we did this, then totaled the dollars spent, and divided by the number of households, the desired results would be obtained. This average is the universe mean, because it is a true measure of the universe. It might also be called a parameter. In most cases, it would be exceedingly difficult, if not impossible, to measure the universe directly and obtain the measurements of various parameters. Consider the difficulty of interviewing every householder in New York City to obtain weekly expenditures for food. Therefore it is necessary to apply sampling techniques to estimate the universe values that are desired.

Another example might be a dress shop that is interested in the average dollar charge sale per customer for the month of July 1975. One way is to obtain the charge records for each customer and record the dollar sales for the month of July for each one. All of the charge sales for July would be totaled, then divided by the number of customers. The resulting average would be the universe mean.

1.	Dollar total of all charge sales for July	\$55,542
2.	Number of customers who charged merchandise in July	3,200
3.	Number of active charge customers	8,810
4.	Universe mean $= \dfrac{\$55{,}542}{8{,}810} = \$6.30$	

The value of the universe mean could have been approximated by taking a sample of the charge accounts. The time spent in computing the desired average would thus have been simplified. The results would not be significantly different if proper sampling procedures were used.

There are many types of samples that can be taken, but it is important to know that whatever sample is used be truly representative of the universe from which it is taken. In other words, the sample must have the same attributes and be in the same proportion or distribution as exist in the universe. One might say that the sample should be an exact replica of the universe. It is difficult to know whether or not the sample is representative of the universe, because one would need to know all the facts about it. If these were known, then there would be no need for a sample. Consequently, a sample is judged on its methodology or selection and its size rather than its representativeness. Many samples are alleged to be representative when in reality they are biased.

Random Sample Is Representative of the Population. A sample is said to be biased if it is not representative of its universe. Bias must naturally be avoided if the results are to have meaning. Most researchers prefer to use a random sample because they are confident that it is without bias, and hence representative. When the universe is sampled by random technique, each variable has an equal chance of being selected. Therefore if a large enough sample is taken, one can be reasonably assured that the sample is indeed a replica of the universe from which it is taken.

Consider this example: An interviewer, wishing to sample the preferences of 100 women in a given city concerning black cocktail dresses, decides to choose as her sample the first 100 women passing Bobbi's Dress Shoppe in the center of downtown. This would not be a random sample, because those ladies who were not passing by Bobbi's Dress Shoppe could not be selected. This type is best called a haphazard sample. In order to obtain a random sample, each woman in the area must have an equal chance of being selected. One of the principal advantages of a random sample is that estimates of measurements can be made mathematically and the results may be tested.

How Large a Sample? The rule is that it should be large enough to give reliable results. In general, one might be guided by the following principle: the more uniform the data, the smaller the sample need be in order to give reliable results. Do you know your blood type? Better yet, do you recall the procedure which the doctor followed in typing it? If you do—perhaps you remember that he withdrew only a small drop from your finger, and from this single drop the laboratory was able to classify the blood reliably as A, B, or some other type. The reliability of this sample could not have been improved even if the sample of your blood had been increased to include all of it. The reason, of course, why a single drop of blood is a reliable sample is because of the uniformity of the blood within any individual. Most universes that are sampled are not this uniform; therefore the sample size has to be relatively large.

Fortunately, a little knowledge of statistics is helpful in understanding the theory of sampling. More and more students are required to learn quantitative methods and techniques in their college curriculum, so that as they are employed in retailing positions they are able to employ sampling with confidence. There are certain formulas which are helpful in choosing the correct sample size, and any standard text of statistics explains them. Most are beyond the scope of this text.

Probability Samples

Simple Random Sample. There are all types of probability samples; the simple random sample, and the two that follow it, are the major ones. Assume that there are 10,000 food stores of a certain type in the United States. The researcher wishes to sample 100 of them. One method would be to place the names of all the stores in a barrel, mix them thoroughly, and withdraw one name at a time. Theoretically, one should replace the name into the barrel after each drawing. One continues in this manner until all 100 names of food stores are selected. This is a cumbersome procedure; instead, specially prepared tables of random numbers should be used. From these tables, a researcher can confidently select 100 numbers that correspond to the stores, and come up with the sample. A sample selected in this manner is a simple random sample.

Stratified Random Sample. The 10,000 food stores may be classified by sales volume. Assume that there are three classifications and 3,000 stores have sales volumes over $1,000,000 weekly. Next assume that 5,000 stores have sales volumes between $500,000 and $1,000,000 weekly, while the remaining 2,000 stores have less than $500,000 sales weekly. From the table of random numbers, select 30 from the first classification (or strata), 50 from the second, and 20 from the last. This is called a stratified random sample. Note that the sample is proportionate to the number of stores in each strata. However, some samples are purposely disproportionate.

Area or Cluster Sample. It is often difficult to identify individuals or stores to be sampled. In this case, one could take the map of a city that is laid out by blocks, identify each block, and then by means of the table of random numbers choose the blocks that are to be sampled. A predetermined design of the respondents in the block to be interviewed should be made. This type of sample is properly called a cluster or area sample.

Which Type of Sample Is Best? The type of probability sample that the researcher should use depends upon budget, skill in statistical techniques, and the purpose of the study. Some types of samples yield results that are statistically more efficient, while others are economically more efficient. A good researcher will use the type of probability sample that will give the most satisfactory results in terms of budget, time allocation, and reliability of the answers.

The purpose of taking a probability sample is that certain claims can be made about the survey data regarding its reliability. Tests can be made attesting to the significance of the conclusions. It is beyond the scope of this chapter to describe the statistical techniques of significance tests and other advanced techniques.

In sheer numbers there are far fewer probability samples taken than the other kinds. The reasons are: (1) lack of technical know-how by people taking samples, (2) lack of time and resource to do the job properly, and (3) no demand by users of samples that they be the probability type. The small retailer especially should become knowledgeable about samples, so that he or she will insist on probability samples whenever possible.

Nonprobability Samples

Some samples are not probability samples. In many cases they should be called *haphazard samples* because the techniques employed are haphazard at best. An example of this type would be to interview every man wearing a blue tie who enters the local drugstore between 2 and 3 p.m. of a given day. The greatest number of samples taken are of this variety and any conclusions are not subject to statistical tests. They should be avoided.

The *quota sample* is a nonprobability sample that can be quite good. In this case, known facts of the universe are selected for the sample in the same proportion as they exist in the universe. For instance, the sample will carry the same proportion of males and females as in the universe, the same proportion of Catholics, Protestants, and Jews, and so on. After assembling the sample, the researcher will test for its representativeness by comparing a factor in the sample with a known statistic of the universe. Suppose that the sample contained 9.7 percent of adults over the age 65, and the proportion of these people in the universe was 9.8 percent. Then the researcher would say the sample was representative.

Sample Terms. The careful student will want to know the difference in the meaning of sampling terms such as reliability, precision, validity, and accuracy. These terms are often, but incorrectly, used interchangeably.

1. *Reliability* measures the presence of random error, and random errors are expected. In more complicated language one could say that reliability measures the predictability that some estimate of a parametric value will be about the same if repeated samples are taken. Generally, one is saying something about reliability when terms such as levels of significance and confidence limits are used. To clarify, consider the following example: A survey was just completed using 400 respondents. The problem was to find the percentage of families in a certain city who intended to buy color television sets in the next year or two. A random sample was taken, and 62.5 percent of the respondents indicated that they intended to purchase color sets within the prescribed time period. Assume that the standard error of proportion was computed and found to be 3 percent. Then one could say that the true proportion of householders in this particular city is $62.5 \pm 2(3\%)$, and we could be 95 percent certain that this would be the case. Another way of stating the results—if thousands of samples were taken, one could be 95 percent certain that all results would fall somewhere in the range of 56.6 to 68.5 percent. Fortunately one need not take thousands of samples in order to predict the results. A single sample with a statement of reliability will suffice.

2. *Precision* relates to the size of the interval that one wishes the statistic to differ from the parameter that is being measured. In the above example—the true proportion was said to be 62.5 percent plus or minus 6 percent (reliability of 95+ percent).[5] The precision in this example is 6 percent. The researcher might wish to improve the precision. In the illustration of the color television sets, let us assume that with a reliability of 95 percent one wishes the precision to be 3 percent rather than 6 percent. A sample of 400 was used for the original results. To achieve a 3 percent precision the sample will have to be quadrupled so that 1,600 would then be the sample size. A handy rule of thumb is to quadruple the sample if the precision is to be halved.
3. *Validity* is concerned with the presence of constant error. Actually, there are different aspects to the concept of validity; consequently, the term is somewhat elusive. Perhaps these simplified explanations will help to clarify it. Does the model actually measure what it is intended to measure? Are the inferences sound? A yes answer to these two questions indicates a valid proposition. Validity is unlike reliability in that it cannot be measured by statistical techniques. One must always examine the entire theory in search for the truth of the underlying mechanisms. Most readers have heard the statement expressed that a proposition looks good in theory but does not work in practice. If this is true—then they are attacking the theory on pragmatic validity. If, however, the research is satisfied that the research is valid, then he or she can use it for decision making. The student must always bear in mind that two of the major purposes of science are:
    a. To explain phenomena in relation to a problem context.
    b. To make predictions.
4. *Accuracy* is simply that the data is correct; thus $3+3=6$, not 5.

Editing and Tabulating

Once all the information has been gathered, it becomes necessary to edit and tabulate it. Experienced people will go over the questionnaires to be certain that each question has been answered appropriately, and that errors and inaccuracies are reduced. In short, the entire return must be checked for validity.

After careful editing, the information is ready to be tabulated. This involves tallying and summarizing the data into meaningful totals. In more recent years the data are punched on IBM cards and the counting is done quickly by a computer. The advantage of computer counting is self-evident. It is both accurate and speedy. However, it may require many hours in expensive programming. One authority puts it this way:[6]

> Although once the data are ready for electronic data processing the machines perform their operations at fantastic speeds. The reality is that the hours spent in programming the machine may be 10 or 20 times the minutes used in computation.

[5] A reliability of 95 percent is in reality 1.96 sigmas away from the mean; however, 2 sigmas are used to simplify the arithmetic. The reliability is slightly better than 95 percent.

[6] Robert Ferber, Donald Blankertz, and Sidney Hollander, Jr., *Marketing Research* (New York: Ronald Press Co., 1964), p. 398.

MARKET RESEARCH FOR RETAILERS

The research projects undertaken by one retailer differ from another retailer if the needs of the two retailers differ significantly. The large department stores, the chains, and other large independent retailers do extensive research, and more often than not they have their own marketing research departments. In other instances they buy their research from outside research firms. The small independent retailer frequently engages in no research at all because of the misguided assumption that he or she cannot afford it. These retailers are singularly in need of good research and often they might be surprised to find that the dollar cost is negligible.

Some types of research that retailers may engage in are:

1. Consumer research
   a. traffic counts
   b. demographic studies
   c. analysis of internal data
2. Store layout
3. Advertising analysis

Consumer Research

The simplest research is an actual count of people. This may be the number of people who actually pass by a retailer's place of business in a given time period. The count may be repeated each day until a pattern of store traffic is discerned. Tuesday may emerge as the poorest shopping day of the week, and special promotions should be used to increase patronage on that day. In many metropolitan areas Fridays and Saturdays are the busiest days in the food supermarkets. An examination of Thursday's newspapers reflects this. All retailers should know the traffic flow of their particular business classified by day, month, and season. After this information is established, decisions can be made to exploit this knowledge.

All types of head counts can be summarized as traffic counts. They are also useful in determining the original location of the retailer. It must be remembered that a traffic study indicates very little about the nature of attitudes of people—it is simply a count. An individual store may establish its trade boundaries with the help of the customers themselves. A large map of the area (laid out in blocks) could be mounted in a conspicuous part of the store with a supply of colored pins. The customer would be invited to place a pin on the map indicating the block in which he or she lives. Some measure of control would have to be set up so that pins would not be placed on the map indiscriminately.

Research studies of a qualitative nature which classify customers by age, income, sex, and educational levels are even more useful. These studies should then be related to such matters as store policies and merchandise stocked in order to maximize their usefulness. Such studies are called demographic studies. Consider the proprietor of a candy store close to an elementary school. He will probably notice the type and kind of candy that appeals most to youthful shoppers, and will stock those that move the fastest. Just as the candy proprietor stocks the store with candies that appeal to children, so the proprietor of a men's clothing store will stock the types that appeal to his clientele. A study of his clientele will be helpful in every aspect of merchandising.

Store Layout

Marketing research can be helpful in determining the traffic within the store, and aid the proprietor in having an effective store layout. Research will be helpful in positioning goods on the shelves. Some merchandise sells better if it is placed on a shelf at eye level (toothpaste), while other merchandise (kitty litter) is best located on the floor. (See Figure 18.9.) The next time you visit a supermarket note the shelf extenders that are used to increase the number of facings. These allow more goods to be offered at the favored location.

Advertising Analysis

The effectiveness of the advertising message is a prime subject for research. Most retailers attempt to relate their sales to advertising, although not everyone is

FIGURE 18.9
Mock stores are sometimes used in market research surveys

Source: Mid-America Marketing Research Company, Chicago, Illinois.

sufficiently acquainted with the more sophisticated tools that measure the effectiveness of various media. Chapter 12 on promotion discusses this topic in greater detail.

In no way does this chapter exhaust all the types of research that could be employed by a retailer. Rather these are only suggestions to supplement the research being turned out by national manufacturers, wholesalers, other middlemen, and private sources.

SUMMARY

Marketing research has come of age since World War II, and a steady stream of information is being generated all throughout the United States. The application of good marketing research techniques is not used by small retailers in any significant manner. This is partly due to the lack of technical know-how and a status quo psychology on the part of the retailers.

Retailers should be familiar with the scientific method of obtaining information that is useful in solving problems and making decisions.

The methodology of obtaining good primary data starts with an understanding of the problem, a statement of the objectives of the research, and setting the boundaries of the universe to be studied. Next, one must plan the research design. This begins with choosing the sample. The advantages of the probability sample are so overwhelming that this choice should be almost automatic. It is necessary that retailing executives understand thoroughly the philosophy underlying statistical techniques that are employed.

The actual mechanics of obtaining the information begins with the creation of the questionnaire. This involves the type of data to be gathered, whether confidential or not, and the kind of interview the researcher plans to use. Good research is the result of great care and skill. Its usefulness to anyone depends upon two factors: (1) Does it explain the relationship of the variables within the framework of the problem context? and (2) Is it useful in making predictions for future courses of action?

All retailers, large or small, can apply research techniques. At least they should be research oriented and apply what they can, even though it be only a simple traffic count.

QUESTIONS FOR DISCUSSION

1. What is the scientific method of inquiry and how does it differ from common sense?
2. Explain the steps that the market researcher employs in the scientific method of inquiry.
3. State the rules for creating a good questionnaire.
4. Compare and contrast the telephone interview, the personal interview, and the mail interview. Under what conditions would you use each?

5. Distinguish between attitude and opinion.
6. Give at least four examples using projective techniques.
7. What is a random sample, and how does it differ from a haphazard sample?
8. Discuss the means of determining the size of a sample.
9. Compare and contrast these terms: reliability, precision, accuracy, and validity.
10. Explain how a traffic count might be useful to a suburban dress shop.

19 CAREERS IN RETAILING

A young man whose father owns an automobile dealership has known for as long as he can remember that he would go into his father's business. The manufacturer is anxious to make the transition from father to son as smooth and orderly as possible and has established a training school for sons of its dealers. The formal training at the home office plus experience on the job should mean that the change will not be too wrenching.

A high school dropout takes a job in the stockroom of a large department store. His prospects there are limited, but he earns a living wage, is covered by the firm's health and accident insurance, takes an annual vacation, and is accumulating rights to a small pension if he stays with the company until retirement. He is well liked and his job performance is reviewed every six months; he may later be asked if he would like to enter the company's sales training program.

A bright young woman with an M.B.A. from a well-known university has taken a position with the central staff of a major midwestern food chain. The firm pays well but it imposes a very demanding work schedule, including weekend work and considerable travel, all of which interfere with her personal life. She fully expects to be an officer in the firm within 20 years.

A retired military officer and his wife invest their savings in a fast-food franchise where they spend almost every waking moment. It is hard work and their first experience in retailing, but they believe that they will soon begin to earn a profit from their operation. One of their friends invested in a different type of franchise and lost his entire life's savings to a "hit-and-run" franchiser in less than two years; and it was all very legal.

A young woman with an Associate Arts degree who took two years of accounting started her career in the home office of a regional chain furniture retailer. She took no retailing course in college but that is only a minor hindrance to her career, at least at first. Her present job revolves exclusively around accounting problems, and she thinks of herself more as an "accountant" than as a "retailer."

In Chapter 6 we discussed some of the problems that retailers have in recruiting employees. Among the obstacles that the retailer must face are the low average pay of most retail workers, particularly when contrasted with those in construction or manufacturing; the physical demands of the job; and the often unusual working hours to accommodate the shopping preferences of customers. So we already have several strong hints about what a new employee should expect from a career in retailing. The focus of this chapter is from the point of view of the jobseeker rather than the employer, as was the case in Chapter 7.

The above examples point out the diversity in retailing, but these stories can do little more than hint at the range of possible careers. Indeed, retailing employed 12.4 million workers in January 1975, a total equal to 14.6 percent of the labor force (84,500,000).[1] This total is exceeded only by the manufacturing industries, which in 1974 employed 19.7 million persons. For further comparison, consider the fact that there are only 13.9 million people employed in all areas of government, federal, state, and local.[2] It is only logical to assume that many job opportunities exist in any industry employing a large number of persons, and retailing is no exception. A more detailed breakdown of jobs by type of retailer is as follows:[3]

	Workers in 1974
Department store	2,066,000
Mail order	162,700
Variety store	382,800
Other general merchandise	435,000
Food stores	1,980,800
Apparel and accessories	828,600
Furniture and home furnishings	524,000
Eating and drinking	3,109,000
Other retail trade	3,836,600
Total Retail Workers	13,325,500

Merely citing statistics about the number of retailing jobs and where they are located does not give sufficient insight into the career opportunities that exist. Therefore we shall first discuss the kinds of talents needed to insure a successful career in retailing.

TALENTS AND SKILLS

Many people think of the salesperson when retail careers are discussed. This is because salespeople are the most visible of all retailing employees, and the ones with whom the general public comes into closest contact. Certainly they are the most numerous among those employed in the retail trade. The first talent these people should have in abundance is, obviously, the *ability to sell*. In retailing, selling merchandise is what it is all about, and therefore people with selling talent are especially in demand. This is true whether we think of the clerks who are involved in actual face-to-face dialogue with the customer or the executives who are buying the most salable merchandise and supervising the selling operation. The entire store

[1]*Employment and Earnings*, U.S. Department of Labor, 21, no. 8 (February 1975), pp. 50, 58, 63, 64.

[2]*Survey of Current Business*, U.S. Department of Commerce, 54, no. 2 (February 1974), S-13.

[3]*Employment and Earnings*, pp. 63–64.

must be sales oriented and the talents of everyone should be directed toward accomplishing this major function.

Montgomery Ward recognizes that the ability to sell is an essential talent needed in the operation of its retail stores. On the occasion of opening its first computerized store in Rockford, Illinois on November 17, 1970, Ward said:[4]

> The heads of the department teams will be designated as department merchandisers. Since the computer will have the assigned task of reordering, billing, and handling other data, the floor staff will be primarily sales oriented and sales trained.

Like other employers, retailers are seeking individuals who have *leadership talent*. The Illinois Retail Merchants Association estimates that one out of every five retail employees is in an executive role. Assuming that the estimate is correct, then in a total of 12,000,000 retail workers, 2,400,000 may be considered managerial in nature. With an emphasis on youth in retailing jobs, this provides an excellent opportunity for younger workers to demonstrate leadership talents, and consequently earn promotions. On this point, the Illinois Retail Merchants Association says:[5]

> Retailing has placed great emphasis on youth. Over half of the executives in retailing are under age 35. There are many junior executive positions and training programs designed to give the employee an opportunity to develop and demonstrate managerial skills.

Leadership talents are needed in a variety of managerial jobs both in selling and nonselling. Exactly what constitutes this particular talent is difficult to pinpoint. However, it involves the ability to make other employees work together, cooperatively and harmoniously in achieving the store's objectives. Individuals with leadership ability come in various sizes, ages, sex, color, and aptitudes. Inasmuch as retailing is such a large employer of people, there is a need for individuals whose leadership qualities are available immediately or whose talents can be developed and used at a later time.

Numerous nonselling jobs in the course of operating a retail store require *analytical skills*. There are accounts to be kept, inventories to be managed, sales records to be analyzed, customers to be billed, and payrolls to be made. Analytical skills generally associated with an accountant are needed to perform these assignments. Moreover with the adaptation of the computer to more and more retail operations, a more sophisticated type of analytical ability is needed to process the data in an integrated system. A greater analytical talent is needed to interpret the meaning of all the data generated by the computers.

Creativeness is a fourth necessary talent. Creative people are employed in a

[4]News of Interest to You," Public Relations Department of Montgomery Ward, November 17, 1970, p. 3.

[5]"Retail Fact Sheet," Illinois Retail Merchants Association, Chicago, Ill. (undated but distributed in 1970).

wide assortment of retailing jobs. Some are used to create effective window displays. Others are employed in retail advertising departments where they prepare ads and write copy. Mail-order houses employ creative people to prepare the merchandise catalogs. As in many large organizations, individuals with writing skills are used to publish company newspapers.

All of these talents are essential for many other jobs, not just those in the retail trade. For that reason, retailers have to compete actively in the job market for individuals who possess the essential talents of selling ability, leadership, analytical skill, and creativeness. Those individuals—separately or in a combination—will find opportunities in retailing for personal development.

VITAL STATISTICS

Assuming that a person has one or more of the four talents just described, are there any additional requirements for a career in retailing? In particular, what about age, sex, education and training, and race?

Age

Age is not a barrier to a career in retailing. Opportunities exist for the young person who is seeking his or her first job; for the mature individual who is at the peak of productivity; and for the retired worker who wishes to spend part of his or her free time in productive work. It is, however, the young person with whom we are concerned in this chapter. Young people are actively being sought for careers in retailing. One writer on retail careers has this optimistic note.[6]

> The demand for young people in retailing so far exceeds the supply that salaries are on the rise, and geography has far less influence than the desirability of the talent. The salary range for beginners who have just finished two years of junior college is competitive with many jobs requiring a B.A. in other fields. Stores respond rapidly both to any inflationary spiral and to competition from other industries for promising candidates.

Sex

Sex is no obstacle to a career in retailing. The retailing industry is a major employer of women, and career opportunities exist for females in a variety of challenging positions. In October 1974 the retail trade employed 6,100,000 female workers, a total equal to 41 percent of all retail employees. In January 1975, 228,-000 females, 20 years old and over were self-employed in the retail trade.[7]

Harriet Wilinsky writes that being female is an advantage for a retail employee because the majority of store customers are women. Specifically she says:[8]

[6]Harriet Wilinsky, *Careers and Opportunities in Retailing* (New York: E. P. Dutton & Co. Inc., 1970), p. 13.

[7]*Employment and Earnings*, pp. 40, 71.

[8]Wilinsky, *Careers*, p. 24.

> One of their strongest assets is the very fact that they are female. So are the majority of department store customers. Who is better qualified to prejudge the tastes of women than another woman?

Women are accepted by retail management and there is every opportunity for a woman to reach the executive level. Statistics indicate that half of the buyers in stores are women.[9] It is still difficult to achieve the job of store president, but there probably are more women at or near the top in retailing than in any other industry. Indeed, Sears, Roebuck indicated that almost 53 percent of its work force in 1974 was women; more important, 27.6 percent of its management group was women, up from 19 percent in 1969.[10] (See Table 19.1.)

TABLE 19.1

Job Categories of Female Employees
Sears, Roebuck & Company, for 1973

	Percentage of Females Employed		
*Job Category**	*February 1969*	*February 1973*	*Change (in percentage points)*
Officials and managers	19.7	27.6	+ 7.9
Professionals	14.7	48.7	+34.0
Technicians	13.4	34.1	+20.7
Sales workers	58.7	60.5	+ 1.8
Office and clerical	86.9	88.5	+ 1.6
Craftswomen	5.4	4.3	− 1.1
Operatives	12.9	26.3	+13.4
Laborers	40.4	24.2	−16,2
Service workers	35.6	28.8	− 6.8

*Total males and females employed = 100%
Source: *Sears, Roebuck Annual Report, 1973* (April 1974).

Education and Training

The retailing industry provides career opportunities for individuals with different levels of education. College graduates are eagerly sought to fill the many positions of leadership and responsibility. Top retailers actively recruit individuals on college campuses. Wilinsky writes that a college degree is almost a necessity in order to be recruited for a management training program, such as the one used by Filene's in Boston. Filene's employs 3,850 persons, of which 515 are executives. The store selects 45 men and women in January and again in July for its management training program. At the end of two years, graduates of this program are executives.[11]

[9] Ibid., p. 24.

[10] *Sears, Roebuck Annual Report, 1973* (April 1974).

[11] Ibid., p. 35.

Minority Status

At the present time, graduates of community colleges are especially attractive to retailers. Many potential retail workers are disadvantaged in regard to education, training, or racial background. Many retailers are more and more conscious of this, and they sincerely wish to help all minority groups. An example is Jewel Foods Company, a food supermarket chain headquartered in Melrose Park, Illinois. In 1968 Jewel set up special employment offices in Chicago's inner city for the purpose of hiring black employees. Jewel reported on this effort as follows:[12]

> After two years of effort, we are optimistic about our approach to successful employment of the disadvantaged. In Chicago, we have found it not too difficult to recruit and employ the disadvantaged, particularly after we opened an employment office in the Chicago Inner City. For instance, two years ago, less than 5 percent of the full-time staffs of Jewel Food Stores were members of minority groups. Today the total exceeds 10 percent.

Jewel does not hire the disadvantaged and then let them sink or swim. They are guided and directed by coach-counselors. They have a head coach and five field coaches whose job is to smooth the transition of the new employees from his or her previous environment to a successful work career at Jewel. Each of the field coaches is assigned 15 trainees for a minimum period of three to four months. This is how Jewel describes the function of the coaches:[13]

> He relates problems of individual trainees to the managers, supervisors, and personnel people. He makes recommendations on the utilization of the trainees. He counsels trainees on their work habits and productivity and on their home situations. In brief, he sponsors them in their new job.

Jewel believes that the coaches are prepared professionally to handle this sensitive assignment. All of the coaches are college graduates with degrees in education or social science. They all are black and well acquainted with ghetto life.

Jewel Foods Company is, of course, not the only retailer to launch programs to help minority groups. Jewel's program, however, is representative of efforts in this area by many retailers. For example, Sears, the nation's largest retailer, says:[14]

> Through an Affirmative Action program, your company is working to inform the minority community of your philosophy and desire to foster equal employment opportunity. The Company is making a special effort to attract minority employees and when their present level of skill and knowledge might not be sufficient, to assist them through training programs to improve their skills so that they may compete successfully in the market place.

In 1973, 15.3 percent of Sears' employees were from minority groups.[15]

[12]*The Jewel Companies: Diversified Retailers, Annual Report, 1968*, p. 10.

[13]Ibid., p. 11.

[14]From "Notice of Annual Meeting of Shareholders," Sears, Roebuck and Co., April 6, 1970.

[15]*Sears, Roebuck Annual Report, 1973* (April 1974).

DISTRIBUTIVE EDUCATION

The Distributive Education Program is so important to retailing that it must be discussed separately. It is a cooperative plan between a school and a business to provide both education and on-the-job training for an individual in a distributive occupation. Retailing businesses are major partners with schools in this venture. Federal funds are made available to train people through the provisions of the George-Barden Act of 1946 and the Vocational Act of 1963. It has programs for high school students, community college students, and adults. The high school program is the largest.

High School Programs

An important adjunct of Distributive Education is DECA (Distributive Education Clubs of America), a youth organization which was first organized in 1948 to provide a program to enrich the distributive curriculum. All of the 50 states have clubs today. In 1970 DECA had a total membership of over 100,000.[16]

Students who enroll in the program must be of employable age and have at least junior standing in high school. However, most student-trainees are seniors. Students attend classes at their schools for half a day and work with a cooperating business called a training station for a limited number of hours. All trainees must work at the training station (the job) at least 15 hours weekly, half of which should be on days that school is not in session. Student-trainees are urged not to exceed 24 working hours weekly. Retailers pay trainees the going rate for people performing their kind of work. (See Figure 19.1.)

At school the trainees are instructed by teachers who are both educationally and vocationally qualified. The training station (retail business) supplies a sponsor who cooperates with the teacher in setting up a training plan benefiting the student. The goal is to coordinate the trainee's classroom work with learning experience. Students obtain high school credits for participation in the program.

The purpose of the Distributive Education Plan is to educate and train personnel in retail practices so as to increase the productivity of the workers. This is highly useful because it facilitates the students' transition into businesses that do not have formal training programs. For example, in Illinois almost 25 percent of all workers are engaged in the marketing and distribution of goods and services; yet less than one-half of 1 percent of these workers are educated in distribution.

Training in distribution may lead to a career as a buyer, a salesperson, a department head, a personnel manager, a store manager, or something equally challenging. Graduates of such programs may go on to college for more formal education if they choose. A more normal route is to go directly into the business world and begin a career. In Illinois, to mark the twenty-fifth anniversary of distributive

[16]Lucy C. Crawford and Warren G. Meyer, *Organization and Administration of Distributive Education* (Columbus, Ohio: Charles E. Merrill Publishing Company, 1972), p. 183.

FIGURE 19.1
A trainee on the job

Source: Distributive Education Clubs of America, Falls Church, Virginia.

education, a booklet was issued giving biographical sketches of 25 graduates of the program. The sketches are interesting because they highlight the variety of jobs each of these graduates eventually assumed. Of the 25 individuals whose careers are summarized, only four had gone on to college. All had risen to the executive level. Some of the jobs they held at the time the booklet was written are store manager of a Robert Hall unit, owner of a florist shop, advertising manager for Jupiter Stores, buyer for an H. Hyman and Sons store, assistant manager for an F. W. Woolworth store, manager of main floor for a J C Penney store, store manager for an A & P supermarket, assistant buyer for Charles A. Stevens Company, and department manager for Goldblatts, Inc. The others were equally impressive.

Community College Programs

There is increasing emphasis on post high school distributive education programs, and many community colleges are participating to a greater extent. Only 10.7 percent of all enrollments in distributive education were in post high school programs, but the number of trainees increased by 35.7 percent in 1969. Although there are fewer students enrolled in distributive programs offered by community colleges than participating in high school programs, the types of programs are exciting. Each year new ideas are converted into new programs. The Department of Health, Education and Welfare describes one such program at Portland Community College in this way:[17]

> At Portland Community College, Oregon, a large separate and modern facility is being constructed to house a campus fashion store to be operated by the director of marketing education. The entire store operation will involve a multitude of occupational areas including law enforcement for store security, office education for secretaries, clerks and accountants for the store, journalism for printed store publicity, advertising and others.

Other states are also involved in expanding their programs. For example, Minnesota has programs of distributive education in five area technical schools and three junior colleges. In Minnesota retailing enrollees may take Retail Floristry, Fashion Merchandising, and Home Furnishings Marketing. Michigan has added a program in Automatic Retailing. Massachusetts has built a million-dollar center for distributive education at Essex Agricultural and Technical Institute in Danvers. It offers programs in Food Distribution, Horticultural Businesses, Fashion Retailing, and General Merchandising. Programs have been added in Mesa College, Arizona; Harrisburg Area Community College, Pennsylvania; Highline Community College in Washington; and Atlantic County Community College, New Jersey. Distributive education programs are becoming more important and popular at the post high school level.

Many of the nation's largest retailers participate in distributive education programs. Among them are Grant, Kresge, Kroger, Penney, Sears Roebuck, Woolworth, and Carson Pirie Scott. Many small retailers also participate. All in all, the distributive education program is important for both high school and community college students.

A RETAILING CAREER—LOW STATUS OR NOT?

Traditionally, retailing has been characterized as a low-status occupation. This was true as long ago as ancient Greece. A colorful description of this fact is the following:[18]

> Historically, retailing has been a low-status field of endeavor. In Ancient Greece a sharp distinction was made between wholesaling and retailing. Owners of wholesale businesses (emporia) ranked high in the social structure. They frequently were suppliers of capital, owners of ships, and importers of foreign goods. On the other hand, there was a marked lack of esteem attached to retailing. The term "kapelos,"

[17]From a program memorandum prepared by the Department of Health, Education and Welfare, Office of Education, Bureau of Adult, Vocational and Technical Education, August 13, 1971, p. 10.

[18]Douglas J. Dalrymple and Donald L. Thompson, *Retailing: An Economic View* (New York: The Free Press, 1969), p. 156.

which normally referred to a retailer, could also mean "petty," "tradesman," "huckster," "tavern keeper," "cheat," "rogue," "knave." So despised was retail trade by the Athenians that the staffing of retail stores was relegated largely to slaves.

Even today, a person's occupation is a clue to social class. James Engel states that the first question asked of a stranger relates to the individual's occupation.[19] Social scientists agree that a person's occupation is the best single indicator of social status. Furthermore, almost all individuals are able to rate various job titles in terms of prestige. Rating lists purport to measure the prestige ratings of various occupations in the United States. From these lists one can compare the prestige of retail jobs with other occupations. One such list shows that a United States Supreme Court justice ranked first in a list of 90 rankings.[20] For comparative purposes, a physician is second, a college professor is in eighth position, and a manager of a small store tied for 54th and 55th place. A retail clerk is ranked 70th, a restaurant waiter ties for 80th and 81st place. A soda fountain clerk ranked 86th. A shoe shiner is ranked 90th—last place.

However, these rankings of occupations do not indicate the prestige or lack of prestige in retailing. This is because one generally does not respond to a question concerning occupation by answering "retail employee." For example, a senior accountant for Sears, Montgomery Ward, or another retailer would probably respond to a question about occupation by answering "accountant." This position is tied for 25th place on the prestige list, considerably higher than the ranking of a retail clerk. Suppose an individual is employed in the legal department of a large food chain. He would list his occupation as attorney, 11th on the list. The point is simply that one does not automatically lose status by being employed in some capacity in the retailing industry. Furthermore, this particular ranking does not include many retail positions, such as buyer for a large department store, merchandising manager of a chain of variety stores, or simply store manager. Clerking is still rated as low status, but there are many managerial positions in retailing, some of which have high rankings with the general public.

Public Attitude

The attitude of the general public to a retail salesperson depends to a large extent on the social class of the individual who is making the assessment. Let us assume a class structure consisting of three groups—high, middle, and low. A member of the low social class might look up to the status of retail salesperson, while a member of the high social class would likely look down on the job. In short, the attitude of the public toward any specific retail job is affected by the social status of the individuals making the assessment.

Salespeople offer cues as to whether or not a retail store caters to a particular social class. The late Pierre Martineau points out:[21]

[19]James E. Engle, David T. Kollat, and Roger D. Blackwell, *Consumer Behavior*, 3rd ed. (New York: Holt, Rinehart and Winston, Inc., 1973), p. 116.

[20]Ibid., pp. 117–18.

[21]Pierre Martineau, *Motivation in Advertising* (New York: McGraw-Hill Book Co., 1957), p. 165.

> Regardless of her ability to pay, each individual wants to feel that she will be "comfortable." If the store is too high style, the blue collar worker's wife's sixth sense tells her that she will be subtly humiliated by the clerks and other customers because she is out of her depth classwise.

We can say that a retail employee's social status is a function of many factors other than his or her connection with the retailing industry. The important fact is for the individual concerned to be happy with his or her social role, whatever it may be. Unlike in ancient Greece, retailers are not automatically despised or distrusted, although it would be unreal to deny their social standing. Salespeople are, of course, not the whole of retailing. The industry is so large and diverse that it embraces individuals at every social level.

Working Conditions

It is sometimes said that the retailing industry is characterized by high turnover, unusual work hours, and a large portion of female employees, part-timers, and inexperienced workers. A more important consideration should be tenure and opportunity, and whether the job is personally challenging to the individual. Management's responsibility is to portray jobs accurately to prospective employees. Those seeking part-time jobs should understand that retailing offers them this opportunity to work. Inexperienced workers should understand that they can be employed some place in retailing without experience. And women should understand that discrimination because of sex is not only illegal but historically has probably been less severe in retailing than in other industries.

Perhaps every job has some aspects that are considered undesirable. Some executives travel extensively and are away from their homes overnight or a week or more at a time. Manufacturing employees work nights, split shifts, and perhaps on weekends and holidays. Retail clerks work nights, Saturdays, and some Sundays. In all these cases, the important factor should not be the stress on the hours worked or on the days, but whether the employee has the opportunity to grow and develop according to his or her talents and capacities.

Monetary Rewards

Everyone presumably wishes to be rewarded for work with an excellent salary. Retailing employees are no different. The Department of Labor statistics report the average weekly wage of a worker in the retail trade was $121.55 weekly as of January 1975. For the same period, a construction worker earned $252.40, a miner $235.90, and a transportation worker $225.94.[22] This indicates that retailing employees are being paid substantially less than workers in other industries. This is true for the salespeople. However, when one considers managerial salaries, the disparity in wage levels is largely eliminated. For example, buyers earn $10,000 to $20,000 annually; store managers $9,000 to $35,000; and division heads $50,000 and over.[23]

[22]*Employment and Earnings*, p. 89.

[23]"Retail Fact Sheet," p. 1.

Some of the largest salaries are paid to retailing executives. For example Sears reported in 1974 the following salaries for its executives: chairman of the board, $345,000; president, $245,833; senior vice-president for merchandising, $235,000; vice-president of Midwestern territory, $170,000. Salary ceilings for retail's top executives are practically unlimited.[24]

Progressive Grocer estimates that a typical chain supermarket manager earns $19,000. When one considers there are approximately 40,600 supermarkets throughout the United States, each with a manager, one can see that there are opportunities in chain food retailing to earn good salaries. Moreover in 1972, independent supermarket owner-managers averaged $34,400 in salary and net profit with sales of $1 million annually and earned on the average $59,500 if sales were $2 million or more annually.[25]

Security, Stability, and Mobility

Full-time workers are practically guaranteed continuous employment within the retailing industry. Inasmuch as retail sales are relatively stable regardless of business conditions, retail employment is subject to a minimum of cyclical layoffs, as employment figures for 1975 demonstrate.[26] Other industries, notably construction, are subject to considerable cyclical and seasonal unemployment. For example, during those periods when mortgage funds dry up and the construction of new buildings is curtailed, many construction workers are laid off, as was true in 1974 and 1975. The layoffs may persist for a number of days, weeks, or even months. Erratic employment practices are also present in the construction industry because of the influence of climate and weather. Retailing employees can expect a more stable job market than is true in many other industries.

Furthermore, a retailing employee has mobility and need not limit employment to one store. The experience gained in one retailing job is useful if one must change retail employers. The assurance of mobility is an advantage for a career in retailing.

Personality Traits

People differ from one another in a number of ways, including personality, temperament, attitude, and ambition. Consequently it is difficult to assess the desirable personality traits for those seeking careers in retailing. Harriet Wilinsky believes the following are highly desirable.[27]

1. A liking for things such as pretty clothes.
2. A liking for people (extroverted).
3. A positive feeling for change whether it is a change of scenery or activity.

[24]From "Notice of Annual Meeting of Shareholders," Sears, Roebuck and Company, April 8, 1974, p. 3.

[25]"40th Annual Report of the Grocery Industry," *Progressive Grocer* (April 1973), p. 154.

[26]In January 1974 manufacturing employed 20,355,000 workers and one year later employment dropped to 13,200,000 people. On the other hand retailing employed 12,473,000 in January 1974 and employed 12,400,000 in January 1975.

[27]Wilinsky, *Careers*, pp. 22–23.

4. Being inquisitive.
5. Being an energetic, active person.
6. Enjoy making decisions.
7. Prepared to work hard.
8. Ready to accept risk.
9. Yearn to accomplish something.
10. Expect to earn a good salary.

There is no guarantee that a person with all ten of the above stated traits will be a success in retailing. It is a distinct possibility, however, that such a person would enjoy a retailing career, and consequently should seriously consider this option. It should be added that anyone who possesses all or most of these traits might be successful in a number of different vocations.

Personal Development

People who have the talents, the personality traits, and the education will find that a retailing career offers an employee the chance to advance professionally to the full extent of his or her capabilities. Retailers cannot make people grow and develop, but they can provide the environment to make such growth possible. Furthermore, management can provide the intelligent leadership to aid each individual in his or her personal development.

FRANCHISING

One of the better career opportunities in retailing is obtaining a franchise and becoming an independent businessperson. Ray Kroc, chairman of McDonald's Corporation, has said: "Franchising has become the updated version of the American dream."[28] Kroc believes that franchising is the vehicle through which an independent businessman can succeed in a world of corporate chains. Yet, there is some doubt as to the degree of independence a businessperson may exhibit as the owner of a franchised outlet. Most customers probably cannot identify a particular business outlet as a franchised operation.

Definition

It is impossible to define franchising in simple terms. However, the following definition is both comprehensive and accurate.[29]

> Franchising is a system for the selective distribution of goods and/or services under a broad name through outlets owned by independent businessmen called "franchisees"; although the franchisor supplies the franchise with know-how and brand

[28]Charles G. Burck, "Franchising's Troubled Dream World," *Fortune*, 81, no. 3 (March 1970), p. 117.

[29]Robert M. Rosenberg and Madelon Redell, *Profits from Franchising* (New York: McGraw-Hill Book Co., 1969), p. 41.

identification on a continuing basis, the franchisee enjoys the right to profit and and runs the risk of loss. The franchisor controls the distribution of his goods and/or services through a contract which regulates the activities of franchisee, in order to achieve standardization.

Although comprehensive and accurate, this definition is somewhat cumbersome. The following elements appear most significant: (1) a contractual agreement, (2) a branded product or service that is highly standardized, (3) operated by an independent businessman for the purpose of making a profit, and (4) controlled by the franchisor through standardized operating procedures.

Franchising History

Many people believe franchising to be of recent origin, yet this is not so. One of the earliest pioneers was Louis K. Liggett, who permitted the franchising of the Rexall name for drugstores as early as 1902. Two years before that, Coca-Cola supplied its syrup to franchised bottlers. (See Figure 19.2.) Other early pioneers were the automobile and gasoline industries. Auto manufacturers in the early days simply lacked the capital to set up their own retail outlets; therefore they turned to

FIGURE 19.2
The first home of the Atlanta Coca-Cola Bottling Company, an early pioneer in franchising

Source: The Coca-Cola Company, Atlanta, Georgia.

franchising. (See Figure 19.3.) Moreover the auto manufacturers lacked the trained personnel to operate the retail outlets even if they had the capital. In 1973 the auto industry sold approximately 9.6 million cars through franchised dealers, and they accounted for sales of $50 billion.[30]

Gasoline companies entered the franchising field in a big way in 1930. Rosenberg comments on this bit of history as follows:[31]

> The stuff that makes the car go, namely gas, went into franchising sometime later—about 1930, to be precise. Up until then the oil companies had been operating their own stations. A few of them began to license dealers and in the period from 1930 to 1935, the practice spread until it became for all intents and purposes the sole method employed to distribute gasoline.

In the 1920s and 1930s the retailing industry saw the emergence of such early enthusiasts for the franchise system as Butler Brothers, with their Ben Franklin

FIGURE 19.3
An early Ford dealership, circa 1903–4

Source: The Ford Archives, Henry Ford Museum, Dearborn, Michigan.

[30] *1975 The U.S.Fact Book, The American Almanac, and The Statistical Abstract of the U.S.* (New York: Grosset & Dunlap, 1975), pp. 555, 560.

[31] Rosenberg and Redell, *Profits from Franchising*, p. 12.

FIGURE 19.4
Franchising is important in the motel industry

Source: Holiday Inns, Inc., Memphis, Tennessee.

variety stores, the Rexall Drug outlets, Independent Grocers Alliance (IGA), the Super Value stores, Western Auto Supply Company, and Hertz Corporation; franchising is especially important in the motel industry (see Figure 19.4).

Hertz, as can be seen in Figure 19.5, has always been involved in franchising. On this point, Rosenberg says:[32]

> Another maverick, of course, is the Hertz Corporation, which has been owned or affiliated at various times in its long but always successful history with General Motors, the Omnibus Corporation, and just lately, none other than the Radio Corporation of America. Despite its somewhat bewildering pattern of corporate structure, Hertz has not changed in one respect. It began as a franchise and still is one. It's pretty impossible these days to buy a Hertz franchise in the U.S.: they're just about sold out.

In the 1950s franchising really exploded. An article in *Fortune* magazine stated that of all the franchised outlets currently in operation, 90 percent have been started since 1954.[33] According to a recent U.S. Dept. of Commerce booklet, franchise sales of goods and services are expected to reach a total of $176.9 billion in 1975,

[32]Ibid., p. 12.
[33]Burck, "Franchising's Troubled Dream World," p. 118.

FIGURE 19.5
Hertz began renting cars in Miami as early as 1925

Source: The Hertz Corporation, New York, New York.

an increase of 9.3 percent over the 1973 reported sales of $161.9 billion. In 1975 retail franchising is expected to account for 27 percent of all U.S. retail sales, about one-fourth of all sales receipts made in eating places, and to employ 3.3 million people.[34] (See Figure 19.6.) Table 19.2 lists the kinds of franchised businesses currently operating in the United States and their numbers; Table 19.3 shows their sales volume in 1973–75; and Table 19.4 depicts the division of establishments between company ownership and franchise ownership.

Perhaps the most visible of the franchised outlets is found in the food industry, especially those dealing with fast foods. During a short drive down any major highway close to a major population area, one can see franchised dealers serving hot dogs, hamburgers, fried chicken, fish and chips, tacos, and much more (see Figure 19.7). McDonald's has practically become a household word (see Table 19.5), and Colonel Sanders has become symbolic of fried chicken that is "finger lickin' good."

Fried chicken outlets have become so numerous that Charles Burck suggests that it may be difficult to find enough hungry customers to go around. He says:[35]

[34]*Franchising in the Economy, 1973–75*, U.S. Dept. of Commerce, Domestic and International Business Administration/Bureau of Domestic Commerce, pp. 1–3.

[35]Burck, "Franchising's Troubled Dream World," p. 118.

TABLE 19.2
Franchising in the Economy, 1975*

Kinds of Franchised Business	Establishments (Number)			Sales (000)			Percent Changes 1974–1975		Percent Changes 1973–1975	
	Total	Company-owned	Franchisee-owned	Total	Company-owned	Franchisee-owned	Estab.	Sales	Estab.	Sales
Total—All Franchising	460,720	81,586	379,134	176,949,374	28,776,821	148,172,553	3.8	7.3	1.6	9.3
Automobile and truck dealers1/	32,692	301	32,391	85,282,000	5,818,000	79,464,000	−0.3	5.2	−0.5	−4.2
Automotive products and services2/	49,108	5,372	43,736	5,444,350	2,067,569	3,376,781	6.4	7.9	13.2	19.4
Business aids and services	21,332	4,554	16,778	1,595,759	385,290	1,210,469	14.5	21.5	25.9	35.3
Accounting, credit, collection agencies, and general business systems	2,586	86	2,500	125,639	15,168	110,471	16.6	8.8	28.5	17.1
Employment services	3,440	693	2,747	622,162	244,887	377,275	16.0	15.5	23.9	25.9
Printing and copying services	1,574	89	1,485	111,842	6,227	105,615	24.6	37.1	66.9	100.5
Tax preparation services	7,810	3,579	4,231	168,618	90,061	78,557	6.8	15.0	13.7	43.7
Miscellaneous business services	5,922	107	5,815	567,498	28,947	538,551	21.5	31.8	36.1	40.2
Construction, home improvements, maintenance, and cleaning services	14,257	233	14,024	880,436	77,854	802,582	14.6	13.6	24.9	20.6
Convenience stores	14,376	8,644	5,732	3,775,948	2,145,210	1,630,738	12.4	12.4	25.0	24.2
Educational products and services	1,362	281	1,081	188,821	31,328	157,493	13.5	10.0	14.4	5.5
Fast food restaurants (all types)	44,724	11,121	33,603	11,488,224	3,729,303	7,758,921	11.6	17.8	23.1	34.6
Gasoline service stations1/	193,000	38,600	154,400	43,023,000	8,604,000	34,419,000	−1.6	5.0	−10.6	25.0
Hotels and motels	6,463	1,485	4,978	4,603,971	1,505,767	3,098,204	12.7	11.0	28.3	23.3
Campgrounds	1,474	51	1,423	96,376	10,102	86,274	17.2	29.7	36.2	55.3
Laundry and drycleaning services	3,932	117	3,815	254,374	11,103	243,271	5.0	4.9	8.5	8.1
Recreation, entertainment and travel	3,155	82	3,073	139,505	6,420	133,085	15.4	29.8	7.2	19.8
Rental services (auto-truck)	7,321	1,932	5,389	1,407,011	964,938	442,073	5.4	10.6	−8.1	21.2
Rental services (equipment)	1,798	154	1,644	164,877	51,758	113,119	14.2	13.5	22.6	23.3
Retailing (non-food)	46,902	7,290	39,612	9,764,627	2,748,104	7,016,523	4.7	12.0	3.6	25.7
Retailing (food other than convenience stores)	13,511	1,096	12,415	1,222,644	293,735	928,909	13.9	17.0	19.1	30.9
Soft drink bottlers1/ 3/	2,570	100	2,470	7,211,000	267,000	6,944,000	−1.2	12.5	−4.1	26.6
Miscellaneous	2,743	173	2,570	406,451	59,340	347,111	8.6	8.9	2.0	11.0

*1975 data estimated by respondents.
1/Estimated by BDC based on Bureau of the Census and trade association data. 2/Includes some establishments with significant sales of non-automotive products such as household appliances, garden supplies, etc. 3/Includes soft drinks, fruit drinks, and ades; syrups, flavoring agents, and bases. Data do not include figures for independent private label and contract-filler bottling companies which accounted for 22 percent in 1973, 22 percent in 1974, and 24 percent in 1975 of the value of shipments of the total industry.
Source: *Franchising in the Economy, 1973–75*, U.S. Department of Commerce, p. 21.

FIGURE 19.6

Franchising is predicted to encompass 27 percent of retail sales in 1975

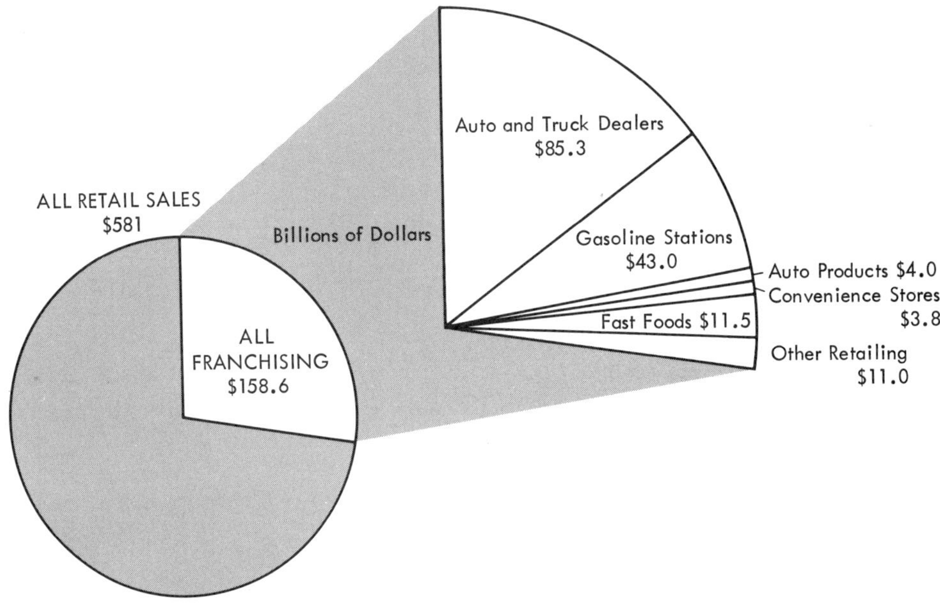

Source: *Franchising in the Economy, 1973–75*, U.S. Dept. of Commerce.

> If all the fried chicken stores projected for the next three years survive (Kentucky Fried Chicken says it will have 4,000) it seems improbable all the hamburger stands or fish and chip stores—to say nothing of pizza, roast beef, and manifold varied menu restaurants—will have enough hungry customers to go around.

The franchised fast food outlets are truly ubiquitous, and it is difficult to believe their sales constitute only two percent of all franchised sales. Burck is fearful for the future of many of these fast food franchises because of the intense competition. In spite of this, some of the most sophisticated American companies are in the franchised food business. For example, General Foods franchises Burger Chef; Pillsbury has Burger King; and United Fruit Company has A & W Root Beer.

Trend Toward Company-owned Units

Some units in chains such as McDonald's or Colonel Sanders are owned by the company itself. In fact, there are good reasons for companies to operate their own units, one of which is that the company-operated and -owned units are more profitable. An article in the *Journal of Retailing* states that Kentucky Fried Chicken earns more profit from 300 company-owned stores than they do from 2,100 franchised units. The article also states that two-thirds of McDonald's profits come from the units it owns. Other factors favoring company-operated units are greater

FIGURE 19.7
Food franchisors handle many different types of products

Source: Dunkin' Donuts of America, Inc., Schiller Park, Illinois.

managerial control, fewer legal problems, and avoidance of restrictive legislation. Table 19.6 shows a slight trend by Fast Food chains to rely more on their own units.[36] However the number of franchised units predominates.

Franchises Everywhere. To point out how common franchised outlets are, let us visit the Martin family in suburban Illinois.

John Martin is the proprietor of *Village Buick.* He is middle-aged, and the father of two teen-aged children in high school. On the morning in question he left for work unusually early and had no time for breakfast, so he stopped at *Mr. Donut* for coffee and rolls.

After the children had left for school, Irene Martin was enjoying her second cup of coffee, and the doorbell rang. It was the *Culligan* man delivering salt for her soft water unit.

After breakfast, Mrs. Martin gathered up her husband's suits and took them to the cleaners, *One-Hour Martinizing.* On her way home, she stopped at a *Shell* service station to fill the gasoline tank, for she had promised to drive her neighbors to the airport that afternoon. On the way out to the airport, the conversation turned to the number of outlets serving snacks and fast foods that have opened in the past five years, Mrs. Martin counted thirteen: *A & W Root Beer, Burger Chef, McDonald's, Burger King, Chicken Unlimited, Kentucky Fried Chicken, Dunkin' Donuts,*

[36]Shelby D. Hunt, "The Trend Toward Company-operated Units in Franchise Chains," *Journal of Retailing*, 49, no. 2 (Summer 1973), pp. 3–12.

TABLE 19.3
Sales ($000), 1973–1975

	1973			1974*			1975*		
Kinds of Franchised Business	*Total*	*Company-owned*	*Franchisee-owned*	*Total*	*Company-owned*	*Franchisee-owned*	*Total*	*Company-owned*	*Franchisee-owned*
Total—All Franchising	161,903,183	24,354,281	137,548,902	164,971,958	26,395,300	138,576,658	176,949,374	28,776,821	148,172,553
Automobile and truck dealers 1/	89,040,000	6,157,000	82,883,000	81,041,000	5,541,000	75,500,000	85,282,000	5,818,000	79,464,000
Automotive products and services 2/	4,559,120	1,794,216	2,764,904	5,045,024	1,953,442	3,091,582	5,444,350	2,067,569	3,376,781
Business aids and services	1,179,361	324,576	854,785	1,313,096	342,752	970,344	1,595,759	385,290	1,210,469
Accounting, credit, collection agencies, and general business services	107,257	12,156	95,101	115,521	13,399	102,122	125,639	15,168	110,471
Employment services	494,314	213,357	280,957	538,877	218,858	320,019	622,162	244,887	377,275
Printing and copying services	55,793	4,281	51,512	81,600	5,125	76,475	111,842	6,227	105,615
Tax preparation services	117,333	67,830	49,503	146,608	78,398	68,210	168,618	90,061	78,557
Miscellaneous business services	404,664	26,952	377,712	430,490	26,972	403,518	567,498	28,947	538,551
Construction, home improvement, maintenance, and cleaning services	730,302	66,860	663,442	775,038	67,364	707,674	880,436	77,854	802,582
Convenience stores	3,039,509	1,751,580	1,287,929	3,358,173	1,926,014	1,432,159	3,775,948	2,145,210	1,630,738
Educational products and services	178,953	28,222	150,731	171,705	25,977	145,728	188,821	31,328	157,493

Kinds of Franchised Business	1973			1974*			1975*		
	Total	*Company-owned*	*Franchisee-owned*	*Total*	*Company-owned*	*Franchisee-owned*	*Total*	*Company-owned*	*Franchisee-owned*
Fast food retaurants (all types)	8,534,094	2,604,851	5,929,243	9,756,383	3,076,538	6,679,845	11,488,224	3,729,303	7,758,921
Gasoline service stations [1/]	34.432,000	6,886,000	27,546,000	40,974,000	8,194,000	32,780,000	43,023,000	8,604,000	34,419,000
Hotels and motels	3,733,927	1,311,301	2,422,626	4,146,906	1,411,218	2,735,688	4,603,971	1,505,767	3,098,204
Campgrounds	62,061	5,241	56,820	74,297	7,055	67,242	96,376	10,102	86,274
Laundry and dry-cleaning services	235,306	10,514	224,792	242,473	9,535	232,938	254,374	11,103	243,271
Recreation, entertainment, and travel	116,444	9,929	106,515	107,478	5,447	102,031	139,505	6,420	133,085
Rental services (auto-truck)	1,161,178	827,372	333,806	1,271,882	890,952	380,930	1,407,011	964,938	442,073
Rental services (equipment)	133,693	41,011	92,682	145,328	46,722	98,606	164,877	51,758	113,119
Retailing (non-food)	7,768,813	2,086,206	5,682,607	8,721,080	2,385,873	6,335,207	9,764,627	2,748,104	7,016,523
Retailing (food other than convenience stores)	934,104	190,935	743,169	1,044,744	223,725	821,019	1,222,644	293,735	928,909
Soft drink bottlers [1/] [3/]	5,698,000	211,000	5,487,000	6,410,000	237,000	6,173,000	7,211,000	267,000	6,944,000
Miscellaneous	366,318	47,467	318,851	373,351	50,686	322,665	406,451	59,340	347,111

*1974 and 1975 data estimated by respondents.

[1/]Estimated by BDC based on Bureau of the Census and trade association data. [2/]Includes some establishments with significant sales of non-automotive products such as household appliances, garden supplies, etc. [3/]Includes soft drinks, fruit drinks, and ades; syrups, flavoring agents, and bases. Data do not include figures for independent private label and contract-filler bottling companies which accounted for 22 percent in 1973, 22 percent in 1974, and 24 percent in 1975 of the value of shipments of the total industry.

Source: *Franchising in the Economy, 1973–75*, U.S. Department of Commerce, p. 22.

TABLE 19.4

Number of Establishments, 1973–75

Kinds of Franchised Business	1973 Total	1973 Company-owned	1973 Franchisee-owned	1974* Total	1974* Company-owned	1974* Franchisee-owned	1975* Total	1975* Company-owned	1975* Franchisee-owned
Total—All Franchising	453,632	78,850	374,782	443,994	78,206	365,788	460,720	81,586	379,134
Automobile and truck dealers 1/	32,855	301	32,554	32,797	301	32,496	32,692	301	32,391
Automotive products and services	43,377	4,941	38,436	46,148	5,120	41,028	49,108	5,372	43,736
Business aids and services	16,950	4,011	12,939	18,630	4,270	14,360	21,332	4,554	16,778
Accounting, credit, collection agencies, and general business systems	2,013	67	1,946	2,218	77	2,141	2,586	86	2,500
Employment services	2,776	641	2,135	2,965	633	2,332	3,440	693	2,747
Printing and copying services	943	67	876	1,263	77	1,186	1,574	89	1,485
Tax preparation services	6,866	3,142	3,724	7,310	3,391	3,919	7,810	3,579	4,231
Miscellaneous business services	4,352	94	4,258	4,874	92	4,782	5,922	107	5,815
Construction, home improvement, maintenance, and cleaning service	11,411	232	11,179	12,439	210	12,229	14,257	233	14,024
Convenience stores	11,501	7,161	4,340	12,793	7,808	4,985	14,376	8,644	5,732
Educational products and services	1,191	227	964	1,200	220	980	1,362	281	1,081
Fast food restaurants (all types)	36,340	8,316	28,024	40,084	9,643	30,441	44,724	11,121	33,603
Gasoline service stations 1/	215,880	43,176	172,704	196,130	39,226	156,904	193,000	38,600	154,400
Hotels and motels	5,038	1,198	3,840	5,737	1,331	4,406	6,463	1,485	4,978
Campgrounds	1,082	38	1,044	1,258	38	1,220	1,474	51	1,423
Laundry and drycleaning services	3,623	141	3,482	3,744	109	3,635	3,932	117	3,815
Recreation, entertainment, and travel	2,944	65	2,879	2,735	68	2,667	3,155	82	3,073
Rental services (auto-truck)	7,963	1,816	6,147	6,949	1,855	5,094	7,321	1,932	5,389
Rental services (equipment)	1,466	138	1,328	1,574	145	1,429	1,798	154	1,644
Retailing (non-food)	45,294	5,881	39,413	44,785	6,593	38,192	46,902	7,290	39,612
Retailing (food other than convenience stores)	11,347	961	10,386	11,865	1,016	10,849	13,511	1,096	12,415
Soft drink bottlers 1/ 3/	2,680	100	2,580	2,600	100	2,500	2,570	100	2,470
Miscellaneous	2,690	147	2,543	2,526	153	2,373	2,743	173	2,570

*1974 and 1975 data estimated by respondents.

1/Estimated by BDC based on Bureau of the Census and trade association data. 2/Includes some establishments with significant sales of non-automotive products such as household appliances, garden supplies, etc. 3/Includes soft drinks, fruit drinks, and ades; syrups, flavoring agents, and bases. Data do not include figures for independent private label and contract-filler bottling companies which accounted for 22 percent in 1973, 22 percent in 1974, and 24 percent in 1975 of the value of shipments of the total industry.

Source: *Franchising in the Economy, 1973–75*, U.S. Department of Commerce, p. 23.

TABLE 19.5
Sales of McDonald's Corporation

Year	Stores	Sales
1974	3,232	$1.940 billion
1973	2,717	1.507 billion
1972	2,272	1.032 billion
1971	1,904	784 million
1970	1,592	587 million
1969	1,298	450 million

Source: *Chicago Tribune* (February 24, 1975).

Shakey's Pizza, International House of Pancakes, Arby's Roast Beef, H. Salt's, Lum's, and *Mr. Steak.*

Mrs. Martin's neighbors were flying to California for a vacation. They had arranged their trip with *Vacations International, Inc.*, a travel agency. They expected to stay at a *Howard Johnson Motor Lodge*, a *Sheraton Inn*, and a *Ramada Inn.* They also planned to rent a car from *Hertz* or *Avis* while in California.

On the way home from the airport, Mrs. Martin had a few errands to run. She needed milk so she stopped at the *Convenient Food Store.* She also had to stop at *General Pool* to obtain chlorine for their swimming pool. Her last stop was *Coloramic Tile Company* to chat with the assistant manager, who was dating her sister.

After she arrived home, Mrs. Martin saw a *Mayflower* van across the street. She surmised that the new neighbors were in the process of moving in. Then the phone rang; it was *Puppy Palace* calling about the collie she was buying for her son's thirteenth birthday.

Later that night, Mrs. Martin was preparing a list of things she had to do the next day. On her list were the following: meet with *Weight Watchers, Inc.*, call *Service Master* to wax her floors, pick up cosmetics at *Merle Norman*, call *Kelly*

TABLE 19.6
Fast Food Units Classified by Ownership

Type	Number of Outlets 1960	1968	1970	1971
Franchised unit	16,200	31,100	38,100	41,000
Company-owned	200	2,200	4,000	5,200
Total	16,400	33,300	42,100	46,200
Percentage of Company-owned units to total	1.2	6.6	9.5	11.3

Source: *Journal of Retailing*, 49, no. 2 (Summer 1973), p. 5.

Girl for a temporary secretarial replacement for her husband's business, arrange to pick up a champagne fountain at *A to Z Rentals*, and pick up a bicycle tire from her *Schwinn* dealer. That ended Mrs. Martin's day.

Typical Franchise Agreements

Perhaps there is no such thing as a typical franchise contract. However, all franchises do have some common points. The purchaser of a franchise probably pays an initial fee, and then a continuing royalty in the form of a monthly percentage of the gross sales. In exchange, the franchisee obtains the right to sell a product or service. The franchisor usually provides initial training in the operation of the business, and frequently offers continuing advice throughout the life of the business. Various degrees of control are exercised by the franchisor in order to assure the success of the operation.

Capital Requirements. In almost every case, the purchaser of a franchise must invest a certain amount of personal money in the business. The amount can vary from a few thousand dollars to many thousands. For example, it takes almost $180,-000 to obtain a typical McDonald's franchise. McDonald's requires a down payment of $85,000 to $100,000 cash. This down payment covers the following:

License fee	$10,000
Site development fee	2,500
Security deposit	15,000
Down payment on equipment	28,000
Down payment on signs	4,000
Landscaping and opening costs	30,000–45,000
	$89,500 to $104,500 (cash)

The balance of $81,000 owed to McDonald's is financed through private sources, since McDonald's does not lend money or guarantee a loan. McDonald's provides the site and builds the outlet, complete with parking lot. The operator of the franchise pays rent on a 20-year lease.

Another example is Kentucky Fried Chicken.[37] An individual who purchases such a franchise needs $22,600 in cash. This includes a franchisee fee of $3,000. However, this investment does not pay for everything. The owner of the outlet must provide the site and building, although the store must be built according to Kentucky's Fried's specifications.

Royalty on Income Guarantee. The heart of the franchise agreement is the income guaranteed to the franchiser. Both parties to the franchise agreement hope the business will be successful. The franchisee must operate the business profitably to obtain an income. However, the franchisor makes his income in a variety of

[37]Robert Metz, *Franchising: How to Select a Business of Your Own* (New York Hawthorne Books, Inc., 1968).

ways. To start, there is usually a franchise fee included in the cash down payment. A continuing royalty fee is sometimes required. For example, McDonald's requires a 3.0 percent royalty on gross sales. A Kentucky Fried Chicken franchisee pays 5 percent of gross sales as royalty. Another example of income guarantee is the one used by Sheraton Inns, Inc. They charge an initial franchise fee ranging from $7,500 to $12,500. For an inn with 125 guest rooms, the initial fee is $7,500. For each room in excess of 125, the innkeeper pays $100 up to a maximum of $12,500.

The royalty payment is not always paid cheerfully, because the franchise holder experiences some pain when seeing some of the profits going to someone else. Rosenberg comments on this point as follows:[38]

> Royalties have one negative aspect—a psychological one. It is only human nature for a man to feel some pain when he sees part of the fruit of his labor go to someone else. Paradoxically, this pain may become more intense as the franchise operation gets more successful. The franchisee may be making many thousands of dollars, but so is the franchisor. It may hurt.
>
> The franchisee should remember the psychosomatic character of his pain. No matter what method of return is used, as the franchisee's income increases, the franchisor's income will also increase. Isn't that precisely the point of the whole system?

Often the franchisor makes a profit on the supplies sold to the operator. For example, a gasoline station franchise holder receives a royalty of 1½¢ to 2½¢ per gallon of gasoline sold. Metz points out that profit on the sale of supplies is a major source of income for many franchise companies.[39] This is true of such fields as ice cream, carpet cleaning, glass tinting, and certain fast foods.

Control

Those who choose a career as a franchisee are "their own bosses," but there are limits to their freedom. Franchisor control over franchisee is maintained in five important ways: (1) through real estate ownership, (2) through cancellation provisions, (3) through restrictions on territory, (4) by exclusive handling, and (5) through financial controls.

The franchisor who owns the facilities and leases them to the operator is in a position of maximum control. Dalrymple and Thompson say:[40]

> Maximum control of franchises is obtained by owning the facilities and leasing them to operators, but this requires a great deal of capital. Approximately the same degree of control may be obtained by the use of third party leases where the supplier controls the master lease and then subleases to the retail operator. This is an attractive arrangement when the outlets are in good locations, because if the operator is lost, the operation reverts to the franchisor.

Examples of this type of control are the major oil companies who sometimes

[38]Rosenberg and Redell, *Profits from Franchising*, p. 105.

[39]Metz, *Franchising*, p. 31.

[40]Dalrymple and Thompson, *Retailing*, p. 84.

select the site and build the station. As mentioned, McDonald's also owns the site and building.

A second method of control is through the cancellation provisions which are part of the contractual agreement. Gasoline companies frequently grant the operators of stations only a one-year franchise. In the event the operator does not meet the standards expected, the franchise agreement is not renewed. Whenever a franchisee is subject to a short-term franchise agreement, he or she has a very strong incentive to operate the business in the manner suggested by the franchising company. Although the franchising companies like cancellation provisions, this is not true of the franchisees. They believe these provisions limit their independence as owners. Occasionally this results in legal action. Franchisors generally point to cancellation clauses in their contracts and the right to protect the trademarks and trade names that they use in commerce. The Lanham Act permits the owner of a mark or name to register it in order to indicate ownership. The owner, in turn, can stipulate the circumstances under which others may use such industrial property. During the gasoline shortage of 1973–74, many franchised service stations were terminated by their suppliers even though the stations claimed they had performed loyally for many years. Suits were brought against Mobil, British Petroleum, Shell, Texaco, and several other suppliers for either terminating their franchisees for insufficient reason or for favoring their own wholly owned outlets during the period of shortage. One of the greatest dangers that those beginning careers in franchised businesses must face is that the franchisor may abruptly terminate the relationship.

A third method of control is through restrictions on the franchisee's selling territory. In recent years it has become almost impossible for a supplier to limit the area within which a merchant reseller can operate. In a celebrated case involving the Schwinn Bicycle Company, the Supreme Court ruled against territorial restrictions when title to the merchandise passed to a middleman, but permitted it to continue when the middleman was acting as an agent.[41] And in another important case, an agreement among large retail grocers not to enter each other's territory was declared illegal. The food retailers, whose aggregated sales made them the fourth largest retailing group in the United States, cooperatively owned Topco Associates, a large buying organization whose main asset was ownership of a number of different trademarks and trade names. Since each member-retailer agreed not to sell any Topco brand in another member-retailer's operating area without permission, the Court held that competition was lessened in a line of commerce. Such Court decisions as the Schwinn or Topco case have discouraged suppliers from imposing strict limits on their reseller's trading territories. However, this has not prevented them from defining areas in which their middlemen should direct most of their marketing attention; such territories sometimes are called "areas of prime responsibility." Most of the protection that suppliers have accorded retailers consists of spacing them far enough apart so that consumer lethargy will minimize customer raiding. Since consumers are mobile, there are few ways to assure that buyers will not visit several retailers selling the same brand in order to compare values. Where

[41]*U.S.* v. *Arnold Schwinn and Company*, 388 U.S. 365 (1967).

there is strong channel discipline—well-known brands of men's suits are a good example—the customer is likely to shop at the most convenient outlet for a particular brand.

A fourth type of control is exclusive handling. The franchised outlet is not permitted to handle branded products other than those permitted by the franchisor. This type of control has a long history of court battles. Exclusive dealerships are illegal per se, and are not permitted where competition is substantially lessened in a line of commerce. One of the most famous early cases on this point involved the Standard Oil Company of California. Dealers of Standard Oil were not allowed to buy tires, batteries, and accessories from suppliers that were not approved by Standard Oil. The United States Supreme Court held that this agreement substantially reduced competition, and hence was illegal.

The increased freedom of the franchisees is suggested by a more recent case in which Chicken Delight, a fast food franchisor, was declared in violation of the law when it obliged its outlets to purchase cooking and frying equipment, dips, and barbecue and other spice mixes from it. The franchisees argued that similar products could be purchased from other sources at lower prices. Chicken Delight argued that such requirements were not tying contracts that were declared illegal by the country's antitrust laws; it pointed out that when a customer buys a left shoe he must also take the right shoe or when the buyer purchases an automobile he cannot buy the engine without also taking the wheels. And even if it were a tying contract, Chicken Delight argued, such a contract would be legal because (a) it was a legitimate means of protecting the product's quality and thus the company's trademarks, (b) the company was rather new in the industry and thus could hardly be large enough substantially to affect commerce, and (c) the tied arrangement was nothing more than a convenient method for the franchisees to compensate the franchisor for use of the Chicken Delight license. Although all of the arguments may seem persuasive, the Supreme Court held for the franchisees, declared the system illegal, and awarded the franchisees the triple damages they are entitled to under the law. Indeed, the Chicken Delight case is considered a landmark case in that it indicated that franchisees have more freedom from dominant franchisors than had been suspected. The direction that legal cases seem to be going would suggest that those embarking on a career in franchising must increasingly be prepared to make business decisions that are independent of the franchisor.

Professional Requirements

The owner of a franchise need not have a college education to obtain a franchise; however, it certainly helps to assure success. Some owners of franchises are college graduates and others are not. Some are young and inexperienced, and others are of retirement age and quite experienced in business.

There are certain qualifications a successful franchise owner seems to share with other such successful operators. Most have an unusual desire to be their own bosses. This desire seems to ignite the drive to make their businesses financially successful. Initially, most of these owners sacrifice themselves to the business. They work long hours, take few days off, and skip vacations. Their business truly becomes a way of life. Most of the successful franchise operators are also talented in business practices. This talent may or may not be sharpened by experience elsewhere. It is almost a certainty that the franchise owners are "savers," because of the high investment requirements needed to acquire a franchise. A good portion of this investment is personal savings. There is no guarantee that all people of this background will succeed, but perhaps the odds are better.

Earnings

There are a variety of reasons why an individual chooses to go into business —perhaps the pleasure associated with being one's own boss is paramount. However, many owners are convinced they can earn more income for themselves than would be the case if they worked for someone else. The lure of profits is the magic attracting many individuals to the world of franchising.

Actually, the profits any individual franchise owner can expect to earn depend upon such factors as: (1) the nature of the business, (2) the amount of the investment, (3) the location of the outlet, (4) the strength of competition, (5) the types of managerial aids offered by the franchisor, (6) the skills of the franchise owner, and (7) the economic climate of the times.

The operator of a franchise is more likely to succeed because he or she is handling a product and/or service with high consumer identity. Furthermore, the product or service is nationally advertised and promoted. He or she uses business techniques which are proven to be successful. The individual operator is also usually an enterprising individual with a strong desire to succeed.

Government Regulation

There is a movement to subject franchising to federal rules. One reason is the numerous complaints made against the franchising companies by franchise holders. Some of the complaints are:[42]

1. misrepresenation of earnings to prospective franchise buyers.
2. misrepresentation of investment requirements.
3. dislike of franchisor's control over such functions as purchases, prices, and management.
4. objections to cancellation clauses.
5. objections of franchise holders over inability to sell the businesses to whomever they wish.

Some of these complaints are expected to be satisfied by the Federal Trade Commission, which will probably set down guidelines to curb malpractices. Furthermore, there are several bills pending in Congress to force franchisors to disclose all relevant facts to prospective franchisees before a deal is made and to regulate and control competition by franchisors.

[42]"Movement to Subject Franchising to Federal Rules," *Modern Franchising* (December/January 1971), p. 8.

SUMMARY

Opportunities exist for careers in retailing for individuals with diverse backgrounds and experience. As an industry, retailing employs more individuals than any other except manufacturing. Almost one out of every five retailing employees is functioning in an executive role at one level or another. A retailing career is characterized by rapid advancement, emphasis on youth, promotion from within, long tenure, and stability and security. Most employees acquire skills which permit them to move from city to city, if they choose, with good prospects of obtaining employment.

Most retail employers do not discriminate against the young, the inexperienced, the aged, the minority groups, or because of sex. In fact retailers actively recruit its employees from among these people. Some of the largest retailers are inaugurating programs designed specifically to help the disadvantaged.

Schools and businesses are cooperating to offer instruction in distribution and marketing in distributive education programs. This route has helped many individuals to achieve successful careers in retailing. At the same time it aids in improving distributive techniques—aiding both the retailer and the individual.

One of the better career opportunities in retailing is for an individual to invest in a franchise and become his or her own boss. Almost 25 percent of all retail sales are made by franchised outlets. They are important in a variety of trades—notably automobile sales, gasoline service stations, fast food, motels, and rental businesses.

Franchising is successful because it handles a product or service that is nationally known and accepted. The franchising agent controls the franchise through various techniques, which assures the operator the greatest chance for success. Franchise operators are usually individuals with business talents who are motivated to achieve success through personal sacrifice and initiative. Through franchising some individuals make the "American dream" come true.

QUESTIONS FOR DISCUSSION

1. "A policy to promote from within the organization is a good solution to obtaining superior executives." Show whether you agree or disagree and why.
2. What measures do you think a retailer should take to provide the ideal environment so that growth and development of employees can take place?
3. Why do you think the average weekly wages are so low for workers in the retail trade as compared with workers in other industries?
4. Do you believe the retailing industry is doing enough to employ the socioeconomically disadvantaged? If not, what would you suggest?
5. Discuss distributive education. How do you evaluate its significance?
6. Comment on the following: "Retailing jobs are low status, and therefore they attract workers with low skills and aptitudes."

7. What are the major elements in a franchise contract? Who do you think benefits the most, the franchisor or the franchisee?

8. Charles Burck suggests that there are too many franchised food outlets for all to survive. Do you agree?

9. Some franchisors sell supplies to their franchised outlets and make a profit on these supplies. Do you think this is ethical?

10. Discuss the various ways the franchisors control their outlets.

20 A LOOK INTO THE FUTURE

Improved communications systems combined with the computer should make inventory control more efficient. Many stores have linked their cash registers to computers so that management can know instantly the amount and types of goods that have been sold at a particular time. And it is technologically possible for an automatic vending machine operator to bypass a stop if his information system—linked to each machine—tells him that all the machines at that location have ample supplies.

Many retailers advertise over cable television; the customer places an order by telephone for the goods that are shown. But there are no technical reasons why customers cannot someday have consoles in their homes through which they can order goods by typing in the necessary information.

Improved physical distribution systems will surely bring great changes to retailing. A packer in Iowa slaughters, dresses, and packages various meat cuts and ships them directly to eastern retailers. Such a practice substantially reduces the number of butchers in those areas where the unions have not prevented the practice.

Astute retailers are watching very closely the impact of such issues as consumerism and energy consumption on their businesses. Throughout the country food retailers have improved their labeling, hoping that it will help the customer make a more efficient purchase. Oregon retailers must take back soft drink bottles. And just about everywhere, retailers have experimented with less lighting and lowered heat and air conditioning.

It appears as if retailers cannot be as haughty toward consumers as was once possible. Such organizations as the Better Business Bureau, the Major Appliance Consumer Action Panel, the Furniture Industry Consumer Advisory Panel, the Advertising Review Boards in many American cities, and the Federal Trade Commission devote either all or much of their attention to the small band of retailers who would put profits ahead of service to the community. Such organizations usually try to influence retailers through moral suasion, but they often have legal power to wield if persuasion does not work.

Throughout the United States, downtown retailers have increasingly recognized that they must compete not only with the store next door but with stores in other shopping areas. In Zeckendorf Plaza in Denver, Nicollet Mall in Minneapolis, Illinois Center Plaza in Chicago, Rittenhouse Square in Detroit, and many other places, those who make up the central city business system have sponsored fashion shows, boxing matches, art shows, "meet the author" hours, concerts, hobby shows, and just about anything else that will bring in customers or keep them longer. To be successful, future shopping areas may be obliged to perform social and political as well as economic roles.

Retailing is a dynamic industry, subject to many uncertainties. Economic and social patterns forecast CHANGE in the future in capital letters. Retailers who wish to survive and prosper must have their eyes on the future as they adapt to these changes. A good crystal ball would be helpful. However, since none is available, retailers must rely on more prosaic methods of predicting what the future has in store. Fortunately, the future emerges from the present, and much can be learned by thoughtful analysis of what is happening today. The above examples illustrate a few present-day business practices. Some ideas will prosper while others will wither and die. But they certainly will be watched.

Retailers need not start their long-term planning with any mystical tools. Rather, among the best guides to the future is an analysis of publicly available demographic data. This data can supply the answers to such questions as: What are the trends in population, income, and education? What do we know about the shopper of the 1980s? How many shoppers will there be? How well educated are they likely to be? What will be the average American's family income? Answers to these questions and others like them partially tell retailers what to expect in the future.

THE FUTURE MARKET

Population

Markets are people with money who are willing to spend it on goods and services to satisfy their needs. Statistics about population and its composition are the first clues to investigate for long-range planning. While population is increasing, it is doing so at a decreasing rate. For instance, population increased from 180.7 million persons in 1960 to 213.5 million in 1975, a gain of 32.8 million people. In the period 1960 to 1965, the population was growing at an average rate of 1.5 percent. Since that time it has declined to an average increase of 1 percent. It is expected to stabilize at this rate for at least the foreseeable future. The United States Census Bureau anticipates the population to total 222.8 million in 1980.

Table 20.1 indicates the population projections of the Bureau of the Census for 1975, 1980, and 1990. Short-term forecasts can be remarkably accurate for older age groups because the people included in those groups have already been born. There is no need to forecast the national birth rate, an extremely difficult phenomenon to predict. For example, we know that logically the same individuals who were counted in the 10 to 19 year-old group in 1970 will be in the 20 to 29 year-old group in 1980; only minor adjustments have to be made for death and net immigration.

The alert retailer can observe the aging of the American public and learn much about the kinds of products and services that will be demanded in the future. Table 20.1 suggests several things: (1) There will be a substantial increase by 1990 in the number of children under 10 years of age as a result of the large number of family formations that took place during the preceding ten years. But for the shorter term

TABLE 20.1
Projections of the Population of the United States by Age: 1975, 1980, and 1990 (in thousands)

Age	*Year* 1975	1980	1990
Under 9	33,240	33,398	40,115
10 to 19 years	41,405	38,393	34,774
20 to 29 years	36,145	39,841	38,113
30 to 39 years	25,610	31,251	40,155
40 to 49 years	22,979	22,689	31,146
50 to 59 years	22,503	22,929	21,645
60 and over	31,568	34,268	39,128
Total	213,450	222,769	245,075

Source: "Current Population Reports: Population Estimates and Projections," Series P-25, no. 541 (February 1975).

future, children's products are not expected to be a growth industry. (2) The very important 30 to 39 year-old group will grow by 57 percent during the fifteen years from 1975 to 1990. Many major expenditures on durable goods take place during these years. (3) The number of aged—defined here as over 60 years—in American society will grow by 20 percent between 1975 and 1990. Retailers will cater to this specific market because it shows no sign of slower growth. Residents of such cities as Sun City, Arizona, are now limited to senior citizens, and shops located there cater to older citizens' wants. Not all older people move to retirement villages, but sufficient numbers are found in Florida, California, and Arizona to influence the character of some cities in those states.

Meaning of Youthfulness

Engel, Kollat, and Blackwell point out the change in American culture due to an increased emphasis on youthfulness.[1] Most young people are physically and sexually active. These characteristics affect the values of younger Americans, and are admired by older people. The products they purchase reflect this admiration, and will probably continue to do so.

Marketers seek acceptance of their products by young people because they expect youth to influence the taste patterns of older people as well. For example, it is well known that young people are sometimes among the first to adopt new products. Therefore, if they are pleased, the younger shoppers may urge older shoppers to try the new product also. Much of this influence comes about in the family. In the many day-to-day contacts that members of a family have with each other, there is considerable opportunity to discuss products and possibly to influence a person's purchasing habits. For example, a nineteen-year-old daughter may very well be the

[1]James F. Engel, David T. Kollat, and Roger D. Blackwell, *Consumer Behavior*, 2nd ed. (New York: Holt, Rinehart, and Winston, Inc., 1973), p. 101.

one most responsible for her mother's latest fashion tastes. The influence of younger family members on purchase decisions cannot be overstated.

Affluence

Markets are not only people; they are people with purchasing power. In Chapter 1 we pointed out the significance of Gross National Product, national income, and disposable personal income as indicators of a nation's affluence. On December 15, 1970, at 11:13 a.m., the United States GNP clock signaled the first trillion dollar GNP in history. This fact was announced by the president and was a newsworthy achievement. A trillion dollars represents a vast amount of goods, much of which is handled by retailers on its way to the consumer.

Some experts predict a $1.6 trillion GNP by 1980.[2] To accomplish this, a growth rate of 5.8 percent per year is necessary. However, much of this growth is not more goods but simply higher priced goods, the result of inflation.[3] It seems realistic to assume a real growth rate of 3 percent annually for the long run. At this rate of increase, the GNP will total $1.3 trillion by 1980 (measured in 1970 dollars), an increase of $300 billion.

Just as GNP is expected to grow, so must national and disposable income. In the final analysis, it is not in the aggregative totals that a nation's affluence is seen. Rather, it is in statistics relating to individual or family income. In 1974, for example, 52 percent of families in the United States had incomes between $10,000 and $25,000 annually. Another 9 percent had incomes over $25,000 annually.[4] By 1980 these same families can expect to increase their purchasing power by an additional 33⅓ percent as measured in 1970 dollars.

Another favorable sign is the decline both absolutely and relatively in those who are judged below the poverty income level as defined by the Social Security Administration. For example, in 1966 11 million families, representing 18 percent of all households, had incomes at the poverty level or below. By 1973 the number of families at the poverty income level or below had declined to 5.07 million, or 9.3 percent of the total families.[5] These statistics are encouraging, but do not imply that poverty will be eliminated by 1980, nor that all segments of the economy will prosper equally. However, expectations are for most families to experience a rise in real purchasing power.

Federal government projections suggest that the per capita income of Americans will increase 74 percent between 1971 and 1990, while wholesale and retail trade will grow by 88 percent.[6] But retailers will not prosper equally in response to consumers' higher incomes. Greater affluence will bring higher expenditures on

[2] *The Impact of Environmental Change on the National Automatic Merchandising Association and Its Members, Management and Economics*, Research Incorporated, 1968, p. 7.

[3] In 1974 the American economy was experiencing a double-digit inflationary rate and real growth was at a standstill. *U.S. News and World Report* (October 14, 1974), p. 45.

[4] *U.S. News*, p. 45.

[5] *Information Please Almanac*, 1974, p. 2.

[6] *Area Economic Projections* (Washington, D.C.: U.S. Department of Commerce, 1974), Table 1.

luxury goods, leisure time activities, housing, education, and travel. In 1968 when many people were optimistic about the future, retailers were urged to stock more goods for the affluent customer. It was suggested that the customer may not want the extra money that can be saved by careful shopping.[7] Figure 20.1 is visual evidence of the growing affluence of the middle class.

FIGURE 20.1

The growing affluence of the American consumer can be seen in the rapidly increasing number of swimming pools in surburban backyards

Source: C. M. Larson, Arlington Heights, Illinois.

[7]Eugene R. Beem, "Retailing in the 1980's," *Marketing Insights*, 3, no. 8 (November 18, 1968), p. 11.

Inflation

The economic picture turned pessimistic in 1974, with the inflationary rate averaging 10 to 12 percent. Secretary of Agriculture Earl L. Butz estimated that family food costs would rise by 15 to 17 percent, and he forecasted another 8 to 10 percent rise in 1975. It became a major objective of President Gerald Ford and the Congress to bring under control the inflation that was rapidly eroding Americans' purchasing power. The effect of inflation upon retailers is, of course, traumatic.

The Middle Class

The middle class in America, which has such a great impact on retailing, came upon hard times in the mid-1970s, because of hard economic times and changing moral values. An article in a news magazine summed up the situation as follows:

> An era of self-doubt and change is dawning for the great American Majority that calls itself middle class.
>
> This critical mass of U.S. voters a few years ago sustained attack on its treasured values from a broad range of dissenters—intellectuals, black militants, young radicals, and "hippies." . . .
>
> An economic surge that brought unparalleled advances in means and status during the 1960s has turned down on them as inflation erodes their savings, their plans for educating their children, and their own security in old age. . . .
>
> Disaffection with its fiercely held values from the past—patriotism, hard work, respect for authority and dogged faith in the future—is spreading from its more affluent sections into the middle class "hard core," composed of white collar and blue collar workers.[8]

Changes in the life of the middle class will make great changes in retailing. History shows that middle class values are highly resistant to substantive changes, and therefore any changes are likely to be evolutionary rather than revolutionary.

The New American Woman

One cannot forecast the trend of retailing for the 1980s without taking into account the American woman. It is said that 85 percent of all discretionary income is spent by women. To the extent that this is even partially true, it is essential for the retailer to understand the value system of the American woman. Since the 1960s the self-image of the American woman has been changing, due partially to the revolution spearheaded by women's liberation groups. While no one can be certain of the changes still to come, it is possible to make certain predictions, some of which are likely to affect retailing. First, an increasing number of women are likely to be working wives and mothers. Currently, there are 34.6 million women in the

[8] *U.S. News and World Report*, October 14, 1974, p. 42.

work force, of which approximately 60 percent are married. Altogether 44 percent of all women of working age are employed. This should increase to 50 percent or more by 1980. The median age of the present working woman is high—forty years. This is because many young women get married, quit their jobs to raise families, and then return to work after their children are in school. Others return to the work force after their families are grown. The work is therapeutic as well as a means to increase family income.[9]

The attitude of the working woman toward shopping is considerably different from the attitude of the nonworking woman. For one thing, she has less time to invest in shopping. Some shopping must be shared by her husband or other members of the household. This is especially true of food shopping. Consequently, products will more and more have to appeal to men as well as women. Dr. Dorothy Gregg, an assistant director of public relations at United States Steel, is quoted as saying:[10]

> Working women particularly resent advertising in terms of sex identity. In other words products are going to have to appeal to both sexes, and that means that the women's audience is going to lose any validity it might have had. And that goes for soap powders as well as anything else because men are going to be buying them too. You already find that, but I don't think that manufacturers have caught on to it.
>
> For example in a working family such as mine, sometimes I do the shopping and sometimes my husband does. It depends on which one of us is tied up at that time when we need to shop.

The marketing team of manufacturer and retailer must find new ways to communicate with the woman of the 1970s and 1980s. Traditional concepts are no longer valid. Commenting on the new woman and her new freedom, Ralph Leezenbaum said:[11]

> With the advent of the pill, more liberal abortion and divorce laws, more universal higher education, more women in business and all the ramifications for changing values these phenomena bring with them, advertisers and their agencies, more than ever before, are having to reevaluate the traditional concepts on which they base their communication to women.

Another change, according to forecasters, is the emphasis placed on dining out. More families are eating out than ever before. It has been reported that meals and beverages consumed outside the home increased 50 percent between 1955 and 1965,[12] a trend that continued into the 1970s. One source indicates that Americans will eat 60 percent of their meals away from home by 1980.[13]

Furthermore, the same families are also buying more prepared foods and con-

[9]Ralph Leezenbaum, "The New American Woman and Marketing," *Marketing/Communications*, 298 (July 1970), p. 22.

[10]Ibid., p. 24.

[11]Ibid., p. 22.

[12]Ibid., p. 22.

[13]"Aiming at the Eating-Out Market," *The New York Times* (February 5, 1975), p. 54.

suming them at home. *Progressive Grocer* reports that food retailers see a big potential in fast foods. They say:[14]

> Impressed by the sensational growth in the sale of prepared hot goods through new outlets such as Kentucky Fried, McDonald's, Burger Chef, and scores of others, food retailers in 1969 began to plan in earnest to capture their share of the take-out food business.

The working woman also spends a great deal more on clothing and personal care items than her nonworking counterpart. Leezenbaum comments on a special report made by Young and Rubican, an advertising agency.[15] It stated that working women spend 20 percent more on food, 40 percent more on alcoholic beverages, 33 percent more on recreation, 40 percent more on clothing, 20 percent more on medical/personal care, and 33 percent more on auto purchases and maintenance than nonworking women. The significance of these statistics to retailers is self-evident.

Urbanization

The American population is becoming more urban. In 1965, 138 million people, out of a total population of 194.6 million, lived in an urban environment. By 1970 the total population had increased to 205 million, and 149.3 million of them lived in an urban setting. By 1980 it is anticipated that 185 million individuals will live in an urban environment.[16] One source estimates that by 1980 there will be 194 individual cities with populations in excess of 100,000, compared with 98 cities of like size in 1940.[17] The 1970 census showed that there were 153 cities that already had grown to that size. One result of an increasing population is the scarcity of land to build on within established communities, and consequently there has been a shift from building single family units to constructing multiple-dwelling units. In 1970 of the total of 63 million dwelling units, 37 percent were occupied by renters. Moreover, new apartment units are increasing annually as a percentage of total units started, increasing from 34.6 percent in 1965 to 44.6 percent in 1973. It is expected to remain near this level through 1980. The fact that the number of apartment dwellers is increasing is important because apartment dwellers have different consumption patterns from homeowners. One example of this is garden supplies: single family homeowners invest a great amount of money and time in taking care of their lawns: apartment dwellers are not usually occupied with garden activities.

American culture will be affected by a largely urban population. James Engel sees a greater interaction between individuals in an urban environment than occurs

[14]"37th Annual Report of the Grocery Industry," *Progressive Grocer* (April 1970), p. 7.

[15]Leezenbaum, *The New American Woman*, p. 26.

[16]Philip M. Hauser, *Implication of U.S. Population Changes* (American Association of Advertising Agencies, 1967), p. 1.

[17]*The Impacts of Environmental Change on the National Automatic Merchandising Association*, p. 5. Also see *1975 The U.S. Fact Book, The American Almanac, and The Statistical Abstract of the U.S.* (New York: Grosset & Dunlap, 1975), pp. 696, 701.

in a rural setting. This also brings about an increase in social disorganization. He puts it this way:[18]

> Compared to rural areas, cities permit greater interaction with people of different subcultures, they promulgate higher educational levels, they foster less religious observance and more crime of all types. They encourage fewer marriages than under similar circumstances in rural areas, and they result in new forms of social disorganization such as divorce, illegitimate birth, and suicides.

A change in culture usually results in a change in the value system of the people. Different value systems will affect the products consumed and may result in new shopping patterns. For example, fewer marriages means fewer new households established. This adversely affects the sale of furniture, appliances, and all other products essential to housekeeping. Crime in downtown shopping areas can cause shoppers to stay away and restrict their shopping to safer areas. Riots and threats of riots also may affect the shopping patterns of millions of people.

Education

Americans continue to attain higher levels of education. In 1972–73 almost 51.6 million students were enrolled in either elementary or high schools. There were 3,240,000 high school graduates in 1973 and the budget totaled $43.4 billion.[19] The impact of such a vast number of school children on the nation's retailers is significant. For example, in late August millions of women shop for children's clothes and all the other items needed for school. Back-to-school sales are traditional. A declining birthrate, such as the U.S. is currently experiencing, can seriously affect the sales of all products associated with school children.

A more important result of a higher education level will be the increasing sophistication of shoppers. They will demand and expect more quality products. The growing participation of the consumer in various consumer movements is partially due to the improved education of the population in general. Younger people especially tend to be concerned about environment, ecology, and pollution. They believe that American businessmen are sacrificing natural resources indiscriminately while turning out a greater abundance of goods. The quality of life is said to be deteriorating. Much of the drive of the consumer movement is being supplied by those who share this concern.

Consumerism

The consumer movement became a phenomenon in the late 1960s and continues to be influential. In the fall of 1969, President Richrd Nixon affirmed that "the buyer has the right to register his dissatisfaction and have this complaint heard and weighed when his interests are badly served."[20]

[18]James F. Engel, David T. Kollat, and Roger O. Blackwell, *Consumer Behavior* (New York: Holt, Rinehart and Winston, Inc., 1968), p. 250.

[19]*Information Please Almanac*, p. 750–51.

[20]Sheila Wolfe, *Chicago Tribune* (July 19, 1970), p. 4.

Consumerism identifies all the activities purporting to safeguard the consumer from being exploited by the complexities of modern society. Forty-two federal agencies administer at least 400 separate consumer programs. Many states have also expanded their consumer fraud programs. Volunteer consumer groups have been organized. Many individuals acquired nationwide reputations for their work in behalf of the consumer. Foremost among them was Ralph Nader, usually identified as the "consumer advocate," who made his reputation in fighting for safer automobiles. A former Miss America, Bess Myerson Grant, was appointed New York City's Commissioner of Consumer Affairs, and Virginia Knauer was appointed the Director of the Office of Consumer Affairs for the federal government. Many prominent people, as well as private citizens, are involved in consumerism.

The consumer movement is reported to be a thrust for economic justice meant to balance the scale between buyer and seller. Consumers, it is said, cannot make rational decisions if they are perplexed about the options offered. As an outgrowth of the consumer movement, the federal government passed the Truth-in-Packaging and the Truth-in-Lending laws. Both are designed to remove uncertainties from decision making in the marketplace. Some products have already felt the pressures of the consumer movement. Cyclamates have been banned from foods, D.D.T. is outlawed, and phosphates in detergents are banned in some states or cities.

Today the consumer movement is much concerned with pollution, ecology, and environment. Howard Frazier, president of the Consumer Federation of America, is quoted as saying:[21]

> The consumer movement is unique because of its scope. From the realization that it involves all people, it has discovered that there is scarcely an area of human endeavor that is not its concern. Today the consumer movement has a scientific concern with atomic energy, ecology, medicine, chemistry, environment, conservation, economics, manufacturing, advertising, among other things.

It is likely that the emphasis on consumer protection will accelerate in the future. Congress, in February 1971, created the Office of Consumer Affairs to look after the interests of the American consumer; this agency represents the consumer and is empowered to argue both in courts and governmental agencies on behalf of the consumer. It is a safe assumption that the federal government will become more involved than ever before as the consumer movement demands laws safeguarding the public from economic injustices and unfair trade practices.

LIFE STYLE

Forecasting the future of retailing is based partially on demographics and partially on the anticipated behavior of the individuals who comprise the market. This behavior is determined to a large extent by the way an individual chooses to live his or her life. This philosophy of living has been termed *life style*. There are many

[21]Ibid., p. 4.

forces at work shaping the life styles of all of us. Some of these forces are economic, others are environmental, while others are moral and philosophic.

Changes in life styles profoundly affect the American retailer. The long-haired bearded young man in faded jeans probably lives his life differently, and chooses to buy far different products, than does a conservative middle-aged man. Their differences in life styles must be interpreted, because people with similar life styles tend to purchase similar goods. A retailer who has some understanding of the nature of his or her customers' life styles can devise strategies on such things as types of merchandise to stock, prices, and promotion. The retailer's interpretation may be imperfect but strategies based on thoughtful interpretation are superior to those based on intuitive judgment only.

Leisure Activities

A predominantly young and affluent society spends a lot of time in leisure-type activities such as camping, boating, fishing, golfing, swimming, and bowling. It has been estimated that industries catering to leisure activities account for a total of about $300 billion annually.[22] The future looks good for retailers handling sports and leisure equipment.

One reason for the increase in leisure time activities is the free time that many workers enjoy. Three-week vacations are commonplace and three-day weekends are popular. In fact, a federal law was passed in 1971 which provides five three-day weekends a year. Moreover, many companies are opting for the four-day work week. Some believe that by 1980 the 30 hour work week will be typical. All of this free time plus increasing discretionary income suggest that retailers who provide the leisure time goods and services will prosper.

Hobbies represent another booming industry. Manufacturers, wholesalers, and retailers have formed a trade association called Hobby Industry Association of America. Its purpose is to serve better the needs of those engaged in hobbies. The trade association estimates that 75 percent of the nation's population spend their leisure time on hobbies.

THE DECADE OF MORE

A look into the future of retailing would be incomplete without investigating specific forecasts made for particular segments of the industry. For example, what is likely to happen in the food industry, the vending industry, or to discounting? Is it true that the retail store will be eliminated? How will the computer change the face of retailing? Answers to these questions are enlightening and interesting. A. J. Clausi, manager of creative development for General Foods Corporation, says the key word for the '70s is *more*. As he puts it:[23]

[22]Herbert V. Prochnow, "American's Leisure Industries in the Years Ahead," *Chicago Tribune* (July 19, 1970), Section 4, p. 15.

[23]A. J. Clausi, "Convenience Foods and Our Changing Social Patterns," *Marketing Insights*, 3, no. 7 (November 11, 1968), p. 15.

> More people, more affluence, more leisure, more second incomes, perhaps third cars, more mobility, more variety of foods, more convenience in goods, more sophisticated tastes, more eating out.
>
> More old people, but also more emphasis on youth—and, in health, more medicines. More museums, more culture, more education, particularly higher education. More desire for service, service, service. And more technological advances.

The significance of more of everything is what makes the predictions so optimistic. An assumption underlying these predictions is the expectation of little change in the value system of the American culture. However, the unrest one finds on college campuses, and the many sit-ins occurring throughout the nation indicate that values might be changing and rather quickly. The retailers will have to adapt to these changes as will everyone else.

FOOD RETAILING IN THE SEVENTIES

The grocery industry is gigantic, accounting for sales totaling $113 billion in 1973. This represents approximately 22 percent of all retail sales. Without question more householders visit food stores than any other single type of retail outlet. Therefore, a specific forecast of retailing should begin here. Knowledgeable people of the grocery trade have made extensive and interesting predictions for this vital area of retailing.[24]

The new food supermarket will avoid the standardized styles of the immediate past. New stores will be built to harmonize with the character of the community where they are located. The supermarket will be more conservative in appearance. Garish colors are out, and subdued colors will prevail; the architecture will be simple and feature clean lines.

One of the most noticeable changes of the new supermarket is its overall size. After ten years of rather stable size, supermarkets opened in 1973 expanded almost 50 percent to cover 32,000 square feet of area, in contrast with the supermarket of the sixties which covered 22,700 square feet of area. New superstores of 50,000 square feet are now emerging.[25] Figure 20.2 is an interior view of a superstore.

A 50 percent increase in overall size represents a drastic change in thinking by the major food chains, a change which occurred because of a return to price competition. The housewife's revolt against high prices is playing a major role in changing the attitudes of retailers. A growing resistance to stamps, games, and other promotional strategies also is contributing to a greater emphasis on low prices as the stimulus.

Most store operators know they must become more productive and efficient if they are to implement their new philosophy on price competition. Increasing the store size seems to be the best answer, because more items can be stocked and sold

[24]This portion of the chapter is based on an address by Robert W. Mueller, editor and publisher of *Progressive Grocer*, to the Annual Convention of the Supermarket Institute at Atlantic City, N.J., May 14, 1969. The address is titled: "Food Retailing in the 1970's."

[25]*Progressive Grocer* (April 1974), p. 69.

FIGURE 20.2
Interior view of a "super" supermarket in Denver

Source: Safeway Stores, Inc., Oakland, California.

without a corresponding increase in expense. Not only is the overall store size to be increased but the sales area will also be increased in its ratio to overall store area. This represents a departure from the past because the selling area had remained at 68 percent of the total area for the past few years. The new supermarket of the late '70s will increase its selling area to 74 percent of the total area, as shown in Figure 20.3.

Space Allocation. Important changes are to occur in the allocation of space. Because of a decline in the sale of produce as a percentage of total sales, produce is the only selling department destined to suffer a reduced share. On the other hand, frozen foods will require more selling space. New selling departments are to feature flowers and plants, garden supplies, prescriptions, delicatessen items, bake-off goods, and fast foods.

There are some noteworthy changes forecast for the nonselling departments also. Grocery storage area will decline as the computer does a more efficient job of warehousing. Meat processing areas are to be reduced as well. The big change, however, will be the expansion of the consumer and employee service areas. There will be restrooms, lounges, and luncheonettes. The store manager will be given an office designed specifically to increase the store manager's status and prestige. This new office will be off the selling floor, and the store manager will finally have the privacy to receive salesmen, customers, and employees, and to conduct the store's business more effectively.

Parking. Automobiles, although perhaps smaller, will be more numerous in 1980 than they are now; therefore it is necessary to plan for additional parking

FIGURE 20.3
The variety of products and services offered by a super store of the 70s is tremendous

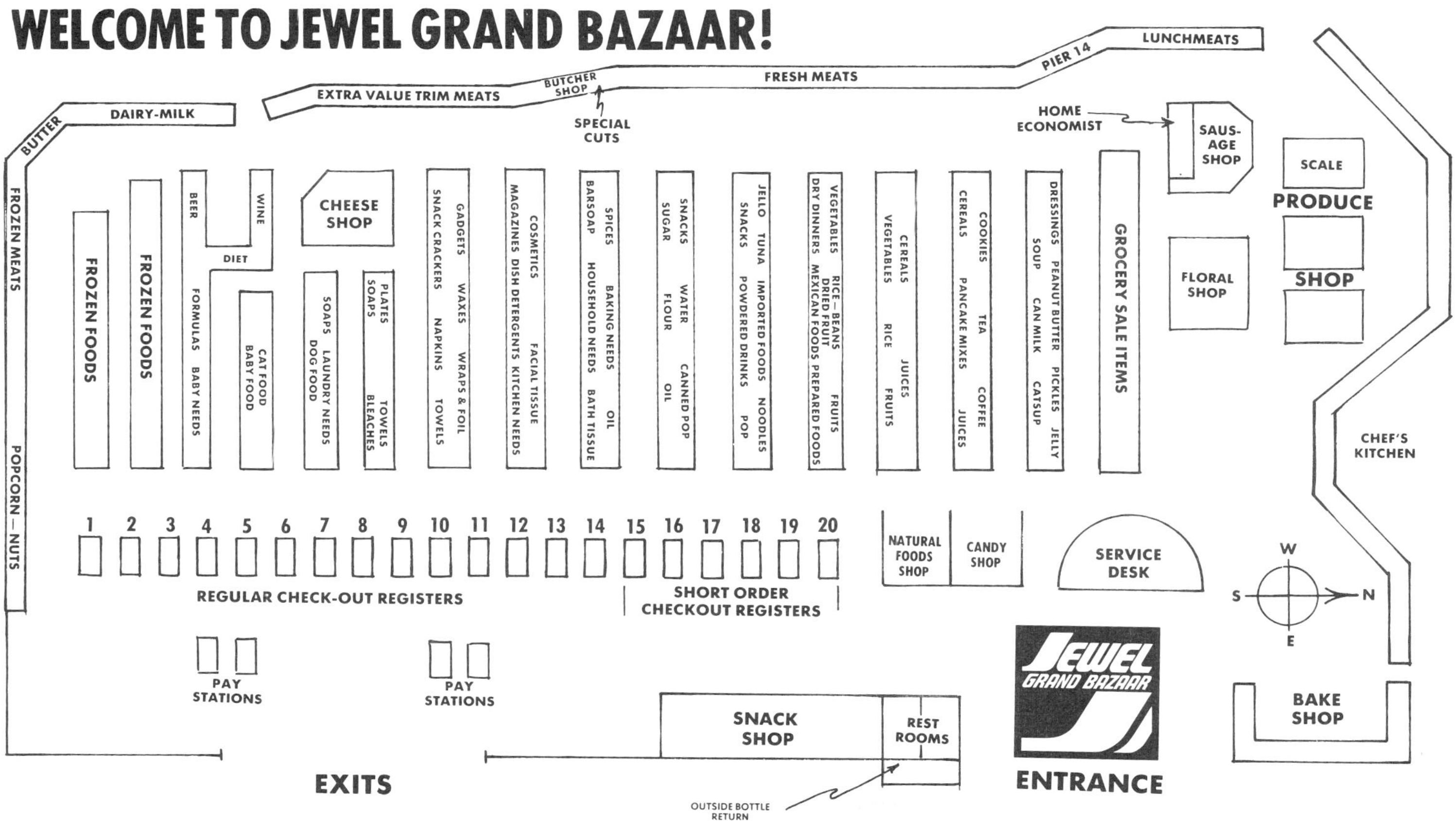

Source: Jewel Food Stores, Melrose Park, Illinois.

space. There is a relationship between parking space and the overall store size. According to the present rules, a supermarket provides parking space equal to an area 3.1 times the store's overall area; this ratio will increase to 3.6 to 1 in the future. According to this ratio, then, the new supermarket will provide 112,000 square feet of parking.

Merchandising. The typical supermarket operator will be under pressure to add more items. The growth in the number of items will be especially noticeable in general merchandise. In 1974 nonfood sales totaled 7.3 billion. Note in Table 20.2 that health and beauty aids contribute the largest sales volume. Furthermore, 95 percent of all stores handled this category. There is a tendency for the sale of nonfoods to increase faster than overall grocery store sales.

Fast Foods. Consumers may find the biggest change in supermarkets is in the offering of fast foods (prepared hot foods). Supermarket operators have begun to realize the many advantages they have to compete in the prepared hot food market. For one thing, supermarkets are located in prime locations and as a result they have considerable consumer patronage. Furthermore, they have the knowledge about foods and their purchasing power is unmatched.

Some years ago Theodore Levitt wrote a classic essay titled "Marketing Myopia," in which he pointed out examples of industries who endangered their future by not properly defining their purpose. Railroads, although limited by government regulation, failed to see themselves in the transportation industry. Specifically, Levitt said:[26]

TABLE 20.2
Nonfoods in Grocery Stores

Item	*1974 Sales in Dollars*	*% Increase in Sales over 1973*
Health and beauty aids	$3,666,000,000	5.6
Housewares	1,556,000,000	9.1
Soft goods	570,000,000	10.1
Magazines and books	413,000,000	14.9
Photo film, flash, finishing	124,000,000	12.9
Stationery, school supplies	193,000,000	12.7
Sewing needs	97,000,000	10.1
Pet supplies	146,000,000	21.5
Greeting cards	64,000,000	22.5
Seasonal and all other	468,000,000	8.4
	$7,297,000,000	8.1

Source: "42nd Annual Report of the Grocery Industry," *Progressive Grocer* (April 1975), p. 165.

[26]Theodore Levitt, *Innovation in Marketing* (New York: McGraw-Hill Book Co., Inc., 1962), p. 40.

> The railroads are in trouble today not because the need was filled by others (cars, trucks, airplanes, even telephones), but because it was not filled by the railroads themselves. They let others take customers away from them because they assumed themselves to be in the railroad business rather than in the transportation business. The reason they defined their industry incorrectly was because they were railroad-oriented instead of transportation-oriented; they were product-oriented instead of customer-oriented.

Just as Levitt argues that the railroad industry defined its industry incorrectly so did some supermarket operators. They defined themselves narrowly as being in the grocery industry instead of the food industry. However, perceptive supermarket managers are adaptable and are now redefining themselves as being part of the food industry. Fast foods are part of their responsibility. They wish to sell the food whether it is already prepared or in the "raw" stage.

In 1969 *Progressive Grocer* estimated that retail grocery sales would reach a total of $150 billion by 1980. Moreover, it forecast that the average weekly sales of the supermarket would be $100,000. At the time of the prediction the average weekly sales were $48,000. As it turns out, the estimate was a bit conservative, for in 1973 the new superstores were already over the $100,000 weekly sales level. *Progressive Grocer* surveyed the superstores and found they averaged $128,960 weekly. By 1980 this could climb to the $200,000 level.[27] Figure 20.4 shows additional statistics on a supermarket's operating results.

Convenience Stores

The number of convenience stores (bantam supermarkets) had increased from a modest beginning of 500 stores in 1957 to 20,300 in 1974. In the same time span, sales increased from $75 million to over $4.3 billion. These small stores accounted for 3.8 percent of all total U.S. grocery store sales. Their major advantages are: (1) the personal attention of the owner-manager, (2) the longer operating hours when other stores may be closed, (3) the small size that eases shopping, and (4) the short walk from the automobile to the store. These advantages were somewhat neutralized when many traditional supermarkets initiated late night operations and when A & P stores began their WEO low price drive. Still, forecasters are optimistic about their future growth. It is expected that by 1980 there will be 25,000 of these junior supermarkets and they will have sales totaling $7.5 billion. This would represent a spectacular growth for a five-year period.

DISCOUNTING

We have discussed the discount store in other sections of this book, notably in Chapter 2. However, there is a need now to assess its future. Some say the major reason for its existence is the psychological need for customers to save money.[28]

[27] *Progressive Grocer* (April 1974), p. 179.

[28] "The Great Shoe Discounting Trial," *Marketing Insights* (November 18, 1968), p. 16.

FIGURE 20.4
Inflation erodes the productivity of supermarket operations

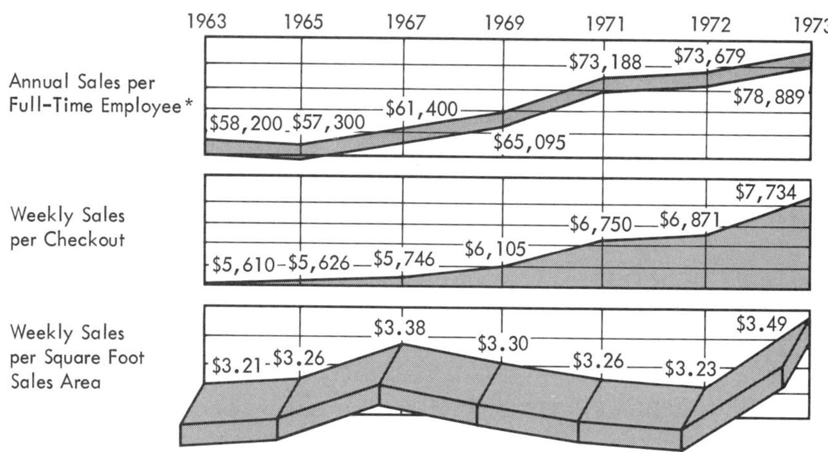

*Based on full-time and part-time employees assuming 2 part-time = 1 full-time. Example: Store with 40 full-time and 20 part-time = 50 full-time employees.

Source: "41st Annual Report," *Progressive Grocer*, April 1974, p. 177.

This psychological need is not likely to diminish even though people are now more affluent and are likely to be more so in the seventies and eighties. Perhaps that is why the discount store is still flourishing. There have been some changes, perhaps the most notable of which is the discounters' change of image from that of cheap merchandisers to that of movers of great quantities of goods. It is for this reason that discounters prefer the terms mass merchandisers or merchandising department store. As they put it, mass merchandisers do not give discounts; rather they use a lower markup.

Davidson, Doody, and Lowry, writing in the *Journal of Marketing*, point out that the leased department will no longer dominate the discount store as it once did.[29] They further say that the trend for firms to open their own self-standing unit is likely to continue. This will give the discounter more control over where they locate and how they operate.

In the late 1960s there was a trend for large merchandising units to enter the discounting field. Examples are Kresge, L. J. Ayres, Woolworth, and Dayton-Hudson Corporation. These merchandisers as well as other large discounters are

[29]William R. Davidson, Alton Doody, and James Lowry, "Leased Departments as a Major Force in the Growth of Discount Store Retailing," *Journal of Marketing*, 34, no. 1 (January 1970), pp. 39–46.

organized to have strong control over all phases of their operation. In spite of the large volume of sales made by major discounters, almost three-fourths of the sales volume was still being done by firms operating fewer than 35 units.

VENDING

The vending industry is expected to grow through the 1970s and into the 80s. One forecast believes there will be greater growth opportunities for full food service than there will for the vending of snacks, beverages, and cigarettes. They see their markets as government offices, colleges and universities, hospitals, airports, and other high-density areas. Expectations are for a slower growth rate in factories.

THE NONRETAIL FUNCTION OF RETAILING

E. B. Weiss, a respected observer and writer of the retail scene, says that the retailer of the future is likely to deemphasize the basic retail function of moving goods off shelves and tables into the customer's shopping bag.[30] Weiss, using Sears as the example, believes greater stress will be placed on nonretail activities.

Sears earns a profit on the product lines supplied by manufacturers who are wholly owned by Sears. This factor alone will account for profits substantially larger than Sears' retail profit. Sears also has sizeable investments in other manufacturers.

Sears also earns a substantial income from credit sales, its Allstate Insurance business, its allowances from suppliers, and its real estate investments. The company recently built a new 110 story office headquarters in Chicago costing $100 million.[31] This new building has a total of 3.7 million square feet of rental space. Sears itself occupies less than 2 million square feet. The remainder is leased to tenants, who thereby contribute to Sears' overall profit.

COMPUTERS

In our look into the future, we would be remiss without mentioning the computer and its impact. The automated checkout at many supermarkets will be in full operation by 1978. Manufacturers have agreed on a Universal Product Code so that optical scanners can be used to transfer the pertinent data of each item to the cash register. The customer will receive a register tape identifying the product, its brand name, and its unit price, as well as the grand total price for the entire purchase. There will be less chance of human error at the checkout station.

Perhaps the greatest breakthrough will be the instant audits that the computer will perform. Management will know precisely the sales of all items both in physical

[30]E. B. Weiss, "Sears: Leader in Non-Retail Functions," *Advertising Age* (March 9, 1970).

[31]Alvin Nagelberg, "Sears to Construct Tallest Building in World, 110 Stories," *Chicago Tribune* (July 28, 1970), p. 1.

units and dollar value. Store managers will have at their fingertips data identifying the brands that are selling and those that are shelf-sitters. Warehouses will have central computers connected to each store, so that ordering will be automatic and tied in with actual needs. An "out-of-stock" situation will become less likely.

The computer will enable each individual store to cater to its customers according to their unique tastes. For example, supermarkets with a Latin American clientele will feature foods appealing to Latino tastes. Other supermarkets will cater to the tastes of their customers whatever their race or national origin.

The computer also will measure the sales and profits of displays, coupons, advertising, and special promotions. From this monitoring, managers will be able to use promotional activities more effectively in the new supermarket.

Some of the complications to automated checkouts at the present time are the high costs involved, the lack of adoption of the Universal Product Code, and customer fears of automation. These problems are expected to be nearer solution by 1978.

RETAILING ABROAD

The subject of international retailing is much too complex to be covered in a portion of this chapter. Therefore our objective is merely to suggest some of the similarities that exist between American retailing institutions and their counterparts abroad. Furthermore, we shall limit our discussion to the developed countries of the free world, although in Figure 20.5 we have shown the Gum department store in Moscow.

An interesting question about international retailing is whether it differs from retailing in the United States. One writer says:[32]

> The perceptive international observer is likely to notice about as many similarities as differences in the practices of retailers in the developed countries. He will probably be about as comfortable in a department store in Paris, London, Tel Aviv, or Tokyo as in a large American city. The services that he is accorded such as credit, delivery, exchange privileges or guarantees will be roughly the same, although the details may differ.

Observed similarities may be due to American influence. On the other hand, similarities could be due to German influence, French influence, or the influence of any other developed country. However, certain aspects of retailing are universal, and consequently are found in most developed countries. Due to the extensive traveling done by citizens of all countries, it is likely that all retailers throughout the world will borrow successful practices regardless of their origin. That is to say, American retailers will be expected to adopt techniques from foreign retailers if it

[32]Robert E. Weigand, "Aspects of Retail Pricing in Japan," *MSU Business Topics* (Graduate School of Business Administration, Michigan State University, Winter 1970), p. 29.

FIGURE 20.5

Department stores are important in the Soviet Union

Source: *Sales Management*, New York, New York.

seems beneficial to them. The same is true of retailers abroad. Our concern, however, is to relate retailing practices abroad with their American counterparts. And many American retailers have units in Europe as Figures 20.6 and 20.7 illustrate.

It is difficult to generalize on such a complex subject as retailing, an industry which is affected by nationalism, tradition, culture, and the political climate of the time. Nevertheless, we are prepared to make a few generalizations. First, retailing is much more fragmented (many more stores) abroad than it is here. This fact is true in England, France, Spain, Italy, and all the other Western European countries. It is also true of Israel, Japan, and the other developed countries of the Near and Far East. As an example consider France, which has 60 percent more retail shops per 10,000 people than has the United States. Moreover, Italy is more fragmented

FIGURE 20.6
Safeway opened this store in Birmingham, England, in September 1973

Source: Safeway Stores, Inc., Oakland, California.

than France—primarily because of the high degree of itinerant vendors found there.[33]

French retailing is a good example of how culture affects institutions. French consumers tend to dislike both mass production and standardization. Consequently, the French are slow to accept mass marketing techniques. Moreover, the French people are highly individualistic and this trait is shown in the physical make-up of the French store. The French retailer selects his merchandise, then arranges it within his store, and determines his interior display according to his own tastes. Inasmuch as men's taste is infinite, French stores have a good deal more individualism than American stores.[34]

The department store is common to most developed countries. However, except for size, those in Israel resemble their counterparts in the United States:[35]

> A walk through any of Israel's largest department stores would not seem substantially different from a small American retail outlet. The type of merchandise often

[33]S. Watson Dunn, "French Retailing and the Common Market" in *Comparative Marketing Systems*, ed. Montrose S. Summers and Jerome B. Kernan (New York: Appleton-Century-Crofts, 1968), pp. 224–30.

[34]Ibid., pp. 224–30.

[35]Robert E. Weigand, "Department Stores in Israel," *Journal of Retailing*, 44, no. 2 (Summer 1968), pp. 50–60.

would be much the same, the display fixtures would seem identical, although perhaps older, the store might have escalators, and there would be an adequate number of salespeople trying out points they learned in their sales training courses.

Japanese retailing has much to remind one of American retailing, although there are many differences. Japanese retailers are at the end of a long channel of distribution, but in spite of the fact have a close relationship with their suppliers, much more so than American retailers. An American visitor to Japan would find discount houses, installment buying, credit buying, and resale price maintenance.[36]

American retailers also place resident buyers in various foreign countries to select merchandise from the suppliers. For example, Macy's has resident buyers in Japan who keep in close contact with Japanese suppliers. In this way Macy's assures itself of fresh merchandise of the kind that satisfies Macy's customers.

From a functional point of view, retailers abroad are both similar and different. For example, foreign retailers, regardless of country, are similar in that there is a store, hours are maintained, merchandise is stocked, prices are determined, goods

FIGURE 20.7

Woolworth's is an important retailing store in England

Source: *Sales Management*, New York, New York.

[36]Ibid., pp. 23–30.

are promoted, and customers partake of various services. They differ from American retailers in the scope of their operations and in the detailed application of these functions. Tradition, culture, nationalism, and regulatory laws are important determinants of functional details. Considering all of these factors, we can make these observations:

1. The productivity of retail workers abroad is lower than that of American retail workers.
2. Pricing strategy seems to be more common to American retailers. Foreign retailers often are less aggressive in using price as a competitive weapon.
3. Multistop shopping is more common abroad than it is in the United States.
4. Some European retailers use sophisticated tools, especially the computer. We discussed a German mail-order house in Chapter 17.
5. Vending by machine is popular in many countries.
6. Retailing practices such as discounting, self-service, scrambled merchandising, and installment selling are utilized more or less, depending upon the country.
7. There seem to be far more speciality shops abroad, and they are more individualistic in their approach to retailing.

We have not discussed retailing in developing countries, because of the scarcity of information relative to them. Charles C. Slater writes that in most developing countries, family incomes are so low that a high proportion must be spent on food. Consequently, food marketing systems predominate. He also writes that these systems are ancient and inefficient. Slater sums it up this way:[37]

> A critical step in the process of reform of agriculture and food channels must take place at the retail level. Most developing societies are characterized by a multitude of small specialty merchants in public markets, who often sell small amounts daily at low margin, but do little to encourage suppliers by offering to buy large quantities of products of uniform quality at stable prices.

We do not wish to infer that all retailing in developing countries takes place in public marketplaces. Sears has had stores in Latin American countries for many years, and they are successful operations. Because of their Latin American experience, Sears began its European expansion in Spain. They believe their retailing experience with the Spanish culture of Latin America will serve them well.

OPERATIONAL PROBLEMS AND OPPORTUNITIES

Retailers are likely to face a number of problems in the near future that are unrelated to their relationship with the final consumer. These include (1) neutralizing the powerful supplier, (2) effectively utilizing human resources such as women and minorities, and (3) maintaining the right to use private property.

[37]Charles C. Slater, "Marketing Processes in Developing Latin American Societies," in *Environment of Marketing Behavior*, 2nd ed., Robert J. Holloway and Robert S. Hancock (New York: John Wiley and Sons, Inc., 1969), p. 394.

The Powerful Retailer

In American business history, the power of the retailer has seldom been as great as that of the wholesaler or manufacturer. With the exception of the large retail chains, individual retailers have needed the supplier far more than the supplier has needed any single retailer. This imbalance of power in the channel has led to such abuses—often illegal—as dictation of the retailer's selling price, forbidding the retailer to buy from other suppliers, establishing minimum buying amounts, specifying that retailers are obliged to purchase and resell less popular products in order to obtain the more popular items, and promises of promotional assistance that are not forthcoming. Some of the greatest abuses took place when retailers were aligned with a single source, finding it difficult or even impossible to turn to another supplier. Several solutions—FTC rules, state legislation, and arbitration—may put the retailer in a stronger position than he historically has been, vis à vis those from whom he buys.

Trade Regulation. The Federal Trade Commission proposed a rule in 1971 that would oblige franchisors to disclose the material facts concerning their offers to franchisees. There have been many instances where businessmen have cheated other businessmen by promising much and giving little. More specifically, they charged a flat franchise fee for the right to do business in the future under the franchisor's name, usually in a particular territory. The franchisor sometimes pocketed the fees collected from all over the country and did little to fulfill the terms of the contract. The proposed rule would require the franchisor to reveal such matters as the success rate of other franchisees, the role of celebrities in the operations, and the financial standing of the franchisor. The Commission's rule is scheduled to go into effect in 1975.

State Legislation. Many states have enacted legislation that is designed to protect the retailer, largely because the federal government has been slow to respond. Eight states with different disclosure laws—California, Illinois, Minnesota, Oregon, Rhode Island, South Dakota, Washington, and Wisconsin—have agreed on a single statement that a franchisor may file instead of eight separate statements. The Uniform Offering Circular obliges the franchisor to list the experience of the franchisor, the officers and director, the firm's financial history, the duties of both franchisor and franchisee, termination and renewal rights, and the role of public figures and celebrities in the operations.

Arbitration. Business disputes between retailers and their suppliers often have been resolved either by resolving to stop doing business with each other, or in more serious cases, by litigation. Arbitration is a third alternative that seems to be growing in importance.The use of an independent arbitrator means that solutions are arrived at faster than when determined by litigation, they are more secret, less expensive, confront the problem sooner, and are resolved by industry experts.[38] The

[38]Robert E. Weigand and Hilda C. Wasson, "Arbitration in the Marketing Channel," *Business Horizons* (October 1974), p. 40.

Federal Trade Commission has shown increasing concern over the abrupt and unilateral termination of retail dealerships in the petroleum industry and has indicated it will require cancellations to be submitted to arbitration.

Human Resources Management. Retailers increasingly must face the task of bringing women and minority groups into the mainstream of American economic life. The historic tendency to underutilize such groups has been a serious drain on the country's national product. An increasing proportion of women participate in the nation's work force; by the mid-1970s about 44 percent of women of working age were employed in a paying position. The proportion of black women who work approaches 60 percent.[39] Furthermore, there is only a modest difference in the proportion of young men and women who presently are attending America's colleges and universities. About 27 percent of the men and 20 percent of the women in the 18- to 24-year-old group are presently in school. And over 18 percent of the country's minority population is enrolled in a college or university. Thus the differential between the sexes and the races is quite small and probably is growing even smaller.

Retailers must recognize that women and minorities will not be satisfied with the roles to which they traditionally have been assigned. They will want jobs commensurate with their abilities. The larger firms—those that are most visible—will feel the greatest pressure from government agencies and political groups. One study suggests that retailers have a poor record in regard to promoting women and other minorities into managerial positions. Although there are ample opportunities at the entry level, few women or minority persons move to higher echelons. More specifically, women account for 67 percent of total employees, 80 percent of the salespeople, and 89 percent of the clerical staff. But women generally account for less than one-third of the managerial group in even the largest retailing firms.[40] Pressure to hire more women and minority employees is likely to continue or grow stronger, creating both problems and opportunities for the retailer. One of the more serious problems may be the loyal employee who finds himself passed over for promotions, perhaps working for a woman or minority manager. For at least some employees—long accustomed to traditional roles—this is likely to be a wrenching experience with which the retailer must deal.

The Right to Use Property. A number of recent incidents suggest that there is much doubt about the definition of "private property" and the manner in which the owner can use it. For example:

> City officials in Saint Petersburg, Florida, voted that the last 25,000 people to move to the city would have to move out. They believed that the city's facilities were already overburdened, so newcomers were not welcome. The vote was revoked, but few were happy at the thought that the city would grow larger. And all over the

[39] *Social Indicators: 1973* (Washington, D.C.: U.S. Department of Commerce), Charts 4/11 and 4/12.

[40] Esther Dyson, "Help Wanted: Minorities and Women in the Retail Industry," *Economic Priorities Report* (Council on Economic Priorities, 1974).

country, land owners have been prevented from building homes and commercial establishments by strong zoning laws.

Striking veterans of the National Football League picketed a Packer-Bear football game being played at Lambeau Stadium in Green Bay; it was being played by each team's rookie squad. The protestors were arrested for trespassing; the stadium is in a city park but is leased to the Packer team for each game, so no one was quite sure whether or not the protestors were on private property.

In New York City, the Fifth Avenue Association—funded by such retailers as Saks Fifth Avenue, Lord and Taylor's, Tiffany's, and Brooks Brothers—brought suit to prevent the city from converting Madison Avenue into a shopping mall. It alleged that the mall would turn the avenue into a "carnival" area. City streets are considered open to the public, but the way they are used clearly can affect nearby retailers.

American law has generally been sympathetic to the protection of private property rights. Owners have been able to use their property as they see fit and seldom have had it confiscated by government bodies. However, the right to usage has limits. In an early legal case, (*Marsh* v. *Alabama*, 1946) the Supreme Court held that a labor union had the right to enter a privately owned shopping center in an attempt to unionize employees. The center owners argued that the organizers should be restricted to public roads and land some distance away. The Court held that Alabama's "no trespassing" law could not be used to prevent the union from exercising its right to free speech. In a more recent case (*Lloyd Corp.* v. *Tanner*, 1972) involving Lloyd's Center, a large shopping plaza in Portland Oregon, the Court held that antiwar marchers could legally be kept off the property. It pointed out that, unlike *Marsh v. Alabama*, the marchers had other ways to reach their audience and that the marchers' message was general in nature rather than directed at a specific retailer. The retailer of the future is likely to be faced with the dilemma of trying to attract large crowds by offering social and political events while simultaneously maintaining its private property character.

HOPE FOR THE FUTURE

Retailers throughout the world have had to deal with such complex issues as massive shifts in population; changing tastes of their customers; differences in cultural norms within their communities; new value systems; accelerated technological discoveries; occasional abuses of power from their suppliers, government bodies, and consumer groups; inflation and recession; changing views on the nature of private property; and demands that they play a role in redressing racial and sexual injustices of long standing. In many instances, retailers have been unable to cope with such problems and statistically become business failures. But America, like many countries of the world, does not promise the right to succeed, only the right to try. The astute retailer has studied, thought, read, and worked hard to adjust to the world, and has in turn affected the world. There is no reason for this to change. Indeed, there is hope for the world.

SUMMARY

Retailing is expected to change remarkably during the next ten years. These changes will be due to a variety of reasons: increasing population, greater family affluence, changing life styles, and increased consumerism.

One should begin an appraisal of retailing's future with a comprehensive analysis of demographic data. First of all, population is increasing in absolute numbers, but at a declining rate. Presently the increase is 1 percent, and the Bureau of the Census forecasts a total population of 223 million people in 1980. However, it is the composition of the population that is interesting. Young people will continue to be the dominant group, and their tastes are to be reflected in the kinds of products offered and the character of the institutions offering them.

Another very important demographic factor is family income. There is every indication that people are becoming more affluent individually and collectively. The first trillion dollar gross national product was realized in 1970. Indications are that it will continue to grow in real terms and that all segments of our society will enjoy a high standard of living.

Retailing will be affected by the changes occurring in American culture. Values are expected to change as a result of the consumer movement, the activities of the women's liberation movement, and the fact that individuals are better educated, increasingly live in urban environments, and have higher incomes. Leisure-time activities are already affecting retailing.

There are many changes affecting the retailing institutions themselves. The supermarket will become larger and play an increasing role in the retail industry. They will grow in size, in number of items stocked, and in the variety of goods offered. Fast foods are one of the new products to be added.

Discounting and vending are to continue to play a part in American life. Mass merchandisers are movers of large quantities of merchandise. There is every indication they are to be even more important in the future.

Many people are interested in retailing in foreign countries, especially in comparison with American retailing. The answers are not pat because tradition, nationalism, culture, and government regulations affect retail practices differently in different countries. It is fair to generalize that most of the practices resemble American practices; however, there is a difference in degree and scope. Retailing is much more fragmented abroad than it is in the U.S., which of course lends it to more individualistic approaches. American retailers utilize mass marketing techniques to a greater extent.

And finally, the retailer must learn how to countervail the powerful suppliers he must face, to develop and use the underutilized knowledge and skills of women and minorities, and to earn a profit with his assets while simultaneously maintaining its private character.

QUESTIONS FOR DISCUSSION

1. What clues do population and its composition give us concerning the retailing industry of the future?
2. Marketers are enthusiastic about the future because most family units are becoming more affluent. Discuss this point pro or con.
3. Discuss the impact of the American woman on retailing in the 1970s.
4. Do you think the value system of the population is changing? If so, explain how it affects retailing.
5. The consumer movement is a phenomenon of the 1960s. Discuss this statement.
6. What are some of the major changes the supermarket is expecting for the 1970s?
7. How do you think the computer will affect retailing? Give examples.
8. What is "marketing myopia"? Do you think the grocery industry is myopic? Why? How about other forms of retailing?
9. What is meant by the nonretail function of retailing?
10. Write a short essay giving your own forecast of retailing for the year 1980.

REFERENCES

BOOKS

ALBAUM, GERALD, and M. VENKATESAN, *Scientific Marketing Research.* New York: The Free Press, 1971.

ANDREASON, ALAN R., ed, *Improving Inner-City Marketing.* Chicago: American Marketing Association, 1972.

BACH, GEORGE LELAND, *Economics: An Introduction to Analysis and Policy* (8th ed.) Englewood Cliffs, N.J.: Prentice-Hall, Inc., 1974.

BEARCHELL, CHARLES A., *Retailing Today: An Introduction.* New York: Harcourt Brace Jovanovich, Inc., 1975.

BERELSON, BERNARD, and GARY A. STEINER, *Human Behavior: An Inventory of Scientific Findings.* New York: Harcourt Brace and World, Inc., 1964.

BLOOM, GORDON F., *Productivity in the Food Industry.* Cambridge, Mass.: The M.I.T. Press, 1972.

BOYD, HARPER, and RALPH WESTFALL, *Marketing Research and Analysis* (3rd ed.) Homewood, Ill.: Richard D. Irwin, Inc., 1972.

BRITT, STEWART HENDERSON, ed., *Consumer Behavior in Theory and in Action.* New York: John Wiley & Sons, Inc., 1970.

BROWN, MILTON P., WILLIAM APPLEBAUM, and WALTER J. SALMON, *Strategy Problems of Mass Retailers and Wholesalers.* Homewood, Ill.: Richard D. Irwin, Inc., 1970.

BUCKLIN, LOUIS P., *Competition and Evolution in the Distributive Trades.* Englewood Cliffs, N.J.: Prentice-Hall, Inc., 1972.

BUTCHER, BENJAMIN C., and JAMES R. MCANELLY, *Fundamentals of Retailing.* New York: The Macmillan Co., 1973.

CARMAN, JAMES M., and KENNETH P. UHL, *Phillips and Duncan's Marketing Principles and Methods* (7th ed.) Homewood, Ill.: Richard D. Irwin, Inc., 1973.

CHISHOLM, ROBERT, *The Darlings: The Mystique of the Supermarket.* New York: Chain Store Age Books, 1970.

DALRYMPLE, DOUGLAS J., and DONALD L. THOMPSON, *Retailing: An Economic View.* New York: The Free Press, 1969.

DAVIDSON, WILLIAM R., ALTON F. DOODY, and DANIEL J. SWEENEY, *Retailing Management* (4th ed.) New York: The Ronald Press Co., 1975.

DESAUTEL, BRUCE L., JOSEPH A. KREUTLE, MICHAEL J. WALTON, and WILFRED R. MALSCHICK, *Accounting by Computer*. Corte Madera, Calif.: Rinehart Press, 1974.

DOCTORS, SAMUEL I., and SHARON LOCKWOOD, eds., *Minority Economic Development*. New York: Holt, Rinehart & Winston, Inc., 1974.

DUNCAN, DELBERT J., and CHARLES F. PHILLIPS, *Retailing Principles and Methods* (7th ed.) Homewood, Ill.: Richard D. Irwin, Inc., 1967.

EDWARDS, CHARLES M., and RUSSEL A. BROWN, *Retail Advertising and Sales Promotion* (3rd ed.) Englewood Cliffs, N.J.: Prentice-Hall, Inc., 1959.

EMMET, BORIS, and JOHN E. JEUCK, *Catalogues and Counters: A History of Sears, Roebuck and Company*. Chicago: Chicago University Press, 1950.

ENGEL, JAMES F., DAVID T. KOLLAT, and ROGER D. BLACKWELL, *Consumer Behavior* (2nd ed.) New York: Holt, Rinehart and Winston, Inc., 1973.

ENTENBERG, R. D., *Effective Retail and Market Distribution*. Cleveland and New York: World Publishing Co., 1966.

ERICKSON, MAYNARD L., and RICHARD F. CURTIS, *A Primer of Computer Utilization*. Park Ridge, Ill.: General Learning Press, 1974.

FERRY, JOHN WILLIAM, *A History of the Department Store*. New York: The Macmillan Co., 1960.

GAMBLE, STEPHEN H., *The Despensa System of Food Distribution: A Case Study of Monterrey, Mexico*. New York: Praeger Publishers, 1972.

GILLISPIE, KAREN R., and JOSEPH C. HECHT, *Retail Business Management*. New York McGraw-Hill Book Co., 1970.

GIST, RONALD R., ed., *Management Perspectives in Retailing* (2nd ed.) New York: John Wiley & Sons, Inc., 1971.

GIST, RONALD R., *Retailing: Concepts and Decisions*. New York: John Wiley & Sons, Inc., 1968.

GREEN, PAUL E., and DONALD S. TULL, *Research for Marketing Decisions* (3rd ed.) Englewood Cliffs, N.J.: Prentice-Hall, Inc., 1975.

GREER, THOMAS V., *Marketing in the Soviet Union*. New York: Praeger Publishers, 1973.

GROSSMAN, LOUIS H., *Department Store Merchandising in Changing Environments*. East Lansing, Mich.: Michigan State University, 1970.

HARTLEY, ROBERT F., *Retailing: Challenge and Opportunity*. Boston: Houghton Mifflin, 1975.

HAVENGA, J. J. D., *Retailing: Competition and Trade Practices*. The Netherlands: A. W. SIJJ Hoff International Publishing Co., 1973.

HOWER, RALPH MERLE, *History of Macy's of New York*. Cambridge, Mass.: Harvard University Press, 1946.

JACOBS, LAURENCE W., *Advertising and Promotion for Retailing: Text and Cases*. Glenview, Ill.: Scott, Foresman and Co., 1972.

JENKINS, HAROLD L., *Action Marketing for Savings Institutions*. Chicago, Ill.: Savings Institutions Marketing Society of America.

JOHNSON, GLENN L., and JAMES A. GENTRY, *Finney and Miller's Principles of Accounting, Introductory*. Englewood Cliffs, N.J.: Prentice-Hall, Inc., 1970.

JONES, FRED M., *Retail Merchandising*. Homewood, Ill.: Richard D. Irwin, Inc., 1957.

KATONA, GEORGE, *The Powerful Consumer*. New York: John Wiley & Sons, Inc., 1969.

KINTER, EARL W., *A Primer on the Law of Deceptive Practices: A Guide for the Businessman*. New York: The Macmillan Co., 1971.

Kissel, Irwin R., and Ann Kissel Grun, *How to Handle Claims and Returns: A Manual for Manufacturers and Retailers.* New York: McGraw-Hill Book Co., 1973.

Kleppner, Otto, *Advertising Procedure* (6th ed.) Englewood Cliffs, N.J.: Prentice-Hall, Inc., 1973.

Kotler, Philip, *Marketing Management: Analysis, Planning, and Control* (3rd ed.) Englewood Cliffs, N.J.: Prentice-Hall, Inc., 1976.

Krieger, Murray, *Decision-Making in Retailing and Marketing.* New York: Fairchild Publications, Inc., 1969.

Levitt, Theodore, *Innovations in Marketing.* New York: McGraw-Hill Book Co., 1962.

Logan, William B., and Herbert Freeman, *Merchandising Mathematics.* New York: McGraw-Hill Book Co., 1973.

Luck, David J., Hugh J. Wales, and Donald A. Taylor, *Marketing Research* (4th ed.) Englewood Cliffs, N.J.: Prentice-Hall, Inc., 1974.

Marcus, Stanley, *Minding the Store.* Boston: Little, Brown and Co., 1974.

Markin, Rom J., *Consumer Behavior: A Cognitive Orientation.* New York: The Macmillan Co., 1971.

———, *Retailing Management: A Systems Approach.* New York: The Macmillan Co., 1971.

Martineau, Pierre, *Motivation in Advertising.* New York: McGraw-Hill Book Co., 1957.

McConnell, Campbell R., *Economics, Problems and Policies* (6th ed.) New York: McGraw-Hill Book Co., 1975.

McNair, Malcolm P., and Anita Hersun, *The Retail Inventory Method and Life.* New York: McGraw-Hill Book Co., 1952.

McNeal, J. U., *An Introduction to Consumer Behavior.* New York: John Wiley & Sons, Inc., 1973.

Metz, Robert, *Franchising: How to Select a Business of Your Own.* New York: Hawthorne Books, Inc., 1969.

Meyers, James H., and William H. Reynolds, *Consumer Behavior and Marketing Management.* Boston: Houghton Mifflin Co., 1967.

Mills, Kenneth H., and Judith Edison Paul, *Create Distinctive Displays.* Englewood Cliffs, N.J.: Prentice-Hall, Inc., 1974.

Newman, William H., Charles E. Summer, and E. Kirby Warren, *The Process of Management: Concepts, Behavior, and Practice* (3rd ed.) Englewood Cliffs, N.J.: Prentice-Hall, Inc., 1972.

Nicosia, Francesco M., *Consumer Decision Processes.* Englewood Cliffs, N.J.: *Prentice-*Hall, Inc., 1966.

Pintel, Gerald, and Jay Diamond, *Retailing.* Englewood Cliffs, N.J.: Prentice-Hall, Inc., 1971.

Rachman, David J., *Marketing Strategy and Structure.* Englewood Cliffs, N.J.: Prentice-Hall, Inc., 1974.

———, *Retail Strategy and Structure* (2nd. ed.) Englewood Cliffs, N.J.: Prentice-Hall, Inc., 1975.

Robinson, O. Preston, Christine H. Robinson, and George H. Zeiss, *Successful Retail Salesmanship.* Englewood Cliffs, N.J.: Prentice-Hall, Inc., 1961.

Rosenberg, Robert M., and Madelon Redell, *Profits From Franchising.* New York: McGraw-Hill Book Co., 1969.

SAMUELSON, PAUL A., *Economics: An Introductory Analysis* (9th ed.) New York: McGraw-Hill Book Co., 1973.

SANDERS, DONALD H., *Computers in Business* (3rd ed.) New York: McGraw-Hill Book Co., 1975.

SCHIFF, MICHAEL, *Accounting and Control in Physical Distribution Management.* Chicago: National Council of Physical Distribution Management, 1972.

SCHWARTZ, GEORGE, ed., *Science in Marketing.* New York: John Wiley & Sons, Inc., 1965.

SCHWARTZMAN, DAVID, *The Decline of Service in Retail Trade: Analysis of the Cost of Sales per Man Hour, 1929–1963.* Pullman, Wash.: Bureau of Economic and Business Research, 1971.

SEXTON, DONALD E., JR., *Groceries in the Ghetto.* Lexington, Mass.: D. C. Heath & Co., 1973.

SLAVIN, ALBERT, ISAAC N. REYNOLDS, and JOHN T. MILLER, *Basic Accounting for Managerial and Financial Control.* Hinsdale, Ill.: The Dryden Press, 1972.

STANTON, WILLIAM J., *Fundamentals of Marketing* (4th ed.) New York: McGraw-Hill Book Co., 1975.

STAUDT, THOMAS A., and DONALD A. TAYLOR, *A Managerial Introduction to Marketing* (2nd ed.) Englewood Cliffs, N.J.: Prentice-Hall, Inc., 1970.

THOMPSON, DONALD N., *Franchise Operations and Antitrust.* Lexington, Mass.: D. C. Heath & Co., 1971.

WALKER, BRUCE, DONALD JAMES, and MICHAEL ETZEL, *Retailing: A Professional Approach.* New York: Harcourt Brace Jovanovich, Inc., 1975.

WALTERS, C. GLENN, *Marketing Channels.* New York: The Ronald Press Co., 1974.

WEISS, E. B., *Marketing to the New Society.* Chicago: Crainbooks, 1973.

WILINSKY, HARRIET, *Careers and Opportunities in Retailing.* New York: E. P. Dutton & Co., Inc., 1970.

WILL, R. TED, and RONALD W. HASTY, *Retailing: A Mid-Management Approach.* San Francisco: Canfield Press, 1973.

WINGATE, ISABEL B., *Textile Fabrics and Their Selection* (6th ed.) Englewood Cliffs, N.J.: Prentice-Hall, Inc., 1970.

WINGATE, JOHN W., and JOSEPH FRIEDLANDER, *The Management of Retail Buying.* Englewood Cliffs, N.J.: Prentice-Hall, Inc., 1963.

WINGATE, JOHN W., ELMER O. SCHALLER, and ROBERT W. BELL, *Problems in Retail Merchandising* (6th ed.) Englewood Cliffs, N.J.: Prentice-Hall, Inc., 1973.

WINGATE, JOHN W., ELMER O. SCHALLER, and F. LEONARD MILLER, *Retail Merchandise Management.* Englewood Cliffs, N.J.: Prentice-Hall, Inc., 1972.

WINKLER, ROBERT L., *An Introduction to Bayesian Inference and Decision.* New York: Holt, Rinehart and Winston, Inc., 1972.

WRIGHT, JOHN S., DANIEL S. WARNER, and WILLIS L. WINTER, Jr., *Advertising,* (3rd ed.) New York: McGraw-Hill Book Co., 1971.

WRIGHT, RICHARDSON LITTLE, *Hawkers and Walkers in Early America: Strolling Peddlers, Preachers, Lawyers, Doctors, Players, and Others, from the Beginning of the Civil War.* Philadelphia: J. B. Lippincott Co., 1927.

YODER, DALE, *Personnel Management and Industrial Relations* (6th ed.) Englewood Cliffs, N.J.: Prentice-Hall, Inc., 1970.

YOSHINO, M. Y., *The Japanese Marketing System: Adaptations and Innovations.* Cambridge, Mass.: The M.I.T. Press, 1971.

JOURNAL ARTICLES

"Advertising Gets Families Out of the House and into Your Restaurant," *Restaurant Business* (August 1974), 55–66.

BERKMAN, H. W., and C. C. GILSON, "Consumer Life Styles and Market Segmentation," *Journal of the Academy of Marketing Science* (Winter 1974), 189–200.

"Bicycle Stores," *Small Business Reporter*, xii, no. 1 (1974), 16 pp.

BIRD, MONROE M., and JAMES W. ROBINSON, "The Value of 'Buy Union' Campaigns for Retail Sales Promotion Activities," *Journal of Retailing* (Summer 1973), 65–68.

BOGART, LEO, "The Future of Retailing," *Harvard Business Review* (November-December 1973), 16–32.

BONWICH, WILLIAM T., and EDWARD B. CONWAY, "Pricing in Food Chains: Poverty Area Versus Non-poverty Area Stores," *Journal of Retailing* (Summer 1970), 60–63.

"Bookstores," *Small Business Reporter*, II, no. 6 (1973), 20 pp.

BRITT, S. H., and J. D. GORDON, "Congressional Acts that Affect Your Marketing Decisions," *Journal of the Academy of Marketing Science* (Winter 1974), 201–12.

CAMPBELL, ROSS W., "Stages of Shopping Center Developments in Major Latin American Metropolitan Markets," *Land Economics* (February 1974), 66–70.

CARUSONE, PETER S., "A Shift in the Point of Patronage," *Business Topics* (Autumn 1970), 61–69.

"Convenience Store Study," *Progressive Grocer* (September 1972).

COOPER, PHILIP D., "Will Success Produce Problems for the Convenience Store?" *MSU Business Topics* (Winter 1972), 39–43.

COTTRELL, JAMES L., "An Environmental Model for Performance Measurement in a Chain of Supermarkets," *Journal of Retailing* (Fall 1973), 51–63.

CRAWFORD, C. MERLE, "Needed: A New Look at Retailer Horizontal Cooperation," *Journal of Retailing* (Summer 1970), 64–76.

"Credit Card and Check-Credit Plans at Commercial Banks," *Federal Reserve Bulletin* (September 1973), 646–53.

CUNNINGHAM, ISABELLA C. M., and WILLIAM H. CUNNINGHAM, "The Urban In-home Shopper: Sociometric and Attitudinal Characteristics," *Journal of Retailing* (Fall 1973), 42–50.

CURHAM, RONALD C., and EDWARD G. WERTHEIM, "Consumer Food Buying Cooperatives—A Market Examined," *Journal of Retailing* (Winter 1972–1973), 28–39.

DANA, M., "Retailers—An Important Link in Consumer Product Safety," *Stores* (June 1974), pp. 16ff.

DARLING, JOHN R., "Capital Investment in the Retail Industry and Cyclical Business Fluctuations, 1948 to 1968," *The Southern Journal of Business* (July 1971), 49–57.

DAVIDSON, WILLIAM R., ALTON F. DOODY, and JAMES R. LOWREY, "Leased Departments as a Major Force in the Growth of Discount Store Retailing," *Journal of Marketing*, 34, no. 1 (January 1970), 39–46.

"Department Stores—A Booming Market," *Commerce Today* (June 1971), 9–11.

DEUTSCH, CLAUDIA, "Automated Mass Merchandising," *Stores* (July 1971), 8–9

"Don't Write Off the Senior Citizen Market," *Media Decisions* (July 1973), 64–67.

"Downtown in the Cornfields," *Sales Management* (November 1, 1970), 34–36.

FABIAN, DICK, and GEORGE DICKSTEIN, "Who is Making it in the Inner City?" *Chain Store Age* (February 1973), 53–62.

FENVESSY, STANLEY J., "Importance of Fulfillment in Keeping Customers Happy," *Direct Marketing* (February 1974), 22–24.

FITZELL, PHILIP B., "Eating Out in the Inner City," *Fast Food* (January 1974), 37–39.

"40th Annual Report of the Grocery Industry: 1972 Sales up 7.7%, Top $100 Billion Mark," *Progressive Grocer* (April 1973), 91–106.

"Gearing up for the Automated Front End," *Progressive Grocer* (February 1973), 66ff.

GOLDMAN, ARIEH, "The Role of Trading-up in the Development of the Retailing System," *Journal of Marketing*, 39, no. 1 (January 1975), 54–62.

GOTTLIEB, LEON, "Franchise vs. Company Operations," *Fast Food* (June 1972), 44.

"Grand Union, Pathmark, Giant Food Join Catalog Store Boom," *Progressive Grocer* (May 1973), 140–44.

"The Green Stamps Sing the Blues," *Forbes* (September 1, 1973), 44–45.

"Growing Growing Grown," *Fast Food* (August 1973), 51–55.

"H&BA Report/73: Merchandising the Merchandise of Health and Beauty Aids," *Progressive Grocer* (part 2) (August 1973), 123ff.

"Health Food Stores," *Small Business Reporter*, II, no. 2 (1973), 16 pp.

HENSEL, JAMES S., "Environmental Change and the Future Structure of Retailing," *Arizona Business* (February 1973), 14–20.

HOLLANDER, STANLEY C., "Consumerism and Retailing: A Historical Perspective," *Journal of Retailing* (Winter 1972–1973), 6–21.

"How Products Perform in the Super Store," *Progressive Grocer* (July 1973), 40–45.

HUNT, SHELBY D., "The Trend Toward Company-Operated Units in Franchise Chains," *Journal of Retailing* (Summer 1973), 3–12.

"Independent Drug Stores," *Small Business Reporter*, ix, no. 12 (1971), 16 pp.

"Independent Liquor Stores," *Small Business Reporter*, II, no. 4 (1973), 16 pp.

"It's All in the Cards," *Stores* (November 1972), 36–39.

JOLSON, MARVIN A., "Standardizing the Personal Selling Process," *Marquette Business Review* (Spring 1974), 16–22.

———, and WALTER F. SPATH, "Understanding and Fulfilling Shoppers' Requirements: An Anomoly of Retailing?" *Journal of Retailing* (Summer 1973), 38–50.

JUDELLE, BEATRICE, "Creative Merchandising," *Stores* (May 1971), 15, 36–38.

KOHN, ROBERT, "Present Retailer Reaction to Consumerism—Death or Hope?" *Journal of Retailing* (Spring 1973), 3–9.

KOTLER, PHILIP, "Atmospherics as a Marketing Tool," *Journal of Retailing* (Winter 1973–1974), 48–64.

"Last Lap," *Forbes* (April 1, 1971), p. 21.

LINK, JOE, "Convenience Groceries Build Profits for Gasoline Marketers," *National Petroleum News* (August 1973), 58–66.

LITTLE, ROBERT W., "The Supra-firm: Key to Small Retailer Survival," *University of Washington Business Review* (Winter 1971), 32–47.

MALLEN, BRUCE, and RONALD ROTENBERG, "The Benefits and Costs of Evening Shopping to the Canadian Economy: An Exploratory Study," *Journal of Retailing* (Summer 1971), 14–27.

MARTIN, CLAUDE R., JR., "The Contribution of the Professional Buyer to a Store's Success or Failure," *Journal of Retailing* (Summer 1973), 69–80.

MASON, JOSEPH BARRY, and DANNY BELLENGER, "Analyzing High Fashion Acceptance," *Journal of Retailing* (Winter 1973–1974), 79–88.

MCKELVEY, ROBERT A., "Retailing's Future in Downtown," *Stores* (April 1973), 16–33.

MCLAUGHLIN, DANIEL J., JR., and PAUL J. REILLY, "Retail Experiments in Frozen Food Merchandising," *Quick Frozen Foods* (August 1973), 34–36.

"The Media, Money and the Manufacturer—1969," *Supermarketing* (July 1970), 19–28.

MERTES, JOHN E., "A Store is a Store is a . . .," *Oklahoma Business Bulletin* (March 1970), 3–7.

"Mirror, Mirror on the Wall . . .," *Forbes* (November 1, 1970), 21ff.

"More Space for Frozen Foods," CSA Special Report, *Chain Store Age* (June 1973), 39–50.

"New Facts on New Items and Private Label," *Progressive Grocer* (July 1972), 36–40.

OAKLEAF, ROBERT B., "The Mall: Treasure Trove or Trap," *Management Accounting* (June 1970), 41–43.

O'NEILL, ROBERT E., "Inside the Hypermarket," *Progressive Grocer* (May 1974), 42–48.

PARTCH, KEN, "U.P.C. is Here—Time for the Second Revolution," *Chain Store Age* (May 1973), 5, 75–78.

PENNER, IRVIN, "The College Credit Market," *Stores* (September 1970), 14–16.

PETERSON, ESTHER, "Consumerism as a Retailer's Asset," *Harvard Business Review* (May-June 1974), 99–101.

PETROF, JOHN V., "Attitudes of the Urban Poor Toward Their Neighborhood Super Markets," *Journal of Retailing* (Spring 1971), 3–17.

PICKERING, J. F., "Economic Implications of Hypermarkets in Britain," *European Journal of Marketing*, pp. 257–69.

PINTO, ALLEN, "What Makes Warehouse Markets Go," *Progressive Grocer* (August 1972), 60–68.

"Planners Confront the Cost Crisis," *Chain Store Age* (March 1971), E24–29, 68–78.

PRASAD, V. KANTI, "Store Perception Factors and Multi-Store Food Shopping," *The Southern Journal of Business* (November 1972), 73–78.

"Restaurants in Retaildom: A Fight For Every Foot," *Fast Food* (July 1973), 56–66.

REYNOLDS, JOHN J., "The Future of the Bank Credit Card," *Credit World* (December 1973), 19–21.

ROY, H. J. H., and R. D. SANDERSON, "Human Judgment Versus Credit Scoring," *The Credit World* (November 1972), 8–11.

RUBIN, R. S., "Franchising: A Marketing System to Improve Inner Cities Conditions," *Journal of the Academy of Marketing Science* (Winter, 1974), 278–89.

RUBNER, H. J., "The Impact of Point of Sales," *Stores* (August 1974), 2.

RUDELIUS, WILLIAM, ROBERT F. HOEL, and ROGER A. KERIN, "Assessing Retail Opportunities in Low-Income Areas," *Journal of Retailing* (Fall 1972), 96–114.

SALMON, WALTER J., ROBERT D. BUZZELL, and STANTON G. CORT, "Today the Shopping Center, Tomorrow the Superstore," *Harvard Business Review* (January-February 1974), 89–98.

SAUNDERS, JOSEPHINE R., A. COSKUN SAMLI, and ENID F. TOZIER, "Congruence and Conflict in Buying Decisions of Mothers and Daughters," *Journal of Retailing* (Fall 1973), 3–18.

SCHIELE, GEORGE W., "How to Reach the Young Consumer," *Harvard Business Review* (March-April 1974), 77–85.

"Second Annual Convenience Store Study," *Progressive Grocer* (September 1972), 156–61.

SEGALL, MAURICE, "Mailers and Retailers Revving up for Marketing Revolution," *Direct Marketing* (July 1973), 25ff.

"73 H & BA Superstars," CSA Special Report, *Chain Store Age* (April 1974), 59–74.

SEXTON, DONALD E., "Do Inner City Chain Stores Charge More?" *The Journal of Consumer Affairs* (Winter 1973), 145–55.

"Sharp Eyes on Shoplifting," *Department Store Management* (September 1970), 16–19.

SIMONS, PETER L., "The Shape of Suburban Retail Market Areas: Implications From a Literature Review," *Journal of Retailing* (Winter 1973–1974), 65–68.

SMALLBROOK, WILLIAM A., and ULRICH C. TOENSMEYER, "Analysis of Prices among Discount Food Stores," *Journal of Food Distribution Research* (September 1973), 43–46.

SMITH, BERNARD W., "The Continuity of Retail Problems," *Journal of Retailing* (Summer 1970), 48–59.

SMITH, SPENCER B., "Automated Inventory Management for Staples," *Journal of Retailing* (Spring 1971), 55–62.

SNYDER, GLENN H., "The Boom is for Expanded General Merchandise," *Progressive Grocer* (January 1974), 40–46.

———, "General Merchandise on the Move: Housewares Ring up New Profits for Supers," *Progressive Grocer* (January 1973), 38–42.

———, "The Health and Beauty Aids Study: New Growth for Supers in Fabulous Category," *Progressive Grocer* (October 1972), 136–39.

SPAR, EDWARD J., "Restaurant Growth Index—Part II: Sixth Annual Restaurant Growth Index—1973," *Fast Food* (September 1973), 124ff.

STEPHENSON, P. RONALD, and ROBERT G. HOUSE, "A Perspective on Franchising," *Business Horizons* (August 1971), 35–42.

SWAN, J. E., "A Functional Analysis of Innovation in Distribution Channels," *Journal of Retailing* (Spring 1974), 9–23ff.

SWAN, JOHN E., "Patterns of Competition for Differential Advantage in Two Types of Retail Institutions," *Journal of Retailing* (Spring 1971), 25–35.

SWART, J. CARROLL, and ROBERT B. CARTER, "Negroes in Franchising," *Journal of Retailing* (Fall 1972), 81–88.

TAYLOR, EILEEN F., "Food Prices Before and After Distribution of Welfare Checks . . . Low Income Areas, Seven Cities, 1969," *Marketing Research Report No. 907*, Economic Research Service, USDA, September 1970, 22 pp.

"3rd Annual Report on the Convenience Store Industry," *Progressive Grocer* (September 1973), 66–68.

THORNHILL, WILLIAM T., "Bank Credit Cards: Past, Present and Future," *Credit World* (November 1972), 15–19.

TIGERT, DOUGLAS J., RICHARD LATHROPE, and MICHAEL BLEEG, "The Fast Food Franchise: Psychographic and Demographic Segmentation Analysis," *Journal of Retailing* (Spring 1971), 81–90.

VON RIESEN, R. DALE, "Toward Staffing Optimality in Retail Selling," *Journal of Retailing* (Winter 1973–1974), 37–47.

VORZIMER, L. H., "Rx Small Retailer Survival: Community Demand Analysis," *Journal of the Academy of Marketing Science* (Fall 1973), 180–88.

WALKER, ORVILLE C., JR., and RICHARD F. SAUTER, "Consumer Preference for Alternative Retail Credit Terms: A Concept Test of the Effects of Consumer Legislation," *Journal of Marketing Research* (February 1974), 70–78.

"What's Wrong with the U.S. Super Markets?" *Progressive Grocer* (May 1973), 120–22.

"Why Marketers Turn to Convenience Store Tie-ins," *National Petroleum News* (April 1971), 48–54.

YETTER, GENE, "Franchisors and Franchisees—Partners in Profits," *Fast Food* (March 1974), 89–94.

———, "Restaurant Growth Index, Part I: The $44.7 Billion Food-Service Market," *Fast Food* (September 1973), 77–92.

INDEX

K

L

M

Q

R

T

U